VOLUME 1

COUNTRY WALKS

52 WALKS NEAR LONDON

Time Out Guides Ltd
Universal House
251 Tottenham Court Road
London W1T 7AB
United Kingdom
Tel: +44 (0)20 7813 3000
Fax: +44 (0)20 7813 6001
Email: guides@timeout.com
www.timeout.com

Published by Time Out Guides Ltd, a wholly owned subsidiary of Time Out Group Ltd.
Time Out and the Time Out logo are trademarks of Time Out Group Ltd.

© **Time Out Group Ltd 2011**

10 9 8 7 6 5 4 3 2 1

This edition first published in Great Britain in 2011 by Ebury Publishing.
A Random House Group Company
20 Vauxhall Bridge Road, London SW1V 2SA

Random House Australia Pty Ltd 20 Alfred Street, Milsons Point, Sydney, New South Wales 2061, Australia

Random House New Zealand Ltd 18 Poland Road, Glenfield, Auckland 10, New Zealand

Random House South Africa (Pty) Ltd Isle of Houghton, Corner Boundary Road & Carse O'Gowrie,
Houghton 2198, South Africa

Random House UK Limited Reg. No. 954009

Distributed in USA by Publishers Group West
1700 Fourth Street, Berkeley, California 94710

Distributed in Canada by Publishers Group Canada
250A Carlton Street, Toronto, Ontario M5A 2L1

For further distribution details, see www.timeout.com.

ISBN: 978-1-84670-221-1

A CIP catalogue record for this book is available from the British Library.

Printed and bound in India by Replika Press Pvt. Ltd.

The Random House Group Limited supports The Forest Stewardship Council (FSC), the leading international
forest certification organisation. All our titles that are printed on Greenpeace approved FSC certified paper
carry the FSC logo. Our paper procurement policy can be found at http://www.rbooks.co.uk/environment.

Time Out carbon-offsets its flights with Trees for Cities (www.treesforcities.org).

Published by

Time Out Guides Limited
Universal House
251 Tottenham Court Road
London W1T 7AB
Tel +44 (0)20 7813 3000
Fax +44 (0)20 7813 6001
email guides@timeout.com
www.timeout.com

Maps John Oakey

Cover photography Photolibrary.com

Back cover photography Bela Struzkova and Stuart Leeds

Photography Bela Struzkova; except pages 12, 89, 108, 109, 111, 193, 248/249, 328 Stuart Leeds; pages 19, 20, 30, 37, 56,
64, 70, 73, 80, 102, 105 Jon Combe; page 38 Catherine Ames; pages 44, 182 Sean O'Neill; pages 86, 160, 170, 190, 191,
209, 225, 238, 264, 283, 314, 347, 348 Ian Trotter; pages 116, 382/383 Claire Lau; pages 219, 296, 404 Peter Conway;
page 259 Ayla Bedri; page 273 Andrew Murphy.

Contents

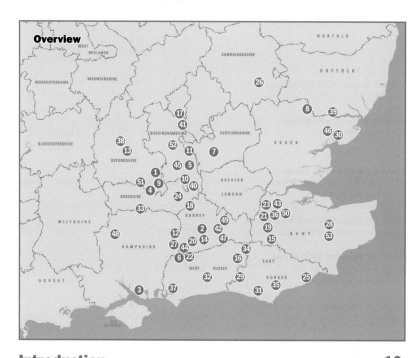

Overview

Contents

Contents

Contents

Contents

Introduction

The walks in this book grew out of the experiences of a group of friends – and friends of friends – who went walking together every Saturday.

They came to the conclusion that there was no better way to have an inexpensive party each week than for a dozen or so people to go out for a walk together in beautiful countryside. The walks were between 7 and 13 miles long, included a pub for lunch and a stop for cream tea, and always started and finished at a railway station.

The walks were created using Ordnance Survey maps and designed to take in places that looked interesting – those with National Trust land or buildings, or those which led through woods and along streams.

Thinking of all the Londoners and tourists of different ages who would really enjoy getting out of the city for the day, one of the group – Nicholas Albery – was inspired to write this book.

The result was a collection of walks – one for each week of the year and one to spare – that covers the whole of the south-east of England, from Kent to the Chilterns and from Hampshire to Essex. Each one introduces a beautiful corner of the countryside in this lovely part of England.

In selecting walks for this book, Nicholas endeavoured to provide plenty of variety, to cater for all tastes: Winchelsea to Hastings (Walk 25) is a strenuous but exhilarating cliff walk; Otford Circular (Walk 43) is a nice, hilly, short walk, close to London; Princes Risborough to Wendover (Walk 52) has the Chilterns and the Ridgeway path; Milford to Haslemere (Walk 27) explores the surprisingly remote Surrey Heathland and the Devil's Punchbowl; Henley Circular (Walk 1) is a gentle walk that follows the Thames Path before taking you up into the Great Wood; and Glynde to Seaford (Walk 31) follows the South Downs Way via picturesque Alfriston to the sea. All these delights are contained within the following pages, just waiting for you and your friends and family to discover them.

The author and the researchers

Nicholas Albery was a self-styled social inventor and, for the original editions of *Time Out Country Walks,* he had the idea of creating a self-organising walking club – the Saturday Walkers' Club – that would do the walks in the book every week, following a rota published in the book. The idea was that any person who bought the book could turn up on the walks, which would need no leader because every walker would have the directions for the walk with them.

Tragically, Nicholas died in a car accident in 2001 at the age of 52. Saturday walkers combined to research and write a second volume of *Country Walks* as a tribute to Nicholas, and the two volumes remain his legacy. These books have proved to be a way for many people from all walks of life to discover the beauties of the English countryside.

In keeping with Nicholas's ideals, the authors' royalties from both volumes go to fund another of his enduring legacies: the **Natural Death Centre**, a registered charity founded by Nicholas and his wife, which gives advice on alternative and ecological funerals, as well as seeking to 'inform, empower and inspire' the public about all aspects of death and dying. As part of its work, the charity publishes *The Natural Death Handbook* and offers a directory of natural burial grounds on its website, www.naturaldeath.org.uk.

Saturday Walkers' Club

The Saturday Walkers' Club remains a self-organising group of walkers and all readers of this book are welcome to join it. There are no joining fees, you do not need to reserve a place, and everyone is welcome, especially visitors to London. Just turn up.

Despite the club's name, walks take place not only on Saturdays but also on Sundays, bank holidays and in midweek slots. Each week sees several walks posted on the website, giving you a changing range of options – for current details, see 'This Week's Walks' on the club's website (www.walkingclub.org.uk). An extra advantage is that the poster will have already checked the train connections for you.

All we ask is that you bring a copy of the instructions (*Country Walks* volume 1 or 2, as appropriate, or a downloaded free walk), since the walks are 'self-led' – that is, the walks do not have leader with insurance, so you are responsible for yourself at all times. On the plus side, if you want to leave the main groups to walk faster or slower, or to spend longer in the pub or stop for a swim, that's perfectly fine.

Planning a walk

Putting one foot in front of the other is one of the simpler leisure activities, but even so a little planning and preparation can make a difference to your enjoyment of the experience. This section contains some practical advice and tips.

What to bring

There are no high mountains in the south-east of England, so you do not need expensive equipment.

Footwear is the most important piece of gear to think about. In summer, on even paths, trainers can be fine, but most of the time you will be more comfortable in proper walking boots. Do wear them in before tackling long walks and wear proper walking socks.

Keep a **waterproof** jacket and lightweight overtrousers in your backpack, just in case it rains during your walk.

In the summer you will need a **hat and sunscreen** (you will be outside for several hours) and a large water bottle. On hot summer days, drink plenty of water, more than you think you need – it makes a big difference.

One **walking pole** or a pair can be a useful addition to help you go up steep ascents, down steep descents and over slippery terrain.

Walking equipment can be purchased from high-street chains like Millets and Blacks. For specialist retailers, the best concentration in London is in Covent Garden, where you will find Ellis Brigham, Field and Trek, The North Face, Kathmandu and Rohan.

This book includes all the directions you need without having to refer to a map. That said, we recommend the excellent **Ordnance Survey (OS) Explorer Maps** (with orange covers). The OS Landranger series are less detailed but also useful.

Many of the walk directions include compass bearings and you should bring a **compass** with you to be able to confirm your route in places where there are few other landmarks.

New walkers

We recommend you start with the shorter walks, and ones with a lower toughness rating. Don't go from no walking to walking 13 miles a day every Saturday and Sunday – build up to it.

Getting to the walks

Train times: www.nationalrail.co.uk or 08457 48 49 50
Bus times: www.traveline.org.uk or 0871 200 22 33

By train

The walks in this book all start and end at a railway station. See the **Travel** section at the start of each walk for details of where to catch the train if you're starting from London and an idea of what time to set off from the city if you aim to reach the suggested pub by lunchtime.

Introduction

Train times and ticket prices can be checked at a local train station, online or by phone. Be sure to confirm the return journey times as well, since a few stations only have a two-hourly service. Finally, check for planned engineering works, when slow buses, with lengthy waits for connections, replace trains.

If the walk starts and finishes at different stations on the same line, you just need to buy a day return ticket to the more distant of the two stations.

That does leave some walks where the start and finish are on different railway lines. For these walks there is no easy advice to offer. While ticket inspectors often accept a day return to the station furthest from London, some railway companies take a harder line and make you buy a separate ticket. The safest (though not always the cheapest) approach is to buy a day return to the station at the start of the walk, and then a single from the station at the end of the walk to the point where the return route merges with the outbound one.

Where the train journey is not straightforward, the walk's **Travel** section contains specific advice on which ticket(s) to buy from the London terminus.

The cost of train tickets can be reduced by using a railcard. Information on the various types of railcard can be obtained from most stations and can also be found on the Saturday Walkers' Club website.

For non-railcard holders, there are other options, including Groupsave, where four people travel for the price of two (but you must travel together). It is also worth checking the websites of the individual rail companies (see links on the National Rail Enquiries website) for advance fares and temporary special offers, which can sometimes give substantial savings.

By car

We have given brief details on possible parking places near the start or end of some walks, but car drivers are advised to check this information locally.

For non-circular walks, we have given brief details on how to get back to the start of the walk by train. There are a

few walks where the start and finish stations are on different rail lines and do not connect, which makes these walks unsuitable for drivers.

It is possible to combine the car and train travel, especially if you live in outer London – drive to a station on the train's route, and take the train from there.

Following the walks

To make our instructions as useful as possible, we have followed a set format for describing each walk in this book.

Toughness ratings

Each walk has been given a rating between 1 (undemanding) and 9 (the most effort required). They take into account the amount of climbing, if there are exceptionally steep sections, and the length of the walk. These ratings are only relevant to the walks published here (all of them would be considerably lower if put in the context of hillier parts of Britain), but they can help you choose which walk to do depending on how fit you are or whether you feel like more of a workout.

The walk directions

Unlike some other walking books, the *Time Out Country Walks* books set out to give you all the information to follow a walk without having to refer to a map.

You may not always need all the detail provided in the text, however, and for this reason essential directions are in italics. With experience, you may well find that you can rely on the italics for stretches of the walk, dipping into the detail only when you are unsure.

Note that the seasons can make a difference to how easy it is to follow a walk. In summer, vegetation can obscure footpath posts or arrows on trees and, in winter, paths through woods can sometimes become confusing. Ploughed fields in winter also test navigational skills, and you may have to decide in summer whether to wade through a field of corn, or walk around the field

edge. We have taken these factors into account when devising our walk directions, however, and given you as many navigational clues as possible.

Frequent compass bearings are given in the directions. They can reassure you that you are on the right route – for example, in a wood, when crossing a newly ploughed field where you are unsure about your onward way, or when you face a choice of paths.

Using a compass is not complicated. Simply align the needle of the compass with north (usually helpfully marked by a red arrow on the compass base) and then face in the direction of the bearing given in the text using the numbers around the edge of the dial. This, and the instructions in the text, should make the onward route obvious.

Many directions have distances. If you are uncertain about these, it can help to have a mental image of some known distances for comparison: 100 metres is about the length of a football pitch, for instance. For longer distances, most people's walking speed is between 60 and 80 metres per minute, so 'in 300 metres' should be after about 4 or 5 minutes of walking.

Each chapter includes a sketch map, with numbers – for example, **[7]** – referring to points in the text, so that you can check your progress along a route. Where a turning is less obvious or more complex, we alert you in the directions with a **[!]**.

What to do if you get lost

All these walks have been checked several times and at all times of the year. Although things do change, the most likely explanation is that you missed a turning or hard-to-see signpost, read the same instruction twice, or perhaps skipped one.

The best thing to do if you are unsure, or the instructions no longer seem to make sense, is to retrace your steps until you reach a point you were sure of and try again.

Introduction

Accuracy

To ensure the walks follow rights of way, we have relied on OS Maps, particularly the excellent Explorer series. To the best of our knowledge, all routes follow public rights of way, permissive paths (paths where the landowner – usually the National Trust or a local authority – has given formal permission to use the path, but may withdraw it: such paths are usually marked on OS maps too), or are on common land. Still, it is impossible to guarantee that this book is free from errors in this respect.

Our experience has been that the vast majority of rural landowners and inhabitants are perfectly friendly and accommodating to walkers so long as the walkers keep to legitimate paths. Be civil to them and respect their rights and they are likely to reciprocate your courtesy.

Web resources

The internet has allowed us to offer additional services that complement the *Country Walks* books.

Updates

All walks in this book were fully revised in 2010, with information on pubs and attraction opening times updated at the same time.

If you have used previous editions of this book, you will be familiar with the walks. Generally, the routes are the same except for minor changes to accommodate diverted routes, different lunch options and changes in land-use.

However, changes do inevitably occur after publication. Stiles collapse (some local authorities maintain them well, others don't) or get replaced by kissing gates. Footpath signposts fall over, are removed, or get covered by foliage. Pubs close or stop serving food, or (a worrying modern trend) are turned into upmarket restaurants. Rural tea rooms, alas, often go out of business at short notice.

Where such changes come to the attention of the walking club, it records them on its website, www.walkingclub.org.uk. In the separate 'Time Out Country Walks 1' section of the website, you will find a web page for each walk in this book; an 'Updates & Feedback' button is at the top of the page for each walk.

Where necessary, updated versions of the walks will be posted on the site.

Feedback

You can post your own updates using the 'Updates & Feedback' button on each walk page – the walking club greatly appreciates your comments.

New options

Our website also has alternative routes, not available in the books, for some of the walks, as well as ideas about how to combine them with other walks.

Photos

Each walk has a photos page, which can give you a better idea of what each walk is like. If you would like to share your own photos with the world, upload them to the SWC group on Flickr (www.flickr.com/groups/swc).

GPS data

We are starting to collate GPS data for the walks. If you have a GPS-enabled smartphone (or walker's satnav), check the website for GPS data. If you have recorded the route of a walk, the walking club would be grateful to receive a copy.

Volume 2

If you enjoyed this book, there is a second volume with 30 new walks. These walks are more car-friendly, and many of them have shorter options for new walkers.

When to walk

The first volume of *Country Walks* provided a walk for every week of the year – and even a 53rd walk as a substitute for one that could not be done when engineering works made travel arrangements difficult. Rotas were included in the book, translating this order of play into specific Saturday dates for years ahead: Walk 1 was to be done in the first week of January, Walk 2 in the second, and so on.

The establishment of **www.walkingclub.org.uk** has reduced the need to provide rotas in the book, as comprehensive information on the following week's walks, including changes to accommodate engineering work, are posted there.

Some walkers, however, might still find a schedule of walks for the year ahead to be a helpful guide to enjoying the walks at an appropriate time of year. The one below is based on many years' experience of trying out the walks at all times of the year, marrying increasing daylight hours and longer walks, and noting flowering seasons, such as the bluebells in early May.

Do try out the walks at other times of the year, though: you will be surprised how different – but equally enjoyable – a walk can be in different seasons.

January to March
Week 1	1 Henley-on-Thames Circular
Week 2	2 Wanborough to Godalming
Week 3	43 Otford Circular
Week 4	4 Pangbourne Circular
Week 5	5 Great Missenden to Amersham
Week 6	6 Liphook to Haslemere
Week 7	33 Mortimer to Aldermaston
Week 8	8 Bures to Sudbury
Week 9	15 Leigh to Tunbridge Wells
Week 10	10 Beaconsfield Circular
Week 11	11 Tring to Wendover
Week 12	12 Farnham to Godalming
Week 13	13 Oxford Circular

April to June
Week 14	14 Gomshall to Guildford
Week 15	19 Hever to Leigh
Week 16	16 Balcombe Circular
Week 17	17 Bow Brickhill to Woburn Sands
Week 18	18 Sunningdale to Windsor
Week 19	9 Shiplake to Henley
Week 20	20 Milford to Godalming
Week 21	21 Leigh to Sevenoaks
Week 22	22 Haslemere Circular
Week 23	23 Otford to Eynsford
Week 24	3 Netley to Botley
Week 25	25 Winchelsea to Hastings
Week 26	26 Shelford to Cambridge

July to September
Week 27	27 Milford to Haslemere
Week 28	28 Chilham to Canterbury
Week 29	29 Hassocks to Lewes
Week 30	30 Wivenhoe Circular
Week 31	31 Glynde to Seaford
Week 32	32 Arundel to Amberley
Week 33	50 Yalding to Borough Green
Week 34	34 Balcombe to East Grinstead
Week 35	35 Crowhurst to Battle
Week 36	36 Borough Green to Sevenoaks
Week 37	37 Southbourne to Chichester
Week 38	38 Hanborough to Charlbury
Week 39	39 Manningtree Circular

October to December
Week 40	46 Wakes Colne to Bures
Week 41	51 Henley to Pangbourne
Week 42	42 Holmwood to Gomshall
Week 43	48 Whitchurch to Andover
Week 44	44 Witley to Haslemere
Week 45	45 Princes Risborough to Great Missenden
Week 46	40 Gerrards Cross to Cookham
Week 47	47 Ockley to Warnham
Week 48	24 Cookham to Maidenhead
Week 49	49 Box Hill to Leatherhead
Week 50	41 Bow Brickhill to Leighton Buzzard
Week 51	7 Garston to St Albans
Week 52	52 Princes Risborough to Wendover
sub walk	53 Wye Circular

Walk 1

Henley Circular

Temple Island, Hambleden and the Great Wood.

Start and finish: Henley station

Length: 16.1km (10.0 miles)

Time: 4 hours 30 minutes. For the whole outing, including trains, sights and meals, allow 7 hours 50 minutes.

Transport: Take the train nearest to **10am** from **Paddington** station to **Henley-on-Thames**, changing at Twyford (journey time 65 minutes). At Twyford you have to cross over to the other platform. Be quick if the London train is late, as there is an hour's wait if you miss the connection. Trains back from Henley are hourly.

If you are driving, Henley station has a car park (£3.90/day Mon-Fri), or there is free parking a little way outside the town.

OS Landranger Map: 175
OS Explorer Map: 171
Henley-on-Thames, map reference SU764823, is in **Oxfordshire**, 10km north-east of Reading.

Toughness: 2 out of 10

Walk notes: Route-finding is easy on this mainly flat walk along the Thames, or up on the wooded geological terrace above it. The walk starts in Henley (famous for its rowing regatta in late June or early July) and goes along the Thames towpath, with rowing instructors on bikes shouting instructions to their crews, past Temple Island to the 250-metre footbridge over the weir at Hambleden Mill, where canoeists practise in the stormy waters. From there the route is northwards to the suggested lunchtime pub in the well-preserved hamlet of Hambleden, which has a huge church out of all proportion to the population. After lunch, the walk for the next 2.5km is through the Great Wood, the endlessness of which gives an inkling of how most of Britain must once have been. From the village of Fawley, with its church and mausoleum, the walk returns along the Oxfordshire Way, past the manor of Henley Park, to Henley for tea.

Walk options: You could get a bus back to Henley from Mill End (there are about three buses each hour) or a taxi from the pub in Hambleden.

History: **Henley**, with its 300 listed buildings, is said to be the oldest settlement in Oxfordshire; a Roman grain store and the skeletons of 97 supposedly unwanted children were excavated at **Mill End** in 1911.

Fawley Temple, the neoclassical folly on Temple Island, is maintained by the Henley Regatta on a 999-year lease. It was built back in 1771 by James Wyatt for a local landowner, Sambrooke Freeman, and has some Etruscan-style murals inside.

Hambleden Mill, mentioned in the Domesday Book, was used for grinding corn until 1955.

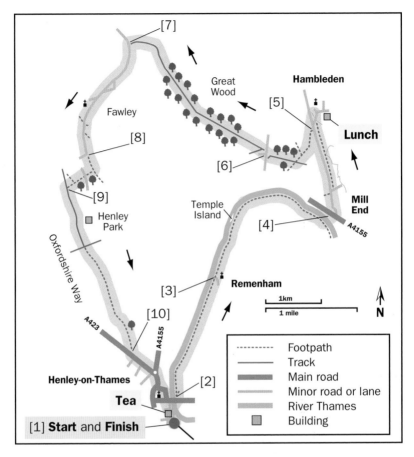

Hambleden means 'village in a valley'. Charles I spent one night at the manor house in Hambleden during his flight from Oxford to St Albans in 1646.

St Mary the Virgin Church, Hambleden, has a memorial with alabaster figures representing Sir Cope D'Oyley (who died in 1633), his wife and their ten children – with the children shown carrying skulls if they died before their parents. To the left of the monument is the oak muniment chest used by the Earl of Cardigan in Balaclava, where he led the ill-fated Charge of the Light Brigade in 1854. And to the left of this chest, tucked in an alcove, is a reusable stone coffin. The churchyard contains the grave of the bookseller WH Smith, who became (posthumously) Lord Hambleden.

The village of **Fawley** (from the Old English for 'clearing') is listed in the Domesday Book as having 13 villeins, one cottager and five slaves. In 1086 it was given to a Norman, Herbrand de Sackville, as a reward for guarding his master's estates in Normandy during the invasion of England. The churchyard in Fawley contains a large, circular, neoclassical **mausoleum**, built by John Freeman for his family around 1750.

Walk directions

**[1] [Numbers in square brackets
refer to the map]**
Coming out of **Henley station**, *turn
right,* your direction 305 degrees, and
walk 50 metres to the main road.

Here, with the Imperial Hotel opposite
you, *turn right on the road,* your direction
45 degrees.

After 125 metres bear left, passing
the 'Boats for Hire' place on your right-
hand side.

Keep the River Thames on your
right until you reach the bridge, *which
you cross.*

40 metres from the other end of the
bridge **[2]**, *turn left on a footpath
signposted Thames Path, then take the
left fork* beside the Tollgate, on a tarmac
lane with a concrete bollard guarding
its centre, your direction 350 degrees.

In 55 metres, you come to the river
and turn right, with the river on your
left-hand side, your direction due north.

After 1.75km **[3]**, you come to a
footpath sign to the right. You may wish
to go through the wooden swing gate and
take a detour of 100 metres here to see **St
Nicholas Church** in **Remenham**. (You
may only be able to see the exterior and
churchyard, as the doors are often locked.)

Back on the towpath, in 500 metres you
pass **Temple Island**. In another 1.25km
you come to **Hambleden Lock [4]**.

Here you pass through a wooden
kissing gate and, in 70 metres, *go left
over the far lockgates* (following the
public footpath sign).

Then you are on a tarmac path on
the right-hand side of the lockhouse,
your direction 60 degrees, which, in
30 metres, leads you *over the footbridge
across the weir.*

At the other end of the bridge go
straight on, staying on the tarmac and
bending left with it, following the white
arrow painted on a fence in front of you,
your direction 20 degrees. Your path takes
you through a short alley between two
white cottages (Old Millgate Cottage to
your left) on to the A4155 at **Mill End**.

Turn right on this A road, your
direction 115 degrees. In 30 metres, by
he bus stop, *turn left* on a road signposted
Hambleden, heading northwards.

In 350 metres, cross a car road that goes
right to Rotten Row, to take a signposted
footpath through a metal kissing gate into
a field and continue straight on, parallel
to your previous direction.

Continue for 600 metres, exiting
the field through a metal kissing gate
to the right of a bridge over a stream.

Cross the earth road and enter
the next field through another metal
kissing gate, heading towards
Hambleden Church.

In 500 metres, the path comes out
by a metal kissing gate beside another
small bridge.

Turn right on the road into **Hambleden
Village**. The suggested lunchtime pub, the
Stag & Huntsman, is 140 metres along
on your right-hand side.

After lunch and any exploring of the
village and church, retrace your steps
on the village's approach road, passing
the bridge and metal kissing gate by
which you arrived.

Continue straight on, in 20 metres
passing cottage no.57 on your right-hand
side and, in a further 35 metres, coming
to the main road.

Cross the main road, slightly to the left,
to go up a tarmac path, signposted as a
public footpath **[5]**, a metal railing on its
left-hand side, your direction 195 degrees.

Continue on this main path, ignoring
turn-offs and passing buildings to enter
the wood.

After 25 metres, take a right fork uphill
(which is marked by a white arrow on
a tree), your direction 190 degrees, and
keep to this main uphill path, following
white arrows.

After 270 metres, you come to the
top of the hill (and, depending on the
amount of foliage, you should be able
to see the Thames ahead of you). In
15 metres, ignore a path to your right
to carry straight on downwards, your
direction 240 degrees.

Henley.

In a further 160 metres, and 20 metres before the edge of the wood (marked by a wooden swing gate at the exit), *turn right on a bridleway,* your direction 285 degrees.

Your route is straight on thereafter until you come to an earth car road. In 165 metres, you ignore a fork to the right and, in 75 metres, another going very sharply right. In 125 metres you leave the wood to continue along a tree-lined bridleway.

In a further 250 metres, you come out on to an earth car road T-junction.

Turn right on this road, your direction 350 degrees, in 55 metres passing houses nos.6 and 7 on the left-hand side. Ignore a left turn immediately after these but, in a further 10 metres **[6]**, *turn left on a signposted bridleway,* initially a car-wide earth road. Your direction is now 310 degrees.

At a sign that reads 'Strictly no riding without permits', take the right fork, keeping close to the right-hand edge of a field, steeply uphill, your direction 310 degrees.

Just by the entrance to the wood, ignore a car-wide earth fork to the right to go uphill into **Great Wood** (as marked on the OS map) following a public bridleway sign, your direction 305 degrees.

Your route is more or less straight on through this wood, ignoring all turn-offs, for over 2km, following relatively clear white arrows on trees.

In more detail: In 450 metres, you reach the flatter terrace land above the Thames and ignore a way off to the right. Ignore more ways off (in 210 metres one to the left, in another 45 metres one to the right, and in a further 120 metres one to the left). But then, in 90 metres, bear left for 30 metres, following white arrows on trees, before regaining your initial direction, now 325 degrees. In 250 metres, ignore a fork sharply to the left and, in 85 metres, one to the right.

When the wood ends on your left-hand side, continue on a path with a fence on your left, with **Roundhouse Farm** (as marked on the OS map) visible ahead of you, slightly to the left. This is a potentially muddy stretch, particularly in winter, of narrow bridleway.

In 500 metres, you come to a bench by **Orchard House**, from which you have a fine view of the far slopes.

Hambleden Mill.

In 90 metres, continue along an earth driveway. In 100 metres **[7]**, you come out on to a tarmac road by the **Round House**, where you *turn left,* your direction 190 degrees.

Keep on this road, ignoring all ways off, for 1.5km. In 270 metres you pass on your right-hand side the boarded-up and disused building that was once the Walnut Tree pub.

In 230 metres ignore a left turn signposted to Marlow. In 280 metres, keep straight on, following the sign to Henley.

In 80 metres, you come to the lychgate of **St Mary the Virgin Church**, **Fawley**, which is worth a visit.

Continuing on the road, ignore a footpath to the left by a house called Mavoli. In a further 250 metres **[8]**, *take a public footpath signposted to your left,* by a yellow water marker (H100/2), your direction 145 degrees.

You pass Five Gate House on your left-hand side. In a further 175 metres, you pass the gates of Homer House on your left-hand side.

In a further 40 metres, at a three-armed footpath sign, just before a set of overwrought high iron gates *take the footpath branching right* from your road, your new direction 230 degrees.

In 140 metres, you go through a metal barrier, cross a tarmac road and continue straight on, uphill, passing through a small wooden swing gate in 15 metres.

In 80 metres, you go through a small wooden swing gate and onwards. In a further 140 metres, you go through another small wooden swing gate and over a car lane (passing the gates of a water station on your left-hand side), then through a small wooden swing gate to continue straight on.

In another 100 metres go through a small wooden swing gate into a field and continue straight on, with the field edge on your right-hand side.

In a further 200 metres, go through a small wooden swing gate to a T-junction with a gravel car road **[9]** *where you turn left,* your direction 150 degrees.

Thereafter it is more or less straight on into Henley. But in more detail: In 300 metres, you come to a white post announcing 'Henley Park Private' but carry straight on. In 270 metres, you pass **Henley Park**, a white manor house, on your left-hand side. In a further 100 metres, you leave the car road (which bears left) to go through a wooden kissing gate, marked **Oxfordshire Way** (a metal fieldgate on its left-hand side), to continue straight on, your direction 150 degrees. In 450 metres pass a metal kissing gate on your left-hand side to continue straight on, your direction 165 degrees. In 500 metres you pass through a metal kissing gate to go down into a wood.

In 430 metres, ignoring all other ways off, you come out on the A423 **[10]** and *turn left,* your direction 135 degrees.

In 50 metres, you pass the **Old White Horse** pub on your left-hand side. In a further 250 metres, at the roundabout, keep straight on.

In 220 metres, you come to **New Street** with the **Teddy Bear Shop** on the corner.

Keep straight on along **Bell Street** passing **Caffè Nero** on your left.

In 100 metres, turn left into **Hart Street**. (**Maison Blanc**, a potential tea stop, is on the opposite corner.)

In 75 metres, you pass the **Old Rope Walk** tea place on your right-hand side and, in a further 35 metres, **Café Rouge** on your left-hand side.

In a further 40 metres you come to the **Parish Church of St Mary the Virgin**. (In summer you may find teas are served in the Chantry House here.)

Turn right just before the bridge to retrace your earlier steps along the riverfront. In 50 metres you come to the **Henley Tea Rooms** (another potential tea stop) on your right-hand side.

Continue along the riverfront until you come to 'Boats for Hire', where you bear right with the road, taking the second left to **Henley station**, opposite the Imperial Hotel.

Lunch & tea places

Stag & Huntsman *Hambleden, RG9 6RP (01491 571227, www.stagand huntsman.com).* **Open** 11am-2.30pm, 6-11pm Mon-Thur; 11am-11pm Fri, Sat; noon-3pm, 7-10.30pm Sun. *Food served* noon-2pm, 7-9.30pm Mon-Sat; noon-2pm Sun. Some 6km (3.7 miles) into the walk, this is the suggested lunch stop. Food with a local and seasonal emphasis is served.
Henley Tea Rooms *Henley-on-Thames, RG9 1BH (01491 411412).* **Open** 9am-5pm daily. Situated on Thames Side, overlooking the river, this cafe is a good spot for hot drinks and cakes.

There are a number of tea options, restaurants and pubs in Henley to suit most tastes, including – on Sunday afternoons in summer – the church of **St Mary the Virgin** on Hart Street, which serves tea with home-made cakes.

Walk 2

Wanborough to Godalming

Watts Gallery and Chapel.

Start: Wanborough station
Finish: Godalming station

Length: 12.0km (7.5 miles)

Time: 3 hours 30 minutes. For the whole outing, including trains, sights and meals, allow at least 8 hours 40 minutes. In winter, it's best to be on your way from Watts Chapel by 3pm, so as to reach Godalming before dark.

Travel: Take the train nearest to **9.40am** from **Waterloo** station to **Wanborough**, changing at Guildford. Journey time is around 50 minutes.

There are trains back from **Godalming** every half hour (hourly on Sundays), with a journey time of about 45 minutes. Buy a day return to Wanborough and, on the return journey, also buy a single from Godalming to Guildford. If you're driving, there is free parking by Wanborough station, just off the A34 road.

OS Landranger Map: 186
OS Explorer Map: 145
Wanborough station, map reference SU931503, is in **Surrey**, 6km west of Guildford.

Toughness: 2 out of 10

Walk notes: The route's original author was enchanted by this walk – first by Wanborough Manor and its tiny church, then by the tea shop in Compton, with its 50 varieties of tea, but, above all, by Watts Gallery and Chapel, the monuments left by Mary Fraser-Tytler to honour her husband George Frederick Watts, a Victorian painter and sculptor, 'England's Michelangelo' ('that's a bit rich', a visitor was overheard to comment). Later, the walk is along the River Wey, followed by tea in the ancient town of Godalming. The path beside the River Wey can be waterlogged or very muddy in winter, so don appropriate footwear. The path shortly after the start of the walk, as you enter a common, is also often waterlogged in winter.

Walk options: The hourly Guildford–Godalming bus service from Watts Gallery will resume once work on the road bridge is completed. Until then, the bus stop is some five to ten minutes away. The Watts Gallery staff may also be able to help you call a taxi.

History: **Wanborough** ('bump-barrow') may be named after a Bronze Age burial site on the Hog's Back. A Wanborough manor and chapel are said to have belonged to King Harold's brothers and to have been ransacked by William the Conqueror's army, marching up the Hog's Back. The present **manor house** was built in the 18th century. During the war it was a training centre for 'the members of the European Resistance

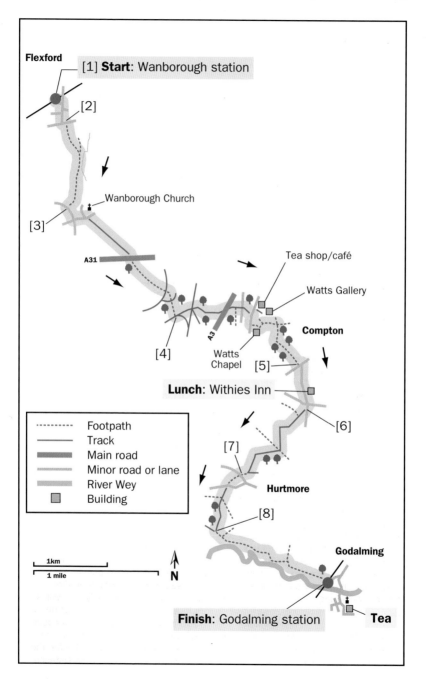

Flexford

[1] **Start**: Wanborough station

[2]

Wanborough Church

[3]

A31

Tea shop/café

Watts Gallery

Compton

[4]

A3

Watts Chapel

[5]

Lunch: Withies Inn

[6]

[7]

Hurtmore

[8]

Godalming

Finish: Godalming station

Tea

Footpath
Track
Main road
Minor road or lane
River Wey
Building

1km
1 mile

N

Movement who served behind enemy lines in special operations, facing loneliness and unknown dangers in the cause of humanity'.

Wanborough Church, one of the smallest in Surrey, was rebuilt by the Cistercian monks of Waverley Abbey in 1130, and was visited by pilgrims passing along the Pilgrim's Way.

Railway bridge with crosses. Brian Beaumont-Nesbitt writes: 'When Surrey CC wanted to build a bypass through the Watts property, Mary Watts refused, then finally agreed – if the bridge was designed by Lutyens. It dates from 1931; the Vic Soc says it is "an excellent example in miniature of Lutyens' interest in geometry. The tunnel surrounds, created with a sequence of stepped arches, are skilful exercises in perspectival adjustment – the vertical walls are battered, the centres of the arches are not the same, and the horizontal planes also taper." The original railings of oak cantilevered out had to be replaced by metal safety rails, but the two crosses over the Pilgrim's Way have been renewed.'

Watts Gallery, Down Lane, Compton (01483 810 235) has been undergoing restoration and is due to reopen in spring 2011. The gallery is recommended: look out for a vast sculpture of Watts' lifelong friend Tennyson (with his wolfhound), allegorical paintings of Time, Death and Judgement, political paintings of hunger and some coy nudes. Watts' most famous painting is a Rossetti-like portrait of the actress Ellen Terry, called *Choosing* (would she give up the stage for him?). Their marriage, in 1864, is said never to have been consummated; he was 46 and she just 16.

Watts Chapel was the project of his second wife, the artist and potter Mary Fraser-Tytler. She designed this art nouveau masterpiece without previous architectural or building experience, inspired by the Home Arts and Industries Association, and with the help of local villagers. Every interior surface is covered with what Mrs Watts called 'glorified wallpaper' – angels and seraphs made out of gesso, a material which her husband used when rheumatism meant he could no longer handle wet clay. He is buried in the cloister behind the chapel. Admission is free, and the chapel is open dawn to dusk daily.

Godalming is thought to mean 'field(-ing) of Godhelm' (the putative first Saxon to claim the land). It was a coaching town between London and Portsmouth, and a centre of trade in wool, stone-quarrying, timber, leather, paper, corn and brewing. The High

Street has many half-timbered and projecting buildings.

On the north side of the churchyard of St Peter and St Paul in Godalming there is the **Phillips Memorial Cloister**, designed by Thackeray Turner in 1913 with a garden by Gertrude Jekyll. Phillips was the chief wireless operator of the *Titanic*, who went down at his post on the ship.

Walk directions

[1] [Numbers in square brackets refer to the map]
Turn left out of **Wanborough station** and in 80 metres *turn right* on the main road in a southerly direction for 200 metres to the junction where the main road continues – *but you turn left* on to Flexford Road.

In 50 metres, opposite Little Hay Cottage **[2]**, *take the public footpath to the right,* your direction 160 degrees, over a stile with a metal fieldgate on the left-hand side, into a gravelled area. In 30 metres go over another stile on to a potentially waterlogged or muddy path between fences, towards a little concrete bridge and stile visible some 200 metres away.

Go over the stile and continue on, your direction 150 degrees, for a further 200 metres to the field hedge. Go through the gap in the hedge and straight on, southwards, with a hedge and stream on your left-hand side. In 400 metres you go over a stile, then left for 30 metres, following the field edge on your left-hand side. Bend right with the field edge, your direction now 215 degrees, to continue straight on, still with the stream on your left-hand side, passing a black wooden house further away to your left.

You reach a car road **[3]** with a footpath sign and a house (Pear Tree Cottage) on your left-hand side. *Turn left* on to this road and in 150 metres *go left* on a road with a footpath sign directing you to **Wanborough Church**, your direction 100 degrees. **Wanborough Manor House** is to the left of the church. To continue the walk, take the signposted

bridleway just to *the left* of a red-brick gabled house opposite the churchyard entrance, your direction 140 degrees. The bridleway is soon overarched by mixed evergreens and goes uphill to the A31 for 800 metres. With care, cross the first carriageway, go slightly to the left and then over the second carriageway.

Continue on a signposted footpath, over a stile, your direction 130 degrees, along the left-hand edge of the field. In 300 metres go over a stile and straight on, still with the hedge on your left-hand side, and, in 100 metres, go over another stile. Cross over a farm track, then head through a gravelled overflow car park and over the next stile, to go half right across a small field, your direction 135 degrees, to a gap in the hedge near an old barn.

15 metres brings you to another stile and then on to a farm track. Go right and then, after 10 metres, go onwards, your direction 130 degrees. Continue beyond a golf-course tee on your right-hand side to reach a fence by a wood. Go straight ahead for 80 metres through the wood, your direction 165 degrees. Emerging from the wood, go across the golf course (any golf balls will be coming at you from the left), your path between white posts. Exit the golf course via a narrow path to the left of a largish house, to arrive at a T-junction **[4]** where you *turn left* on the **North Downs Way**, an earth car road, your direction 70 degrees.

Keep left at a fork in the road in 20 metres, and carry on downwards past a house called Questors on your left-hand side. In 100 metres, at a crossing of the ways in the wood, you carry straight on for 800 metres, still on the North Downs Way, your direction 65 degrees towards the noise of traffic on the A3, ignoring ways off. Go under the A3 on a tarmac lane. In 40 metres, under a second bridge (this is the one designed by Lutyens), keep straight on, ignoring forks to the left to a road T-junction. *Turn left* on the road and, in 40 metres, *turn right* at a sign to Watts Gallery. The Watts Gallery Tea Shop is the alternative place to have lunch and when the **Watts Gallery** reopens, a visit is highly recommended. After visiting the tea shop or gallery, to get to **Watts Chapel**, return to the car road and *turn left* along it, your direction 230 degrees. In 160 metres you pass Coneycroft Farm on your left and in another 100 metres you reach the cemetery, with the chapel up above you on the hillside.

After visiting the chapel, return downhill through the cemetery to the road and *turn right* (in the reverse direction you came from). In 100 metres turn right at the footpath sign just before Coneycroft Farm. Keep to the right edge of the barn beyond the farm, following the path left at the end of the barn, then through a metal fieldgate and, in 10 metres, right through another metal fieldgate, following arrows. You are now on a concrete road, your direction 110 degrees.

Ignore ways off. At the end of the concrete, in 200 metres, by a fieldgate, *turn right* through a gate and then ignore a path immediately to your left to continue on a path due south. In 40 metres, you have the edge of the wood on your left-hand side. Carry on down the path for 600 metres, ignoring ways off, to come out of a wood on to a tarmac lane where you *turn left.* **[5]** In 10 metres, you *turn right,* past some houses on your left-hand side (one called Waterhaw), your direction now 200 degrees.

You arrive at the **Withies Inn**, the suggested pub lunch stop. After lunch, turn left on the road and continue ahead until you come to a T-junction with the main road, the B3000, called New Pond Road. *Go straight over (slightly to the right)* and continue on a lane called The Avenue, fringing the wood on its right-hand side, your direction 200 degrees.

In 250 metres **[6]**, *take the first right* on to a signposted bridleway to go into a wood. In 30 metres **[!]** *carry straight on* at a four-way signpost. In another 30 metres go ahead on a bridleway between hedges.

You pass a house on your left-hand side in 80 metres and your way merges with a farm track to carry straight on, your

direction 220 degrees. In a further 125 metres, by a large old ash tree to your left, *turn right,* following the blue bridleway signpost, your direction 265 degrees. A field edge is on your left. In 120 metres, follow the path as it bends sharp left to go due south, with the field hedge still on your left and a fence on your right.

At the top of the field, in 350 metres, turn right, and keep the edge of the wood on your left-hand side, on a footpath going due west. In 380 metres, *turn right* with the path for 15 metres and then *left again,* to continue gently uphill, your direction 215 degrees, ignoring two gates into a wood on your right. In 60 metres you pass a large house on your right and, 200 metres beyond it, you come out into its driveway and go straight on between houses, with Broomfeld Manor on your right. 100 metres past this manor, you come to the main road where, ignoring a yellow-marked footpath alternative uphill to your left, **[7]** *go straight over* on to another bridleway, your direction 250 degrees.

200 metres down this path (which is like a flood drain in wet weather) you go straight across another car road on to another path, your direction 230 degrees, soon between wooden fences on both sides. After 250 metres, you come to the end of the fence on your left-hand side and carry straight on downwards, ignoring a left turn.

In a further 60 metres, at a T-junction, *go left,* following a blue bridleway arrow, due south. Then in 15 metres **[!]** ignore a yellow-arrowed footpath uphill to your left (which goes off at 130 degrees) to keep on due south, still downwards, along a wide path.

In 450 metres, you pass a dry stone wall on your right-hand side, with a lovely 16th-century mansion house with varied window styles beyond it. **[8]** Just past this house *turn left* on a tarmac lane, your direction 145 degrees. In 80 metres you go through a wooden swing gate (a wooden fieldgate and the entrance to Milton Wood on its right-hand side).

Withies Inn.

In 150 metres go through a metal barrier, now alongside the River Wey.

In 500 metres, go through another metal barrier. In 40 metres, one metre before the start of a tarmac road and a housing estate, **[!]** follow the public footpath signpost *right,* your direction due south. In 75 metres go over a concrete bridge and straight on. In 10 metres ignore a footpath to the left and, in another 10 metres, *turn left* under the pylons, your direction 140 degrees, with the River Wey on your right-hand side. In 30 metres you pass under more pylons and *fork left,* your direction 170 degrees. In 40 metres, *continue to the left,* your direction 100 degrees, alongside the River Wey on your right.

In 120 metres you once more go under pylons and again in 55 metres. In a further 120 metres your way merges with a tarmac path coming from the left and you continue ahead. In 150 metres cross a stream on a bridge. In a further 280 metres, you cross a bridge with scaffolding pole railings. In 5 metres *go through a metal barrier across an entrance drive and straight on,* passing offices on your right-hand side, with the stream still on your left-hand side.

In 65 metres, at a tarmac road, *go right,* your direction 170 degrees. In 20 metres *go under the railway line.* 10 metres after the bridge, *fork right* on a signposted public footpath. In 110 metres, having kept parallel to the road, cross the river on a wooden bridge with wooden railings.

In 35 metres you are back on the main Borough Road and *go straight on,* in 65 metres reaching the entrance to the Church of St Peter and St Paul. If you want to go straight to the station without tea, turn right here down Deanery Place but, instead of following Station Road, take the passageway straight ahead. This takes you to the station.

For tea, *go left* up Church Street, which is a car road made of bricks (signposted 'To the High Street'), your direction 125 degrees. Going uphill, in 130 metres you come to the High Street, Godalming. Turn left and, in 140 metres, **Caffè Nero** is on the right-hand side of the road; continue a bit further and **Costa Coffee** is on your left. The Slug & Lettuce and Wetherspoon's are a little further on.

After tea, *retrace your steps to the church.* Go back down the High Street and, at the Old Town Hall, turn right down Church Lane. When you reach the church *go straight on to pick up the passageway ahead, leading to the station.*

At **Godalming railway station**, go under the subway for the London-bound platform.

Lunch & tea places

Watts Gallery Tea Shop *Down Lane, Compton, GU3 1DQ (01483 813590, www.wattsgallery.org.uk).* **Open** 10.30am-5pm Tue-Sun & bank hols. A good alternative for lunch, this tea room has remained open during the gallery's restoration.

Withies Inn *Compton, GU3 1JA (01483 421158, www.thewithiesinn.com).* **Open** 11am-11pm Mon-Sat; noon-4pm Sun. *Food served* noon-2.30pm, 7-9.30pm Mon-Sat; noon-2.30pm Sun. This popular pub – our suggested lunch stop – is about 7km (4.3 miles) into the walk. Large groups are advised to phone ahead to book.

On the High Street in Godalming, tea options include **Caffè Nero** and **Costa Coffee**; the **Slug & Lettuce** and **Wetherspoon's** open late at weekends and serve food daily until 10pm.

Walk 3
Netley to Botley

Southampton Water and the River Hamble.

Start: Netley station
Finish: Botley station

Length: 14.5km (9.0 miles)

Time: 4 hours 15 minutes. For the whole outing, including trains, ferry, sights and meals, allow 9 hours 45 minutes. In summer, allow an extra 30 minutes if you're visiting the Netley Chapel visitor centre and Manor Park Farm.

Transport: Take the train nearest to **9am** from **Waterloo** station to **Netley**, changing at Southampton Central (allow at least 5 minutes to change trains). Journey time is about 2 hours, depending on the connection. There are hourly direct trains back from **Botley** to Waterloo, which take about 1 hour 35 minutes. You can also return in the other direction, changing at Fratton, but this takes over 2 hours. Buy a day return to Netley, which in practice is accepted for the return journey.

OS Landranger Maps: 196
OS Explorer Maps: OL 22 & 119
Netley, map reference SU464086, is in **Hampshire**, 5km south-east of Southampton.

Toughness: 1 out of 10

Walk notes: The walk goes down through the Royal Victoria Country Park, past Netley Chapel, down to the shore at Southampton Water, with a dramatic view of the vast Fawley oil refineries opposite. Then the way is along the stony beach for a couple of kilometres (or, if you prefer, parallel to the beach for part of the way, in and out of scrub woodland), followed by an inland path through the woods and Hamble Common to the ferry in the delightful village of Hamble. The Warsash Ferry (0238 045 4512) runs on request from 9am-6pm daily (9am-4pm daily in winter, closed for Christmas week). It costs £1.50 per person and has space for a maximum of 12 people. On the other side of the river, the walk continues up alongside the River Hamble, with its marinas for yachtsmen and mudflats for birds – every variety from grey herons and

kingfishers to redshank and lapwing is here (binoculars are worth bringing). Lunch is in Lower Swanwick. Then it is up the other side of the river and through woodlands and fields to Manor Farm (01489 787055), an open farm run for visitors by the council. It has a tea room that opens daily (last orders 4.45pm) through the summer until the end of October. The route ends in a pleasant footpath called Lovers Lane, over a stream and up into Botley, where there is a newish tea room. It is then a not-very-pleasant kilometre along the main road to the station, which has a good pub opposite (across a very busy road) that serves food all afternoon.

Walk options: To shorten the walk, take one of the hourly trains (seven days a week, summer and winter) from Burlesdon after lunch, either

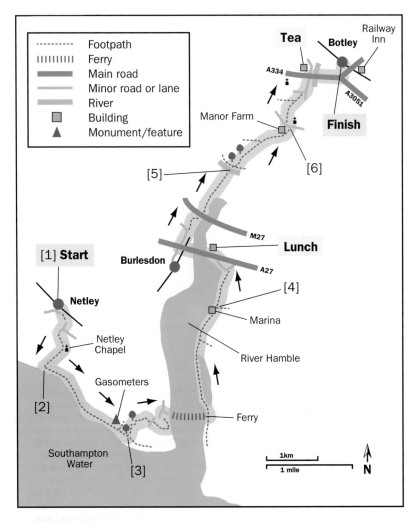

Legend:
- - - - - - - Footpath
|||||||| Ferry
━━━━ Main road
──── Minor road or lane
River
▢ Building
▲ Monument/feature

Tea

Botley

Railway Inn

A334

Manor Farm

Finish

[5]

[6]

M27

Lunch

A27

[1] **Start**

Burlesdon

Netley

[4]

Netley
Chapel

Marina

Gasometers

River Hamble

[2]

|||||||| Ferry

Southampton
Water

[3]

1km
1 mile

N

via Southampton or Fareham. Or, much earlier in the walk, you could get one of the regular buses from Hamble (nos.16 or 16a) to Netley station or Southampton town centre.

History: Netley Chapel, in the Royal Victoria Country Park, was at the centre of the Royal Victoria military hospital that opened in 1863 and was demolished in 1966. Now the Heritage Visitor Centre,

it houses an exhibition and a shop, and visitors can go up to the top of the tower. Phone 0238 045 5157 for opening hours and further information.

The hospital pier was begun in 1865 and was 190 yards long. Now, only the **pier head** remains. Inscribed on the spit slate to the right of the pier is a poem by Frank Thompson: 'Write on the stones no words of sadness,/ Only the gladness due/That we who asked the most of living,/Knew how to give it too.'

Manor Farm (01489 787055), with its wheelwright and blacksmith's forge (and tea room), is open daily until 5pm from Easter to 31 October, and only on Sundays (until dusk) from 1 November to Easter (and during February half-term). The building of the parish church next to the farm started in 1282. The church was damaged by a tree that fell in the 1700s.

Hamble.

Walk directions

[1] [Numbers in square brackets refer to the map]
Coming off platform 2 at **Netley station**, cross over the footbridge, go out of the station on the other side for 20 metres, then *turn left* on the road, signposted Royal Victoria Country Park, your direction 145 degrees. In 120 metres this becomes a narrower tarmac path as you continue to the left-hand side of house No.30, past a 'No Cycling' sign, soon with a steep wooded valley below to your right-hand side.

200 metres down this narrower path, *turn right* on a tarmac road, your direction 235 degrees, past No.4 Taylor Cottage on your left-hand side. In 100 metres, just before a noticeboard with a map of the Royal Victoria Park, **[!]** take the *middle fork road, slightly to your left,* bearing a 'No Entry' sign, your direction 165 degrees, marked 'Police and Residents Only'. In 120 metres, having ignored ways off, go between two wooden posts on the path, your direction 205 degrees, with the tower of Netley Chapel visible ahead to the south. In 70 metres, go through a wooden barrier and *turn left* on a tarmac road, your direction 145 degrees. In 60 metres, *take a right fork.*

In 80 metres, enter the park proper, with the Cedar Tea Room (open April to September 10am-5pm daily, and October to March 10am-4pm daily), a YMCA (which opened in 1940) and toilets to your right-hand side. Head for the chapel, due south, with a miniature railway track running parallel to your

path. In 200 metres you come to **Netley Chapel**, now the Heritage Visitor Centre.

From the front of the chapel, *head straight* on for 140 metres to Southampton Water, down the path between lamp posts, your direction 235 degrees.

At the pier head there, **[2]** *turn left* along the shore and, in 90 metres, by the sailing club entrance, continue along the beach for the next two kilometres to the pier, its pipes and crane visible in the distance.

On the way, you will in due course see ways up into the trees that border the shore. You can follow paths there (including 'Hamble Valley' and the 'Strawberry Trail') that run parallel to the beach, if you so prefer. These are, however, rather zig-zaggy paths and can be difficult to follow.

On reaching the oil terminal fencing, you will need to leave the beach up stone steps to follow the concrete path next to the fence, still along the shoreline.

Go down steps and so under the pier (with its oil pipelines) to continue straight on until you reach the end of the fence. Here you continue along the shoreline for another 100 metres (ignoring earlier ways off to the left that are unmarked in any case) until **[!]** you reach a wide grassy bank with a bench, which you 'climb' to leave the beach. You will notice (half left, on a bearing of 65 degrees) some 15 metres away a board marked 'Hamble Common – The Defence of the Realm'. If you were to go left for 20 metres, just after this board, you would come to a wooden gate with a kissing gate to its left (and a green arrow indicating the Solent Way). Do *not go this way* but instead, from the bench take the path going back towards the oil terminal, your direction 330 degrees.

In 60 metres ignore a kissing gate on your right-hand side. In 25 metres, by a post marked Hamble Common Circular Trail **[3]**, *bear right* with the path over an open grassy area, your direction 20 degrees, the refinery now close and visible to your left, as you re-enter a wood. Soon the path becomes clearer again and you follow the trail signs.

In 70 metres, cross over a two-plank footbridge. In 45 metres, *fork left* with the main trail. In a further 80 metres, by a footpath-signed post by a rustic wooden bench, go right (where to continue would lead you in a few metres to a rustic totem pole). **[!]** *Do not take the path going more or less back the way you came, on a bearing of 175 degrees, but take the less-obvious path bearing 140 degrees.*

Stay with this twisty trail (houses are visible to your left), in 180 metres going over wooden boards (by water) leading to a tarmac road. *Turn left* on this road, your direction 30 degrees. In 40 metres *turn right* into a car park (by a hidden sign for Hamble Common), your direction 120 degrees, to follow a path through the wood.

In 90 metres, ignore a 'Hamble Common' sign to the left and keep to the Strawberry Trail. In a further 90 metres, keep straight on over wooden boards, *then bear left*, now beside the **River Hamble**. In 50 metres, *bear left* with the path and over a covered water pipe. Ignore a kissing gate to your left-hand side; keep going through the copse, even when the path thins.

In 160 metres, as you leave the woods, go over boards past a noticeboard and follow the car track onwards. In 50 metres, by the 'No Entry' signs for cars, *turn right downhill* on the road, passing Oyster Cottage on your right and other **Hamble Village** houses, your direction 75 degrees.

By the water's edge, *go left* towards the white metal pier, at the end of which you can catch the distinctive pink-painted **Warsash Ferry** (for details, *see p28*).

Once over on the other side (after a five-minute ride), *turn left* and follow the riverside causeway, heading north, for 3km, through mudflats, ignoring ways off, passing the **Crableck Marina** (and Nautical Nellie's Café-Bar & Restaurant) **[4]**, making your way through yachts on the slipways. Keep parallel to the shore and on designated footpaths where indicated.

On reaching the tarmac road at the far end, *go left,* your direction 340 degrees, soon passing Swanwick Shore Public Hard to your left-hand side. Ignore ways off and you come in due course to the main road, the A27. Cross the road at the lights *and turn left,* your direction 305 degrees. In 200 metres along the road you come to the **Spinnaker** pub and restaurant, the suggested lunchtime stop.

Coming out of the pub, continue on the main road. In 150 metres, go over the bridge, and then under the railway bridge. At this point, those ending the walk here can turn left to **Bursledon station**, opposite the Yachtsman's pub. The main walk *turns right here*, up Blundell Lane, your direction 50 degrees.

In 250 metres, where the tarmac public road goes left, carry straight on through **Brixedone Farm** (a boat repair yard). Soon you go under the motorway and in 20 metres **[!]** *fork right* over a stile and *turn left,* your direction 50 degrees, to keep alongside the shore. In 60 metres go over another stile.

In 80 metres, pick up the footpath forking *half left diagonally* across the field, your direction 20 degrees. In 200 metres, you are beside a channel of water to your right-hand side that joins the river, your direction 330 degrees. In 80 metres go through a potentially muddy hedge gap and, in 50 metres, *go over a stile on your right-hand side* to cross the channel. **[5]**

At the other side, in 40 metres, at the T-junction, *turn right,* your direction

140 degrees. In 90 metres, by a bench at a fork, *turn left* on a path, your direction 50 degrees, following yellow-ringed wooden posts and occasional signs for Manor Farm.

In 600 metres, your path opens up and there is now a car-wide track with a wooden fence and field to your right-hand side, your direction 30 degrees.

Ignoring ways off, in 1km you come to Manor Park Farm. Here *bear leftwards* through the farm (ignoring the right fork with the large Manor Park sign). Head downhill, marked 'No Unauthorised Vehicles', past a post ringed blue and yellow, your direction 25 degrees, with buildings to your right-hand side. Soon you pass the fieldgate to the **Manor Farm** and café entrance on your right-hand side, and then the wheelwrights on your left-hand side, and soon a pond on your right-hand side; emerge through a wooden gate on to an earth road **[6]**, with **St Bartholomew's Church**, the old Botley parish church, to your right-hand side. *You go left on this road,* your direction 15 degrees.

In 60 metres, you come to a T-junction with the tarmac road, where you *go left,* your direction 300 degrees. In 120 metres, just 30 metres past the Old Rectory on your right-hand side, *go right* on a sign-posted footpath, your direction 30 degrees.

In 350 metres, ignore a concealed and overgrown metal kissing gate to your right-hand side. In a further 70 metres, *turn half right* at the end of the hedge on to a broad way across pumpkin fields, your direction 60 degrees.

This brings you through an old metal kissing gate and 25 metres down on to a tarmac road. You *turn right* for 10 metres, and *then left* through a metal kissing gate, your direction 35 degrees, on a footpath known as **Lovers Lane**.

In 40 metres, you cross water on a concrete bridge with metal railings and go up the other side, in a further 100 metres to a road, where you *turn right,* eastwards.

In 25 metres, *turn left* by the 'No Entry' sign, to go northwards, on Church Lane,

into the centre of **Botley**, coming to the main road in 200 metres.

On the other side of the road is **Delicieux Café**, the suggested tea stop. There are at least three pubs on or close to the main street, as well as a restaurant on the corner.

Coming out of the café, *turn left* on the main road to go (via the crossroads) up the A334. Your direction is 105 degrees for 1km, heading over the stream and past Botley Mills Craft and Business Centre on your left-hand side, to **Botley station**, ignoring the A3051 right turn. By the station is the **Railway Inn**.

The near platform is for Winchester, Basingstoke and London, although the opposite platform can get you to London via Fareham or Fratton.

Lunch & tea places

Spinnaker *Bridge Road, Lower Swanwick, SO31 7EB (01489 572123, www.thespinnakerinn.co.uk).* **Open** noon-11pm Mon-Thur; noon-midnight Fri, Sat; noon-10.30pm Sun. *Food served* noon-2.30pm, 5.30-9pm Mon-Fri; noon-9pm Sat, Sun. Some 8.5km (5.3 miles) into the walk, this is the suggested lunch stop. The pub serves food that is slightly above average in quality and often offers lunchtime and evening meal deals from Monday to Saturday, as well as bar snacks. The Spinnaker gets crowded on Sundays, so book in advance; book ahead on other days if you are a group of 10 or more.

Deliceux Café *6 High Street, Botley, SO30 2EA (01489 790463, http://delicieuxcafe.co.uk).* **Open** 8.30am-4pm daily. In season, an early tea can be had at the Manor Farm (*see above*), but otherwise this is the suggested tea place.

Railway Inn *Station Hill, Botley, SO30 2DN (01489 799746).* **Open** 9.30am-11pm Mon-Thur; 9.30am-1am Fri, Sat; 9.30am-10.30am Sun. *Food served* noon-9.30pm Mon-Thur; noon-10pm Fri, Sat; noon-8.30pm Sun. This more-than-adequate pub is conveniently situated opposite the station.

Walk 4

Pangbourne Circular

River Thames and Crays Pond.

Start and finish: Pangbourne station

Length: 13.6km (8.5 miles)

Time: 4 hours. For the whole outing, including trains, sights and meals, allow at least 7 hours 30 minutes.

Transport: Take the train nearest to **9.30am** from **Paddington** station to **Pangbourne**. Journey time is just over an hour on the direct, stopping service to Oxford. You can save about 15 minutes by taking a fast train to

Reading and changing there for the stopping service. Return trains are every half hour (hourly on Sundays), either direct or changing at Reading for the faster service.

OS Langranger Map: 175
OS Explorer Map: 171
Pangbourne, map reference SU633766, is in **Berkshire**, 8km west along the River Thames from Reading.

Toughness: 3 out of 10

Walk notes: Pangbourne and its companion Whitchurch (on the other side of the River Thames – and in Oxfordshire rather than Berkshire) are delightful villages, spoilt only by too much traffic. Passing on a toll bridge over the river, you come to St Mary's Church, with the route continuing along part of the Thames Path National Trail (which opened in 1996) past Coombe Park, to a wood with views down to the Thames. From there it is up through a nature reserve and Great Chalk Wood, from which the route heads to a pub for lunch by Crays Pond. After lunch you pass the entrance to Oratory Preparatory School and go through woods and fields, before heading back down through Whitchurch and into Pangbourne for tea.

Walk options: At point **[6]** in the walk you could head south to Coldharbour and reduce the length of this walk by about 3 km. Or you could call for a taxi from your

lunchtime pub. An alternative route, also starting at point **[6]**, takes you to another lunch pub option at Hill Bottom. For the directions and other walk options, refer to the Saturday Walkers' Club website (www.walkingclub.org.uk).

History: The earliest mention of **Pangbourne** is in a Saxon charter of the year 844 as Paegingaburnam (meaning 'streams of sons of Paega'). In 1919, DH Lawrence stayed in Pangbourne, commenting: 'Pleasant house – Hate Pangbourne – Nothing happens'. Kenneth Grahame, author of *The Wind in the Willows*, lived in Church Cottage, Pangbourne.

An Act of Parliament in 1792 allowed the building of **Whitchurch Toll Bridge**, designed to replace the ferry. The ten proprietors were given the right to charge tolls – for instance, one halfpenny for every sheep and lamb. The present iron bridge of 1902 replaced two previous wooden toll bridges. Today, pedestrians cross the bridge toll-free; the 2010 toll charge for cars is 40p.

St Mary's Church in Whitchurch dates from the 12th century. St Birynius is said to have landed at the ferry crossing at Whitchurch and, on seeing how fine the place was, decided to build a church there.

Walk directions

[1] [Numbers in square brackets refer to the map]
From platform 1 at **Pangbourne railway station** go down into the tunnel, turn left and go up steps on the other side to platform 2, exit the station and *turn right* downhill along the station approach road, your direction 100 degrees.

In 100 metres at a T-junction with the A329 road, cross over the road and continue straight on along a car-wide road, The Wharf, signposted as a public footpath, your direction 60 degrees.

In 90 metres you cross the Pang, a tributary river, and, with Waterside House ahead of you, *turn left* on a path between railings, with the River Thames on your left-hand side. In 100 metres cross a gravel road to continue straight on, between walls. In a further 25 metres, at a T-junction with the B471 road, turn left, your direction 55 degrees, to pass the Boathouse Surgery on your left-hand side.

In 110 metres you begin to cross the **Whitchurch Toll Bridge** on the River Thames. 5 metres beyond the toll booth on the far side of the bridge **[2]** *turn left* on the signposted Thames Path, up a drive beside a gatepost marked 'The Mill. Private Drive. Church Cottages', your direction due west, with the river on your left-hand side.

In 65 metres, just past Church Cottages on your right, *turn right* on to a tarmac path marked 'Thames Path and Footpath to the Church', your direction 5 degrees, to enter **St Mary's Church**, Whitchurch.

Coming out of the church, go straight ahead through its lychgate and keep straight on, now on a tarmac road (or if not visiting the church, pass the church

and its lychgate on your left-hand side and turn half right on to the tarmac road). Bear right with this road and in 100 metres rejoin the B471 road where you *turn left,* and follow the Thames Path sign, your direction due north.

In 45 metres you pass the Greyhound pub on your right-hand side. Keep ahead along the road, uphill, in 200 metres passing Manor Road on your left and in a further 155 metres passing Hardwick Road on your right. *Veer left* with the road as it narrows and goes more steeply uphill and in 110 metres *turn left* on a bridleway signposted 'Thames Path – Goring 3.5 miles' and 'Hartslock Bridleway'. You now keep ahead along this bridleway, a surfaced road, for some 1.2km, initial direction 275 degrees.

In more detail: The road soon goes gently uphill with a fence and hedge on your left and a fence and fields to your right. In 350 metres you pass the entrance to Avoca Farm on your right and in a further 130 metres you pass a turn on your right to Long Acre Farm. Keeping ahead, the road dips and rises again and in 160 metres you pass Rivendell Farm on your right. In a further 200 metres you begin to get a good view of **Coombe Park** (as marked on the OS map) over to your left.

Stay on this road for a further 350 metres, passing cottages and farms, then as the road swings left into Hartlock Farm **[!]** leave the road **[3]** to follow a blue arrow straight on (to the left of a metal fieldgate), your direction 325 degrees, *to go down* a set of 23 wide earth steps. At the bottom of the steps keep ahead along an earth path and in 80 metres you go up another flight of earth steps, 16 in total, to continue ahead, uphill, between wire fences and hedges.

In 250 metres you enter Hartslock Wood by a 'Private Woodland' sign and a Thames Path blue arrow. Now follow Thames Path blue arrows on posts along this path above the River Thames (below on your left) as the path winds its way through the wood, along the hillside, gradually descending towards the river.

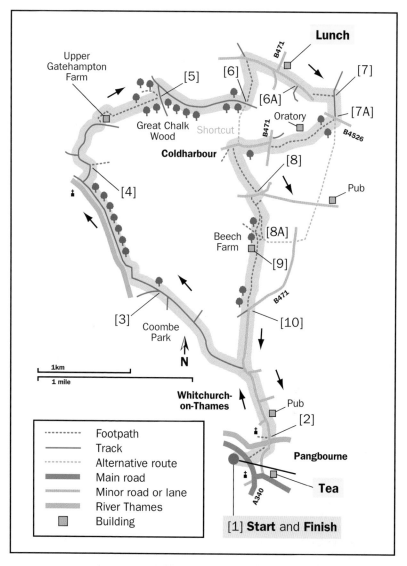

In 250 metres you begin to have fine views of the river on your left. In a further 700 metres you pass a pillbox on your left-hand side. In a further 250 metres, and 5 metres before the end of the wood, by a blue arrow on a post, and with a large beech tree overhanging the

way, **[!]** *turn right uphill,* quite steeply, your direction 20 degrees. In 20 metres go through a metal swing gate to exit the wood into **Hartslock Nature Reserve**; there is an information board about the nature reserve on your left.

Turn right and ascend steeply up a small hill, your direction 60 degrees. In 110 metres, at the top of the hill, you pass a bench on your right, from which there are fine views of the Thames below. Now drop down the other side of the hill on a clear grassy path and at the bottom, in 100 metres, you exit the reserve through a wooden swing gate to the left of a metal fieldgate, to *turn left* on to an earth road, your direction 285 degrees. **[4]**

The road swings to the right and after 150 metres you come out to a T-junction with a tarmac road, where you *turn right,* uphill, your direction 30 degrees.

In 400 metres, as the road emerges from woods, **[!]** *turn left* over a stile marked with yellow arrows, to follow the public footpath, your direction 70 degrees.

In 20 metres cross another stile to pass wooden stables on your right. Now bear half left uphill over grass, in the direction of yellow arrows and, in 35 metres, *bear right* to go between fences, following more yellow arrows, your direction 70 degrees. In a further 30 metres, **[!]** with a wooden fence panel directly ahead of you, turn *sharp left* to follow the path around an earth pile, soon joining a farm track coming in from your left.

Keep on the farm track around the earth pile but, before you reach the farmyard to **Upper Gatehampton Farm** (so marked on the OS map), cross a stile on your left and *turn half left* to go diagonally across a field, your direction 60 degrees, making for a stile visible in the distance.

In 230 metres, cross over this stile into **Great Chalk Wood** (so marked on the OS map) and in 5 metres turn half right to follow the footpath, your direction 85 degrees. In 35 metres cross a path (marked 'Permitted Footpath – Not a Public Right of Way – Persons may use at own risk') and keep ahead on the public footpath, now a broader way, following yellow arrows.

[5] In 150 metres cross a car-wide track to continue ahead, now downhill. In a further 125 metres, at a T-junction with another path, and with a footpath post on your left with blue and yellow arrows, *turn right,* downhill, your direction 115 degrees.

In 45 metres, at another path T-junction *turn left* (by hinges for a missing swing gate), following a blue bridleway arrow, your direction 5 degrees, downhill on a path with an uneven footbed. In 105 metres, at the bottom of the slope, at the edge of the wood, cross a path and *veer right,* now gently uphill, your initial direction 100 degrees.

In 400 metres go through a wooden swing gate marked **Bottom House Farm**. In a further 100 metres, just after you pass a small wooden horse stable in the paddock on your right-hand side, go through another wooden swing gate. In 80 metres you pass the farm cottage on your left-hand side and keep ahead, now on the farm driveway. In 100 metres you pass through the main entrance gate to the farm.

Continue along the farm access road through woodland, gently uphill, your direction 75 degrees. In 350 metres, as you emerge from the woodland, before reaching a large house on the left and 5 metres before a bridleway to the right, *turn left uphill,* to follow a public footpath marked by a yellow arrow on a post. **[6]**

[The **shortcut to Coldharbour** starts here: Take the bridleway to the right and follow the path uphill, then the road, to rejoin the main directions by Laurel Cottage.]

Continuing on the main route, in 15 metres *fork right* to follow the path round with the fence on your left. In 100 metres bend *sharp left* with the path, between hedges, your direction 20 degrees.

In 160 metres, at the end of the hedges, you emerge on to a path to go across an open field, your direction now 345 degrees. In 250 metres cross a stile to exit the field on to the B4526 road where you *turn right.*

In 500 metres you come to a road junction with a pond on your right-hand side. The **White Lion**, Crays Pond, is just off to your left. This pub is the suggested lunchtime stop.

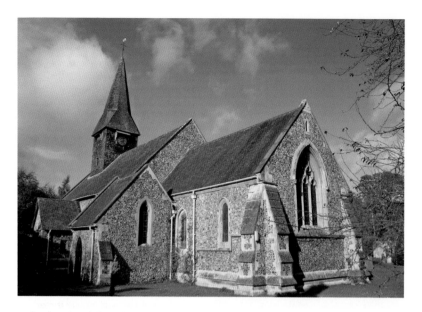

Coming out of the pub on to the tarmac road, turn left and, in 50 metres, turn left on to the B4526 road, your direction 130 degrees. In 225 metres you pass on your right-hand side the path next to the gated exit road from the Oratory School. **[6A]**

In 80 metres, and 10 metres beyond a metal barrier on your left, **[!]** *turn left* on to a footpath into woodland. In 5 metres, at a path T-junction, turn right, your direction 80 degrees. Now follow white arrows on trees as the path winds downhill through woods.

In 400 metres you pass to the left of an earth-aggregate mound (with new fencing around its perimeter). **[7]** At its end, you reach a path and car-wide track crossing where you *turn right* on to the car-wide earth track (named as Eastfield Lane on the OS map), uphill, your direction due south. In 200 metres the track comes out through anti-fly-tipping barriers on to the B4526 road, which you cross.

[7A] On the other side of the B4526 road, **[!]** *take the right-hand footpath of two,* signposted to Coldharbour, your direction 220 degrees. In 30 metres you reach an open space with a concrete base.

Keep ahead over it and in 80 metres you have a rusty iron fence on your right as you head up through the wood in a south-westerly direction.

Ignore ways off and in 300 metres go through a metal kissing gate to leave the wood. Keep ahead along the right-hand edge of a field (Coombe End Farm) to follow a fence on your right-hand side. In a further 100 metres bear right with the fence to follow a yellow public footpath arrow on a post.

In 300 metres go over a tree-trunk stile to the right of a metal fieldgate, to come out on to a car-wide earth road, your direction 260 degrees. In 150 metres, pass a timber-framed house on your right-hand side and go through a metal swing gate to the left of a metal fieldgate, to come out on to the B471 (with the entrance to Oratory Preparatory School some 20 metres over to your right).

Cross over the road and continue along the tarmac road opposite, your direction still 260 degrees. In 125 metres you pass under mini pylons. In a further 225 metres you pass a bridleway on your right-hand side beside Laurel Cottage. **[!]**

[The **shortcut to Coldharbour** rejoins here **[!]**.]

Turn left and in 85 metres, as the road bends to the right and opposite Coldharbour Farm, go through a new metal kissing gate on your left-hand side and take the footpath in the direction of Whitchurch, your bearing 165 degrees, across an open field.

Pass to the left of a clump of trees and in 300 metres, at a field boundary, go through a new metal kissing gate into the next field. In 200 metres you cross a stile to emerge on to a tarmac road opposite a house called Pine Paddock. **[8]**

Turn right on the road, your direction 250 degrees. In 75 metres, by a footpath sign to Whitchuch, *turn left* through a wooden swing gate to the left of a wooden fieldgate to Boundary Farm, down a earth car road, your direction 165 degrees.

In 115 metres you pass the farm and in 20 metres, as the earth road swings to the right towards a hay barn some 25 metres away, **[!]** *turn left* into the wood, following a yellow arrow on a post, your initial direction 145 degrees.

Follow the path as it winds through the wood. In 100 metres the path becomes enclosed by chestnut paling fences on either side. Continue along the enclosed path as it meanders on through the wood, following yellow arrows.

In 300 metres go through a metal kissing gate and come out to a T-junction with a path, where you *turn left* following a Chiltern Way sign, your direction 150 degrees, keeping close to the left-hand edge of the wood.

In 135 metres leave the wood by a metal kissing gate. **[8A] [!]** Keep ahead over a field with its fence on your right-hand side, your direction 170 degrees.

In 95 metres go through a wooden swing gate and over the concrete driveway of **Beech Farm** (so marked on the OS map). **[9] [!]** Beware of a boisterous dog here, which has bitten walkers in recent times. **[!]** Pass between a gap in the trees and follow the footpath sign around to the right, along the edge of a lawn, with a fence and hedge on your right-hand side, your direction 195 degrees.

In 40 metres pass through a metal kissing gate with an metal fieldgate on its left-hand side to continue on a wide grassy path between fences, your direction now 200 degrees.

In 260 metres go through another metal kissing gate to follow the field edge on your right, with open fields to your left. Keep ahead, roughly parallel to a power line some 65 metres over to your left, along a path that in winter can be muddy.

In 500 metres, as the power line converges with your way, you pass a pylon on your left (where the electricity cable goes underground) and go through a metal kissing gate. Drop down a woodland path, keeping ahead (slightly right) and in 75 metres you come down on to the B471 road. **[10]**

Continue on the B471 into Pangbourne, your direction 190 degrees. In 40 metres you pass Whitchurch War Memorial on your right-hand side. A short distance beyond this you can pick up the path parallel to the B471 and above it, on the left-hand side. 350 metres along this path, you drop down to rejoin the road (opposite the Thames Path, which you took on your outward journey).

Opposite the turning on the left to Hardwick Road you pass the interesting **Modern Artists Gallery** (0118 984 5893) on your right-hand side: They are open to walkers dropping in and are tolerant of muddy boots.

Retrace your morning route, passing the **Greyhound Inn** on your left-hand side. Cross back over Whitchurch Toll Bridge and pass Pangbourne Working Men's Club on your right-hand side. Go under the railway bridge and in 50 metres, at the mini roundabout junction with the A329 (Reading Road), you pass the **George Hotel** on your right-hand side, a possible tea/late meal stop. Turn left along Reading Road and in 25 metres you come to **Lou La Belle Café** on your left-hand side, the suggested tea place.

Coming out of the café, turn right, cross over the mini roundabout and keep ahead, in 85 metres coming to another mini roundabout at the junction with the A329. The **Elephant Hotel** – another possible tea/late meal stop – is opposite. If you turn left, you come to the **Cross Keys** pub on your left-hand side in 60 metres.

But to get to the railway station, at the road junction opposite the Elephant, *turn right,* to pass the Parish Council Offices and Village Hall on your left-hand side (with a useful WC block in the front of the car park).

In a further 100 metres, just before the railway bridge, *turn left* up the lane to **Pangbourne railway station**. Pass under the tunnel to reach platform 2 for trains to London. (Alternatively, you can walk under the railway bridge and take the access road on your left-hand side, which leads to the station. Platform 2 is now on your near side.)

Lunch & tea places

White Lion *Goring Heath, Crays Pond, RG8 7SH (01491 680471, www.thewhite lioncrayspond.com).* **Open/food served**
8am-midnight Mon-Fri; 10am-midnight Sat; 10am-10pm Sun. The suggested lunchtime stop is here, some 8km (5 miles) into the walk; the pub reopened in September 2010 after a year's closure. It offers a good choice of main meals, sharing platters and sandwiches.

Sun Inn *Hill Bottom, Whitchurch, RG8 7PU (0118 984 2260).* **Open** noon-3pm, 6-11pm Mon-Thur; noon-midnight Fri, Sat; noon-11pm Sun. *Food served* noon-2.30pm, 6-9pm Mon-Sat; noon-7pm Sun. This homely pub makes a good alternative lunch stop, serving home-cooked food – main meals or light fare – at reasonable prices. The surroundings are comfortable, and there are outdoor dining areas. The pub is in Hill Bottom, however, so you'll need to download directions from the Saturday Walkers' Club website (www.walkingclub.org.uk).

George Hotel *The Square, Pangbourne, RG8 7AJ (0118 984 2237, www.thegeorge hotelpangbourne.com).* **Open** 10am-11pm Mon-Thur; 10am-midnight Fri, Sat; 10am-10.30pm Sun. *Food served* 10am-7.30pm daily. One of several tea or late meal stops in Pangbourne.

Opposite the George Hotel, a **Co-op convenience store** can provide you with sandwiches and snacks.

Lou La Belle Café *3-5 Reading Road, Pangbourne, RG8 7LR (0118 984 2246, www.loulabellefinefoods.co.uk).* **Open** 8am-5pm Mon-Sat. Another of the possible tea stops in Pangbourne.

Elephant Hotel *Church Road, Pangbourne, RG8 7AR (0118 984 2244, www.elephanthotel.co.uk).* **Open** 11am-11pm Mon-Thur, Sun; 11am-midnight Fri, Sat. *Food served* noon-3pm, 6-10pm daily. Another option for late refreshments, the Elephant serves cream teas from 3pm to 6pm daily.

Cross Keys *Church Road, Pangbourne, RG8 7AR (0118 984 3268).* **Open** noon-10.30pm Mon-Wed, Sun; noon-midnight Thur; noon-1.30am Fri, Sat. *Food served* noon-3pm, 6-9.30pm Mon-Sat; noon-6pm Sun. Another possibility for tea or a late meal in Pangbourne.

Walk 5

Great Missenden to Amersham

Little Missenden and Penn Wood.

Start: Great Missenden station
Finish: Amersham station

Length: 16.3km (10.1 miles)

Time: 5 hours. For the whole outing, including trains, sights and meals, allow 8 hours.

Transport: Take the train nearest to **9.55am** from **Marylebone** station to **Great Missenden** (journey time 42 minutes). Great Missenden is one stop outside Transport for London (TfL) Zone 9 and Network Card holders can get a discounted TfL Zones 1-9 travelcard at weekends and on bank holidays from any Underground ticket office up to a week in advance. You then only need to buy a one-stop extension from Chiltern Railways

to travel from Great Missenden to Amersham.
   This approach has the advantage that on the return journey from **Amersham** you can use the four Underground trains an hour (45 minutes to Baker Street) as well as the twice hourly Chiltern Railway trains to Marylebone (journey time 39 minutes; note that there's only one train an hour on Sundays). By contrast, a normal day return to Great Missenden is only valid on Chiltern Railways.

OS Langranger Map: 165
OS Explorer Maps: 172 & 181
Great Missenden, map reference SP893013, is in **Buckinghamshire**, 8km north-west of Amersham.

Toughness: 5 out of 10

Walk notes: Only 40 minutes from London by train, this route makes an easy outing at any time of year, although note that in January and February one section of the bridleway just before point [6] is invariably flooded. The route is more open than most Chilterns walks, but there is one large beech wood, Penn Wood, which produces fine autumn colours. Other attractions include four interesting churches, the ancient village of Little Missenden, and Amersham's surprisingly unspoilt old town, which is approached over a ridge with fine views. After tea, it is a

20-minute walk up through a wood to reach the station.

Walk options: The easiest way to shorten the walk is to carry on along the road past the Crown Inn at point **[5]** and follow the well-waymarked South Bucks Way into old Amersham, a distance of 3.6km (2.2 miles) compared to 9.4km (5.8 miles) by the main walk route. The only disadvantage of this shortcut is that it is close to the busy A413 throughout. It does, however, reduce the overall walk length to 10.5km (6.5 miles).

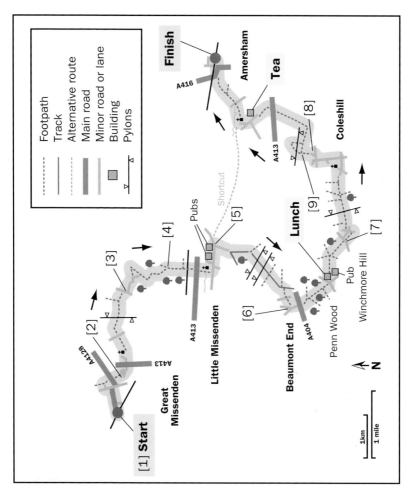

There is an hourly bus into Amersham from point **[6]**, but this is a disappointing place to finish the walk. Another option would be to get a taxi from one of the lunch pubs.

History: The **Parish Church of St Peter & St Paul** in Great Missenden was built mainly in the 14th century. It is located on a hill outside the town because, when it was built, Great Missenden was only a collection of scattered farms and the hilltop location made a good focal point.

St John the Baptist Church in Little Missenden has a giant 13th-century mural of St Christopher carrying the Christ child across the waters. Part of the church was built in the 10th century. The gatepost is in memory of the Dunkirk evacuation of 1940.

All Saints Church in Coleshill is a neo-Gothic church designed by George Edmund Street, whose work was praised by Betjeman. The stone for the church, completed in 1856, was brought by river to Windsor and then by cart.

The building of the **Parish Church of St Mary** in Amersham started in the early 1100s. The window glass is mainly from the 19th century.

Walk directions

[1] [Numbers in square brackets refer to the map]
Coming off the train, cross the footbridge and, leaving **Great Missenden station** building, *turn left,* your direction 20 degrees. At the T-junction, *turn right downhill,* your direction 50 degrees.

In 60 metres, at the next T-junction, *go left,* your direction 320 degrees (to the right is the High Street).

In 25 metres, *turn right* on to Walnut Close, your direction 50 degrees. In 60 metres, at the end of this, take the tarmac path going to the left of the double garage of house number 18.

In 40 metres ignore a footpath to the left and a car park to the right to keep straight on, initially with a green metal fence to your left. In a further 100 metres, pass through a metal kissing gate and *turn right,* your direction 160 degrees.

In 40 metres go through a metal kissing gate to the right of a wooden fieldgate. Cross the main road and continue *straight on,* using a tarmac path down the left-hand side of a green space, signposted South Bucks Way, your direction 160 degrees.

In 300 metres you emerge on to a road, with a residential cul-de-sac to your right. Keep straight on and in 70 metres you come out into an oval-shaped green. **[2]**

Turn right to follow the edge of the green for 40 metres until you are in front of a brick and flint house on its far side (bearing 160 degrees from the point you entered the oval-shaped green). Pass to the *right* of this house *up a tarmac lane* signposted South Bucks Way (Church Lane, though the signpost is not that visible; the first cottage on the left is called The Pound).

Follow this lane as it climbs uphill. In 200 metres, ignore the South Bucks Way footpath off down to the right to continue on a bridge over the A413 to the **Parish Church of St Peter & St Paul**.

If you want to visit the church, the entrance is on its left-hand side. Otherwise, *pass to the right* of the church. 30 metres up its right-hand side, look out for a rusted kissing gate in the fence to the right (it may be hidden by foliage in summer).

[!] *Turn right* through this kissing gate and then *turn left uphill,* ignoring a faint path straight ahead if you can see one. Aim to the right of a clump of three large trees 80 metres ahead and towards an electricity pylon high on the ridge in the far distance (again, this may be less visible in summer), your direction 80 degrees.

In 450 metres, at the top of the field, go over a stile (there's a nice view backwards here), across a car-wide track, and over another stile to continue in roughly the same direction as before (now 100 degrees) across an open field, heading to the right of the nearest pylon ahead.

In 250 metres, go over a stile to continue with a hedge on your left-hand side, your direction 130 degrees. In 250 metres, pass under electricity pylons and in 300 metres, at the far end of the field, cross another stile to continue straight on, now with the hedge on your right.

In 160 metres, go over another stile to continue along the field edge, with a house visible ahead. In 100 metres, before you get to this house, turn right over a stile, and carry on down the path, with a garage shed on your right-hand side. In 50 metres, you emerge on to a road opposite Rowen Farm, and *turn right,* your direction 200 degrees. **[3]**

Pass on your right the timber-framed Chapel Farm, which has lighthouse lamps on either side of its front door. 20 metres beyond this, *turn left* on a concrete track, signposted Circular Walk, your direction 100 degrees.

Follow this track for 300 metres all the way to the bottom of the dip, ignoring ways off, and carry on uphill as it bears right and starts to climb again, by which time it has become a gravel track.

In another 180 metres, at the top of the hill and just before the wood ends (right), ignore a stile to the left, but *turn right* opposite it, following an arrow on a post, on a path just inside the woodland edge, your direction 220 degrees.

In 60 metres *veer left* to leave the *wood* (there's a decaying stile, but it may not last long) and *turn right* along the edge of a field, with the wood now to your right.

Keep to the edge of this field as it *turns left* in 80 metres (it can be very muddy here in winter) and *then right* in another 40 metres. In another 30 metres, at a footpath post, *veer left* on a faint path between fields, your direction 120 degrees.

In 60 metres, just before you get to the wood edge on the far side, *turn right* along the field edge, your direction 200 degrees. Keep to this field edge, with the wood to your left, as it descends the hill.

In 300 metres, where the wood edge ends at a line of mini pylons, *turn left* with the path across the open field, your direction 130 degrees. In 150 metres, stay on a car-wide track upwards into the wood, your direction due south.

In 200 metres, you come to a track crossroads [4] with a sign 40 metres ahead saying 'Strictly private: No thoroughfare' and large farm sheds beyond. *Turn right here,* your direction 210 degrees.

Stay on this track, ignoring ways off, for 400 metres, until you come to a car-wide wooden barrier. Here *turn right* to cross the railway on a footbridge. On the far side, follow the path to emerge into an open field in 30 metres. Carry straight on downhill, heading just to the left of the first mini pylon, your direction due south.

In 150 metres, cross the A413 with great care and go over a stile on the other side to continue down the left-hand edge of the field. In 90 metres, cross a stream on a concrete footbridge. In 140 metres, cross a stile and *turn left* on the road, into **Little Missenden**. Immediately on your left is **St John the Baptist Church**, which is well worth a look inside.

Carry on along the road, past the church. In 100 metres, ignore a road to the right, and in a further 20 metres ignore Taylors Lane to the left. In a further 90 metres you pass the **Red Lion pub**, a possible early lunch stop.

Carrying on along the road, in 170 metres you pass Missenden House on your left: ignore a stile and footpath on the right here. In another 250 metres, the **Crown** pub is on your left, another possible early lunch stop. **[5]**

[[!] For the **shortcut to Amersham**, continue along the road for about 85 metres and take the footpath on the right-hand side, signposted South Bucks Way.]

Your onward, main route is to *turn right* on the bridleway 10 metres before the Crown, between Jug Cottage and the village hall, your direction south. In 60 metres, you pass Tobys Lane Farm on your left-hand side.

You now stay on this bridleway between hedges all the way up the hill, ignoring ways off. At the top of the hill, the bridleway levels out, with open fields either side. 1km from Little Missenden it passes under a line of electricity pylons and, after a further 250 metres, another. The section after this second set of pylons seems to be invariably flooded in January and February, though it can be passed with difficulty by invading nearby fields.

400 metres after the second line of electricity pylons, ignore footpaths left and right (a metal fieldgate to the left, a wooden fence to the right). But in another 250 metres, with the main road not far ahead, you come to a second crosspaths. [!] Here there are metal gates left and right and you *turn right,* following the footpath arrow across a field on a slightly raised bank, your direction 250 degrees. A main road, the A404, can be seen and heard away to your left.

In 250 metres, cross a stile and continue on past a white bungalow. In another 200 metres, you come to a driveway between houses and, 90 metres later, this comes to a tarmac road, with the gates of Beamond

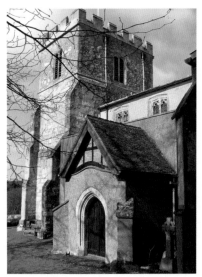

Lodge ahead of you. **[6]** *Turn left* on this road, your direction 200 degrees.

In 70 metres, go straight on at a road junction. [To **shorten the walk** by getting the bus to Amersham mentioned in Walk options, turn *sharp right* here, to find the bus stop on the right-hand side of the road.] To continue with the main route, in 50 metres cross the A404 with care, to enter **Penn Wood**.

Keep *straight on* into the wood, ignoring a fork to the left in 60 metres, and passing through a wooden gate to the left of a wooden fieldgate in another 30 metres. In 40 metres more, ignore a fork to the right.

After this, keep straight on through Penn Wood. This path is broad and muddy in winter, and it can be a bit of an obstacle course. Be careful when walking round the morasses of mud not to stray off the path.

In 1km, you come to the end of the wood and a road where you *go left*. The **Squirrel**, the suggested lunchtime pub, is straight ahead across the green.

If you're not stopping at the Squirrel, keep to the road along the right-hand edge of the green. In 80 metres, *turn right* on a road signposted to Winchmore Hill and Amersham. (To reach this point from the

Squirrel, come out of the pub and turn left for 40 metres, and then left on the road to Winchmore Hill.)

The **Hit or Miss Inn** is 100 metres along this road on the left. To continue the walk, however, in 30 metres, *turn left* up a signposted footpath.

In 80 metres, cross a stile, and curve right along the edge of an overgrown open space, with buildings to your right. In 180 metres, cross a stile and carry straight on across an open field, your direction 90 degrees.

In 100 metres, at a path junction, *turn half right* towards a wood. Enter the wood and go straight on, with its edge to your right, your direction 120 degrees. In 300 metres, exit the wood by a metal kissing gate, and *go half right* across a field, your direction 150 degrees.

In 130 metres go through a metal kissing gate and carry straight on. In 170 metres, you come to a tarmac road with a bus shelter opposite (it isn't served by any useful buses). **[7]**

Cross the road to continue straight on up an open space, keeping the hedge to your left, your direction 140 degrees. In 160 metres, merge with a tarmac road. You are now in the village of **Winchmore Hill**.

Keep on along the road, passing the Memorial Hall on the left in 100 metres. 40 metres beyond this, *turn sharp left* down a road called The Hill, signposted to Amersham.

In 80 metres, opposite the Methodist church on your left, **[!]** *turn right* on a signposted footpath, your direction 80 degrees. In 130 metres, keep straight on along the right-hand edge of a field, and in 200 metres carry on down the right-hand edge of the next field.

In 400 metres, enter a wood and keep straight on along a car-wide track, your direction 100 degrees. In 80 metres, you emerge from the wood and keep straight on, heading to the right of a copse 120 metres ahead.

Beyond the copse keep straight on for 130 metres to cross a stile. Beyond this, follow the path with a wooden fence and open field to your left.

In 200 metres, pass through a gate and keep straight on up a broad grassy strip. In 80 metres this becomes a concrete drive. In 80 metres more, cross a stile to the right of a wooden fieldgate and carry on down a gravel driveway between gardens. In 80 metres, go through a gate and, in 60 metres more, *turn left* on to a road.

On your right is **All Saints Church, Coleshill**. Carrying on past the church, in 80 metres merge with the inventively named Village Road to your right, and carry straight on, passing Coleshill First School on your right.

In 500 metres you pass a bus stop and Coleshill Cottage on your left-hand side and Village House to the right. Stay on the road and, in a further 150 metres, you come to a three-way junction, where you *fork right* with the main road, Tower Road. **[8]**

In 40 metres, **[!]** *fork left* up a concrete road, marked Cherry Tree Farm (*not* the tarmac drive to its left), your direction 30 degrees. In 150 metres, where the concrete ends, continue *straight on* along a path between fences, your direction still 30 degrees. In 70 metres, go over a stile.

In 40 metres, the path emerges into a field. Keep on along its right-hand edge. In 120 metres, cross a stile and, in 20 metres more, emerge into a field, with a view of Amersham (and a large electricity pylon) ahead. **[9]**

Bear right before the electricity pylon, keeping the field edge to your right-hand side, your direction 60 degrees. In 160 metres, at the end of the field (marked by a slight ridge), keep on down *the right-hand edge* of the next field, on a bank raised above the field to the right.

In 200 metres, *turn sharp right* where the bank ends, heading to the left of a lone tree at the bottom edge of the field (or, if you prefer, just to the left of a circular tower on the hill behind), your direction 160 degrees. In 90 metres, at the field edge, *turn left,* your direction 10 degrees, soon passing to the left of a line of bushes.

Follow this path along the valley bottom, with a ditch to your right. In 600 metres, houses start to the right and, in another 300 metres, you come to the far corner of the field.

Here *turn left* on a tarmac path, following a footpath sign. In 40 metres, cross the A413 on a footbridge. 30 metres after the bridge, at a tarmac path T-junction, *turn left.*

In 100 metres, ignore a road right, and *veer left* into a field. Immediately *turn right* down its edge, heading for the tiled roofs of Old Amersham ahead, your direction 310 degrees. In 40 metres, *curve right* on a faint path, heading to the right of the church tower, to come to a fieldgate 120 metres away, your direction north.

Pass through a gate to the right of the fieldgate and *turn left* on a road. In 60 metres this brings you into **Old Amersham**. *Turn right* on the road (unless you want to visit the **Saracen's Head Inn**, a possible tea stop, which is to your left).

Passing the **Nags Head** on your left, the road brings you in 100 metres to a junction with a roundabout with the churchyard ahead. The suggested tea stop, **Seasons Café Deli**, is immediately to your left on this corner.

For other tea choices and a look at the picturesque main street of Old Amersham, turn left: The **Crown Inn Hotel** is in 50 metres on your left, and the **Kings Arms** another 100 metres further along. Alternatively, turning right from the roundabout facing the church brings you in 100 metres on the left to **Il Bertorelli**.

Your onward route, however, is to cross the road and **[!]** *take the path directly across the road* from Seasons into the churchyard, your direction 20 degrees. (If it is dark by this point, you can instead follow the road that starts in front of the old market building, 70 metres to the left (west) at this point, and climbs uphill. This brings you up to the railway bridge mentioned in the directions below.)

Passing to the right of the **Parish Church of St Mary** on the path, you come to a tarmac lane and *turn right,* with a stream on your left, your direction 80 degrees. In 60 metres, at a T-junction with a cemetery ahead, *turn left* and in 30 metres *turn right* on a tarmac path, *uphill*, with the cemetery wall to your right and allotments to your left.

In 250 metres, you enter **Parsonage Wood** and keep *straight on*, ignoring all turnings off and keeping some 25 metres from the edge of the wood and the road on your left-hand side.

In 500 metres, with the railway bridge visible some 100 metres ahead, **[!]** *take an unmarked right fork*. In 100 metres, *turn right* along the railway embankment. (If you miss the fork, easy to do in summer, go to the railway bridge and turn right before it on a footpath.)

The path by the railway embankment passes houses on the right and, in 70 metres, comes to a main road. Cross the road carefully, *go left* under the railway bridge and *turn right* just beyond it for **Amersham station**, 60 metres away. The near platform has trains to London.

Lunch & tea places

On this walk there's a great choice of pubs, all of which have some outdoor seating.

Red Lion *Little Missenden, Amersham, HP7 0QZ (01494 862876, www.redlion lm.co.uk)*. **Open** 11am-2.30pm, 5.30pm-midnight Mon-Thur; 11am-midnight Fri-Sun. *Food served* noon-2.30pm, 5.30-9pm daily. Some 5.5km (3.4 miles) into the walk, Little Missenden's pair of characterful old pubs are good for slower walkers or late starters, but their food offering is more limited than other pubs on the route.

Crown *Little Missenden, Amersham, HP7 0RD (01494 862571, www.the-crown-little-missenden.co.uk)*. **Open** noon-3pm, 6-11pm Mon-Sat; noon-3pm, 7-10.30pm Sun. *Food served* noon-2pm Mon-Sat. The second of the early options in Little Missenden, this pub serves pies, baked potatoes, sandwiches and soup.

Squirrel *Penn Street, Amersham, HP7 0PX (01494 711291, www.thesquirrel pub.co.uk)*. **Open** noon-3pm, 5.30-11pm

Mon-Thur; noon-3pm, 5pm-midnight Fri; noon-11pm Sat; noon-10.30pm Sun. *Food served* noon-2pm Tue; noon-2pm, 6.30-9pm Wed, Thur; noon-2pm, 6-9pm Fri, Sat; noon-2.30pm Sun. The recommended lunch stop, some 9.5km (5.9 miles) into the walk.

Hit or Miss Inn *Penn Street, Amersham, HP7 0PX (01494 713109)*. **Open** noon-11.30pm Mon-Sat; noon-10.30pm Sun. *Food served* noon-2.30pm, 6.45-9.30pm Mon-Sat; noon-8pm Sun. 100 metres down the road from the Squirrel, the Hit or Miss has a broader menu, and plenty of seating. It's open in the afternoon for drinks, including tea and coffee.

Saracen's Head Inn *38 Whielden Street, Old Amersham, HP7 0HU (01494 721958, www.thesaracensheadinn.com)*. **Open** 11am-11pm Mon-Sat; noon-11pm Sun. *Food served* noon-2pm, 6-9pm Mon-Sat; noon-2pm Sun.

Seasons Café Deli *6 Market Square, Old Amersham, HP7 0DQ (01494 728070, www.seasons-cafe-deli.com)*. **Open** 8am-6pm daily. The recommended tea stop for this walk is open until 6pm daily, but has limited seating.

Crown Inn Hotel *16 High Street, Old Amersham, HP7 0DH (01494 721541, www.thecrownamersham.com)*. **Open** noon-11pm Mon-Sat; noon-10.30pm Sun. *Food served* noon-3pm, 6-10pm. 50 metres to the west of Seasons, the Crown provides afternoon tea.

Kings Arms *30 High Street, Old Amersham, HP7 0DJ (01494 725722, www.zolahotels.com/kingsarms)*. **Open** 5-11pm Mon-Sat.

Alternatively, **Il Bertorelli** (27 The Broadway, 01494 729749, www.ilbertorelli. co.uk), is a chain restaurant that also offers tea and coffee in the afternoons.

There are slim pickings up by Amersham station, but if you are desperate, the **Tesco Express** (London Road West, 0845 677 9000, www.tesco. com) just up the road sells snacks or you can get a tea at the **Subway** (6 Sycamore Place, 01494 431231, www.subway.co.uk), not far beyond.

Walk 6

Liphook to Haslemere

Shulbrede Priory and its woods.

Start: Liphook station
Finish: Haslemere station

Length: 15km (9.3 miles)

Time: 4 hours 30 minutes. For the whole outing, including trains and meals, allow 8 hours.

Transport: Take the train nearest to **9.45am** from **Waterloo** station to **Liphook** (journey time 1 hour 15 minutes). You can sometimes save 15 minutes by taking a faster train and changing at Haslemere. There are four trains an hour back from **Haslemere**, two an hour on Sundays

(journey time 50-60 minutes). Buy a day return to Liphook.
  Parking at Haslemere station costs £5.50 Mon-Fri, £3 Sat and £1 Sun. Parking is easier at Liphook station (it costs £2 Sat and after 10.30am Mon-Fri; free Sun), but trains back from Haslemere are only hourly.

OS Langranger Map: 186
OS Explorer Map: 133
Liphook, map reference SU842309, is in **Hampshire**, 15km south of Farnham. Haslemere is in **Surrey**.

Toughness: 5 out of 10

Walk notes: This walk can be muddy, especially the part after lunch, and has plenty of relatively mild uphill and downhill sections. It is almost entirely through full-grown mixed woods – mainly oak, beech and chestnut trees. After passing Shulbrede Priory in the middle of the woods, you come to the pub and church by the village green in Fernhurst. In the afternoon, you cross over streams in the forest before passing through Valewood Park and heading up into Haslemere, a town surrounded by beautiful countryside.

Walk options: You could shorten the walk by using the hourly Monday-to-Saturday bus service from Fernhurst, the halfway-mark lunchtime village, back

to Haslemere; the bus goes from the top of Hogs Hill Road in Fernhurst, along the A286.
  Walk 22 (Haslemere Circular; see p168) uses the same Fernhurst pub for lunch. For a longer and more energetic walk, you could substitute Walk 22's afternoon route, climbing Black Down on the way back to Haslemere.

History: **Shulbrede Priory** is the remains of a priory for Augustinian regular canons dating from about 1200. It was dissolved in 1536, with the King's Commissioner alleging that 26 whores were found at the priory. It is now a private house. The prior's chamber, above a vaulted undercroft, contains 16th-century wall paintings. The priory is open to visitors by appointment (01428 653049) and also on the Sunday and Monday of the late May and August bank holidays (admission is usually around £2.50).

In Tudor and Stuart times, **Haslemere** was a centre for the iron industry. With the coming of the railway in the mid 19th century, it became a popular spot for literary people. The poet Tennyson's house, Aldworth, is on the slopes of Black Down, where he loved to walk, and George Eliot wrote *Middlemarch* in Shottermill.

Haslemere has an interesting **museum** up the High Street, 100 metres north of the Georgian Hotel. The museum is open 10am to 5pm Tuesday to Saturday, and has important natural history collections. Other highlights include an Egyptian mummy, Zulu beadwork and Eastern European peasant art.

Walk directions

[1] [Numbers in square brackets refer to the map]

Coming off the London train, cross the footbridge. On leaving the **Liphook station** building, *turn right* into the station car park, go under the road bridge and immediately *turn left up some steps*. At the top, *turn left* and cross the railway bridge, your direction 140 degrees.

Follow the road for 650 metres, ignoring all ways off (including Churchers School), until you come to a road on the left, signposted Highfield School, where you *turn left,* your direction 50 degrees. **[2]** In 20 metres *turn right* on to a bridleway into the wood, your direction 105 degrees. Follow this path, ignoring ways off. There is a single post after 100 metres, with a ditch and fence to your left, and a two-arm sign in 230 metres. In 40 metres after the two-arm sign the wood opens out a little and the path becomes less distinct and curves slightly left. Follow another sign straight on. In a further 40 metres, *take the left-hand of two virtually parallel paths* (the right-hand path is sunken), your direction 105 degrees.

In 280 metres, where the two paths reunite, at a post follow the blue arrow

to turn slightly uphill, your direction 40 degrees.

In 100 metres, go straight on to join the broad track that has come in from behind you on your left-hand side. The track immediately curves left and crosses a cattle grid. In another 140 metres, at a three-armed footpath sign (with a metal gate away to the left), leave the Sussex Border Path to *turn right* on to a broad track designated the **New Lipchis Way**, your direction 130 degrees.

Go straight on along this broad track for 900 metres. Just before you exit the wood, there is a four-armed footpath sign where the New Lipchis Way goes right, but you go straight on over a cattle grid, your direction 105 degrees. In 100 metres you come to a farmhouse.

Keep to the right of the farm buildings, cross the stile and in 50 metres, as the main track turns left, go straight on following the footpath sign, your direction 100 degrees.

In 130 metres, with good views of Marley Common on your left-hand side, follow the track half right downhill, your direction 140 degrees. Ignore another track forking right uphill.

In 180 metres, the path curves in a hairpin to the left. 40 metres after the bend *turn sharp right* on an easily missed, unmarked path, steeply downhill through a chestnut coppice, your direction initially 70, then 95 degrees.

In 150 metres, at the T-junction at the bottom, *turn left,* your direction 40 degrees.

In 220 metres, by a large beech tree with a dozen trunks and an almost hidden two-armed footpath sign, follow the sign straight on, a path having joined yours from above on your left.

In a further 80 metres, at an easily missed two-armed sign propped against a tree, leave your main path to follow the public footpath sign by *forking right,* your direction 80 degrees.

[3] In 120 metres you pass a house and garden, keeping their wooden fence on your right-hand side. Then in 20 metres, by a three-armed footpath sign,

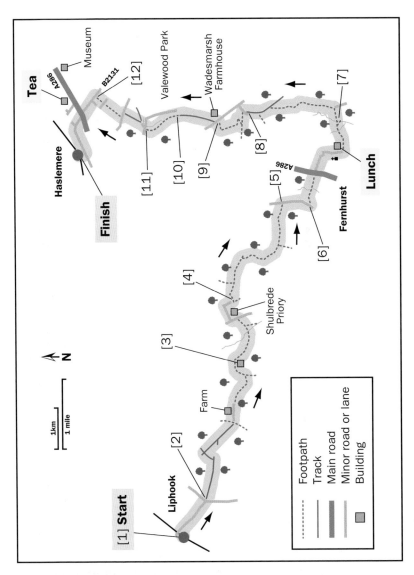

N

1km
1 mile

Legend
Footpath
Track
Main road
Minor road or lane
Building

Tea

A286

Museum

B2131

[12]

Valewood Park

Wadesmarsh Farmhouse

[11]

[10]

[9]

[8]

[7]

Haslemere

Finish

A286

[5]

[6]

Fernhurst

Lunch

[4]

Shulbrede Priory

[3]

Farm

[2]

Liphook

[1] **Start**

go through a wooden fieldgate and *turn right,* with the house fence still on your right-hand side, your direction 150 degrees. In 25 metres, go over wooden planks and through two fenced wooden fieldgates to go down a wide grassy path, your direction 95 degrees.

In 100 metres, at the bottom of the slope, the path bends to the right, your direction initially 150 degrees.

Follow the wide grassy path through the plantation, ignoring all turn-offs, and in 400 metres you come to the edge of the plantation and a two-armed footpath sign, which you follow by turning left, your direction 70 degrees, on a car-wide earth track.

In 40 metres, cross a stream. In a further 70 metres, ignore a path off to the right and continue towards **Shulbrede Priory** (as marked on the OS map), just visible through the trees ahead of you.

In 125 metres, at the tarmac road T-junction, *turn left,* your direction 355 degrees, passing Shulbrede Priory on your right-hand side. 50 metres beyond the white gates to the building, *turn right* on a car-wide earth road, with a cottage and large bird house on your left-hand side, your direction 70 degrees.

In 200 metres, go over a stream and follow the earth road round to the right, your direction now 140 degrees.

[4] In 150 metres, by the three-armed footpath sign, *turn left gently uphill* into **Greenhill Wood** (so marked on the OS map), your direction 45 degrees.

In 130 metres, ignore a fork off to the left (marked 'Private') to keep straight on, uphill.

In 150 metres, by a three-armed footpath sign, *take the right-hand fork,* your direction initially 90 and then 110 degrees.

Follow the main path, ignoring ways off, for 900 metres, following footpath signs at intervals until you come to a signed path going downhill, which you ignore to go straight on.

In a further 450 metres, bear slightly left, following the footpath sign, as the main track descends downhill.

In 180 metres you come to a stile with a metal fieldgate to its left, then to a four-armed footpath sign. 1 metre beyond the stile, *go right downhill* on a path, your direction 140 degrees. (There is another path a few metres further on, should this first path be excessively muddy.)

[5] In 50 metres, you come out on to a tarmac road by Updown Cottage. *Go to the right* down this road, your direction due south, and in 350 metres you come to an old house and garden called Thrae (on your left-hand side).

100 metres beyond Thrae's entrance take a footpath signed *to the left* across green open space, with oak trees, your direction 150 degrees. [6]

In 50 metres fork right into the woods proper and down steps across a stream and up the other side (ignoring turn-offs, and now with gardens on your right-hand side). In 450 metres go across the main road (the A286), straight over and down Hogs Hill Road, keeping to this tarmac road for 400 metres down to the **Red Lion** pub, which is the suggested lunchtime stop.

After lunch the route is relatively gently uphill for the first 2.5km, on bridleways that can be very muddy. *Turn left* out of the pub and *left again* down the side of the pub and alongside its back garden, following the footpath sign's direction (85 degrees). In 20 metres pass Manesty Cottage on your right-hand side, and in a further 40 metres you enter the woods.

Keep to the main path. In 115 metres, you cross a stream and in a further 30 metres you ignore a fork off to the right. In a further 105 metres, ignore two metal fieldgates and a stile off to your left.

In a further 225 metres, bend right with the main path to cross a stream where the water falls down from a storm pipe, with the stream soon on your left-hand side. [7]

In 165 metres, at the next T-junction, with a wooden barn opposite, *turn left,* following the footpath sign, on a car-wide earth track, your direction 30 degrees.

In 80 metres, at a crossing of paths, take the wide *left fork uphill,* your direction due north, a potentially muddy path.

Follow the track as it winds uphill, ignoring turn-offs. 380 metres further uphill, after a crossing of paths, follow the public footpath as it bends to the right, still uphill, your direction 60 degrees.

In 150 metres fork left, following the footpath sign, your direction 345 degrees.

In 340 metres, with a ditch stream on your right-hand side, ignore a fork down to the left, to keep straight on.

In 150 metres, you come to a bridleway T-junction. Take the level way to the left, virtually straight on, your direction 315 degrees (ignoring the grass avenue uphill to its right). Ignore all ways off and in 120 metres, at a major crosspaths, take the fork, not straight on, but slightly to the right, a signposted bridleway, your direction 350 degrees. (The grass avenue uphill to its immediate right is again marked 'Private'.)

Keep to this path and, in 150 metres, you come to a wooden fence, on your left-hand side, with a thatched converted barn beyond.

In 200 metres, by a two-armed footpath sign, fork left, your direction 15 degrees, down to a tarmac road 20 metres below.

[8] Cross straight over the tarmac road to take the signposted footpath downwards, your direction 315 degrees.

[!] In 120 metres, by a post on your left-hand side (which may be easy to miss in summer) with a yellow and a green arrow, follow the yellow arrow and climb the bank by going very *sharp right* on a faint footpath steeply uphill, your direction due east.

In 100 metres, you come to a fence where you follow the footpath sign to the left, with the fence on your right-hand

side. In 30 metres, go over a stile and turn right along the edge of a field, a wooden fence on your right-hand side, your direction 345 degrees. In 100 metres, go over a stile and straight on. (These horse paddocks can be very muddy – it is possible to make your way on the other side of the electric fence to point [9], replacing removable poles where you cross back.)

In 200 metres, at the far-right corner of the field, go over a stile and follow the footpath sign on a path with fences on both sides, your direction 90 degrees.

[9] In 100 metres, come out through a broad opening on to a tarmac road by **Wadesmarsh Farmhouse**.

Cross over the road, slightly to the left, to continue on a bridleway, your direction 10 degrees. In 30 metres, you enter the National Trust's **Valewood Park**. There are good views of **Black Down** on your right-hand side.

Keep straight on for 500 metres until you come to a large and isolated oak tree with a three-armed footpath sign next to it, at which point you leave the main track to *fork left,* your direction 330 degrees. **[10]**

Shulbrede Priory

In 100 metres go through a gate into the wood. Keep to the main way straight on. In 300 metres, ignore a fork to the right and, in a further 35 metres, ignore one sharply to the left. In another 125 metres, by a three-armed footpath sign, and 40 metres before a building with many outhouses, *turn right downwards* on the Serpent Trail, your direction 50 degrees. Go on a series of planks over a potentially muddy zone, to veer left with the path at the bottom of the hill and continue with the stream on your right-hand side.

In 75 metres, go on two planks over the stream and, in 25 metres, you come out on to a road near the entrance to Valewood Farm House. **[11]** *Turn left* on the road and then *immediately sharp right* to go past Stedlands Farm on your left, your direction 40 degrees.

Go past the entrance drive on your right that leads to 'The Stables', a large new brick house with diamond-paned windows. At a fork in the track marked with a footpath sign, take the *left-most bridleway uphill,* your direction 20 degrees. Then go fairly steeply uphill, ignoring turn-offs. In 500 metres, you come to a tarmac road at the top, with a house called Littlecote on your left-hand side. *Turn left* and in 20 metres *turn right* up a tarmac path marked 'Neighbourhood Watch Area', with an anti-motorbike barrier at its start, the direction 20 degrees, and soon with playing fields on your left-hand side.

In 350 metres, cross another tarmac road and keep straight on, down a path with steps between high hedges, to the main road, the B2131. **[12]** *Turn left* and then in 150 metres *turn right* into **Haslemere** High Street. In 40 metres, you pass the **Swan Inn** on your left and the **White Horse Hotel** on your right-hand side. 100 metres beyond this, you come, on your left-hand side, to the suggested tea place, **Darnleys** tea room.

Coming out of Darnleys, *turn right* and, in 25 metres, *turn right again* down West Street, signposted to the police station. In 120 metres, where the

main street curves to the right past the police station (which is on your right-hand side), take the street *straight on* to the fire station, but then not the tempting path straight on; instead, *turn left* in front of the fire station and take the footpath that goes *down the left-hand side* of the building, signposted 'Footpath to the station', your direction 315 degrees.

Follow this path, with a stream to your right and later a playground to your left, until you come out on to a tarmac road with Redwood Manor opposite. *Turn left* and, in 40 metres, *turn right* on to the B2131, leading in 260 metres to **Haslemere station** on your right-hand side. **Metro Café** is on your right just before the station and **Inn on the Hill**, with its bar, is opposite the station. The London platforms (2 and 3) are over the footbridge.

Lunch & tea places

Red Lion *Fernhurst, GU27 3HY (01428 643112).* **Open** 11.30am-3pm, 5-11pm Mon-Thur; 11.30am-11pm Fri, Sat; 11.30am-10.30pm Sun. *Food served* noon-2.30pm, 6.30-9.30pm daily. The suggested lunch stop has quality home-cooking. Book ahead.

Swan Inn *High Street, Haslemere, GU27 2HG (01428 641747, www.jdwetherspoon. co.uk).* **Open** 9am-11.30pm Mon, Sun; 9am-11pm Tue, Wed; 9am-midnight Thur; 9am-1am Fri, Sat. An alternative tea stop.

White Horse Hotel *High Street, Haslemere, GU27 2HJ (01428 661276).* **Open** noon-11pm Mon, Sun; noon-11.30pm Tue; noon-midnight Wed-Sat. *Food served* noon-9.45pm daily. Another option for tea.

Darnleys *High Street, Haslemere, GU27 2JZ (01428 643048).* **Open** 9.30am-5pm Mon-Fri; 9am-5pm Sat; 10am-4pm Sun. The suggested tea stop.

Metro Café *Lower Street, Haslemere, GU27 2PD (01428 651535).* **Open** 6.30am-3pm Mon-Fri; 7.30am-3pm Sun. Early closing café by the station.

Inn on the Hill *Lower Street, Haslemere, GU27 2PD (01428 642006).* **Open** 7am-11pm Mon-Thur; 7am-midnight Fri; 8am-midnight Sat; 8am-10.30pm Sun. Hotel bar handily located opposite the station.

Walk 7

Garston to St Albans

River Ver, Moor Mill and Verulamium.

Start: Garston station
Finish: St Albans Abbey or St Albans City stations

Length: 14.0km (8.7 miles)

Time: 4 hours. For the whole outing, including trains, sights and meals, allow at least 7 hours.

Transport: Take the train nearest to **10am** from **Euston** station to **Garston**, changing at Watford Junction to platform 11 (journey time 32 minutes). Trains back from **St Albans Abbey** station to Euston via Watford Junction

run every 45 minutes (hourly on Sundays), with a journey time of 40-45 minutes. There are much more frequent trains from **St Albans City** station to St Pancras (journey time 20-35 minutes). Buy a day return to St Albans (all stations).

OS Langranger Map: 166
OS Explorer Maps: 173 (for the first 100 metres) & 182
Garston, map reference TQ118999, is in **Hertfordshire**, 2.5km north of Watford Junction.

Toughness: 1 out of 10

Walk notes: This walk, although not the most beautiful in the book, is surprisingly unspoiled by 21st-century civilisation, despite being close to London and squeezed between Watford and St Albans, the M1 and M25.

From Garston the walk is through Bricket Wood Common (which tends to be very muddy in winter and after periods of heavy rain) to Lord Knutsford's park and manor at Munden, passing the impressively converted Netherwylde Farm, to go along the River Colne and River Ver to Moor Mill Inn, a possible early lunchtime stop. The walk then follows Ver Valley Walk arrows almost all day, up through woods and blackberries, beside lakes, along the River Ver to a mobile home park and on into Park Street, where you find your second option for lunch. Next it's onwards, at times beside the River Ver and over water meadows (which

can be waterlogged), as you head into the Roman town of Verulamium (which derived its name from the river) and so to St Albans Cathedral and its cloisters. To finish, you can either go back into the Cathedral grounds, down to the Roman walls, to head for the Abbey station, or make your way through the old town to the City station.

Walk options: You could call a taxi from your lunchtime stop, or take a train from Park Street railway station back to Watford Junction. Near the end of the walk, as you approach St Albans, you also have the option of heading straight for Abbey station without sightseeing in St Albans.

History: **Munden House** is owned by Lord Knutsford.

The current **Moor Mill**, at Bricket Wood, was built in 1762 and remained a working mill until 1939. A mill has stood on this site for over 1,000 years, known as Moremyll in Norman times. For 500 years it was under the control of the abbots of St Albans and was rebuilt in 1350. Its giant revolving waterwheel has recently been restored.

In its heyday, the **River Ver** powered 11 waterwheels and sustained the Hertfordshire watercress industry. Steps are being taken to increase its flow once more.

The **Catuvellauni** tribe, in the Ver Valley, were defeated by Julius Caesar in 54 BC. **Boadicea** destroyed Verulamium in AD 61 while the Roman legions were in north Wales. In AD 209, the Roman **Alban** was beheaded for refusing to sacrifice to the Roman gods, on the orders of Geta Caesa, son of Emperor Severus, during the latter's visit to Britain to put down a rebellion.

St Albans Abbey (01727 860780) and its monastic buildings were completed in 1088 with bricks from the Roman town (dismantled because it had become a hiding place for robber gangs). In 1381, the Abbey's **Great Gateway** was besieged during the Peasants' Revolt; it was later used to imprison the rioters. In 1455, during the Wars of the Roses, **Henry VI** was wounded in the neck by an arrow and took refuge in the Abbey, while drunken Yorkists ransacked the town. The Abbey, now a Cathedral, is open daily until 5.45pm; outside these hours you can enter for evensong at 5pm weekdays, 4pm Saturdays and 6.30pm Sundays.

Walk directions

[1] [Numbers in square brackets refer to the map]

Coming off the train at **Garston railway station**, *turn left* off the platform down a tarmac path between fences, your direction 20 degrees, with the railway track on your left-hand side.

In 160 metres you come down to a car-road T-junction. Cross the road here by pedestrian traffic lights and *turn right,*

your direction 85 degrees. In 35 metres *turn left* on the road, Falcon Way, signposted as public bridleway no.16, your direction 70 degrees. Keep on this road, ignoring turn-offs.

In 180 metres, when this road comes to an end, continue straight on. In 15 metres you go through a tunnel under the M1 Motorway. At the other end of the tunnel, take the tarmac fork up to your left, your direction 70 degrees, steadily uphill.

Ignore ways off and, in 400 metres, you pass the Old Fox pub on your left-hand side and keep on the tarmac road. 50 metres beyond the pub, *fork left* on a signposted public footpath, your direction 10 degrees.

In 70 metres cross a gravel drive, keeping ahead past cottages on your left-hand side and then go slightly to the right of a gated driveway. After a further 40 metres, you pass through a metal barrier to continue straight along a tarmac lane, with a thatched cottage and pond on your left-hand side.

Some 45 metres beyond this cottage, pass through a wooden kissing gate into **Bricket Wood Common** (as marked on the OS map). [!] The route ahead for the next kilometre can be very muddy.

In 70 metres, at a multiple junction, you have a choice of parallel paths – choose the one that looks least muddy. Either keep ahead, to follow a series of yellow arrows on marker posts, or *fork right* to then *immediately turn left* to continue ahead, following a yellow arrow, your direction 20 degrees. [2] In 400 metres, at a path T-junction (and in the case of the right-hand path, by a four-armed footpath sign) [!] *turn right,* your direction 130 degrees.

In 180 metres, you go over a series of four car-wide wooden plank bridges. In 200 metres you come to a tarmac road, which you cross, to continue straight on, along a car-wide road marked 'Munden. Strictly Private (bridle and footpath only)', your direction 140 degrees.

In 40 metres you pass house no.18, ignoring a stile on your left-hand side,

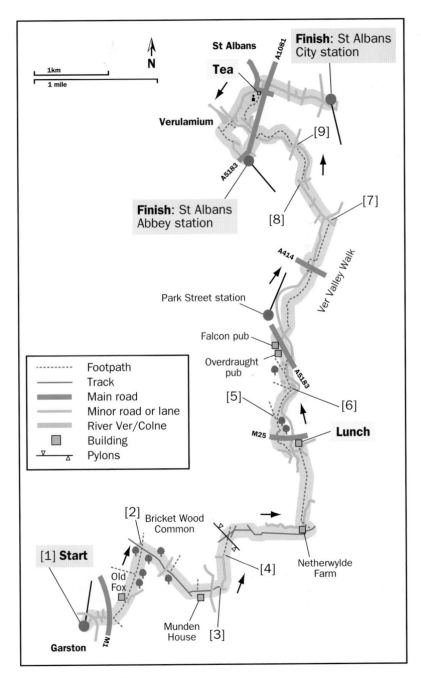

St Albans

Tea

Verulamium

Finish: St Albans
City station

A1081

A5183

Finish: St Albans
Abbey station

[9]

[8]

[7]

1km

1 mile

N

A414

Ver Valley Walk

Park Street station

Falcon pub

Overdraught
pub

A5183

[5]

[6]

M25

Lunch

- - - - - - Footpath
———— Track
━━━━ Main road
━━━━ Minor road or lane
━━━━ River Ver/Colne
▢ Building
▽—△ Pylons

[2] Bricket Wood
Common

[1] **Start**

Old
Fox

Munden
House

[3]

[4]

Netherwylde
Farm

M1

Garston

River Ver.

and go straight on past a wooden fieldgate and cattle grid on bridleway no.9, a car-wide road.

In 300 metres ignore a wooden gate and footpath signpost to the right. In 50 metres *fork left* on a gravel car-wide road, which is signposted as a bridleway, your direction 100 degrees.

In 90 metres ignore a wooden kissing gate to your left. Then, in 5 metres, go through a wooden gate (with a wooden fieldgate to its right-hand side) to go down a car-wide track, soon with **Munden House** visible on your right-hand side.

In 180 metres, with a ford on your left-hand side, go over a wooden bridge with railings over the **River Colne**. On the other side, follow the path to the left, your direction 70 degrees. This path is subject to flooding, which may entail wading with your boots off, or climbing along the wooden fence on your right.

In 150 metres you pass River Lodge on your right-hand side and go through a wooden gate. In 10 metres **[3]**, *go left* on a bridleway, your direction 40 degrees. In 40 metres you pass by a metal field-gate and go through a trough to continue straight on. In a further 350 metres ignore a turn left to Little Munden Farm **[4]** and continue straight on.

In 180 metres you pass under pylon cables. Ignore ways off and in 950 metres *bear right* on a new permissive bridleway,

Bridleway 72, your direction 70 degrees, initially uphill.

In 250 metres you pass a private fieldgate entrance to the splendid **Netherwylde Farm** on your left-hand side, to continue straight on, your direction 50 degrees. In a further 125 metres you pass a main gated entrance to this farm on your left-hand side. In another 30 metres, by a footpath signpost, at times half-hidden in the hedge **[!]**, *turn left,* your direction 320 degrees, with a hedge and tennis court on your left-hand side. In 60 metres go across the river on a wooden bridge with railings. In 6 metres **[!]** *turn right* along a potentially muddy footpath, due north.

Some 150 metres along this winding path go over a two-plank bridge (with wooden railings on its left-hand side). At the other end of this little bridge, *go right,* your direction 40 degrees, following the riverbank on your right-hand side and passing under mini pylon cables in 15 metres.

In 170 metres you pass a pumping station on your right-hand side (situated on the other bank). In a further 20 metres **[!]** *turn left,* following the yellow arrow, with the field boundary on your right-hand side, your initial direction 330 degrees.

In 500 metres go over a stile (or through the open gate on its right-hand side) and follow the blue bridleway left along an earth farm road, your direction 300 degrees. In 180 metres you come to a tarmac road, which you cross to enter the tarmac driveway signposted bridleway and Moor Mill, your direction 350 degrees, a mill stream (River Ver) on your left.

In 170 metres you come to **Moor Mill Inn**, the suggested lunch stop. If you visit this pub, retrace your steps for the 170 metres back to the car-road T-junction. Here you turn right over the bridge, your direction 260 degrees. 5 metres beyond the bridge, *turn right* on a signposted public footpath (the Ver Valley Walk), going through a wooden kissing gate and uphill, your direction 320 degrees.

In 350 metres cross the M25 motorway on a footbridge. From the other end of the bridge follow the arrows to the right, down alongside the motorway. In 35 metres **[!]** follow the arrow on a post *to the left,* your direction 350 degrees, in a further 25 metres with the edge of the wood on your right-hand side.

In 150 metres ignore a fork down to the right. In a further 500 metres, as the main path swings to the right, and by a notice on your left-hand side noting the site of Park Street Roman Villa, *bear left* to continue along the Ver Valley walk, with the field fence on your left-hand side, your direction 350 degrees. **[5]** Now continue ahead with the lake down below to your right, on a narrow and at times muddy path, following the field fence to your left. You come to a T-junction, where *you turn left*. At the next junction, **[!]** you *turn right* to descend with the path, down to the lakeside, to continue ahead with the lake on your right-hand side, passing anglers' stations, your direction 110 degrees.

In 150 metres, just before the end of the lake on your right-hand side, *turn left,* cross a main path and a grassy triangular area to *bear left* (ahead) on the Ver Valley Walk. **[6]** You are again between two lakes, your direction 320 degrees, on a path of fine gravel.

Ignore ways off. In 250 metres, your way rejoins the River Colne on your right-hand side. There, *fork right* with the Ver Valley Walk path, hugging close to the

river on your right-hand side, towards a closely packed town of mobile homes with aerials, your direction 50 degrees.

In 70 metres go over a plank bridge and follow the riverbank, ignoring other ways off. In 220 metres you come to the A5183 road, with what used to be the Old Red Lion pub, now a self-drive centre, on the other side of the bridge.

Turn left on this main road, your direction 340 degrees. In 150 metres you pass the **Overdraught** pub at **Park Street** on your left-hand side (which may have closed down). In 90 metres you come to the **Falcon** pub on your left-hand side (a watering-hole option). Here *you turn right* to go down Burydell Lane, opposite the pub, a tarmac road, your direction 45 degrees. In 80 metres, you go over the **River Ver** on a brick bridge.

In 110 metres, by Toll Cottage, follow the public footpath sign *sharply to the left,* your direction 340 degrees, with allotment fences on your left-hand side. In 100 metres, at the end of the allotments, go through a metal kissing gate to follow the Ver Valley Walk arrow straight on across open fields, your direction 350 degrees, a line of thorn trees on your right-hand side. The way across the fields ahead can be water-logged in winter.

In 150 metres *veer right* to follow a footpath with a lightly wooded field boundary on your right-hand side, your direction 70 degrees. In 100 metres ignore a fork off to the left to keep on, following the mini pylon poles. The simplest route, so as to keep dry, is to follow the mini pylon poles for about 200 metres, until you can clearly see the arch of the bridge in the far corner of the field, 200 metres away. Head towards this bridge on any not-so-wet route you can find.

Go through a metal kissing gate (to the right of a wooden fieldgate) to cross the bridge, then *turn right* to follow the path with the river now on your right-hand side.

In 35 metres, go under a bridge carrying the A414 road. In a further 25 metres, go through a metal kissing gate (with a metal fieldgate to its left). In 80 metres, ignore a metal kissing gate ahead *to turn right* over the river on a concrete bridge with scaffolding-pole railings. Now follow the river-walk arrow *to the left,* with the river on your left-hand side, your direction 30 degrees.

In 550 metres go through a metal kissing gate. In a further 80 metres you come to a tarmac road, with a wooden barn on your right-hand side. **[7]** *Go left* on this road, Cottonmill Lane, your initial direction 330 degrees.

In 10 metres, you go over a brick bridge over water and, in a further 40 metres, you go over another brick bridge. In 45 metres ignore Butterfield Lane to your left and keep on up through the estate, your direction now 320 degrees. In 270 metres, ignore Old Oak (road) to your right. You can now see the Cathedral ahead.

In 300 metres, by house no.63, take the tarmac lane *to your right* **[8]**, signposted Sopwell Mill Farm, your direction 70 degrees. In 50 metres, *fork left* through barriers to go on a parallel path, with a children's playground to its left, following the river-walk arrow. At the end of the playground fence, *go half left* across the field, your direction 20 degrees, towards the far left-hand corner of the playing field, 130 metres away. Once there, continue on the path to the next waymark post, 30 metres ahead by a concrete sluice, *where you go left.*

In 35 metres you pass under a bridge and continue on a potentially muddy way, staying on the riverside path, ignoring all ways off, initially with allotments on your left.

In 500 metres you come up to a tarmac road **[9]** by St Peter's School. Go across the road and over the bridge, then *turn left down steps* to continue on the river walk, with the river and allotments on your left-hand side, your direction 290 degrees.

In 200 metres go through gate posts and follow the path as it forks to the right, away from the river, your direction 290 degrees, to rejoin the river in 130 metres. In a further 50 metres, go over the river on a metal bridge with scaffolding-pole

railings, to continue with the river now on your right-hand side.

In 80 metres you come to the main road. **[!]** Going left here will take you, in 200 metres, to St Albans Abbey railway station. But the suggested onward route is *to go right,* over a bridge, your direction 20 degrees.

In 30 metres, *turn left,* on a tarmac road, just before the **Duke of Marlborough** pub, your direction 300 degrees initially. In a further 40 metres, you pass the left-turn into Pondswick Close. Then, in 45 metres, *turn left* on to Lady Spencer's Grove, a footpath lined with horse chestnut trees, your direction 295 degrees, gently uphill.

In 140 metres, after passing the buildings of Abbey CE Primary School over to your right, the path comes out to an open green space where you *turn right* up the hill towards the Cathedral (or you could go straight on for 150 metres for a drink at **Ye Olde Fighting Cocks**, a tea stop option). In 220 metres *turn right* along the modern outcrop of St Albans Abbey, in 7 metres coming to the entrance.

After visiting the Cathedral, come out by this same door and *turn left.* Now follow the Cathedral buildings all the way round to the other side. Then go uphill away from the Cathedral, your direction 40 degrees, passing Buon Amici and Lussmanns restaurants on your left-hand side. Opposite the latter, *turn right* uphill over a green for 50 metres towards the Village Arcade to come to the suggested tea place, **Abigails**, the last unit on the right in the arcade ahead of you.

Coming out of the tea room, keep ahead (right) down the arcade. In 45 metres you come to the High Street, where you *turn left.* In 30 metres you come to the **Clock Tower** on the other side of the road. If you have the time, the Clock Tower is a good starting point for a wander through the alleys of the old town, starting with French Row to its left.

For St Albans City station: Go to the left of the Clock Tower, with the Fleur-de-lis pub (now branded 'The Snug') on your left-hand side, to go up French Row, your direction 30 degrees.

In 100 metres you come out into Market Square. Continue ahead and in 75 metres *go right* through an archway (Sovereign Way), your direction 130 degrees. In 40 metres cross the main road by pedestrian traffic lights nearby on your left to turn under the archway into the Maltings Shopping Centre.

Swing right, then left, through this centre and in 250 metres, at its far end, turn left to exit the Maltings on to a main road (opposite the police station). *Turn right* on the main road, downhill, your direction 105 degrees.

In 650 metres, as the road goes uphill, you go over the railway bridge. Before the bridge ends, go down the steps to your left, to **St Albans City station**. Platform 1, for trains to London, is on this side.

For St Albans Abbey station: Continue along the High Street. In 45 metres you come to the Thai Square Restaurant (formerly the Tudor Tavern) on your right-hand side. Go straight on and in 100 metres *fork left* on a tarmac road signposted 'Cathedral West Gate'.

In 110 metres go through the **Great Gateway** of the monastery. Carry on down Abbey Mill Lane. In 150 metres *take the left fork,* with a house on your left-hand side.

In 80 metres turn right to pass the front door of **Ye Olde Fighting Cocks** pub. The water is on your left-hand side. 30 metres beyond the pub, *turn left* over the bridge into **Verulamium Park**, your direction 245 degrees, with the ponds to your right. (25 metres beyond the bridge, turning right leads to the museum). The suggested route is straight on, along the edge of the pond on your right-hand side, to carry on beyond the ponds for 30 metres to the remains of the **Roman Wall**.

Bear left along the line of the Roman Wall, your direction 185 degrees. In 85 metres, cross a tarmac path to carry straight on, your direction now 120 degrees, on a tarmac path. You pass a sports ground on your right-hand side.

In 300 metres you come to a tarmac road, a larger leisure centre complex ahead, where you *go left,* your direction 100 degrees. Follow the line of the road, but just inside the park railings.

In 260 metres exit the park by the main road T-junction. Cross the road by pedestrian lights and *turn right* along it. The entrance road to **St Albans Abbey station** is in 35 metres on your left, under a yellow metal gate.

Lunch & tea places

Moor Mill *Smug Oak Lane, Bricket Wood, AL2 3PN (01727 875557, www. beefeater.co.uk).* **Open** 6.30am-11.30pm Mon-Fri; 7.30am-11.30pm Sat, Sun. *Food served* noon-10pm daily. The setting of this Beefeater – beside a mill stream – would be ideal if it wasn't also almost directly beneath the M25. Nonetheless, it is our suggested lunchtime stop. Groups of more than ten should phone ahead.

Falcon *72 Park Street, St Albans, AL2 2PW (01727 873208).* **Open** 11am-midnight daily. A useful watering-hole for beer drinkers, but it doesn't serve food.

Abigails Tea Rooms *Village Arcade, 7 High Street, St Albans, AL3 4ED (07970 219957).* **Open** *Summer* 9.30am-5pm daily. *Winter* 11am-5pm daily. **No credit cards.** The suggested place to take tea on this walk.

Café at the Abbey *St Albans Cathedral, St Albans, AL1 1BY (01727 890214, www.stalbanscathedral.org).* **Open** 8.30am-4.30pm Mon-Fri; 10am-4.30pm Sat; 1-4pm Sun. Another option for tea.

Ye Olde Fighting Cocks *16 Abbey Mill Lane, St Albans, AL3 4HE (01727 869152, www.yeoldefightingcocks.co.uk).* **Open** noon-11pm Mon-Thur; noon-midnight Fri, Sat; noon-10.30pm Sun. *Food served* noon-3pm, 6-9.30pm Mon-Fri; noon-9.30pm Sat; noon-9pm Sun. Lovers of fine ale might like to call in at this pub, below the Cathedral. It is one of several in the country that claim to be the oldest public house in England. A good range of real ales and guest ales, plus bar snacks and full meals keep customers happy.

Walk 8

Bures to Sudbury

Gainsborough country.

Start: Bures station
Finish: Sudbury station

Length: 16.0km (9.9 miles)

Time: 4 hours 30 minutes. For the whole outing, including trains, sights and meals, allow at least 9 hours 30 minutes.

Transport: Take the train nearest to **9.30am** from **Liverpool Street** station to **Bures** (pronounced 'Bewers'), changing at **Marks Tey** (journey time about 1 hour 10 minutes). If you're doing the short walk, you can take a later train. Trains back from **Sudbury** to Liverpool Street are hourly, again changing at Marks Tey (journey time 1 hour 15 minutes). Buy a day return to Sudbury (Suffolk).

OS Langranger Map: 155
OS Explorer Map: 196
Bures, map reference TL903338, is in **Essex**, 13km north-west of Colchester and 8km south of Sudbury, which is in **Suffolk**.

Toughness: 4 out of 10

Walk notes: This walk has few hills and some pleasant scenery. It should be quite easy going, with simpler route-finding once a couple of farmers en route have been persuaded to maintain their overgrown footpaths. Sudbury lies at the heart of the Stour Valley, designated an Area of Outstanding Natural Beauty. Much of the walk is along the Stour Valley footpath, which is well waymarked. On the final approach into this historic town, you cross the Sudbury Common Lands – a traditional pastoral landscape that has the longest recorded history of continuous grazing in East Anglia, where the painter Thomas Gainsborough is said to have played as a child – to tea in a converted millhouse on the banks of the river.

Walk options: If you are not having lunch in the suggested pub, you can avoid the detour to Bulmer Tye by carrying on northwards up the road at point **[5]** to rejoin the route in 200 metres, at the asterisk **[*]** below.

You can shorten the walk by taking the delightful Stour Valley – St Edmund Way path from the church at Great Henny **[4]** to rejoin the route at point **[6]**. This reduces the walk to 12.6km (7.8 miles).

If you would like a long walk, you can add the short walk version of this route to Walk 46, Wakes Colne to Bures (*see p351*), making an excellent long ramble of more than 30km (some 20 miles).

History: **St Mary's Church** in Great Henny has a tower with parts dating back to the late 11th century, although most of the church was rebuilt in the middle of the 14th century.

Thomas Gainsborough, the 18th-century portrait painter, was born in Sudbury in 1727, the youngest son of a wool manufacturer. He studied in London under Gravelot and Francis Hayman. On his marriage in 1746,

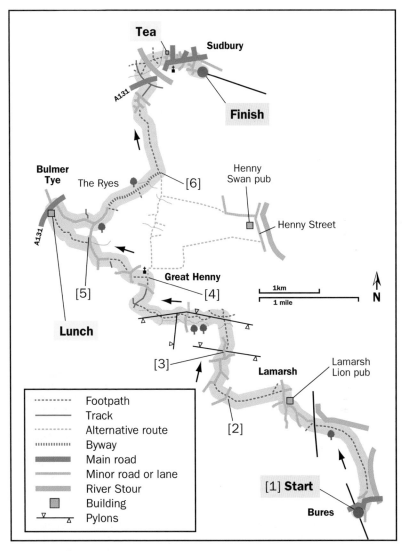

Tea

Sudbury

A131

Finish

Bulmer
Tye

The Ryes

[6]

Henny
Swan pub

A131

Henny Street

Great Henny

[5]

[4]

1km

1 mile

N

Lunch

Lamarsh
Lion pub

[3]

Lamarsh

[2]

	Footpath
	Track
	Alternative route
	Byway
	Main road
	Minor road or lane
	River Stour
	Building
	Pylons

[1] Start

Bures

he moved to Ipswich, where he remained until his move to Bath in 1760. **Gainsborough's House** (01787 372958, www.gainsborough.org) in Sudbury is now a museum with the most extensive collection of his paintings, drawings and prints in the world (the house is open 10am to 5pm Monday to Saturday, but

closed on Sundays). The entrance fee (2010) is £4.50.

Walk directions

[1] [Numbers in square brackets refer to the map]

Coming off the platform at **Bures station**, go down steps, walk through the station car park and bear left down The Paddocks. In 30 metres, you come to a T-junction where you *turn right* into Station Hill, due east. In 100 metres, you pass Water Lane on your left-hand side. 40 metres further on, the **Swan Inn** is on your right-hand side, just before the T-junction with Colchester Street. Opposite the pub, *turn left* off the road and follow the public footpath sign down the wide gravelled lane along the left-hand side of a building, your direction 20 degrees.

Keep following the high brick wall on your left-hand side, ignoring other ways off. In 180 metres, the path comes to an end of the hedge on your left-hand side, where there is a wooden post with public footpath arrows on it. *Turn right* and follow the Stour Valley Path along a car-wide track, your direction 350 degrees.

Follow this track for the next 1km until it brings you down to the River Stour. Where the track swings to the right towards a bridge with metal railings, ignore the bridge and **[!]** *keep ahead*, to follow the direction of a footpath post along a narrow path into a clump of trees. 40 metres further on, the path wends its way down to a stile, which you cross over into a field. Ahead of you and over to your right is the **River Stour**.

Once over this stile, *keep ahead* and follow the riverbank, keeping close to the fence on your left, your direction 280 degrees. In 300 metres, you will see a concrete pillbox down by the river below and directly ahead a wooden stile. Cross over the stile, which leads you on to and over the railway track, and over a stile the other side. 70 metres up the footpath ahead, there is a wooden telegraph pole on your right-hand side, with footpath signs on it. Take the footpath going *straight ahead* along the car-wide track, heading in the same direction as before.

Along the track you pass a thatched cottage, a barn and a tiled house, all on your right-hand side, and the foundations and slab of a demolished property on your left-hand side. After 370 metres you come out on to a road. *Turn right* along the road, in 60 metres passing the **Lamarsh Lion** pub, in **Lamarsh**, on your left-hand side (this is a lunch option if you have started late). In 150 metres follow the road as it curves around to the right, past the turning on the left signposted Horne's Green. In 110 metres you pass a turning on the left signposted to Alphamstone and Pebmarsh. Continue *straight on* for Sudbury and Henny.

250 metres further on, there is Lamarsh Village Hall on the right-hand side and a house called Green Hills on your left-hand side. 10 metres beyond, **[!]** *turn left off the road,* following the direction of a concrete public footpath sign down a car-wide track to the right-hand side of the house, your direction 260 degrees. In 270 metres, going uphill alongside a tall hedge, with a field on your left-hand side and a large house over to your right, where the hedge ends and by a footpath post, the path takes a *sharp turn to the right,* following the right-hand edge of the field. 50 metres further on, it takes a *sharp turn to the left* to follow the direction of the footpath post along the right-hand edge of field, initially uphill.

In 200 metres, by a footpath post, you come to a small dip where the path goes down into the next field. Follow the left-hand edge of this field, your direction 250 degrees initially. In 200 metres go under the overhead cables and down through a wooden kissing gate into the next field, and follow the left-hand edge of this field, in the same general direction as before.

In 350 metres you come to the far left-hand corner of this field and head out through a wooden fieldgate on to a country lane. **[2]** On the other side of the lane, you will find a public footpath sign; ignore the stile to the right and follow the directions of the footpath sign, going gently uphill in the same general direction as before, now 310 degrees, on a wide grassy track.

In 80 metres you pass a wooden fieldgate on your right-hand side and go straight ahead beneath some overhead cables, on a narrow path, now with hedges to your left-hand side and a low wire fence to your right-hand side.

180 metres further on, you come to the corner of the field and go over a wooden stile into the next field.

In 70 metres, cross over a stile on to a single carriageway country lane. *Turn right* up the hill, your direction 50 degrees. In 300 metres you come to a T-junction at the top of the hill, with a farm building on the right-hand side. *Turn left*, your direction 355 degrees. In 150 metres you come to another T-junction, signposted left to Twinstead, and right to Lamarsh. *Go straight* over the road, following the public footpath sign, through gateposts and in 10 metres over a stile.

You then go *half right* across the field, your direction 20 degrees. **[3]** In 30 metres the field dips sharply downhill. Aim for the wooden stile that is now visible ahead of you, in the far right-hand corner of the field. In 130 metres down the hill, you go under some overhead cables. 20 metres further on, cross over the stile and *turn left* along the car-wide track, gently downhill, your direction due north. In 130 metres take the right-hand fork, to follow the direction of the footpath sign more or less straight ahead, your direction 350 degrees, towards the farm.

Continue down the track and in 100 metres go directly past the farmhouse. Beware of a boisterous dog at this point. 45 metres further on, go through a gap where previously there was a stile and fieldgate and walk straight ahead, downhill, following the left-hand edge of the field, your direction due north.

In 140 metres, and 25 metres before you reach the end of the field, *turn left* and *cross over* three wooden planks, then over a stile with a public footpath marker on it, and finally over three more planks across a small stream.

On the far side, *turn right*, following the direction of the footpath along the bank of the stream. In 30 metres the stream turns sharp right, but you continue straight ahead across and up the field, towards a stile on the far side, your direction due

north. The path takes you directly under electricity cables on pylons. 65 metres beyond the pylons you come to the top of the field, to go up steps up the bank and over the stile at the top.

Turn left, following the yellow pointer on the post for the Stour Valley Path, your direction 280 degrees. The path now follows the direction of the electricity pylons off to your left. In 140 metres cross over another stile and follow the path on the other side in the same direction as before. Keep as close as possible to the hedge on your left-hand side and, in 150 metres, you come to a car-wide track.

Cross the track, *turn left* and follow the path around the right-hand side of a house. Follow the edge of the garden for 25 metres until you come to its far corner, under electricity cables, and by a footpath post. *Branch right* in the direction of the footpath post, diagonally across the field, following the line of the pylons, your direction 265 degrees.

When you reach the first pylon, the field splits into two levels (originally two fields, with the bank as the hedge). Follow the edge of the lower field, in the direction of the footpath post, along the foot of the bank. Note: this lower field is often waterlogged.

340 metres further on, you come to the far end of the field. The official route down on to the tarmac road is to *go left* down the ridge, parallel to the road on your right-hand side, and then down on to the road itself. *Cross over* it to go up a car-wide gravelled track, following the public footpath sign, in the same general direction as previously (320 degrees). 35 metres up this track, you pass Loshes Woodland visitor car park on your right. (If you wish, you can enter Loshes Woodland through the gate in the deer-protection fence some 25 metres to the right of the car park and walk on a permissive path through this Forestry Commission conservation area, to exit through another, similar gate some 250 metres away in the far left-hand corner of the woodland, to rejoin the route.) Otherwise, *keep ahead* up the track, pass under overhead cables and,

in 50 metres, you come to another Forestry Commission gate. (Again, you can enter the woodland at this point and walk parallel to the public footpath on a permissive path.) The public footpath is to the left of this gate. Follow this narrow, often overgrown path, with the Forestry Commission fence on your right.

In 250 metres you come to the far left-hand corner of the field, where you go over cross poles and over a stile to the right of an electric fence. Ignore the stile on your left, with 'Private' painted on it, and continue *straight on* along the left-hand side of the field, your direction 280 degrees.

In 400 metres pause and look right, where 85 metres across the field you can see where your way ahead continues, **[!]** uphill through a wooded area. *But the official route* is to continue down the left-hand edge of the field for a further 100 metres until you come to the far left-hand corner. Cross the overgrown stile (or go through the metal fieldgate to its right), and *turn right*, your direction 20 degrees, with a wooden fence on your right-hand side. In 80 metres, keep to the fence and the path as they veer right. **[!]** In a further 125 metres, where the fence does a 4-metre dog-leg left, *you go left uphill,* initially quite

steeply, on a potentially overgrown path, your direction 50 degrees. Keep the line of conifer trees on your left.

In 100 metres you come to the end of the trees and to a crossroads with another path.

Go straight on up the hill, ignoring paths to the side, and carry straight on, aiming always for the church spire (your interim destination) with your direction 15 degrees, soon keeping the wooden fence to your left-hand side.

In 60 metres, where the wooden fence goes sharp left, carry straight on downhill along the left-hand edge of the field, towards the church spire that you can soon see in front of you. 120 metres further on, you come down to a stile that you cross on to a road (if the stile is overgrown, climb over the wooden slat fence to the right of the nearby fieldgate). *Turn right* along the road and, in 40 metres, *turn left* uphill, following the public footpath sign towards the church spire. You pass **Great Henny Rectory** on your right-hand side.

150 metres further on uphill you come to a wooden gate. On its left there is a smaller wooden gate.

[4] This is the entrance to **St Mary's Church, Great Henny**. To visit the church – or if you are taking the short walk – go through this gate into the churchyard.

River Stour.

Here you have a choice of two routes. [To take a **shortcut** avoiding Bulmer Tye, just enter the churchyard, walk through it and exit by the lychgate. Cross a concrete drive and take the signposted footpath opposite, and follow the St Edmund Way/ Stour Valley Path (which you have been following from time to time earlier in your walk) in a northerly direction for just under a mile, through delightful, open countryside, to rejoin the main route at point [6]. There, coming from the shortcut, you keep directly ahead at the four-arm footpath sign. For an **optional detour** to take lunch at the **Henny Swan** pub: Having walked through St Mary's churchyard, follow the direction of the concrete footpath sign to your right, and continue in an easterly direction, downhill, to the main road, where you turn left, coming in 250 metres to the pub on the banks of the River Stour. After lunch either retrace your steps to the churchyard or, armed with OS Explorer Map 196, turn left out of the pub and plot a route to join the shortcut walk.]

But to continue on the main route to Bulmer Tye: *Turn left immediately before the entrance gate to the church,* your direction 275 degrees. In 15 metres, the hedge on your right-hand side goes sharp right. But you head *straight on* across the field, on what may be a clear path (depending on the time of year) and aiming for the two houses on the far side. (If the field is in crop or looks very muddy, go back to the churchyard, go through it and *turn left* on to a road. Walk along it in a westerly direction for 300 metres to rejoin the route by Henny Parish Room.) In 250 metres you come to the perimeter fence around the houses. Follow the direction of the footpath sign around to *the left,* along the fence, to another footpath sign 40 metres ahead, where you *turn right.* In 60 metres you come out on to the road.

Turn right along the road. In 60 metres, you pass the Thatched Cottage on your right-hand side and, 15 metres further on, ignore a turning to the right signposted 'Henny Church'. Follow the road as it

curves *around to the left,* past Henny Parish Room on your right-hand side. In 140 metres further on, *turn right* down two steps, following a public footpath sign, along the right-hand side of the field, your direction due north.

In 300 metres [!] you come to an oak tree. 20 metres ahead, cross a ditch and by a footpath post *turn left,* following the right-hand edge of a line of trees, your direction 295 degrees. In 200 metres you pass a farmhouse on your left-hand side (on the other side of the hedge) and, 30 metres further on, pass through a gap in the hedgerow straight over into the next field. Walk along the edge of this field in the same direction as before. [!] In 140 metres, *turn left over the ditch, then turn right* along a car-wide gravel drive, continuing in the original direction, now within the well-maintained grounds of a farming business. 125 metres along this drive, you come out to a T-junction, and *turn right into* **Little Henny**. In 160 metres, as the road swings to the right, you pass a house on your left-hand side called Pitfield Green. 200 metres further on, the road curves around to the right, heading towards some trees. Just 5 metres beyond the curve, there is a public footpath sign on the left-hand side of the road. [5]

(If you are not having lunch in Bulmer Tye, keep on the road northwards for 200 metres to rejoin the route at the asterisk [*] below.)

For the main route *turn left* off the road and [!] *follow the direction* (300 degrees) of the concrete footpath signpost across the field (which can be very muddy when not in crop) on a path that you may find poorly maintained and/or scarcely visible at some times of the year. (If this field is very muddy and looks too unpleasant to cross, stay on the road for 200 metres, and at the road junction with Ryes Lane, *turn left* – then reverse the walk directions from the Bulmer Fox pub, your lunchtime pub. That is, head along Ryes Lane in a north-westerly direction for 1km until you reach the T-junction with the A131. *Turn left* along the road and, in 170 metres, you come to the Bulmer Fox pub on your left-hand side.)

In 150 metres, halfway across the field, *turn quarter right* and [!] aim for the short footpath post with a yellow arrow in the first gap in the hedge from the right by a large oak tree, some 40 metres from the right-hand edge of the hedgerow ahead.

By this footpath post, cross over two wooden planks into the next field. Continue straight on across the field, your direction 315 degrees.

In 150 metres you come to the far side of the field, where there is another wooden footpath post. Cross on two planks over a ditch to go straight across the next field, in the same direction as before, for 250 metres, [!] *aiming for the trees* with a long red-brick building behind them. Once at these trees, *turn right,* following the left-hand edge of the field, with the trees on your left-hand side.

150 metres further on, go through a wooden swing gate, following the direction of the wooden footpath post just before the gate. Keep ahead on a grassy path through a field with young fruit trees and, in 70 metres, exit the field by another wooden swing gate. *Turn left,* following the direction of the arrow on the gatepost, into the car park of the **Bulmer Fox** pub-restaurant, the suggested lunch place.

Coming out of the pub after lunch, *turn right* along the road (the A131). In 100 metres you pass Church Road on your left-hand side. 70 metres further on, *turn right* into Ryes Lane, which takes you back to Little Henny. Walk down Ryes Lane for 1km, until the road enters some trees and curves sharply around to the right. Directly opposite is the entrance to Henny Lodge (formerly known as The Hall).

Turn left on a road at this junction [*] following the sign for Ryes House, your direction 55 degrees. In 60 metres you pass Lodge Farm on your left-hand side. 100 metres further on, where a small postbox faces you, *take the left-hand fork,* which is signposted as a public byway. Walk straight down this car-wide track,

your direction 35 degrees, past two brick cottages on your left-hand side.

In 800 metres the path leads down and out of the trees, and on your right-hand side there is a wooden post with various yellow markers on it. Ignore this and continue straight along the existing path.

[6] In 600 metres, having gone down the hill and up the other side, at the crest of this hill you have a fine view of Great Henny Church. At this crest you also come to a four-armed footpath sign (where the path straight on goes through trees). *The short walk from Great Henny Church rejoins the main walk here. Turn left* along the car-wide public footpath, going due north. This car-wide track takes you steadily downhill. In 500 metres you come to the foot of the hill (where there are extensive farm buildings off to the right of the path) and to a footpath sign. Ignore the way to the right and go straight ahead along a car-wide track, due north uphill, along the right-hand edge of a field. In 110 metres, where the hedge turns right, keep ahead, a quarter left, uphill. In a further 100 metres, at the top of the field, pass between a gap in the fence into the next field.

Walk straight down this field on a path between low fences and bushes to a dip and then up the other side, your initial direction 340 degrees. From here you have a good view of **Sudbury** away to your right-hand side. In 250 metres, you come to the far side of the field and exit it.

Follow the path through some trees, your direction 300 degrees, as it winds its way downhill. You are now on the outskirts of Sudbury and can see some houses down on your right-hand side. Ignore ways off and, in 200 metres, the path takes you up to the back of a row of houses and you follow the path *sharp right down the hill,* parallel with the row of houses.

In 100 metres you come out on to a residential street, by a public footpath sign. *Turn right* down the street, your direction 60 degrees. In 100 metres, you come down to the bottom of Pinecroft Rise and *turn left*. In 100 metres follow the road as it curves around *to the right,* past Hall Rise (road) on your left-hand side. 70 metres further on, you come to the bottom of Meadow View Road, where you reach a T-junction with the main road.

Cross over the main road and, on the far side, go through a wooden kissing gate near a sign saying Kone Vale. Go straight ahead down the path through lawns and into the trees. In 250 metres take the *right-hand fork* in the path, next to a Babergh District Council sign. 15 metres further on, fork left up the slope with metal railings on to the disused railway line.

(At this point, if you wish to go directly to the station without having tea, *turn right* and follow the path along the top of the disused railway line for just over 1km, passing over a number of bridges, until the path descends, narrows and exits on the flat through a sports centre's car park, at the end of which you turn right for the railway station.)

For the main route: *Turn left* on top of the disused railway line, your direction 310 degrees initially. In 65 metres a bridge takes you over the main road. 125 metres further on, continue straight on over a metal bridge. 250 metres beyond that, you come to a brick bridge with a metal railing and [!] *take the steps* (with a wooden banister on their right-hand side) *down to the right* before the bridge.

Go round the wooden barrier at the bottom of the steps and head straight across the field towards the bridge across the river ahead, your direction 80 degrees. In 120 metres cross the bridge (with metal gates at both ends) and, on the far side, *turn half left,* heading for the Mill Hotel, the large white building to the right of the church tower, your direction 60 degrees. In 300 metres, having crossed two minor streams, you come across the field to a gate leading on to a brick bridge, going alongside a large duck pond and out to the **Mill Hotel, Sudbury,** on your left-hand side, the suggested tea stop.

Coming out of the Mill Hotel, go straight up to the top of Walnut Tree Lane. *Turn left* on the main road, going

into town. In 200 metres ignore the road left to Bury St Edmunds and Colchester. Carry on down Gainsborough Street. In 170 metres, down on your left-hand side, is **Gainsborough's House**. 100 metres further on, you come out into the Market Square. To get to Sudbury railway station, *turn sharp right* and, in 40 metres, with the **Anchor** pub on your right-hand side, turn left into Station Road. At the bottom of Station Road, the **Eastern Station Lounge** is on your left-hand side and you follow the signs straight across for **Sudbury station**.

Lunch & tea places

Lamarsh Lion *Bures Road, Lamarsh, CO8 5EP (01787 227918).* **Open** noon-11pm daily. *Food served* noon-2.30pm, 6-9.30pm Mon-Sat; noon-2.30pm, 6-9pm Sun. Late starters can stop here, early in the walk. If you're doing the short walk, there are no pubs or facilities once past Lamarsh until you arrive in Sudbury (unless you detour off the route to the Henny Swan).

Henny Swan *Henny Street, Great Henny, Sudbury, CO10 7LS (01787 269238, www.thehennyswan.co.uk).* **Open** 11.30am-11pm Mon-Sat; 11.30am-10.30pm Sun. *Food served* noon-8.30pm daily. Reopened in August 2010, this pub has a lovely riverside setting.

Bulmer Fox *Bulmer Tye, Sudbury, CO10 7EB (01787 312277, www.thebulmerfox. com).* **Open/food served** noon-2pm, 6-9.30pm Mon-Sat; noon-3pm, 6-9.30pm Sun. This pub-bistro welcomes walkers and is the suggested lunch stop.

Mill Hotel *Walnut Tree Lane, Sudbury, CO10 1BD (01787 375544, www. elizabethhotels.co.uk).* **Open** 10am-11.30pm daily. *Food served* 10am-9pm daily. The suggested tea place, offering scones, pastries and toasted teacakes. The hotel bar is open in the afternoon. Allow 20 minutes to get to the station after tea.

Eastern Station Lounge *30 Station Road, Sudbury, CO10 2SS (01787 374241).* **Open** 6pm-midnight Mon-Thur, Sun; 6pm-3am Fri, Sat. One of several Sudbury pubs and handy for the station.

Walk 9
Shiplake to Henley

River Thames, Rotherfield Greys and Greys Court.

Start: Shiplake station
Finish: Henley station

Length: 17.7km (11.0 miles)

Time: 5 hours 15 minutes. For the whole outing, including trains, sights and meals, allow 8 hours 45 minutes.

Transport: Take the train nearest to **9am** from **Paddington** station to **Shiplake**, changing at Twyford (journey time 1 hour). Trains back from **Henley** station are hourly (journey time 65 minutes). Buy a day return to Henley-on-Thames.

OS Langranger Map: 175
OS Explorer Map: 171
Shiplake, map reference SU776797, is in **Oxfordshire**, 9km north-east of Reading.

Toughness: 4 out of 10

Walk notes: This walk is a bit like the scenery in a cowboy film: as soon as you are more than a few feet up, you have magnificent views over the unspoilt Thames Valley. From Shiplake Lock, the route follows the Thames, then heads up to the church beside Shiplake College and through bluebell woods beside Crowsley Park (the grandiose site for the BBC's listening masts), before reaching the church and pub in Rotherfield Greys. The cherry trees and cricket green in the hamlet of Greys Green lead you on into the National Trust estate of Greys Court, and from there into the beech woods of Lambridge and past Friar Park, with its splendidly over-opulent Gothic gatehouse, to a teahouse in Henley beside the river. Note that if there has been sustained heavy rain, the river may be flooded, which makes the first stretch along the river impassable.

Walk options: After lunch at the Maltsters Arms pub in Rotherfield Greys, you could take a direct footpath to Henley (see the asterisk [*] in the main walk directions),

and so avoid the extra 4km (2.5 miles) involved in visiting Greys Court; or you could call a taxi from the pub. Earlier in the walk, on Shiplake Row, there are hourly buses from near the White Hart pub (point **[3]**) into Henley or Reading.

History: **Shiplake** was as close as the Vikings could get their ships to their main encampment in Reading – hence, possibly, the name 'Ship lack'. There were vineyards on the riverside slopes during Tudor and Stuart times.

Shiplake College was built in the 1890s by a stockbroker. It was used by the BBC in World War II, and became a school in 1959.

Shiplake Church dates from the 11th century and contains stained glass from the Abbey of St Omer in France. The poet Tennyson was married here in 1850 – he wrote: 'The Peace of God came into my life before the altar when I wedded her.' Four times a week Shiplake College uses the church for its assemblies.

St Nicholas Church in Rotherfield Greys contains the ornate tomb of

Shiplake to Henley

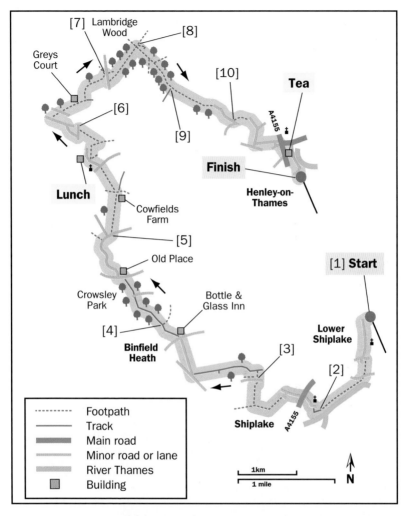

Robert Knollys, Elizabeth I's treasurer, who took charge of Mary Queen of Scots during her imprisonment; and of Robert's wife Katherine, a first cousin to Elizabeth I; and the effigies of their 16 children. The church curate reported in 1738 that, so poor were his parishioners, of the 'Absenters from ye Church there are a great many yet come but seldom [for] want of clothes'. The church's Reverend J Ingram wrote of his

experiment in 1823 to create jobs by cultivating opium: 'From its purity it was found of superior efficacy to that bought from Turkey or the East Indies, and I obtained a high price for it from the Society of Apothecaries Hall.'

Greys Court (01491 628529), owned by the National Trust, is a 16th-century house of brick, flint and stone. Erected in the ruins of a vast mansion, it was castellated by the first Lord Grey in

1347 – with a licence from Edward III, in recognition of loyal service at the Battle of Crecy. Until recently the house was the home of Lady Brunner, a granddaughter of the actor Sir Henry Irving. The estate has a maze, two possibly Tudor towers, ruins and a large donkey wheel and horse wheel that were used for pumping up water. The house (2-5pm) and gardens (11am-5pm) are open from April to September, Wednesday to Sunday and Bank Holiday Mondays. Admission (2010) is £7.10 (with a free cup of tea for walkers).

Henley, with its 300 listed buildings, is said to be the oldest settlement in Oxfordshire.

Walk directions

[1] [Numbers in square brackets refer to the map]

Coming off the train at **Shiplake station**, *head left* towards the end of the platform (away from Henley) and go down steps with grey railings, your direction 250 degrees. In 3 metres go through a white swing gate and *straight on*; in 85 metres *turn left* on a tarmac road, your direction 160 degrees.

Ignore ways off. In 425 metres, by a brick postbox, *take a road to the left*, marked Lashbrook Farm and Thames Path (with Crowsley Road going off to the right), your direction 120 degrees. In 15 metres, go over the stream and, in a further 20 metres, *turn right* on a footpath signposted 'Thames Path, To Shiplake Lock', your direction 165 degrees, down steps and through a metal kissing gate.

In 45 metres go through another metal kissing gate and straight on, with a fence on your right-hand side, your direction now 190 degrees. In 150 metres cross a gravel track and in 40 metres you reach a gravel road, opposite Mill House, where you *go right,* your direction 250 degrees. In 20 metres *turn left* on to a tarmac lane, following a Thames Path signpost to Sonning, your direction 195 degrees.

In 35 metres go through a wooden kissing gate on your right-hand side, with **Shiplake Lock** and the River Thames on your left-hand side, your direction 245 degrees.

In 300 metres go through a metal swing gate with high lever mechanism and continue ahead. In a further 350 metres you go through a metal kissing gate and continue along the edge of the river, now with a hedge on the right-hand

Shiplake Church.

side. In 150 metres go over a wooden bridge (made of six railway sleepers) with wooden handrails. In a further 200 metres [2] you come to a small bridge on your left-hand side, [!] but you stay on this side of the river, about 20 metres from the bank, *to take the car-wide gravel path* (which has the Shiplake College boathouses on its right-hand side) *straight on*, your direction 240 degrees. (Chalk cliffs are 50 metres away on your right-hand side.)

In 90 metres *turn right uphill* on a narrow bridleway (not the earth car-wide track to its left), your direction 10 degrees, soon with the occasional concrete step.

In 150 metres you enter the churchyard of **Shiplake Church**, with **Shiplake College** off to your right. After looking around the church *turn right* out of the church door, leaving the churchyard by the cedar of Lebanon.

Turn right on the car lane (Church Lane), your direction 310 degrees. In 250 metres cross the A4155, slightly to the left, to continue on Plough Lane, past the Plowden Arms pub on your left-hand side; ignore two roads going off to the right.

In 200 metres, just past the timber-framed Tudor Cottages on your left-hand side, *go left* on a signposted footpath, your direction 230 degrees (a concrete road).

In 40 metres do not veer left with the concrete road, *but go straight on* through a metal kissing gate, crossing a farm track and squeezing between a gap in electric fences. Keep ahead, gently uphill, with the field fence on your left-hand side, your direction now 330 degrees.

In 350 metres go over a stile with stone steps and a footpath sign, where you *turn right*, the field fence on your right-hand side.

In 150 metres you come to the end of the field. There is a redundant footpath sign on your right. *Turn left* and follow the edge of the field for 85 metres. By the first of two copses and a mini pylon, *turn right* over a stile and continue north for 50 metres.

Go over another stile and then continue on the path in the same direction, towards a cluster of three houses. In 200 metres *veer right* along the field edge, keeping the fence on your left, until you reach a road. [3] You are next to the **White Hart** pub (but this is not the lunchtime stop). There are buses from here to Henley or Reading once an hour.

Cross the road, slightly to the right, and pick up the signposted footpath to the right of Waylands House, your direction 5 degrees, and follow a line of telegraph poles, with a hedge on your left.

In 200 metres you come to an earth car road (Kiln Lane) by a bungalow, where you *go left,* your direction 260 degrees.

Ignore all turnings off. In 760 metres you come to a car T-junction, at which you *turn right,* your direction 350 degrees.

In 650 metres you come to the **Bottle & Glass Inn** in **Binfield Heath**. The suggested lunchtime stop is still 4km away, so try this place if you cannot get to that next pub by 2pm or simply want to have your lunch now.

Go past the pub (on your right) on a car-wide track. In 40 metres ignore a right-hand turn into a farmyard and take the lesser path, *continuing straight on,* your direction 290 degrees.

In 350 metres *bear right* with the path. In a further 100 metres [4], by a post with a blue arrow left and a yellow arrow right, follow the blue bridleway arrow *to the left,* into the wood, your direction 295 degrees. Keep to the main path.

Ignore all turnings off and follow the arrows on trees as the bridleway descends. In 350 metres you cross an earth car-wide track marked with 'No horses' signs on either side. The bridleway swings to the right and, in a further 80 metres, levels out before narrowing and starting to go uphill, your bearing now 300 degrees. In 200 metres you reach the battered iron railings of the BBC's Crowsley Park (with listening masts) on your left-hand side and you *bear right,* your direction now 345 degrees.

Ignoring ways off, in 300 metres you cross the drive to Keeper's Cottage and you keep ahead, now downhill. In a further 250 metres, you leave the wood to a car road T-junction, where you *turn left,* your direction 255 degrees.

You pass a timber-framed mansion, **Old Place** (marked on the OS map), on your right-hand side, then *take the road right* at the end of the building, signed 'The Chiltern Way Extension', your direction 355 degrees. In 85 metres, *fork left* with the road, still uphill, your direction 320 degrees.

In 550 metres, by Kingsfield House, ignore a footpath sign off to the left. In a further 100 metres, just before the road veers left, **[!]** *take the path to the right of two cottages,* following the footpath sign, and go over a stile (a metal fieldgate to its left), your direction 80 degrees, on an earth car-wide road.

[!] In 35 metres, by the back of a garage, by a concealed yellow arrow on a post, *go left over a stile* **[5]** and straight on, your direction 20 degrees, between fences.

In 135 metres go over another stile and straight on, across a grass road and then between fences. In a further 200 metres leave the paddocks through a line of trees and go straight on across open fields.

In 125 metres, at a path junction, follow the arrow on a telegraph pole, ahead and onwards, and follow arrows on posts as you proceed between fields. In 150 metres a wire fence starts on your left-hand side. In a further 150 metres pass through a gap in the fence ahead. In 175 metres go through a wooden fieldgate on to a worn tarmac road, with **Cowfields Farm** (so marked on the OS map) on your right-hand side.

In a further 75 metres **[!]** follow the yellow arrow *half left,* your direction 325 degrees, on a tractor way across the field (the right-hand of two paths across this field), heading slightly to the right of St Nicholas Church, which is just visible in the distance. In 350 metres exit the field between a gap in the hedge and come out on to a small road. Cross it and in 10 metres you reach a larger road T-junction, where you *turn left,* your direction 290 degrees (you can see Greys Court House 1.5km ahead of you, at 340 degrees).

In 360 metres you come to **St Nicholas Church** in **Rotherfield Greys** and, 35 metres beyond the church, the **Maltsters Arms**, the suggested lunchtime stop.

Coming out of the pub door after lunch, *turn right* and, a little beyond the church, just after a bus stop on the left, *turn left* through a wooden kissing gate. Here there are two options. **For the short walk** mentioned in the introduction **[*]** *take the right-hand footpath* signposted to Henley and follow the signs to get back to Henley (compass and map advised). **For the main walk** *take the left-hand footpath,* your direction 20 degrees.

In 135 metres go over a stile and straight on into a wood, following a clear path, downhill, your direction 35 degrees.

In 170 metres exit the wood over a stile and *turn left,* your direction 305 degrees, and walk with the edge of the wood on your left-hand side, gently uphill.

In 120 metres you pass a stile with an ex-vicarage on your left-hand side. In 80 metres go over a stile (or pass it, if it's still broken). The path winds uphill and in a further 120 metres you come out to a minor car road **[6]**, where you *turn left,* due south, in 35 metres passing Green Place House on your right-hand side. 60 metres beyond the house's driveway, at a T-junction, *go right,* your direction 295 degrees.

In 100 metres, by a war memorial, you join a more major road lined with cherry trees. *Bear left* following the signpost direction to Nettlebed, your direction west.

In 240 metres you pass the wooden village hall of **Greys Green** on your left-hand side. 20 metres beyond the village hall *turn right* on to an earth car road, with a signpost to Greys Court, due north, and the cricket green on your left-hand side.

In 85 metres, *turn left* in front of a row of cottages and at their further end pick up a footpath signposted 'The Chiltern Way Extension' *to the right,* your direction 65 degrees. In a further 50 metres you pass a broken stile and go down into a wood on a clear path.

In 50 metres you go over a stile and descend steeply. In 60 metres exit the wood over a stile and go straight on across a field, downhill to a dip then uphill, your direction 45 degrees, towards **Greys Court**, in winter visible across the valley. In 80 metres cross a stile to leave the field. In 5 metres cross a tarmac lane and keep ahead, and in 20 metres you cross another stile to enter the Greys Court estate, your direction 55 degrees.

In 40 metres join a tarmac drive to go straight on uphill. In a further 160 metres, you pass the manor house on your left-hand side (with some of the medieval ruins visible to its right). After passing the visitor site hut and ticket kiosk, **[!]** *bear left* off the entrance drive to go along the left-hand side of the visitor car park, following yellow arrows, your direction 15 degrees.

In 100 metres go through a wooden gate and continue with pine trees on your left-hand side. In 120 metres go through another wooden gate (a wooden fieldgate on its left-hand side) and continue. In a further 70 metres go over a stile in the left-hand fence and *turn right* on to a path going in the same direction as before.

In a further 25 metres go over a wooden bridge structure with a wooden railing and a pond on the right-hand side. In 35 metres ignore a yellow-arrow path up some steps to the left. In 40 metres go through a wooden gate and *turn left.*

In a further 5 metres, go over a stile (with a metal fieldgate on its left-hand side and a farm shed ahead of it) *to go right,* and continue in your previous direction, 50 degrees, with the fence on your right-hand side.

In 130 metres you come to a tarmac lane and ignore the two visible sets of onward footpath arrows **[7]**, then *turn right downhill* on a lane, your direction 105 degrees.

In 55 metres you come to a tarmac road T-junction by Broadplat Croft, where you *turn left uphill* and, in 10 metres, *take the footpath right,* signposted Lower Assenden, *bearing left* after 7 metres into the beech wood marked on the OS map as **Lambridge Wood**, your direction 55 degrees.

Following yellow arrows on the trees, you come in 290 metres to the start of open fields visible off to your right-hand side. (You remain in the wood, parallel to the fields.)

In 200 metres, at the end of these fields on your right-hand side, cross a minor path and follow yellow arrows straight on, deeper into the wood, your direction 55 degrees. In 320 metres you come to a crossing **[8]** marked with crossed yellow arrows on a tree. **[!]** Here, 10 metres beyond the first marked tree, take path

no.25 *to the right,* your direction 125 degrees, gently downhill.

In 140 metres ignore a fork marked no.27 to the left. In a further 30 metres you come to a T-junction, *at which you turn left.* You are now on the edge of the wood again, with fields on your right-hand side, your direction now 135 degrees.

In a further 75 metres, *bear slightly left* with the main path to a yellow arrow on a tree 30 metres away, with a small crater to its right. In 40 metres ignore path no.51 (to the left) to keep on with path no.25, now uphill.

In 525 metres, as you pass a large industrial corrugated shed off to your right-hand side, stay on path no.25 (rather than forking right on to path no.49). In 50 metres at a junction *bear right* and in 30 metres exit the wood over a low stile **[9]** on to a golf course, coming out between the greens for hole 13 to your left and 12 to your right. *Go straight on,* your direction 145 degrees.

By green 12 you come to a line of trees, which you thereafter keep on your right-hand side. Follow the posts with orange or yellow directional arrows across the golf course. In 500 metres you come to a stile (with a wooden fieldgate to its right) and cross it, *to go straight on,* along a tarmac lane with brick bands, your direction 105 degrees.

In 60 metres go over a stile (a wooden fieldgate to its left) and straight on. In 45 metres you join a tarmac road coming in from the left, going through an open gate in the same direction, past the entrance to Lambridge House on the left-hand side.

In a further 80 metres you pass a folly, (The Temple), screened by fences on your right-hand side. In a further 150 metres you come to Croft Cottage on your left-hand side (recently redeveloped) **[10]**, where *you turn left* as the road bends to the right, on to a signposted footpath, your direction 80 degrees. (The house where George Harrison used to live, Friar Park, is on the other side of the high fence topped with razor wire to your right.)

In 200 metres you come to a housing estate road (Crisp Road), where you *turn right,* your direction 120 degrees. In 165 metres *turn right uphill* into Hop Gardens.

In 400 metres you come almost to the main road T-junction. Just to your right is the Victorian Gothic splendour of **Friar Park's lodge house**. *Turn left* on to the minor road, 5 metres before the main road (West Street), which has a one-way sign, your direction due east.

In 120 metres you pass Row Barge pub on your right-hand side and keep on, heading for the church, crossing the main road junction with Kings Road, down the pedestrianised Market Place and crossing Bell Street. Just beyond the church, with the Red Lion Hotel on your left, *turn right along the riverfront.* In 50 metres you reach the **Henley Tea Rooms** on your right-hand side, the suggested tea place. After tea *turn right* and continue to the Boats for Hire place, where you bend right with the road, *taking the second left* to **Henley station** by the Imperial Hotel.

Lunch & tea places

Bottle & Glass Inn *Binfield Heath, Henley-on-Thames, RG9 4JT (01491 575755, www.thebottleandglassinn.com).* **Open** noon-3pm, 6-11pm Tue-Fri; noon-11pm Sat; noon-8pm Sun. *Food served* noon-2pm, 7-9pm Tue-Sat; noon-3pm Sun. A thatched pub that makes a useful alternative lunch spot 4km (2.5 miles) earlier in the walk than the Maltsters.

Maltsters Arms *Rotherfield Greys, Henley-on-Thames, RG9 4QD (01491 628400, www.maltsters.co.uk).* **Open** 11.45am-3pm, 6-11pm Mon-Sat; 11.45am-11pm Sun. *Food served* noon-2.15pm, 6.15-9.15pm Mon-Sat; noon-2.30pm Sun. This pub, 10.3km (6.4 miles) from the start of the walk, is the suggested lunch stop.

Henley Tea Rooms *Henley-on-Thames, RG9 1BH (01491 411412).* **Open** 9am-5pm daily. *Food served* 11am-2pm daily. The suggested tea place for the end of the walk. It faces the river, with the railway station just 5 minutes' walk away.

There are also a large number of pubs in Henley if you fancy a stronger drink.

Walk 10

Beaconsfield Circular

Milton's Cottage and a Quaker hamlet.

Start and finish: Beaconsfield station

Length: 19.5km (12.1 miles)

Time: 5 hours 30 minutes. For the whole outing, including trains, sights and meals, allow at least 9 hours.

Transport: Take the train nearest to **9.30am** from **Marylebone** station to **Beaconsfield** (journey time 30-40 minutes); in summer you can take a train up to an hour later. There are about three trains an hour back from Beaconsfield.

OS Landranger Map: 175
OS Explorer Map: 172
Beaconsfield, map reference SU940912, is in **Buckinghamshire**, 7km south-east of High Wycombe.

Toughness: 4 out of 10

Walk notes: This walk passes the cottage of the poet John Milton in Chalfont St Giles and comes to Jordans, a hamlet with Quaker links. In between, there is typical Buckinghamshire countryside to enjoy – gently rolling wooded hills – enough to provide interest without being too tiring!

Walk options: Instead of completing the loop back to Beaconsfield, from Jordans you could take the short detour to Seer Green & Jordans railway station (see the asterisk [*] in the main walk directions) and catch the return train from there. You can so cut out 750 metres of road walking by taking the shortcut at point [7] in the directions. You could also enquire at the lunchtime pub about buses or taxis back to Beaconsfield or (going in the opposite direction) to Gerrards Cross.

History: **Bekonscot Model Village & Railway** (01494 672919, www.bekonscot.co.uk) in Beaconsfield is the world's oldest original model village (1929). The 1.5-acre site comprises six model towns of 1930s vintage, a Gauge 1 model railway, a ride-on railway and other attractions. The Model Village is open mid February to October, 10am to 5pm daily, including bank holidays. Admission (2010) is £8.50.

The village of **Chalfont St Giles** is largely unspoiled, with many listed buildings and lying mostly within a Conservation Area. (The village was used as Walmington-on-Sea in the film of *Dad's Army.*)

It was a Quaker, Thomas Ellwood, who acquired a cottage in Chalfont St Giles as a refuge from London for **John Milton**. The plague was a serious threat in the city and, as Milton was a high-profile supporter of the republican cause, his liberty was at risk following the Restoration. During the short time he lived here, Milton completed his epic poem *Paradise Lost* and was inspired (by a question from Ellwood) to begin *Paradise Regained*. The cottage was probably built in the late 16th century, and has an interesting history – it is now a museum, containing the first edition of *Paradise Lost*. Incidentally, Milton was himself a keen walker. **Milton's Cottage** (01494 872313) is open from March to October, Tuesday to Sunday (plus bank holiday Mondays), 10am-1pm and 2-6pm; admission (2010) costs £5.

The **Friends Meeting House** was built within the grounds of **Old Jordans Farm** in 1688. (The Farm was sold to a private owner in 2006.) The Meeting House was the first to be erected following James II's Declaration of Indulgence, which gave the Society of Friends the freedom to congregate. **William Penn** is buried next to the Meeting House, along with his wives Gulielma and Hannah, and 10 of their 16 children. Penn founded Pennsylvania, a state without a military presence, with no religious or aristocratic group in control, and where Native Americans were fairly treated. As Voltaire commented: 'William Penn could boast of having brought forth on this earth the Golden Age.' The Meeting House suffered a major fire in 2005 and, following a lengthy period of restoration, reopened for its first meeting in September 2008. It is now open to the public 2-5pm daily from March to October. Admission is free, although donations are welcomed.

The **burial ground** at Jordans has several hundred more burials than there are headstones, the reason being that for a hundred years, from 1766, the Quakers believed that even a simple headstone with inscription was too ostentatious.

On the south side of the farm building is a large wooden barn, which is reputed to have been built from the timbers of the **Mayflower**, the ship of the Pilgrim Fathers – those Puritan pilgrims who in

New England persecuted the Quakers, cutting off their ears and having them flogged, branded and executed.

Walk directions

[1] [Numbers in square brackets refer to the map]
From platform 2 cross over the footbridge to platform 1 and exit **Beaconsfield railway station** through the ticket barriers. Take the surfaced footpath opposite (a few metres to your left), uphill; it's signposted Model Village. At the top of this footpath, in 100 metres, *carry straight on* along Caledon Close. In 40 metres take the road to the left – St Michael's Green – your direction 345 degrees.

In 100 metres you pass the **Parish Church of St Michael & All Angels** on your right-hand side. For **Bekonscot Model Village & Railway** take the road to your left, following the sign to the Model Village. To continue the main walk, follow the road as it bends round to the right into Grenfell Road.

In 300 metres – and 10 metres before the road curves round to the right into Wilton Road – *turn left* into a road that has no street sign (but is also Wilton Road), your direction 350 degrees.

[2] In 120 metres you come to the end of what you can now see is Wilton Road, and to a traffic island planted with trees and bushes. Go round the left of this island, *straight over* the main road (slightly to the right) and down the enclosed public footpath dead ahead, your direction 20 degrees initially.

Ignore ways off and keep straight ahead, initially between back gardens. In 325 metres the gardens end on your right. *Bear left* with the path, your direction 5 degrees, with a wooden fence on your left and a wooded area now on your right.

In 350 metres **[!]** *ignore* a footpath to your right, marked by a footpath post, and keep ahead (slightly to your left), your direction 300 degrees.

In 75 metres you pass a Penn House Estate Notice Board. **[!]** 8 metres beyond

Beaconsfield Circular

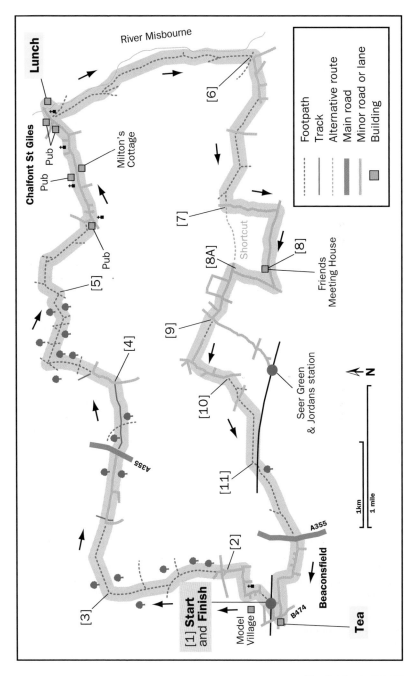

Beaconsfield Circular

River Misbourne

Lunch

Chalfont St Giles

Pub Pub

Pub

Milton's Cottage

Pub

[5]

[6]

[7]

[8A]

[8]

Friends Meeting House

Shortcut

[9]

[4]

A355

[10]

[11]

Seer Green & Jordans station

N

1km
1 mile

A355

Beaconsfield

[3]

[2]

[1] Start and Finish

Model Village

Tea

B474

Legend:
- Footpath
- Track
- Alternative route
- Main road
- Minor road or lane
- Building

it, at a footpath post, *take the right-hand fork,* your direction 345 degrees, gently uphill, into the wood. Keep to this path and, in 260 metres, by a post with a yellow arrow, ignore the paths you cross *to continue straight on,* along the same path, due north, and gently uphill.

320 metres further on, you come to a point where another path crosses the path you are on. At this juncture, there is a single white arrow on a tree pointing straight ahead. Continue straight on, for another 20 metres, until you come to another tree with a white arrow pointing left and right, and here **[!]** *turn right off the path,* your direction 70 degrees initially. **[3]**

At another (unsigned) path junction in 25 metres, *bear right* on the main path and keep to it, ignoring ways off, for the next 500 metres, initially gradually uphill, following footpath posts. At this point (almost a T-junction) a wide track comes in from the left and you *bear right,* your direction 110 degrees initially, now following the edge of a field on your right-hand side.

In 250 metres the path passes between two gaps in fences and, in a further 20 metres, you pass by a redundant kissing gate and exit on to a lane with a three-armed footpath sign on your left. What was Wood Cottage on your right-hand side has recently been redeveloped.

Turn left into the road and follow it as it immediately *curves right* and down the hill. Walk down the road for 750 metres until it brings you out on to a road (the A355) with fast-moving traffic. Cross this road with care and walk *straight ahead* along the car-wide track ahead of you, your direction 125 degrees initially. In 125 metres ignore the fork left to a metal fieldgate and *swing right* with the track, downhill.

In 300 metres, ignore a stile on your left and at a crossroads, by a four-way footpath sign, *keep straight ahead,* on the same track, now going up a hill, your direction east. 200 metres brings you out to the top of this hill, with views through

gates to left and right. Just follow the path between hedgerows and underneath overhead cables.

In 200 metres the path brings you down on to a road **[4]** where you *turn left,* your direction 40 degrees, and walk along the road. In 250 metres the road curves sharply round to the right and you *turn left* off the road, to go *straight ahead.*

In 20 metres you pass a barrier and enter **Hodgemoor Woods**. In 40 metres, at a footpath post, ignore a turn to the left *and keep ahead,* your direction 20 degrees initially. Keep to this path, ignoring all ways off and path crossings – for instance, at the first junction, in 140 metres, *take the left fork,* more or less straight on, your direction due north.

In 250 metres cross a main horse-riding track and keep ahead. In a further 150 metres, uphill, you come to a T-junction with a corrugated barn dead ahead. Here you *turn right.* In 30 metres, walk past the entrance gate to the barn on your left. 25 metres beyond that, there are two paths going off to the right.

[!] *It is easy to get lost during the next 500 metres or so, so please follow these directions carefully.* Take the *first path* sharply to the right, signed by a no-horses symbol on a white-topped post, up into the trees, your direction 140 degrees initially. This path soon becomes a car-wide track.

In 70 metres *keep ahead* at a path crossing. In a further 80 metres, *bear right* with the track, now due south, through a potentially muddy stretch.

In 75 metres, *bear left* on the track through a grassier area, your direction now 110 degrees. In 70 metres you come out to a path junction. **[!]** *Turn left* on to the gravel track, your direction 80 degrees. In 25 metres you pass a post with a yellow band on your left-hand side, then in 5 metres a permitted horse-riding post on your path (with no horse-riding posts to the minor crosspaths ahead).

In 120 metres you pass another post with a yellow band, this time on your right-hand side. In 8 metres, *ignore* a path to the right (heading off at 150 degrees and marked by a post with a yellow band) and *keep on,* your direction 50 degrees.

In 100 metres, at a minor path crossing, with a no horse-riding post over to your left, [!] *go right,* your direction 100 degrees, slightly downhill. In 35 metres, at a T-junction, [!] *go left,* your direction 10 degrees, and immediately in 5 metres [!] *go right,* on a narrow path, slightly downhill, your direction 120 degrees, in a further 5 metres passing on your left-hand side a no-horse-riding post.

Keep to this path, downhill, ignoring all ways off and following posts with yellow bands. In 315 metres, as the path curves sharply around to the left, going uphill, follow the narrower path curving off to your right, your direction 140 degrees initially.

Ignore ways off and, in 130 metres, you come to a T-junction near to the wood, and *turn left* along the path as it follows the tree line, your direction 50 degrees initially.

[5] In 5 metres ignore a fork right. In a further 30 metres, *turn right* through the trees, with an open field visible ahead. This takes you out, around a wooden barrier, on to a car-wide earth track, where you *turn left,* gently uphill, with the edge of the wood on your left-hand side, and a new post and wire fence to the open field on your right, your direction 20 degrees.

In 175 metres the track levels out and opposite a metal farm gate, *it swings left, then right,* your direction now 45 degrees. In a further 100 metres, where the track swings left, *keep ahead* to go through a wooden barrier. Now *turn right* down the left-hand side of the field, your direction 120 degrees.

At the bottom of the field, in 300 metres, ignore the stile in the left-hand corner with a footpath going off to the left, and *instead, turn right,* your direction now 190 degrees. Continue along the bottom edge of the field for 40 metres and go through a gap in the hedge into the next field.

Continue along the left-hand edge of this field, your direction 175 degrees. In 150 degrees go through a field boundary and keep ahead on this grassy path, still following the left-hand edge of this field.

In 350 metres at the far left-hand corner of the field, *turn left* through a metal kissing gate, to follow the fenced-in path. In 150 metres you come out beside a metal fieldgate on to the corner of a residential street. *Turn right* up this street (Back Lane) and in 50 metres you come to a T-junction with the main road, at **Three Households**, where you *turn left.* (The White Hart pub is on your right at this junction.)

Carry on down this road (Dean Way) into **Chalfont St Giles**. In 400 metres you pass the **Milton's Head** pub on your left. 90 metres beyond this pub, on the other side of the road, is **Milton's Cottage** – a museum well worth visiting, if time permits. Keep on down Dean Way and, in a further 250 metres, you pass the **Feathers** pub on your left-hand side. Almost next door to it is the **Crown** pub. In a further 75 metres, on the other side of the road and across the village green, is **Merlins Cave**, the suggested pub for your lunchtime stop.

After lunch, coming out of Merlins Cave, turn left. Opposite the Crown pub, [!] *turn left* through the beamed archway, leading to the (sometimes locked) **Parish Church of Chalfont St Giles**. Follow the footpath that goes along the right-hand side of the lychgate, along metal railings bordering the churchyard, your direction 120 degrees.

The path swings right then left and, in 130 metres, brings you down to a bridge with metal railings going over the dried-out riverbed. [!] 5 metres before this bridge, *turn right* and head half right on a path beside a new residential estate on your right, your direction 230 degrees.

In 70 metres this path *swings left,* away from the estate, your direction now 165 degrees initially, and continue ahead now between lines of trees.

Quaker House.

In 125 metres go through a metal kissing gate and continue in the same direction as before, now with an open field on your right. In 250 metres go through another metal kissing gate and continue straight on.

The path leads out into an open field. You are now going to walk south for the next 1.5km, through a series of five fields, keeping to the left-hand edge of each field in turn. This path generally follows the route that was taken by the **River Misbourne** before it dried up completely due to over-extraction of water from the valley.

In more detail: Follow the path along the field's left-hand edge. In 80 metres ignore a stile on your left. In 275 metres, ignore a farm gate, then a stile and another farm gate on your left, but keep ahead close to the left-hand edge of this field. In 60 metres you come to a metal swing gate (off its hinges) in the far left-hand corner of the field and pass through, to continue along the left-hand edge of the next field.

On your right is now a new training track cum horse gallops, with a tarmac base covered at times with a sand bed, 3 metres wide, between new fences.

In 300 metres you pass a row of trees going uphill to your right, on the other side of the gallops. Continue on in the same direction along the left-hand edge of the field on a grassy path. In 200 metres cross a track with a metal farm gate to your left.

In 200 metres you come to the far left-hand corner of this field, to go through a gap into the next field. Continue ahead, with the left-hand edge of this field over to your left, following the gallops over to your right.

In 250 metres ignore a stile on your left. In a further 100 metres go through a metal swing gate, then immediately a metal kissing gate, into the next field, to continue along the left-hand edge of this field, in the same direction as before.

In 70 metres pass through a metal kissing gate between a timber frame, and keep ahead, aiming for *either* of the two metal kissing gates, 40 metres apart, in the boundary ahead. In 125 metres pass through one of these gates: If you go through the right-hand kissing gate, ignore the metal swing gate 8 metres ahead, but bear left and take the well-defined path ahead, between trees to left and right, your direction 190 degrees initially.

In 200 metres, the trees on the right peter out and the path is bordered by a wooden fence on your right-hand side. In another 130 metres go through a metal kissing gate into a lightly wooded area and, in 5 metres, the path ahead forks. **[!]** *Take the right-hand fork,* which meanders past a tennis club on your left-hand side, your initial direction 200 degrees.

In 140 metres you come out from the lightly wooded area into playing fields. Continue along the right-hand edge of the playing fields on an indistinct path, passing a pavilion structure on your right. 50 metres past the pavilion **[!] [6]** *turn right,* up a fenced-in footpath between houses, your direction 250 degrees. 70 metres brings you up to a road. Go *straight ahead* uphill along Boundary Road.

In 200 metres, where the road becomes Lovel End, continue straight on up the hill. In 250 metres, having passed Chalfont St Peter First School on your right, Lovel End curves off to the left. Just before the cul-de-sac dead ahead, you *turn right* down a footpath, which goes between the school and the houses, your direction 345 degrees. This is signed as a public footpath and there is a 'No cycling' sign.

In 70 metres the path swings left. In another 250 metres you come out to a main road. Go straight across this road into woods on the far side, and walk dead ahead through the trees into the grounds of Chalfont Grove.

In 30 metres the path forks **[!]** and you *take the right-hand fork.* Keep ahead, your direction 275 degrees, *either* on the narrow path that follows the chain-link fence on your right *or* along the broader track, 5 metres to its left: both ways eventually merge.

In 400 metres you come to a (fading) silver-painted metal fieldgate. *Go through it* and *bear half left* across the grass, your direction 300 degrees. In 80 metres you pass between two large lime trees whose lower branches look as though they've been filled up with twigs for some enormous bird's nest.

In 100 metres pass through a gap in trees and in 20 metres follow the direction of the footpath post into the trees, your direction 305 degrees. In 110 metres cross over a stile and follow the white pointer on to the footpath heading *to your left,* your direction 265 degrees.

In 140 metres you come to a stile in the left-hand corner of the field. **[7]** Go over this on to a surfaced track.

[At this point there is a **shortcut** that saves 750 metres of road walking, but bypasses the Friends Meeting House. To take the shortcut, cross over the track and continue along field edges and a fenced-in path for some 800 metres, eventually coming out on the road opposite Seer Green Lane, at point [8A] below.]

But to continue on the main route, *turn left,* due south, down this car-wide track, following the direction of overhead cables on your right-hand side.

Continue down the car-wide track and in 450 metres you come out to a road, by the entrance to Grove Farm. *Turn right* along the road, your direction 285 degrees.

In 450 metres you pass Welders House and Gate House on your left-hand side. 300 metres beyond that you come down almost to the end of the road, where on your right is the **Friends Meeting House** (which is well worth visiting).

[8] After visiting the Meeting House, come out of its entrance, turn right around its front and turn right again, along its left-hand side, uphill into the **Quaker Burial Ground**, your direction 10 degrees. Walk through the burial ground and, in 115 metres, you come to a new path diversion (as a result of the sale of the Guest House and Mayfair Barn to a private owner). Go through the wooden gate and *turn left* down the path, following the sign to Jordans Village, with a new high timber fence on your right. In 50 metres the path *swings right* and continues with the road below and parallel to you. In 85 metres the path ends and you pass through a wooden swing gate to come out on to the road.

Continue up the road and, in 30 metres, you pass the entrance to what was the Jordans Quaker Guest House and the entrance to the **Mayflower Barn**. Keep on up the road for about 100 metres until you reach the road junction with Seer Green Lane. **[8A]** *Turn left* down this lane.

Go down Seer Green Lane, following the sign to Jordans Village.

In 30 metres you pass a house called One Ash on your left. Keep ahead and ignore ways off. In 170 metres, at the end of the village green, where the road curves around to the right, continue straight on down the road dead ahead, your direction initially 300 degrees.

[!] Note: to visit the Village Store and Post Office in Jordans, bear right with the road at the end of the village green, down Green West Road for 80 metres. The store is on your left-hand side.

Continuing with the main route: 170 metres down this road you come to a junction with Copse Lane. **[9][*]** If you want to catch the train back from **Seer Green & Jordans station**, turn left down the hill and follow the road for 650 metres for the railway station.

To continue the loop back to Beaconsfield, cross straight over on to a car-wide track going steeply downhill, dead ahead. 115 metres brings you to the bottom of the hill, where another path crosses your path. Continue straight on, following the public footpath sign, through the metal railings, on a path uphill, between hedges. Go through a second set of metal railings, and straight on as the path leads you through some trees.

Ignore ways off as you keep ahead, with woods on your left and fields over to your right. In 400 metres the path brings you out on to a car-wide track, with wooden gates leading into a courtyard on your right. Here *turn left* along this track, your direction 265 degrees initially. In 50 metres you pass the entrance to Hall Place on your left-hand side. 30 metres further on, you come out to the roadside in the village of **Seer Green**, opposite the Parish Church Hall. *Turn left* into School Lane, your direction 210 degrees.

In 150 metres you pass Stable Lane on your right. In 130 metres you walk past the entrance to Seer Green CE Combined School, which is on your right-hand side. 20 metres further on **[!] [10]** *turn right off the road,* your direction 215 degrees, down the footpath going to the left of Vicarage Close. In 180 metres, cross straight over a residential street, continuing on the footpath on the other side. 30 metres down the tarmac path going straight down the hill, **[!]** take the path *going off to the right,* your direction 245 degrees initially. 185 metres brings you down to the main road, alongside Weathering House on your right-hand side.

Cross this busy road to go *straight on,* through a metal kissing gate, into trees, your direction 245 degrees, in 40 metres coming out on to a golf course. Follow the direction of the public footpath sign. (Note the warning about 'flying golf balls' – keep watching the direction of play.) Head half right across the fairway, towards the green-and-white striped pole that marks the continuation of the footpath, your direction 225 degrees. When you reach this pole, go straight on towards the footpath sign dead ahead. In 70 metres follow the direction of this sign and *turn right* along the side of a fence that borders the railway on your left, your direction 310 degrees, along the left-hand edge of the golf course.

[11] In 500 metres you come to another public footpath sign, this time pointing left, and you follow the path *left, over* the bridge across the railway track. Over the bridge, there are three paths **[!]** and you *take the rightmost path,* which is signposted public footpath, your direction 250 degrees.

Walk straight across the golf course for the next 500 metres, following the directions and the green-and-white striped poles, at times going through trees.

At the edge of the golf course, go through a gap in a fence and out into a field. Go *straight ahead* across this field towards the far side on a distinct path, your direction 245 degrees. 400 metres brings you to the far side of the field and out on to the A355. Cross this busy road at the traffic island, slightly to your left, and go down Ronald Road, straight ahead. This leads into Fernhurst Close.

In 240 metres there is a parking area in the semicircle of houses on the right, and you continue straight on down the road. 90 metres brings you down to the bottom of Candlemas Mead, and you continue slightly left, your direction 280 degrees.

In 150 metres, the road curves sharply round to the left. (If you are interested in visiting the Old Town of Beaconsfield, follow the road round to the left, turn right at the first T-junction and left at the second one, which takes you on to the road linking the Old and New Towns.)

To go directly to the railway station, *turn right here,* pass through a metal barrier and go down the footpath which takes you between houses, your direction 10 degrees.

In 80 metres you come out on to a road, which you cross over to walk *straight ahead* along the left-hand side of the green. 170 metres brings you to the bottom of Chesterton Green, where you *turn left* into Maxwell Road, your direction 280 degrees.

In 200 metres you pass Sainsbury's on your left-hand side and **Revolution** (formerly Bar Med) on your right – a refreshments option.

In 100 metres you come to the road junction with Station Road, where you *turn right.* Pass two mini roundabouts – **Costa Coffee** is between them on your left-hand side – and continue along Station Road, your direction 340 degrees. In 60 metres you pass **La Cape** cafe on your left-hand side.

Cross the railway bridge and *turn right* down the road to **Beaconsfield railway station**. The nearside platform, platform 1, is for trains back to London.

Lunch & tea places

You are spoilt for choice for lunch stops in the village of **Chalfont St Giles**,

particularly if you enjoy real ale. The **Village Store** in Jordans serves hot drinks and cold snacks, while **Costa Coffee** (on Station Road in Beaconsfield) is a back-up option for tea.

Milton's Head *Deanway, Chalfont St Giles, HP8 4JL (01494 872961, www. miltonshead.co.uk).* **Open** 9am-midnight daily. *Food served* noon-3pm Mon-Wed; noon-3pm, 6-10pm Thur, Fri; noon-5pm, 6-10pm Sat; noon-4pm Sun. A real ale specialist that also serves coffee and cake.
Crown *High Street, Chalfont St Giles, HP8 4QQ (01494 875156, www.the-crown-csg.co.uk).* **Open** noon-11pm Mon-Thur; noon-midnight Fri, Sat; noon-5pm Sun. *Food served* noon-3pm, 6-10pm Mon-Sat; noon-5pm Sun. Not far from Merlins Cave, the Crown has a bar menu and serves a two-course set lunch from Monday to Saturday.
Merlins Cave *Village Green, Chalfont St Giles, HP8 4QF (01494 875101).* **Open** 10.30am-midnight Mon-Sat; 10.30am-10.30pm Sun. *Food served* noon-3pm Mon, Tue, Sun; noon-3pm, 6-9pm Wed-Sat. The suggested lunch stop is at the lower, eastern end of Chalfont St Giles, by the village green. This unostentatious pub serves inexpensive meals, and on Sundays often has a jazz club in one of the outbuildings.
Revolution *Maxwell Road, Beaconsfield, HP9 1QX (01494 677808, www. revolution-bars.co.uk).* **Open** 11am-11pm Mon, Tue, Thur; 11am-2am Wed, Fri, Sat; 11am-midnight Sun. *Food served* 11am-10pm daily. Formerly Bar Med, this bar is on Maxwell Road as you enter Beaconsfield.
La Cape *Burkes Parade, Station Road, Beaconsfield, HP9 1NN (01494 681137).* **Open** 7.30am-5pm Mon-Sat; 9.30am-4pm Sun. A cafe handily located just before the railway bridge.
Jungs *6 The Broadway, Beaconsfield, HP9 2PD (01494 673070, www.hpjung. com).* **Open** *Summer* 8am-6pm Mon-Sat; 9am-4pm Sun. *Winter* 8am-5.30pm Mon-Sat; 9am-4pm Sun. A continental bakery and patisserie, just past the Waitrose.

Walk 11

Tring to Wendover

Reservoir nature reserves and Wendover Woods.

Start: Tring station
Finish: Wendover station

Length: 21km (13 miles)

Time: 6 hours 30 minutes. For the whole outing, including trains and meals, allow 9 hours 15 minutes.

Transport: Take the train nearest to **9.20am** from **Euston** station to **Tring**. Trains back from **Wendover** are half-hourly, and return to Marylebone. Journey time is about 40 minutes on the way out, 55 minutes for the return.
   As Tring and Wendover stations are on different lines, you cannot get a return ticket for the full walk. Instead, buy an All Zones Travelcard, plus a single from the Zone 6 Boundary to Tring; on the return journey, you will need to buy a single ticket from Wendover back to the Zone 6 Boundary.

   To avoid getting these two singles, you could get a return to Aylesbury. Go there by train and then take a bus from the bus station to Tring High Street, from where you walk a little under two miles to Tring station to start the walk (or take a bus or taxi). You can return from Wendover on the Aylesbury ticket.
   This walk is not recommended for car drivers unless you are prepared to take a taxi back to your car, as there is no convenient public transport link (train or bus) from Wendover back to Tring.

OS Langranger Map: 165
OS Explorer Map: 181
Tring, map reference SP952122, is in **Hertfordshire**, 13km east of Aylesbury. Wendover is in **Buckinghamshire**.

Toughness: 6 out of 10

Walk notes: This walk has plenty of variety. It is completely flat for the first half of the day, starting along the quiet tree-lined banks of the Grand Union Canal, then past 'twitchers with bins' (aka birdwatchers with binoculars) beside nature reserves-cum-reservoirs. In the afternoon, the public footpath passes alongside RAF gliders being whipped into the air by a whirling wheel on a stationary lorry. For the last 3km (nearly 2 miles) the land changes completely, as you make your way up into a popular part of Wendover Woods (complete with

exercise bars and gargantuan signposts) nearly to the highest point in the Chilterns, and then descend steeply into Wendover.

Walk options: After lunch, you could get a bus from Aston Clinton to the centre of Tring (from where you can walk around 3km or nearly 2 miles or take a bus or taxi to the station). Or, to avoid hills at the end of the day, turn left at the Wendover Arm Canal (see the double asterisk [**] in the walk directions) and follow it all the way into Wendover.

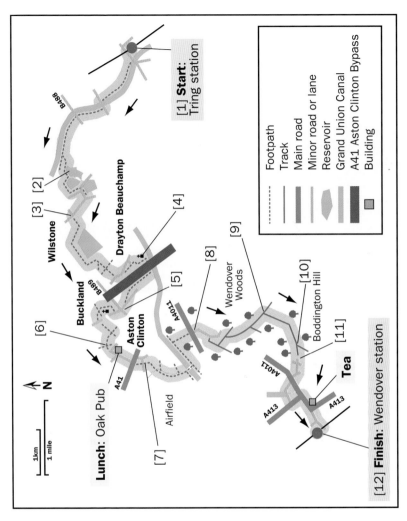

Map labels:

[1] **Start:** Tring station

B489

[2]

[3]

Wilstone

Drayton Beauchamp

Buckland

B489

[4]

[5]

A4011

[6]

Aston Clinton

A41

Lunch: Oak Pub

[7]

Airfield

[8]

Wendover Woods

[9]

[10]

Boddington Hill

[11]

Tea

A4011

A413

A413

[12] **Finish:** Wendover station

N

1km
1 mile

Legend:
- Footpath
- Track
- Main road
- Minor road or lane
- Reservoir
- Grand Union Canal
- A41 Aston Clinton Bypass
- Building

History: Water from the **Tring Reservoirs** (opened between 1793 and 1805) keeps the Grand Union Canal navigable. The first UK nesting of black-necked grebes was noted here in 1918.

The **Church of All Saints**, Buckland, was built in 1273. At the time, the Lord of the Manor was Hugh le Despenser who, with his son, was executed by his erstwhile friend, Edward II, in 1326. A later Lord of the Manor, the Earl of Warwick ('Warwick the Kingmaker'), was killed by his one-time friend, Edward IV, at the Battle of Barnet in 1471.

After lunch, the route goes through the grounds of the **Halton House estate**. Once owned by the Rothsch family – teams of zebras used to take them to their favourite picnic spot – it has now been given over extensively to the RAF.

Construction of the **Wendover Arm Canal** started in 1793, again to supply

Lock Cottage.

water to feed the Grand Union Canal at Tring. It became known as the leaky canal – despite partial relinings in 1803 and 1856, it had to be closed in 1904.

Boddington Bank is an Iron Age hill fort overlooking your final destination of Wendover.

Walk directions

[1] [Numbers in square brackets refer to the map]
Bear slightly right through **Tring station** forecourt and *turn left* on to the main road, going past the Royal Hotel Posting House. In 250 metres there is a bridge where the road crosses the **Grand Union Canal**. *Do not cross the bridge. Instead, turn right* off the road at the start of the bridge, *and take the steps going down on to the towpath.* You will walk along the towpath for the next 4km, your direction 290 degrees initially.

In more detail: In 1.2km you come to a stone bridge across the canal. Follow the path up on to the bridge, across to the other side and down on to the left-hand side of the canal. 900 metres further on there is a second stone bridge (No.133)

carrying a road over the canal, with the Grand Junction Arms public house next to the bridge. Continue along the path under the bridge, with a home and garden gallery formed from former workshops on your right-hand side.

500 metres further on, a footpath crosses the junction with the Wendover Arm, going off to the left. Go over the footbridge and continue straight along the main canal, signposted 'Braunston, 55 miles'. You are now at Lock 45 (Marsworth Top Lock). Counting this as the first set, continue to the sixth set (Lock 40).

[2] Here *leave the towpath and go up* to continue on a higher parallel path on Marsworth Reservoir bank. In 90 metres bear left and after a further 15 metres, by a Tring Reservoirs information board on your left, *fork right* along the right-hand side of the second (Startops End) reservoir, still parallel with the canal.

Ignore a downwards right fork in 30 metres and continue on a grassy path to the reservoir corner. Facing the Anglers Retreat pub ahead (which is across a road), *turn left* to follow the reservoir bank, parallel with the road. After 200 metres, at the next reservoir corner turn left along its third side for 300 metres, then carry on over a wooden bridge.

Go left with the path, past a 'Tring Reservoirs Walks' guidepost. After a few twists this leads in 20 metres to wooden steps up to a road. With great care, cross directly to the other side, where a new path takes you right along another reservoir (Tringford), your direction 260 degrees initially.

In 50 metres you come to a sign on your left giving information about the area. A further 50 metres on, cross a wooden bridge. In another 60 metres, the path reaches the end of the reservoir and continues in the same direction through some trees, down some steps and curves sharply around to the left. 40 metres further on, *turn right* up a path towards a kissing gate, your direction 250 degrees. Past the gate, walk straight across the small field in the same direction.

In 40 metres go through a wooden kissing gate and *turn left along the road.* In 25 metres you pass Tringford Farm on your left and 100 metres further on come to a T-junction. *Turn right here,* and follow this road for 500 metres. Just before a T-junction, you pass Wilstone cemetery on your right.

[3] *Turn left* down the car-wide track next to the T-junction, passing a metal barrier. In 300 metres you come to a clump of trees, with a sign a few yards ahead for Wilstone Reservoir Nature Reserve. *Turn right,* your direction 340 degrees initially. 70 metres further on, you come to a reservoir.

Walk along the reservoir bank, continuing in the same direction as before. Follow the first corner around to the left and walk all the way along the second side, which initially parallels a road on your right. 100 metres from the end of the second side the path crosses over a concrete bridge. In a further 100 metres cross another concrete bridge and then *veer left* through trees, initially along the third side of the reservoir, with a

wire fence on your left-hand side. 200 metres further on, at a junction in the path, there is a sign with information about Wilstone Reservoir.

At this junction, *take the path to the right, your direction 180 degrees.* In 8 metres ignore a stile going off to the right and, 10 metres further on, pass through the open stile ahead of you, then *take the fork going to the right of the tree dead ahead.* In 15 metres, *branch off right across the field,* your direction 195 degrees initially, towards the far corner of the field.

In 30 metres, you pass under electricity lines and, in a further 170 metres, cross the public footpath signed stile. Cross the field diagonally to the left, aiming for a point to the left of the row of houses opposite, your direction 200 degrees. Pass through the metal kissing gate 50 metres to the left of the end house and walk across the next field half left. You come to a stile in 60 metres, which brings you on to a road.

Turn left on to the road and in 40 metres turn right through a rusty kissing gate, following the public footpath sign. Cross the field half left, your direction 170 degrees.

After 180 metres go through a wooden kissing gate on to a drive. *Turn right* and after 20 metres *take the left fork* (ignoring the concrete road to the right). In another 30 metres ignore a wooden kissing gate off to the right and continue through a metal kissing gate to the right of a five-bar metal gate, along the lane to the church of **St Mary the Virgin, Drayton Beauchamp. [4]** (The church is generally kept locked.)

Enter the churchyard through a metal kissing gate. *Turn right* just before the church to walk towards a rusty kissing gate and footpath sign 20 metres away. Pass through the gate and *cross the field,* your direction 260 degrees, to go past a wooden kissing gate in its far left-hand corner.

Beyond the gate, follow the path, which twists and turns through a wooded area to another kissing gate and, after another 40 metres, to steps descending to a canal path. *Turn right,* passing under a bridge (marked with a black plaque stating that the burial site of a Saxon princess was found nearby) and the A41. On the far side of the bridge, *turn right to take steps up the river bank.* At the top of the steps, go straight on and follow the turns of an enclosed path. In 60 metres pass through a kissing gate into an open field.

Follow the footpath sign and keep to the right-hand side of the field beside a fence, then in 80 metres, at two footpath signs attached to the fence, *bear left across the field* keeping 15 metres to the right of a telegraph pole, your direction 300 degrees. In 100 metres you reach a footpath sign and field boundary.

You now walk for nearly 1km directly across the fields. (If you do not want to cross the expanse of potentially muddy fields or you are unsure about the direction to take: At the two footpath signs above, continue along the field edge for a further 80 metres until you reach the field boundary. Here *turn left* and follow the field boundary ignoring all ways off to your right and heading towards houses in front of you. After 600 metres you will reach a road. Here *turn right* and in 700 metres resume the directions at **[*]** below.)

To follow the main route, in more detail: Cross through a broken hedge into the next field on a car-wide section over a ditch. Cross the next field, heading for a 20 metre gap between a telegraph pole and a hedge, your direction 290 degrees. There is a footpath sign on a post to your right. Then keep straight on across another very large field for 700 metres, heading for a house with a white wall which is by the corner of a field leading to a road.

[*] *Turn right* along the road and, in 25 metres, you come to a crossroads, with an old pub sign (the Rothschild Arms) in the garden to your right-hand side.
[5] You go *straight across* the B489 to follow the sign that says 'Buckland village only'.

In 125 metres you pass Nields farm on your left and, in another 50 metres, you pass Manor Farm on your right. In a further 50 metres, *turn right* into Peggs Lane and, in 10 metres, *go left* through the lychgate of **All Saints Church, Buckland**.

Turn right and then *left* around the church (or, after visiting the church, turn left and left again, your direction 330 degrees) through the churchyard. Exit the churchyard through a tall wooden gate with a footpath sign into the field beyond, *to go straight on,* your direction now 340 degrees.

In 25 metres you pass a timber-framed house, 40 metres away on your left-hand side. In a further 35 metres go over a stile and turn left in the field, your direction 315 degrees. In 20 metres *take the left fork,* ignoring a path to the right leading to a locked metal gate, and continue with the field fence to your left to the corner, your direction 230 degrees.

In 80 metres go over a stile on to a tarmac road and *turn right,* your direction 350 degrees. After 150 metres **[!]** *turn left* down a signposted path that is hidden by a hedge as you approach it, which goes along the side of Juniper Cottage (to the right of the tall hedge that separates it from Moat Farm), your direction 300 degrees.

In 30 metres, go over a stile, then half left, your direction 270 degrees, keeping on towards the left-hand corner of the field. At this corner, carry straight on, coming to the hedge ahead. Here you bear left, with the hedge now on your right-hand side, your direction 240 degrees.

Carry on to the far corner (ignoring the pair of disused stiles on your right) and go over a stile and under mini pylons. The field hedge is now to your left-hand side, your direction 235 degrees. In 130 metres, ignore a one-plank footbridge with a metal railing and *turn sharp right,* your direction 335 degrees, walking along the second side of the field.

In 200 metres you cross a two-plank footbridge and stile directly in front of you into a large open meadow with the village of Aston Clinton on the far side.

Go forward and slightly left to another stile in the hedge ahead. After 120 metres cross a further stile and go diagonally towards the far left-hand corner of the field to reach a wooden signpost pointing in many directions. **[6]** Take the enclosed path left, your direction 255 degrees, signed to Green End Street and the Oak Inn. Walk down this path with a hedge on the right and a wooden slatted fence on the left. 100 metres down the path, you come out next to **Sunny Brook Close**, *where you turn left* for 15 metres to reach the road. Across on the other side to your left is the **Oak** pub, the suggested lunchtime stop.

After lunch, walk through the pub car park to the road and *turn left*. Follow this road for 500 metres, ignoring College Road off to the right. When you get to the T-junction at the A41 you will see the village memorial straight ahead of you on the other side of the road, with a bungalow behind it. There is a pedestrian crossing 20 metres to your left, which you should use to cross the road. Head back a few metres and walk down a marked

public footpath that goes down the left-hand side of the bungalow.

In 80 metres the path curves around to the left, your direction 170 degrees initially, and 70 metres further on you come out into an open space and continue with new buildings on your right. After a further 100 metres, you come to a house with a wooden fieldgate (saying 'Rookery Farmhouse').

[7] *Turn right just before the gate,* following a footpath sign, into an enclosed path, your direction 250 degrees initially. In 50 metres you enter a field. Carry on in the same direction as before for a further 150 metres until you reach the edge of a large airfield. Walk out into the open. You will see a sign saying 'Caution. Ministry of Defence airfield.' *Turn left* to follow the public footpath, your direction 170 degrees initially.

Continue with a small brook on the left-hand side of the path. Ignore a small bridge with a footpath sign to your left. At the corner of the airfield, after 750 metres, ignore a small bridge (made of wood and metal) crossing the brook to the left. Instead, you follow the narrow path that continues along the right-hand side of the brook, your direction 120 degrees.

Carry on for 450 metres, passing first trees and a sewage works on your right, then a patch of trees to your left, before meeting trees on both sides. Pass between two large wooden posts, *bear right* and in 70 metres cross over a brick bridge (Harelane Bridge), which spans the **Wendover Arm Canal**.

On the far side of the bridge, *descend to the left* down steps to the towpath. (**[**]** At the bottom of these steps, turn left at this point if you want to take a **shortcut** along the canal into Wendover.)

The main route is to *turn right* along the towpath and walk along with the waterway on your left-hand side. In 750 metres the waterway narrows markedly and, 100 metres further on, you come to a wooden post with 'Green Park' written on it and a sign entitled 'The Wendover Arm', which gives information about

Cobblers Pits and the woodland that you are about to enter.

Turn right off the towpath, through a galvanised-iron kissing gate leading you into the wood (due south initially).

Keep straight on, ignoring ways off. After 200 metres you reach a fork. *Take the left path* and continue on up the hill. In another 300 metres you go through a disused gate gap at the top of the path, and come out on to the A4011.

[8] Directly opposite, a road leads straight ahead up a hill, with a green Forestry Commission sign next to it saying 'Chiltern Forest Wendover Woods'. Cross the A4011 and walk straight up the road ahead. In 25 metres *turn right off the road* through a gap in the metal fence on to a path leading into the forest (due south initially).

In 250 metres, *fork left uphill,* following a horseshoe on a post. In 250 metres, cross a gravel track, and keep on, again following a horseshoe on a post, your direction 200 degrees initially. In 100 metres, a faint footpath crosses your path going straight up and down the hill. Ignore this *and continue straight on.* 40 metres further on, you pass on your right a children's pond-dipping area bordered by a wooden fence.

Continue and, 400 metres further on, you come to a crossing with a wider path marked by a horseshoe sign. Cross straight over, continuing down for a further 40 metres until you come to a car-wide track.

Turn left on to the car-wide track, your direction 120 degrees initially. In 200 metres the path bends round to the right and starts to go uphill. You are now ascending the eastern flank of Aston Hill. After 400 metres of walking uphill, you come to a wooden post indicating footpaths going off to the left, right and straight ahead. Ignore this post and continue walking *straight up the hill.*

100 metres further on, you come to a fork with a wooden post indicating a footpath to the left. *Take the left-hand fork.* 300 metres further on, the path curves round to the left at the top of

the climb and, 60 metres further on, you come to a wooden swing barrier leading out on to a tarmac track.

[9] *Turn right* and walk along the tarmac track. In 60 metres, you come to a large two-armed wooden sign pointing left to the Chiltern Hills' highest point and straight ahead for information and parking. *Go left* on to the gravel pathway running parallel to the tarmac.

In 80 metres you pass just to the left of the Café in the Wood and, a further 30 metres on, you meet a tarmac road. Cross the road and take the righthand one of two paths ahead. Follow it round to the right, passing a scenic viewing spot after 30 metres. When you reach a junction with a tarmac road, [!] *turn left on to a track,* your direction 230 degrees, passing a 'Go Ape' hut immediately on the left.

Carry on along this track, past various tree ladders on your right-hand side, until after 200 metres you reach a sharp right bend. 20 metres before a wooden post marked 'Caution: cables overhead' a footprint sign on a post marks a small path off to the left. [!] *Take this footpath* (the Firecrest Trail), your direction 200 degrees.

After 250 metres this becomes parallel to a broader track 10 metres to the right. Cross over to this track, your direction 220 degrees initially.

In 250 metres, you come to a small grass roundabout and a wooden barrier, dead ahead, with a marker saying 'Boddington Hill ¾ mile'. [10]

Go straight on past this barrier. 10 metres beyond it, ignore a fork to the left. In 70 metres [!] by a footpath marker, there is a path going off to the right diagonally down the hill. Take this path, your direction 280 degrees initially. (If time permits, you can continue along the main track to explore the remains of the fort and, in 150 metres, enjoy the views from the hilltop over the Vale of Aylesbury, but you will need to retrace your steps to this point.)

10 metres on, you reach a fork. *Take the right-hand option* and, after a steep

descent of about 300 metres on a potentially very slippery path, you come to a crossing with a bridleway. Continue *straight across* down the hill, your direction 305 degrees initially. In 30 metres you come to a tarmac lane with the entrance to a house on your right.

Turn left on to the car-wide track, your direction 270 degrees initially, with a fine view of Coombe Hill and its monument ahead to your left. In 300 metres the track comes out into a residential estate **[11]**, and you continue straight on in the same direction along Barlow Road.

In 40 metres you cross over Wolverton Crescent to your left and continue straight on. In 100 metres you come to a crossroads, again with Wolverton Crescent to your left (and with Hampden Road going straight on) and you *turn right,* down Colet Road. In 100 metres, this takes you down to a service road running parallel to the A4011.

Cross the service road and cross over the main road (the A4011). *Turn left* on the A4011, your direction 225 degrees, and in 15 metres *turn right* on Manor Road, your direction 310 degrees. Follow this road, ignoring all ways off. In 250 metres cross the bridge over the southern end of the Wendover Arm Canal. In a further 160 metres, at the A413 junction, *turn left,* your direction 150 degrees.

In 200 metres you pass the George Inn on your left-hand side (which serves tea) and, in a further 10 metres, by the clock tower, follow the A413 right, your direction 230 degrees. This is Wendover High Street. In 70 metres you pass the **Red Lion Hotel** on your left-hand side (which also serves tea).

Continue up the hill, ignoring a road to the left in 50 metres (signposted 'Library'). 50 metres beyond this, **Rumsey's Chocolaterie**, one of the suggested tea places, is on the right-hand side (located in an old brick building that used to house a bank).

80 metres on, you reach a road to the left signposted 'A413, London and Amersham'. On the corner is Wendover

Book Shop and on the other side is **Le Petit Café**, the other suggested place for tea. To get to the station, continue on up the High Street, and in 70 metres you pass the **Shoulder of Mutton** pub on your right. Immediately after that, Station Approach leads down to **Wendover station. [12]** The platform nearest to you is the one for London.

Lunch & tea places

Oak *119 Green End Street, Aston Clinton, Aylesbury, HP22 5EU (01296 630466).* **Open** noon-2.30pm, 5-11pm Mon-Thur, Sat; noon-2.30pm, 5pm-midnight Fri; noon-10.30pm Sun. *Food served* noon-2.30pm, 6-9pm Mon-Thur; noon-2.30pm, 6-9.30pm Fri, Sat; noon-4pm Sun. This suggested lunch stop is 12km (7.5 miles) from the start of the walk, so allow enough time to reach it. The pub provides excellent and reasonably priced home-cooked food – with some dishes taking 45 minutes to prepare. Groups of more than ten should book in advance.
Red Lion Hotel *High Street, Wendover, HP22 6DU (01296 622266, www.redlion hotelwendover.co.uk).* **Open** 10am-11pm Mon-Thur, Sun; 10am-midnight Fri, Sat. *Food served* noon-9.15pm Mon-Thur, Sun; noon-9.30pm Fri, Sat. A 17th-century pub that's worth considering as a tea option.
Rumsey's Chocolaterie *26 High Street, Wendover, HP22 6EA (01296 625060, www.rumseys.co.uk).* **Open** 8.30am-6.30pm Mon-Sat; 10am-6pm Sun. Cocoa aficionados may succumb to Rumsey's, which also serves plain old tea and coffee.
Le Petit Café *South Street, Wendover, HP22 6EF (01296 624601).* **Open** 9.30am-4.30pm Tue-Sun. The suggested tea place, five minutes from Wendover station.
Shoulder of Mutton *20 Pound Street, Wendover, HP22 6EJ (01296 623223).* **Open** 11am-11pm Mon-Thur, Sun; 11am-11.30pm Fri, Sat. *Food served* noon-10pm daily. Another tea possibility, this pub is also close to the train station.

Walk 12

Farnham to Godalming

River Wey, Waverley Abbey and Peper Harow Park.

Start: Farnham station
Finish: Godalming station

Length: 20.6km (12.8 miles)

Time: 6 hours. For the whole outing, including trains, sights and meals, allow at least 9 hours.

Transport: Take the train nearest to **9.30am** from **Waterloo** station to **Farnham**, perhaps changing at Woking (journey time about one hour). There are trains back from **Godalming** every half hour (hourly on Sundays).

The return journey takes about 50 minutes.
Buy a day return to Farnham. For the return journey you will need to buy a single from Godalming to Woking. If you are travelling by car, you can park for free near Farnham railway station at weekends.

OS Landranger Map: 186
OS Explorer Map: 145
Farnham, map reference SU846455, is in **Surrey**, 15km west of Guildford.

Toughness: 6 out of 10

Walk notes: This walk starts and ends along the River Wey. In between, it passes close to the ruins of Waverley Abbey and goes through woods to the suggested lunchtime pub in Charleshill. After lunch, there are further sandy bridleways through woods before entering the parklands of the Peper Harow estate, which has its own church and cricket pitch. Then it's onwards to tea in Godalming's ancient centre.

Walk options: There are no longer buses from Tilford, but to shorten the walk you could get a taxi from the lunch pub to Farnham or Godalming.

History: The town of **Farnham** (the name derives from the Saxon for 'ferny water meadows') prospered through trade in corn, wheat and hops. Its Norman castle

was built by Henri de Blois, a grandson of William the Conqueror.

Moor Park House is the site of the 1897 Moor Park Riot, during which a crowd successfully forced open the gates to maintain the right of way against the intention of the owner, Sir William Rose. During World War II, Moor Park was part of the General Headquarters Line of defence built against an expected German invasion: remains such as pillboxes and gun emplacements can still be seen in the Park and surrounding area.

The 12th-century **Waverley Abbey** – now in ruins – was the first Cistercian monastery to be built in England.

The Peper Harow **Church of St Nicholas** is a Norman building restored by Augustus Welby Pugin, the Victorian architect. It contains a memorial to Vice

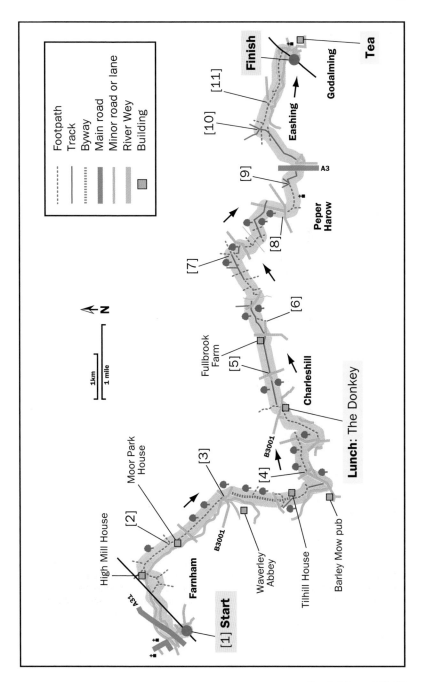

Admiral Thomas Brodrick; Brodrick helped to court-martial Admiral Byng, who in 1757 was shot on the quarterdeck of his own ship as a scapegoat for the navy's failure to save a besieged garrison on Minorca – or, as Voltaire put it, *'pour encourager les autres'.* The church was gutted by fire on Christmas Eve 2007, but restoration should be completed for Easter 2011. It can only be visited by arrangement a week in advance (phone the warden on 01483 810 526).

Godalming is thought to mean 'field(-ing) of Godhelm' (the putative first Saxon to claim the land). It was a coaching town between London and Portsmouth, and a centre of stone-quarrying and brewing, as well as trade in wool, timber, leather, paper and corn. The High Street has many half-timbered buildings.

Walk directions

[1] [Numbers in square brackets refer to the map]
Coming off platform 2 at **Farnham station**, with the Waverley Arms on your right-hand side, *cross over the railway lines,* your direction 330 degrees. In 20 metres you pass a petrol station on your right and head down Station Hill.

In 100 metres you reach the A31 dual carriageway. *Turn right here,* your direction 250 degrees, and, in 150 metres, *fork right on a track* signposted the **North Downs Way**. In 220 metres you come to a minor road. *Turn right here* and follow the road round to the left. There is a BP garage on your left with an M&S shop where you can buy a sandwich or bottled water.

In 350 metres you are beside the River Wey (on your left-hand side). In a further 200 metres, you pass the entrance drive to Snayleslynch Farm on your right.

In 100 metres, *at the entrance of a house called The Kiln, go sharp right,* following the North Downs Way, your direction 120 degrees. In 35 metres you go under the railway line. In a further 85 metres, ignore a footpath signposted

to the right to go straight on with open fields on your left-hand side.

In a further 220 metres, *at a path T-junction, follow the North Downs Way footpath sign to the left,* your direction 60 degrees.

In 65 metres ignore the gate to your right, to go straight on. In 60 metres you *cross the river* on a wooden bridge with railings. Continue ahead and in a further 140 metres *go through the gateway of High Mill* (marked 'Private'), following the white-painted arrow. In 25 metres go over a small stream. In another 30 metres, you exit the property. In a further 65 metres, at a T-junction, *go right on a bridleway,* heading due east.

In 480 metres ignore a tarmac lane uphill to your left and follow the lane half right, your direction 150 degrees. In 160 metres **[2]** *cross a tarmac road to go through the kissing gate* to the left of the entrance gateway to **Moor Park House**, your direction 135 degrees.

In 50 metres notice the ornate gatehouse to Moor Park House on your right but keep straight on; you are now on the Moor Park Heritage Trail. In 700 metres you pass a machine-gun nest on your right-hand side and a noticeboard about Moor Park in World War II. In 450 metres you pass Mother Ludlam's Cave on your left. In 85 metres go through a wooden kissing gate. In 40 metres you pass Stella Lodge on your left-hand side to come out on to Camp Hill road. **[3]**

Go right on this road downhill for 20 metres, then left on the road signposted to Godalming, your direction 145 degrees. In 185 metres *take a public byway on your right,* your direction 185 degrees.

In 200 metres, in winter, you can see **Waverley Abbey House**, away on your right-hand side, and the ruins of **Waverley Abbey**, due west (300 metres to the left of the house).

(If you would like to detour for a closer view of the abbey, in 110 metres take a path down to your right between yew trees and rhododendrons; in 150 metres, you are beside the River Wey, with the abbey ruins opposite to the left.)

Continue on the main path. **[!]** *In 115 metres, where the path starts to descend and there is a metal gate on the left go sharp right up the hill, following a public byway sign, your direction 230 degrees.*

In 370 metres you *cross a tarmac road* (with a brick postbox opposite) to continue on a gravel road with a public byway sign, your direction 230 degrees.

In 40 metres, fork left following a red arrow, your direction 190 degrees. In 10 metres you pass Sheephatch Farm (marked on the OS map) on your left. Keep to this path, ignoring ways off. In 450 metres you pass the entrance drive to Tilhill House on your left-hand side, to continue straight ahead, now on a tarmac lane.

In 130 metres, just before the entrance to Wey Cottage, *fork right off this lane on a signposted public bridleway,* your direction 170 degrees. In 15 metres ignore a stile on your left-hand side. You are back near the River Wey on your right. In a further 185 metres, ignore a path going up to the left.

In 285 metres you come to the main road, with Tilford Village Shop (where you can buy hot drinks and sandwiches) on your left-hand side. (If you want a meal now, turn right, over the bridge, to the **Barley Mow** pub, Tilford, on your right-hand side.)

The main route is to *go left,* your direction 45 degrees, passing the Village Shop on your left. In a further 210 metres, ignore Whitmead Lane to the right. *In 75 metres, as the road bends left, cross over to take the tarmac lane to your right,* your direction 125 degrees, passing a house on your left.

[4] In 75 metres *take the public footpath signposted left* (a tarmac road), your direction 60 degrees.

In 150 metres, at the end of this driveway, by the entrance to a house, *fork right on a public footpath,* following a yellow arrow.

In 400 metres, you reach a metal gate. Immediately turn left and follow the path around a garden to emerge on tarmac road next to Pooh Corner House. *Go right on the road downhill,* your direction 190 degrees, with Highmead House on your left-hand side.

In 240 metres, *by the entrance drive to Whitmead House, fork left* on a vehicle-wide byway, your direction 95 degrees, with a timber-framed lodge house on your right-hand side.

In 950 metres you pass the entrance to West Wey House on your right-hand side. In 80 metres, at a *crossing of lanes, fork right,* downhill, your direction 95 degrees. In 30 metres you pass the entrance to Riversleigh Farm on your right. In a further 55 metres, you come to the suggested lunchtime stop, **The Donkey** pub in **Charleshill**, on your right.

Coming out of the pub after lunch, turn right. In 55 metres you reach the main road. *Cross this and take the public bridleway signposted tarmac lane straight on* (the entrance to Foxhill is on your right-hand side), your direction being 345 degrees.

In 35 metres *turn right, following the bridleway sign,* to go uphill, your direction 65 degrees. In a further 215 metres, your way becomes a tarmac drive. In 210 metres you pass black iron gates on your right-hand side, to *fork left,* your direction 60 degrees, on a tarmac way. There is a low column with an entry phone on your left-hand side.

[5] In 80 metres you exit through the Three Barrows gateway to *cross the tarmac road and go straight on,* your direction 70 degrees, along a signposted public bridleway, ignoring field gates off to the left- and right-hand sides.

In 800 metres, by the entrance drive to Fullbrook Farm, you come out on to a tarmac road and cross it to continue straight on towards Broomfield Cottage (private), your direction due east.

[6] In 170 metres, by a turning circle or parking area on your right-hand side, *go through a swing gate on your left,*

following a wooden public bridleway sign, and then go half right, diagonally across the field. In 25 metres you pass the first oak tree, on your left-hand side, your direction 60 degrees, and keep going in this direction, ignoring all ways off. *Aim for 30 metres to the left of the right-hand corner of the wood, some 400 metres ahead of you.*

Enter the wood by a wooden swing gate, and continue on, your direction 65 degrees, along a potentially muddy way. In 60 metres cross a stream on a bridge

with wooden railings. In a further 170 metres, you come *to a tarmac road by a bridleway sign where you turn right,* your direction 110 degrees.

In 60 metres go over a stream. In a further 30 metres, by a footpath sign opposite Brookside House, *turn left,* your direction 20 degrees.

In 190 metres you come to a *tarmac road T-junction where you go left,* with Kingshott Cottage on your left-hand side, your direction 55 degrees. In 45 metres follow the blue arrow straight on, ignoring a fork left to Broad Firs. In a further 220 metres, ignore a way off to the right (with a fieldgate also on your right-hand side). In 200 metres ignore ways off to the right and left. In 150 metres ignore a post with a blue arrow to the left (indicating a bridleway) to follow the blue arrow straight on. In 30 metres ignore a way to the right.

[!] In 275 metres **[7]** *(5 metres before a post with red arrows to the left and ahead), go right on an unmarked path,* your direction 190 degrees.

In 60 metres *fork left.* In 260 metres you come out *on to a tarmac road where you go right,* your direction 215 degrees. In 40 metres you pass the entrance to Prospect House.

In a further 55 metres, *go left on a sandy road,* signposted public bridleway, your direction due south.

In a further 240 metres, ignore a path to the left. In 65 metres cross a stream.

In a further 70 metres, *at a T-junction,* with a cottage on your right-hand side and a wooden fieldgate ahead, *go left,* your direction 80 degrees.

In 240 metres *go straight on,* where an unmarked track crosses. In 85 metres, *within 20 metres of the end of the wood, at a junction, go right,* your direction 125 degrees, staying just within the edge of the wood on your left-hand side.

Keep to this main path, ignoring all ways off. In 360 metres you come to a *tarmac road where you turn right,* your direction 195 degrees.

In 45 metres you pass Headlands House on your right-hand side. In a further 240 metres, you come *to the main tarmac road.*

Turn right and, in 40 metres **[8]**, *turn left* off the road, following the public footpath sign down the tarmac road into the **Peper Harow** estate (which is marked on the OS map).

In 160 metres ignore a kissing gate and signposted path to the right. In 30 metres, ignore a fork to the right by a postbox. After walking a further

200 metres, you come to the (locked) **Church of St Nicholas**, Peper Harow.

In 30 metres *take the stile* (with a metal fieldgate to its left) signposted public footpath, *going to your left,* heading due east. In 30 metres you pass close to a wooden farm shed on your left-hand side and *head to the left of the green pavilion* ahead, with no clear path.

In 135 metres you pass the pavilion on your right-hand side and keep parallel and to the left of the mini pylons. *Enter the wood, some 30 metres to the left of its right-hand edge,* going over a stile.

[9] At the other end of the wood, *at a T-junction,* ignore a footpath straight on and *turn right,* in 8 metres going through a small metal swing gate with a bridleway sign *where you go left,* with the field fence on your left-hand side, your direction 70 degrees.

In 150 metres veer right with the bridleway, a field fence still to your left.

In 235 metres go through a metal fieldgate to *cross the A3 on a bridge.* On the other side, go right downhill towards a petrol station. In 80 metres *turn left on Lower Eashing Road,* your direction 120 degrees.

In 40 metres *turn left between Greenways and Lower Eashing Farm Cottage* on a tarmac road, which is a signposted public bridleway, your direction 40 degrees.

In 40 metres this tarmac road becomes a concrete road, passing Greenways Farm and Stable on your right-hand side. In 120 metres, with a pillbox down on your right, ignore a path off uphill to your left. In 75 metres, you pass under pylons.

In a further 110 metres, where the concrete road turns left, *go straight ahead through a wooden fieldgate on a car-wide earth bridleway,* your direction 55 degrees, in 10 metres passing a pillbox on your left.

In 230 metres go under pylons (a potentially muddy area). In 110 metres you pass under two lots of pylon cables. In 245 metres ignore a path to the left, marked by a post.

[10] In 30 metres you reach a T-junction, with a garden wall ahead. *Here turn right,* following a public footpath sign, your direction 145 degrees.

In 80 metres go past the entrance to a house called Milton Wood (on your right). In 150 metres go through a metal barrier, now back alongside the **River Wey** which is below to your right.

In 500 metres go through another metal barrier. In 40 metres, **[11]** *1 metre before the start of a tarmac road, follow the public footpath signpost right,* your direction due south.

In 75 metres go over a concrete bridge and straight on. In 10 metres ignore a footpath to the left and, in another 10 metres, you *turn left under the pylons,* your direction 140 degrees, with the River Wey on your right-hand side.

In 30 metres you *pass under more pylons* and fork left, your direction 170 degrees.

In 40 metres continue to the left, your direction 100 degrees, *alongside the River Wey on your right-hand side.*

In 120 metres you go under pylons, and again in 55 metres.

In a further 120 metres, your way merges with a tarmac path coming from the left and you continue ahead. In 150 metres cross the stream on a bridge. In a further 280 metres, cross a bridge with scaffolding pole railings. In 5 metres go through a metal barrier, *across an entrance drive and straight on,* passing offices on your right-hand side, with the stream still on your left.

In 65 metres, *at a tarmac road, go right,* your direction 170 degrees.

In 20 metres *go under the railway line. 10 metres after the bridge, fork right on a signposted public footpath.* In 110 metres, having kept parallel to the road, cross the river on a wooden bridge with wooden railings.

In 35 metres you are *back on the main Borough Road, and go straight on,* in 65 metres reaching the entrance to the Church of St Peter & St Paul. If you want to go straight to the station without tea, turn right here down Deanery Place but, instead of following Station Road, take the passageway straight ahead which takes you to the station.

For tea, *go left up Church Street,* which is a car road made of bricks, your direction 125 degrees. Going uphill, in 130 metres you come to the High Street, **Godalming**. Turn left and in 140 metres **Caffè Nero** is on the right-hand side of the road, or continue a little further and **Costa Coffee** is on your left. The **Slug & Lettuce** and **Wetherspoon's** are a little further on.

After tea, *retrace your steps to the church.* Go back down the High Street and, at the Old Town Hall, turn right down Church Lane. When you reach the church, *go straight on to pick up the passageway ahead leading to the station.*

At **Godalming station**, go under the subway to reach the platform for London-bound trains.

Lunch & tea places

Barley Mow *Tilford Green, Tilford, GU10 2BU (01252 792205, www.the barleymowtilford.com).* **Open** *Summer* 11am-11pm daily. *Winter* 11am-3pm, 6-11pm Mon-Thur; 11am-11pm Fri-Sun. *Food served* noon-2pm, 6-9pm Mon-Sat; noon-2pm Sun. An early lunch option, 6.5km (4.0 miles) into the walk. It is by the green and has a riverside garden. In summer, lunch is served until a bit later – and there's dinner on Sundays (6-9pm). Groups of more than 12 should book.
The Donkey *Charleshill, Tilford, GU10 2AU (01252 702124, www.donkeytilford. co.uk).* **Open** 11.30am-3pm, 6-11.30pm Mon-Fri; 11.30am-11.30pm Sat; noon-10.30pm Sun. *Food served* noon-2.30pm, 6-9.30pm Mon-Sat; noon-3.30pm, 6-8.30pm Sun. This pub, 9km (5.6 miles) into the walk or about 50 minutes past the Barley Mow, is the suggested lunch spot. Booking is recommended for seats indoors.

There are several chain options for tea on Godalming High Street: a **Caffè Nero** (01483 420826), a **Costa Coffee** (01483 527589), a **Slug & Lettuce** (01483 527134) and a **Wetherspoon's** (01483 521750). The latter both open late on Sundays.

Walk 13

Oxford Circular

Port Meadow, the river, canal and colleges

Start and finish: Oxford station

Length: 15.2km (9.4 miles)

Time: 4 hours 15 minutes. For the whole outing, including trains, sights and meals, allow as much of the day and evening as possible – a minimum of 9 hours.

Transport: Take the train nearest to **10am** from **Paddington** station

to **Oxford** (journey time about 1 hour). There are usually two direct trains an hour back to London from Oxford, and two CrossCountry services where you can change at Reading.

OS Landranger Map: 164
OS Explorer Map: 180
Oxford is 90km west of London.

Toughness: 1 out of 10

Walk notes: This is not so much a country walk as a day out exploring the historic university city, with an undemanding but enjoyable walk thrown in as an hors d'oeuvre before you start a tour of Oxford University's colleges.

The route is easy and entirely level, but can be muddy along the path beside the River Cherwell after Wolfson College; after periods of heavy rain, paths beside both the Rivers Isis and Cherwell can be flooded. The walk starts along the River Isis to Binsey, a favourite walk for the poet Gerard Manley Hopkins (the 'wind-wandering, weed-winding bank'), who lamented the felling of aspens along the towpath here in his 1879 poem 'Binsey Poplars' ('the sweet especial rural scene'). You can take a dip here if you want. Passing the ruins of Godstow Nunnery, you come to the Trout Inn at Wolvercote (a lunch option) then take in a bit of Port Meadow before coming to the Plough Inn (a second option for lunch).

After lunch the walk heads south along the Oxford Canal, past a

community of houseboats, then across town and via a footbridge by Wolfson College to go along the River Cherwell through its nature reserve, where buttercups are abundant in May. Going through the University Parks, you come to the Pitt Rivers Museum. From here you start your walking tour of Oxford's historic colleges and famous buildings, winding in and out of small streets as the walk fits in many of the colleges before you stop for tea and finally head for the railway station.

Walk options: There are buses from near the Plough Inn back to Oxford, by point **[4]** in the walk directions. Alternatively, you could miss out the leg beside the River Cherwell and instead walk along Banbury Road back into Oxford, or take one of the many buses that go along this road. And if you wish to omit or curtail the tour of the colleges, you can head straight for the railway station at any time once you're back in the city centre.

History: The Saxons fording the River Thames with their oxen gave this place the name 'Oxen-ford'. Robert d'Oilly took over Oxford in 1066, creating a Norman stronghold. Possibly the first college to be founded was **Merton** in 1264, although there had been a university for at least a century before this. A tavern argument between townspeople and scholars in 1354 resulted in a massacre, during which 14 inns or halls were ransacked and a number of chaplains scalped. **Christ Church College** in Oxford was Charles I's headquarters during the Civil War, with **New College** cloisters used as a gunpowder store. In the 16th century, Cranmer, Ridley and Latimer were burnt at the stake in **Broad Street**. Gates at Balliol College still show scorch marks from the flames and there is a **memorial** to these Protestant martyrs in St Giles. The men's colleges started admitting women in 1974.

There are too many places to visit in one day, but you might like to stop at the **Pitt Rivers Museum** (01865 270927, www.prm.ox.ac.uk), which offers free admission until 4.30pm daily and contains shrunken heads and artefacts from around the world. Many of the University Colleges are open to visitors, but most charge for admission. If you attend evensong at **Christ Church College** (usually 6pm), there is no entry fee.

Walk directions

[1] [Numbers in square brackets refer to the map]
Coming off the London train at **Oxford station** on platform 2, cross over the pedestrian bridge to platform 1 and exit the station through its ticket barriers and main ticket office. Outside, *turn right* and in 40 metres cross over a pedestrian bridge signposted to Botley Road. You turn left on the bridge and left again to go down steps to Botley Road, where you *turn left,* your direction due west.

Head up Botley Road, passing Micks Café on your right at a road junction. In a further 30 metres you pass on your right the White House Sports Bar and pub (formerly the Old Gate House pub). Cross the road here by the pedestrian lights and *turn left,* continuing along Botley Road, soon passing the junction with Abbey Road.

In 20 metres, just before the road bridge, *turn right* at the sign for the Thames Path, your direction 310 degrees, to go through bollards and down to the towpath beside the River Isis (Thames).

You now walk along this towpath, with allotments over to your left on the other side of the river and the back gardens to houses on your right. In 330 metres go over a footbridge with metal railings and at the end of the bridge, swing left then right with the path *to keep ahead,* ignoring the paths beside the Oxford Canal going off to the right.

Continuing along the path you soon have water on both sides: [!] after heavy rain at certain times of the year this next leg of the walk can be flooded and impassable. In 550 metres cross a platform bridge with handrails. In a further 300 metres, ignore a bridge on your right-hand side with a path heading towards **Port Meadow** and instead *go straight on* over the larger concrete footbridge with wooden railings ahead of you.

In 120 metres, as the path comes to an end, *turn left to cross over* a mini Brunel-style iron bridge over the river. On the far side, *turn right* to follow the Thames Path sign to continue, now with the river on your right-hand side, your direction 345 degrees. In 20 metres you pass Bossom's Boatyard on your left-hand side and, in 180 metres, you ignore a fork left towards Binsey. In a further 15 metres go through a metal swing gate to the right of a metal fieldgate and keep ahead, now with fields to your left and the river on your right.

Keep ahead beside the river and, in 280 metres, there is a path on your left signposted to the **Perch Inn**. **[2]** [Here,

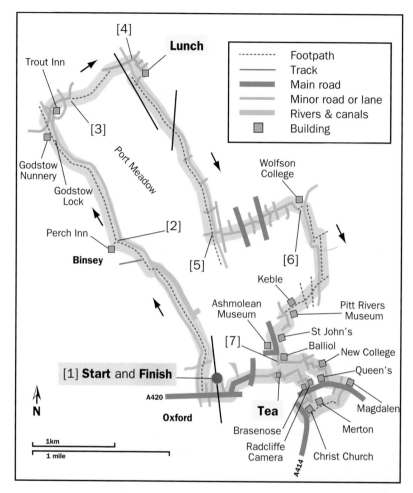

if you would like to make a brief tour of the village of **Binsey**, take this path, which leads out in 50 metres to the pub's garden. The Old School House in Binsey has a number of doll's houses in its windows, including one with a thatched roof. If you continue on the tarmac road beyond the Old School House, in 750 metres you come to **Binsey Church** and St Margaret's Well in the churchyard. Return from Binsey to the riverside.]

Back at the path leading to the Perch Inn, in 10 metres you go through a metal gate to continue your walk beside the river. In 1.6km cross a bridge with wooden handrails and wooden swing gates at either end and head onwards towards a lock. In a further 100 metres go through a wooden swing gate beside **Godstow Lock**. On your left-hand side is Lock Cottage, where you can buy ice-creams and cold drinks.

In 80 metres, at the end of the lock, go through a wooden swing gate to the right of a wooden fieldgate and take the gravel track *half left*. In 100 metres you come to the remains of **Godstow Nunnery** (the entrance is round the far side).

Keep ahead beside the stone wall of the Nunnery and in 70 metres, as the wall turns left and the track swings left, *keep ahead* to cross the grass, your direction 340 degrees. In 80 metres go through a wooden swing gate to come out on to a road. *Turn right,* to cross a road bridge over the river and, in 25 metres, cross another. The **Trout Inn**, Wolvercote, your first lunch pub option, is on the right-hand side, next to the river.

Keep ahead along this road and in 200 metres cross another bridge. Note the memorial at the end of the left-hand parapet wall to two Royal Flying Corps flying officers who were killed in a plane crash some 100 yards from this spot in September 1912.

Some 50 metres past the bridge, with a car park on your right-hand side, and as the road bends to the left by a thatched cottage, *go right through a wooden swing gate,* with the Port Meadow toilets on your right, into **Port Meadow. [3]** Here you *turn half left,* your direction 105 degrees, across the meadow on a faint path, heading towards a low stone bridge over concrete water pipes in the middle of the field.

Cross over this bridge and follow the path *slightly left,* your initial direction 30 degrees, towards the car bridge visible ahead in the distance. In 100 metres the path swings right, past two small trees and a post on your right, your direction now 60 degrees. You have allotments some 25 metres away on your right and houses 90 metres to your left.

In 220 metres, at the end of the houses over to your left and at a path crossing, *turn left,* your direction due north. Avoiding as best you can muddy sections and flooded patches, you head towards the Jubilee Gate, which you go through to leave Port Meadow. *Turn right* along the road and go over the footbridge, which runs parallel to a long road bridge over the railway and then the Oxford Canal.

Some 80 metres from the end of the footbridge, by the bus stop (where those who want a bus into Oxford can drop out of the walk), *turn right* on Wolvercote Green Road. **[4]** Keep straight down this road and, in 230 metres, you come to the **Plough Inn**, the suggested lunch pub option for this walk.

Coming out of the pub door, go *straight ahead* for 50 metres to cross the bridge over the Oxford Canal. On top of the bridge, *turn left* down to the canal and *then turn right* along the towpath, your

Godstow Nunnery.

direction 130 degrees, with the canal on your left-hand side and the railway over to your right (the railway crossing shown here on old OS maps is long gone).

Walk along the towpath beside the canal and in 500 metres you pass under a railway bridge (no.236A). In a further 150 metres you come to a community of houseboats. There are now playing fields (rugby pitches) on the left-hand side of the canal.

You now pass along the way one swing bridge, then two brick road bridges over the canal (nos.238B and 239A). Continue along the towpath and, just before the next bridge (no. 240), go through a wooden fieldgate and head up to a road where you *turn left* over the bridge. On its far side, after 35 metres, you come to a road T-junction with the Anchor pub directly ahead. **[5]**

(If you want to shorten the walk, you can turn right here and keep on going to Walton Street, which leads into Worcester Street and comes out just before the main walk turns right into Hythe Bridge Street, close to the railway station.)

The main route is to *turn right* in front of the pub and in 15 metres to *turn left* up Polstead Road, your direction 75 degrees, now with the pub on your left-hand side. In 200 metres cross Woodstock Road, slightly to the left, to continue straight on along Rawlinson Road.

In 240 metres you come to Banbury Road (where you can take a bus into the centre of Oxford). But continuing on the walk, *cross* Banbury Road, *turn left* up it, then in 30 metres, *turn right* into Linton Road. In 150 metres you pass St Andrew's Church on your right-hand side.

Continue down Linton Road, ignoring all turnings off, and in 210 metres at the end of the road you come to **Wolfson College. [6]** *Turn right* in front of the college and follow the tarmac road through its car park to go through iron gates into the garden. Here you follow the tarmac road *round to the left,* with the college buildings on your left-hand side, and continue straight on, now on

a gravel path, to the end of the buildings. The path swings left and you *turn right* to go over an arched metal footbridge over the **River Cherwell**.

On the far side of the footbridge go through a metal swing gate and in 10 metres, at a path T-junction, ignore the stile ahead, *and turn right,* your direction 195 degrees, on the riverside walk through **Wolfson College Nature Reserve**, with the river on your right-hand side.

In 120 metres you pass the War Memorial Cross on the opposite bank. Your way ahead is now potentially muddy and is prone to flooding. Go over a stile and in 90 metres go over a stream on a small wooden bridge. In a further 50 metres go over a stile and two planks with a wooden railing over a ditch, *then turn left,* following the footpath arrow, away from the river, your direction 60 degrees.

In 45 metres go through another potentially muddy area and go over a plank bridge, to continue ahead on a clear path, your direction now 145 degrees, rejoining the river on your right-hand side. In 90 metres you come to another area liable to flooding, with the Dragon School on the opposite side of the river. In a further 120 metres, you pass tennis courts on the opposite bank, with **Lady Margaret Hall** beyond them.

You go over a concrete humpback bridge with metal railings and, in 240 metres, cross another such bridge and come immediately to a more substantial, and much larger, concrete pedestrian bridge with metal railings, on your right. Cross over this bridge over the river to enter the **University Parks**.

On the far side of this bridge *keep ahead,* your direction 240 degrees, on an earth path. In 100 metres you cross a path and go straight on, now on a surfaced path. In a further 100 metres, at another path crossing, continue ahead, now back on an earth path. Continue through the University Parks and, in 300 metres, leave through **Keble Gate**, *to turn left* on Parks Road, your direction 145 degrees.

[!] You are now about to embark on a walking tour of Oxford University's principal colleges. [!]

You pass **Keble College** on your right-hand side, with its lively yellow-patterned brickwork. Just before the end of the college, you pass **Pitt Rivers Museum** on your left-hand side (its entrance is through the University Museum).

At the far end of Keble College, cross Parks Road by the pedestrian lights and go down Museum Road. In 75 metres, where Blackhall Road goes off to the right, *keep straight on,* passing to the side of a wooden barrier, between houses, along a passageway that in 75 metres goes through another barrier and winds to the right to become the Lamb and Flag Passage. In a further 60 metres pass under an archway and come out on the main road of St Giles.

Turn left, with **St John's College** on your left-hand side and the **Ashmolean Museum** on the other side of the road. 150 metres past the main entrance of St John's, you pass the **Martyrs' Memorial** on your right-hand side. You are now on Magdalen Street East.

In 100 metres *turn left* into Broad Street. [7] Keep ahead and you pass **Balliol College** on your left-hand side and the Oxford Story exhibition on your right, and later two sections of Blackwell's Bookshop on your left-hand side (with the White Horse pub in between). You pass the **Sheldonian Theatre** on your right and in 65 metres *turn right* into Cattle Street.

In 30 metres *turn left* on New College Lane and go under the **Bridge of Sighs**. You now zigzag round with the lane, with **New College** on your left-hand side. This lane becomes Queens Lane, with **Queen's College** on your right-hand side, to come out eventually on to the High Street. Here cross over the road and *turn left* along it.

You pass Merton Street going to the right. In 85 metres, with **Magdalen College** on your left-hand side, *turn right* on Rose Lane. In 120 metres go through **Christ Church Gates**, with Meadow Cottages on your right-hand side.

20 metres beyond the gates, *go right* on Dead Man's Walk, along the side wall of Meadow Cottages, your direction 305 degrees, with Christ Church private playing fields over to your left and walls on your right-hand side. In 20 metres you pass **a notice honouring James Sadler**'s balloon ascent in 1784.

In 120 metres you come to **Merton College** on your right-hand side. At the far end of this college, do not exit the gates on your right *but turn left,* with the wall and **Christ Church College** on your right-hand side, and the playing fields still on your left-hand side, your direction due south.

In 100 metres you come to a broad sandy avenue *where you turn right,* your direction 265 degrees. In 120 metres you pass the visitors' entrance to Christ Church College on your right and, in a further 90 metres, [!] *ignore the fork to the right* and instead *keep straight on* to go through the **War Memorial Garden**, in 80 metres coming out on to the main road, called Aldgates.

Here you *turn right,* your direction due north. In 110 metres you pass the main entrance to Christ Church College. In a further 100 metres *you turn right,* by the **Museum of Oxford**, into Blue Boar Street. In 100 metres you pass the Bear pub on your left-hand side to continue straight on along Bear Lane. At the end of this road go through bollards to come out on to a bend in King Edward Street. Go across it (Oriel Square) for 30 metres and then pick up the passageway, Oriel Street, *on your left,* your direction 5 degrees, with **Oriel College** on your right-hand side.

In 80 metres *cross over* the High Street (going through bollards on either side). The **University Church of St Mary the Virgin** is on your right-hand side as you continue along a passageway into Radcliffe Square, passing **Radcliffe Camera** on your right-hand side and the entrance to **Brasenose College** on your left. 25 metres beyond this entrance, *you*

turn left, signposted to the Covered Market on Brasenose Lane, your direction 255 degrees.

In 120 metres pass a wooden barrier and *turn right,* on Turl Street. In 20 metres you pass the entrance to **Jesus College** on your left-hand side and, in a further 10 metres, the entrance to **Exeter College** on your right-hand side.

In 30 metres *turn left* into Ship Street, at the end of which you pass the **City Church of St Michael** on your right-hand side. Cross over the Cornmarket and *go straight on* along St Michael's Street. 20 metres along this street on your right-hand side is the suggested tea place, the **Nosebag**, on the first floor of nos.6 to 8. (Note: the railway station is about 10 minutes' walk from here.)

Coming out of the Nosebag, *turn right* along St Michael's Street. In 120 metres *turn right* into New Inn Hall Street and, in a further 50 metres, *turn left* into George Street.

In 160 metres, at the crossroads, *go straight across* at pedestrian lights into Hythe Bridge Street. In 80 metres go over a bridge over the river and pass the Oxford Retreat pub (formerly called the Antiquity Hall) on your left-hand side.

In 130 metres, at a main road junction (with Frideswide Square on your left and the new **Said Business School**, University of Oxford, ahead and over to your right), *go straight on,* now along Park End Street, and in 70 metres you come to **Oxford station** over to your right. The Reading and London platform (platform 1) is on the near side of the station.

Lunch & tea places

In the city centre, you are spoilt for choice for cafés, restaurants and pubs, but the following are our suggestions.

Trout Inn *Godstow Road, Wolvercote, OX2 8PN (01865 510930, www.the troutoxford.co.uk).* **Open** 11am-11pm daily. *Food served* noon-10pm Mon-Thur; noon-10.30pm Fri, Sat; noon-9.30pm Sun. One of the two possible lunch stops on this walk. A popular pub that enjoys a lovely Thameside setting and has plenty of indoor and outdoor seating. Sunday walkers should book ahead.

Plough Inn *The Green, Wolvercote, OX2 8BD (01865 556969, www.theplough oxford.co.uk).* **Open** 11am-3pm, 6-11pm Mon-Sat; noon-10.30pm Sun. *Food served* noon-2pm, 6-9pm Mon-Sat; noon-2.30pm, 6-8.30pm Sun. This homely pub, furnished with comfortable sofas and armchairs in the dining area, is our suggested lunch stop. There is a library room and outdoor dining area, and one restaurant space was previously a morgue. Pub favourites, snacks and specials are served, with traditional roasts on Sundays.

Nosebag *6-8 St Michael's Street, Oxford, OX1 2DU (01865 721033, www.nosebagoxford.co.uk).* **Open** 9.30am-9.30pm Mon-Thur; 9.30am-10pm Fri, Sat; 9.30am-8.30pm Sun. The recommended tea stop for this walk.

Walk 14

Gomshall to Guildford

Blackheath forest and River Wey.

Start: Gomshall station
Finish: Guildford station

Length: 15.6km (9.7 miles)

Time: 3 hours 50 minutes. For the whole outing, including trains, sights and meals, allow 7 hours 30 minutes.

Transport: Trains to Gomshall, whether departing from **London Bridge** (changing at Redhill) or from **Waterloo** (changing at Guildford), are very infrequent, so you will have to decide whether to make an early start around **9am** or a late one nearer **11am**. Journey time by either route is a little over one hour. Returning, there are frequent trains from **Guildford** to

London, taking 34-40 minutes if you catch a fast one (avoid the stopping trains, which take twice as long). Whether to buy a day return to Gomshall or to Guildford depends on your departure station: consult station staff. If you are driving, there are direct but infrequent trains between Guildford and Gomshall. Guildford station is closer to London and has a large car park, but you can park near Gomshall station for free.

OS Landranger Maps: 186 & 187
OS Explorer Map: 145
Gomshall, map reference TQ089477, is in **Surrey**, 10km east of Guildford.

Toughness: 3 out of 10

Walk notes: There is much that is ancient, beautiful and surprising to be enjoyed on this walk. It starts in Gomshall, passing some of the pleasant buildings on its outskirts, before crossing fields to the interesting church and village of Shere on the Tilling Bourne stream, a place packed full of 15th- and 16th-century timber-framed buildings. The walk then continues past massive gnarled trees in Albury Park and through the pine woods of Blackheath Common. From there, the route follows the Downs Link path and the River Wey into Guildford for tea at the Yvonne Arnaud Theatre. Short stretches of the Downs Link can be muddy.

Walk options: To shorten this walk, you could call a taxi from the lunchtime pub, or, at the double asterisk [**] (map point [11]), go along the A248 to catch a train back to London from Shalford.

History: **Gomshall station** is where it is because, in the 1840s, the site for a railway station was decided on a given day by whichever shortlisted spot had the greatest number of people waiting. The publican at the Black Horse, Gomshall, provided free beer for those willing to wait at his premises, as he wanted the station to be at Gomshall.

    Gomshall is detailed in the Domesday Book (1086) as having 'land for 20

Gomshall to Guildford

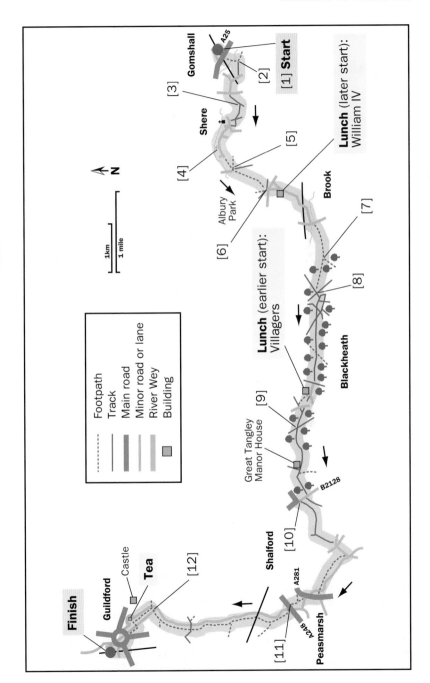

ploughs, 30 villagers, 8 smallholders with 18 ploughs, 6 slaves'. Of **Shere**, it reports: 'Queen Edith held it. Now it does not pay tax – 19 villagers and 6 smallholders with 12 ploughs. A church. 6 slaves.' By the 16th and 17th centuries Shere had grown into a small township of perhaps 40 houses (most of which remain today) housing weavers, blacksmiths, wheelwrights and tailors.

St James's Church, Shere, was built in 1190. It is a rare example of a church in the Early English Transitional Style (with the round Norman arches giving way to pointed ones), but its lychgate was designed by architect Edwin Lutyens. The nave pews have numbers – at one time people paid rent to the church for them.

In 1329, anchoress **Christine Carpenter** was enclosed in a cell on the north wall of the church (receiving food through a grating on the outside wall) for three years. She then returned to the world before petitioning to be re-enclosed. The bishop consented: 'The said Christine shall be thrust back into the said enclosure that she may learn how nefarious was her committed sin.'

The **Alms Chest** in the church dates from about 1200 and was used to collect money for the crusades fought in the Holy Land.

Walk directions

[1] [Numbers in square brackets refer to the map]

Leave **Gomshall station** from platform 1 (the side with the caravans on display) and turn left downhill on the station approach road, your direction 240 degrees.

In 110 metres, at the T-junction with the A25, *cross over and turn left under the bridge* using the pedestrian tunnel on the right, your direction 155 degrees.

10 metres past the bridge, *go right on the signposted public footpath,* a lane called Wonham Way, your direction 225 degrees.

In 80 metres go across a bridge over the Tilling Bourne stream. In a further 80 metres you pass a house called Badgers Oak on your left.

[2] In a further 50 metres *turn right on an unmarked bridleway* (just before the gateway of Twiga Lodge and with the bridleway parallel to an earth farm road on its left), your direction 265 degrees.

In 200 metres you pass a manor house on your right and a farm on your left.

In 40 metres at a road T-junction *turn right* and in 20 metres go back under the railway line.

In 10 metres, at a car road T-junction by a house (no.4), *turn left,* your direction 290 degrees.

Ignore ways off and in a further 190 metres, at the T-junction, *go to the right of the grass triangle, cross over the road and continue more or less straight on* along Gravelpits Lane, your direction 295 degrees, on a signposted public bridleway. In 35 metres the lane swings left, your direction 220 degrees.

[3] In a further 65 metres at a junction of paths, *take the bridleway to your right,* with Gravel Pits Farmhouse on your left, your direction 290 degrees.

Keep to the path, ignoring ways off. You can see Netley manor house (as marked on the OS map) to your right, northwards.

In 500 metres, at the corner of a field, with a footpath post on your right, *turn right through a swing gate, downwards on a minor path towards the church,* your direction 310 degrees.

In 120 metres you come out through another wooden swing gate and *keep straight on along the car road,* your direction 290 degrees, past the **Church of St James, Shere**, on your right-hand side (a church that is well worth a visit).

[4] In 100 metres your onward route is to *cross over the main road* (slightly to the right) to *continue on Lower Street,* with the stream on your right, your direction 305 degrees. (You might like to explore the village a bit first, by turning right over the stream into Middle Street.)

Continuing on, in 80 metres ignore the Orchard Road turning on the left. Go straight on, past the sign saying 'No entry except for access'. In 20 metres you pass the Old Prison House on the left.

In a further 65 metres, with Summerdown Cottage on your left and a ford and footbridge on your right, carry straight on, along a signposted public footpath, your direction 250 degrees, the river still on the right.

In 90 metres ignore a turning on the right across the river. In 20 metres you come to a wooden swing gate on the right. Go through it to continue ahead,

the river still on your right and your direction 250 degrees.

[5] In 110 metres go through another wooden swing gate (it has another ford and wooden footbridge on its right) and *turn half left to cross a trail and go through a kissing gate ahead.* Continue through parkland on a wide grassy path with fences on both sides, your direction 205 degrees.

In 600 metres, exit the park through a wooden swing gate with South Lodge on your right and *go across the car road (slightly to your left) to continue on an earth car road,* your direction 170 degrees. **[6]**

Go straight on for 220 metres, passing several houses on your right-hand side. You will reach a road where you *turn right.* In 20 metres you come to the **William IV** pub, Albury Heath, on your right, the suggested place for lunch if you made a later start. Coming out of the pub after lunch, turn right along the road.

If you are not stopping at the pub, continue along the road. In 225 metres go under the railway bridge, ignoring footpaths to the right and left, to continue on the car road.

In 320 metres you come to a car road T-junction and *turn left,* signposted to Farley Green, your direction due south.

In 45 metres *turn right on to a broad track,* signposted as a public footpath and also 'Surrey Hacking Centre', your direction 215 degrees.

In 40 metres you pass the horse-riding centre on your right. Continue on uphill and slightly to the right. In a further 50 metres keep straight on across a track.

[7] In a further 70 metres, where the track bends left, *go right,* following a footpath sign, along an enclosed path with a fence on your left and hedge on the right, your direction 265 degrees.

In 340 metres go over a stile and continue along the field with a fence on your right, towards woodland ahead.

[8] In 60 metres cross another stile to enter the wood, marked Blackheath

on the OS map. Keep straight on this path, ignoring ways off.

In 210 metres go over a stile. In 25 metres, at a junction of paths, keep straight on (the footpath post is numbered 235), your direction 285 degrees.

[!] In a further 160 metres you come to a multiple path junction in a large open area. Imagine this space as a road junction roundabout and *take the second left path* (this is narrow, while the third left is within a metre of it and broader), your direction 245 degrees.

In 40 metres your way merges with one on your right. Continue on, your direction now 205 degrees.

In 40 metres you come to a T-junction with a wide bridleway, with a blue arrow on a post pointing right. Here you *turn right,* your direction 280 degrees. Your way goes straight off into the distance, almost as straight as a Roman road.

Ignore all ways off through **Blackheath Common**. In 1.2km keep straight on through a car park.

The other side of the car park, with some houses on your left, continue ahead on the tarmac road (Blackheath Lane), your direction 255 degrees. In 145 metres you come to the **Villagers** pub on your right, the suggested lunchtime stop if you took an early train.

After lunch, *turn right out of the pub* into its car park and *cross it, veering to the right to enter a path* marked with a blue-painted post, your direction 305 degrees.

In 100 metres *take the left fork,* marked by a blue-painted post, your direction 295 degrees. In a further 80 metres you pass a house on your left.

[9] In 55 metres cross over a car road to continue straight on, following a footpath sign, your direction still 295 degrees. In 70 metres cross over a path to continue on.

In 25 metres you come to a T-junction with an unasphalted car lane marked **Downs Link** and you turn left, your direction 280 degrees. In a further 80 metres you pass Tangley Way, wooden buildings round a courtyard, on your left.

In 120 metres keep straight on at a junction, passing a large wooden gate on your left, your direction 295 degrees.

In a further 360 metres the village of Chilworth is visible away to your right. In another 280 metres you pass two large hay barns on your right.

In 45 metres you come to a *T-junction, where you continue to the left (virtually straight on),* your direction 280 degrees. You can glimpse **Great Tangley Manor House** through the hedging on your right. In 80 metres you pass the entrance drive of this house.

240 metres further along the lane, with a car road T-junction 40 metres ahead, *turn right at a three-armed wooden sign saying 'Downs Link',* your direction 305 degrees. This stretch can be muddy.

Until the asterisk **[*]** *below, your route is to follow the Downs Link.*

In more detail: Ignoring ways off, in 160 metres cross over a car road to continue on a bridleway marked 'Downs Link', your direction 245 degrees initially. **[10]**

In 20 metres ignore a path to the right to continue on past a house on your left through another potentially muddy zone. In 280 metres you pass a post informing you that the South Downs Way is 305 metres ahead. Continue 30 metres to the path junction.

Villagers.

(At this point you could detour to the Tower – a 19th-century folly – and Chinthurst Hill for a good view. Go straight ahead uphill and up some steps. Ahead is a footpath post signed to the Tower. Follow a series of footpath signs to go steadily uphill to the top. Then retrace your route back to the path junction.)

Continuing the main route, turn right on the Downs Link bridleway, your direction 255 degrees (or, if you're coming back from Chinthurst Hill, turn left).

In 345 metres ignore a stile and footpath off to the right and continue downhill on a left bend with the main path, your direction 200 degrees. Visible ahead of you are the outskirts of Shalford village.

In 345 metres, amid more potential mud, you pass Southlands with its horses on your left and come down to a car road. Cross it to continue ahead along a tarmac road, Tannery Lane, signposted Downs Link, your direction 225 degrees.

In 20 metres by a Downs Link post, *go up left on a tarmac path towards a pair of houses where you turn right.* In 40 metres cross Drodges Close to continue on the tarmac path to the left of the phonebox, parallel to the road below you on the right.

In 80 metres go down to the left of the bridge and in 20 metres *fork right to go over a mini bridge* that is below and to the left of the main bridge.

[*] You come to a path T-junction. *Go right, under the bridge* on a clear path, your direction 330 degrees, with industrial buildings on your right and the **River Wey** on your left.

Here you can choose to pick up the meandering path closer to the river on the left, although it may be overgrown with nettles in summer. After 265 metres it crosses a side stream on some concrete bars – at this point it is best to return to the main path.

345 metres on from the concrete bars, continue on the main path on a bridge crossing the river and keep straight on towards the A281, reaching it in 65 metres.

Turn right on the pavement of this A road and in 35 metres cross the bridge over the river. After 80 metres, with Somerswey Cul-de-Sac on your right, *cross the road.* 10 metres beyond a brick wall on the left, *turn left on a signed path,* your direction 310 degrees.

In 180 metres you emerge from the path with Wharf Cottages at your left. Continue ahead along a tarmac path, your direction 300 degrees.

In 80 metres continue on a gravel path with an extensive office and industrial estate on your right. In a further 145 metres you come to the A248 and a bridge. **[11] [**]** If you want to end the walk at this point, go right on the A248 to the station at Shalford.

For the main route, *go left over the bridge and immediately right to pick up the riverbank path* on the other side by the National Trust sign, your direction 335 degrees. The River Wey is now on your right.

Keep straight on along the riverbank, ignoring all ways off, in due course going under a pair of bridges, passing St Catherine's Lock and eventually going under another bridge.

After 2.5km of this riverbank walk, the path crosses a mini weir by a bridge. *Immediately turn left* with this branch of the river now on your left, your direction 350 degrees. **[12]**

In 150 metres go over a bridge with metal railings and another mini weir. Now the canal is on your right and the river on your left.

In 80 metres you reach Millmead Lock. For tea at the **Yvonne Arnaud Theatre**, *go right over a bridge.* In 70 metres you come out to the entrance of the **building**. After tea, turn right out of the theatre to return to Millmead Lock and go straight on. In 25 metres cross another bridge.

If you are not going to tea at the theatre, turn left at Millmead Lock and cross the bridge.

Turn right with the river now on your right-hand side, your direction 335 degrees.

In 130 metres *fork right off the car road to follow the riverside terrace path.* In 75 metres, by the bridge, bear left with the path up beside the **White House** pub on your left; this is an alternative tea stop, especially useful for those doing the walk on a Sunday, when the Yvonne Arnaud Theatre is shut.

With St Nicholas Church ahead, *turn right, following the pedestrian sign to the station.* Continue along the path to go under the bridge, then *ahead up a short flight of steps. Turn left at the top,* soon reaching the main road where you *turn right.*

In 50 metres you come to an underpass that takes you to **Guildford station** on the other side of the road for trains back to London.

Lunch & tea places

William IV *Little London, Albury, GU5 9DG (01483 202685, www.william ivalbury.com).* **Open** 11am-3pm, 5.30-11pm Mon-Fri; 11am-11pm Sat; noon-11pm Sun. *Food served* noon-2pm, 7-9pm Mon-Thur; noon-2pm, 7-9.30pm Fri; noon-2.30pm, 7-9.30pm Sat; noon-2.30pm Sun. This is the suggested pub for lunch for those taking a later train.

Villagers *Blackheath Lane, Blackheath, GU4 8RB (01483 893152).* **Open** noon-3pm, 6-11pm Mon-Sat; noon-9pm Sun. *Food served* noon-2.30pm, 7-9.30pm daily. The suggested lunch stop for those who have made an earlier start.

Yvonne Arnaud Theatre *Millbrook, Guildford, GU1 3UX (01483 569334, www.yvonne-arnaud.co.uk).* **Open** 10am-11pm Mon-Sat. If you're doing the walk from Monday to Saturday, we recommend taking tea at the theatre.

White House *8 High Street, Guildford, GU2 4AJ (01483 302006).* **Open** noon-11.30pm Mon-Sat; noon-10.30pm Sun. *Food served* noon-9pm Mon-Sat; noon-7pm Sun. An alternative tea stop for Sunday walkers, the White Horse is close to both the river and St Nicholas Church.

Walk 15

Leigh to Tunbridge Wells

Penshurst Place and the Medway Valley.

Start: Leigh station
Finish: Tunbridge Wells station

Length: 18.9km (11.7 miles)

Time: 5 hours 20 minutes. For the whole outing, including trains, sights and meals, allow 10 hours 30 minutes.

Transport: Take the train nearest to **9.45am** from **London Bridge** station to **Leigh** (Kent), going via East Croydon and Redhill (journey time 1 hour). On Sundays there is only a direct service in summer; at other times of the year you would need to change at Redhill, with a longer journey time. An alternative route is to travel out via Tonbridge, changing there for a connecting service to Leigh; this indirect route is sometimes quicker. There are frequent direct trains from **Tunbridge Wells** back to Charing Cross (journey time about 55 minutes). Buy a day return to Tunbridge Wells.

If you are driving, you can park near Leigh station and return by train, changing at Tonbridge for the hourly service to Leigh.

OS Landranger Map: 188
OS Explorer Map: 147
Leigh, map reference TQ546462, is in **Kent**, 4km west of Tonbridge.

Toughness: 5 out of 10

Walk notes: The route of this walk is through a landscape of great beauty, confirming the description of Kent as 'the Garden of England'. It proceeds through the grounds of Penshurst Place, with fine views of the house, taking in a truly pastoral landscape of rivers, lakes, woods and rolling hills, and passes through the lovely village of Penshurst. The walk then makes its way along the River Medway and into historic Royal Tunbridge Wells, through woods and parks that extend right into the heart of the town. The suggested tea place is in the colonnaded Pantiles.

Walk options: You can reduce the length of the walk by 4km, by more or less following the River Medway from point **[5]** to point **[8]** on the map – missing out the steepest hill, but also the suggested lunchtime stop and the best view. This would be a good option if you set out late and stop for lunch at one of the alternative places in Penshurst. Except on Sundays, you can also get a 231 or 233 bus about once an hour going to Tunbridge Wells or Edenbridge, from either the bottom of Smart's Hill (a ten-minute walk from the suggested lunchtime pub) or from Penshurst. For bus information, call 0871 200 2233.

History: The stately home of **Penshurst Place** (01892 870307) is a perfectly preserved, unfortified manor house that has been the home of the Sidney family since 1552, when Edward VI gave it to his old tutor, Sir William Sidney. The poet Sir Philip Sidney was born here in 1554. The oldest part of the building dates from the 14th century, but the present house represents a curious blend of five centuries of architectural styles. Penshurst Place is open on weekends from mid February to the end of March (10.30am-4.30pm), and daily from the end of March to the end of October, when the gardens open from 10.30am to 6pm and the house from noon to 4pm. Admission (2011) is £9.80; or £7.80 for the gardens only.

On the south side of **St John the Baptist Church**, Penshurst, are timber-framed cottages that form part of **Leicester Square** (named after a favourite of Elizabeth I) and include a post-office house from 1850. In the Sidney Chapel of the church are many memorials and the effigy of the top half of Stephen de Penshurst, Warden of the Cinque Ports and Constable of Dover Castle, who died in 1299. The fine armorial ceiling in the chapel was restored in 1966. By the side altar is the Luke Tapestry (in Greek), made by Penshurst's former village doctor: it honours the partnership between medical science and Christianity.

The spa town of **Royal Tunbridge Wells** had its beginning in 1606, when a courtier, Dudley, Lord North, discovered a chalybeate (iron-bearing) spring that made good the damage he had done to his health through dissolute living. At the town's zenith, William Pitt, Dr Johnson, David Garrick and Sir Joshua Reynolds were regular visitors. Queen Victoria frequented Tunbridge Wells as a child, but the 'Royal' prefix was added in 1909 by Edward VII. The colonnaded **Pantiles** are named from the small clay tiles that Princess Anne paid for in 1698, after her son fell on the slippery ground.

Walk directions

[1] [Numbers in square brackets refer to the map]

From either platform at **Leigh station**, take the path down to the road. *Turn left* and walk up the road, your direction 200 degrees. In 100 metres, you pass an oast-house conversion called Paul's Farm Oast. 150 metres further on, to the right of Paul's Hill House, there is a signpost indicating a link to the Eden Valley Walk, with a concrete public footpath sign at ground level.

[2] *Turn right up this car-wide track,* your direction 240 degrees initially. In 150 metres you come to a metal fieldgate with a black sign saying 'Penshurst Place Estate Public Footpath'. Cross over the stile to the left of the gate and continue along the track. In 100 metres you come to a wooden post on the right of the path. Go slightly left here, to the far-left corner of the field, 250 metres away.

Continue in the same direction down an avenue of plane trees, ignoring a footpath off to the right after 100 metres. In a further 300 metres you come to a metal fieldgate and go through the adjacent squeeze gate, to continue on the Eden Valley Walk.

In 100 metres, where the Eden Valley Walk goes off to the left, you continue ahead on the wide grassy path, soon with a fine view of Penshurst Place, Penshurst village church and the sylvan dales of **Penshurst Park** on your left.

In 550 metres, by a three-arm signpost **[3]**, *turn left down the hill,* between the trees, on a broad grassy path, aiming towards Penshurst Place. 350 metres down the hill, pass through a squeeze gate and follow the wide grassy path as it turns slightly to the right, aiming for the far end of the fence on your right.

In 200 metres go through a gate in this fence to follow the fence on your left-hand side, with the lake beyond it. In 150 metres, where the fence turns left, continue straight on towards a kissing gate in the fence 180 metres ahead. Go through this gate and walk straight

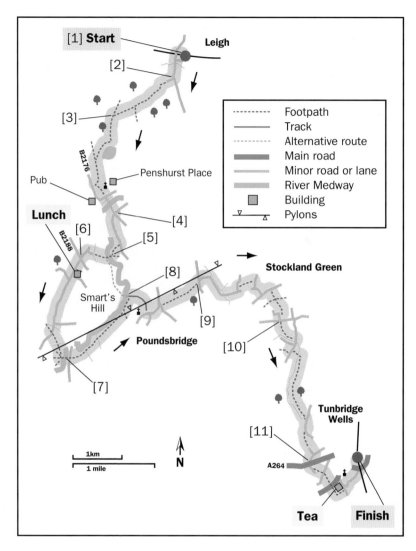

towards the right-hand side of Penshurst Place, your direction due south.

In 450 metres go through a pair of kissing gates to cross a tarmac road and continue south on a grassy path. In 150 metres you come to a projecting piece of Penshurst Place's hedge-topped stone wall and continue ahead with the wall on your left-hand side. In 80

metres go through a gate leading into the churchyard of **St John the Baptist Church**, Penshurst.

Walk through the churchyard (the church is worth visiting – enter through the second door on your left). Continue out of the churchyard, underneath a cottage that stands on stilts (in a line of remarkable ancient cottages), into

Leicester Square and down past the 1850 **post office**. Some stone steps take you down to the road.

(If you want an early lunch – for example, when planning to take the **shortcut** later on – turn right here for the **Leicester Arms** or **Quaintways** tea room. Afterwards, return to this point.)

To continue on the main walk, *turn left* and follow the road as it curves around to the right. The entrance to Penshurst Place is on your left, on the corner. You cross a backwater on a small stone bridge and then, 150 metres beyond this, the **River Medway** itself on a second stone bridge.

[4] 150 metres further on, going slightly uphill, you come to a sign pointing left to the 'Enterprise Centre' and a green footpath sign on the other side of the road. *Turn right on to the footpath,* along a grassy car-wide track.

In 350 metres ignore a track leading into the field on your right. In a further 350 metres, you come to a hedge with some disused hop-poles on your right.

Go past the hedge and **[!]** *turn right along the field edge* (even though there may be no indication of a footpath here). You are aiming for a large footbridge, which you can see in the opposite corner of the field. Halfway down, follow the field edge round to the left and then cut diagonally across the field to the bridge (this is the route shown on the OS map, but you could walk all the way around the field edge if you prefer). Cross over the **River Medway** on this footbridge. **[5]**

(Once over the bridge, you have the option of *turning left for a* **shortcut**. Follow the field edge for 600 metres, keeping the river close by on your left, then go through a gap in the hedge and over a plank into the next field. *Turn left* and go along the field edge, following it round to the right towards a stile in the barbed-wire fence. Cross over the stile, *turn right* and follow the field edge up and round to the left; when you go over the brow of the hill you will see a large metal footbridge in the bottom right-

hand corner of the field. Go down to this bridge, cross back over the River Medway and take the path straight ahead across the field, your direction 100 degrees; this is [8] below.)

[5] To continue the main walk: On the other side of the bridge, *turn right* to go along the field edge. In 50 metres, where the river curves off to your right, continue straight on across the field, towards a red-brick building in the distance, your direction 290 degrees.

In 220 metres you come to the far side of the field and see a 'Penshurst Estate public footpath' sign. Cross over the ditch and head up the grassy car-wide track.

In 200 metres you come to a T-junction with an unmade-up lane, with Ford Place (marked on the OS map) on your right-hand side. *Turn left along this track,* your direction 220 degrees initially.

[6] In 300 metres you come to a T-junction with the B2188. Directly opposite you can see the old wooden buildings of South Park Farm, with the house of South Park in the background. *Turn left* on to the road and then immediately *take the right fork,* signposted 'Smart's Hill, half mile'.

In 650 metres, having ignored a bridleway to the left, you come to a T-junction, where you have a choice. For the suggested lunchtime stop, *turn left,* following the sign for Fordcombe and Tunbridge Wells. In 150 metres you come to the **Spotted Dog** on your left-hand side. (For an alternative lunch stop, *turn right* and in 30 metres fork right again. In another 350 metres you come to the **Bottle House Inn**.)

After lunch at the Spotted Dog, turn right out of the pub, retracing your steps up the road. In 150 metres, continue past the road you ascended before lunch. 30 metres further on, *fork left along Nunnery Lane.* In 150 metres ignore a footpath on the right.

(After lunch at the Bottle House Inn, go back down the road you came on for 25 metres, then *take a footpath on the right.* In 200 metres you come out on to Nunnery Lane and turn right.)

Follow this road steeply downhill, ignoring ways off, for the next 500 metres. At the bottom of the hill go straight past the turning to the left, signposted Fordcombe and Tunbridge Wells, following the sign for Walter's Green and Blackham. In 50 metres *turn left off the road,* where public footpath signs point to both left and right. Cross over the stile and follow a line of oak trees, your direction 140 degrees.

100 metres further on, you come to the last oak in the row and continue straight on down the hill, for 120 metres, to a wooden bridge with a scaffolding pole railing, crossing a stream through the hedgerow.

On the other side, head half right across the field on a faint path, your direction 190 degrees, aiming for the right-hand end of a hedgerow on the banks of the River Medway. On reaching it, keep the river on your left as you bear left with the bend of the river. In 120 metres you come to a footbridge on your left. *Cross the river on this bridge* and bear half left along a path, heading north-east towards a metal fieldgate 100 metres away.

[7] Cross the stile to the right of the gate, which brings you out to the B2188. Cross over the road but ignore a footpath directly opposite and turn left along the road. In 15 metres *take another footpath on the right,* over a stile. Head across the field, your direction 70 degrees. In 50 metres cross over a stile and a ditch, and continue along the side of the next field, in the same direction as before, with oast houses on your right-hand side.

In 350 metres you come to the corner of the field. Follow the path as it bears around to the left. 20 metres further on, turn right across the wooden bridge with a scaffolding-pole railing, which takes you into the next field, where you continue on a faint path, your direction 70 degrees.

In 150 metres you come to a bend of the river on your left. Ignore a path leading off between trees into the field on your right and continue ahead through a squeeze gap in the wire fence. Head slightly left, your direction 40 degrees, eventually passing under some pylons and meeting the river again in 500 metres. Continue with the riverbank close by on your left-hand side for the next 700 metres, going through hedges and across ditches as necessary.

[8] You then come to a bridge with high metal railings, going over the River Medway. Do not cross the bridge. Instead *turn right* and go along the left-hand field edge towards a row of trees and an electricity pylon in the distance, your direction 100 degrees. In 250 metres go

through a wooden gate to the right of a metal fieldgate and *turn half right* uphill.

Ahead of you is a tiny (locked) **chapel** and graveyard (used because Penshurst churchyard is full), and the path goes up the side of a row of oak trees towards the left-hand edge of the graveyard. You come to a metal fieldgate and go through the wooden gate on its left. 40 metres further on, you pass the wooden gate leading into the churchyard and come out on to the road.

Turn left on to the road (Coopers Lane). In 120 metres you come to a T-junction, with Poundsbridge House opposite. *Turn left,* down the hill. In 150 metres, at the bottom of the hill, go over the bridge that crosses a small brook. 50 metres beyond the bridge, you come to another T-junction, signposted Penshurst and Leigh to the left, with a 1593 house and walled garden on your right. *Turn right* and, in 20 metres, **[!]** *turn left off the road,* over the stile which is marked by concrete and wooden footpath signs. Head straight up the hill, with the edge of the field on your right-hand side, your direction at this point 65 degrees.

For the next 1km you will be walking more or less parallel to the pylons away on your left-hand side.

In more detail: In 300 metres the path goes underneath two parallel sets of overhead cables. Continue along the edge of the pond on your right-hand side. 80 metres further on, at the far end of the pond, cross over a stile into the next field. Continue in the same direction, with the field edge on your right-hand side. In 60 metres the overhead cables take a sharp right-hand turn, but you continue straight on, to cross a stile that you can see directly ahead of you, your direction 95 degrees.

Continue along the path, with another pond on your right-hand side. In 50 metres *go over a stile into the next field and turn right uphill,* heading in the same direction as before, with trees and the edge of the field on your right-hand side.

In 150 metres cross over a ditch into the next field and continue ahead. In 200 metres, over the brow of the hill, you again have the field edge on your right-hand side. In another 120 metres, cross over the stile in the corner of the field (with a metal gate on its left-hand side) to follow the footpath between a fence and a copse.

[9] 120 metres further on, you come out on to a road. *Turn left down the road.* In 35 metres, turn right down a car-wide track, marked by a concrete public footpath signpost and a wooden sign for Squirrelsmead and Barden Mill Cottage. In 160 metres cross a stile to the left of a metal fieldgate. Beyond this, follow the track sharply round to the right. In 180 metres ignore the turning off to the left and continue ahead. 160 metres further on, the track curves around to the left, across a brook.

450 metres further on, you come to the top of the hill, with a barn on your left-hand side and a large house with an oast chimney on your right. At the end of the track, just beyond the barn, there is a metal fieldgate. Cross over the stile made of steps next to it and go half right across a concrete yard for 15 metres. Go to the left of the large horse chestnut tree and cross over the stile to the right of the wooden fieldgate, and walk straight ahead with the edge of the field on your right-hand side, your direction due east. In 120 metres cross over the stile into the next field. Follow the path half left, slightly downhill at first, to skirt a tall hedge up ahead on the right-hand side of the field.

In 150 metres, at the far side of the field, cross over a stile that brings you out on to a tarmac lane. *Turn right up the hill.* In 90 metres there is a house on your right-hand side called Hollanbys. In another 250 metres along this winding road you come to a T-junction.

Turn left on to the road through the village of **Stockland Green**. In 120 metres you pass Birchetts Lodge on your left-hand side (and a white sign pointing to various other Birchetts). Immediately opposite the drive going off to the left here, there is a public footpath sign on the right-hand side of the road. *Turn right here* through the metal kissing gate, down the path leading between the houses. (If you see Birchetts Cottage on your right-hand side, you have gone too far down the road.) In 20 metres cross over the stile and continue along the left-hand side of the field.

In 60 metres, at the corner of the field, cross over the stile on your right-hand side. Turn left and resume your previous direction along the left-hand field edge. In 100 metres, at the top corner of this field, *turn left* through the kissing gate.

Go straight down the path, between the hedgerows, your direction 80 degrees. In 25 metres there is a wooden post on your left, pointing straight ahead for the High Weald Walk, but you *turn right* here through a metal kissing gate and follow a narrow path, heading due south.

[10] In a further 200 metres you come down through another kissing gate on to a road.

Go straight over the road and on to the narrow footpath opposite. This is a potentially muddy little path that makes its way between hedgerows, steeply downhill. In 500 metres you come out on to a busy minor road, where you *turn right.*

In 20 metres the road crosses over a small brook and passes the Redsheen Kennels at Mill Farm. 200 metres further on, the road curves around to the right, and there is a public footpath sign off to the left.

Turn left off the road here on to a track going downhill, your direction 135 degrees. In 120 metres cross over a fast-flowing stream and follow the path as it starts to make its way back uphill. 50 metres up the hill, the path forks. *Take the right-hand fork,* your direction due south. In 60 metres you come to wooden fieldgates with signs saying 'Keep Out'. Continue along the track, towards the woods.

80 metres further on, you come to a metal fieldgate and go over the stile on its left-hand side, into the wood, to continue along the woodland path. In 200 metres you come to a Forestry Commission sign saying 'No admittance to vehicles'. Ignore the paths to left and right and continue straight on, ignoring all ways off.

In 500 metres you come down to a wooden fieldgate. Go through the kissing gate on its left. 200 metres further on, you come to the end of the public footpath. Ignore a track leading down to the right and continue ahead on a wide track that passes to the left of a brick building belonging to Southern Water Services.

40 metres further on, you come out on to a residential street, on the outskirts of **Tunbridge Wells**. You are on a corner with Coniston Avenue heading left and Bishops Down Park Road ahead, with a footpath between them. *Go up Bishops Down Park Road*, your direction 145 degrees. In 150 metres you come to a T-junction and *turn right,* still on Bishops Down Park Road, past a house called Charlcombe on your left-hand side. There is a golf course on your right-hand side as you go along this road.

300 metres further on, [!] *turn half right on to a path,* still alongside the golf course and now heading due south. In 450 metres, with Grange Cote on your right-hand side, you come to a road T-junction. *Turn right,* your direction 240 degrees.

[11] At the end of this cul-de-sac, *turn half left on to a small grassy area* and go up to the A264 at a junction, with the Major Yorke pub on the other side. Cross the main road carefully and go down Major Yorke Road opposite, *then immediately turn half left past some low wooden posts* on to a wide path leading into the woods of Tunbridge Wells and Rusthall Common, your direction 100 degrees.

In 150 metres cross over a path to go straight on. In another 180 metres go past a scaffolding-pole barrier and over a tarmac road (Fir Tree Lane) to continue ahead, with a cricket pitch on your left-hand side.

Ignoring ways off, in 200 metres you come to a tarmac path, where you *turn right downhill,* your direction 155 degrees. Continue to ignore ways off.

In 350 metres you come to the A26 by a mini roundabout. Cross this busy road carefully and go down steps to the left of the **Swan Hotel** to reach the **Pantiles**. The bar at the back of the hotel is a possible tea place; **Woods Restaurant & Wine Bar**, which does cream teas, is a short distance off to the right. For more alternatives, and to continue the main route, *turn left* into the Pantiles: **Slossies** (the former Picnic Basket) is in the parade of shops on the left; **Gastronomia G** is near the end on the right.

After tea, continue north-east along the Pantiles to reach Neville Street, with **King Charles the Martyr Church** opposite. Cross Neville Street by the pedestrian lights to your right. On the other side of the street, *turn left and then immediately right by a sundial into Cumberland Walk.* In 30 metres *turn left* up some steps and a brick alleyway to the start of the High Street. Continue along the length of the High Street, about 300 metres, to its intersection with Vale Road. On the other side of Vale Road you can see signs for **Tunbridge Wells station**.

You can enter the station from either side, but trains to London depart from platform 1 on the left. **Continental Flavour**, a coffee shop, is up ahead on Mount Pleasant Road, opposite the back entrance to the station (on the same side as platform 2). There is also a snack bar in the parade of shops just past this entrance, and the **Opera House** (now a JD Wetherspoon pub) is up the hill on the right, 400 metres past the station.

Lunch & tea places

Leicester Arms *High Street, Penshurst, TN11 8BT (01892 870551, www.leicester armspenshurst.co.uk).* **Open** 11am-midnight Mon-Sat; 11am-11pm Sun. *Food served* noon-9.30pm daily. A good lunch

option for late starters – or those planning to take the shortcut – this pub serves à la carte and bar meals all day.

Quaintways *High Street, Penshurst, TN11 8BT (01892 870272).* **Open** 10am-5pm Tue-Sun. This highly regarded, 16th-century tea room serves Kentish cream teas. However, there's no hot food after 2pm on Sundays and bank holidays.

Spotted Dog *Smarts Hill, Penshurst, TN11 8EP (01892 870253, www.spotted dogpub.co.uk).* **Open** *Summer* 11am-11pm Mon-Sat; noon-11pm Sun. *Winter* 11am-11pm Mon-Sat; noon-7pm Sun. *Food served* noon-2.30pm, 6-9pm Mon-Fri; noon-9.30pm Sat; noon-6pm Sun. This is the suggested lunch stop. It's a large and very popular pub, with good food, log fires in the winter and sweeping views across the Medway Valley. There are plenty of outside tables, but call ahead if you want a table inside for lunch.

Bottle House Inn *Coldharbour Road, Penshurst, TN11 8ET (01892 870306, www.thebottlehouseinnpenshurst.co.uk).* **Open** 11am-11pm Mon-Sat; 11am-10.30pm Sun. *Food served* noon-10pm Mon-Sat; 11.30am-9pm Sun.

Woods Restaurant & Wine Bar *62 Pantiles, Tunbridge Wells, TN2 5TN (01892 614411, www.woodsrestaurant. co.uk).* **Open** 8am-5pm Mon, Sun; 8am-midnight Tue-Sat. *Food served* 8am-5pm Mon, Sun; 8am-9pm Tue-Sat. One of several restaurants and wine bars in the Pantiles that serve excellent cream teas.

Slossies *26-28 Pantiles, Tunbridge Wells, TN2 5TN (01892 527690).* **Open** 9am-4pm Mon-Fri, Sun; 9am-5pm Sat. Formerly the Picnic Basket, this café now has an ice-cream counter.

Gastronomia G *7 Pantiles, Tunbridge Wells, TN2 5TD (01892 618281).* **Open** 9am-5pm daily.

Opera House *88 Mount Pleasant Road, Tunbridge Wells, TN1 1RT (01892 511770, www.jdwetherspoon.co.uk).* **Open** 8am-midnight Mon-Thur, Sun; 8am-1am Fri, Sat. *Food served* 8am-10pm daily. A splendid opera house (but more recently a cinema and bingo hall) that is now a pub.

Walk 16
Balcombe Circular

The gardens of Nymans and the ruins of Slaugham.

Start and finish: Balcombe station

Length: 17.6km (10.9 miles)

Time: 5 hours. For the whole outing, including trains, sights and meals, allow 10 hours.

Transport: Take the train nearest to **9.40am** from **London Bridge** station to **Balcombe** (journey time 40 minutes); on Sundays, the service is from Victoria (journey time 50 minutes). Trains back from Balcombe are hourly.
   If you are driving, Balcombe station has a small car park (£3.50; free on weekends and bank holidays).

OS Landranger Map: 187
OS Explorer Maps: 134 & 135
Balcombe, map reference TQ306302, is in **West Sussex**, 7km south-east of Crawley.

Toughness: 5 out of 10

Walk notes: This is a walk full of small delights: a nature reserve and lake with a Japanese pavilion by the stream below the gardens and park of Nymans, with its part-ruined manor house; a churchyard in Slaugham (pronounced 'Slaffam') with a 600-year-old yew tree that is some 10 metres in circumference; the ruins of Slaugham Manor; then a walk down to the River Ouse – with the incongruous sight of a Roman arch and columns in the middle of nowhere – and later up through fields and woods to the fine old village of Balcombe.
   Note: The original version of this walk included a crossing of the A23 between points **[7]** *&* **[8]** *on the map. With the growth in road traffic, this has become too dangerous to attempt. There are plans to provide an underpass in 2011/ 12 as part of a road-widening scheme, and if this happens the original route will be reinstated. When this occurs details will be posted on the Saturday Walkers' Club website (www.walkingclub.org.uk).*

Walk options: The second half of this walk is less interesting in some ways, so you could go as far as the Victory Inn in Staplefield and catch Metrobus 271 to Haywards Heath or Crawley. You can also catch this service earlier in the walk, from the Red Lion pub in Handcross. For bus information, call 0871 200 2233.

History: **Nymans** (01444 400321) is a National Trust garden. Ludwig Messel, who bought Nymans in 1890, sought to show that a more exotic range of plants could survive outdoors in Sussex than previously thought. Its manor house was part-gutted by fire in 1947, when huge slabs of the Horsham stone roof fell through three storeys, and the firemen were hampered by bitterly cold weather – ladder extensions and standpipes froze. Nymans is open from Wednesday to Sunday, although the house is closed between November and mid March. Admission (2010) is £8, which includes a 'free cup of tea or coffee in restaurant when arriving by public transport'.

The Japanese pavilion in the **nature reserve** was designed by Lord Snowdon, the owner of this country estate.

St Mary's Parish Church, Slaugham, has a Norman font made of Sussex marble with a fish symbol on it. There is a brass in the church to John Covert, who in his will left 200 marks to his daughters, even if they married without consent to men without land – but only if the men 'have virtue and cunning which seemeth as good as 100 marks' worth of land'.

Slaugham Place, now in ruins, was once a great Elizabethan manor house. It was the residence of the Covert family, who in the 16th and 17th centuries held land extending from the English Channel to the banks of the Thames. It is now a popular venue for wedding receptions, complete with helicopter landing space.

Walk directions

[1] [Numbers in square brackets refer to the map]
Coming off the train from London at **Balcombe station**, go over the footbridge and down the platform on the other side. Exit to the right just before the tunnel, then go through the car park, due south. Where this approach road meets the B2036, *take the signposted footpath to the right,* downhill and heading south-west. Go down steps (which are very slippery in wet weather) and across two stiles to join a lane.

Carry straight on towards the cottage for 25 metres (over a stream) and **[2]** *take a signposted footpath to the right* over a stile, heading north-west.

Go uphill near the field edge on your right-hand side. In 75 metres go over a stile and continue uphill. In 125 metres go over another stile at the top of the field and bear left, now with the field edge on your left-hand side.

In 125 metres there is another stile and you go straight on (note the communication towers disguised as trees on your right). This brings you in 175 metres to a car-wide unasphalted road.

Continue along the road, still heading north-west. In 70 metres, just beyond a large wooden shed, *take the road fork to the left* following the footpath sign, heading west.

Keep on this road, ignoring other possibilities. In 170 metres bend left with it (ignoring a signed footpath off to the right). You pass a pond on your right-hand side, then a house on your left, but keep on towards the barn sheds. When you reach these, *veer to the right* of the large shed ahead of you.

In 125 metres keep to the main farm track as it bends right, then in a further 125 metres follow it round to the left.

In 175 metres, 10 metres before your farm track is about to reach the first trees of the wood, *fork left,* your direction due south, on what is soon a footpath parallel to the farm track. (This is the official path, although simply staying on the farm track for the next 75 metres would bring you to the same place.)

[3] In 75 metres go over a stile and *turn right* by a three-armed footpath sign, with the edge of the wood now to your right, your direction 240 degrees.

In 150 metres you have, at least in winter, a large pond below you on your right, and you *bear right,* still keeping the edge of the wood on your right-hand side.

In 250 metres go over a stile next to a horse-jump with a small pond beyond, and continue on, in the direction shown by the footpath sign, still with a line of trees on your right-hand side.

In 150 metres cross a stile next to another horse-jump to continue down a path into the woods.

In 75 metres, at a T-junction, *bear left* following the footpath sign on a wider path, but in 15 metres *turn right downhill*, in more or less your previous direction, now 240 degrees. Go down steps (with a wooden railing on your right-hand side) to cross a stream and follow the path up the other side.

About 100 metres from the footbridge, *turn left* at a T-junction with a wider track, then in 10 metres *veer right* towards

Balcombe Circular

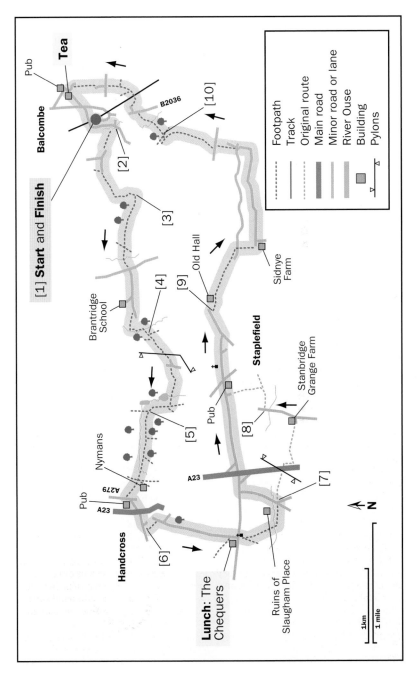

Tea

Pub

Balcombe

Pub

B2036

[1] **Start** and **Finish**

[2]

[3]

[10]

Footpath
Track
Original route
Main road
Minor road or lane
River Ouse
Building
Pylons

Old Hall

Sidnye Farm

[9]

Brantridge School

[4]

Staplefield

Nymans

[5]

Pub

Stanbridge Grange Farm

[8]

A23

A279

Pub

A23

[7]

Handcross

[6]

Lunch: The Chequers

Ruins of Slaugham Place

N

1km
1 mile

a stile 30 metres away. Go over this stile, across a tarmac road and straight ahead on the entrance drive to **Ditton Place** (marked on the OS map), your direction now 260 degrees.

In 250 metres, after passing a new development on your left, and when still 60 metres from the main building, *bear left* on a car road following a footpath sign on your right-hand side, your direction now 240 degrees.

100 metres down this road, take the stile on your right-hand side to continue through the field in more or less the same direction, now due west, with the field edge on your left-hand side.

In 175 metres go over a stile and down into a wood, soon bearing left on this path, which runs parallel to the stream and pylons on your right. In 200 metres cross this stream on a wooden bridge to continue southwards, now on the opposite bank.

[4] In 30 metres *take the right-hand fork uphill,* your direction 210 degrees. In a further 50 metres, at the

Nymans.

top of the slope, *bear left* following the footpath sign.

In 125 metres, exit the wood by a stile. An unofficial path cuts diagonally across this field to the far right-hand corner, but the public footpath turns right and goes around two sides of the field. Either way, exit the field by a metal fieldgate and *turn right* to pass under electricity cables. Continue through another metal fieldgate.

In 40 metres go through a wooden swing gate and *turn left* on to a concrete farm lane, as shown by a footpath sign, to head south-west. (A modernised timber-framed house is on your right-hand side.)

In 80 metres you come to a junction in the farm track; *go across this, slightly to the right,* then *go left on the footpath* by the three-armed footpath sign. Go through a metal gate to continue on a wide grassy path, your direction 240 degrees, with a wooden fence on your right-hand side.

In 100 metres cross a stream on two planks, then go over a stile to continue with the field hedge on your right-hand side, your direction now 300 degrees. Where the hedge ends, continue across the field towards the left of the house ahead of you. Go alongside its garden fence and across its driveway.

At the end of the field, go over a stile and down steps into a wood. Continue along a boardwalk to pass **Lord Snowdon's lake with its Japanese pavilion** on your right-hand side. Cross a footbridge over a stream and go up to a T-junction with a car-wide track.

Turn right here, following the footpath sign, to head north-west. Continue in this direction, soon with another large lake on your right (you are now on National Trust land, part of the **Nymans** estate).

[5] In 300 metres you come to a two-armed footpath sign on your right, and (with the Woodland Walks straight on) you *take the footpath fork uphill to the left.* This path soon bends to the left, with a valley below you to the right.

Follow this attractive path through the woods for 750 metres, ignoring ways off. After climbing gently uphill, a wider path

merges from the left. Follow the 'Short Walk' sign to cross a streambed and then, in 10 metres, *fork left on a narrow path uphill,* as indicated by a public footpath sign.

In 200 metres cross a farm track and continue uphill. (A gate off to the left here would take you into Nymans gardens, but visitors, even National Trust members, are expected to use the official entrance further on.)

In 200 metres, after climbing steeply, you come to **Nymans** car park. If you wish to visit the gardens or the NT restaurant, go through the wooden fieldgate on your left and up to the entrance. Otherwise, continue for another 100 metres to the B2114 and *turn right* to reach a possible lunch stop, the **Red Lion**, at the road junction.

The onward route here is to *turn left* on to the B2110, signposted Cowfold and Horsham (if coming out of the pub, *turn right*). Cross the bridge over the A23, continue past All Saints Church and keep ahead on the B2110 at the mini roundabout, now signposted to Lower Beeding.

[6] In 125 metres, just past the Royal Oak pub on your right-hand side, *turn left* up a driveway with a concrete public footpath marker. 40 metres up this path, follow it round to the left, past allotments on your right. In 50 metres, bend right with the path in front of a hedge, then in 30 metres go through a wooden swing gate and continue ahead between hedges, your direction 140 degrees. In 60 metres you come out on a car lane and *turn right,* initially heading south-west.

Continue on this lane, ignoring turn-offs. In 500 metres you pass a couple of practice starting-gates for horse races, then in 125 metres detour around a set of iron gates to continue on the lane.

In a further 500 metres, go through a side gate to the right of a large white-painted gate blocking the lane to enter the village of Slaugham. In 125 metres you come to the suggested lunch stop, **The Chequers** inn, on your right-hand side.

After lunch, continue across a minor road and through the lychgate into **St Mary's Parish Church**. Go past the (closed) west door and *veer left,* ignoring a footpath that continues straight on. Just past the south door entrance, *veer right* on a path through the churchyard, soon passing the 600-year-old yew tree on your right-hand side.

Where the gravel path ends, continue ahead on a grassy path and leave the churchyard through a kissing gate, entering Church Covert (owned by the Woodland Trust). Follow the footpath sign half right downhill across a field, heading south-east, with the ruins of **Slaugham Place** ahead on your left.

In 180 metres this leads you to a two-armed footpath sign and on to a path between fences, your direction now 160 degrees, with the ruins on your left-hand side. In 75 metres veer right with the path to circumvent the garden of the cottage ahead of you.

On the other side of the garden, cross a wooden bridge over a stream and go up to join Moat House's driveway. Continue ahead, with the stream and ruins to your left. In 100 metres you meet a car lane **[7]**, with a 'No Through Path' sign ahead of you.

(The original walk route continued ahead at this point, but this is not feasible until a safe crossing of the A23 has been provided.)

To avoid this road crossing, *turn left* on to the car lane (the driveway to Slaugham Manor) and continue along it for 300 metres to a T-junction with a minor road (the one you crossed just before St Mary's church).

Turn right on to this road, in 250 metres going underneath two road bridges carrying the A23. Continue on this road for another 1km, eventually going ahead at a crossroads; Staplefield's large village green is on your left-hand side, with the **Jolly Tanners** about 300 metres away on the other side of the green. (The original walk route rejoined from the footpath on the

right here. Point **[8]** comes within the original route).

Continuing ahead, in 100 metres you come to the **Victory Inn** on your right-hand side, another possible refreshment stop. In a further 50 metres, you cross the B2114 to continue straight on, uphill. In 175 metres, you pass **St Mark's Church** (which is usually locked) on your left-hand side.

300 metres beyond the church, you pass Jasmine and Heron Cottages on your right-hand side, to keep on the main road. In a further 190 metres, ignore Rose Cottage Lane to your right and stay on the road, signposted Balcombe.

[9] In a further 250 metres – just past the entrance drive to **Tyes Place** (marked on the OS map) and by a footpath sign on your right – *turn half right* into the driveway of North and South Meadow Cottages, heading south-east.

In 80 metres you pass the cottages and bear left with the driveway. Pass to the right of Old Hall Farm Cottage and *take a narrow path half right* to exit its garden over a stile. Bear left, following the footpath sign, to head east along the left-hand field edge. The intriguing castle-like **Old Hall** is away to your left (but mostly hidden behind trees), with its own mini crystal palace beyond it.

In 300 metres, note the **arch with Roman pillars** in the field to your left. In a further 40 metres, at the bottom left-hand corner of the field, go through the hedge into a lightly wooded area and follow the path to the right.

The path gradually curves back round to the left, later with the **River Ouse** on your right. In 400 metres, cross the river by a wooden bridge, following the footpath sign.

Head uphill on the other side, your direction 150 degrees, towards a gate in the hedge at the top of the field. Go through this and continue along a path between hedges to reach **Sidnye Farm** (marked on the OS map).

At the farm, *bear left,* following the footpath sign. In 25 metres, at a three-

In 250 metres go over a stile and continue uphill towards another stile in a hedge. Cross this and bear left uphill, keeping the hedge on your left as you pass the red-brick house on your left-hand side.

In a further 250 metres, you come to the brow of the hill (with fine views to the south and east). Continue for 50 metres with a hedge on your left, then go gently downhill on a car-wide track into **Pilstye Wood**. 50 metres into the wood, ignore a fork to the left and keep on the main track downhill, with an impressive rock outcrop split by tree roots on your left-hand side.

[!] In another 50 metres, an earth car road merges from the right but instead of joining this, follow a footpath sign to *take a narrow track opposite and slightly to the right,* now going more steeply downhill. In 40 metres, bear right with this path and continue downhill, heading north-east and with a new plantation on your right-hand side.

In 200 metres exit the wood by a bridge with wooden railings over a stream and go over a stile. Here the footpath sign points straight uphill (due north), but if the field is planted with crops with no clear path through them, you may prefer to detour to the left to go around them on the field edge.

On the far side of the field do not go through the metal fieldgate but *take the stile to its right* to go on to a narrow path between fences. In 60 metres you cross another stile to come out on to a main road, the B2036, where you *turn left,* due north. In 75 metres you pass a house on the other side of the road.

(You can shorten the walk here by continuing ahead on the B2036, reaching Balcombe station's approach road in 500 metres.) For the main route through Balcombe village (with its tea room), cross this busy road carefully and *go up a tarmac lane,* following a footpath sign, your direction initially 140 degrees.

In 100 metres you enter the drive of **Kemps House** (marked on the OS map), with the house on your left-hand side. Having gone through a fieldgate and

armed footpath sign, *bear left again,* passing the large corrugated iron shed on your right-hand side and heading due east. Veer slightly left around another farm shed to go straight on past two cottages on your left-hand side.

Keep on the farm's driveway. In just under 1km, you come to a T-junction with Rowhill Lane, where you *turn left downhill.*

In 180 metres you pass the entrance to Hillside on your left-hand side and, in a further 120 metres, you cross the River Ouse.

Instead of bending right with the lane here, go into the field on your left to *continue straight on uphill* (due north, towards a red-brick house visible on the horizon), with the field edge on your left-hand side.

In 250 metres you come up to a lane. *Turn left* here and then in 15 metres *turn right* up a narrow path, passing a redundant stile to continue northwards in a large field.

passed the house, *bear right* to leave the property by a wooden gate. A path brings you in 20 metres to a stile and then the main London–Brighton railway line.

Cross the railway with great care (trains come round the curve at up to 90mph). Continue on the path up the bank on the other side, parallel to the tracks. Cross the stile at the top and *bear right,* with the field edge on your right-hand side, towards the houses ahead, due north.

Once by the houses, follow the footpath sign along the right-hand edge of a small terrace. Go over a stile and across a tarmac road into a cul-de-sac, Jobes. Where this road bears left, go slightly right on to a tarmac path between hedges, heading north, with gardens on your left-hand side.

In 100 metres continue on, now with playing fields on your left-hand side. At the far end of these, continue on a tarmac lane past a pavilion and Balcombe Parish Church Room on your left-hand side. On reaching a road, *turn left.*

At a T-junction in 75 metres, either turn right for the **Half Moon** pub or bear left and cross the road to the recommended tea place, the **Balcombe Tea Rooms**.

To get to the station, continue down the road past the tea room, reaching London Road in 180 metres. (Here you can go directly to the station by turning left on to this main road, reaching the entrance in 350 metres.)

For a more pleasant but circuitous route, cross straight over London Road to continue down Rocks Lane, your direction 210 degrees. Keep on this road as it passes under the railway bridge after 300 metres.

In a further 300 metres, you come to a T-junction by a stream, where you *turn left,* following the footpath sign. Go up the steps you came down at the start of the walk and *turn left* at the top into the approach road to reach **Balcombe station**. Trains to London leave from the near platform.

Lunch & tea places

Nymans restaurant *Handcross, Haywards Heath, RH17 6EB (01444 405250, www.nationaltrust.org.uk).* **Open** 10am-4.30pm Wed-Sun. *Food served* noon-2.30pm Wed-Sun. This National Trust restaurant is a lunch option for those visiting Nymans estate.

Red Lion *High Street, Handcross, Haywards Heath, RH17 6BP (01444 400292, www.redlionhandcross.co.uk).* **Open** 10am-11pm Mon-Thur; 10am-midnight Fri, Sat; noon-10.30pm Sun. *Food served* noon-10pm Mon-Thur; noon-10.30pm Fri, Sat; noon-8.30pm Sun. Another possible lunch stop.

The Chequers *Slaugham, Haywards Heath, RH17 6AQ (01444 400239).* **Open** noon-3pm, 6-11pm Mon-Thur; noon-11pm Fri-Sun. *Food served* noon-3pm, 6-10pm Mon-Thur; noon-10pm Fri, Sat; noon-8.30pm Sun. This upmarket establishment is the recommended lunch stop on the walk, just before the halfway mark. Book ahead, especially on Sundays.

Jolly Tanners *Handcross Road, Staplefield, Haywards Heath, RH17 6EF (01444 400335, www.jollytanners.com).* **Open** 11am-3pm, 5.30-11pm Mon-Thur; 11am-11pm Fri, Sat; 11am-10.30pm Sun. *Food served* noon-2pm, 6-9pm Mon-Sat; noon-8pm Sun.

Victory Inn *Warninglid Road, Staplefield, Haywards Heath, RH17 6EU (01444 400463).* **Open** noon-11pm Mon-Sat; noon-10.30pm Sun. *Food served* noon-3pm Mon; noon-3pm, 6-9pm Tue-Sat; noon-9pm Sun.

Half Moon *Haywards Heath Road, Balcombe, RH17 6PA (01444 811582, www.halfmoonbalcombe.co.uk).* **Open** 11am-noon Mon-Sat; noon-midnight Sun. *Food served* noon-2.30pm Mon-Sat; noon-3pm Sun. A good place for tea-time refreshment if you're after something stronger than a cuppa.

Balcombe Tea Rooms *Bramble Hill, Balcombe, RH17 6HR (01444 811777).* **Open** 10am-4pm Tue-Sat; 10.30am-4pm Sun. A good selection of cakes are on offer here, the recommended tea stop. The owners prefer large groups to call in advance, but are happy to stay open a little later if necessary.

Walk 17

Bow Brickhill to Woburn Sands

Woburn Abbey and Safari Park.

Start: Bow Brickhill station
Finish: Woburn Sands station

Length: 18.7km (11.6 miles)

Time: 5 hours 30 minutes. For the whole outing, including trains, sights and meals, allow at least 10 hours.

Transport: Take the train nearest to **9.50am** from **Euston** station to **Bow Brickhill**, changing at Bletchley (journey time about 1 hour). Trains back from **Woburn Sands** to Euston are about once an hour, again via Bletchley. If your ticket allows it, you could also take the train in the other direction and return via Bedford to St Pancras. Buy a day return to Woburn Sands. Note that there is currently no train service on the Bletchley–Bedford branch line on Sundays and Bank Holidays.

OS Landranger Maps: 165, 153 & (for the last 750m) 152
OS Explorer Map: 192
Bow Brickhill, map reference SP896348, is in **Buckinghamshire**, 2km east of Bletchley. Woburn is in **Bedfordshire**.

Toughness: 6 out of 10

Walk notes: Woburn is the main delight of this walk – the ancient town itself, the deer park, Woburn Abbey and the Safari Park (from the public footpath, without paying admission, you may be able to see brown bears, zebras, buck, bison, elephants, giraffes, rhino and wallabies). The route reaches Woburn mainly through woods and via a golf course, with some impressive redwood trees along the way. After the Safari Park, the route is through the pleasant village of Aspley Guise then on to Woburn Sands.

Short bits of this walk can be very muddy in wet weather and there are (relatively easy) uphills and downhills all day. Be careful not to allow dogs to disturb deer in Woburn Park, particularly when they are rutting or giving birth – the deer may leave their newborn calves or give birth prematurely.

Walk options: There are still over 10km to be walked after lunch in Woburn, so you may wish to take a bus to Leighton Buzzard or Bletchley. You can head for the railway station in Aspley Guise instead of continuing the walk to Woburn Sands, but this only saves about 1km. You can also take a detour shortly after entering Woburn Park to visit **Woburn Abbey** or view the Abbey and its outbuildings from the outside.

History: **Woburn Abbey** (01525 290333), set in a vast park about 16km in circumference, is the seat of the Duke of Bedford. It was founded for Cistercian monks in 1145 by Hugh de Bolsbec, a Norman whose father came over with William the Conqueror. Both Elizabeth I and Charles I were entertained here. The Abbey was partially reconstructed and extended in Totternhoe stone, starting in 1744. The house is open to the public from 11am until (last entry) 4pm daily, from April to September. Admission (2010) is £12.50, or £4 for the Abbey Gardens and Deer Park only (there is no charge for walking through the grounds, if you stay on the public footpaths).

Woburn, the town, was almost completely gutted by fire in 1729. **St Mary Old Church**, Woburn, whose tower dates from the 12th century, is now a volunteer-run Heritage Centre (01525 290631) covering local history. From Easter to September, the Centre is usually open 2-4.30pm Monday to Friday, 10am-5pm Saturday, Sunday and Bank Holidays (plus weekends only in October).

The **Parish Church of St Mary**, graced with devilish gargoyles, was built by the eighth Duke of Bedford in 1868 and has a memorial to Mary, Duchess of Bedford.

The village of **Aspley Guise** was originally called 'Aepslea', meaning a clearing in the aspen. Large herds of swine were kept in the surrounding woods. The **Parish Church of St Botolph**, Aspley Guise, has Norman and medieval traces and a brass, from about 1410, that depicts a kneeling priest.

Walk directions

[1] [Numbers in square brackets refer to the map]

Coming off platform 2 at **Bow Brickhill railway station**, *turn left,* southwards, back over the level crossing, on the road 'V10' Brickhill Street.

In 75 metres you come to a mini roundabout. Ignore the left turn towards Bow Brickhill. Cross over and keep ahead along the grass verge on the left-hand side of the busy Brickhill road.

In 80 metres take the signposted footpath to *the left* over a stile, turning right, then immediately left, to continue

ahead, due east, on a car-wide grassy way, with the field edge on your right and a post and wire fence on your left-hand side. In 345 metres cross a farm track to continue straight on through a wooden kissing gate, on to a path between fences and houses.

In 40 metres this path comes out on to an estate road and you keep straight on up this road, gently uphill, ignoring a turn-off to the left.

In 170 metres you come to a T-junction where you *go right,* your direction 150 degrees. In 45 metres pick up a sign-posted path to continue in your previous direction (105 degrees). **[2]**

In 25 metres go through a wooden kissing gate, swing right, then left, to continue in the same direction as before, ignoring the grassy path to your right, across a field of mounds (a remnant of the old ridge-and-furrow field system). In 55 metres, at a path junction, keep ahead with the field edge on your left-hand side, your direction 120 degrees.

In 80 metres go over a stile to the left of a metal fieldgate (or pass through the fieldgate when open) and keep straight on between timber fences. The path soon starts to go uphill.

In 260 metres, by a three-armed footpath sign on your left (obscured by bushes in summer), follow a bridleway sign to *the right,* upwards, on an earth car road, your direction 160 degrees. In 30 metres you come to a path junction **[3]**, *where you have a choice of ways.* The route ahead, slightly right (south-west) is used by **Walk 41** (Bow Brickhill to Leighton Buzzard; *see p318*). It connects with this walk at point [5A].

(The 'middle route', on your left, beside the tree marked No.25, is particularly enjoyable in autumn and follows an undulating, meandering path uphill, over banks and mounds, on an initial bearing of 140 degrees. After 300 metres, at a path crossing, keep ahead, to go up a final steep incline, in 90 metres coming up to join the ridge path, where you *turn right*. This is point [4A] below.)

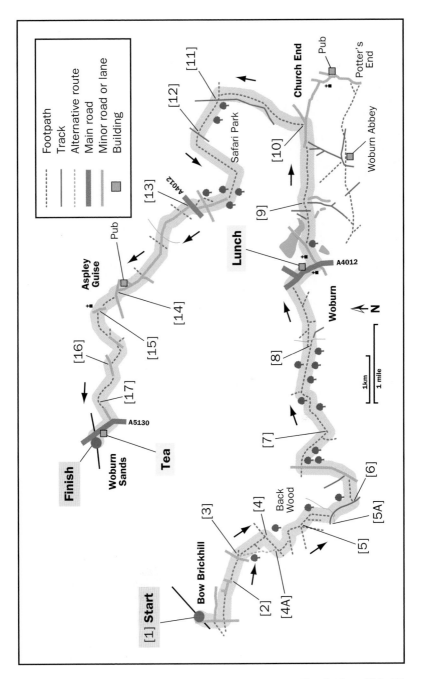

Footpath

Track

Alternative route

Main road

Minor road or lane

Building

[11]

[12]

Safari Park

Church End

Pub

Potter's End

[10]

Woburn Abbey

[13]

A4012

Pub

[9]

Aspley Guise

Lunch

[14]

[15]

A4012

Woburn

[16]

N

[8]

[17]

1km
1 mile

A5130

[7]

Finish

Woburn Sands

Tea

[6]

[3]

[4]

[5A]

Back Wood

[5]

Bow Brickhill

[1] Start

[2]

[4A]

Woburn Park.

To follow the main route: **[!]** *take the leftmost fork,* your direction 145 degrees, uphill into **Back Wood** (as marked on the OS map). In 140 metres you start to have a barbed-wire fence with wooden posts on your left-hand side. The path is now in a cutting as you head steadily uphill.

In a further 230 metres you come to a fence on your right-hand side, with yellow arrows on a corner fencepost. **[4]** Follow the arrow to *the right,* your direction 240 degrees, soon with a glade on your right-hand side. In 250 metres from the fencepost, ignore a fork going steeply downhill on your right and, in 60 metres, **[4A]** ignore another fork (this is where the 'middle route' joins). At this point, you have a fine view out over the valley and Bletchley, unhindered by trees.

In a further 10 metres you come to a corner fencepost on your left-hand side and you follow its arrow *left* to continue on through pine trees, your direction 110 degrees, with the fence now on your left-hand side.

In 45 metres cross over a path junction and keep ahead, now steeply downhill, with gorse on your right-hand side. In a further 110 metres, follow arrows as the path veers right, now due south. Then, in 80 metres, ignore the path to the right and, in 5 metres, veer left with the path, to go uphill, your direction 70 degrees, with a fence on your left-hand side.

After 220 metres going uphill along a sandy channel, you come out on to a sandy earth road heading towards a golf course and, with a footpath post on your right with yellow arrows, *turn right downhill* on a sandy path, your direction 200 degrees.

In 150 metres, at a triangular clearing with a footpath post in its middle, take the fork *left downhill,* your direction 140 degrees. **[5]** In 90 metres cross a set of planks over a swampy area, to carry straight on, now gently uphill.

In 200 metres cross a main path and keep ahead, your direction 145 degrees. Go straight on, now downwards, for 100 metres and at a path junction (with a fence ahead) follow the arrow *right,* your direction 250 degrees, with young trees on your right-hand side.

The path soon heads downhill and in 215 metres you come down to a stream (dried up in summer) on your left-hand side, which you cross by *going left* on a car-wide bridleway (marked with blue arrows) *uphill,* your direction 135 degrees. **[5A]** (Walk 41 – Bow Brickhill to Leighton Buzzard – joins here).

Head uphill towards the **Sierra redwood (Wellingtonia) trees**. The path begins to level out and after 350 metres, and 10 metres beyond the end of the forest on your left-hand side, with a clearing to your right, **[6]** *take the steps on your left uphill* (marked on your right by a yellow arrow on a post), your direction 60 degrees, now with the forest again on your left-hand side. At the top of the slope keep ahead between fences, with a maintained green space on your right.

In 380 metres, exit this enclosed path by going over a stile to *turn left* on to a tarmac road, your direction 20 degrees.

In 340 metres you ignore a possible way into the woods on your right-hand side, but in a further 160 metres – 5 metres beyond the entrance driveway to the Woburn Golf Club clubhouse on your left – go through a wooden kissing gate *on your right* on to a signposted gravelled footpath, a tarmac drive to its right, your direction 105 degrees.

In 175 metres, with a footpath post on your right, as a path joins from the right, *keep ahead* and in 15 metres follow the public footpath sign ahead, ignoring the track off to the left. **Little Brickhill Copse** (as marked on the OS map) is over to your right. In 200 metres, at a path junction, the path *swings to the right,* with a practice driving-range over to your left and golf links to your right, your direction now 145 degrees. Keep ahead and ignore all ways off and path crossings.

In 250 metres, as the open field (driving range) to the left comes to an end **[7]**, follow the Woburn Walk (WW) arrow to *the left,* on a grassy car-wide way, with

the edge of **Charle Wood** (as marked on the OS map) on your right, your direction 30 degrees. In 110 metres the car-wide way comes out on to a new gravel track, where you keep ahead, along it, your direction now 50 degrees.

In 150 metres *fork right* off the gravel track across grass, following the footpath sign, your direction 80 degrees, with a house ahead and over to your left. In 75 metres cross an entrance drive and keep ahead. In a further 90 metres you pass the house on your left.

In a further 75 metres go through an open gateway and continue with the field to your left and the wood to your right, gently downhill, your direction 60 degrees. In a further 130 metres, by a three-armed footpath sign, continue ahead along a concrete path (marked WW). The route is straight on, latterly uphill, and you ignore all ways off.

In 240 metres, as the concrete path swings left, you exit the wood ahead, around a wooden barrier, to follow the WW sign *straight across* open fields, along the line of the telegraph poles, your direction due east. In 175 metres, at the end of the field, you need to continue on, following the footpath arrow, down between woods.

In 220 metres you come to a T-junction, with a stream ahead on the other side of the hedge. **[8]** Here *turn left* following the WW arrow, your direction 20 degrees. In 60 metres *turn right* over the stream, following the WW arrow (your direction 105 degrees) across a field.

In 240 metres go through a gap in the field boundary and follow the WW arrow into the next field, your direction 90 degrees.

In 120 metres go through an archway cut in the hedge and over a wooden footbridge with wooden handrail. Ignore the path ahead and instead **[!]** *turn left,* your direction 5 degrees, now with the ditch on your left-hand side.

In 35 metres follow the WW arrow *right* **[!]** to go *diagonally across the field,* your direction 75 degrees. Aim for the footpath post with a yellow top ahead and, in 325 metres, you go through a gap in the hedge to continue on into the next open field. In a further 275 metres you go over a wooden footbridge with wooden handrail, then through a kissing gate and keep ahead.

In 80 metres go over a ditch and through a wooden kissing gate to go *half left,* your direction due east. In 45 metres go through a wooden kissing gate and up beside the fence of a house on your right-hand side. In 50 metres pass through a barrier and come out on to a road.

Turn right on this main road (Bedford Street) and up into the town of **Woburn**. In 100 metres on your left-hand side you pass the **Bell Inn**, opposite the Bell Hotel, a possible lunch stop. In a further 40 metres on your left-hand side you pass the **Longs Inn**, another possible lunch stop. In a further 120 metres up Bedford Street on your left-hand side is the **Black Horse** pub, the suggested lunchtime stop.

Coming out of the Black Horse pub after lunch, *turn left*, due south. In 35 metres *turn left* on Park Street, your direction 70 degrees. In 100 metres you come to **St Mary**, the parish church of Woburn, with its dreadful gargoyles. Continue down Park Street and in 65 metres you enter **Woburn Park** by the cattle grid and lodge and go *half right* on a signposted footpath, your direction 15 degrees. Soon you pass a lake over to your left.

In 450 metres take the tarmac path *to the left* of cottages nos.2 and 3 (the ones with mock-Elizabethan chimneys) to go straight on, your direction 105 degrees.

In 95 metres go through a swing gate to the left of a cattle grid and keep straight on, with the estate's Bedford office to your right, on a wide tarmac road. In 60 metres pass through a wooden barrier, with a timber-framed pavilion and its ha-ha over to your left and, in 50 metres as the road swings to the right, [!] *turn half left off the road* by a yellow-topped post, to cross the grass, your initial direction 45 degrees. [9]

[At this point you could detour to **Woburn Abbey**. The detour is along public footpaths, to look at the outside of the Abbey buildings without having to pay the Park entrance fee. (**Note**: unless you take the 3.7km walk extension to Potter's End and Church End via the Greensand Ridge Walk path, you will have to retrace your steps to point [9].)]

[To take the **detour**, instead of turning half left off the tarmac road, stay on it as it swings right, with a lake soon on your left-hand side and stables to your right, your direction 195 degrees. Pass the ticket office. In 90 metres, and 5 metres beyond the end of the lake, leave the road *to go straight on,* following the gravelled farm road marked 'No entry', your direction 210 degrees. Woburn Abbey is on your far left-hand side. Follow the fence on your right-hand side for 600 metres. When you come to the four-armed footpath sign by a metal swing gate, take the path signposted Greensand Ridge Walk (left), your direction 75 degrees, heading well to the left of the Abbey, following occasional waymark posts on the way. Head on between lakes and across the estate drive, your direction 80 degrees, in 500 metres joining a gravelled road to go straight on, your direction 100 degrees, with the Abbey garden railings on your right-hand side, to the pedestrian entrance to tea rooms on your right. To visit the Abbey you will have to pay the entrance fee. After looking at the Abbey buildings from the outside, or after visiting the Abbey itself, retrace your steps to point [9]. Do not try to take a shortcut northwards from the Abbey along one of the 'No Entry' estate roads; you will be turned back by a Park Ranger. For the 3.7km walk **extension**: Instead of retracing your steps, you can head east after the tea rooms to follow the Greensand Ridge Walk path. Follow the clear signs, or refer to the OS maps. The path eventually swings south-east after 1.5km to the road at Potter's End, where you head north-east along the road for 400 metres to Church End. You then follow a

Park Cottage.

minor road via Hills End and Froxfield for 1.8km to rejoin the main walk directions at the cattle grid, point [10] below.]

To continue along the main route: Having turned half left off the road, at point [9] above, cross the grass and in 50 metres you pass the end of the lake on your right. Here your route swings to the right on a well-defined grassy path, your direction due east, initially parallel to a main estate road, 100 metres over to your left, which later converges with your path. Follow the 'Keep to Public Footpath' signs and the marker posts with yellow tops as you head gently uphill. Herds of deer are usually seen off to the left and right.

In 825 metres cross a gravel estate road (which heads right to the Abbey) and keep ahead on the grassy path in the same direction as before. In 175 metres the path swings left to cross another estate road with a barrier on your right. Keep ahead on the path, now parallel to the main estate road, just 5 metres to your left.

In 180 metres, as the road on your left comes to a cattle grid and the grassy path comes to an end, cross the road and take the footpath on *your left* just before the cattle grid, your direction 20 degrees. **[10]**

Follow this grassy path, mostly uphill, ignoring all ways off, marked by regular posts, for 600 metres until your path is parallel to the road on your left beside the high fencing of the **Safari Park**. You now follow the grassy path some 3 metres to the right of this road, northwards. The brown bear enclosure is over to your left.

In 400 metres go over stiles on either side of a cattle grid with Trusslers Hill Lodge on your right-hand side. **[11]** In 35 metres **[!]** *fork left* on a path downhill, following the line of mini pylons, your direction 310 degrees, into **Hay Wood** (as marked on the OS map).

In 250 metres, at the bottom of the path, having passed through some muddy sections, you pass through high metal gates and keep ahead, soon crossing the Safari Park's entrance drive **[12]** (with pay kiosks over to your left) *to go straight on,* your direction 310 degrees, on a tarmac road.

In 100 metres, and 20 metres past the end of the quarantine area on your right-hand side, **[!]** take the signposted public footpath *to your left* through a wooden kissing gate, your direction 210 degrees.

Now follow the path with the Safari Park's high fencing on your left. You should be able to see zebra, buck, rhino, bison and later elephants. After 450 metres you pass the new elephant house on your right and *go through* a high wooden kissing gate to go *down* into a wooded area, your direction 220 degrees (ignoring the path before the kissing gate on your right). You may now see giraffes over to your left.

In 40 metres, at the bottom of the slope, follow the sign on a tree *to go right* and follow the footpath with a stream bed on your left-hand side, your direction 285 degrees. Keep ahead along this path, muddy in places, through a lightly wooded area, as you pass the wallaby enclosure to your left, then the Go Ape adventure area and other attractions: further over to the left is the Dolphinarium.

Ignore all ways off and in 450 metres you come to a tarmac road where *you go right,* your direction 345 degrees.

350 metres down this road (where the simplest route is to go straight on), which leads directly out to the Crawley Lodge exit to Woburn Park, you are meant to take the official footpath but if it is wet and/or you are in a hurry to get to the end of the walk, stay on the road to the Lodge. For the official route **[!]** *fork right* off the road by a footpath post, your direction 5 degrees, along a rough and at times overgrown path. In 220 metres you come out to cross a tarmac road (with an earth road to its right). Continue *straight on,* through a wooded area, towards a (broken) stile, your direction 315 degrees. In 40 metres cross over or pass by this stile *to go left,* your direction 275 degrees, along a partly fenced-in, rough and at times overgrown path. In 125 metres you come out on to the estate road just to the left of a cattle grid in front of Crawley Lodge.

Exit Woburn Park through the gate to the right of the Lodge and *turn right* on to the main A4012 road, your direction 20 degrees. In 40 metres *turn left* into Horsepool Lane, your direction 310 degrees, following the sign to **Aspley Guise** village. **[13]**

Continue along Horsepool Lane, uphill, towards the village, ignoring all ways off. (If you want to avoid road walking, there is a public footpath that runs to the left of the lane across agricultural fields and through a lightly wooded area for 500 metres before it rejoins the lane.) In 1km you reach the top of the hill and, a short distance over the top, you pass the **Wheatsheaf** pub on your right-hand side, an early tea stop option.

In 200 metres you come to a road T-junction where you *turn left,* your direction west. **[14]** In 60 metres you pass two thatched cottages (Park Cottage and Valentine Cottage) on your left-hand side, and in a further 80 metres you cross the road to go through a metal kissing gate on *your right-hand side,* to follow a signposted public footpath, with wooden fences on both sides, your direction 310 degrees.

In 250 metres, at the top of the path, go through a metal gate and out on to a road T-junction where you *go right,* your direction 340 degrees. In 70 metres you pass the **Parish Church of St Botolph**, Aspley Guise, on your right.

(To shorten the walk by going to **Aspley Guise railway station**, continue down this road for 600 metres: the station is on your right).

Continuing on the main route: Opposite the Parish Church, take the signposted footpath uphill (not into the churchyard), your direction 240 degrees, with the hedge and churchyard on your right. **[15]**

In 140 metres, you *veer right* with the path. In 35 metres go through a wooden kissing gate and onwards, on a clear path with an open field on your left and a wooded area to your right, your direction 235 degrees, heading towards some telecommunications masts with outbuildings below.

In 180 metres go through a wooden kissing gate and keep straight on, along a car-wide road. In a further 180 metres you *go right* through a metal kissing gate marked with a yellow arrow, your direction 285 degrees, into playing fields (West Hill Recreation Ground) towards Milton Keynes. Pass by a children's playground on your right, and after 135 metres [!] head slightly left to go down to a wooden kissing gate, which you go through on to a golf course.

Follow the yellow-topped posts over the golf course, your initial direction 330 degrees. In 185 degrees you come out on to an earth car road, where you *go left,* your direction 290 degrees. [16]

In 200 metres you pass Golf Course Cottage on your right and a metal shed on your left. In a further 120 metres ignore the road and footpath off to the right [17] by Radwell Farm.

Continue ahead along the track, soon with golf links to your left and right, and in 260 metres, shortly after the track swings to the left, you exit the golf course and carry *straight on,* your direction 235 degrees, on Mill Lane. In 80 metres this lane becomes a road between houses on both sides (Burrows Close).

In 110 metres you cross Weathercock Close to continue straight on, now along a tarmac path, your direction 230 degrees. In 50 metres this path comes out on to the A5130 road, with the Weathercock pub on your right-hand side. (If you turn left at this point, in 40 metres you come to the **Deep Blue** fish and chip shop on your left-hand side.)

To follow the main route: *Turn right* on the A5130 road, your direction 330 degrees, signposted Wavendon. You pass a new housing development on your left-hand side and, in 250 metres, come to the **Station Hotel**, also on your left-hand side, the suggested tea place.

Some 30 metres beyond the Station Hotel you come to **Woburn Sands station**, with platform 1 for trains to Bletchley on the near side.

Lunch & tea places

Bell Inn *21 Bedford Street, Woburn, MK17 9QB (01525 290280, www.bell inn-woburn.co.uk).* **Open** 11am-11pm daily. *Food served* 7am-10pm Mon-Fri; 8am-10pm Sat, Sun. A comfy and walker-friendly pub that serves main meals at lunch and dinner, and deli platters during the afternoon. The Bell often has very good two-for-one offers on food.

Longs Inn *18 Bedford Street, Woburn, MK17 9QB (01525 290219, www.longs inn.co.uk).* **Open** 11am-11pm daily. *Food served* noon-3pm, 6-9pm Tue-Sat; noon-4pm Sun. Having been the Magpies Hotel, Longs recently reverted to its original name – first recorded back in 1649. A bar menu is served, as well as main meals and Sunday roasts.

Black Horse *1 Bedford Street, Woburn, MK17 9QB (01525 290210, www.black horsewoburn.co.uk).* **Open** 10.30am-11pm Mon-Thur; 10.30am-11.30pm Fri, Sat; 10.30am-10.30pm Sun. *Food served* noon-3pm, 6-9.45pm Mon-Fri; noon-9.45pm Sat, Sun. The suggested lunch stop on the walk is a popular pub and often full. Main meals are served for lunch and dinner, as well as lighter options at other times.

Wheatsheaf *Mount Pleasant, Aspley Guise, MK17 8JZ (01908 583338, www. charleswells.co.uk).* **Open** noon-midnight Mon-Sat; noon-11pm Sun. *Food served* noon-10pm daily. An option for an early tea stop.

Deep Blue *47 Station Road, Woburn Sands, MK17 8RX (01908 583144, www.deepbluerestaurants.com).* **Open** 11.30am-9.30pm Mon-Wed, Sat; 11.30am-10.30pm Thur, Fri; 4-8pm Sun. A fish and chip shop, formerly known as Henry Higgins.

Station Hotel *146 Station Road, Woburn Sands, MK17 8SG (01908 582495).* **Open** 9am-11pm Mon-Sat; 10am-10pm Sun. *Food served* 9am-2.30pm, 6-9.30pm Mon-Fri; 9am-2.30pm Sat; 10am-2.30pm Sun. The suggested tea stop welcomes walkers – and cheers them up with hot drinks and a good range of beers. There's a food menu too.

Walk 18

Sunningdale to Windsor

Windsor Great Park.

Start: Sunningdale station
Finish: Windsor & Eton Riverside station

Length: 16.0km (9.9 miles)

Time: 4 hours. For the whole outing, including trains, sights and meals, allow 8 hours – or 9 hours if you plan to visit Savill Gardens.

Transport: Take the train nearest to **9.50am** from **Waterloo** station to **Sunningdale** (journey time 47 minutes). Trains back from **Windsor & Eton Riverside** station to Waterloo run twice an hour (journey time 58 minutes). If your ticket allows it, you could also return from Windsor Central station to Paddington, changing at Slough. This service is also half-hourly, but with a shorter journey time of around 32 minutes.

The most flexible ticket is a day return to Windsor (all stations). This covers both return routes, but is not sufficient for the full outward journey: you will also need to buy a single from Staines to Sunningdale. If you buy a return to Sunningdale instead, you again have to buy an extra single ticket, this time on the return journey: to Staines if you are returning from Windsor Riverside, but to London if you are departing from Windsor Central.

OS Landranger Map: 175 (nearly all the route is on 176 too)
OS Explorer Map: 160 Sunningdale, map reference SU953667, is in **Surrey**, 15km south-west of Heathrow Airport. Windsor is in **Berkshire**.

Toughness: 2 out of 10

Walk notes: Near the start of this walk, you go through Coworth Park, with its polo fields, to enter the 4,800 acres of Windsor Great Park (no entrance charge), near the Virginia Water lakes and Valley Gardens. These gardens have a vast collection of rhododendrons and azaleas (best visited in May or June). Lunch is in a pleasant cafeteria overlooking the Savill Gardens (you have to pay to enter the gardens). After lunch, the route is up Rhododendron Ride to Cow Pond, which is covered in an array of water lilies. From here, it is through some light woods and on to the Royal Lodge, to pass through gates into Windsor Deer Park. You now have a choice of route onwards: either make for the Copper Horse statue and simply embark on the full 4km of the Long Walk, or follow the original (and more complicated) route through the park, joining it 1km further along. When you eventually reach the gates of Windsor Castle, you turn left into the town to walk through some of its oldest streets, their

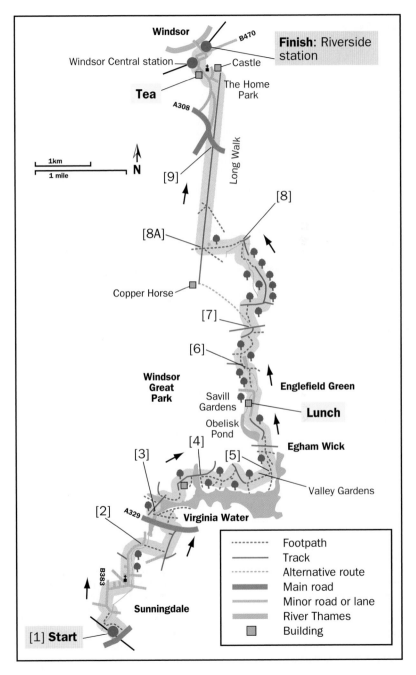

many inns, cafés and restaurants all suitable for a tea stop.

Walk options: You can phone for a taxi to Windsor at lunchtime from the Savill Gardens cafeteria.

History: Sunningdale Parish Church was built in 1840 at a cost of only £1,600.

The 100-foot-high **Totem Pole** in Windsor Great Park was a gift to the Queen in 1958 from British Columbia, and is made from a 600-year-old western red cedar tree. The giant **Obelisk** in the park was put up by King George II to commemorate 'the success in arms of his son, William'.

Savill Gardens (01753 860222, www.theroyallandscape.co.uk) are named in honour of Eric Savill who, with encouragement from King George V, created the gardens on inauspicious, fast-draining sandy soil.

Admission (2010) is £6-£8.50 and the gardens are open 10am-6pm daily from March to October and 10am-4.30pm from November to February.

Later, in 1947, Eric Savill began work on **Valley Gardens**, created on the site of an old gravel pit.

The **Copper Horse** in the park is a huge equestrian statue to King George III, commissioned by his son, George IV.

A **castle** was first built at Windsor by William the Conqueror in 1070. Windsor Castle fell to a siege by John, King Richard I's brother, in 1193, and was captured, without a defence being mounted, by the Parliamentarians in 1642, the first year of the Civil War. It suffered badly in the fire of 1992, Queen Elizabeth II's '*annus horribilis*'. **Windsor Castle** (01753 831118, www.royalcollection.org.uk) is open daily: March to October from 9.45am to 5.15pm, and November to February from 9.45am to 4.15pm. Admission (2010) is £16.

Walk directions

[1] [Numbers in square brackets refer to the map]
Coming out of **Sunningdale station** from platform 2, exit the station by the ticket office and turn left, your direction 125 degrees. In 45 metres turn left again to go over the railway crossing. At the other side of the crossing, *turn left* on a tarmac path parallel to the railway lines, back past the station building on your left-hand side and past new houses on your right.

In 60 metres the tarmac ends and you keep ahead on an earth path, still parallel to the railway lines on your left and soon gently downhill. In 150 metres ignore a path to your right into the recreation ground. In a further 135 metres you cross a bridge over a stream and *turn right* alongside the stream, which is now on your right-hand side, with a playground and tennis court (Broomhall Lane Recreation Ground) coming up shortly on your left-hand side.

Ignore a footbridge to your right and, after 180 metres, you come out through a metal barrier to the B383 road, where you *turn left*. In 100 metres *turn right* on to Station Road.

In 200 metres, and with Holy Trinity Church of England Primary School on your right-hand side, *turn right* on Church Road. You pass the entrance to the school on your right and after 250 metres you come to the entrance of **Holy Trinity Sunningdale Church** on your left. 100 metres beyond the church you *turn half left* up Whitmore Lane (not the sharp left fork, High Street).

In 320 metres ignore a byway sign to the left beside Sunningdale Bowling Club. In a further 200 metres you pass the entrance to Callaly House on your left-hand side and then have Tittenhurst Park behind the wall on your left (the park is not yet visible).

In a further 190 metres, just after the road bends to the left, **[2]** take the signposted footpath *to the right,* through a wooden swing gate (with a wooden fieldgate to its left) and, in 20 metres, cross a bridge over a stream to go straight on, your direction 110 degrees.

In 60 metres, as the wood ends, you enter **Coworth Park**. Cross a gravel track and continue ahead on a grassy way with a wooden fence on your right and a ditch on your left. In 450 metres, with a timber-framed building with a clock tower ahead to your left and the renovated Belvedere Farm ahead to your right, you *turn left,* just before the bridge, on a tarmac car-wide bridleway, your direction 10 degrees.

You pass a lake on your right and then the polo fields of Coworth Park Polo Club on your left, in 450 metres coming out on to the A329 road. *Turn left* down this road. In 150 metres *turn right* into the entrance of Blacknest car park. In 15 metres, just before barriers, *turn left* through the motorcycle entrance to head due north. In 70 metres you enter **Windsor Great Park** through a wooden gate.

Cross a car-wide earth track and with park information boards on your left, go straight on, slightly to the right, your direction 40 degrees. Stay on this main path and make your way, in 200 metres, to **Virginia Water Lake**, where you *turn left,* on to a tarmac path, your direction due west, with the Lake on your right-hand side.

In 220 metres go over a small brick bridge with stone parapet walls and bordered with large rocks. *Turn sharp right* with the path at the end of the bridge **[3]** to keep the water on your right-hand side, your direction now 20 degrees, gently uphill.

In 75 metres fork right, to keep to the water's edge. In 200 metres cross the lake by a large five-arch bridge with stone parapets. 5 metres beyond the bridge **[!]** *turn right on to a faint path,* to go back along the lakeside to your right, your direction 125 degrees.

In 270 metres you come to the fence of a small cottage and a sign saying 'Private Area'. Here, *turn left,* away from the lake, your direction 330 degrees. In 35 metres turn right along the front of the terrace of houses, your direction 45 degrees. In 80 metres, *veer left* at Lakeside Cottage, on to a tarmac path. Then in 20 metres *fork right* over the grass, your bearing 40 degrees.

In 100 metres you pass a 'Crown Estate. Private' entrance gateway on your right and keep on, without a very evident path, with the fringe of the wood on your right-hand side, going due north. 80 metres beyond this gateway, where the wood fringe goes sharply right, you can see the wooden railing on the tarmac lane by the lakes. Head towards this lane, across grass, on a bearing of 40 degrees. In 160 metres join the lane as it swings right, between the upper and lower lakes.

Once on the other side of the lakes **[4]** as the lane swings to the left, *turn right, then left,* your direction 115 degrees, to go uphill on a gravel path signposted **Valley and Savill Gardens**.

[!] Route following is relatively complex in Valley Gardens [!]. Should you be unable to follow the directions suggested below – or if you inadvertently go off piste – simply wander round the gardens to your heart's content, then head down to the lake and *turn left,* which will take you in due course to the Totem Pole (point [5]), where you rejoin the directions.

70 metres past the entrance signs to the gardens, *take a left fork,* uphill, on a gravel path, your direction 100 degrees.

In 20 metres ignore the turn downhill to your right and continue uphill, as the path swings left. In 90 metres near the top, as the path levels out, first ignore a path down to the right (by post no.28) but then at a post with red and yellow bands at its top **[!]** *turn right downhill* on a grassy car-wide track, your direction 175 degrees.

In 6 metres you pass a wooden bench over to your left. In a further 20 metres **[!]** *you fork left uphill* on a grass track, on a bearing of 155 degrees.

In 40 metres *bear right,* merging with a car-wide grassy track, to go downhill, due south. In 45 metres, and 30 metres before a sandy lane T-junction below **[!]** *turn left* on a grassy car-wide track, your direction 85 degrees.

Carry straight on, ignoring other ways off. In 110 metres ignore a grassy car-wide fork going up steps on your left (by post no.53) and keep on, now downhill, on a bearing of 80 degrees.

In 25 metres, as you come out into the open, **[!]** *bear half right* from the oak tree and a bench, downhill, your direction 140 degrees, to cross a gravel path then head for a wooden bridge. In 80 metres go down steps to cross the bridge, go up steps on the other side and then keep ahead, uphill, your direction now 110 degrees.

Keep on uphill across the open grass of **Azalea Valley**, between a near bench to your right and a far bench to your left. **[!]** Once the left-hand bench is facing you, 30 metres over to your left, *go half right* on to a car-wide earth road, gently uphill, on a bearing of 145 degrees.

In 60 metres, by a post with a yellow band on its top, you cross a path, to continue straight on. In 30 metres, at another path crossing, keep ahead (slightly left) now gently downhill as the path swings to the left. The lake is now visible through the trees below on your right-hand side, and your path onwards will be roughly parallel to its edge.

In 100 metres you come down into a green valley, **Valley Garden**, with the **Plunkett Memorial** (a little pavilion with four columns) some 250 metres away to your left at the top of the valley.

Cross the valley bottom *to go up the other side* on railway-sleeper steps, your direction east. At the top of these steps keep straight on (slightly right). Then in 20 metres at a T-junction, *go left* on to a grassy path, your direction 350 degrees.

In 15 metres ignore a fork downhill to the right and in a further 60 metres ignore forks downhill to the left then right. Your path is now a gravelled car-wide track.

In 90 metres you come to a three-way junction, all car-wide tracks. **[!]** *Go sharp right*, on the rightmost (gravel) one, your direction 130 degrees, to head gently downhill as the path swings left. In 45 metres you pass a bench on your left-hand side and in a further 30 metres another bench, with the lovely grassy valley of the **Punch Bowl** falling away to your right. 55 metres past the second bench ignore a fork off to the right and keep ahead on the car-wide earth track.

In 40 metres cross a car-wide earth road by a giant Wellingtonia tree to keep straight on. 15 metres beyond this tree you come to a car-wide earth road *where you turn right*, on a bearing of 95 degrees. In a further 25 metres ignore a fork to the left, to keep ahead, gently downhill.

In 400 metres you come right up to the **Totem Pole**. **[5]** 10 metres beyond it, turn left, with the lake now on your right-hand side, your direction due north, across grass (with no path as such). In 50 metres you cross a stream on a four-plank bridge, with the lake still on your right-hand side.

In 110 metres *do not go over the bridge with white railings* but instead cross a path and go straight on, your direction 10 degrees, through a lightly wooded area. In 115 metres you come out on to a tarmac road (to the right, a signpost indicates 'Vehicle Exit') where you *turn left,* gently uphill.

In 160 metres, at a path crossing, and 80 metres before fingerpost signs ahead, *turn right* on to a gravel and earth car-wide track, between rhododendron bushes, your direction north. In 300 metres your path crosses a stream and starts to ascend. In a further 120 metres, near the top, *go left,* to come out in 35 metres at **Obelisk Pond**. Here you *turn right,* on to a tarmac car-wide path.

In 200 metres *fork left* and in 40 metres you come to the **Obelisk**. To continue on,

return to the tarmac path and, by a sign to 'Savill Garden and Shop', you follow this sign's direction along the tarmac path, in 200 metres coming to the entrance on your left to **Savill Gardens** and the **Savill Garden Restaurant**, the suggested lunchtime stop.

After lunch, return to the tarmac path and *turn left*, to continue in the same direction as before (when approaching the restaurant), on a bearing of 15 degrees. In 70 metres ignore a turn to the right.

In 225 metres, as the path swings left past double-storey greenhouses, *take the gravel, car-wide track ahead,* **Rhododendron Drive**, past a sign saying 'No Cycling'.

In 360 metres cross a stream on a bridge with brick headwalls. In a further 40 metres **[6]** at a crossing of paths, *turn left,* due west, to **Cow Pond** with its water lilies. Carry on around the pond, still keeping it on your right-hand side. Where the gravel track swings to the left, *keep ahead,* now on grass, your bearing 340 degrees. At the far end of the pond, when the wide green path comes to an end, *turn left* over the stream on a tree trunk and continue ahead through light woodland, your direction 300 degrees.

Follow the indistinct path through the trees in this lightly wooded area, heading in the direction of the car road soon visible ahead, and keeping the bogs and marshes over on your right-hand side. In 120 metres you exit the wood and *turn right* immediately, to keep the fringe of the wood to your right, your direction due north.

The path swings right and in 100 metres *you turn right* on to a car-wide horse-ride covered with sand, your direction 50 degrees. In 290 metres, at a faint path crossing, **[!]** *turn left,* to cross a ditch in 10 metres. Now head across the grass towards the pink gatehouses of the **Royal Lodge**, crossing paths on your way.

In 80 metres you come to a tarmac estate road and *turn right* on it as the road swings to the left. In 160 metres you cross the entrance road to the Royal Lodge, over to your left **[7]** and go straight on (slightly left) – the road is clearly marked 'Deer park. No commercial vehicles'.

In 85 metres you go through the gates to the **Deer Park**. Keep ahead on the tarmac estate road. In 55 metres there is a fork to the right.

[For **a simpler route** (the Copper Horse route) ignore the path on your right and keep ahead on this estate road, in 600 metres crossing a stone bridge. Just beyond this, bear left up a grass slope to reach the **Copper Horse** statue. Now simply head downhill and follow the Long walk north to Windsor Castle, joining the main route at point [8A] below.]

For the suggested route, *fork right* off the estate road, your direction 320 degrees, on a narrow but fairly well used footpath.

Keep straight on along this undulating path. In 140 metres *go right* on a path that starts grassy but soon becomes sand and

earth, down towards pine trees, your direction 40 degrees.

In 200 metres, after entering the lightly wooded area, you come to a very wide, gravel and sandy avenue for horses. *Turn right* on this avenue, your direction 85 degrees.

Keep ahead along this avenue. In 240 metres a track joins from the left. In a further 80 metres, at a major crossing of tracks, cross over and keep ahead (slightly to the left) along the sandy, car-wide bridleway, your direction 35 degrees, to pass a Crown Estate notice on your right.

Stay on this sandy bridleway for the next 450 metres. Now look out for two large oak trees on your left-hand side, numbered 880 and 881. **[!]** You now *turn left* off the bridleway **[!]** and walk *between the two trees* **[!]**, ignoring the more obvious path to the left of tree number 880.

Walk ahead on a compass bearing of 260 degrees (half right from the sandy bridleway), through brush and trees, with no obvious path to start with, but you soon pick up a clear, narrow path.

In 100 metres, with the remains of two tree stumps on your left, and some 40 metres before the wood's valley and stream below, *veer right* with the path, your direction now 310 degrees.

In 140 metres *turn left* off the path to cross a ditch where it goes through a concrete pipe under your path. On the far side, *turn right* with the path and head uphill, your direction 320 degrees.

In 130 metres, exit the wood and *turn right* on a car-wide track, your direction 25 degrees. In 160 metres your track joins an access track and you keep ahead. In 60 metres you pass the entrance driveway to scout huts on your left-hand side.

In 70 metres you cross a stream and 5 metres beyond it **[8]**, *fork left,* in 75 metres coming to a notice board for Bear's Rails Pond on your left. A track joins from the right and you keep ahead along it.

In 85 metres go through deer-protection gates and carry on, along the hedge then fence to your right, avoiding muddy areas as best you can.

In 300 metres you have a fine view of the **Copper Horse** on the hillock away to the left and you follow the bend of the fence to the right, your direction 310 degrees.

In 100 metres or so you can see Windsor Castle ahead of you. Now head towards the tarmac path ahead of you, the **Long Walk**, and in about 180 metres you turn right on to (or alongside) it.

[8A] Continue to head north on the Long Walk. In about 1km you exit the park by passing though the swing gate to the left of white double gates, with Double Gates Lodge on your right.

In 750 metres you cross the main road, the A308 **[9]** and continue on the Long Walk (with the unwelcome din of planes overhead as they come in to land at Heathrow Airport).

In 1.1km you reach a set of gates to Windsor Castle. Here you *turn left* to exit Windsor Great Park through side gates on to Park Street, passing the Two Brewers pub on your right-hand side. In 85 metres fork right uphill on St Alban's Street, keeping the castle walls on your right-hand side.

In 90 metres you pass the Parish Church of St John the Baptist on your left-hand side. In a further 25 metres you pass Church Lane to your left, and then in 50 metres, *turn left* and walk 10 metres to be by the Henry VII gatehouse entrance to **Windsor Castle**.

Turn left, exactly opposite the gatehouse, to go down Church Street, coming in a few metres to the Carpenters Arms pub. Continue to the end of the street, with Maloney's Irish Bar directly ahead. Here *turn right* down Church Lane.

At the end of Church Lane *turn right,* by the Three Tuns pub, down the passageway beside Market Street, passing the **Guildhall** on your left-hand side. In 25 metres, by the old, leaning Market House, *turn left* on Queen Charlotte Street – supposedly the shortest street in Britain.

Turn right in the High Street (signposted to Central station and Riverside station). In 35 metres you pass Queen Victoria's statue, to keep straight on. In a further 60 metres, you come to the approach road on your left-hand side to **Windsor Central station** (for trains to Paddington, changing at Slough). For Riverside station, keep straight on along the High Street, in 75 metres passing the King & Castle Wetherspoon's Freehouse on your left-hand side.

In 75 metres ignore River Street to the left to keep on with the castle walls on your right-hand side. 30 metres on, you pass the Theatre Royal Windsor on your left-hand side. In a further 60 metres you pass the statue to Christian Victor, Queen Victoria's grandson.

In 40 metres, cross straight over the main road (Datchet Road) on to Thames Street, with the Bel & the Dragon pub on your right-hand side. In a further 40 metres you pass Sir Christopher Wren's House on your left-hand side.

In 30 metres, just before the bridge over the River Thames, go down steps on the right-hand side, to follow the riverside walk, along the Thames on your left-hand side.

In 40 metres turn right by a modern building marked 'Thameside', up Farm Yard, which leads in 80 metres to the entrance to the Old Ticket Hall Restaurant, and then to **Windsor & Eton Riverside station** (for trains to Waterloo).

Lunch & tea places

Savill Garden Restaurant *Wick Lane, Englefield Green, TW20 0UU (01784 432326, www.theroyallandscape.co.uk).* **Open** *Mar-Oct* 10am-5.30pm daily. *Nov-Feb* 10am-4pm daily. The only lunchtime stop on this walk, serving hot meals, sandwiches and snacks.

No specific tea place is suggested for this walk because there are so many suitable inns, cafés and restaurants in Windsor.

Walk 19

Hever to Leigh

A Kent castles walk.

Start: Hever station
Finish: Leigh station

Length: 14.2km (8.8 miles)

Time: 3 hours 40 minutes. For the whole outing, including trains, sights and meals, allow at least 8 hours 30 minutes.

Transport: Take the train nearest to **10.20am** from **London Bridge** station to **Hever** (journey time 41 minutes). On Sundays there is no direct service from London stations to Hever; you will need to travel from Victoria or London Bridge, changing at East Croydon and/or Oxted, with a longer journey time.

Returning from **Leigh**, you can either take a *westbound* train via Edenbridge and Redhill to London Bridge (on Sundays you might need to change at Redhill), or an *eastbound* train and change at Tonbridge for Charing Cross. The journey time for both routes is about an hour. It is usually best to take

the first train to arrive, so check the timetable when you get to the station in order to decide on the right platform.

Buy a day return to Leigh (Kent). This is valid for both return routes, but on the way out it is only valid as far as Edenbridge Town (on a different line, but tickets via the two Edenbridge stations are interchangeable). In practice, a Leigh ticket is usually accepted to Hever, the next stop, but you might be asked to pay a small supplement.

This walk is not very convenient for car drivers, but you could park somewhere in Edenbridge between its two stations and travel out from Edenbridge Town station and return to Edenbridge station.

OS Landranger Map: 188
OS Explorer Map: 147
Hever, map reference TQ465445, is in **Kent**, 3km south-east of Edenbridge.

Toughness: 2 out of 10

Walk notes: This is a fascinating and very beautiful walk through 'the Garden of England'. It includes two castles, a stately home, rivers, ponds, woods, undulating hills and three lovely villages: the National Trust village of Chiddingstone; Penshurst, with its half-timbered houses; and Leigh (pronounced 'Lie'), with its large cricket green, dominated by the Church of St Mary. The Medway Valley is prone to flooding, so it is possible that parts of this walk may not be passable in extreme conditions.

Walk options: You can shorten the walk by 1.5km by not heading into Chiddingstone when you reach Hill Hoath (see the asterisk [*] in the walk directions). This misses out the lunch stop in this pretty village, but you could stop further on in Penshurst and choose between a late pub lunch or a cream tea in its highly regarded tea room, Quaintways.

If you want to abandon the walk after lunch in Chiddingstone, and you have the OS map, you could head across country

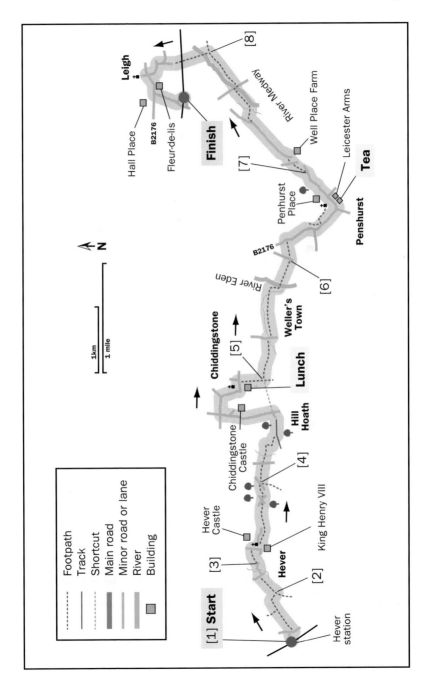

Hever Castle.

to Penshurst station, one stop to the west of Leigh. (It is not worth doing this after tea in Penshurst, because Leigh station is by then almost as close.)

History: **Hever Castle** (01732 865224, www.hevercastle.co.uk) was erected in 1453 by Sir Geoffrey Boleyn, Lord Mayor of London, and was the childhood home of Anne Boleyn (mother of Elizabeth I). She was courted here by Henry VIII. William Waldorf Astor acquired the estate in 1903, and set about restoring the castle. He employed 1,500 men for five years to divert the course of the River Eden and form a large new lake of 35 acres. He also built a new – but surprisingly convincing – Tudor-style village on the north side of the castle to accommodate guests and staff. The compact grounds include a maze, topiary and gardens draped on ruins imported from Italy. There is a cafeteria restaurant by the lake. Opening times vary with the seasons: check in advance. Admission (2010) is £13, or £10.50 for the gardens only.

St Peter's Church in Hever is a part-Norman church with a 14th-century tower topped with a shingle spire. Within the Bullen Chapel, the brass over the tomb of Sir Thomas Bullen (Anne Boleyn's father) shows Sir Thomas in his garter robes.

Chiddingstone Castle (01892 870347, www.chiddingstonecastle. org.uk) is not much of a castle compared with Hever – it is more of a country squire's house, masquerading as a fantasy castle. The present castellated structure dates from the 17th century. Once the ancestral home of the Streatfeild family, it now contains a collection of art and curiosities left behind by its recent owner, Denys Eyre Bower. It is only open on certain days of the week, 11am to 5pm; check in advance. Admission (2010) is £7, or £1 for the grounds only (this used to be free and the charge might be waived if you are just visiting the shop or tea room).

The village of **Chiddingstone** became wealthy as a centre of the iron industry in the 16th and 17th centuries. The Streatfeild family sold the village to the National Trust in 1939, as a consequence of which it remains largely unspoiled. The building that is now a village shop (with a tea room in buildings at the back) was bought, in 1517, by Anne Boleyn's father as the manor house of Chiddingstone.

In 1624, **St Mary's Church** in Chiddingstone was struck by lightning and extensively damaged by fire. Prominently displayed in the church is a **Vinegar Bible** of 1717, so called because in St Luke's Gospel, Chapter 20, 'The parable of the vineyard' is misprinted as 'The parable of the vinegar'! The gazebo in the churchyard covers the vault of the Streatfeild family.

The stately home of **Penshurst Place** (01892 870307, www.penshurstplace. com) is a perfectly preserved, unfortified manor house, which has been the home of the Sidney family since 1552, when Edward VI gave it to his old tutor, Sir William Sidney. The poet Sir Philip Sidney was born here in 1554. The oldest part of the building dates from the 14th century, but the present house represents a curious blend of five centuries of architectural styles. It is open to visitors daily from late March to the end of October, and at weekends only from mid February to late March. Admission (2010) is £9.80, or £7.80 for the gardens only.

On the south side of **St John the Baptist Church**, Penshurst, are timber-framed cottages that form part of **Leicester Square** (named after a favourite of Elizabeth I) and include a post-office house dated 1850. In the Sidney Chapel of the church are many memorials and the effigy of the top half of Stephen de Penshurst, Warden of the Cinque Ports and Constable of Dover Castle, who died in 1299. The fine armorial ceiling in the chapel was restored in 1966. By the side altar is the Luke Tapestry (in Greek), made by Penshurst's former village doctor: it honours the partnership between medical science and Christianity.

Walk directions

[1] [Numbers in square brackets refer to the map]
Coming out of **Hever station**, walk to the top of the approach road and *turn right* on to the country lane.

In 50 metres *turn left* on to a footpath. (Note: this path can be overgrown with nettles and brambles. If you prefer, you can continue on the lane for a further 180 metres, then *turn left* on to a grassy path at a road junction, signed as the **Eden Valley Walk**. The main route joins this path through a gap in the hedge after 350 metres; this is at [2] below.)

For the main route, go along the footpath. In 300 metres go over a stile and *turn right* into a field. Aim for a gap in the hedge 100 metres away; go through this, down steps to a path and *turn left*.

[2] Go along this enclosed path for 150 metres and cross a stile. This takes you on to a road where you *turn right*. In 50 metres, *turn left* down a road signposted for Penshurst, Tonbridge and Hever Castle.

In 150 metres the road curves gently around to the right and, 50 metres further on, you come to a footpath going off to the left. (Note: if you wish, you can simply continue up this road for another 250 metres to meet the King Henry VIII pub and St Peter's Church from the opposite direction.)

[3] For the main route, however, *turn left off the road* on the signposted footpath, crossing over a stile and going along the right-hand side of the field. You can see the spire of St Peter's Church, Hever, on your right-hand side. In 75 metres, *turn right through a wooden fieldgate* into another field. Cross the field, half left, and go through a gap in the hedge in the far left-hand corner of the field. Then walk along the left-hand side of the field.

In 100 metres leave the field and then *immediately turn right* to go along the right-hand side of the next field. In 50 metres cross over another stile, leading you out on to a road, and *turn right* into the village of Hever.

In 150 metres you pass the main entrance to **Hever Castle**, which can be glimpsed through the archway. 30 metres further on, you come to **St Peter's Church** on your left and the **King Henry VIII** pub on your right.

Turn left off the road into the churchyard, following the public footpath sign to Chiddingstone and the Eden Valley Walk. At the bottom of the churchyard, the path curves around into a copse and goes through a small depression, over wooden planks with a wooden railing.

In 150 metres a tarmac lane appears on your left-hand side and beyond it a large field used for the castle's archery and jousting displays. In 400 metres, with the lake belonging to Hever Castle away to your left, the path veers sharply round to the right.

In 150 metres you cross a lane on a wooden bridge. In another 150 metres the tarmac lane that you crossed merges from the right and you continue alongside it. In 350 metres the lane comes to a metal fieldgate.

[4] Pass through a gate in the fence to the left of the fieldgate. *Bear right across the lane and take the footpath on the other side,* your direction 110 degrees. There is a cottage on the right-hand side of the path.

In 300 metres you cross a minor road and go over a stile opposite to continue in the same direction, with a field on your left-hand side and woodland on your right.

In 150 metres cross over a stile and bear right with the path, now with a wood on your left. Continue along the path, veering left across a small brook and up some steps.

The path now crosses a number of wide grassy tracks that are sometimes laid out with horse-jumps. After the second of these, your path veers to the right and then merges with a bridleway coming in from the right.

Continue on this rough track, your direction 80 degrees initially. After climbing gently, the path starts to wend gently downhill through trees. The path is cut through sheer rock and the roots of the beech trees overhanging the path make an interesting sight as they find their way through the rock.

In 200 metres, you cross another grassy track and continue ahead, ignoring a stile and footpath sign 20 metres away to your right. This takes you on to an unmade-up lane, past some houses and then an old wood-beamed cottage, part of the hamlet of **Hill Hoath**, on your left-hand side. Just past the cottage, you come to a T-junction with a country lane.

(**[*]** At the T-junction, you have the option of *turning right for a* **shortcut**. In 70 metres you pass Hill Hoath House on your left-hand side and bear left towards some farm buildings, ignoring another farm track going straight on past some stables. In 60 metres you pass to the left of a large farm shed with a grain hopper and continue ahead (due east). In 80 metres you cross a stile and then go through a gap in a hedge into a field, with Chiddingstone Church now visible away to your left. Continue ahead on a faint path near the left-hand edge of the field. In 80 metres the path heads into a scrubby area and then comes to a stile at a path junction. Cross the stile and continue ahead on the path going across the field; this is at [5] below.)

To continue the main walk, *turn left at the T-junction,* following the tarmac road towards Chiddingstone. As you walk along this track you may be able to glimpse Chiddingstone Castle through the trees on your right, with St Mary's Church, Chiddingstone, to the right of the castle.

In 450 metres you come to Cherry Orchard Cottage on your right-hand side, adjacent to the castle walls. 200 metres beyond that, you reach the main entrance to **Chiddingstone Castle** on your right.

Continue along the road to a crossroads and *turn right,* following the signpost to Chiddingstone. In 250 metres follow the road as it curves round to the right and in another 60 metres goes over a stone bridge. From the bridge you may be able to see the castle behind the trees on the right of the lake.

100 metres further on you pass the tower of St Mary's Church on your left

and then a pedestrian entrance to the castle on your right. Ahead of you is the ancient **Castle Inn**, the suggested stopping place for lunch. (The village stores tea room is further along the street, opposite the entrance to the church.)

From the Castle Inn, continue along the village street. In 40 metres you come to the entrance of **St Mary's Church** on your left, and on your right the village stores and post office (which has a tea room, open at weekends).

50 metres further on you pass the primary school. (Just after the school, you have the option of detouring 150 metres off to the right to see the **Chiding Stone**, an outcrop of local sandstone after which the village is named. The path to it is a dead end and you will have to return to this point.)

30 metres beyond the path to the Chiding Stone, and just past a tarmac driveway, *turn right off the road* at a public footpath sign on to an enclosed path, heading south. In 180 metres you pass a playing field on your left-hand side, with another view across the fields to Chiddingstone Castle on your right-hand side.

100 metres further on, go through a gap into a large field and follow the path straight ahead. The path starts to go gently downhill, passes to the right of a large tree and in 200 metres comes up to a stile in the wooded area on the right.

[5] Do not cross this stile. Instead *turn left* and walk straight across the field towards an oak tree in the hedge on the other side of the field, your direction 80 degrees. In 120 metres go past the oak tree and across a stile into a large field.

Cross the field, slightly to the right and downhill, your direction 105 degrees. If there is no path visible across the field (which can be very muddy), aim for the field's bottom right-hand corner, 450 metres away. In this corner you come out on to a road opposite a sign for **Weller's Town**.

Turn right along the road, crossing over a brook. On the other side, *turn left*

off the road and go over a stile beside a metal fieldgate. Walk along the left-hand side of the field, your direction 75 degrees initially.

In 150 metres, cross a stile to the left of a metal fieldgate to continue ahead along a wide grassy path. 125 metres later, do exactly the same and continue along the left-hand field edge. In a further 500 metres, cross yet another stile to the left of a metal fieldgate and continue with the hedge on your left, your direction now 120 degrees.

[!] In 30 metres *go left over a stile* (or through the fieldgate to its right) into another field and bear right. You will eventually reach a large footbridge visible 200 metres away, but you first need to aim slightly to its left (towards the left of two large trees on the other side of the field) in order to cross a concealed ditch halfway across the field. Having done so, veer right towards the bridge.

Cross this concrete and metal footbridge over the **River Eden** (a tributary of the River Medway). Once over the bridge, *turn right* along the riverbank. In 50 metres *turn sharp left* up the hill through a copse, your direction 120 degrees.

In 100 metres continue straight along the left-hand side of a large cultivated field, climbing gently. In 300 metres you come to two barns at the top of the hill.

[6] Ignore a track off to the left and continue ahead, slightly to the left, along the right-hand field edge, your direction 80 degrees initially. 300 metres further on, just before the end of the field, take a narrow path that veers off to the right and leads you down steps to a main road (be careful as there is no pavement).

Turn right along the road, passing Steamhammer Lodge on your right. In 350 metres you pass Doubleton Lane on your right and, 25 metres further on, a private entrance to Penshurst Place on your left.

60 metres beyond this entrance, *turn left off the road* through a kissing gate and head half right across the field towards the church, your direction

140 degrees. There is a fine perspective of **Penshurst Place** as you cross this field. The walk takes you directly alongside the stone wall and manicured hedge surrounding the south-west side of the house.

In 200 metres go through a squeeze gate into the churchyard of **St John the Baptist Church**. Walk through the churchyard (the church is worth visiting: the entrance is around the corner on your left). Leave the churchyard – underneath a cottage that stands on stilts, in a line of ancient cottages – and go down to the road. On your left is the stone-arched entrance to Penshurst Place, which is the continuation of the route.

For refreshments, however, *turn right* along the road. In 100 metres, where the road curves around to the right, is a late lunch stop, the **Leicester Arms**. 40 metres further on, on the left-hand side, is **Quaintways** tea room, while the alternative tea stop, the **Fir Tree House Tea Rooms**, is another 40 metres along the road to the right.

Afterwards, return along the road and go straight ahead through the brick-and-stone archway to Penshurst Place, following the sign which says 'Public Footpath to Killick's Bank and Ensfield', as well as 'Eden Valley Walk'.

In 225 metres, at the end of the brick wall on your left, ignore the left turn to Penshurst Place car park and continue straight on. In a further 150 metres, ignore two more turns off to the left.

In 100 metres you come to the first of two lakes on your left-hand side. 250 metres later, you come to the end of a second, larger one. Continue along the road for another 50 metres.

[7] Just before the road starts to climb, *turn left off the road* and pass through a wooden squeeze gate, signposted as the Eden Valley Walk. On the other side, *turn sharp right* and walk along the right-hand field edge.

In 75 metres, you pass through another squeeze gate. As you climb uphill, half left, your direction 40 degrees, be sure to

look back for a magnificent view of Penshurst Place, the lakes and the River Medway down in the valley, with its backdrop of trees and hills.

In 250 metres, at the top of the field, go through another squeeze gate (to the right-hand side of a metal fieldgate). Continue straight ahead. In 100 metres you come out on to a concrete lane (the one you left at point [7]). To the right is signed 'Private Road to Well Place only'. Carry straight on, with the River Medway flowing through the valley on your right-hand side, and fields on your left leading up to some woods.

In 600 metres you come to some red-tiled cottages on your right-hand side. Just beyond them, *turn right* down the concrete track and then immediately *cross over the stile on your left*, still following the Eden Valley Walk. Set off half right across the field, heading due east. Follow the marker posts beneath overhead cables as they lead you down the hill towards the river.

In 160 metres cross a wooden bridge with pipe stiles, over a backwater of the River Medway. Over the bridge, head very slightly left across the field towards a wooden post with a footpath sign. In 60 metres you come to the **River Medway**. Turn left and walk along the riverbank, with the river on your right-hand side.

In 450 metres you come to a stone-and-concrete bridge over the river. Go through a squeeze gate on to the road and turn right across this bridge. On the other side, take the footpath going off the road to the left. Pass through a metal squeeze gate and walk along a wide path with a hedge on your left and a large field behind a wire fence on your right.

In 450 metres leave the path by *going right through a wooden squeeze gate* to the left of a metal fieldgate and continue in more or less the same direction along the left-hand field edge.

In 200 metres, go over a stile and across a ditch. Head slightly left across the corner of the field towards a rusty metal gate on your left-hand side, 25 metres away. Go through a squeeze gate to the left of this gate on to a wide track through the trees.

[8] In 30 metres, go straight ahead over the wide path you left earlier and across a brick-and-concrete bridge, which takes you over a backwater. Once over the bridge, fork left and follow the path round to the left. In 50 metres cross a green concrete-and-metal bridge over the River Medway. On the other side, follow the main path straight ahead across the field, your direction 330 degrees.

In 300 metres go through a gap into the next field and continue along its left-hand edge. You can see a car-wide track going up an embankment ahead of you. Go along the left-hand field edge and through a metal kissing gate on to this track, which soon descends to go through a tunnel under the railway.

On the far side of the tunnel the track climbs gently. In 100 metres continue in the same direction on a residential street (Green View Avenue). In 100 metres you pass Lealands Avenue on your right.

100 metres further on, you come to a T-junction leading out on to the village green of **Leigh**. Directly across the green on a small knoll behind and above some picturesque cottages, the **Church of St Mary** dominates the village. *Turn left* and walk around two sides of the village green, past the village school on your left-hand side, and up to the main road, where you *turn left*.

In 150 metres you come to the (closed) Bat & Ball pub and the **Village Stores**, as well as some attractive almshouses. In another 120 metres you come to the **Fleur-de-lis** pub on a corner. *Turn left* down the road towards the station.

In 200 metres you come to a high brick bridge under the railway, with the (unstaffed) **Leigh station** up on your left. Check the timetable displayed here before deciding which platform to head for, as you cannot cross over directly from one platform to the other. To return to London via Tonbridge, go up the path

on *this side* of the bridge; for trains via Redhill, go up the path on the *other side* of the bridge.

Lunch & tea places

Chiddingstone Castle tea room
Hill Hoath Road, Chiddingstone, TN8 7AD (01892 870347, www.chiddingstone castle.org.uk). **Open** *Apr-Sept* 11am-5pm Mon-Wed, Sun. *Oct-Mar* 11am-5pm Sun. A newly refurbished tea room at the castle. Light lunches and afternoon teas can be enjoyed in the Tom Close courtyard during the summer.

At the weekend, an alternative in Chiddingstone is the **village shop tea room**, which serves simple meals through to late afternoon.

Castle Inn *Chiddingstone, TN8 7AH (01892 870247, www.castleinn-kent.co.uk).* **Open** 10am-11pm Mon-Sat; noon-10.30pm Sun. *Food served* 10am-2pm, 7-9.30pm Mon-Fri; noon-4pm, 7-9.30pm Sat, Sun. This is the suggested lunch stop, just over a third of the way through the walk. It serves good but fairly expensive bar food, and has an attractive garden. Groups should phone ahead.

Leicester Arms *High Street, Penshurst, TN11 8BT (01892 870551, www. leicesterarmspenshurst.co.uk).* **Open** 11am-midnight Mon-Sat; 11am-11pm Sun. *Food served* noon-9.30pm daily. Open for tea and coffee all day, but also a good option for a late lunch.

Quaintways *High Street, Penshurst, TN11 8BT (01892 870272).* **Open** 10am-5pm Tue-Sun. This 16th-century tea room, serving fine Kentish cream teas, is the recommended place to stop for tea. No hot food is available here after 2pm Sundays or bank holidays.

Fir Tree House Tea Rooms
Penshurst, TN11 8DB (01892 870382). **Open** *Summer* 2.30-6pm Wed-Sun. Another tea alternative; closed between November and Mothering Sunday.

Fleur-de-lis *High Street, Leigh, TN11 8RL (01732 832235).* **Open** 11am-midnight daily. *Food served* noon-3pm, 6-9pm Mon-Sat; noon-4pm Sun.

Walk 20

Milford to Godalming

The Greensand Way and Winkworth Arboretum.

Start: Milford station
Finish: Godalming station

Length: 17.9km (11.1 miles)

Time: 5 hours. For the whole outing, including trains, meals and a church visit, allow 8 hours.

Transport: Take the train nearest to **9.40am** from **Waterloo** station to **Milford** (journey time 50 minutes).

Buy a day return to Milford (Surrey). There are two trains an hour back from **Godalming** (hourly on Sundays), with a similar journey time.

OS Landranger Map: 186
OS Explorer Maps: 145, 133 & 134 Milford, map reference SU955414, is in **Surrey**, 9km south of Guildford.

Toughness: 6 out 10

Walk notes: This is a relatively strenuous walk, and bits of it can be muddy in wet weather, but it is rewarding and full of interest. From Milford station, you come to the lakes and the magnificent timber-framed Enton Mill – one of the many houses on this walk that have 17th- or 18th-century galleting (black pebbles lining the mortar of the walls, a method much used in those days in Kent and the south). Near a pub and church in Hambledon, you join the Greensand Way, a sandy bridleway through The Hurtwood, offering hazelnuts and blackberries in season. Lunch is at the White Horse pub in Hascombe, a village with a remarkable church covered in wall decoration, so that it looks almost Moorish.

In the afternoon, the walk goes on legitimate rights of way that give free access to the National Trust's Winkworth Arboretum and its lakes – the azaleas and bluebells make it particularly lovely

to visit in springtime – and then along the fringes of its woods to a horse-training course and the rich outskirts of Godalming, with its many imposing buildings. The final approach to the town is along the National Trust's River Wey & Godalming Navigation path along the canal, to the Church of St Peter & St Paul and the ancient High Street.

Walk options: You could call for a taxi from the Merry Harriers pub in Hambledon. Arriva bus 42/44 runs about once an hour (not Sundays) from Hascombe to Godalming, passing Winkworth Arboretum.

If you have a map, you can save about 1km near the end of the walk by heading for Farncombe station rather than Godalming; it is about 750m from the Farncombe Boat House.

History: The timber-framed **Enton Mill** was built in 1757.

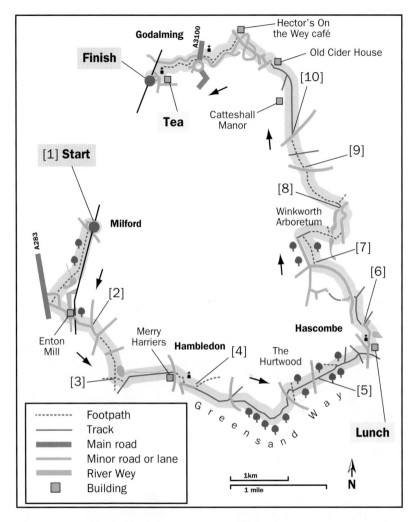

Milford to Godalming

St Peter's Church, Hascombe, was rebuilt in 1863, following the old Saxon design, but slightly larger and incorporating older features such as the 17th-century font. At the same time, Canon Musgrave had almost every inch of wall space decorated 'to make us aware of God's glory shining through the physical world'. Above the altar is an ornate dome, formed from the decorated undersides of the roof's supporting timbers, and allowing a view through to the hallelujahs painted on the roof. John Betjeman called it 'a Tractarian work of art'. (The white button for the lights is just through the curtains, up on the left.)

The Old Cider House, Catteshall, was previously the **Ram Cider House** pub (which took its name from the Ram gravity pump used for raising water). The house is based on a wattle-and-

Time Out Country Walks 155

daub 16th-century building and the pub used to sell 35 different types of cider.

Godalming is thought to mean 'field(-ing) of Godhelm' (the putative first Saxon to claim the land). It was a coaching town between London and Portsmouth, and a centre of stone-quarrying and brewing, and trade in wool, timber, leather, paper and corn. The High Street has many half-timbered and projecting buildings.

Walk directions

[1] [Numbers in square brackets refer to the map]
Coming out of **Milford station**, cross the railway footbridge and exit platform 1 on the station building side by a white gate.

Cross over the main road to *take the footpath opposite,* between fences; this narrow path runs parallel to the railway lines on its left-hand side, your direction 200 degrees.

In 425 metres the path bends right away from the railway lines and in a further 200 metres you begin to see lakes to the left-hand side. Then in 100 metres your path joins a farm track to continue straight on.

In 300 metres cross a road (The Quest and Lakes Cottage are to your left) and *continue ahead* on a footpath, your direction 210 degrees.

In 140 metres you come out on a road T-junction, with Witley Social Club on your left-hand side, and you *turn left,* your direction 110 degrees.

In 210 metres bear right with the road, a stream (visible in winter) now on your left-hand side.

In 150 metres you pass the very lovely **Enton Mill** on your left-hand side, to go under a railway bridge and continue on the road.

300 metres beyond the bridge, you come to a T-junction, by a barn supported on wooden pillars on your right-hand side. **[2]** *Turn right,* your direction 170 degrees. In 140 metres, at a T-junction, cross it to *go straight on,* your direction 120 degrees, on a signposted footpath.

In 130 metres go over a stile bearing half right, your direction 130 degrees.

In 100 metres you pass a metal barrier (a kissing gate minus tongue) to continue straight on. In 200 metres cross a car lane and continue into another field, heading towards a lake (visible in winter). Keep the mini pylons on your right, your direction due south.

In 325 metres you enter the fringes of a wood through a metal swing gate (which has a wooden fieldgate on its left-hand side).

In 40 metres, by a mini pylon, *fork left,* following a yellow footpath arrow on a post, your direction 160 degrees.

In 100 metres you come to a post with arrows and *turn left* **[3]**, your direction 100 degrees, initially following overhead mini pylons.

In 65 metres, at a crossing of paths, keep straight on, your direction 110 degrees. Ignore tracks to the right and, in 100 metres, you come to a potentially muddy zone by a post with multiple arrows, at the edge of the wood. You *go left,* your direction 70 degrees.

In 65 metres you *veer right* with this wide bridleway, out of the wood, your direction now due east, following mini pylons.

In 600 metres you come out to a car road T-junction with the **Merry Harriers** pub to your right, a possible early lunch stop.

Turn right on the road, your direction 165 degrees. In 25 metres *turn left* on to the signposted public footpath opposite the pub, through a metal kissing gate, your direction 75 degrees.

In 145 metres bend right with this path, which in a further 80 metres becomes a driveway for houses. In 65 metres you come out on a tarmac road and *turn left,* uphill, your direction 110 degrees. In 50 metres you come to **St Peter's Church, Hambledon** (kept locked).

Just past the church, but still alongside its churchyard wall **[4]**, *fork right* on a signposted public bridleway (an earth car road), your direction 125 degrees – and with a small parking area on your left-hand side. You are now on the

Greensand Way (so marked on the OS map).

Keep on this road and, in 450 metres, it becomes a narrower path. In a further 370 metres, you come to a T-junction where you *turn right,* on a sandy road, your direction 170 degrees.

[!] In 20 metres *turn left* up an easy-to-miss public bridleway, your direction 150 degrees, to go along the north fringe of the wood. In 170 metres *fork right,* down into the wood, your direction 140 degrees, and ignoring ways off to remain on the Greensand Way.

In 125 metres keep on, following a GW and bridleway sign (with a parallel car road on your right). In a further 75 metres, ignore a lesser car-wide way straight on, to *fork left* with your way uphill, your direction 100 degrees.

Then, in 130 metres, ignore a faint fork off down to the right and towards a house. Keep on the main path, now along the south edge of the wood.

In 85 metres you pass under a mini pylon. In 650 metres, having enjoyed fine views off to the right, ignore a signposted footpath off to the right.

In 160 metres, at a tarmac road, *go left,* uphill, your direction 295 degrees. In 85 metres *turn right* on a bridleway, signposted Greensand Way, your direction 45 degrees, into **The Hurtwood** (as marked on the OS map).

In 80 metres you pass a metal fieldgate to continue in the same direction.

In 200 metres, at the top of the incline, bear slightly left along the main track. In 200 metres cross over a car-wide earth track and in a further 200 metres cross a car-wide earth road to keep straight on along the Greensand Way. **[5]** In 220 metres ignore a fork to the right.

[!] In 150 metres, by a post, *turn right,* your direction 150 degrees, following a GW yellow arrow.

[!] In 25 metres, *turn sharp left* to go downhill on a narrow path, your direction 20 degrees (not the wider track off to the left at a path junction just past this). The main track you left a few moments earlier is now down below on your left, on the other side of a bank.

[!] In 200 metres (with – in winter only – a large house and tennis court visible ahead) and by a post with a yellow footpath GW arrow (on a black background), *turn left,* leaving the bridleway. Go steeply downhill, with wooden handrails on your right-hand side, your direction 50 degrees.

In 40 metres you exit the wood by a stile to continue on with the field edge on your right-hand side.

In 130 metres go over two stiles and through a potentially very muddy area to reach the B2130. Cross the road to come to the **White Horse** pub, **Hascombe**, the suggested lunchtime stop.

Coming out of the pub after lunch, *fork sharp right* into Church Road, your direction 25 degrees, in 75 metres coming to the entrance to the delightful **St Peter's Church, Hascombe** (it is open to visitors).

Continue on the road past the village pond on your right-hand side, and bear left with the road as it passes the School House again on your right. Then, in a

further 200 metres, by a cottage **[6]**, where one bridleway is straight on, you *turn left* on another bridleway, your direction 290 degrees, with the course of a stream still down below you on your left-hand side.

In 75 metres you *go over a stile on your right* (with a metal fieldgate on its right-hand side), your direction now 305 degrees. Continue over two stiles, and after 130 metres you join a bridleway and *turn right* along it, your direction 345 degrees.

In 80 metres your path merges with an earth road and you carry straight on through a metal field gate marked 'The Stables', ignoring a bridleway off to the left. In 45 metres you pass a house on your left-hand side. In a further 175 metres, *fork left* on a path down between fences, following a blue public bridleway arrow, your direction 285 degrees.

In 120 metres, having negotiated this potentially muddy path, go through a metal fieldgate to cross the B2130 and *continue straight on* up a public bridleway (a gravel driveway signed to Leybourne Cottage), your direction 255 degrees.

In 55 metres you pass Elm Cottage on your left and in a further 50 metres Leybourne Cottage, to continue steeply up the bridleway.

In 160 metres ignore an opening and way off to the left. In 145 metres, at the brow of the hill, you pass High Winkworth House on the left-hand side. By a sign for the entrances to Sullingstead and Winkworth Hanger, *turn left* on the tarmac lane, your direction 260 degrees.

In 210 metres, at a tarmac T-junction, *turn right,* your direction due north.

In 400 metres you come to the B2130 where you *turn right* on to the road, your direction due east (be careful as there is no pavement).

[!] In 140 metres **[7]** *turn left* on to a not-very-evident signposted public footpath, just inside Eden House's driveway and forking left off it, your direction 345 degrees.

In 45 metres you pass a partly timber-framed house on your left-hand side, with **Winkworth Arboretum** soon visible beyond the fencing on your right-hand side.

In 500 metres or so, you come to an earth road, with a car park on your left-hand side, and you *turn right,* following

a public footpath sign, through a wooden swing gate to the right of a metal fieldgate, your direction 55 degrees, along a car-wide earth road. In 10 metres you pass a cottage on your right-hand side. In 60 metres, you pass the National Trust's ticket kiosk on your left (entrance to the Arboretum for those leaving the public footpath costs £5).

In 150 metres, at a crossroads, you follow the yellow public footpath arrows going straight on down towards the Azalea Steps and lakes.

In 75 metres *turn left* with the yellow arrow, by a wooden sign saying Fiona Adam Steps. At the bottom of these steps, *turn right,* again following the yellow arrow, your direction 110 degrees.

In 130 metres, at a T-junction, follow the yellow arrow to the right, your direction 200 degrees.

In 35 metres, where the steps go up to the right, *turn left,* with a log cabin then on your right-hand side, your direction due east. You pass a lake on your right-hand side.

Out of the wood you come to a T-junction by a National Trust donation pyramid on your right and you *bear left* with the yellow arrow, your direction 100 degrees.

In 100 metres you go through the car park on to a tarmac road where you *go left,* your direction 345 degrees.

In 300 metres, by a public footpath sign and a sign for Phillimore Cottage, *turn left* uphill on a tarmac lane, your direction 340 degrees. **[8]**

In 100 metres *go over a stile on the right,* marked with an arrow, then *turn left,* your direction 300 degrees, with the field edge on your left-hand side. In 200 metres you go over a stile, then in 10 metres pass a sign saying 'Agricultural and sporting pursuits in progress' to go straight on, in 15 metres crossing a path, your direction 310 degrees.

In 160 metres you pass a bench on your left-hand side to keep straight on (slightly to the right). Then in 45 metres you cross a path, and in a further 350 metres, having ignored all ways off, you come out through a metal kissing gate on to a tarmac

road where you *turn left,* your direction due west.

In 100 metres *turn right off the road* on to a track, your direction 330 degrees, ignoring a gate into a field on your right. **[9]**

In 250 metres, at the end of a tall wooden fence on your left-hand side, cross a bridleway to continue straight on past a metal barrier, between fences.

In 265 metres cross a tarmac road to *continue straight on,* along a signposted bridleway. **[10]**

In 1km you pass the swanky gates to Catteshall Farm on your left-hand side. In a further 250 metres, you pass the entrance to Catteshall Manor (with a sign for 'The Book People') on your left-hand side and bend right with the road. Then in 80 metres you come to a T-junction, with the timber-framed Old Cider House on your right-hand side, where you *turn left,* your direction 245 degrees.

In 65 metres you *turn right* into Catteshall Road, your direction 335 degrees. Then in 80 metres you cross Warramill Road to continue ahead.

In 50 metres, by Brocks Close, you fork left on to the main road to cross the bridge, your direction 300 degrees. Stay on the road and, 175 metres beyond the bridge, you come to another one with **Farncombe Boat House** on the right-hand side.

To visit **Hector's On the Wey** café, go down steps on the right on this side of the river; the café is at the far end of the boat house. Afterwards, return to the road and turn right.

Once over the river, cross the road and *turn left,* going through a small metal swing gate in 5 metres, to pass Catteshall Lock on your left-hand side, continuing on the National Trust's **River Wey & Godalming Navigation** path, your direction 220 degrees.

In 900 metres you pass the partially converted Godalming United Church to come out on the A3100 where you *turn left,* your direction 210 degrees, to cross the Town Bridge over the River Wey.

At the other side of the bridge, *turn sharp right* down some steps to get on to the riverside path, meandering with the river on your right-hand side (and Godalming library away to your left).

In 450 metres, beyond the bowling green and before the church, *fork left* away from the river path towards the back entrance of the churchyard of Godalming's **Church of St Peter & St Paul.** Go through the churchyard and exit it, in 80 metres, into Deanery Place, near the entrance to the church.

If you wish to visit one of the alternative tea places, *turn left* and go up Church Street. In 130 metres you come to the High Street and turn left: **Caffè Nero** is along the High Street to your right, **Costa Coffee** a little further on to your left. Afterwards, head back along the High Street and (by the Old Town Hall) turn right into Church Street to return to the church.

Continue past the church entrance and across a road to pick up a signposted passageway leading to the station, still straight on.

Once at **Godalming station** you need to go under the subway for trains to London.

Lunch & tea places

Merry Harriers *Hambledon, GU8 4DR (01428 682883, http://merryharriers.com).* **Open** 11am-3pm Mon; 11am-3pm, 5.15-11pm Tue-Thur; 11am-midnight Fri; 11am-11pm Sat; 11am-8pm Sun. *Food served* 11am-3pm Mon; 11am-3pm, 6-10pm Tue-Sat; 11am-3pm, 6-8pm Sun. A possible early lunch stop. Groups of more than 15 should book.

White Horse *The Street, Hascombe, Godalming, GU8 4JA (01483 208258, www.whitehorsehascombe.co.uk).* **Open** 11am-11pm Mon-Thur; 11am-midnight Fri, Sat; 11am-10.30pm Sun. *Food served* noon-3.30pm, 7-10pm daily. The suggested lunchtime pub for this walk; the owners prefer large groups to phone ahead.

National Trust tea room *Winkworth Arboretum, Hascombe Road, Godalming GU8 4AD (01483 208477, www.national trust.org.uk).* **Open** *Jan, Feb, Dec* 11am-4pm Sat, Sun. *Mar, Nov* 11am-4pm Wed-Sun. *Apr-Oct* 11am-5pm Wed-Sun. A convenient tea stop if you've had an early lunch at the Merry Harriers, or spent some time exploring the Arboretum.

Hector's On the Wey *Farncombe Boat House, Catteshall Lock, Catteshall Road, Godalming, GU7 1NH (01483 418769, www.farncombeboats.co.uk).* **Open** *Summer* 10am-5pm Wed-Sun. *Winter* 10am-4pm Wed-Sun. Strong tea and an excellent selection of cakes are to be found at the suggested tea stop. Allow 30 minutes after tea to reach Godalming station. Groups of more than 20 are asked to call ahead.

If Hector's is closed, there are several alternatives on Godalming High Street, including **Caffè Nero** (no.91, 01483 420826, www.caffenero.com) and **Costa Coffee** (no.74, 01483 527589, www.costa.co.uk).

Walk 21

Leigh to Sevenoaks

Knole Park and Kent's 'rolling, tidal landscape'.

Start: Leigh station
Finish: Sevenoaks station

Length: 14.5km (9.0 miles)

Time: 4 hours 20 minutes. For the whole outing, including trains, Knole House and meals, allow 9 hours.

Transport: Take the train nearest to **9.30am** from **London Bridge** to **Leigh** station (journey time just under an hour). An alternative is to go from Charing Cross, changing at Tonbridge, which takes just over an hour. On winter Sundays, there are no direct trains. There are frequent trains back from **Sevenoaks**, journey time 35 minutes to Charing Cross, or about an hour to Victoria. Buy a day return to Leigh (Kent).

If you are driving, there are frequent trains from Sevenoaks to Tonbridge, where you change for the one stop to Leigh. Sevenoaks station is closer to London and the M25. It has several large car parks (Mon-Fri: £6; Sat: £2; Sun: £1), but you can park near Leigh station for free.

OS Landranger Map: 188
OS Explorer Map: 147
Leigh, map reference TQ546462 is in **Kent**, 9km south of Sevenoaks.

Toughness: 5 out of 10

Walk notes: You need to start this lovely walk in good time as the bulk of it is before lunch. The route is through what Laurie Lee described as the 'rolling, tidal landscape' of Kent. The walk starts in the village of Leigh (pronounced 'Lie', from the Anglo-Saxon for 'forest clearing') with its many fine old buildings, goes through the churchyard and past the parkland of Hall Place, and carries on through a few too many potentially muddy fields and past many an oast house (the conically roofed buildings used for drying hops) to the church and pub in Underriver, the suggested lunchtime stop. After lunch, it is sharply uphill to then follow the Greensand Way into magnificent Knole Park, passing the front entrance of Knole and leaving the park on a footpath to arrive in the centre of Sevenoaks.

Walk options: There are rare buses (two a day, Mon-Sat) from the lunchtime pub in Underriver to Tonbridge station, or you could take a taxi.

History: **Knole House**, built in the 15th century (and so huge that it has a room for every day of the year), was visited by Elizabeth I in 1573, who granted it to Thomas Sackville. It remained in the Sackville family and was the childhood home of Vita Sackville-West, featuring in Virginia Woolf's *Orlando*. The house, with its tapestries, paintings and collection of 17th-century furniture, is open to visitors from mid March to the end of October, Wednesday to Sunday (plus bank holiday Mondays and Tuesdays in August) with last entry at 3.30pm. Admission (2010) is £9.50. The garden is open on Tuesdays only. The house

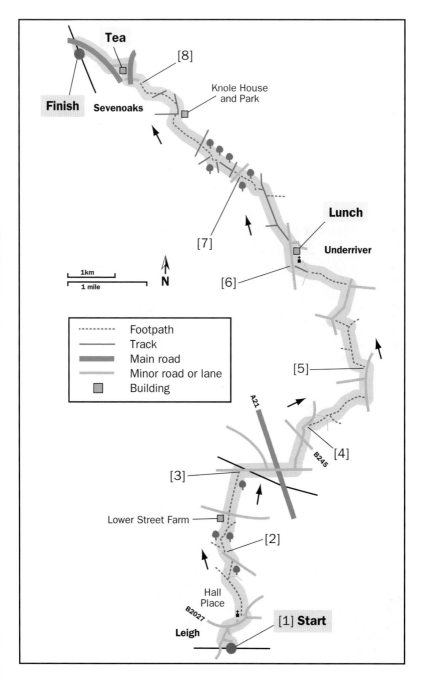

Tea

Finish

[8]

Sevenoaks

Knole House
and Park

Lunch

Underriver

[7]

[6]

1km
1 mile

N

[5]

Footpath
Track
Main road
Minor road or lane
Building

A21

[3]

B245

[4]

Lower Street Farm

[2]

Hall
Place

B2027

[1] Start

Leigh

Knole House.

stands in a park of 1,000 acres. There is no charge for walking in the park – in any case, the route described in the walk directions follows public rights of way.

Walk directions

[1] [Numbers in square brackets refer to the map]
From **Leigh station** platform 2, *exit down the tarmac path,* your direction 285 degrees, to the road and turn right. (If you have come via Tonbridge you will arrive on platform 1; go down its tarmac path to the road where you turn right and go under the railway bridge.)

Continue on the road past the garage and the Fleur-de-lis pub to the main road, B2027.

Turn right and continue for 300 metres. Just before a bus shelter on your left and with a school on your right, cross the road to *turn left northwards to the church* on a tarmac lane. (Public toilets

are available off the main road; follow the sign to the right.)

Go through the gate into the churchyard. Follow the path to the right of the church and exit though the lychgate.

In 10 metres *turn left,* taking the footpath indicated with a yellow arrow, direction 345 degrees, past the impressive gatehouse leading to Hall Place on your left and through a wooden fieldgate marked Porcupine House.

In 80 metres go through a metal kissing gate and straight on, with the field fence and ancient trees and parkland of Hall Place to your left. In 300 metres go though another metal kissing gate and straight on through a potentially muddy area, partially alleviated by some bricks.

In 170 metres ignore the next metal kissing gate at the end of the field and *fork right over a concrete bridge and stream,* your direction 25 degrees. After 100 metres continue on the path on the left-hand side of a field, your direction 15 degrees.

In 260 metres go over a stile to pass through a copse. In 50 metres pass through a gap next to a collapsed stile and turn left down an earth lane, your direction 305 degrees.

[2] 20 metres before the end of this lane, just before a cottage on your left, follow the low footpath sign to go half right northwards with a field fence on your right.

In 40 metres this path enters the wood on a wide earth track. *10 metres into the wood, turn half right,* following a footpath sign, up a wide path, your direction 345 degrees. In 120 metres bend right with the path, your direction initially 35 degrees, along a bridleway.

In 200 metres exit the wood over a stile (a potentially muddy area) and go straight on, with the field edge and ditch on your left.

In 120 metres cross a stream over a concrete bridge and go through a kissing gate to the left of a fieldgate (another possibly muddy area). Carry straight on, your direction 20 degrees, with a stream tributary on your left and an oast house (marked as Lower Street Farm on the OS map) further off to your left.

In 200 metres you come up towards a car road and through a kissing gate to the left of a fieldgate, which may be muddy. *Go straight across the road and continue by a public footpath sign over a stile* straight ahead, with a field boundary on your right down a large field.

At the end of this field go over a stile to the right of a fieldgate, another potentially muddy spot, and continue on with the hedge now on your left, direction 345 degrees.

In 120 metres go over another stile to the right of a fieldgate and then *go half right to cross the field diagonally,* your direction 35 degrees, towards a stile in the far right-hand corner, 10 metres beyond a pond on your right. *Turn right on a car road,* going east. [3]

Continue along the road for 500 metres to the road bridge over the A21 and cross

it. Carry on until you come to a T-junction, where you turn left. Continue ahead for 500 metres, passing a house called Oak Trees on your left to reach the B245.

Turn left and in 70 metres turn right on to Mill Lane.

[4] In 180 metres when the road bends slightly to the left and opposite Meadow House, *take the footpath to your right over a stile,* your direction half left, 65 degrees, aiming at wooden fencing visible in the distance. In 250 metres go over a wooden footbridge and stream.

Continue ahead, your direction 70 degrees. In 130 metres, go straight on across the field to a stile visible to the right of a fieldgate. In 120 metres, *cross this stile, a potentially muddy area, and turn half left to go diagonally across the field.*

In 250 metres exit this field by its far-left corner (near the left-hand edge of the copse) over a stile hidden behind trees on your right. Continue on, your direction 70 degrees, heading well to the left of houses visible ahead (with difficulty in summer), across a potentially muddy field. Leave the field over a stile with a yellow arrow about two-thirds down the side you are walking along.

In 10 metres go over a wooden bridge and through a metal kissing gate to revert to your previous direction, 70 degrees, following the right-hand edge of the field. Turn left at the corner and after 100 metres leave the field by a metal kissing gate close to a track.

Cross the track and turn left. After 10 metres turn right towards a stile marked by a yellow arrow. Cross the stile and continue on the path with the horse training ground on your left. At the end of the path go through a wooden gate and turn left, keeping the breeze-block wall on your left, your direction 50 degrees. After 50 metres go through a fieldgate, along the driveway of Brambles House and out on to the road.

Turn left on the road, northwards, passing Hadlow College Princess Christian Farm on your right. In 120 metres ignore Vines Lane on the left to keep straight on.

[5] After a further 150 metres, *turn left at a public footpath sign* and a sign saying Woodside, your direction 325 degrees. Continue along the wide path with fences on both sides.

After 200 metres, when the wide path ends, go through a gap ahead to the right (hidden by vegetation in summer) and then through a wooded area to pass through another gap into a field. Continue with the fence on your left, direction 350 degrees.

In 400 metres, at the end of this large field, go past a big oak tree on your left and, following a low footpath sign, *cross a track to go straight on across a field,* your direction due north. In 200 metres, leave the field through a gap to carry straight on into a wooded area.

After 30 metres *cross a stile into a field and turn half left,* your direction 270 degrees, following the direction of the mini pylons westwards, to the edge of the back garden of a house. Here turn right, your direction 320 degrees, keeping the edge of the gardens to your left. In 150 metres, *exit the field by a stile and footpath sign on the left, 30 metres before the field corner,* to reach a car road.

Turn right and in 15 metres take the car road to the right, signposted to Shipbourne, gently uphill. In 600 metres, well over the brow of the hill, where a road goes off to the right (again signposted to Shipbourne) you *go left over a stile,* due west, on a signposted public footpath with a field fence and tennis court on your right.

Go straight on and in 350 metres go over a stile with a metal fieldgate to its left and straight ahead up an avenue, your direction 305 degrees. In 200 metres go over a stile and straight on. After 250 metres across a potentially muddy field go over a stile and cross a stream to carry straight on slightly uphill, your direction 315 degrees with a stream on your right. *After 50 metres exit the field through a metal kissing gate on to an earth car lane.*

With Green Lane Cottage on your right, continue ahead.

[6] At a T-junction with a tarmac road, *turn right* (due north), in 65 metres passing St Margaret's Church, **Underriver**. In a further 75 metres you come to the **White Rock** pub, the suggested lunchtime stop.

Coming out of the pub after lunch, *turn right on the road* and in 130 metres ignore the footpath on the right to continue gently uphill. In a further 100 metres, opposite a road to the right signposted Shipbourne, *take the wide lane that is signposted public bridleway to your left,* direction 305 degrees.

In 100 metres you pass Black Charles House on your right to continue up a slightly narrower path. In 320 metres *turn right up a restricted byway* with an oast-house barn visible ahead to your left, your direction 345 degrees. Continue steeply uphill on a potentially very muddy path overarched with trees.

In 500 metres, near the top of the hill, you pass a path on the right marked Greensand Way. 20 metres after this, *fork upwards to the left.* In 10 metres cross a stile marked Greensand Way to the right of a metal gate.

In essence you now just follow the Greensand Way until you come to a car road, but in more detail: Continue on, initially due west, with the field edge on your left. In 130 metres bear right at the corner of the field, your direction 340 degrees. 100 metres on from this bend *turn left across a stile,* your direction 290 degrees, into a wood. In 200 metres you exit the wood at a car road.

[7] *Cross the road to enter* **Knole Park** by a fenced kissing gate. (Ignore the fenced kissing gate to your right just inside the park.)

Continue straight ahead in your previous direction with the fence on your right. In 100 metres you come to a junction of tarmac roads and take the one straight ahead, your direction 325 degrees. In 750 metres, at the top of a rise, at a tarmac path T-junction, *continue ahead through an opening slightly to the right,* direction

315 degrees. In 20 metres you see fences on the left and your path becomes wider. Follow it towards the walled garden of Knole House, soon visible ahead.

About 100 metres from the walls, *fork left on to a wide grassy path that runs parallel to the walls,* your direction 305 degrees. You can get a good view of the side of Knole House through the second set of metal railings along the wall. At the end of the wall, turn right to reach the main entrance of **Knole House**.

If you want tea now, go right and right again to the **Brew House tea room**.

Otherwise continue ahead (or turn right on leaving the house, if you have visited it) on the curved driveway, due north. In 85 metres from the entrance cross another road and immediately *turn half left on the grass* with no clear path uphill, heading for a clump of trees at the top of the rise, your direction 315 degrees (on a line that is a continuation of the line of the side wall of Knole House behind you). You may need to weave your way round parked cars.

Once there, following a footpath sign to the right go downwards, your direction 310 degrees. In 150 metres keep a crater depression on your right. You are now on a clear path marked by a footpath sign that leads to a tarmac drive. *Cross it to carry straight on, along a clear path initially downhill,* your direction 300 degrees.

In 200 metres *leave Knole Park by a fenced kissing gate to go steeply uphill,* your direction 265 degrees. In 5 metres you pass the entrance to Sevenoaks Environmental Park on your right. (If the park is open, a pleasant alternative route is to wend your way up through the park, always choosing the left-hand fork to come out at the car park.)

In a further 200 metres keep to the tarmac path as you pass the Sevenoaks Leisure Centre car park on your right. Continue past the end of the car park with a wall on your right and railings on your left, coming out opposite Waitrose. **[8]** *Cross the road and continue to the right*

of the public toilets (Akehurst Lane), your direction 255 degrees. This leads out to **Sevenoaks High Street**.

(Alternatively cross the Sevenoaks Leisure Centre car park diagonally to the opposite corner, where you turn left, following the sign for the Tourist Information Office. After 50 metres you come to a road; cross it and carry on straight ahead, past the bus stops, to arrive at Sevenoaks High Street.)

There are various possibilities for tea in Sevenoaks. For **Caffè Nero** turn right down the High Street. For **Costa Coffee**, cross the High Street, turn right and continue to Blighs Road.

After tea you will need to get to London Road, which runs west of the High Street for the station. From Costa Coffee, cross the car park to the far side, where steps lead down to London Road; then turn right downhill. From Caffè Nero, carry on along the High Street to the traffic light junction, where you turn left along Pembroke Road; when you reach London Road, turn right.

Continue for about 1km down London Road to reach **Sevenoaks station** on the left for frequent trains to London.

Lunch & tea places

White Rock *Underriver, Sevenoaks, TN15 0SB (01732 833112, www.thewhite rockinn.co.uk).* **Open** noon-4pm, 6-11pm Mon-Fri; noon-11pm Sat, Sun. *Food served* noon-3pm, 6.30-9.30pm Mon-Fri; noon-9.30pm Sat; noon-9pm Sun. The suggested lunch stop, about 9km (5.6 miles) from the start. Book ahead for a table on Sundays or if a large group is coming to eat.
Brewhouse tea room *Knole House, Sevenoaks, TN15 0RP (01732 450608, www.nationaltrust.org.uk).* **Open** times vary; phone for details. You don't have to pay an entrance fee to eat at Knole House's tea room. Cream teas are served.

There are various tea options in Sevenoaks, including **Caffè Nero** (113 High Street, 01732 779050) and **Costa Coffee** (2 Blighs Road, 01732 462159).

Walk 22

Haslemere Circular

Marley Common and Black Down.

Start and finish: Haslemere station

Length: 14.0km (8.7 miles)

Time: 4 hours 15 minutes. For the whole outing, including trains and meals, allow 8 hours 30 minutes.

Transport: Take the train nearest to **10am** from **Waterloo** station to **Haslemere** (journey time 50 minutes). There are four trains an hour back from Haslemere (two on Sundays). Parking at Haslemere station costs £5.50

weekdays, £3 on Saturday and £1 on Sunday. You can also park on residential roads to the east of the station, or by the lunch pub in Fernhurst and start the walk from there.

OS Landranger Map: 186
OS Explorer Map: 133
Haslemere, map reference SU897329, is in **Surrey**, 13km south-west of Godalming.

Toughness: 4 out of 10

Walk notes: The route is through very beautiful countryside. It is mainly National Trust land – mixed woods with blackberries and bluebells, and heathlands of bracken, gorse, heather and bilberry – with fine views from Black Down (280 metres/919 feet), the highest point in both Sussex and the South Downs National Park. It is particularly lovely when the rhododendrons are in flower in late spring, although the heathland is at its most colourful in late summer.

A path just after the lunch pub can be very wet and muddy, even in dry weather: wear appropriate footwear.

Walk options: You could shorten the walk by taking the hourly bus service from Fernhurst (less than halfway through the walk) back to Haslemere; the bus goes from the top of Hogs Hill Road in Fernhurst, along the A286. Walk 6 (Liphook to Haslemere; *see p47*) uses the same pub in Fernhurst for

lunch. You could substitute its easier afternoon ending back to Haslemere, avoiding the climb up Black Down.

History: In Tudor and Stuart times, **Haslemere** was a centre for the iron industry. With the coming of the railway in the mid 19th century, it became a popular spot for literary people. The poet Tennyson's house, Aldworth, is on the slopes of Black Down, where he loved to walk, and George Eliot wrote *Middlemarch* in Shottermill.

The town has an interesting **museum** up the High Street, just north of Darnleys tea room. The museum is open 10am to 5pm Monday to Saturday, and has important natural history collections, as well as a fine explanatory display of local wild flowers in the foyer. Other highlights include an Egyptian mummy, Zulu beadwork and Eastern European peasant art.

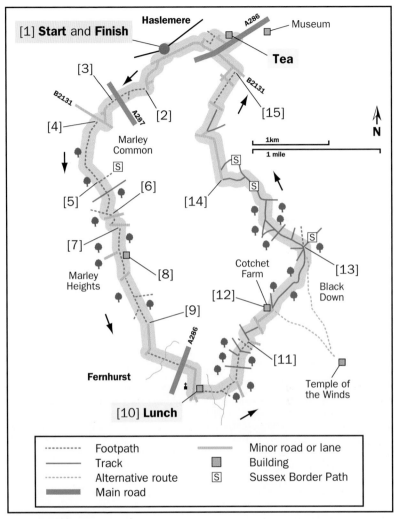

[1] **Start** and **Finish**

Haslemere

Museum

Tea

[3]

B2131

A286

B2131

[2]

[15]

[4]

A287

N

Marley
Common

S

1km

1 mile

[5]

[6]

S

S

[14]

[7]

S

Marley
Heights

[8]

[13]

Cotchet
Farm

Black
Down

[12]

[9]

A286

[11]

Fernhurst

Temple of
the Winds

[10] **Lunch**

- - - - -	Footpath	▬▬▬	Minor road or lane
———	Track	■	Building
- - - - -	Alternative route	S	Sussex Border Path
▬▬▬	Main road		

Walk directions

[1] [Numbers in square brackets refer to the map]

Coming out of **Haslemere station**, *turn right,* cross the main road and take Longdene Road (the lane going uphill, to the right of the pub opposite). After 400 metres up this road, where the road goes sharply left up Courts Hill Road, you *continue straight on* along Hedgehog Lane, signposted as a dead end.

[2] Then, in 30 metres, opposite Ridgeways House, *turn right* along an earth path, your direction 260 degrees, with a fieldgate and kissing gate visible ahead. Once through the kissing gate frame, keep straight down an enclosed footpath. In 450 metres, you cross a stile (to the left of a metal fieldgate) to go down a car-wide shingle track between (former) farm buildings to the main road, the A287.

[3] In 60 metres go across the A287 (very slightly to your right), and carry *straight on,* through iron railings down a tarmac path that becomes a quiet road (heading 250 degrees) between houses. In 150 metres (having ignored a left turn into Orchard Close) follow the road *round to the left,* your direction 210 degrees, leading up to another main road, the B2131.

In 100 metres, at a T-junction, *turn right* on the B2131 and, in 30 metres, there is a sign on the other side of the road saying Marley Combe Road, with a **Marley Combe** National Trust sign to its left. **[4]** Go between these two signs, steeply up some steps then a footpath, your direction 250 degrees, into the woods.

In 50 metres, follow this path round to the left, as it becomes a broader track, your direction now 220 degrees. Continue up this main path through the woods, with houses just visible to your right, with the path going gently leftwards.

[!] Please pay careful attention as the fork in the next paragraph may prove hard to find (if you cannot find it, just keep heading vaguely south, as all such paths take you towards Fernhurst). In 500 metres, at the top of the uphill section, keep going straight – your direction is 160 degrees.

After a level stretch of about 250 metres, the path, having started to go downhill, makes a sharp bend to the left and descends more steeply. **[5]** 15 metres down this hill from the bend, leave the main path to *turn right* down a little path that continues in your previous direction. The path goes between a wooden red-top post on your left and a prominent beech tree on your right, and has an earth bank on its right-hand side; your direction is 130 degrees. 15 metres down this little path, *turn right* through a wooden gate, to continue in more or less your previous direction (160 degrees), to go more steeply uphill.

Ignore ways off. In 250 metres you cross a path signposted Sussex Border Path/ Serpents Trail, but you carry straight on,

Cotchet Farm.

slightly uphill, your direction 160 degrees. Soon you have a small ditch and an earth bank on your left-hand side. 200 metres further on, you temporarily emerge from the woodland as the path *veers to the right* and then, in 70 metres, at a crosspaths *turn left,* your direction 140 degrees. (You can further identify this crossing by the houses just visible 100 metres away to your left, at 120 degrees, houses that become very visible 40 metres further on.)

[6] In 80 metres from this crossing, you go through a wooden gate to reach a tarmac road that leads (off to the left) to a small housing estate.

But you *cross straight over* this tarmac road and carry on, your direction due south.

In 60 metres, turn right (slightly) down an unmarked footpath, your direction 240 degrees, and in another 70 metres you turn left on a public road near a National Trust sign for **Marley Common**.

Go along this road for 200 metres then **[7]** *fork right* (initially due south) on to an earth road that is signposted with a restricted byway sign.

Follow this earth road for 550 metres as it bends in and out, roughly parallel to the minor power lines on your left-hand side, until you come to a fork in the road, with a wooden fieldgate up to your right-hand side. *Take the left fork,* still on an earth road, your direction 160 degrees. **[8]** After 150 metres you come to houses on the left (one of the houses is the Old Orchard) and you carry straight on along a narrower signposted path, initially due south and steeply downwards.

Stick to this footpath as it zigzags down to a tarmac road. After 160 metres cross this and carry on down the signposted footpath, your direction 170 degrees.

In 200 metres, you ignore a turn-off footpath signposted to your left and keep walking parallel to the minor power line on your left-hand side. Then, in 90 metres, at an unmarked footpath junction, *keep left and downwards* on the main fork, your direction 150 degrees (going under

the power line) rather than straight on towards a stile and metal fieldgate.

In 70 metres **[9]**, you come out on to a tarmac road by Updown Cottage. Continue down this road, your direction due south, and in 400 metres you come to a house and garden on your left-hand side.

80 metres beyond, take the footpath that is signed to *the left* through a green open space with oak trees, your initial direction 160 degrees.

In 60 metres, another footpath sign leads you into the woods proper and down shuttered steps across a stream and up the other side (ignoring turn-offs, and now with gardens on your right-hand side).

Go across the main road, the A286, straight over and down Hogs Hill, keeping to this tarmac road for 400 metres down to the **Red Lion** pub **[10]**, the suggested lunchtime stop.

After lunch the route is relatively gently uphill for the first 2.5km, on bridleways that can be very muddy.

Turn left out of the pub and *left again* alongside the pub and its back garden, following the footpath sign's direction, your bearing 80 degrees, in 20 metres passing Manesty Cottage on your right-hand side, and in a further 40 metres entering the woods.

Keep to the main path. In 130 metres, you cross a stream and, in a further 30 metres, you ignore a fork off to the right. In a further 110 metres, ignore two metal fieldgates off to your left.

In a further 220 metres, bend right with the main path to cross a stream where the water falls down from a storm pipe, with the stream soon on your left-hand side.

In 170 metres **[11]**, at the next T-junction, with a wooden barn opposite, *turn left,* following the footpath sign, up a car-wide earth track, your direction 30 degrees.

In 70 metres, at a crossing of paths, by a three-way footpath signpost, *take the path, straight on upwards* (not the fork to the left), your direction 70 degrees. You will be following the overhead electricity cable for some way.

After 100 metres, ignore a fork to the left.

In 220 metres, at the next crossing, again follow the footpath sign straight on, initially 40 degrees.

If it is very muddy at this point, you can normally scramble along the top of the banks to the left or right of the path.

In 200 metres at the next crosspaths, turn right to follow the footpath sign straight on and up (alongside the electricity cable), again the only signed footpath on offer, your direction 80 degrees. Soon you are sharing the path up with a tiny stream coming down to it.

After 300 metres you come up to a tarmac lane with a farmhouse on your right-hand side. Leave the overhead electricity cable to *take a sharp left,* following the signed bridleway *up to your left,* your direction 330 degrees.

150 metres from the farmhouse, at a bridleway path junction, ignore a left turn *to continue, straight up.*

After 200 metres go straight through a fieldgate entrance (it has a bridleway signpost on the right-hand side) and down for 80 metres to a tarmac road. Your direction is 10 degrees.

Turn left on the tarmac road, with the Royal Stables, an Arab stud farm, immediately on your right-hand side (there is a sign in Arabic at the entrance). Just past the farm, *turn to the right* on a tarmac road, signposted as a bridleway, your initial direction 20 degrees.

Go on up to reach **Cotchet Farm** after 270 metres. [12] Here there is a National Trust sign for **Black Down** on your right-hand side.

[For an optional detour to the **Temple of the Winds**, a beauty spot offering fine views, take the bridleway uphill to the right and head in a south-easterly direction for 700 metres to reach this viewpoint. To return to the main route, start by retracing your steps but then fork right after 200 metres, just before the bridleway starts to go back downhill. Follow this winding path on the plateau in a northerly direction for 800 metres to

reach a five-way path junction; this is point [13] below.]

For the main route: Continue ahead, keeping the farm buildings on your left-hand side. In 70 metres go through a wooden gate and, at the three-armed signpost, *fork right* to follow the bridleway *sharply uphill,* your direction 20 degrees.

Follow this bridleway, which is somewhat winding. Continue in a generally north-easterly direction for 800 metres (in due course passing a glorious view out to your left-hand side; the path having levelled out and descended a little) until you reach a five-way path junction, at a small triangular green. [13] Here you *turn sharp left* on to the signposted Sussex Border Path/Serpents Trail (SBP/ST) bridleway, a car-wide track, your direction west, now mainly through the pine forest and rhododendrons.

From here on, follow the SBP/ST signs for 2km almost all the way to Valewood House down in the valley.

But in more detail: In 220 metres ignore a right fork. In 500 metres, at a crosspaths, go through a wooden gate to carry straight on, your direction 320 degrees. In 70 metres, at the next junction, take the SBP/ST *to the left,* your direction 280 degrees (ignoring a path straight on). Go downhill and, after 200 metres near the bottom of the hill, at the T-junction, the bridleway goes left (downhill), but you take the SBP/ST *right,* initially 20 degrees.

In 350 metres, the path *veers left.* Ignoring a turn-off to the right, go through a wooden gate to go down a footpath through what becomes almost a tunnel of over-arching rhododendrons. In 320 metres you go through a wooden gate to enter **Valewood Park** (marked by a National Trust sign), *to veer right* on the signposted SBP/ST track, down across a large open field (initially 310 degrees), in the direction of a large mansion house on the opposite hill.

In 370 metres, at the lower right-hand corner of the field, go through a very wide gate – a fieldgate on the right-hand side, attached to a side pedestrian gate –

and you can see down to Valewood Farmhouse below.

The Sussex Border Path continues straight on round the far edge of the field and down, but the suggested route (a shortcut) is to take the bridleway car-wide track *off to the left,* steeply downhill, its direction 280 degrees.

At the T-junction at the bottom of the field, go left, again signposted SBP/ST, through another wide farmgate with side gate attached, and down 70 metres, keeping right, to turn right along an (initially) car-wide tarmac track, your direction north, **[14]** to carry on past Valewood Farmhouse on your right-hand side in 120 metres. In 160 metres go through Valewood Farmhouse's white entrance gate to cross a stream and *turn right* up a car-wide shingle track.

In 70 metres go past the entrance drive on your right that leads to a large new brick house with diamond-paned windows. At a fork in the track marked with a footpath sign, *take the bridleway uphill to the left,* your direction 20 degrees. Then go fairly steeply uphill, ignoring turn-offs. In 500 metres, you come to a tarmac road at the top, with a house called Littlecote on your left-hand side. *Turn left* and, in 20 metres, *turn right* along a tarmac path marked 'Neighbourhood Watch Area', with an anti-motorbike metal barrier at its start, the direction 20 degrees, and soon with playing fields on your left-hand side.

In 350 metres, cross another tarmac road but keep straight on, down a path with steps between high hedges, to the main road, the B2131. **[15]** *Turn left* and head *straight on* to **Haslemere** Town Hall in 200 metres, and then *turn right* into the High Street. In 40 metres, you pass the **White Horse Hotel** on your right-hand side. 100 metres beyond this, you come, on your left-hand side, to the suggested tea place, **Darnleys** tea room.

Coming out of the tea room, *turn right* and, in 25 metres, *turn right again* down West Street, signposted to the police station. In 120 metres, where the main

street curves to the right past the police station (which is on your right-hand side), take the street *straight on* to the fire station but then *not* the tempting path straight on; instead, *turn left* in front of the fire station and take the footpath that goes *down the left-hand side* of the building (signposted 'Footpath to the station'), your direction 315 degrees. Follow this path, with a stream to your right and later a playground to your left, until you come out on to a tarmac road with Redwood Manor opposite. *Turn left* on this road and, in 40 metres, *turn right* on to the B2131, leading in 260 metres to **Haslemere station** on your right-hand side. **Metro Café** is on your right just before the station and **Inn on the Hill**, with its bar, is opposite the station.

The London platforms (2 and 3) are over the footbridge.

Lunch & tea places

Red Lion *The Green, Fernhurst, Haslemere, GU27 3HY (01428 643112).* **Open** 11.30am-11pm Mon-Sat; 11.30am-10.30pm Sun. *Food served* noon-3pm, 6-9.30pm daily. The suggested lunch stop serves quality home-cooking. Booking is always recommended.

White Horse Hotel *High Street, Haslemere, GU27 2HJ (01428 661276, www.thewhitehorsehaslemere.co.uk).* **Open** noon-11pm Mon, Sun; noon-11.30pm Tue; noon-midnight Wed-Sat. *Food served* noon-9.45pm daily. A possible stop for the end of the walk; the Swan Inn (15 High Street, 01428 641747) is another possibility.

Darnleys tea room *High Street, Haslemere, GU37 2JZ (01428 643048).* **Open** 9.30am-5pm Mon-Fri; 9am-5pm Sat; 10am-4pm Sun. The suggested tea stop.

Metro Café *Lower Street, Haslemere, GU27 2PD (01428 651535).* **Open** 6.30am-3pm Mon-Fri; 7.30am-3pm Sat, Sun. One of two options close to the station.

Inn on the Hill *Lower Street, Haslemere, GU27 2PD (01428 642006, http://tm steaks.co.uk).* **Open** 7am-11pm Mon-Thur; 7am-midnight Fri; 8am-midnight Sat; 8am-10.30 Sun.

Walk 23

Otford to Eynsford

River Darent, two castles and a Roman villa.

Start: Otford station
Finish: Eynsford station

Length: 14.1km (8.8 miles)

Time: 4 hours. For the whole outing, including trains, sights and meals, allow 8 hours 45 minutes.

Travel: Take the train nearest to **10.45am** from **Victoria** station to **Otford** (journey time 35 minutes). Trains back from **Eynsford** are half-hourly, and go to Blackfriars and Kentish Town during the week, Victoria at weekends; these are slower, but you can change at

Bromley South for a fast train to Victoria. Buy a day return to Otford. If you are driving, Otford station car park costs £4 (cheaper at weekends). Alternatively, there is a free public car park in the village, opposite the Bull pub. Eynsford station has a small free car park. There are trains every 30 minutes from Eynsford to Otford.

OS Landranger Maps: 188 & 177
OS Explorer Maps: 147 & 162
Otford, map reference TQ532593, is in **Kent**, 4km north of Sevenoaks.

Toughness: 5 out of 10

Walk notes: The walk has two steep uphill sections and the first half can be very muddy. The suggested route takes in three villages steeped in history, a ruined palace, two castles and a Roman villa. At times the route runs alongside the River Darent, at other times through fields and woods. At the start of the walk, there is the Otford Solar System, which claims to be the only scale model of its kind in the world: it shows the relative position of the sun and planets at the start of the new millennium. In the afternoon, you come to Lullingstone Park with its (early summer) orchids; the Visitor Centre here offers exhibitions and information about the park (and has a cafe). Towards the end of the walk you pass Lullingstone Castle, with its new visitor attraction, the World Garden, and Lullingstone Roman Villa.

Walk options: To avoid the mud on wet days, you could start the walk from the suggested lunchtime stop by travelling directly to Shoreham station (or you could end the walk in Shoreham). You can cut 1.2km off the end of the walk by following the shortcut at [*] in the main walk directions.

History: **Otford** goes back to the 6th century, when the Anglo-Saxons called their settlement Ottanford ('Otta's ford'). The Archbishop's Palace, the remaining fragments of which are on open view here, once rivalled Hampton Court for splendour, until Henry VIII forced Cranmer to surrender it in 1537.

Construction of **St Bartholomew's Church**, Otford, began in 1060, with the tower being added in 1175. The church contains large marble memorials

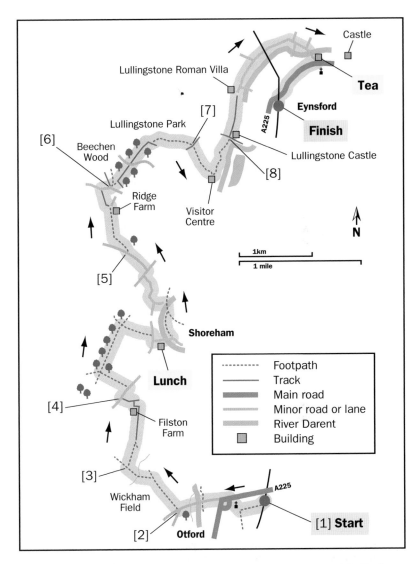

to Charles and David Polhill, great-grandsons of Oliver Cromwell.

The artist **Samuel Palmer** lived and worked in Shoreham from 1826 to 1834. He was leader of **The Ancients**, a group who followed William Blake. Palmer's father, also called Samuel, rented the **Water House** by the river.

The **Church of St Peter & St Paul** in Shoreham has many interesting features, including an outstanding wooden rood screen that spans the entire width of the building and a stained-glass window designed by the Pre-Raphaelite artist **Edward Burne-Jones**.

Lullingstone Park was a deer park from the Middle Ages until World War II, when the park was used as a decoy airfield – the heavy bombing so terrified the deer that they escaped. Species of tree that deer would not eat have been planted through the centuries, thus ancient hornbeam pollards remain.

Lullingstone Castle (01322 862114) is the residence of the Hart Dyke family, having remained in the Dyke family for centuries, with the original house built during the reign of Henry VII. Its gatehouse is one of the earliest all-brick buildings in Britain. In the grounds is the **World Garden**, containing plants from around the globe; it opens in the afternoons from Friday to Sunday, April to September (and Bank Holiday Mondays). The house is only open on Bank Holiday weekends. Admission (2011) is £7.

Lullingstone Roman Villa (01322 863467) was first occupied in AD 80 by a rich Roman who practised pagan worship of the local water sprite in a room that later became a Christian temple. The ruins include two mosaic floors. The Villa opens 10am-6pm daily in summer, and 10am-4pm daily in winter. It closes over Christmas. Admission (2010) is £5.90.

St Martin's Church in Eynsford is unusual in having retained its Norman ground plan with apsidal chancel. In about 1163, Thomas Becket excommunicated Sir William de Eynsford III, the Lord of the Manor who controlled the patronage for this church. The excommunication was cancelled by Henry II and the issue became part of the quarrel which led to Becket's murder.

The 11th-century **Eynsford Castle** (free entry) was vandalised in 1312. John de Eynsford, who lived here, is said to have assisted in Becket's murder.

Walk directions

[1] [Numbers in square brackets refer to the map]

Coming off the London train, go over the railway line and exit the **Otford station** building. Turn left and 40 metres inside the car park, on the right-hand side, *go through the gap in the railings*. Take the tarmac path heading west away from the station, soon with an open field on your left-hand side. Keep to this path through a bend to the right. A wooden kissing gate takes you through to the churchyard of **St Bartholomew's Church**, which is worth a look inside. (The old south door is no longer used: the new entrance is the set of modern doors on the north side.)

From the church, head north-west towards the main road. (A detour to the left here would take you in less than 100 metres to the gatehouse and north-west tower, virtually all that remains of **Otford Palace**.)

To continue the walk, go over to the far side of the village pond; the duckhouse is Britain's smallest listed building. Take the road on the left, westwards, by the Crown Inn, soon passing the Hospices of Hope tea shop (left) and the 17th-century Forge House, now a restaurant (right).

Keep on this road. In 120 metres, by the Bull pub (part of which dates back to 1500), a short diversion to the back of the public car park on the opposite side of the road will take you to a map showing the planetary locations of the Otford Solar System. In 200 metres you pass on the left Pickmoss, a medieval open-hall house, and on your right the Darent Valley Path.

After crossing over the River Darent, you pass the imposing gates of 18th-century Broughton Manor on your left. 200 metres or so later, just beyond a wooden bus shelter on the north side of the road, you come to a concrete pillar representing the planet Uranus.

[2] Immediately after this pillar, *turn right* through a kissing gate to the right of a wooden fieldgate on to a signposted and well-used public footpath, your direction 330 degrees. In 230 metres, having kept to this main path, go through a kissing gate (a potentially very muddy area) to go straight on between a hedge and a wire fence.

In 400 metres the path goes through a hedge and across a ditch. In a further 120 metres, cross a stream on a slab of concrete and, 10 metres later, fork right along a path, with a wire fence on your right. In 100 metres the path curves to the right past a horse chestnut tree (ignore another path close by on the left) and in 130 metres merges with a farm track from the right.

(10 metres ahead, you have a choice of routes, both about the same distance. To go past the concrete pillar representing the planet Pluto, *turn right* along a signposted footpath. In 240 metres you pass this pillar and continue along the field edge. In 180 metres keep ahead on a potentially muddy car-wide track between hedges. In 500 metres you pass an open barn on your left, with **Filston Oast** house ahead. Follow the farm track round to the left, heading for a prominent hopper attached to a large industrial shed. *Turn right* there to reach the farm access-road, then turn left to reach Filston Lane in 140 metres. Pick up the main directions at [4] below.)

To follow the original route, however, keep on this farm track, which in 250 metres comes to the corner of an orchard. **[3]** Instead of veering left and right with the main path towards **Sepham Farm** and its oast houses, *turn right* through a gate to go along the edge of the orchard, your direction 40 degrees, soon passing under mini pylons.

In 100 metres, ignore a left turn through the orchard towards the farm, to continue along the edge of several large fields towards **Filston Farm** in the distance. On nearing the farm, go past an industrial shed up to the farm's access road and *turn left*. Follow this road to reach Filston Lane in 140 metres.

[4] Turn right on this car road. In 250 metres, opposite Water Lane on the right, *turn left* up a trackway between hedges. After climbing steadily, continue through a gate to climb more steeply up the right-hand side of a field, with **Meenfield Wood** on your right. Just before a convenient seat, *turn right* and go over a stile on to a wide path through the wood.

In 600 metres you come to a crossing, with steps up and down, and you *turn*

right downhill towards Shoreham on a potentially slippery path, your direction 120 degrees.

In 60 metres go through a swing gate and continue downwards. On your left, behind you, is a chalk cross commemorating those who died in World War I. In a further 100 metres, go over a stile and down through hedges. In a further 120 metres, go through a metal kissing gate and keep on the main path down, past playing fields on your left-hand side.

You come out on to **Shoreham**'s High Street. (*Turn left* here if you wish to go to the **Two Brewers** pub, 100 metres away on the other side of the road, or the **Village Stores**, a further 50 metres up the road.) For the main route, *turn right,* soon passing the **Honeypot** tea room on your left. Just past this, *turn left* into Church Street. In 180 metres you come to the **King's Arms** pub on your right-hand side, the suggested lunchtime stop for the walk.

(Otherwise, continue on the road, cross the river and follow Church Street up to the right: **Ye Olde George Inne** is on the right 150 metres away, opposite the entrance to the **Church of St Peter & St Paul**.)

On coming out of the King's Arms, turn right and go along the road, cross the river and *turn left* into Darent Way (or, from Ye Olde George Inne, return to this point). Pass to the left of **Water House** and keep to the riverside path, with the River Darent on your left-hand side.

In 500 metres you cross the river by a footbridge with metal railings. 50 metres further on, you leave the Darent Valley Path to *turn left uphill* on a car lane, westwards. At the top of Mill Lane you come to a T-junction with the main road (the **Crown** pub is 80 metres away on your left here).

Cross the road and take a permissive path, the Millennium Footpath, which runs parallel to the road on your right-hand side. In 100 metres cross a stile and follow a grassy path up the right-hand field edge to reach the top corner of the field.

Exit the field over a stile to the left of a fieldgate. Continue out to a road and *turn right downhill.* In 100 metres, continue ahead at a road junction, but in a further 100 metres turn left at another junction into Cockerhurst Road, signposted Well Hill and Chelsfield. (Just before this junction there is an interesting little memorial stone up on the bank: the biblical quotation is from Hosea 2:14.)

After 350 metres of walking uphill between tall beech trees, and opposite a large bungalow (Combe Vale) **[5]**, *take the footpath on the right,* your direction 15 degrees, to follow a clear path steeply uphill, soon with a large field behind a fence on your left-hand side.

300 metres from the road, cross a stile and follow the left-hand field edge northwards, towards **Homewood Farm**. Keep on this path, with trees and then hedges on your left-hand side.

In 400 metres the path bends left beside a small house on the right-hand side. In a further 100 metres, you join a concrete car road and continue on, your direction 350 degrees.

200 metres later, at the T-junction with a car road, *turn right down the road.* In 100 metres, ignore the road to your left, but 10 metres later *cross a stile on the left* into **Home Wood. [6]**

(These woods, and the golf course up ahead, are part of Lullingstone Park. When this walk was devised the directions through this Country Park followed the route of a published trail, but the numbered posts that marked out this route are no longer present. Not all of the paths used are shown on the OS map.)

10 metres inside the wood, *turn right* on to a wide path, your direction 100 degrees. In 40 metres follow it round to the left, your direction now 40 degrees.

In 300 metres, having ignored paths off to both sides, you come to a T-junction. *Turn right and then in 20 metres turn left* into a very wide grassy avenue, going downhill between **Upper** and **Lower Beechen Wood**, still heading north-east.

In 400 metres you come to a permissive bridleway **[7]**, with a wooden gate up ahead leading on to a golf course. The suggested route is to go through this gate

on to the golf course, reaching a gravel track in 75 metres, but as you come out into the open *beware of golfers playing across your route from a raised golf tee on your left.* (You can avoid this hazard by turning left on to the bridleway just before entering the golf course, then following it through the trees and up a short rise, round to the right behind the golf tee and down through the trees to reach the same gravel track a little further along.) Either way, turn right on to this gravel track, heading east.

(If you wish, you could now simply follow this gravel track all the way through the golf course. In 1.25km you would come out on to the Darent Valley Path in front of Lullingstone Castle, resuming the directions at point [8] below. However, this would miss out a nice stretch of the walk and you would bypass the Lullingstone Park Visitor Centre.)

For the recommended route, follow the gravel track for about 200 metres and then *turn half left* on to a wide grassy path going up a slope. After levelling out, the path goes past the 13th tee and a green, then descends to go back across the gravel track, which has curved round to the left in the valley. Aim to the left of a green, up a short slope ahead, and go through a gap in the trees to pass between it and the 8th tee on your left. On reaching some trees, *turn right,* joining a permissive bridleway.

After passing the green, *bear left* through a gap in the trees. This leads to a fine view across the Darent valley, with the brick gatehouse of Lullingstone Castle in the valley on your left and Lullingstone Park Visitor Centre down on your right.

Turn right and go along the ridge on a broad grassy path, taking the left fork at a Y-junction, your direction 210 degrees. In 200 metres the path goes between hedges. In another 100 metres, turn left downhill on a car-wide track, in 200 metres reaching **Lullingstone Park Visitor Centre** (which has a cafe).

Coming out of the Visitor Centre, go through a wooden kissing gate on its northern boundary and *turn right*

Otford to Eynsford

towards the river. *Turn left* in front of the bridge and continue northwards along an attractive path, with the water on your right-hand side. In 600 metres go through a wooden barrier **[8]** and continue straight on towards the gatehouse of **Lullingstone Castle**.

Beyond the castle, continue straight on, still northwards, on a tarmac lane. In 600 metres or so, you come to a large shed on your left-hand side, which houses **Lullingstone Roman Villa**.

(**[*]** You can shorten the walk by 1.2km at this point by turning right to cross the river on a bridge to the left of the car park. In 600 metres this private road – which is also a public footpath – comes to a T-junction with the A225, where you *turn left*. In 300 metres you go under the railway bridge and turn sharp right to reach the station.)

To complete the full walk, continue northwards on the car road. In 600 metres you go under Eynsford Rail Viaduct (built in the 19th century with bricks made in Brick Field, just above the east bank of the river) and go straight on, with the river still on your right-hand side.

After the road curves to the right, keep straight on, signposted Eynsford, at the junction with Sparepenny Lane. In a further 200 metres, you come to the **Plough** pub on your left-hand side (the suggested tea place). Continuing along the road, go over the bridge by the ford and up to the main road.

(To visit the ruins of **Eynsford Castle**, which is about 400 metres away, turn left on the main road and carry on through the village, passing the **Five Bells** pub on your right-hand side. Opposite the **Castle Hotel**, turn left on a tarmac lane signposted Village Hall and follow it round to the right to find the castle's car park and ruins.)

For **Eynsford station**, *turn right* on to the main road, with **St Martin's Church** opposite. You soon pass the **Malt Shovel Inn** on your left-hand side. Go uphill for 800 metres, turning left into the station approach road just over the brow of the

hill. Trains back to London are on the far platform, over the footbridge.

Lunch & tea places

Two Brewers *30 High Street, Shoreham, TN14 7TD (01959 522800).* **Open** noon-11pm Wed-Sat; noon-6pm Sun. *Food served* noon-2.30pm, 6-8.30pm Wed-Sat; noon-4pm Sun.

King's Arms *Church Street, Shoreham, TN14 7SJ (01959 523100).* **Open** noon-11pm daily. *Food served* noon-2.30pm, 6-8pm Mon, Wed-Fri; noon-2.30pm Tue; noon-8.30pm Sat; noon-5pm Sun. The suggested lunch stop. The country's last remaining ostler box (an enclosed sentry box, where the ostler waited to attend to customers' horses) is in the pub's front wall.

Ye Olde George Inne *Church Street, Shoreham, TN14 7RY (01959 522017).* **Open** noon-11pm daily. *Food served* noon-3pm, 6-9.30pm Mon-Sat; noon-6pm Sun.

Crown *84 High Street, Shoreham, TN14 7TJ (01959 522903).* **Open** 11.30am-3pm, 7pm-midnight daily. *Food served* 11.30am-3pm, 7-9pm daily.

Lullingstone Park Visitor Centre cafe *Kingfisher Bridge, Castle Road, DA4 0JF (01322 865995).* **Open** *Jan-Mar, Nov, Dec* 11am-4pm Mon-Fri; 10am-4pm Sat, Sun. *Apr-Oct* 10am-5pm daily.

Plough Inn *Riverside, Eynsford, DA4 0AE (01322 862281, www.theploughinn eynsford.co.uk).* **Open** 11am-11pm daily. *Food served* noon-10.30pm daily. The recommended tea stop, with an attractive riverside location.

Five Bells *High Street, Eynsford, DA4 0AB (01322 863135).* **Open** 5-11pm Mon; noon-3pm, 5-11pm Tue-Fri; 11am-11pm Sat; noon-10.30pm Sun. *Food served* noon-2pm Tue-Sat.

Castle Hotel *High Street, Eynsford, DA4 0AB (01322 863162, www.thecastle hotel-eynsford.co.uk).* **Open** noon-midnight daily. *Food served* noon-9pm daily.

Malt Shovel Inn *Station Road, Eynsford, DA4 0ER (01322 862164).* **Open** noon-midnight Mon-Thur, Sun; noon-1am Fri, Sat. *Food served* noon-3pm, 6.30-9.30pm Mon-Fri; noon-9.30pm Sat, Sun.

Walk 24

Cookham to Maidenhead

Stanley Spencer, *The Wind in the Willows* and Cliveden.

Start: Cookham station
Finish: Maidenhead station

Length: 17.0km (10.6 miles)

Time: 5 hours. For the whole outing, including trains, sights and meals, allow 9 hours.

Transport: Take the train nearest to **10am** from **Paddington** station to **Cookham**, changing at Maidenhead (journey time 48-58 minutes). If you plan to have a very early lunch stop at Cookham Dean

on the short circular walk, leave an hour later. There are four trains an hour back from **Maidenhead** (two on Sundays), with a journey time of 44 minutes. Return trains from Cookham are hourly. Buy a day return to Cookham.

OS Landranger Map: 175
OS Explorer Map: 172
Cookham, map reference SU886850, is in **Berkshire**, 4km north of Maidenhead.

Toughness: 3 out of 10

Walk notes: This walk incorporates most of the Cookham (round walk) – the original Walk 24 from earlier editions of this book – but adds an extension along the Thames Path to Maidenhead.

You start with a circuit of Cookham, heading westwards from the town and passing the very ordinary house where the artist Stanley Spencer lived and worked for some 15 years until his death in 1959. After passing through Cookham Dean, you go past a large free-range turkey farm and into Bisham Woods, where an attractive stretch along an escarpment (with fine views over the Thames Valley) leads to Winter Hill. Mole, Ratty and company of *The Wind in the Willows* fame inhabited the riverbanks and wild woods around here, at least according to their author Kenneth Grahame, who lived nearby.

From here you drop down to the Thames to return by the river to Cookham for lunch, with the opportunity to visit the Stanley Spencer Gallery.

After lunch, you head south on a particularly attractive stretch of the Thames Path, with the hanging beech woods of the Cliveden Estate on the other side of the river. On the outskirts of Maidenhead, you go past Boulter's Lock, a popular spot to watch the river traffic.

Walk options: You can shorten the walk by returning to Cookham station, making a circular walk of 11.3km (7.0 miles) – finish the circle as described after point **[9]** in the main walk directions. Alternatively, 2km before Cookham, you could cross the Thames by the railway bridge to catch a train back from Bourne

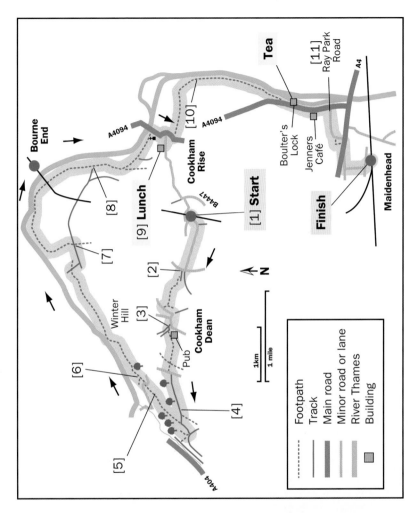

A shorter route into Cookham (which cuts 1.3km from the walk) is also described in the walk directions, after point **[7]**.

History: Cookham was inhabited by ancient Britons, Romans and Saxons, and in the Doomsday Book is listed as containing '32 villagers, 21 cottages, 4 slaves, 2 mills, 2 fisheries and woodland at 100 pigs'. In 1140, a Norman church was built on the site

of **Holy Trinity Church**, Cookham. There is a memorial stone to the artist **Sir Stanley Spencer** in the graveyard.

Spencer was born in 1891 in a Victorian semi-detached house called Fernley in Cookham High Street. He lived and worked from 1944 to 1959 in a house called Cliveden View (passed on this walk) and attended services at the Wesleyan Chapel in the High Street. That chapel is now the **Stanley Spencer Gallery** (01628 471885). From Easter to

October, the gallery is open 10.30am to 5.30pm daily; from November to Easter, it opens 11am to 4.30pm Thursday to Sunday and on bank holidays. There is a small admission fee.

Grade I-listed **Cliveden** was built in 1851 in Italianate style by architect Charles Barry for the 2nd Duke of Sutherland. It was later owned by the Waldorf and Astor family. From the 1920s, it became the centre of high society, culminating with the notorious Profumo affair in the early 1960s. The house is now a luxury five-star hotel. The grounds, these days owned by the National Trust (01494 755562, www.nationaltrust.org.uk), were laid out by John Fleming in 1855 and contain an extensive collection of sculptures. There is limited access to parts of the house and its chapel on Thursdays and Sundays, April to October (admission £9). The gardens are open daily from 11am until 5.30pm (summer), closing at 5pm in spring and autumn, and 4pm in winter; entry costs £8 (£3 in winter).

Walk directions

[1] [Numbers in square brackets refer to the map]
Coming out of **Cookham station** *turn left*. In 15 metres *turn left again* over the level crossing. In a further 25 metres *turn left* into High Road, following it round to the right in 60 metres.

Ignore ways off. In 350 metres ignore Worster Road to the left. **Cliveden View**, the house on the corner, is where Stanley Spencer lived and worked.

Continue on High Road, ignoring ways off. In 380 metres you come to a T-junction. Ignore the footpath sign opposite and *turn right* on this road, due north.

In 80 metres, opposite Whyte Cottage **[2]**, *turn left* on a signposted public footpath, your direction 290 degrees, between wooden fences.

In 180 metres follow the path round to the left and in 30 metres bear right through the wooden gate to cross the field, your direction 310 degrees.

In 180 metres you reach the far side of the field and keep straight on up the wide

track ahead. 100 metres further on pass between gateposts – there is a fine view back over the valley at this point. In a further 75 metres, by Grey Cottage on your left-hand side, follow the footpath sign (on your right) along a grassy track slightly left and onwards, your direction 260 degrees.

In 110 metres you join a tarmac road and bear left going gently uphill. In 100 metres, after the road has curved right, *bear left* at a junction, signposted to Cookham Dean Church.

In 25 metres *turn right* across the green at Cookham Dean, aiming for a pub sign, your direction 290 degrees. In 120 metres, at a multi-directional signpost, *bear left* on a tarmac lane towards **Sanctum on the Green**, 75 metres away. Pick up a footpath to the right-hand side of this country hotel, going through trees. **[3]**

In 100 metres you come to a V-shaped stile on your right. (If you want an early lunch at the **Jolly Farmer** pub, *turn left* just before this stile, through trees and bushes, to reach the pub via its back garden in 200 metres. Afterwards, return the same way.)

To continue the walk, go through the V-shaped stile and follow the clear footpath ahead with a fence on your right, heading west. Soon there are views of a large free-range turkey farm across the valley ahead. In 300 metres, at the bottom of the valley, there is a five-armed footpath post. In a further 25 metres, bear right to climb a broad grassy path past the enclosures.

In 150 metres, go through a kissing gate and *turn left* on to a tarmac road. In 40 metres *turn right* on a signposted public bridleway into **Bisham Woods**.

Walk along the edge of this wood on a partly surfaced track. In 400 metres ignore a public footpath to the right. In a further 120 metres, just past a wooden post on your right, with a faded blue arrow, there are paths branching off on both sides. **[4]**

Fork right here, your direction 320 degrees, and pass through a wooden barrier. Take a wide path ahead through

the trees and gently uphill, in 50 metres following it round to the left and downhill towards another wooden barrier.

Go through the barrier and follow the path round to the right to join a broad track running along the top of the escarpment, your direction 50 degrees. As you go along this permitted bridleway, there are several places where the trees have been cleared to give fine views of Marlow in the Thames Valley below.

In 500 metres the bridleway veers right, with a yellow footpath arrow pointing slightly left. (This footpath is the most direct continuation to Winter Hill, but is not recommended: up ahead you would have to negotiate an awkward little stretch of narrow road with no pavement.)

Instead, follow the bridleway round to the right. The path becomes less distinct, but is marked by tall wooden posts with blue arrows. In 30 metres you pass one post and in 80 metres another. Just 10 metres after this second post **[!]** *turn left* off the bridleway on to a narrow path through brambles, your direction 50 degrees. **[5]**

(If you miss this turning, the bridleway comes to a three-way road junction in 200 metres. In this case, take the signposted footpath on the other side of Quarry Wood Road to go between a fence and gardens, your direction 30 degrees. In 120 metres *turn left* at a T-junction, then in a few metres **[!]** *turn right* at a footpath signpost into the woods. Continue the directions at point [6] below.)

If you take the path through brambles, it leads into an attractive part of the beech wood, with no clear path ahead. Keep ahead for about 120 metres through the wood to reach a road, with houses opposite.

Cross the road and take the signposted footpath going alongside the last house on the left (called Dormers), your direction 100 degrees. In 60 metres **[!]** *turn left* at a footpath signpost into the woods. (If you reach the end of the fence on your right, you have missed the turning.)

[6] Follow a faint path through the woods, your initial direction 20 degrees. The path gradually curves to the right, the way being indicated by white arrows on trees. In 170 metres, bear right with the path through some shrubs. In a further 30 metres you go down a short slope to your right. Continue down the slope and in a further 40 metres you reach a signpost with a footpath coming in from behind on your left – the continuation of the direct route mentioned earlier.

Bear right with the path, a wire fence on your right and then a wall. (The slightly spooky wood down on your left is probably the inspiration for the Wild Wood in *The Wind in the Willows*.)

In 300 metres the path veers right, joining the driveway of a house called Rivendell. Ignore a faint path down to the left in 10 metres, but 10 metres beyond this *turn left* by a post with a yellow arrow to go through undergrowth to the parking area for the National Trust's **Winter Hill**. There are outstanding views and, in summer, there is often an ice-cream van here.

(To detour to **Kenneth Grahame's house**, go sharp right and follow the main road with a wall on your left and a curious disused letterbox set into it. In 120 metres, turn left into Job's Lane. In 200 metres, you come to a road where you turn right. Up on your right-hand side, in 50 metres, is the author's old house, now a prep school.)

On Winter Hill, continue straight on with the road to your right, heading north-east. In 250 metres the footpath strays from the road but then rejoins it. 80 metres along the road you pass Chiltern Court on your right-hand side. In 20 metres *fork left* down a rough path.

In 50 metres you cross two small roads to pick up the continuation of the footpath, a footpath post to your right. There is a private road running parallel on your left-hand side. Where the path joins a track, bear left along it. In 150 metres you pass through a metal kissing gate. Ignore paths to both sides and continue down the main car-wide track, with superb views to your left. In 600 metres you reach the valley bottom and a four-armed footpath sign. [7]

(To **shorten the walk** by 1.3km, go straight on at this path junction. In 900 metres you pass under the railway and turn half right on to a wide path between a ditch and a golf course. In 350 metres, veer left across the grass to join the Thames Path and continue the directions at point [8] below.)

For the main route, *turn left* at the four-armed signpost, heading north. In 65 metres, go through a wooden gate and straight across a huge field.

In a further 160 metres, at a two-armed footpath signpost, *turn right* as indicated, your direction 40 degrees. In 240 metres you reach the River Thames on your left-hand side.

Your route to Cookham more or less follows the Thames. But in more detail: In 300 metres, go through a wooden gate. In 150 metres, fork left to keep by the riverside. In 40 metres, go through a wooden kissing gate and past houses on your right-hand side. In 120 metres, pass (or call in at) **The Bounty** riverside inn, a very walker-friendly pub (one of the few that cannot be reached by road).

In a further 200 metres you go under a railway bridge and keep ahead through the National Trust's **Cock Marsh**. 500 metres beyond the bridge, go through a metal kissing gate. In a further 500 metres ignore a fork to the right.

[8] Carry on along the riverside, now with a distant view of **Cliveden** up on the ridge ahead. In 120 metres you go through a white metal swing gate and past a sailing club on your right-hand side, then another gate.

In 40 metres ignore a tarmac path to your right and continue alongside Bell Rope Meadow on a tarmac path. In a further 250 metres, at a Thames Path sign, *turn right* on to a tarmac path, towards the church visible to your right (but if you are going to the **Ferry** for refreshment, then carry straight on beneath the road bridge up ahead).

In 50 metres you enter the churchyard of **Holy Trinity Church**, Cookham, past a metal kissing gate. The church entrance is on the far side.

Coming out of the church, take the path from the front door, going between yew trees. Spencer's memorial stone is off to the right of this path, near a wooden bench – his ashes were scattered by his wife's grave in Cookham cemetery. At the church gates *turn left* to reach the A4094. Turn right on to this main road and follow it round a bend to the right.

In 60 metres you come to a road junction, with the **Stanley Spencer Gallery** opposite. *Turn right* to go along Cookham's High Street. On the right is a possible refreshment stop, the **Bel & the Dragon**, while a little further along on the left is the suggested lunchtime stop, the **Kings Arms. [9]**

(If you are doing the **short circular walk**, the suggested tea stop, **Culinary Aspirations**, is past the Kings Arms along the High Street, in Cookham Arcade on the right. To get to Cookham station, about 1km away, continue along the High Street, then across **Cookham Moor** on the tarmac path to the left of the road. After 300 metres the path rejoins the road and you go along it for a further 500 metres, passing the **White Oak** and the **Old Swan Uppers** pubs, and then going straight on at a mini roundabout. You pass **Station Hill Deli** on your right and bear left to reach Cookham station.)

For the full walk, continuing to Maidenhead, return to the road junction by the Stanley Spencer Gallery and *turn right* on to the A4094, heading south. In 200 metres *turn left* into Mill Lane, signposted as the Thames Path.

Keep ahead on this lane, passing a cricket pitch on your left. 500 metres from the main road, you come to a group of houses. Opposite the imposing gates to the Sol Mill, *fork right* down a narrow path, following the Thames Path sign. This soon curves back to the left and almost rejoins the driveway (so you could have simply walked past the houses).

Continue along the signposted path to the right of the driveway. In 250 metres the path bends right and you now head south-east along it for a further 400 metres to return to the River Thames. **[10]** On the far bank are several cottages and boathouses on the **Cliveden** estate. (The house itself is high up to your left, but not visible from here.)

Turn right and now simply follow the path south, with the river on your left. This is a lovely stretch of the Thames Path, with the wooded escarpment on the far side particularly attractive in autumn. In 2.4km the path joins the A4094 and shortly after this you reach **Boulter's Lock**, an upmarket tea stop with a splendid view of the river from its terrace bar.

From the lock continue south on the A4094. In 500 metres you pass **Jenners Café** in the gardens on your right, another possible tea stop. In a further 200 metres you pass the River Bar of the Thames Hotel and there is a turning on the right, Ray Park Road. **[11]** You now have a choice of routes to Maidenhead station.

(For a more direct route through the town centre, passing many more tea places, *turn right* into Ray Park Road, heading west. In 500 metres, where the road swings right, bear left briefly into Ray Park Lane and then turn right into a grassy open area. Keep to its left-hand side and, in 200 metres, go down an underpass beneath the busy A4. Turn right on the other side to head west along Bridge Road and then High Street for 500 metres. For the best choice of coffee shops and other refreshment places, keep ahead into the pedestrianised part of High Street, which turns sharp left after 250 metres. In a further 350 metres you come to a major road junction with the A308. Make your way via the pedestrian crossings to the far side of this busy road and go up Station Approach to reach Maidenhead station.)

For the recommended route (which is not possible after dusk as the park gates on this route are locked then), continue on the Thames Path alongside the A4094 for 300 metres to reach a major road junction. Cross the A4 here with great care, to continue along Guards Club Road on the other side of the roundabout, heading south.

In 150 metres, after passing some interesting buildings, enter Guards Club Park through a gate (locked at dusk). You will be leaving the park through a gate on the right 100 metres ahead, by a small car park, but a small detour towards the river on your left will give you a fine view of Isambard Kingdom Brunel's famous brick rail bridge from the footbridge to Guards Club Island.

After leaving the park, head west along a winding residential road, eventually revealing itself as Oldacres. In 350 metres, at a T-junction, turn left into Oldfield Road. In 200 metres pass under a railway bridge. In a further 200 metres cross a road to take a tarmac roadway ahead of you, signed to Brayrick Park.

In 100 metres cross a bridge over a small river to take a concrete path, the Green Way, to your right. The river is on your right. In 300 metres the path reaches a road where you bear left, passing Homebase and other stores in Maidenhead Retail Park on your right.

In 300 metres you reach a major roundabout where you turn right, back towards the railway. Just before the railway bridge, use pedestrian crossings to cross the busy A308. Go under the bridge and turn left along a path to reach **Maidenhead station**. Trains to London leave from platform 4, which also has a refreshment kiosk.

Lunch & tea places

Jolly Farmer *Hills Lane, Cookham Dean, SL6 9PD (01628 482905, www.jollyfarmer cookhamdean.co.uk).* **Open** noon-11pm Mon-Thur, Sat; noon-midnight Fri; noon-10.30pm Sun. *Food served* noon-2.30pm Mon, Sun; noon-2.30pm, 6-9pm Tue-Sat.

Late starters on the circular walk can take an early lunch in this busy, walker-friendly pub. Good food is served at reasonable prices.
Ferry *Sutton Road, Cookham, SL6 9SN (01628 525123, www.theferry.co.uk).* **Open** 11am-11.30pm Mon-Thur; 11am-midnight Fri, Sat; noon-10.30pm Sun. *Food served* noon-10pm Mon-Thur; noon-10.30pm Fri, Sat; noon-9pm Sun. Food and drink can be enjoyed on the fine patio overlooking the river.
Bel & the Dragon *High Street, Cookham, SL6 9SO (01628 521263, www.beland thedragon-cookham.co.uk).* **Open** noon-11.30pm Mon-Sat; noon-10.30pm Sun. *Food served* noon-3pm, 6-9.30pm Mon-Thur; noon-3pm, 6-10pm Fri; noon-10pm Sat; noon-8.30pm Sun. A pub-restaurant in a 15th-century building.
Kings Arms *High Street, Cookham, SL6 9SJ (01628 530667, www.thekingsarms cookham.co.uk).* **Open** 10am-11pm Mon-Sat; 10am-10.30pm Sun. *Food served* 10am-10pm Mon-Sat; 10am-9.30pm Sun. The recommended lunchtime pub, where there is a varied and well-priced menu.
Culinary Aspirations *Cookham Arcade, High Street, Cookham, SL6 9TA (01628 523904, www.culinaryaspirations. com).* **Open** 10.30am-4.30pm Tue-Sat. A nice tea room, with a splendid selection of cakes. Take tea here if you are doing the circular walk and returning to Cookham.
Station Hill Deli *Station Hill, Cookham, SL6 9BT (01628 522202, www.station hilldeli.co.uk).* **Open** 7am-5pm Mon-Fri; 8.30am-3.30pm Sat; 9.30am-1.30pm Sun.
Boulter's Lock *Boulter's Lock Island, Maidenhead, SL6 8PE (01628 621291, www.boultersrestaurant.co.uk).* **Open** 10am-11pm Mon-Thur; 10am-12.30am Fri, Sat; 10am-10.30pm Sun. *Food served: Brasserie* noon-3pm, 6.30-9.30pm Tue-Sat; noon-3pm Sun. *Terrace Bar* noon-3.30pm, 6-9.30pm Mon-Sat; noon-3.30pm, 6-9pm Sun. Boulter's Lock has a terrace bar that makes a particularly attractive tea stop.
Jenners Café *Riverside Gardens Park, Ray Mead Road, SL6 8NP (01628 621721).* **Open** *Summer* 7am-5pm daily. *Winter* 7am-3pm daily.

Walk 25

Winchelsea to Hastings

Fairlight Glen and a dip in the sea.

Start: Winchelsea station (with an alternative start from Rye station, which has more frequent trains)
Finish: Hastings station

Length: 20.3km (12.6 miles)

Time: 6 hours. For the whole outing, including trains, meals, sights and a swim, allow at least 12 hours.

Transport: Take the train nearest to **10am** from **Charing Cross** station to **Winchelsea**, changing at either Ashford International or Hastings. The journey time is about 1 hour 50 minutes via Ashford or 2 hours via Hastings, depending on the connection. For a premium, you can reduce the journey time to 1 hour 20 minutes by taking the High Speed Train from St Pancras and

changing at Ashford. Trains back from **Hastings** to Charing Cross run twice an hour (hourly in the evenings), with a journey time of 1 hour 30-45 minutes. Buy a day return to Winchelsea.

There is currently no convenient train service to Winchelsea on Sundays. Either take Stagecoach bus 100 from Hastings or Rye and start the walk in Winchelsea (town) or Icklesham, or leave one hour earlier and do the extended version of this walk, starting at Rye station.

OS Landranger Maps: 189 & 199
OS Explorer Map: 124
Winchelsea, map reference TQ899184, is in **East Sussex**, 3km south-west of Rye.

Toughness: 9 out of 10

Walk notes: This is a delightful walk along the south coast. It is best done in summer if you would like to swim, otherwise in spring when the woodland floor is covered in bluebells and other wild flowers and, in early May, the gorse is bright yellow.

Starting below Winchelsea (once a coastal port, but storms have since stranded it 2km inland), the walk follows the River Brede and canals to an early lunch at a 17th-century pub near the church in Icklesham. Less than 5km of this walk is before lunch.

After lunch, the route crosses two relatively clear streams, both with ill-fitting names: Pannel Sewer and Marsham Sewer. And so to the coast at Cliff End. A detour off the coastal route through the houses of Fairlight is required, as a result of severe coastal erosion (an average 1.4 metres of cliff-face is lost annually in these parts). Thereafter the walk is along the coast-line through Hastings Country Park, with steep climbs out of the wooded Warren, Fairlight and Ecclesbourne Glens. Fairlight Glen has a nudist beach where you can drip-dry in fine weather, if you don't happen to have a towel. At low tide (but you must follow local advice on this) the adventurous, at their own risk, may be able to walk along the beach between Fairlight Glen and Hastings. Otherwise, there is more steep climbing, then a descent down steps into the old town of Hastings, with its Net Shops on the beach (tall, black, wooden sheds that were built for hanging out fishermen's nets) and, inland, lanes and twittens (narrow alleys) of half-timbered cottages. From here, it is a 20-minute walk through the town and along the seafront beneath the Norman castle to the station.

Walk options: There are two variations to the main route.

i) Shortening the walk: You could get a bus or taxi to Hastings from near the pub at Icklesham, or a taxi from the pub at Pett Level.

ii) Starting from Rye: As Winchelsea has an infrequent train service, you could start at Rye station and follow the 1066 Country Walk to Winchelsea station. This makes a longer walk of 24km (nearly 15 miles). Detailed walk directions for this option are on the Saturday Walkers' Club website (www.walkingclub.org.uk). The OS map for the Rye to Winchelsea leg is Explorer 125.

History: The part-Norman **All Saints Church** at Icklesham contains a variety of architecture styles and has a nave and chancel that are not aligned with each other. A 1592 legacy notice in the church leaves over £3 a year 'for ever' for highway maintenance.

Ex-Beatle Paul McCartney, who lives a few miles from Winchelsea, funded the renovation of **Hog Hill** windmill, which is visible from the walk route.

Iron Age chieftains had fortresses on both the east and west hills of Hastings. When the Romans left, the barbarian

Haestingas tribe gave its name to the place, having to be subdued by King Offa in 771. William the Conqueror built his first **castle** here above the town. In 1287, large parts of Hastings were washed away in the **Great Storm**, the one that left Winchelsea stranded way inland. In medieval times, Hastings was one of the **Cinque Ports**, supplying 25 ships for 15 days a year for the country's defence, in the days before the Royal Navy existed. (The Cinque Ports, pronounced 'sink', were Sandwich, Dover, Hythe, Romney and Hastings, and the two ancient towns of Rye and Winchelsea.)

Walk directions

[1] [Numbers in square brackets refer to the map]
Coming off the only platform at **Winchelsea station**, at the tarmac road *turn right* across the railway line, your direction 170 degrees. There is a tourist information board on the other side of the line, on your left-hand side. Bear left with this road, a waterway to your right. In 450 metres, ignore a concrete car-wide path off to the right (next to a mini pylon pole with a grey transformer box) beside the River Brede. In 220 metres ignore a stile to the left and cross the River Brede bridge.

Looking back from this bridge, the town of Rye can be seen on a hilltop and, on its right, Camber Castle, built by Henry VIII in 1540.

In 180 metres, at the A259, *turn right on a concrete car lane* that is signposted as a footpath, your direction 310 degrees.

Go over a stile (to the left of a wooden fieldgate) to go along a concrete car-wide track. In 50 metres continue along a narrow earth track. In a further 70 metres, go through a wooden gate, and in 25 metres go across a wooden footbridge over a stream and through a wooden gate.

Turn left with the stream (which is often dried up in summer) and trees on your left-hand side, your direction 240 degrees.

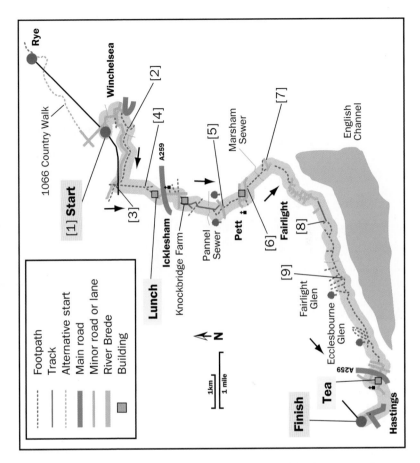

But in 100 metres, **[!]** as the wood to your left begins to bear left, *fork right,* with no clear path, towards an isolated wooden gate visible ahead, at a bearing of 260 degrees.

In 40 metres you pass a sometimes soggy ditch on your right-hand side. In a further 70 metres go through a wooden gate to the left-hand side of a wooden fieldgate to cross a stream. Head across this field aiming for a wooden gate on the far side, your direction 290 degrees.

In 200 metres go through the wooden gate (with a wooden fieldgate on its right-hand side) **[2]** into the next field. Head across this field, your direction 260

degrees. (Depending, however, on the time of the year and the state of the field you may find it easier to continue with the **River Brede** on your right-hand side.)

In 400 metres you go through a wooden gate at the corner fencing on your left-hand side (with a wooden footpath post 'Icklesham') to continue in the same direction on a car-wide track with field fencing on your right.

In 220 metres, by a brick water-pumping hut on your left-hand side, go through a wooden kissing gate (to the right of a metal fieldgate), to carry on with the river on your right-hand side.

In 450 metres go over a stile (a metal fieldgate on its left-hand side).

In 400 metres go over a stile; in a further 40 metres, cross over the railway line.

The other side, *bear left* on a track alongside the river for 30 metres, *then go over a stile and turn left* along the fence, due west.

In 55 metres [3] cross a grassy bridge and go through a metal fieldgate and over a stile and again over the railway line. In 20 metres go over a stile and straight on, with a waterway on your right-hand side and heading directly for Icklesham church, already visible in the distance.

Keep on through stiles and fences and, four fields and 800 metres later [4], you [!] *go over a stile* (with a metal fieldgate and a concrete grid on its right-hand side) and ignore the main left fork (a car-wide grassy road) *to take a fork bearing right,* following a faint path and heading between two mini pylon poles visible on top of the hill ahead, your initial direction 200 degrees.

In 400 metres, on the brow of the hill, go under the mini pylon cables. In a further 35 metres go over a stile into the corner of the car park of the suggested lunch pub, the **Queens Head**, Icklesham (its name is painted on the roof tiles), to reach its back entrance after 50 metres.

After lunch, you go out from the pub on to the passing lane, *and turn left* on this lane, coming to the A259 crossroads in 130 metres. Cross over the A259 into Workhouse Lane. In 40 metres you come to the driveway of Chantry House, marked as a footpath. (To bypass the church, simply continue on the lane. In 60 metres the main route rejoins from the left and you continue at the asterisk [*] below.)

To visit the church, *turn left* on to the driveway of Chantry House, which leads in 130 metres to **All Saints Church**, Icklesham. Coming out of the church door, *turn 90 degrees left* to go through the churchyard, your direction south. In 20 metres ignore a stile 10 metres ahead and *fork right* *through a gap* in the blackberry bushes into an orchard.

Ignoring another stile 8 metres to the left, *you turn right* to go alongside the orchard fence on your left, your initial direction 280 degrees. In 120 metres you *rejoin Workhouse Lane and go left,* heading due south.

[*] In 200 metres, by a tarmac road right (Laurel Lane), *go over a stile* to the left of a metal fieldgate on to a footpath. Go 240 degrees to the far right-hand corner of the field, 120 metres away. Here you go through a metal fieldgate, and on diagonally across this small field aiming for its far corner, your direction 230 degrees.

In 70 metres cross a stile and carry on in the same direction, towards a stile visible ahead (3 metres to the left of the leftmost metal fieldgate), some 100 metres distant.

Go over this stile and slice the corner of the next field, your direction 220 degrees, and in 130 metres go through a metal fieldgate *and turn left* down a car-wide shingle track. You may now be able to see the sea away to your left-hand side. In 120 metres ignore a fork right to the farmhouse.

Go straight on through the farmyard. In 90 metres, at the end of the farmyard, go through a metal fieldgate on your right and *turn left,* your direction 220 degrees, with a field fence on your left-hand side.

In 80 metres you pass a large pond on your right-hand side. In 70 metres go through a metal fieldgate to continue down the farm track, between hedges. Pett church is visible on the far horizon.

In 140 metres go through a fieldgate and head a quarter right, making for a bridge, your direction 210 degrees.

In 150 metres you go through a metal fieldgate to cross this bridge over **Pannel Sewer** to follow a mini pylon cable run in a southerly direction, towards a fieldgate.

In 130 metres go through this fieldgate (there is another one 5 metres to its left). *Go right,* your direction 250 degrees, with the field fence on your right-hand side.

In 70 metres, cross a ditch into the next field. *Go left* up its left-hand side (with the ditch on your left-hand side), your direction 200 degrees.

In 100 metres you come to a fenced wood, where you *go rightwards* along the fence, until, in 60 metres, *you go left* through a metal gate set in the fence and so into the wood, and up a track, your direction 230 degrees.

In 160 metres exit the wood by a stile. *Turn half left* up across a field (there is no distinct path), aiming to pass 50 metres to the left of some farm buildings, to continue across the field towards the far top left corner of the field, your direction 140 degrees. In 250 metres, near a mini pylon pole (with a grey transformer box), you cross two stiles on to a tarmac lane.

Turn left and after 8 metres *turn right* over a stile. **[5]**

Go left for 10 metres, *then right* following the hedge on your left-hand side, your direction 160 degrees.

In 220 metres, at the bottom left-hand corner of the field, go right, your direction 260 degrees, with the field hedge on your left-hand side.

In 60 metres go over a stile on your left, and onwards, uphill, your direction 165 degrees, across the field. Go *straight on*

towards and past a mini pylon pole in the middle of the field (the pole is about 5 metres to the right of the path, although there may be no path maintained in winter).

In 300 metres, go over a stile and *veer left,* your direction 140 degrees, up across a field.

In 160 metres you go over a stile and across a tarmac road to the former Royal Oak Inn, Pett (which has been closed since summer 2010).

Go around the right-hand side of this ex-pub to carry on, down a tarmac road, your direction 140 degrees.

In 200 metres you pass an entrance to Gatehurst Farm to your right.

In a further 100 metres **[6]**, *fork right* up a track to go over a stile that has a post marked to Cliff End.

Go diagonally across the field, your direction 130 degrees, aiming 40 metres to the left of a brick structure. (This was the base of a radar-transmitting tower in World War II, used to guide British planes back home.)

In 170 metres, with a fine panoramic view to admire, go over a stile signposted to Pett Level and continue on in the same direction, down towards a (not initially visible) stile, 50 metres to the right of the far field corner.

In 180 metres you go over the stile and continue in a similar direction, 150 degrees, down towards a (not initially visible) footbridge.

In 190 metres go over the wooden footbridge and cross the **Marsham Sewer** to go straight on towards another footbridge. In 60 metres cross this wooden footbridge over a stream and go straight on, keeping to the left.

In 50 metres *turn left* through a wooden fieldgate (the post marked with a yellow arrow), to go along the bottom of a farmhouse garden for 10 metres, to then go through another fieldgate into the bottom corner of a field. *Go diagonally across this field* for 200 metres, your direction east, and go over a stile in the opposite corner of the field.

Bear left on the tarmac road. In 40 metres you reach a driveway on your right.

If you wish to take lunch at the **Smugglers**, Pett Level, continue along the road for 350 metres to reach the Smugglers pub.

Otherwise *turn right* up the driveway for 8 metres, *to then fork right up four steps on to a path* with the Saxon Shore Way emblem on a post. **[7]** Go up this path for 550 metres, crossing over two driveways (after which you can hear and see the sea below on your left), and enter the National Trust's land at **Fairlight**.

Ignore a stile to the right to keep on the coastal path.

In 450 metres ignore a stile on your right-hand side to go down some steps with wooden railings and then straight on.

In 120 metres follow the path round to the right to continue along a fenced-in path bordering a garden off to your left. In 90 metres the path curves to the right (away from the garden) and, in 20 metres, *fork left* through a wooden horse-blocking barrier. In 15 metres turn right down a car-wide shingle track (Sea Road), your direction 300 degrees.

After 70 metres, at a junction, *turn left* up a lane (Lower Waites Lane), your direction 190 degrees.

In 350 metres *take the first turning left (Cliff Way),* by the 'Sea Road Closed' sign, your direction 160 degrees.

In 100 metres *take the fenced-in footpath right,* 5 metres before the entrance to Fairhaven on your right-hand side, your direction 250 degrees.

In 160 metres you come out on to a T-junction with a tarmac road (Rockmead Road) *and turn left up it,* your direction 150 degrees. In 60 metres, follow the now gravel road round to the right.

At the end of Rockmead Road, in 300 metres, by the 30mph sign, *you keep straight on,* going along Bramble Way, ignoring all possible ways off. In 170 metres, at a T-junction, *go left,* your direction 170 degrees.

In 100 metres, at a T-junction, *turn right* on Channel Way, your direction 250 degrees.

Ignoring all ways off, after 450 metres you enter a narrower path. **[8]**

In 80 metres go through a wooden kissing gate, at last leaving the outskirts of Fairlight Cove village behind you, to enter the **Firehills** of **Hastings Country Park** and *fork left,* your direction 230 degrees.

You now follow the cliff walk for 5.5km to the top of the East Hill funicular railway at the double asterisk **[**]** below.

In more detail: Keep on this main path. In 350 metres, 20 metres before a bench ahead of you, *fork right uphill* with the broad grassy way, your direction 300 degrees.

Keep along the coastal way as much as possible. In 500 metres you have to head uphill towards the radar station. Then in 130 metres, by a bench below this station, *go left to keep on the coastal way,* your direction 240 degrees.

In 40 metres you pass a post (24) saying 'Hastings 3¼ miles' to carry on downhill.

In 400 metres, by a bench and a multi-path junction (marked by a post), *go left down some steps.* In 200 metres you cross a stream at the bottom of **Warren Glen** to go up the other side on a wide grassy way. Ignore ways off. In 300 metres, by post 18 (Hastings 2½ miles), *go up steps.*

At the top of the steps is a stone slab known as 'Lovers' Seat' – the slab has been dragged back inland from the cliffs where two lovers met in secret in the 1780s; their actual clifftop has now been eroded and fallen into the sea. 60 metres from the top of these steps, you pass a post ('Hastings 2½ miles').

In 80 metres, go down some steps. At the bottom of these, *follow the post 17 left* to Fairlight Glen ('¼ mile').

After 150 metres, where a wooden fence blocks the old coastal path ahead, *turn right* down the new path with the wooden fence on your left-hand side, your direction 260 degrees. In 100 metres, go down some steps and turn right to rejoin the old coastal path.

In 140 metres, by a stream **[9]**, the left fork leads to **Fairlight Glen nudist beach**. (**[!]** At low tide, it may be possible to walk along the beach from Fairlight to Hastings, but you do so at your own risk

and you are strongly advised to seek local advice before doing so [**!**].)

The main walk's onward route is straight on. In 40 metres you pass post 16 to emerge from a wooded area after 40 metres, to continue on a wide grassy way uphill, your direction 220 degrees.

In 220 metres it is steeply up steps again. In 35 metres you pass post 14 ('Hastings 2 miles'). 100 metres beyond the top of the steps, you come to a post ('Hastings 1¾ miles') where you keep left.

In 500 metres ignore a fork by post 8 up to the right, to keep on along the car-wide grass path (with a fence on its right-hand side), your direction 240 degrees.

In 600 metres you come to a bench with a view out over the beach ahead and *you go sharp right,* your direction 35 degrees. In 30 metres, *go left,* your direction 340 degrees, soon down steps.

At the bottom of this (**Ecclesbourne Glen**) you cross a stream, by a post, and keep straight on upwards on the main steps, ignoring ways off to the right and left.

At the top of the steps, by a post, *go left,* your direction 210 degrees, with a wooden field fence on your left-hand side.

In 350 metres, **Hastings** can be seen at last. In a further 450 metres, you pass by a replica of the old warning beacons that spread news of the rapidly approaching Spanish Armada in 1588.

[******] In 60 metres you reach the top of the East Hill funicular railway on your left. You now pick up a tarmac path and a *paved stepway going downwards,* soon seeing the black wooden **Net Shops** on the beach to your left.

At the bottom, cross the tarmac Tackleway and continue on down Crown Lane to the next crossing, All Saints Street, where the **Crown Inn** is on your right-hand side. *Turn right* on All Saints Street.

In 90 metres you pass the **Cinque Port Arms** pub. 15 metres beyond it, *go left* down Bourne Passage. In 40 metres cross (via a pelican crossing) the A259 to continue up Roebuck Street.

In 60 metres, by the **Duke of Wellington** pub on your left-hand side, *turn left* into the High Street, your direction 220 degrees.

In 80 metres you pass the **Electric Palace Cinema** on your left-hand side. In a further 25 metres, you pass the **Jenny Lind** pub on your right-hand side and the **Land of Green Ginger Café** on your left-hand side, a possible tea stop.

In 40 metres *turn left* up Swan Terrace, your direction 310 degrees, passing the Church of St Clement on your right-hand side.

Then *turn left* on Hill Street.

In 80 metres, at the end of Hill Street, *go down some steps, bearing right,* past **Ye Olde Pump House** pub into George Street, where *you go right,* your direction 230 degrees.

In 230 metres, at the junction with the A259 coastal road, *turn right* along it. After 250 metres, by the roundabout fountain on your left, *fork right* along a pedestrianised road. In 70 metres you go through a subway and, in a further 160 metres at a six-way crossroads, continue in the same direction up Havelock Road, your direction north-west.

In 200 metres cross over Devonshire Road and *veer left* to go up Station Approach to reach **Hastings station** after 130 metres.

Lunch & tea places

Queens Head *Parsonage Lane, Icklesham, TN36 4BL (01424 814552, www.queenshead.com).* **Open** 11am-11pm Mon-Sat; noon-10.30pm Sun. *Food served* noon-2.45pm, 6.15-9.45pm Mon-Fri; noon-9.45pm Sat, Sun. This suggested lunch stop serves good food, but can get rather crowded.

Smugglers Inn *Pett Level Road, Pett Level, TN35 4EH (01424 813491).* **Open** 11am-11pm daily. *Food served* noon-2.30pm, 6-9pm Mon-Fri; noon-3pm, 6-9pm Sat; noon-3pm Sun. A later lunch option. **Tea** can be taken at any of the many establishments you pass on your way through Hastings.

Walk 26

Shelford to Cambridge

Grantchester – the Rupert Brooke walk.

Start: Shelford station
Finish: Cambridge station

Length: 20.5km (12.7 miles)

Time: 6 hours. For the whole outing, including trains, sights and meals, allow at least 11 hours.

Transport: Take the train nearest to **9am** from **Liverpool Street** station to **Shelford** (journey time 1 hour 15 minutes). Alternatively, you can take a fast train from **King's Cross** station to **Cambridge** and change there for Shelford.

Trains back from **Cambridge** run twice an hour to Liverpool Street and up to four times an hour to King's Cross (journey time 50-80 minutes). Buy a day return to Cambridge; if you travel out from Liverpool Street and intend to return on a fast train to King's Cross, ask for a (more expensive) ticket which will allow you to do this.

OS Landranger Map: 154
OS Explorer Map: 209
Shelford, map reference TL465523, is in **Cambridgeshire**, 6km south of Cambridge.

Toughness: 5 out of 10

Walk notes: This walk is long and flat and gets better as the day progresses after a somewhat dull morning: the route into Cambridge is lovely, particularly after Grantchester.

Near the start, to lessen the amount of road walking that faces you today, you may be able to walk along a farm track beside the River Cam from Shelford and its church, but you need to obtain the farmer's written permission in advance. Write to Mr AF Pemberton, Church Farm, Trumpington, Cambridgeshire CB2 2LG, two weeks before your planned walk, stating the day you would like to cross his land, the approximate time of arrival (15 minutes after leaving Shelford station, plus any church-visit time) and the approximate number of walkers in your group. Your letter should be sent in duplicate with a 'Grant Permission – Withhold Permission' paragraph for the farmer to sign and an s.a.e. for its return. The farmer has previously indicated he would prefer to give consent between the months of February and June, so please do not seek his permission during the harvest period, which is August and September.

The route then passes through the village of Hauxton, with its interesting church, then on to Haslingfield for lunch. From there you head to Grantchester and the Orchard tea rooms, before walking alongside the River Cam into Cambridge. Try to conserve enough energy to take the walk's tour of Cambridge colleges at the end of your day out.

To avoid the less-than-exciting morning, and the need to contact the farmer in advance, as well as giving yourself the chance to spend more time exploring Cambridge, a Cambridge via Granchester circular walk has been devised (*see below* **Walk options**).

Walk options: There are two variations to the main route.

a) **Cambridge via Granchester circular**: This 15km (9.4 mile) version cuts out the morning leg of the main walk and allows you more time for the city centre tour of the University Colleges before you head out to Grantchester on a walk besides the River Cam. You stop for refreshment at the famous Orchard tea rooms and then have a choice for the return walk to Cambridge, heading either via Trumpington or back beside the River Cam. Gardeners among you may like to visit the Cambridge University Botanic Gardens at the end of the route, before taking the short walk that remains to Cambridge railway station. As most of this walk is on footpaths and paved paths, you may prefer to wear stout walking shoes or well-cushioned trainers instead of boots. For directions for this walk, refer to the Saturday Walkers' Club website (www.walkingclub.org.uk).

b) **Shortening the walk**: In addition to the Cambridge–Grantchester option, you can shorten the main walk by taking a taxi from your lunch stop to Grantchester or Cambridge. Alternatively, catch a bus into Cambridge from Hauxton or Haslingfield: for bus information call Traveline on 0871 200 2233.

History: Perhaps Friends of the Earth should employ poets. Writing a famous poem must be as effective a way as any of ensuring that a place is preserved forever. Rupert Brooke's poem 'The Old Vicarage' – he had rooms as a student at the Orchard, and later at the Old Vicarage, Grantchester – was written in a mood of nostalgia in a Berlin café, in May 1912. The poem celebrates not only **Grantchester** and the river ('Laughs the immortal river still/Under the mill, under the mill?'), but the surrounding countryside ('And sunset still a golden sea/From Haslingfield to Madingley'). Augustus John camped in Grantchester meadows with, as Keynes put it, his 'two wives and ten naked children'; Brooke and Virginia Woolf (who dubbed his friends the 'Neo-Pagans') swam naked by moonlight; EM Foster visited the Orchard; Wittgenstein would come there by canoe; AN Whitehead and Bertrand Russell worked on their *Principia Mathematica* at the Mill House, next to the Old Vicarage. As for the church clock ('Oh! Yet/Stands the Church clock at ten to three?/And is there honey still for tea?'), it appears in Brooke's first draft at half past three – the actual time it was stuck at for most of 1911.

The **Church of St Mary the Virgin**, Great Shelford, was rebuilt at the expense of its rector, Thomas Patesley, in the early 15th century. It contains a mural of the Last Judgement that was painted about then, showing the devils on the left of Christ dragging away the damned in a chain.

St Edmund's Church, Hauxton, is renowned as one of the oldest and most interesting small churches in Cambridgeshire, with Norman windows, doors and chancel arch; a 13th-century font bowl; a 15th-century pulpit and nave roof. It also contains a rare 13th-century fresco of St Thomas Becket, which survived Henry VIII's depredations; and, having been previously walled up, this fresco also survived the vandalism of the notorious puritan William Dowsing (who, in 1643, destroyed 'three popish pictures' in this church). St Edmund became King of East Anglia in 856 at the age of 15, and was killed 13 years later by the Danes for refusing to renounce his Christian faith.

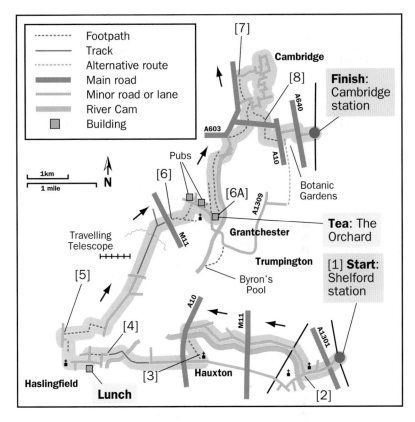

Legend:
- - - - - - - Footpath
———— Track
- - - - - - Alternative route
———— Main road
▬▬▬▬▬ Minor road or lane
———— River Cam
☐ Building

1km
1 mile
N

[7]

Cambridge

[8]

Finish: Cambridge station

A640

A603

A10

Pubs

[6]

[6A]

A1309

Botanic Gardens

Tea: The Orchard

Travelling Telescope

M11

Grantchester

[5]

Trumpington

[4]

Byron's Pool

[1] **Start:** Shelford station

A10

M11

A1301

[3] **Hauxton**

Haslingfield

Lunch

[2]

The oldest surviving building in Cambridge is **St Bene't's Church**, which has a Saxon tower. **Cambridge University** was founded in the early 13th century by students and academics fleeing riots in Oxford, where the townsfolk felt imposed on by the academics. Within a couple of centuries, the university dominated the Cambridge townsfolk too: in 1440, Henry VI had a large part of medieval Cambridge demolished to make way for **King's College**, intended for students from his new Eton school; in 1496, a 12th-century nunnery became **Jesus College**; in 1542, a Benedictine hostel was transformed into **Magdalene College**; and, in 1596, **Trinity College** was endowed by Henry VIII with funds from the monasteries he had vandalised.

The **Orchard Tea Rooms** date from 1897, although the orchard's apple trees were planted 11 years earlier. Soon after opening, the tea rooms became a favourite upriver cafe of college students. In the tea rooms' early years, the owners took in lodgers to supplement their income, one being Rupert Brooke. Today, college students punt up to the Orchard for tea – or a champagne breakfast after May Balls. During Cambridge's Fringe Festival, summer evening performances of Shakespeare are held at the Orchard.

Walk directions

[1] [Numbers in square brackets refer to the map]

Coming off platform 2 at **Shelford station**, *turn right* to cross the level crossing on to the main road, Station Road, your direction 215 degrees. In 40 metres you pass the **Railway Tavern** on your left, which serves morning coffee.

In 115 metres you cross the A1301, Tunwell's Lane, to continue *straight ahead* on Woollards Lane, ignoring ways off. In a further 325 metres, you come to a T-junction (with house no.90 opposite), where you *go left,* on Church Street.

In 160 metres you come to the **Church of St Mary the Virgin**, Great Shelford, which is worth a look inside.

In 50 metres you pass Kings Mill Lane on your left-hand side.

[2] Now there are two alternatives:

a) The road route: Continue on the main road (Church Street). In 125 metres cross a bridge over the river to enter **Little Shelford**. In 60 metres cross another bridge. You are now on Bridge Lane, with an old red-brick wall on your right-hand side. Continue for a further 250 metres to a junction. Here swing right on Church Street, signposted Hauxton and

Harston, and in 35 metres you pass on the left-hand side of **All Saints Church**, Little Shelford. In a further 250 metres you come to a T-junction by the Sycamore House Restaurant. Here *turn right* along Hauxton Road.

Ignore ways off and in 550 metres you pass over a level crossing. In another 250 metres you pass under the M11. In a further 500 metres, you enter the village of Hauxton and pass the bus stop. Continuing along Church Road, ignoring turn-offs, in 440 metres you come to the **Church of St Edmunds** (worth a visit inside), rejoining the route at point [3] below.

b) The farm-track route: 10 metres beyond Kings Mill lane, there is a gravel road *to your right,* due north, into **Rectory Farm**, through double wooden gates, and towards a silo and barns, with an onward route that keeps the River Cam away on your left-hand side. **[!]** As noted on p199, this is not a public right of way and you should only take this route if you have obtained the farmer's permission beforehand.

The route into the farm *bears left* with the lane as it continues on through outbuildings.

In 165 metres keep on the concrete road, with wooden fencing on your left-hand side, and ignore a grassy farm track fork left that goes down beside the river. In 45 metres ignore another fork left to continue on, your direction 310 degrees. In a further 180 metres, go through metal fieldgates and *across the railway line* to continue on.

In a further 750 metres bend with the road to the left to continue on, your direction 260 degrees, still with the river on your left-hand side, ignoring a turn-off to the right.

In 305 metres *go under* the M11 motorway bridge.

In 730 metres *veer right,* with a field hedge on your right-hand side, your direction 340 degrees, following the main track.

In 290 metres you come to some farm buildings where you *veer left* with the road, your direction 315 degrees, towards the cottage. In 170 metres you pass this building.

In a further 175 metres, you come to within 25 metres of the A10. But here you *turn sharp left* on a driveway, past car-blocking posts, on a signposted public footpath, your direction 175 degrees, towards a timber-framed house. In 65 metres go over a bridge and straight on. In 40 metres go over a mill stream. At the end of the **Hauxton Mill** building *you go left,* your direction 120 degrees, with the river on your left and a chemicals factory on your right.

In 40 metres ignore a footpath to the right. In a further 135 metres, ignore a bridge with a fishing-club sign to your right. In 45 metres ignore a public footpath to the right. In a further 200 metres, your path leads to a concrete bridge with wooden railings, which you cross to continue on.

In 100 metres take the wooden kissing gate *to your left,* your direction 165 degrees. In 20 metres go through another kissing gate, continuing towards the church.

In 150 metres you come out to the road and to the **Church of St Edmund**, Hauxton. **[3]**

Continuing on the main walk: Turn right on to this road (Church Road) from **b) the farm-track route** or keep ahead on **a) the road route**.

Ignore all ways off. In 300 metres you come to the A10 where you *turn left.* In 35 metres there is a bus lay-by, with buses to Royston and 50 metres further down the road, on the opposite side, buses to Cambridge. Opposite the nearside bus lay-by, take the public bridleway signposted to Haslingfield, your direction 285 degrees, on to a wide earth road with a large open field on the left.

In 260 metres ignore a fork to the left towards **Rectory Farm** (marked on the OS map). In 50 metres ignore another fork to the left, to carry straight on, your direction 300 degrees; the church in Haslingfield is already visible ahead to your left.

In 180 metres ignore a turning to the right marked 'Private Farm Road'.

In 100 metres the earth track becomes grassy. In 200 metres the track swings gently left between vast fields and over a stream, with a small coppice on your left. Keep ahead, on a bearing of 245 degrees. In 150 metres pass through a part tree-lined field boundary. Follow the grassy track with a ditch and field boundary on your right. In 400 metres pass through another field boundary and at a path junction, *bear right,* your direction 305 degrees.

In 200 metres go on a bridge over the River Cam and *turn left,* with the river alongside on your left-hand side, your direction 235 degrees. In 230 metres you come to a farm track. **[4]**

In 50 metres cross a farm track and keep ahead on a stony track, with a play area to the left, your direction 200 degrees. In 30 metres, with a playing field on your right-hand side **[!]** *turn right,* your direction due west, along the right-hand edge of the playing field.

In 100 metres you pass a thatched cottage on your right-hand side. In a further 100 metres, you come out through metal barriers (with wooden posts) to a road (New Road) where you *go left,* your direction 200 degrees.

Stay on this road, ignoring Fountain Lane to the right, coming to the High Street T-junction in 80 metres. Here you *go right.* In 55 metres *go left* on Baldock Road and immediately right, to the modern building that is the **Little Rose** pub, the suggested lunchtime stop.

After lunch return to the High Street and *turn left,* your direction 285 degrees. Ignore ways off. You pass the village shop on your right and then Haslingfield's Millennium Sun Dial and Village sign. After 330 metres, where the High Street veers left, you *go straight on,* along Church Way, with a thatched house on your right-hand side. In 80 metres you come to the Parish church of **All Saints**, Haslingfield.

Coming out of the church door, *go straight ahead* on a stony path through the churchyard, your direction 340 degrees. In 110 metres you come out to a tarmac road where you *continue straight on.* In 25 metres you pass the thatched Oak Cottage on your left-hand side. In a further 35 metres, *fork right* on Dodds Mead. In a further 45 metres, pick up the tarmac path to the left of a house called Adelaide (no.1), *straight on,* your direction 15 degrees.

In 85 metres you come out on to a road (New Road) by house no. 118 (opposite), where you *turn left,* your direction 320 degrees. In a further 95 metres, you come out on to Barton Road, with a thatched house opposite where you *turn right.*

In a further 175 metres, opposite house no.31, take the signposted public footpath *to the right* **[5]**, your direction 95 degrees (the pub marked here on old OS maps is long gone).

In 45 metres go over a wooden footbridge with railings over a stream on a gravel path and in 20 metres dogleg left then right with the path. In a further 60 metres go under mini pylons and in 70 metres the gravel path becomes a wide grassy path. In a further 140 metres cross a farm track and go over a ditch. With a farm gate directly ahead, *turn left,* your direction 10 degrees.

In 80 metres veer right with the path, your direction due east. In a further 240 metres, go over a wooden bridge with railings over a ditch-stream, to go straight on.

In a further 175 metres dogleg left then right over a ditch, then pass a corrugated shed on your right-hand side (part of Lesania Farm) and in 90 metres you come to a tarmac lane T-junction, *where you go left,* your direction 25 degrees.

Continue ahead, ignoring all ways off. In about 300 metres radio telescopes are visible off to your left-hand side. After 1.75km along this lane, with cottage no.6 on your left-hand side, cross a track junction and ignore a lane to your right to Cantelupe Farm (marked on the OS map) to continue straight on, along the concrete lane serving as a bridleway, your direction 20 degrees.

In 250 metres you pass some 75 metres to the right of the end of the railway track for the **travelling telescope**, usually parked about 1km down the track away to your left.

Continue straight on, now on a wide grassy way, with Grantchester Church just visible behind the trees to your right (60 degrees on your compass) and Barton Church away ahead to your left.

In 550 metres go over Bourn Brook, on a concrete bridge with high wooden railings. In 55 metres *fork right,* your direction 65 degrees.

In a further 120 metres, go over the M11 footbridge, the top of which offers a panoramic view of the landscape. **[6]** On the other side of the bridge, *turn half right,* on a grassy path, with Grantchester Church ahead of you, your direction 95 degrees. In 50 metres, *swing left,* your bearing now 60 degrees.

In 500 metres, at a four-way footpath sign and crossing of ways, go straight on along a tarmac path, your direction 25 degrees. In 60 metres you pass a children's adventure playground on your left-hand side.

In 100 metres you come on to an estate driveway, Burnt Close, and in a further 120 metres to Cotton Road, where you *turn right,* your direction 105 degrees, by the thatched Grant Cottage on your right-hand side. Keep ahead on Cotton Road to the T-junction with the main road (High Street), with the **Rupert Brooke** pub opposite (a possible late lunch stop).

Turn right on the High Street, your direction 150 degrees. In 120 metres you pass the thatched **Red Lion** pub on your left-hand side, another possible late lunch stop. Continuing along the High Street, you next pass the **Green Man** pub, a third possible late lunch option.

In 100 metres you come to the **Parish Church of St Andrew & St Mary**, Grantchester, on your right-hand side. Coming out of the church, turn right (to continue in your direction as before down the High Street) and you pass the entrance to Manor Farm on your right.

In 40 metres, as the road swings right, go down a gravel track to go through a wooden swing gate into the garden of the suggested tea place on this walk, the **Orchard**. After tea, if not taking the detour to the Old Vicarage, your route continues at point [6A] below – the path by the low-level sign 'To the River' is *on your left,* almost opposite the entrance to the tea rooms.

(After tea in the Orchard's garden, it is worth your while taking a short detour to view the outside of the **Old Vicarage** where Rupert Brooke used to lodge. Walk through the Orchard's car park in a southerly direction and pass the Rupert Brooke Museum buildings on your right, to exit the car park back on to the main road, where you *turn left.* In 50 metres, the road swings to the right, and there is a footpath ahead between high walls. The Old Vicarage is the house on your left, with a postbox in a wall. The property is now owned by Lord Jeffrey Archer and Lady Mary Archer. The large

conservatory where Lord Archer wrote many of his novels is clearly visible. In the front garden of the house is a **statue of Rupert Brooke in military uniform**. *Retrace your steps,* through the Orchard's car park, to the entrance to the Orchard tea room building.)

[6A] Returning from the Old Vicarage detour, opposite the entrance to the tea rooms, [!] there is a low-level sign on your right 'To the River'. Go right down this path, your direction 100 degrees, in 40 metres going through a metal kissing gate. *Keep ahead* over a field and in a further 100 metres go through another metal kissing gate, to the banks of the **River Cam**.

Your onward route is more or less to follow the River Cam to the outskirts of Cambridge.

In more detail: Bear left and in 80 metres go through a metal kissing gate. In a further 120 metres go over a stream. In 110 metres go through metal kissing gate no.19 and onwards along the bank. In a further 200 metres go through a metal kissing gate. In 80 metres go through a gate and over a wooden footbridge with wooden railings. In dry weather, follow the path to the right and along the banks of the River Cam; in the wet, take the tarmac path some 50 metres over to your left.

Continuing by the river, in 240 metres go over a wooden footbridge with wooden railings. In 130 metres go through a metal gate and over a wooden footbridge with wooden railings. In 150 metres go over another wooden footbridge with wooden railings, and in 55 metres yet another.

In 100 metres go over another wooden footbridge with wooden railings. The path now swings left and in 300 metres joins the upper (tarmac) path. *Turn right,* through a metal kissing gate to join the tarmac path, your direction 40 degrees.

In 200 metres, having passed Grantchester Meadow on your right, *keep ahead* along a badly maintained car road, your direction 65 degrees, with a car parking area on your left.

In 100 metres your way becomes a tarmac road.

In 115 metres, at a three-way road junction, [!] ignore Marlowe Road on your left and *turn down* Eltisley Avenue (the middle junction), your direction 30 degrees. In 200 metres *turn left* to go northwards up Grantchester Street.

In 160 metres, you come to the junction with the A603. [!] Your way ahead depends on whether you intend to tour the Cambridge colleges; if not, take the direct route to Cambridge railway station (passing the entrance to Cambridge University Botanic Gardens, which you may like to visit).

To go to the railway station: *Turn right* at the junction with the A603 and head just south-of-east, on a surfaced path on the southern edge of Lammas Land, to cross a stream on a bridge after some 350 metres. Where a path joins you on your left, continue ahead; then follow the directions at [8] below.

To continue on the main walk – which includes the 'City Tour' (NB: if you have never visited Cambridge before, it is a shame to miss out on the tour of the colleges): At the junction with the A603, *cross over* and *go straight ahead* on Newnham Road with the A603 on your left-hand side, your direction 40 degrees. Keep to the bike path, parallel to the road on the right of the pavement and, in 45 metres, with pedestrian traffic lights on your left, *fork right* with the bike path, your direction 70 degrees, across **Lammas Land** (open grass).

In 240 metres *cross over* the main road, Fen Causeway, diagonally to the right, to go across the bridge and *turn left,* on a bearing of 350 degrees, to pick up the path beside the Old Mill stream on your left-hand side. In 10 metres go through a metal swing gate (with a cattle grid to its right-hand side).

In a further 100 metres, by the Bella Italia restaurant on your left-hand side, *fork right* over a footbridge with white metal railings and continue on the tarmac path, your direction 45 degrees.

In 70 metres go over a similar bridge. In 40 metres bear left and you are beside the River Cam on your right-hand side and you continue on, your direction 350 degrees, with the Hilton Double Tree Hotel on the other side of the river. In 50 metres go over a weir. In 80 metres cross a bridge to your right, towards the Mill pub. On the other side of the bridge, *turn left,* and in 15 metres *go left* down Laundress Lane, which has bollards at its entrance.

In 50 metres you come to a T-junction, Silver Street, with **Queens' College** opposite you. Turn left, your direction 230 degrees, passing the Anchor pub on your left, and in 30 metres go on a bridge *back over the river.*

For a **Tour of Cambridge Colleges** follow this suggested route:

In 80 metres *fork right* following the signpost to 'The Backs', your direction 290 degrees.

In 120 metres, having just gone past the white pyramid building on your right-hand side, go straight on away from the river, your direction 330 degrees. In a further 180 metres you come to the main road where you *turn right,* your direction 345 degrees.

In 25 metres, do not go through the gates on your right-hand side into the grounds of **King's College**, but keep to the wide path with the river on your right-hand side. In a further 150 metres you pass the gateway to **Clare College**. In 85 metres **[7]** *turn right* on to Garret Hostel Lane, eastwards, on a long tarmac lane between railings, with the **Wren Library** away to the left. *Go over the bridge* (with **Clare Bridge** visible to the right).

In 140 metres, at Trinity Lane T-junction, *turn right,* your direction 190 degrees.

In 40 metres, having passed **Trinity Hall** on your right-hand side, *turn left* into Senate House Passage, passing on your left the **Gate of Honour**, topped with sundials (the gateway through which

undergraduates pass on their way to receiving their degrees).

At the main road, Trinity Street, *turn left,* your direction 5 degrees, passing an entrance to **Gonville & Caius College** on your left-hand side and **St Michael's Church** on your right. In a further 100 metres you pass the gatehouse to **Trinity College** on your left-hand side.

In 55 metres you come to **St John's College** on your left. Here *turn right* on All Saints Passage, your direction 110 degrees. In 60 metres, at the T-junction, *go left,* your direction 50 degrees. In a further 45 metres, at the Bridge Street T-junction, *go right,* your direction 145 degrees. In 20 metres continue *straight on,* now on Sidney Street. In 70 metres you pass **Sidney Sussex College** on your left.

In 75 metres you pass Market Passage on your right-hand side. In a further 40 metres *turn right* on Market Street, your direction 240 degrees. In 35 metres you pass **Holy Trinity Church** on your left-hand side. In 90 metres you come to the back of **Great St Mary's Church**, where you *go left,* your direction 170 degrees, with market stalls on your left-hand side. In 35 metres, *go straight on* along Peas Hill.

In 25 metres, at the end of the HSBC Bank building, *go right,* signposted to 'G David Bookseller', your direction 290 degrees. In 50 metres you pass the front of the **Church of St Edward** and in 10 metres, at the T-junction, *go right* on St Edward's Passage.

In 30 metres you come on to the main Kings Parade, where you *go left,* with **King's College** opposite.

Continuing south on King's Parade, you pass in 30 metres the **Rainbow Café** on your left-hand side. In a further 55 metres, *turn left* on Bene't Street, your direction 85 degrees. In 35 metres you pass the **Eagle** pub on your left-hand side and **St Bene't's Church** on your right.

Go right on Free School Lane, your direction 150 degrees. **Corpus Christi College** is on your right-hand side and the **Old Cavendish Lab** is to your left.

In a further 65 metres you come out on to the main road, Pembroke Street, with **Pembroke College** opposite and you *go right,* your direction 245 degrees.

In 100 metres you come to Trumpington Street *where you go left,* your direction 150 degrees. In 15 metres you pass the entrance of Pembroke College. In 35 metres go right on Little St Mary's Lane, your direction 250 degrees, passing **Little St Mary's Church** on your left-hand side. This ends the College Tour.

You are now heading for the railway station. In 80 metres continue straight on, along a narrow lane. In 50 metres, at the T-junction (Granta Place), by the modern Cambridge University Centre on your right-hand side, *turn left,* your direction 150 degrees.

In 50 metres, with the Hilton Double Tree Hotel on your right-hand side, go through the railings and over the cattle grid to *fork left,* with the wall of **Peterhouse** on your left, your direction 130 degrees. (Founded in 1284, Peterhouse is the oldest Cambridge college.)

In 120 metres you pass the **Fitzwilliam Museum** (behind the wall on your left-hand side). In 230 metres go through a metal swing gate **[8]** and *across* the Fen Causeway (A10) to continue straight on, through a metal swing gate and across the **Coe Fen**.

(The **station shortcut** rejoins here.) In 310 metres at a T-junction *go left,* your direction 125 degrees, with a stream on your right. In 190 metres *fork left,* due east, with a wall on your left-hand side.

In 120 metres you come to the A10 (Trumpington Road) where you *go left.*

In 110 metres *turn right* on Bateman Street, due east. In 70 metres you pass the entrance to **Cambridge University Botanic Gardens** on your right-hand side. For the next 450 metres ignore all ways off.

You come to the A640 T-junction, *where you turn right,* your direction 155 degrees. In 55 metres, by the war memorial, *fork left* on Station Road. Ignore all ways off

and in 360 metres you come to **Cambridge railway station**.

Lunch & tea places

Little Rose *7 Orchard Road, Haslingfield, CB23 1JT (01223 870618).* **Open** noon-2.30pm, 5-11.30pm Mon-Thur; noon-11.30pm Fri-Sun. *Food served* noon-2pm, 5-8pm Tue-Sat; noon-2pm Sun. The suggested lunchtime pub. Steaks are served on weekdays and roasts on Sundays, alongside standard pub fare. You should phone ahead to check the pub is still open, since it has closed down at least once in recent years.

Rupert Brooke *2 Broadway, Grantchester, CB3 9NQ (01223 840295, www.therupertbrooke.com).* **Open** 11.30am-11pm Mon-Sat; noon-10.30pm Sun. *Food served* noon-3pm, 6-9.30pm daily.

Red Lion *33 High Street, Grantchester, CB3 9NF (01223 840121, www.redlion-grantchester.co.uk).* **Open** 11am-11pm Mon-Sat; 11am-10.30pm Sun. *Food served* 11.30am-10pm Mon-Sat; 11.30am-8pm Sun.

Green Man *59 High Street, Grantchester, CB3 9NF (01223 844669, www.thegreen mangrantchester.co.uk).* **Open** 11am-11pm Mon-Fri; 11am-12.30am Sat; noon-11pm Sun. *Food served* noon-3pm, 6-9pm Mon-Sat; noon-6pm Sun.

Orchard Tea Garden *45-47 Mill Way, Grantchester, CB3 9ND (01223 551125, www.orchard-grantchester.com).* **Open** *Jan, Feb, Dec* 9.30am-4.30pm daily. *Mar-May, Sept-Nov* 9.30am-5.30pm daily. *June-Aug* 9.30am-7pm daily. The suggested tea stop on this walk. Although touristy, these tea rooms are steeped in history and retain a great atmosphere, keeping them popular with locals and visitors alike. At weekends, the place is packed: if you want a table under the apple trees, you will have to queue – be patient, as the wait is worthwhile.

If you are in need of a cuppa after finishing the college tour, there are numerous options in the city centre of Cambridge.

Walk 27

Milford to Haslemere

Thursley, Hindhead and the Devil's Punch Bowl.

Start: Milford station
Finish: Haslemere station

Length: 18.6km (11.6 miles)

Time: 5 hours 15 minutes. For the whole outing, including trains, sights and meals, allow at least 9 hours.

Transport: Take the train nearest to **10am** from **Waterloo** station to **Milford** (Surrey). The journey takes 50 minutes.

There are up to four trains an hour back from **Haslemere** (journey time 50-60 minutes). Buy a day return to Haslemere.

OS Landranger Map: 186
OS Explorer Maps: 133 & 145
Milford, map reference SU955414, is in **Surrey**, 3km south-west of Godalming.

Toughness: 6 out of 10

Walk notes: A long walk along a road out through Milford is rewarded by the beauty of the landscape beyond. Bagmoor Common Nature Reserve's heathland of purple moss, grass and heather, and woodland of oaks and Scots pine, leads on to the lakes of Warren Mere and across to the village of Thursley, which has a fine old church. The Three Horseshoes pub, closed for a long time in the early 2000s, reopened in 2005. At point [7] below, there is a 300-metre-long fenced path where nettles in summer make you grateful for long trousers. Mainly you are walking through National Trust land, sandy bridleways through ancient established woodlands and the heather, gorse and bilberry of the heathland. Thursley Common suffered from a major fire in 2006, leaving a burnt-out moonscape that is eerie to walk through, although the Common is slowly recovering back to

a more natural state. After walking through the Devil's Punch Bowl, you ascend to its cafe, for a late lunch or an early tea stop. From there you follow the Greensand Way with fine views out towards the South Downs, with finally a footpath into the High Street in Haslemere for tea. Note: the paths at the head of the Punch Bowl may change, as a road scheme due to open in mid 2011 will bury the current A3 in a tunnel while the current busy road becomes a cycle path.

Most of the country walks in this book are as enjoyable when walked alone as they are when walked in the company of a group of walkers. However, due to the bleakness of the commons, this walk is eerily lonely when solitary, so it is best walked in company.

Walk options: Three major variations to the main route are possible.

a) Keeping to the Punch Bowl's rim: After lunch, instead of going down and up through the valley of the Punch Bowl, this route goes along its rim, with a fine view – it is the same length and easier walking. For directions, refer to the Saturday Walkers' Club website (www.walkingclub.org.uk).

b) Gibbet Hill and Sailor's Stone: After tea at the NT cafe, instead of going through the next valley, this alternative heads out to Gibbet Hill (viewpoint) and the Sailor's Stone memorial; after this, the onward route follows the rim of the next valley. It is again an easier route than the main walk, but a little longer. For directions, refer to the Saturday Walkers' Club website (www.walkingclub.org.uk).

c) Shortening the walk: You could order a taxi from Thursley or could catch a bus near the cafe in Hindhead.

History: The **Church of St Michael & All Angels**, Thursley, has heavy-duty wooden roof beams, added in Henry VII's time to support a new tower. Its Saxon windows, up by the altar on the north wall, are the only ones in England with their original timber frames (thin horn or oiled linen was used for window panes).

Legend has it that the **Devil's Punch Bowl** was formed when the Devil scooped up earth to hurl at Thor, the God of Thunder, who lived in **Thor's Lie** (Thursley); the punch bowl refers to the mist that seems to flow over the rim of the bowl.

The **heathlands** here were among the UK's earliest cultivated areas, clearings in the forest that were abandoned as the nutrients leached away into the sandy soil. The spring line between the sandstone top layer and the impermeable clay beneath led to erosion of the sandstone, thus creating the Devil's Punch Bowl.

A sailor in 1786 bought drinks for three men at the pub in Thursley. Later, they were seen murdering him at the

Devil's Punch Bowl. Found guilty, they were hanged in chains on a hill nearby, now known as **Gibbet Hill**. The outraged and doleful headstone erected for the sailor can be read in the north-west edge of Thursley churchyard. There is also a memorial to the sailor, **Sailor's Stone**, near Gibbet Hill.

Only the tower of **St Bartholomew's Church** in Haslemere is ancient, the rest having been boldly demolished by the Victorians. There is a stained-glass window dedicated to the poet Tennyson.

In Tudor and Stuart times, **Haslemere** was a centre for the iron industry. With the coming of the railway in the mid 19th century, it became a popular spot for literary people. The poet Tennyson's house, Aldworth, is on the slopes of Black Down, where he loved to walk, and George Eliot wrote *Middlemarch* in Shottermill.

The town has an interesting **museum** up the High Street, just north of Darnleys tea room. The museum is open 10am to 5pm Monday to Saturday, and has important natural history collections, as well as a fine explanatory display of local wild flowers in the foyer. Other highlights include an Egyptian mummy, Zulu beadwork and Eastern European peasant art.

Walk directions

[1] [Numbers in square brackets refer to the map]

Coming off platform 2 at **Milford station**, exit by the grey gate and cross over the railway line at the level crossing (or use the footbridge) to continue on a tarmac road, your direction 345 degrees, passing the railway station building on your right-hand side. Keep on the road, ignoring all ways off, as you head towards the village of Milford, passing Milford Golf Club on your way, with golf links either side of the road.

In just over 1km at the T-junction, *go right* and in 10 metres *go left* on the main road, signposted Guildford, with

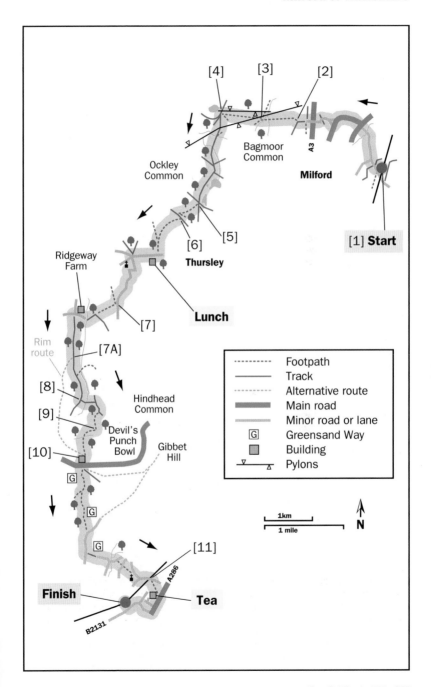

the Co-operative convenience store on the corner to your left.

Ignore all ways off as you walk through **Milford**, going past Whitley Parish Council's offices on your left and a Farmer's Market on your right. In 450 metres, at the traffic light T-junction, where right is signposted to Guildford, cross before *going left* (taking care as there is no pedestrian crossing), your direction now 230 degrees.

In 50 metres you *go right* on Lower Moushill Lane. In a further 225 metres, you pass Moushill Court on your left-hand side.

Stay on this tarmac lane and ignore all ways off (including signposted footpaths and bridleways to your left and right) and in 170 metres you pass Chimneys House to continue on a bridge over the A3. Ignore the public footpath to the right, immediately on the other side of the bridge.

In 100 metres, as the tarmac road becomes an earth road, follow the public bridleway sign straight on. In 70 metres you pass the entrance to Dairy Farm House on your right-hand side and in 25 metres you take a *fork to the right,* a car-wide track that is a public footpath **[2]**, your direction 300 degrees initially.

In 80 metres *go over a stile on your right-hand side* that has a yellow arrow on it (with a wooden fieldgate to its left) to continue straight on, along a car-wide earth track, along the fence of a house on your left-hand side, your direction 315 degrees.

In 225 metres go over two stiles, 2 metres apart (a metal fieldgate to their left) with a wooden pole pylon to your right. Follow the line of these pylons straight on, due west, between fenced-off new plantations of Christmas trees (Norway spruce).

In 220 metres go over a stile to go through a potentially muddy area between streams and then ahead through a waterlogged field. In 130 metres go over a stile and a wooden bridge with railings across a stream.

[!] Beside a three-armed footpath post *continue straight on* across a grassy area with a house away to your right-hand side, ignoring more obvious ways off to the left, your direction 285 degrees. You pass between wooden posts by a sign welcoming you to the **Bagmoor Common Nature Reserve** where you are soon following the line of wooden pylons into the common. **[3]**

Walk along a fern-bordered narrow pathway, at some times of year ill-defined, with birch trees all around until in 500 metres you leave the nature reserve over a grass-covered earth bank, with more Bagmoor Common welcoming signs on either side of the bank, to continue on a not very clear path that follows the line of wooden pylons, avoiding any boggy bits as best you can.

In 300 metres you come to a green sward where the line of pylons bears off to the right. Keep straight on here towards a tarmac road 50 metres further on, with a lake beyond. **[!]** At the road **[4]**, *turn 135 degrees to your left to look back over the green sward, towards a footpath post with yellow and blue arrows, some 40 metres away,* on a compass bearing of 170 degrees **[!]**. Walk to the post and 20 metres beyond it, at a path junction, **[!]** *bear right,* following the direction of the blue arrow, 205 degrees, along a bridleway, which soon has a drainage ditch on its right.

In 200 metres the path *swings to the right* and in a further 60 metres, at a path crossing, you go under pylons, to keep ahead, through heather, to follow a faded arrow on a white disc on a low-level post to your left. In 10 metres cross a broad track and *keep ahead,* your direction due south, towards **Thursley National Nature Reserve**. Continue to follow blue arrows and ignore any ways off for 450 metres, your direction now 200 degrees, along a potentially muddy bridleway with drainage ditches to left and right, until you reach a clearing with an island of trees in the middle, containing a Ministry of Defence training

area warning notice and a Byelaws notice post.

Go straight on for another 10 metres to a pair of wooden posts to the left, one with blue arrows pointing ahead, to join a track coming in from the right. Now keep ahead half left, down a dip and up the other side. In 180 metres is an HR sign on a blue-topped post, and a path joins from the right. Go on down for another 75 metres to another HR sign on a post and keep ahead slightly right, ignoring a bridleway off to the left through a wooden swing gate with a metal fieldgate on its right.

In 140 metres, at a path junction, with a steel-clad warehouse (coloured green) over to your left, *fork right,* your direction 220 degrees, further into the pinewood.

In 150 metres there is a lake 40 metres to your left. In 70 metres, for a pleasant detour to the lake, *fork left,* at a dip in the main path, your direction 165 degrees, to walk beside the lake.

In 190 metres, at the end of the lake and 25 metres before the end of the wood (marked by a fence line – with a house and lake some 250 metres away over to your left), you bear right with the potentially overgrown path until in 80 metres you

turn left to rejoin the bridleway, still with fencing on your left-hand side, your direction 220 degrees. In 75 metres bear left with the path, keeping beside fencing, and ignore a fork to the right.

In 25 metres you pass under mini pylons. In 15 metres, by a post to your left with a faded blue arrow on a white disc, *fork right,* your direction 215 degrees.

In 40 metres you come to a track junction (there is a house visible away to your left). *Go right.* In 20 metres by a post with blue bridleway arrows, *turn left* on a car-wide earth track **[5]**, your direction 190 degrees.

In 30 metres *fork right,* your direction 240 degrees, following a blue arrow on a post. Follow this sandy bridleway, initially uphill, before it levels out, then heads gently downhill. For the next mile you walk through the area of heather, gorse and bracken which was devastated by fire in 2006.

In detail: In 500 metres you come to a bridleway junction with a waymark post ahead. You *turn left* along a broad sandy track, your direction 155 degrees, to keep on this main way, ignoring the fork first left in 5 metres.

In 100 metres **[6]**, *turn right* on to a sandy way by a burnt signpost, your direction 240 degrees. In 40 metres ignore a faint path to the right and keep ahead on a path that descends then starts to go uphill. In 250 metres ignore a path that goes up a hill to your left.

In 125 metres go through wooden fence poles to continue uphill, now steeply, on a sandy way. Keep ahead, steeply uphill, and you soon have the remnants of a fence line to your right. In 100 metres at the top of the hill you pass burnt-out fire paddles on your left-hand side. Continue ahead, now on the level, on a broad track, your direction 220 degrees.

In 400 metres, at a bridleway junction, ignore a footpath post directly ahead with its blue bridleway arrow pointing to the right. **[!]** *Bear left* and in 6 metres cross a wide bridleway *to go straight on, slightly to the left.* In 15 metres pass to the left-hand side of a wooden fieldgate to go onwards, your direction 220 degrees.

In 235 metres you come to a tarmac road T-junction (with the entrance to Foldsdown Cottage on your left-hand side). Here you *go right* to cross the road to the **Three Horseshoes** pub just along on the left-hand side, the suggested lunch stop.

Coming out of the pub after lunch, *turn left.* In 80 metres, by the Old Vicarage, *fork left* on The Street. In 250 metres *turn right* on a signposted public footpath, an earth drive, leading towards Church Cottages, your direction due west.

In 65 metres *go left,* up steps, into the churchyard to visit the **Church of St Michael & All Angels**. Coming out of the church door, go straight on to exit the churchyard by the wooden swing gates (or over a stone step built into the wall, with a two-way footpath sign on its other side) to *go right uphill* on the tarmac road, your direction 245 degrees.

In 15 metres you pass Hill Farm House on your right-hand side. Keeping to the left-hand side of the road, your pavement is parallel and above the road. In 100 metres go through a metal barrier and in a further 100 metres, rejoin the road.

Keep ahead, gently uphill, and in a further 225 metres, you pass Hill House on your left-hand side. In 200 metres ignore a public footpath to the right by a sign for Hedge Farm.

In 35 metres, at a bend in the road, [7] *branch right* to take the signposted narrow footpath, over a stile, your direction 250 degrees, with a field fence on your left-hand side and a hedge on your right.

In 300 metres, having zigzagged with the path (often overgrown with nettles in the summer), go over a stile and continue straight on, now steeply downhill. In 110 metres, having veered left with the path, go over a stile. In 25 metres, cross over an earth road, pass between low wooden bollards and head down to turn right over a bridge over a stream. On its other side, turn left up a car-wide track, quite steeply uphill, your direction 225 degrees.

In 200 metres ignore a fieldgate opening to the left to go straight on, along an earth farm track, now on the level. In 75 metres you pass **Ridgeway Farm** house (marked on the OS map), to continue on its tarmac driveway, now gently downhill. In 135 metres, at a road junction with a sign to Upper Ridgeway Farm pointing to the right, *turn left* on a signposted public bridleway, a sunken path, your direction 175 degrees. In 15 metres ignore an entrance through metal double fieldgates on your right. In a further 15 metres ignore a left turn and a metal fieldgate on your left-hand side to keep straight on uphill on this sunken path.

Ignore ways off as you progress uphill and in 440 metres you pass a National Trust sign on your right. In 10 metres go through a wooden swing gate with a blue arrow on its gatepost and keep straight on, still uphill, your direction 190 degrees.

In 200 metres, as the path levels out, ignore a path to the left. In 125 metres, as the path swings to the right, ignore a fork to the left.

In 10 metres, at a path crossing and by a post with blue arrows on top [7A], *turn left,* downhill, your direction 145 degrees, keeping on this main way.

In 12 metres ignore two ways off to the left as the path swings to the right. Your direction is now 185 degrees. In 300 metres you pass a bridleway down to the left by a part-timbered cottage. Keep ahead, your way now being a car-wide earth track.

In 500 metres, go through a wooden fieldgate, ignore the second wooden fieldgate immediately on your left *and take a kissing gate* beside the third wooden fieldgate on your left [8] to go on a footpath steeply downhill, your direction 105 degrees.

In 70 metres go across a stream on a new wooden bridge with wooden railings and go up the steps on the other side. In 100 metres, at the top, go through wooden posts and *bear left,* with Hindhead Youth Hostel off to your right. Continue uphill on a track with a ditch on your right-hand side, your direction 80 degrees.

In 100 metres join a tarmac lane coming in from your left to *go straight on* (slightly right), your direction now 100 degrees.

In 100 metres you come to the tarmac entrance driveway to a house on your right-hand side and carry on uphill, on a tarmac lane, which swings to the left. In 60 metres take a footpath fork *off to the right* by a post with one yellow and two red arrows on its top, next to a yellow grit and salt bin, your initial direction 185 degrees.

In 45 metres go through a wooden kissing gate (to the left of a wooden fieldgate). Keep to this main path for 800 metres as it meanders and undulates down into the Devil's Punch Bowl. At the bottom of the bowl, with its western escarpment directly ahead, you come to a track junction [9] with a small stump on your left-hand side (its former markings long gone). Here *cross over the junction and bear a quarter right for 15 metres. Now take the left-hand stony path of the two paths uphill,* your initial direction 170 degrees. In 35 metres the path swings right past a single pine tree, your direction now 230 degrees, and the path goes steadily uphill.

In 200 metres the path becomes stepped. In a further 100 metres you reach the top, with the noisy A3 road only 10 metres to your left-hand side (until the completion of the tunnel scheme, *see p205*), *bear right* along a level path, your direction 300 degrees. There are fine views north to the Hog's Back and beyond.

In 150 metres, you go through a kissing gate and 20 metres further on, *fork left*, slightly uphill, your direction 200 degrees. Follow this path out over a grassy area and on to reach the car park, at the far end of which is the **Devil's Punch Bowl Cafe [10]**, a possible early tea stop. Coming out of the cafe keep ahead and cross the A3 with great care at a small pedestrian traffic island.

Cross a grassy area and follow the footpath **[!]** *nearest to the left-hand side* of the Devil's Punch Bowl Hotel, your direction due south. Ignore the more obvious – and signposted – paths to your left.

Follow this broad and often muddy path and in 80 metres, at the end of the fence on your right-hand side, *bend left* with the main path and stay on it, ignoring all ways off. Continue due south, parallel to the back gardens away to your right-hand side, gently downhill, just inside woods.

In 250 metres you pass the entrance gate to The Shieling on your right-hand side and ignore a path to the left, *to follow the direction of the blue arrow on the footpath post, and go straight on* downhill, your direction 130 degrees.

In 95 metres you go through a wooden swing gate and in 110 metres, as you come out to open heathland on your left-hand side, you are joined by a path from behind on your left. Here bear right, gently downhill, your direction 190 degrees.

In 200 metres you come to crosspaths, with a footpath post on your left and with a wooden swing gate and a fieldgate on your right-hand side. Follow the **Greensand Way** arrow straight on,

uphill, on a sandy path, your direction 170 degrees.

In 210 metres cross over a path crossing by a footpath post to keep straight on, going through heather, with a magnificent view of a valley out to the south-west.

In 150 metres, as the path descends, you cross a rough track to continue straight on and, in 20 metres, at another path crossing, with a footpath post on your right, continue straight on, steeply uphill, on an uneven path with a tree-root bed. In 110 metres you cross a path to keep straight on (slightly left), your direction now 170 degrees.

In 145 metres you go through a wooden kissing gate and in a further 30 metres you come out on to a tarmac road with Little Scotstoun House opposite. Here you *go right,* on this road, Farnham Lane.

In 100 metres ignore a bridleway to the right.

In 255 metres you pass the entrance to Thursley House on your left-hand side and *turn left* on a signposted public byway, your direction 130 degrees, passing the entrance to Beech House on your right-hand side.

Head down this access road as it swings to the right. In 95 metres, with the entrance to Pucksfold House on your right, *keep left downhill* along a path in a gully (muddy in winter), your direction 120 degrees. In 150 metres continue straight on, now along a tarmac driveway, with Little Stoatley House on your right.

In 300 metres, having passed Little Stoatley Horse Farm on your left, you swing right with the tarmac way and come out to a tarmac road T-junction, with Anchor House opposite and a signpost on your left, *to go left* on this road. In 40 metres you cross a stream.

In a further 25 metres *you go right* on a narrow public footpath, signposted Greensand Way, steadily uphill, between fences.

In 300 metres you cross a tarmac road to continue on between hedges, the signposted public footpath marked GW. In a further 250 metres you come out on to a tarmac road, with Ventnor House opposite and *turn right downhill,* your direction 130 degrees.

In 180 metres you come to **St Bartholomew's Church**, Haslemere, on your right-hand side. *Keep left* with the road so that the triangular green is on your right-hand side. **[!]**

For a direct route to the railway station and the hotel bar opposite it, you *bear right* here and follow Tanners Lane until you reach the railway station.

On the main route, in 80 metres, you go over the railway bridge. **[11]** In 15 metres you follow the public footpath sign on Pathfields, your direction 190 degrees, on a tarmac path. Ignore all ways off as you pass houses, flats and a community pavilion on your right-hand side.

After 275 metres along this tarmac path, ignore a footpath to the right signposted 'footpath to town'. Bear half left on the path, now between brick walls, your direction 140 degrees.

In 65 metres you come out on to the High Street. Turning left would take you to the **museum**, in 70 metres. Turning right takes you, in 80 metres, to the suggested tea place, **Darnleys** tea room, on the right-hand side (or to other possible tea places or pubs in the same street).

Coming out of Darnleys, *turn right* and in 25 metres *turn right again* down West Street, signposted to the police station.

In 120 metres, where the main street curves to the right past the police station (which is on your right-hand side) take the street *straight on* to the fire station but then not the tempting path straight on; instead, *turn left* in front of the fire station and take the footpath that goes down the left-hand side of the building (signposted 'Footpath to the station'), your direction 315 degrees.

Follow this path, with a stream to your right and later a playground to your left, until you come out on to a tarmac road with Redwood Manor opposite. *Turn left* on this road and, in 40 metres, *turn right* on the B2131, leading in 260 metres to **Haslemere station** on your right-hand

side. The **Metro Cafe** is on your right just before the station and the **Inn on the Hill**, with its bar, is opposite the station. The London platforms (2 and 3) are over the footbridge.

Lunch & tea places

Three Horseshoes *Dye House Road, Thursley, GU8 6QD (01252 703268, www.3hs.co.uk).* **Open** noon-3.30pm, 5.30-11pm Mon-Fri; noon-11pm Sat; noon-10pm Sun. *Food served* 12.30-2.15pm, 7-9.15pm Mon-Sat; noon-3pm Sun. The suggested lunchtime stop, this pub serves a variety of main meals and snacks. The owners request that walkers phone in advance if on a Sunday, when a classic roast is served.

Devil's Punch Bowl Hotel & Restaurant *London Road, Hindhead, GU26 6AG (01428 606565, www.devils punchbowlhotel.co.uk).* **Open** 11am-11pm daily. *Food served* 7-10am, noon-9pm Mon-Fri; 8-10.30am, noon-9pm Sat; 8-10.30am, noon-6pm Sun. An alternative for a later lunch, with the carvery open until 5.15pm.

Devil's Punch Bowl Cafe *London Road, Hindhead, GU26 6AB (01428 608771, www.nationaltrust.org.uk).* **Open** 9am-4pm daily. Allow 80 minutes from this possible early tea stop to Haslemere station.

Darnleys tea room *High Street, Haslemere, GU27 2JZ (01428 643048).* **Open** 9.30am-5pm Mon-Fri; 9am-5pm Sat; 10am-4pm Sun. The suggested tea stop.

Georgian House Hotel *High Street, Haslemere, GU27 2JY (01428 656644, www.georgianhousehotel.com).* **Open** 11.30am-11pm daily. *Food served* noon-2pm, 7-9.30pm Mon-Sat; noon-2pm, 7-9pm Sun.

Metro Cafe *Lower Street, Haslemere, GU27 2PD (01428 651535).* **Open** 6.30am-3pm Mon-Fri; 7.30am-3pm Sat, Sun.

Inn on the Hill *Lower Street, Haslemere, GU27 2PD (01428 642006, http://tmsteaks. co.uk).* **Open** 7am-11pm Mon-Thur; 7am-midnight Fri; 8am-midnight Sat; 8am-10.30 Sun. *Food served* check website for details.

On Haslemere High Street, **Costa Coffee** (no.42, 01428 645479, www.costa.co.uk) is another option for tea.

Walk 28

Chilham to Canterbury

Canterbury Cathedral and the Great Stour River.

Start: Chilham station
Finish: Canterbury East or Canterbury West stations

Length: 17.7km (11 miles)

Time: 5 hours. For the whole outing, including trains, sights and meals, allow at least 10 hours 45 minutes.

Transport: Take the train nearest to **9.10am** from **Charing Cross** station to **Chilham** (journey time 1 hour 35 minutes). For a premium, you can reduce the journey time to just over 1 hour by taking the High Speed Train from St Pancras and changing at

Ashford International. Trains back from **Canterbury East** station to Victoria run twice an hour (journey time 1 hour 35 minutes). Alternatively, return from **Canterbury West** station, where there is an hourly High Speed Train direct to St Pancras (taking less than an hour) and half-hourly services to Charing Cross (taking 1 hour 45 minutes). Buy a day return to Canterbury.

OS Landranger Map: 179
OS Explorer Maps: 137 & 150
Chilham, map reference TR077535, is in **Kent**, 8km south-west of Canterbury.

Toughness: 3 out of 10

Walk notes: This particular pilgrimage to Canterbury starts beside the Great Stour River and its attendant lakes, visits the church and green at Chartham, and passes through hop fields and apple orchards to the suggested lunch pub in Chartham Hatch. In the afternoon the way is through Church Wood and Blean Woods Nature Reserve to the parklands of the University of Kent, with fine views down over Canterbury Cathedral. The entrance to the city is along the River Stour, through the Norman Westgate and down the medieval high street and alleys, entering the cathedral precincts through its ornate Christ Church Gate.

Walk options: There are buses into Canterbury, three times an hour,

from near the Plough Inn in Upper Harbledown. There are also buses into the city from near the Hare & Hounds pub on the A290 and from the University of Kent. The route passes near Canterbury West station on entering the city, for those who wish to go home without visiting the city centre, and there is a suggested shortcut in the walk directions, once you are within the city, to Canterbury East station.

History: Attacked by marauding Picts, Scots and Saxons, the Britons could not defend the walled city of **Durovernum Cantiacorum** once the Romans had abandoned it. When St Augustine and his followers arrived in 397 – at the instigation of King Ethelbert and his

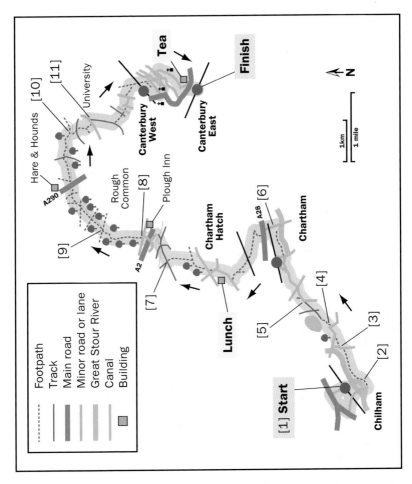

Map legend:
- Footpath
- Track
- Main road
- Minor road or lane
- Great Stour River
- Canal
- Building

Map labels: Tea, Finish, University, [11], [10], Hare & Hounds, A290, Rough Common, [8], Plough Inn, Canterbury West, Canterbury East, [9], Chartham Hatch, A28 [6], Chartham, A2, [7], Lunch, [5], [4], [3], [2], [1] Start, Chilham, N, 1km, 1 mile

French Christian wife, Bertha – the walls were repaired and the overgrown streets cleared. The city was now called **Cautwaraburg**.

The **Cathedral** that St Augustine founded was sacked by the Danes in 1011. It was within the cathedral, on 2 December 1170, that **Thomas Becket**, Archbishop of Canterbury, was murdered by four of Henry II's knights. The city became a place of pilgrimage, as is celebrated by Chaucer in his Canterbury Tales, although these pilgrimages were interrupted in 1538, when Henry VIII had St Thomas declared a traitor. His shrine was pillaged and all references to him were destroyed.

Entrance to **Canterbury Cathedral** (01227 762862, www.canterbury-cathedral.org) is free if you attend evensong, which normally takes place at 5.30pm Monday to Friday, 3.15pm Saturday, and 5.15pm Sunday. Otherwise admission (2010) is £8. The Cathedral is open until 5.30pm in summer, and 5pm in winter.

Huguenots fleeing France after the St Bartholomew Massacre of 1572 settled in Canterbury. The **Weavers' House** in the High Street is an example of one of their high-gabled houses, with loft doors for lifts.

The **Westgate** is the only surviving gateway into the city, built by Archbishop Sudbury before the Peasants' Revolt of 1381. It was used as a gaol. The **medieval wall** around the city follows the line of the 3rd-century wall in Roman times.

The mainly medieval church of **St Peter**, in St Peter Street, may be of Saxon origin.

Walk directions

[1] [Numbers in square brackets refer to the map]
Coming off the platform from London at **Chilham station**, walk through the car park, your direction 340 degrees, and up the tarmac road away from the station. In 50 metres you come to the A28 where you *go left*.

In 80 metres *take the left fork,* the A28 signposted to Ashford (take care here because there is no pavement on this stretch of road).

In 140 metres, just before the Ashford Road service station, *turn left,* your direction 135 degrees, on a tarmac lane to the railway crossing.

In 80 metres cross the railway lines and continue on the tarmac lane the other side.

In 80 metres go on a bridge over a river and bear right with the lane on the other side. In 65 metres you pass **Chilham Mill** on your left-hand side. In 20 metres go over a second bridge, with Setford Lake on your right-hand side. On the other side of the bridge, *go left,* your direction 150 degrees, on a gravel car road. Then, just before a house gate, *bear left* on a path, soon going uphill, with the **Great Stour River** on your left-hand side.

In 80 metres **[2]**, at the top of the incline, by a broken wooden barrier and a post marked with yellow arrows pointing ahead and to the left, **[!]** you turn *left,* your direction 30 degrees, with

the river below you on your left-hand side. Walk along a grassy, car-wide track following the edge of the trees which are on your left-hand side.

In 560 metres, ignore the farm gate ahead. *Bear right,* then in 20 metres *left,* to follow the farm hedge on your left-hand side. In 150 metres you come to the start of the sheds of **Stile Farm** (marked on the OS map) on your left-hand side. In a further 85 metres, go over a stile (a metal fieldgate on its left-hand side) on to a tarmac lane **[3]** where you go left.

Stay on this tarmac lane and in 50 metres, go over a dilapidated stile *on your right* (or through the metal fieldgate to its left), to continue on, a quarter right, your direction 70 degrees, keeping a band of alder and ash trees 40 metres away to your left-hand side.

In 150 metres, where the field narrows, go over the stile ahead of you and keep straight on, your direction still 70 degrees, with the fence of the previous field by your left-hand side. In 150 metres, by a pole with a yellow band at the top, the fence ends and you go straight on across a field, your direction 70 degrees, heading to the right of Pickelden House Farm ahead.

In 160 metres, beside the farmhouse, exit the field through a gate or over the overgrown stile to its left and out on to a tarmac lane where you *go right,* gently uphill, your direction 70 degrees.

In 150 metres **[4]** as the lane swings right, you follow the footpath sign ahead, to go *straight on,* through a wooden fieldgate, with Lake House on your left-hand side, your direction 50 degrees.

In 15 metres ignore the gate on your left and continue straight on, with a hedge on your left and in 40 metres you start going across a vast open field, with lakes away to your left-hand side, your direction 55 degrees. In 280 metres at a path crossing marked by a footpath post, keep ahead.

In 270 metres, you come to a tarmac road **[5]** where you continue *straight on.* In 30 metres you ignore a public footpath to the left. Continue uphill and in 135 metres ignore the Stour Valley Walk sign to the left.

In a further 175 metres, you come to the end of this road (Bobbin Lodge Hill) and cross Shalmsford Street to *go straight on,* down Bolts Hill.

In 170 metres ignore a public footpath sign to the right by the Royal British Legion building.

In a further 200 metres, by Rose Cottage, you ignore the public footpath to the left across the railway line and *continue* with the tarmac road, now Parish Road, towards the church.

In 300 metres go over the river bridge and in 80 metres you follow the right-hand edge of **Chartham** village green, past a timber-framed building away to your left-hand side. At the far side of the green, go into the churchyard of St Mary's, passing the church entrance (the church is open 3-5pm daily, May to September) and keeping on, along a tarmac path. In 40 metres you come to the road by a house called The Glebe where you *go right,* your direction 125 degrees.

In 40 metres, just before the bridge over the river, you follow the Stour Valley Walk sign *to your left,* on a tarmac path, your direction 65 degrees, with the river on your right-hand side. (If you want an early lunch at a pub here, continue over the bridge instead of going left. Pass Chartham Paper Mills on your right-hand side, coming in less than 200 metres to the part timber-framed **Artichoke** pub.)

In 325 metres, where the tarmac ends, go through a gap and onwards, now on a stone and gravel path, with the river still on your right-hand side and a barely visible lake on your left.

In 340 metres, by a derelict bridge on your right-hand side and with a metal kissing gate ahead of you **[6]**, **[!]** *go left* on a grassy car-wide way, your direction 330 degrees. In 180 metres go across the railway lines via metal swing gates on either side.

Continue ahead on a driveway and in 75 metres you go across the A28, to *go left* along its pavement.

[!] In 50 metres a discreet concrete public footpath marker on your *right-hand side* (to the right of the driveway of Carlton Lodge) and a green footpath sign (potentially overgrown) on a pole indicate your narrow path, marked with a yellow arrow, between hedge and fence, your direction 25 degrees.

In 65 metres go through a gap and on, with an orchard on your left-hand side. Keep ahead along an unmarked path at the bottom of the orchard, bearing *left then right,* until in 100 metres you come to a post on your left-hand side, marked with a yellow band. **[!]** Here *turn left,* up between the rows of orchard trees, your direction 315 degrees. At the top of the field *turn right* and almost immediately *left* into a wood, at a footpath sign.

In 150 metres go over a stile to exit the wood. *Keep ahead,* now with the wood on your right-hand side. In 150 metres go over a stile and up over the railway lines. On the other side, swing left and in 20 metres go over a stile on your right, to continue with the field fence on your right-hand side, gently uphill, your direction 305 degrees. In a further 620 metres, go through a gap in the hedge ahead, with a tall aerial mast on your left-hand side, to carry straight on through an orchard.

In 110 metres you exit the orchard over a stile (or through the open gate 15 metres to its left) to come out on to a tarmac road, where you *go right,* uphill – this is signposted the North Downs Way.

In 140 metres you come to the **Chapter Arms** in **Chartham Hatch** on your left-hand side, the suggested lunchtime stop.

After lunch, go straight ahead from the pub door to regain the tarmac road, where you go left, your direction 25 degrees, on New Town Street.

In 150 metres you come to a T-junction where you *go left* on Howfield Lane.

In 35 metres, as the road swings left, take the North Downs Way signposted footpath *straight on,* your direction 355 degrees, between fences.

In 100 metres cross over a tarmac road to follow the North Downs Way sign onwards, up a concrete driveway. In 15 metres you *fork to the right.* In 8 metres you pass a wooden barrier (a metal gate on its left-hand side) to continue on, following the North Downs Way sign, with a playground on your left-hand side and house fences on your right, your direction 60 degrees initially. Keep along the part-enclosed path by the right-hand boundary beside a fence and hedge.

In 145 metres go through a wooden gateway down into **Petty France Wood** (as marked on the OS map), following the North Downs Way arrow and ignoring ways off, initially downhill.

In 310 metres, as the wood comes to an end, [!] take the stile on *your left-hand side* (at the beginning of a line of poplars, also on your left-hand side), to follow a path ahead up and over the top of a hillock, your direction 15 degrees. In 125 metres you pass under mini pylons. Continue ahead, now down the hill, your direction 350 degrees. In 140 metres go over a stile and on two planks over a stream.

In 5 metres you come to a track at the edge of a hop field, where you *turn left, then right,* to follow the left-hand edge of the hop field, your onwards direction 310 degrees. In 110 metres you pass under mini pylons to continue with the field edge on your left-hand side, gently uphill, your direction now 325 degrees, with an orchard now to your right.

In 270 metres you come to a grassy track to your right (there is bridleway off to the left, through a gap in the hedge between fields, marked by a white metal post on the left). **[7] [!]** Take the track to the *right,* your direction 80 degrees, up through the orchard.

In 220 metres, at a crossing of the ways, with a footpath post on your right, continue *straight on,* gently downhill, ignoring ways off, with hop fields and orchards on either side.

In 350 metres you pass industrial sheds on your right. In a further 100 metres you pass primitive staff quarters on your right. Now pass around the right-hand side of a metal gate and *bear left,* your direction 35 degrees, on to a surfaced road. Over to your left behind a hedge are new houses/farm conversions.

In 160 metres you pass the three-storey China Farm Barn on your right-hand side (a residential conversion) to *bear left, uphill,* with the tarmac road.

In 215 metres you come to the A2 bridge, which you cross, ignoring the bridleway sign to the right on the other side.

In 70 metres, at a T-junction, **[8]** take the footpath to the right-hand side of St Mary's Hall, **Upper Hambledown**, your direction 320 degrees, into **Church Wood** (marked on the OS map), with a stream on your right-hand side. (But if you want to get to the pub in Upper Hambledown, turn right on this road, and you come in 110 metres to the **Plough Inn**, which may no longer be open. Just beyond the pub premises is the bus stop.)

In 185 metres you *fork right* to keep near the edge of the wood. In 15 metres you cross a ditch on two planks. In 50 metres you pass a ruined stile. In 300 metres the field away to your right ends and you are walking though a wooded area with heather beside the path.

In 300 metres you reach an earth road T-junction where you *go right,* your direction 75 degrees. In 30 metres ignore the suggestion of a way to your left. In 85 metres, at a major junction **[9]**, *turn left,* your direction 30 degrees, with Scots pine trees on your left-hand side, beyond a ditch.

In 85 metres you ignore a path to the right.

In 270 metres you cross a major car-wide gravel track to continue on, along a car-wide earth way into **Blean Woods Nature Reserve**, your direction 45 degrees.

In 150 metres cross a path to continue on your way, signposted 'Short cut'. In 385 metres you come to a major junction of paths. You go *straight on,* through a lightly wooded area. In 20 metres you

Canterbury Cathedral.

cross a stile, then pass by a redundant stile, to follow a faint overgrown path, *half left,* your direction 50 degrees.

In 100 metres go through a metal fieldgate, *turning right* on a path on the other side, eastwards, with the trees now on your right-hand side. In 110 metres go through a metal fieldgate and cross a ditch on a dozen planks, to continue on with the edge of the wood on your right-hand side.

In 150 metres cross a stile to the right of a metal fieldgate. In 200 metres cross a stile to the left of a metal fieldgate. In a further 100 metres go over a stile to the right of a metal fieldgate and come out on to the A290, where you *turn left.*

In 80 metres (and 50 metres before the **Hare & Hounds** pub), *turn right* on a signposted footpath, down steps, your direction 40 degrees.

Bearing left in 40 metres you pass a scaffolding-pole stile and go through a

wooden kissing gate and in 5 metres fork *right,* your direction 130 degrees, away from the stream to your right-hand side.

In 60 metres *keep ahead, then swing left,* now following a fence to your right-hand side, your direction 100 degrees.

In 220 metres, having had a fence to your right all this way, you go over a wooden bridge with a scaffolding-pole railing and over the stile on the other side, and 10 metres further on you follow along the right-hand edge of the field, your direction east.

In 125 metres you come to a bridge with curvaceous metal railings and an earth road. But you continue straight on, still with a stream on your right-hand side and with a large field to your left.

In 275 metres go over another wooden bridge, to continue on (the right-hand fork), your direction 120 degrees, with the stream still on your right-hand side.

In 400 metres you come to a wooden bridge on your right-hand side with wooden handrails over the stream **[10]**, which you cross *to go left* on the other side, with the stream now on your left-hand side.

In 20 metres pass under the mini pylons. In 10 metres go over a two-plank bridge, ignore a right fork and go *straight on,* gently uphill, following yellow blazes on trees, your direction 160 degrees. In 120 metres ignore a scaffold-and-wooden pole bridge on your left. In a further 40 metres, at a path T-junction, *turn left,* your direction 120 degrees, still gently uphill.

In 120 metres you come to a tarmac road **[11]**, with the **University of Kent** Electronics Department opposite. Go over this road and carry *straight on,* your direction 195 degrees.

In 50 metres you begin to pass the Electronics block (with a large white metal pyramid on its roof) on your right-hand side. Walk ahead through its car park.

20 metres past the end of the block, *fork left* to pass down the left-hand side of the Sports Centre.

35 metres from the start of the side of the Sports Centre, you come to a little windowless hut made of brick on your right-hand side, to pick up a footpath *straight on* (to the hut's left-hand side) into the trees, your direction 145 degrees.

In 90 metres you come to a tarmac road junction. Go straight across and, in 35 metres, with the Kent Union Venue in front of you, you *turn right,* on University Road, following a road sign to Canterbury.

In 150 metres you pass a bus terminus on your right-hand side. In a further 40 metres you have an unobscured view of Canterbury Cathedral visible below on your left-hand side. [!] Here you *fork half left* off the tarmac road to follow a clear path across the grass, heading down halfway between the Cathedral and the road you have just left, your direction 170 degrees. In 10 metres you pass a lone oak tree immediately on your right-hand side.

In 400 metres you cross an earth road to continue *straight on,* diagonally across the grass, on a clear path, your direction 155 degrees. In 200 metres you pass through a gap in the hedges. In a further 30 metres you come on to a tarmac path where you *go right,* your direction 225 degrees. In 20 metres, at a path crossing, *go left* on a tarmac path, between bollards, your direction 120 degrees. In 150 metres, you continue *straight on,* now on Salisbury Road.

In 250 metres, ignoring all ways off, you come to a T-junction (Forty Acres Road) and carry *straight on,* along a signposted public footpath.

In 55 metres pass through barriers and in a further 55 metres you come to playing fields on your left-hand side where you keep straight on, through barriers, with hedges on your left-hand side.

In 85 metres, at the end of the playing fields, go through a metal barrier and follow the tarmac path to the *right,* your direction 175 degrees. In 60 metres go through a tunnel under the railway.

In 50 metres cross a road (The Spires) and go *straight on* along the path

opposite, leading past new houses. In 80 metres join Station Road West and continue straight on. [If you intend to return home from **Canterbury West station** and do not wish to visit the city and the Cathedral, *turn right* on Station Road West: the railway station is some 220 metres along on the right-hand side.]

In 100 metres you come to the main road (North Lane), which you cross over to continue on a tarmac road, past Deans Mill Court on your left-hand side and across a mill-stream bridge.

On the other side *turn right,* signposted Riverside Walk, with the water on your right-hand side.

In 80 metres, ignore the lock bridge straight ahead, to go *right* on an arched bridge. On the other side *turn left,* now with the water on your left-hand side.

In 80 metres you pass the Riverside restaurant on your left-hand side across Guys Bridge. In 80 metres you come to the Westgate, with the Guildhall just beyond and the **Café des Amis du Mexique** opposite. Go *left* through the **Westgate** and *straight ahead* on the pedestrianised St Peter's Street.

In 100 metres, you pass **St Peter the Apostle Church** on your left-hand side. In 75 metres you pass the **Weavers' House** on your left-hand side. (To shorten the walk at this point, continue ahead following signs to Canterbury East station and the bus station, passing the Cathedral entrance to the left-hand side.) You now pass **Patisserie Valerie**, a possible tea stop, on your left-hand side.

In 40 metres the main suggested route is to *turn left* on Best Lane. In 80 metres you pass the Thomas à Becket pub on your right-hand side. In 15 metres you cross The Friars to continue on King Street, then take the first tarmac road left to the old **Blackfriars Gallery**.

At the gallery *turn right* between terraces of houses, through concrete bollards. In 50 metres *pass through* a second set of concrete bollards. In 5 metres, *take the lane sharp right* (Mill Lane), your direction 145 degrees.

In 75 metres you come to a T-junction where you *go left* (despite a sign to the right for the Cathedral), your direction 35 degrees.

In 40 metres you pass the **Old Synagogue**. In 20 metres ignore Knotts Lane to your left. In 40 metres, with the entrance to **Kings School** ahead, *turn right* on Palace Street.

In 170 metres, with the Seven Stars pub away to your right-hand side, *turn left* on Sun Street.

In 70 metres you reach the main entrance to **Canterbury Cathedral**. After visiting the Cathedral – it is also worth walking round the outside, through the cloisters – you come out of the same gate to go *straight on down* narrow Mercery Lane, your direction 220 degrees.

In 50 metres you cross the main street (The Parade) *to go straight on* along St Margaret's Street. [The remaining directions take you to Canterbury East station. For **Canterbury West station**, turn right along The Parade and return to the Westgate, where you cross over the road junction to keep ahead along St Dunstan's Street. In 130 metres turn right down Station Road West. The railway station is some 210 metres along, on the left-hand side.]

In 65 metres you pass Cy's restaurant on your right-hand side. In 70 metres you pass the Three Tuns pub on your left-hand side and go straight on, walking along Castle Street.

In 140 metres, by St Mary's Street on your left-hand side, *you fork left* through the bollards to go through the gardens and the old churchyard, your direction due south. In 60 metres you come to the **White Hart** pub on your left-hand side, the last pub before the station and a suggested refreshment stop.

Afterwards, continue on The Crescent, your direction 210 degrees. In 80 metres, with the remains of the Norman Castle to your right, *turn left,* opposite Don Jon House, your direction 120 degrees, with the flint **city wall** on your right-hand side.

In 35 metres, with the **Dane John Mound** ahead of you, *go up steps* to cross the bridge. **Canterbury East station**, with its snack bar, is directly ahead. For the London trains, go to platform 2 (via platform 1, turning right to go under the tunnel).

Lunch & tea places

Artichoke *Rattington Road, Chartham, CT4 7JQ (01227 738316).* **Open** noon-11pm Tue-Sun. *Food served* noon-2.30pm Tue-Sat; noon-4pm Sun.

Chapter Arms *New Town Street, Chartham Hatch, CT4 7LT (01227 738340, www.chapterarms.com).* **Open** 11am-3pm, 6-11pm Mon-Sat; noon-4.30pm Sun. *Food served* noon-2.30pm, 6.30-9pm Mon-Sat; noon-3pm Sun. The suggested lunchtime pub. In addition to its indoor dining spaces, the pub has covered and open dining areas outdoors. The food menu covers a good variety of light lunches, main courses and specials, including a fish menu on Fridays and Saturdays. Groups of more than eight people should phone to book.

Patisserie Valerie *23 High Street, Canterbury, CT1 2AY (01227 760450, www.patisserie-valerie.co.uk).* **Open** 8.30am-7pm Mon-Thur, Sun; 8am-7.30pm Fri, Sat. A newly opened branch of the London mini chain, good for those who like their gateaux and cakes.

Café des Amis du Mexique *95 St Dunstan's Street, Canterbury, CT2 8AD (01227 464390, www.cafedez.com).* **Open** noon-10pm Mon-Thur; noon-10.30pm Fri, Sat; noon-9.30pm Sun.

White Hart *Waresgate Place, Canterbury, CT1 2QX (01227 765091).* **Open** 11am-midnight daily. *Food served* noon-3pm Mon-Fri; noon-5pm Sat; noon-4pm Sun. The recommended tea stop for this walk. The pub is happy to supply a ploughman's lunch or sandwiches on request.

There is also a friendly **station snack bar** offering hot drinks and snacks, open until 7.30pm daily.

Walk 29

Hassocks to Lewes

The South Downs Way via Plumpton.

Start: Hassocks station
Finish: Lewes station

Length: 18km (11.2 miles)

Time: 5 hours 30 minutes. For the whole outing, including trains, sights and meals, allow at least 9 hours 30 minutes.

Travel: Take the train nearest to **9.20am** from **Victoria** to **Hassocks** (there are also direct trains from

London Bridge). Journey time is about 50 minutes. Trains back from **Lewes** to Victoria run twice an hour (hourly on Sundays) and take 1 hour 7 minutes. Buy a day return to Lewes.

OS Landranger Map: 198
OS Explorer Map: 122
Hassocks, map reference TQ304156, is in **West Sussex**, 9km north of Brighton. Lewes is in **East Sussex**.

Toughness: 4 out of 10

Walk notes: This is an exhilarating walk along the South Downs Way, a ridge of South Downs chalk grassland with panoramic views inland and out to the sea by Brighton. This is also an easier walk, with far fewer ups and downs, than Walk 25 from Winchelsea to Hastings (*see p187*). On the way up to the ridge, the route passes Butcher's Wood and visits a church in Clayton and a still-working Clayton Windmill. On the South Downs Way, you pass medieval dew ponds and an Iron Age fort at Ditchling Beacon. After lunch, down below in Plumpton, you climb back up on to the Downs, before a final walk into Lewes along the River Ouse, then up to the Norman castle and through its gateway into the ancient High Street.

Walk options: From the lunch pub in Plumpton, you could catch a bus to Lewes, but the buses do not run on Sundays (for bus information phone 0871 200 2233). Plumpton railway station is about 3km from the lunch pub.

History: The Saxon **Church of St John the Baptist** in Clayton has 11th- or 12th-century wall paintings and an entrance path whose rippled effect comes from stone quarried from the fossilised bed of a sea or a river.

One of the **Clayton Windmills** ('Jill'), a post mill, with its 1852 'Sussex Tailpole' on wheels for changing direction, is normally open to visitors from 2pm to 5pm on most Sundays from May to September, and also at certain other times; check on www.jillwindmill.org.uk for information.

Ditchling Beacon, once an Iron Age fort (traces of the ramparts are still visible), was a site for one of the beacons that gave warning of the Spanish Armada.

Lewes Castle (01273 486290), and the Barbican House Museum nearby, are open to visitors until 5.30pm daily (last entrance 5pm); admission £6 (2010). The castle was built by William de Warenne, who fought alongside William the Conqueror at the Battle of Hastings.

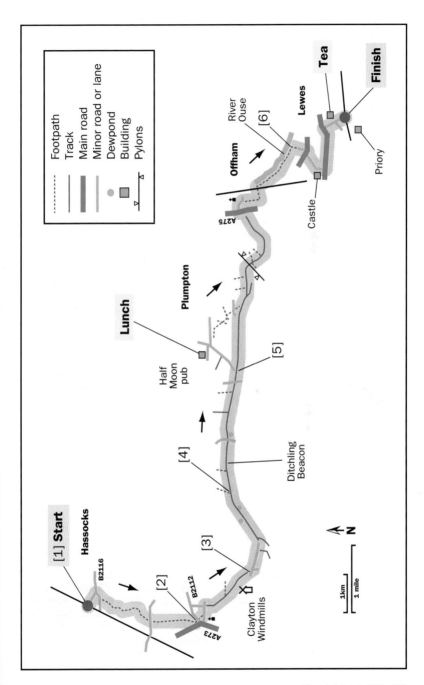

Its towers were added about the time of the **Battle of Lewes**. In this battle in 1264, the rebel earl, Simon de Montfort, with an army of Londoners and 5,000 barons, defeated Henry III, who had two horses killed under him and was forced to seek refuge in Lewes Priory. The Mise of Lewes was signed next day, which led to England's first parliamentary meeting at Westminster in 1265.

The church at **Lewes Priory** was larger than Chichester Cathedral but was demolished during Henry VIII's dissolution of the monasteries. Only ruins of the priory remain.

The churchyard of **St John Sub Castro** ('Under the Castle') has an obelisk commissioned by Tsar Alexander II to commemorate the 28 prisoners of war who were captured during the Crimean War and died in Lewes Gaol in the 1850s.

Tom Paine (1737-1809), author of *Rights of Man*, lived in Lewes, and his political debating society, the Headstrong Club, often met at the White Hart Hotel. He subsequently participated in both the American and French Revolutions.

Walk directions

[1] [Numbers in square brackets refer to the map]
Coming off platform 2 at **Hassocks station**, go down the station approach road, your direction 105 degrees. In 35 metres you pass The Hassocks pub on your left and *take the tarmac path to your right, signposted South Downs Way.*

In 25 metres you come to the B2116 and *go right,* due west, towards the railway bridge but before you reach it, in 40 metres, *go left* on a signed footpath. (An alternative, somewhat more straightforward route is to go past this footpath and after 10 metres turn left through brick pillars on an unmarked path that continues with the railway on your right for 250 metres until you rejoin the main route at **[*].**)

For the main route, go ahead on the first path, your direction 190 degrees. Ignore ways off and in 125 metres you

cross a tarmac road to go on, slightly to the right, following a footpath sign, your direction due south.

In 90 metres you come to a T-junction where you *go left,* your direction 205 degrees with the railway embankment wall on your right. **[*]**

In 150 metres a pleasant detour (unless muddy underfoot) is to go through a gate to your left into the Woodland Trust's **Butcher's Wood** (marked in the OS map) and then to keep on, in the same direction as your previous route. In 250 metres go through a kissing gate to rejoin the previous path. 25 metres after rejoining the route, ignore a footpath to the left.

In a further 150 metres ignore the path on the right, which goes over the railway line.

[2] After 200 metres you leave the wood and can see the Downs ahead with the Clayton Windmills to the left. In a further 400 metres you come to the A273 where *you go left,* your direction 185 degrees. (There is an interesting turreted house to your right on the far side of the main road.) In 25 metres cross the B2112 and go through the stile opposite, heading due south towards the **Church of St John the Baptist, Clayton**. Turn left at the hedge and walk past the back of a building on your left for 10 metres to go through a gap in the hedge on your right on to a road, opposite the church.

Go left on the tarmac road (or, if you visit the church, come out of the lychgate and *turn right*).

In 120 metres *turn right on a signposted bridleway* through a gap with a wooden fieldgate to its right, your direction 185 degrees on a wide track, uphill towards the windmills.

In 150 metres go though a wooden swing gate and continue on the uphill path. When you reach the top of the ridge continue ahead until you reach the nearest, white **Jill Windmill, Clayton**. Its car park is on your right.

Go past the gate giving access to the car park and on to a fenced path along the

left-hand side of the windmill gardens, your direction 130 degrees. Veer right with the path beyond the top, black **Jack Windmill** and cross over a farm track to an earth road T-junction with a signpost. *Turn left,* your direction 115 degrees.

[3] In 120 metres *take the left fork,* your direction still 115 degrees. In 15 metres go through a metal fieldgate.

In 750 metres ignore a bridleway to the right and go straight on through a wooden swing gate.

Continue along the ridge with extensive views both to the left and towards the sea over on your right. In 500 metres pass a footpath post on your left. In a further 100 metres you pass a four-armed sign in a field on the left, pointing onwards to Eastbourne; this is the Keymer post, which also points left to Keymer village. Shortly afterwards go through a wooden swing gate and continue straight on.

In a further 200 metres, go through another wooden swing gate and past

a **dew pond** on your left, then in 250 metres another one on your right. **[4]**

Continue straight on and after 315 metres go through a gate. In 300 metres you pass a footpath post but ignore the path going right and continue straight on. In a further 200 metres you pass a triangulation point over to your right (marked on the OS map).

In 150 metres you reach **Ditchling Beacon**, the site of an early Iron Age fort. There is a car park with a notice about the site and usually an ice-cream van. Walk past the car park to the road, which you cross. Pass through the gate on the far side, following the South Downs Way sign, with a **dew pond** on your right.

In 400 metres ignore a bridleway down to the right and in 50 metres another bridleway to the left. In 160 metres you may be able to see Brighton and the sea beyond it to your right.

Continue for a kilometre. Ignore a path to the left and, in a further 250 metres, cross a tarmac lane and go straight on.

[5] In a further 330 metres you reach a fork on the left where you have a choice: you can go down to the pub in Plumpton for lunch or stay on the Downs. If you do not want a pub lunch, you can continue to walk along the ridge and there are many places where you could stop for a picnic. (One good one is just before the fork, where you can go through a kissing gate to a grassy bank with great views.) If not going to the pub, continue ahead for 1.5km, when you reach a five-way footpath sign at a gate. Go through the gate and continue ahead for about 400 metres to the triangulation point, where you are again on the main route marked [**].

For a pub lunch and the main route, *take the left fork and head downhill* on an unasphalted road, your direction 75 degrees. In 440 metres ignore a bridle-way off to the left and ignore all other ways off.

In a further 370 metres you come to the B2116 and *turn left*. The suggested lunch stop, 40 metres away on the other side of the road, is the **Half Moon** pub in **Plumpton**.

If you do want to reduce the walk at this stage by taking a train from Plumpton, go on the footpath from the top corner of the pub's garden and it will take you all the way to the station.

For the main route, coming out of the pub after lunch, *go left on the B2116*. In 40 metres ignore the bridleway on which you came down before lunch. In a further 50 metres *veer right to pick up the path parallel to the road*.

In 70 metres go over a stile and *half right on a clear path,* your direction 140 degrees, heading towards the Downs. In a further 220 metres go over another stile

and after 80 metres yet another one to enter a wood.

In 20 metres you come to a larger path T-junction where you follow the path arrow right uphill, your direction 140 degrees.

After 65 metres take the left fork. In 150 metres as you go up on the edge of the wood, enjoy the view at the opening to your left and carry on up. After another 150 metres, ignore the footpath marked with a yellow arrow to your left.

In a further 170 metres go through a metal fieldgate and on upwards. In 135 metres you cross a chalk road to go on up, your direction still 140 degrees.

After 80 metres you reach a bridleway and have returned to the South Downs Way. *Turn left,* your direction 100 degrees.

[**] In 130 metres you pass a triangulation point (marked on the OS map) on your left.

Continue on but after 50m, [!] *fork left* on a faint grassy path towards some low trees. After 100 metres the path turns half left and begins to go uphill. At the top of the slope pass a beacon post and then a signpost with blue arrows, both on your right. Continue ahead, due east.

In 450 metres go through a swing gate and continue ahead, your direction 130 degrees. You can now see ahead of you the outskirts of Lewes.

In 250 metres go under pylons and on through a swing gate, your direction 120 degrees.

In 110 metres you come through a belt of trees and in 20 metres you continue in the direction of a cluster of buildings ahead, your direction 155 degrees.

In 50 metres ignore a path to the left and continue on. *Keep the edge of the wood on your left* and ignore all ways off. In 220 metres go through a wooden swing gate and follow the blue arrow ahead, the wood now further away to your left and your direction 120 degrees.

200 metres beyond the gate, ignore a blue arrow on a post pointing into the wood. Continue for a further 200 metres,

keeping to the edge of the wood on your left-hand side to a T-junction. *Go left into the wood,* following the blue arrow, your direction 30 degrees. *In 40 metres, you turn right* on to the main path, your direction 80 degrees.

In 150 metres go through a wooden swing gate and ahead. In 50 metres, ignore a footpath leading to a stile on your right. 60 metres further on, go *through a wooden swing gate on your right* to continue along a chalky road in the same direction as before, 30 degrees.

Carry on for 450 metres until you reach the A275. Here *turn left.* In 50 metres *cross the road and turn right* on The Drove road. In 15 metres you pass the entrance to **St Peter's Church, Hamsey** (the church is usually locked).

In a further 35 metres *take the signed footpath ahead,* going due south. In 180 metres go under pylons. In 25 metres ignore a path to the left. In a further 320 metres *go left through a kissing gate* (a wooden fieldgate to its left) and across a waterway, your direction 95 degrees, with a waterway on your right.

In 280 metres go through a wooden swing gate (with a metal fieldgate to its left). In 20 metres go under a railway line and after 20 metres go through another swing gate.

In 15 metres *turn right to go through a pair of swing gates.* Continue on along the bank of the River Ouse which is on your left. You can now see Lewes Castle ahead of you.

In 150 metres go through a V-stile and continue along the riverside raised path. After 200 metres you pass Old Malling Farm (marked on the OS map) on the opposite bank.

In a further 470 metres you glimpse the 17th-century **St Michael's Church** on the other bank. In another 120 metres, go through a V-stile.

After 230 metres ignore the footbridge crossing the river to your left. Instead, *go right, with a wall on your left.*

In 80 metres you begin to pass a body of water on your right. In a further 80 metres you pass the entrance to Pells Open Air Pool and a children's park on your left. At the end of the park, cross the tarmac road (Pelham Terrace) *and continue up the road in front.* In 80 metres *turn left past the entrance to* **St John Sub Castro Church**. Go right on Abinger Place, towards the Elephant & Castle pub visible ahead.

In 100 metres, with this pub on your right, cross the main road and *continue straight on up along a tarmac lane* (Castle Banks), your direction 220 degrees, with scaffolding-pole railings on your left.

In 80 metres you come to the top of this lane and at the T-junction with The Maltings opposite, *turn right,* your direction 255 degrees. In 15 metres you pass a notice away on your right about the Battle of Lewes and then, under a beech tree, a plaque commemorating Tom Paine. Follow the tarmac lane going around to the left towards the castle, your direction 195 degrees.

In 80 metres you pass the entrance to an ancient Bowling Green, formerly the Castle Tilting Ground on your left. In 25 metres you pass through the **Barbican Gate** and then go past the entrance to Lewes Castle on your right and **Barbican House Museum** on your left.

10 metres beyond these you come to the High Street. (Turning right here leads in 110 metres to the 15th-century Bull House where Tom Paine lived and beyond it on the right the Casbah café). But on the main route, *turn left.*

In 130 metres you come to the **White Hart Hotel** on the right-hand side of the road. A little further up, on the left-hand side, is **Ask** restaurant.

At the traffic lights *turn right* on Station Street. In 110 metres you reach the **Garden Room Café**, the suggested tea place. From there, the road leads straight on to **Lewes station**, visible ahead (platform 2 for trains to London).

But if you have half an hour to spend before the train goes, you might care to

visit **Lewes Priory**. Coming out of the Garden Room Café, instead of going straight ahead to the station, turn right on Southover Road. Pass Garden Street on the left and immediately go left into Grange Gardens and wander through these (parallel to Southover Road) to emerge again on Southover Road at the far end. Then turn left into Southover High Street. At the T-junction turn right, soon passing St John's Church on your left. Then turn left on Cockshut Road, go under the railway line and turn left towards the priory ruins. Pass to their right. Leave the site through a gap in the wall on the right and then follow a wall on your left. After passing a mound on your left, turn left into a path. Then go left over the railway and right to the station.

Lunch & tea places

If you feel like something before lunch, ice-cream is usually available from a van parked at Ditchling Beacon.

Half Moon *Ditchling Road, Plumpton, BN7 3AF (01273 890253, www.halfmoon plumpton.com).* **Open** noon-11pm Mon-Sat; noon-10.30pm Sun. *Food served* noon-9pm Mon-Thur; noon-10pm Fri, Sat; noon-8pm Sun.
This is the suggested lunchtime pub. It welcomes walkers with a Ramblers Menu, but groups of 20 or more should phone ahead to book.
White Hart Hotel *55 High Street, Lewes, BN7 1XE (01273 476694, www.whitehartlewes.co.uk).* **Open** *Café* 9am-6pm daily. *Restaurant* noon-3pm, 6-9.30pm Mon-Thur, Sun; noon-3pm, 6-10pm Fri, Sat.
An alternative tea stop in Lewes.
Garden Room Café *14 Station Street, Lewes, BN7 2DA (01273 478636).* **Open** 10am-5.30pm Mon-Sat.
The suggested tea stop for this walk.

You could also get a coffee on Lewes High Street at the **Ask** (no.186, 01273 479330, www.askcentral.co.uk).

Walk 30
Wivenhoe Circular

To Rowhedge by ferry across the River Colne.

Start and finish: Wivenhoe station

Length: 14.8km (9.2 miles)

Time: 4 hours 15 minutes. For the whole outing, including trains, sights, meals and ferries, allow at least 9 hours 30 minutes.

Transport: The timing for this walk is complicated because of the need to fit in with the varying tide times on the River Colne – for more details on when to walk this route, see **Walk notes** below. To work out the right train to catch, consult the Wivenhoe Ferry timetable. To obtain your own copy of the timetable, write to The Secretary, Wivenhoe Ferry Trust, 1 Trinity Close, Wivenhoe, Colchester CO7 9RA and enclose £1.20 (plus a donation, if you wish). The timetable is also available from Wivenhoe Bookshop by credit card (01206 824050). Or you could phone the Wivenhoe Ferry Trust enquires line, 01206 808704, an answerphone, and one of their volunteers will call you back.

Catch the latest train from **Liverpool Street** station to **Wivenhoe** that will arrive at least two hours before the official printed timetable start of the ferry-operating period (in the example below, by 12.15pm). This will allow you to do the Wivenhoe leg of the walk first,

before catching the ferry. However, if this would mean catching a train that leaves Liverpool Street before 8.45am, then catch the latest train that will get to Wivenhoe at least 5 minutes before the start of the ferry-operating period and catch the ferry straightaway on arrival: do the Rowhedge leg first, on the far side of the river, and the Wivenhoe leg later.

The fare per passenger is £1.50 from Wivenhoe to Rowhedge and £1 for the return; £1 and 50p for the over-60s. This is less than the ferry's upkeep cost and the ferry relies on donations to keep it going.

Allow at least two hours for the Rowhedge leg and leave plenty of time to get back to the ferry before the last crossing back to Wivenhoe. If you miss the ferry back, you could catch a bus or a taxi into Colchester.

Note that on some weekends there is no ferry service due to tide times, so it will not be possible to do the full walk.

The train journey takes about 1 hour 9 minutes.

OS Landranger Map: 168
OS Explorer Map: 184
Wivenhoe, map reference TM036217, is in **Essex**, 5km south-east of Colchester.

Toughness: 2 out of 10

Walk notes: This walk is made up of two loops, one on the Wivenhoe side of the River Colne and one on the Rowhedge

side. However, there is no bridge – you need to take a ferry. This means the full walk is only possible at weekends and on bank holiday Mondays between Easter and the middle of October when the ferry at Wivenhoe is working (although you might be lucky enough to thumb a lift across from a boat at other times). You also need to get there at a time to suit the tides (see **Transport** above). But it is well worth making the extra effort to fit in this unusual walk. Both parts of the walk are about 7km, so allow 2 hours for each.

Wivenhoe, perhaps because of its proximity to the University of Essex, is a remarkable village, bursting with community spirit, with volunteers out there constantly manning the ferry, re-roofing the boat house or washing down the slipways. There are always half a dozen dinghies being made by amateurs in the riverside's Nottage Maritime Institute. From the church and town, the morning's walk is along the mudflats of the River Colne past zones of former dereliction (now in the course of regeneration through new housing), past a £14.5 million flood-surge barrier, and past sand-extraction works and lakes created in old extraction craters. Returning to Wivenhoe, catch the ferry over to the village of Rowhedge.

Rowhedge must be the only village in the UK where swans frequently block the main high street. But having circumvented this fearsome obstacle, you go via the church into a wood controlled by the Ministry of Defence and used on occasions as a firing range. The last part of the return journey is, for us, the highlight of the day: passing the lovely Norman church of St Andrew in Fingringhoe, with its chequerboard design of banded flint, to the former Fingringhoe Mill and on along the John Brunning Walk – mudflats and saltmarshes beside Roman River that are a haven for heron, redshank, lapwing, shelduck, kestrels and barn owls.

Walk options: Both in the morning and the afternoon, shorten the walk or retrace your steps as necessary to ensure that you do not miss the ferry. A shortcut for the morning walk is given in the walk directions (see the asterisk [*] below). It is also possible to do just the first or just the second half of the walk. The printed ferry timetable (see **Transport** above) also contains several suggested shorter walks. Buses from Head Street in Rowhedge leave for Colchester every 15 minutes or so.

History: In the 15th century, the twelfth Earl of Oxford was **Lord of the Manor** at **Wivenhoe**. He and his comrade-in-arms Viscount Beaumont held out in the last castle to surrender to the Lancastrians. They were imprisoned for over a decade. Beaumont later went insane, was looked after by Oxford and died. Oxford then married Beaumont's young wife Elizabeth. The fine brasses to Elizabeth and Beaumont lie in the chancel of the parish church.

In the 1750s there was a **health spa** at Wivenhoe, with fashionable folk taking sea-water baths at a fee of one guinea for the season.

An **earthquake** on 22 April 1884 damaged over 200 buildings, with nearly two tons of brickwork crashing through the roof of Wivenhoe Hall.

The **Nottage Maritime Institute** (01206 824142) in Wivenhoe was founded in 1896 by Captain Charles Nottage to 'improve navigation skills'. It has information on the area's maritime heritage, and welcomes visitors from 11am to 4.30pm daily from late April to mid May, 2-5pm Sundays between mid May and September, and by arrangement at other times.

The **flood-surge barrier** was completed in 1993 and is designed to resist the highest tide likely to be seen in a thousand years. Sluices ensure the tidal flow is unchanged except when the barrier is closed.

The north wall of the **Church of St Andrew** at Fingringhoe dates from

Wivenhoe Circular

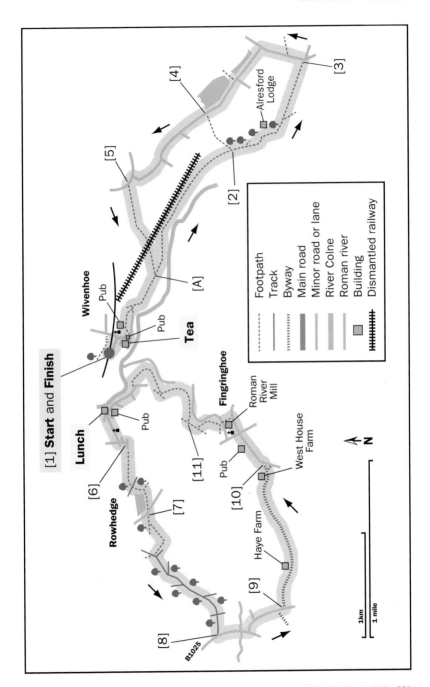

1100. The church originally belonged to a French priory in Mersey and was dedicated to their St Ouen, who was Archbishop of Rouen. St Ouen has since been corrupted to St Andrew. Items hidden within the church at the time of the Reformation have recently been uncovered, including a Trinity crucifix.

Fingringhoe Mill closed in the early 1990s. It was a tidal mill in the 16th century, with a wheel underneath, but was converted to steam in the 1800s.

Walk directions

[1] [Numbers in square brackets refer to the map]

Coming off platform 2 at **Wivenhoe station**, do not go over the bridge but take the tarmac path on its left-hand side, your direction 115 degrees. In 30 metres you pass the Station pub on the other side of the railway tracks. 45 metres further on *turn left, go up steps* to an earth car road, with King Georges Field opposite. Here you *turn right,* your direction 80 degrees, keeping straight on, ignoring ways off.

In 70 metres the road becomes tarmac and you keep ahead, passing a car park with public WCs on your left. In 60 metres, at the High Street T-junction, with the Greyhound pub opposite, you *turn right downhill.* In 85 metres you pass the entrance to **St Mary's Church**. In a further 50 metres, bend right with the main road for 10 metres, to continue down to the banks of the **River Colne**.

The walk on the Wivenhoe side of the river:

Turn left, along The Quay.

In 20 metres you pass the **Nottage Maritime Institute** on your left-hand side and in a further 10 metres the **Rose & Crown** pub.

Continue straight on, along a gravel track next to the riverbank, in 50 metres going over a concrete ramp with a wooden jetty on its right. The route ahead through the former Cook's Shipyard) is now

diverted, permanently – or temporarily until the new residential development is completed.

Turn left up Bethany Street and in 30 metres *bear left* around the **Black Buoy** pub ahead. In a further 30 metres you reach the junction with East Street where you *turn right* down Brook Street. Bear left, then right, down Brook Street and pass St John Road (cul-de-sac) on your right.

20 metres further on, *turn right* along a footpath, left of the Estate Road, with temporary metal barriers on your right-hand side and continue along this diverted footpath as it winds through the Bryant Homes development of Cook's Shipyard. In 200 metres your route continues by the Environment Agency's Colne Barrier Flood Control HQ and the barrier itself.

In 30 metres you are back on the riverbank. In 25 metres you pass the Wivenhoe Sailing Club on your left-hand side. A dismantled railway line runs parallel away on your left-hand side. You walk on the gravel- and stone-surfaced sea-wall path, in 50 metres going through a wooden swing gate and barrier.

In 100 metres ignore steps down to your left **[A]** (this is where the walk rejoins the sea-wall path towards the end of the 'Wivenhoe side' leg of the walk – *see opposite*). In a further 50 metres, you pass the sand-extraction workings on the other bank.

280 metres past these workings, you go through a wooden kissing gate, some 10 metres past a wooden plank seat on your left, and continue on the sea-wall path. In another 280 metres you pass a wrought iron metal bench on your left-hand side. In 270 metres, just as your path is entering trees, ignore a wooden kissing gate to the left. **[2]** (If you want a shortcut back to town, take this path and in 400 metres you come to a lane T-junction where you go left – see the asterisk **[*]** below – rejoining the main walk.)

But continuing with the main walk: The path bears right and you continue ahead, ignoring ways off and in 330 metres you cross a path with a footpath post on your left and continue onwards. In 140 metres *you have a choice of either* forking right on a path (between 8-inch-wide lichen-covered concrete gateposts), your direction 210 degrees, back down to the riverbank, to continue for 200 metres by the riverbank before rejoining the 'upper' path, or just staying on the 'upper' path.

If you have kept on the 'upper' path, continue ahead, ignoring ways off and in 500 metres, with the red-brick **Alfresford Lodge** (marked on the OS map) on your left-hand side, at 50 degrees from you, *fork left* at a path junction through concrete posts, your direction 120 degrees, to continue with a fence and field on your left-hand side. In 125 metres ignore a grassy way to your left. In a further 240 metres, you pass the remnants of a derelict pier on your right-hand side, with abandoned towers with pulleys which once carried overhead conveyors away to your left.

In 100 metres **[3]** *turn left* on an earth car road, your direction 50 degrees. Go straight on, as the road surface becomes tarmac, ignoring ways off, gently uphill. In 170 metres you pass sand extraction works to your left-hand side, and then a giant sand extraction crater to your right. 250 metres further uphill, **[!]** take the signposted public bridleway *left,* by a house called Broomlands, your direction 295 degrees, on a concrete road. In 80 metres go under a red-and-white height-restriction barrier to continue along the concrete road, with a lake away to your right-hand side. In a further 230 metres, **[!]** 5 metres before a pedestrian sign, *fork left,* avoiding Alfreston Lodge Road, to continue parallel to the quarry road, going through a metal fieldgate in 25 metres.

In 190 metres, where your track begins to have hedges on both sides, *fork left* to continue in the same direction, now with the hedges on your right-hand side. In 150 metres **[4]** *turn right* through a wooden swing gate and *turn left* **[*]** to rejoin the

tarmac lane and continue on towards town, your direction 335 degrees.

In 400 metres you go through or around a metal fieldgate; there is a house, Alfresford Grange, to its left-hand side.

In 200 metres ignore a private road to the left. In a further 270 metres, you come out on to a main road where you *turn left,* your direction 305 degrees.

In 110 metres **[5]**, opposite the driveway of a house called The Chase, *go left* through a metal kissing gate, your direction 260 degrees, on a path gently downhill through trees and bushes. In 280 metres go through another metal kissing gate and onwards. In 220 metres go over a stile and turn half right over the disused railway bank and along a grassy path across a water meadow, heading back towards the riverbank.

In 225 metres climb up steps (point **[A]**, *see p232*) and *turn right* back along the sea-wall path and you need to retrace your steps into town, to the Rose & Crown pub. The ferry is 25 metres beyond the pub.

The walk on the Rowhedge side of the river:

Take the ferry to Rowhedge. From its jetty turn left across a green to the **Anchor** pub, the suggested lunch place this side of the river. **Ye Olde Albion** pub is another 100 metres further down the High Street.

To continue the walk: Opposite the Anchor pub, *turn uphill* on Church Street. In 120 metres you *bear left* into the churchyard of the **Church of St Lawrence**.

In 45 metres you pass the church on your left-hand side and in 25 metres you go on out of the church gates on the other side, to continue along Church Hill. In 50 metres, at a road crossing, with house no.17 on your left-hand side, *go left,* due south, on Taylors Road.

In 70 metres you come to a T-junction **[6]** where you *go right* on Parkfield Street. In 50 metres you go through a metal swing gate on a signposted public footpath, *straight on,* with a sports field and a line of trees ('each a living memorial to those in the village who died in the war') on your right.

In 200 metres go through a metal barrier into the wood and onwards, ignoring ways off.

In 60 metres, having swung left with the path, ignore a path down to the left and *bear right.* In another 60 metres, at the start of a wooden fence and houses to your right-hand side, ignore the narrow path down to the left and steps down to the right. Then in 50 metres, by a footpath post, ignore a path to the right and fork left, your initial direction 230 degrees.

In 75 metres you come to a concrete road, with a public footpath signposted right but you go *straight across,* your direction 230 degrees. In 12 metres you pass between two concrete bollards and *bear left.*

In a further 65 metres by a footpath post *fork right* (where going left would lead to a burial ground in 35 metres), your direction 260 degrees. There is a large and rather lovely lake down off to your right-hand side.

In 150 metres you come to a tarmac road **[7]**, *which you cross* and then pass through a wooden kissing gate and into Ministry of Defence land. You nevertheless *continue on,* following the public footpath sign, your direction 295 degrees initially. In 30 metres the path *bears left* and in a further 70 metres ignore a signposted fork to the right and keep on the main path, your direction 240 degrees.

In 220 metres you come to a path crossing where you *go straight on,* along a more minor path, marked by a (possibly overgrown) low post on the left with yellow paint on top, your direction 260 degrees initially, soon swinging left then right.

In 60 metres, at a clearing, you ignore the way your path seems to be going right, to carry *straight on. Bear right* with your main path 35 metres later, your direction 325 degrees. Keeping

straight on, in 50 metres you come to a car-wide earth track and path junction where you *go left* on this track, your direction 265 degrees.

In 30 metres you cross a car-wide track to continue more or less straight on (slightly to your left), your direction 230 degrees and with a fence on your left-hand side.

Ignore all ways off to stay on the main way. In 100 metres ignore a stile on your left and in a further 40 metres ignore a track to the left, to keep straight on. In a further 400 metres, having ignored several ways off, ignore a grassy car-wide *fork left* to keep on your main track. In 145 metres you cross a path (by a sign warning of the Military Firing Range) to keep on the main track. In 200 metres you pass a heavy metal fieldgate, to go out through bollards on to a lay-by of the B1025 **[8]**, *where you go left,* in 25 metres joining the B road. Continue ahead along the left-hand verge of the road and in 200 metres you cross over **Roman River** to go *immediately left* on Haye Lane, signposted Nature Reserve.

In 400 metres, towards the top of the hill, **[9]** with Woodside Cottages on your right, you need to *go left* on a gravel car lane, signposted 'Byway', your direction 80 degrees, in 30 metres passing the entrance to Haye Cottage on your right.

In 320 metres you pass **Haye Farm** on your left-hand side and in 750 metres **West House Farm** (both marked on the OS map).

In 80 metres at a triangular green with a sign in its middle for Fingringhoe, *fork left,* your direction 75 degrees, coming to the main road **[10]** in 35 metres, where you *go left,* your direction 45 degrees.

In 25 metres you pick up a path parallel to (and to the right of) the road, to continue on.

In 150 metres you rejoin the main road to go onwards. In 120 metres you pass the **Whalebone** pub on your left-hand side, to keep straight on to the **Church of St Andrew**, Fingringhoe.

In 100 metres take the public footpath signposted to your *left,* your direction 350 degrees, down the private drive of Mill House. In 125 metres you walk down the right-hand side of **Roman River Mill**, on the tarmac road. At the end of its garden, on the right-hand side, go down steps and over a stile, to go downwards on to the **John Brunning Walk**, your direction 10 degrees, on a grassy path between wire fences.

In 60 metres go over a stile on to a wooden footbridge with two handrails, by Roman River. In 60 metres swing left with the path and in a further 50 metres, ignore the stile to the left, to *keep right* on the John Brunning Way, following its arrows and keeping beside the river.

Ignore ways off. In 200 metres, with a footpath post on your right, ignore the path ahead and *bear right* down to the river, your direction 120 degrees. In a further 200 metres go over a bridge with metal handrails. In 130 metres ignore a signposted fork to the left.

In 70 metres **[11]** *go up three steps ahead* (by a sign saying 'Danger. Proceed with caution'). *Bear right* and in 60 metres at a T-junction, with a warehouse directly ahead, *turn right,* then bear left with the path. In 275 metres you are now back beside the River Colne, and your right of way is straight along the riverbank. After 100 metres you proceed along the edge of a concrete wharf, with warehouses to your left. In 160 metres, at the end of the wharf, **[!]** you see a half-hidden public footpath sign on your right, behind a raised metal water tank. Go down three steps and continue on, with the river immediately on your right-hand side, your direction 280 degrees initially.

In 85 metres, by the entrance to (what was) Northern Wood Terminals Ltd, *go right* on their driveway, your direction 335 degrees, and proceed down the road ahead, in 150 metres passing Ye Olde Albion pub on your left, then on to the ferry in Rowhedge. Take the ferry back to Wivenhoe.

From the ferry back to the station: At the quay in Wivenhoe, if you wish to stop for tea, head for one of the suggested places, then make your way back to Wivenhoe railway station, initially reversing your outward route back to the High Street, then *turning left* on Station Road, in 225 metres, passing the **Station** pub on your left-hand side, with **Wivenhoe station** on your right. The nearside platform is the one for trains back to London.

Lunch & tea places

On the **Wivenhoe** side of the river:

Rose & Crown *The Quay, Wivenhoe, CO7 9BX (01206 826371).* **Open** 11am-11pm daily. *Food served* noon-9pm Mon-Sat; noon-8pm Sun. The suggested lunchtime stop on the Wivenhoe side.
Greyhound *62 High Street, Wivenhoe, CO7 9AZ (01206 825573).* **Open** noon-11pm Mon-Fri; noon-midnight Sat, Sun. *Food served* noon-3pm, 6-9.30pm Mon-Sat; noon-5pm Sun.
Black Buoy *Black Buoy Hill, Wivenhoe, CO7 9BS (01206 822425).* **Open** 11am-11pm Mon-Sat; noon-10.30pm Sun. *Food served* noon-9pm daily.
Station Hotel *27 Station Road, Wivenhoe, CO7 9DH (01206 822991).* **Open** 2-11pm Mon-Fri; noon-11pm Sat; noon-10.30pm Sun.

On the **Rowhedge** side of the river:

Anchor *High Street, Rowhedge, CO5 7ES (01206 728382, www.theanchor-rowhedge.com).* **Open** noon-3pm, 5.30-11pm Mon-Fri; noon-11pm Sat, Sun. *Food served* noon-2pm, 6.15-9pm Mon-Fri; noon-9.30pm Sat; noon-8.30pm Sun. The suggested lunchtime stop.
Ye Olde Albion *High Street, Rowhedge, CO5 7ES (01206 728972).* **Open** 5-11pm Mon; noon-3pm, 5-11pm Tue, Wed; noon-11pm Thur-Sat; noon-10.30pm Sun. No food is served at this former CAMRA Pub of the Year, but walkers are welcome to eat sandwiches if they are buying drinks.

Walk 31

Glynde to Seaford

Alfriston and the Seven Sisters.

Start: Glynde station
Finish: Seaford station

Length: 23km (14.3 miles)

Time: 7 hours. For the whole outing, including trains, sights and meals, allow at least 12 hours.

Transport: Take the train nearest to **8.45am** from **Victoria** station to **Glynde** (change at Lewes). The journey time is 1 hour 27 minutes, longer on Sundays because of poor connections. Trains

back from Seaford generally run twice an hour, again changing at Lewes. The return journey takes just over 1 hour 30 minutes, longer on Sundays – it is quicker at certain times to change at Brighton. Buy a day return to Seaford, which in practice is accepted to Glynde.

OS Landranger Maps: 198 & 199
OS Explorer Map: 123
Glynde, map reference TQ457087, is in **East Sussex**, 12km east of Brighton.

Toughness: 8 out of 10

Walk notes: Near the start, the route goes through Firle Park and then follows the South Downs Way for much of the day, with not as much climbing as Walk 25's arduous route into Hastings (*see p187*), and with marvellous views across the lush valleys to the north and down to the sea. There are three lovely villages to enjoy during the course of the day, all with open churches: West Firle, West Dean and (the suggested lunch stop) the old smuggling village of Alfriston, which likes to call its church a cathedral. There is slightly further to walk after lunch than before it. From Alfriston, the route follows the riverbank through the Cuckmere Valley and through Friston Forest down to Exceat, an extinct village on the edge of the Seven Sisters Country Park, where there is a Visitors' Centre. The Vanguard Way then leads through the Seaford Head Nature Reserve – hoopoe, bluethroat and wryneck have been seen here – to the beach at Cuckmere Haven. This is, in season,

a good enough place to take a dip or just to enjoy a front-stalls view of the white cliffs of the Seven Sisters. Finally, there is a walk along the coastal path and down into Seaford, a seaside town with a long esplanade and reconstructed shingle beach.

Walk options: There are some buses linking Alfriston with Lewes, Glynde, Firle and Seaford. The best option, however, is the frequent bus service from outside the suggested early tea place in Exceat to either Eastbourne or Seaford.

History: **Firle Place** was the seat of Sir John Gage, who helped Henry VIII with the dissolution of the monasteries, despite retaining the old religion himself. During the walk you get a good view of Firle Tower, a watchkeeper's residence. The house itself is open to visitors on Sunday, Wednesday and Thursday afternoons from June to September and also on the Sunday and Monday of the

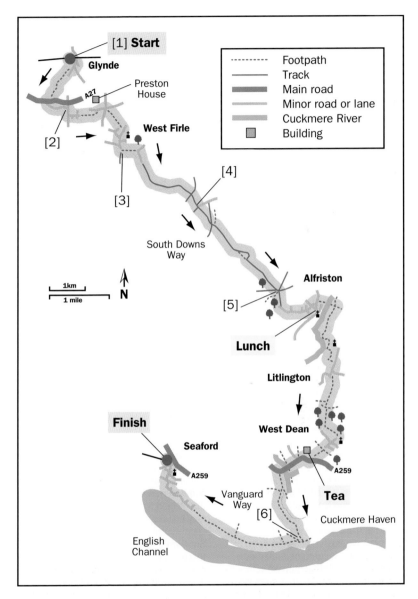

Easter and Spring Bank Holidays, admission £6.50 (2010).

The **Church of St Peter**, Firle, contains an alabaster effigy of Sir John Gage wearing his Order of the Garter and lying beside his wife Philippa. It also has a John Piper stained-glass window in warm colours, depicting Blake's Tree of Life.

Alfriston was once a Saxon settlement. In 1405, Henry IV granted

the town the right to a market, hence the old market square cross (now without its crosspiece), which was supposed to help ensure honest and fair trading. The narrow streets are lined with 14th- and 15th-century houses. In the early 1800s smugglers would run contraband via Alfriston and Cuckmere Haven, with farmers driving their sheep to help cover the smugglers' tracks.

The **Parish Church of St Andrew**, Alfriston – known as the 'Cathedral of the South Downs' – was built about 1360, all at one time and with no later additions. But because there were no local squires and manors the church is rather bare inside, with few memorials. It has a basin and ewer on the Sepulchre at the north side of the chancel that came from the Holy Land.

The **Alfriston Clergy House** (01323 870001) was the first building to be acquired by the National Trust, in 1896, for £10 (which makes the £4.50 entrance fee seem rather steep). A Wealden hall house with thatched roof, it contains a medieval hall and has a cottage garden with some rare specimens. It is open from March to the end of October until 5pm and then to mid December until 4pm (closed Tuesday and most Fridays).

West Dean Church has probable Saxon elements, and next door to it is a medieval parsonage with a colourful garden. The parish priest from 1891 was the Reverend George Lawrance, who believed in captive audiences – it is said that he used to lock the church door before delivering his sermons.

The chalky cliffs of the **Seven Sisters** developed under the sea, 70 to 100 million years ago – the chalk is mainly made up of microscopic fossils. Later the chalk cliffs dipped beneath the sea again and came up covered in silt and sand, still visible as the top layer. There are also layers of flint – the supercooled liquid leached out of chalk to form globules. The Exceat Visitors' Centre has an exhibition on the development of the cliffs and river.

The **Martello Tower**, on the front at Seaford, is the most westerly of a chain of 103 similar fortifications running from Aldeburgh on the east coast. It was built in 1806 against a threatened Napoleonic invasion and now houses the Seaford Museum of Local History. The museum is open on Sundays and Bank Holidays from 11am to 1pm and 2.30pm to 4.30pm (4pm in winter) and also on Wednesday and Saturday afternoons in summer.

Walk directions

[1] [Numbers in square brackets refer to the map]
From platform 2 of **Glynde station** walk up the steps from the station to the road

and turn right across the bridge *over the railway line,* direction 165 degrees.

Curve round to the right with the road past the Trevor Arms pub on your right. 50 metres beyond the pub **[!]**, *just beyond nos.11-16 Trevor Gardens turn right off the road* marked by a half-concealed footpath post with a yellow arrow (Beddingham 1 mile).

[An alternative is to continue on the road to rejoin the route at the asterisk **[*]** below, as one section of the footpath may be very muddy in winter or smothered in high crops in summer.]

Walk down the path with a metal link fence on your left-hand side your direction 260 degrees. In 15 metres you come into a garden where you walk straight ahead along the grass. After 20 metres cross a driveway. Keep straight on and after 50 metres cross a stream over a plank bridge and continue ahead with a hedge on your right and a football pitch on the left.

After 50 metres go straight through the gap in the hedge and walk along the right-hand edge of the field in the same direction.

After 150 metres at a wooden footpath post on the right follow the yellow arrow across the field, your direction 225 degrees. After 400 metres fork left and in another 100 metres you reach a stile with a metal fieldgate to its right.

Cross the stile and turn half left across the field towards the concrete underpass under the A27. Cross it and on the far side walk straight ahead through the farmyard, passing to the left of a telegraph pole. 30 metres beyond the pole you come out on to a minor road.

Turn left down the road, your direction 75 degrees and in 70 metres you pass a white house called Comps on your left. After 450 metres you come to a T-junction (where there is a junction with the A27 on your left). **[2]** *Turn right* your direction 195 degrees. (If you stayed on the road instead of taking the path beyond the Trevor Arms you will come to the A27; cross with care and go straight ahead). **[*]**

In 300 metres *turn left* down the driveway, signposted Preston Court, going due east.

Continue ahead for 190 metres, When the concrete road curves right, you go slightly left to a stile to the right of two painted metal fieldgates.

Cross the stile and *turn three-quarters right into the field,* heading towards a metal fieldgate 200 metres away on the far side, your direction still east.

Go through the gate and walk along the right-hand edge of the field. At the top, go through the small wooden gate (or over it if padlocked) and straight ahead upwards, your direction initially 75 degrees.

In 150 metres, the path, now car-wide, skirts some trees shielding a barn on your left. Follow the path as it bends around to the left and after 80 metres *turn right on to the concrete car-wide track,* your direction 75 degrees.

In 190 metres you pass the entrance to **Preston House** (marked on the OS map) on your left. Continue along the track for another 100 metres to reach the road at a junction.

Cross the road and take the road ahead going half right following the footpath yellow arrow. 50 metres takes you through a white wooden gateway into **Firle Park** with the driveway for **Firle Place** ahead. Immediately through the gate, *turn right off the drive* following a hedge on your right, your direction due south. Off to your left you can see **Firle Tower** on the distant hilltop.

In 100 metres go through a kissing gate and *head half left towards the left of the tennis court ahead* (also to the left of the church), your direction 145 degrees; in summer you may not be able to see these until you get closer. 280 metres brings you to a kissing gate directly to the left of the tennis court, past some young trees.

Once through the gate, go half right towards a car-wide track. Here *turn right* between seven-foot-high walls. In 100 metres you come out on to the roadside with the **Ram Inn** on your right. *Turn left* along the tarmac road into **West Firle** village, heading due south.

In 110 metres you pass Firle Stores and Post Office on your left and *bear right* with the road. 25 metres further on *turn left off the road up the passageway* leading to the **Church of St Peter**, Firle (the entrance is to the right).

With the church entrance behind you, go straight ahead to exit the churchyard and *turn right down the road* your direction 295 degrees. After 65 metres you come to a T-junction.

Turn left, your direction 190 degrees initially, into the private road which has a notice 'Bridleway. No motor vehicles.'

In 85 metres you come to the end of the brick and stone farm building on your left. Keep straight on, ignoring ways off until in 150 metres, at a fork in the paths, *fork to the left,* following a red arrow on a wooden post. **[3]**

Follow the track with a stone wall on your left. After 500 metres there is a stone gateway with a wooden gate to the left. Ignore the path to the right going off through the trees and walk 15 metres further on to a set of double fieldgates with a wooden post on your left with a blue arrow. *Turn right through the gates, down a wide track* following the line of trees on your right towards the ridge ahead, your direction due south. Firle Tower is now much closer, behind and to the left.

Ignore ways off and 550 metres up this track go through the wooden gate to the right of a metal fieldgate and walk straight ahead uphill. After 90 metres, before getting to the top of the hill, the path veers left towards the top of the ridge, your direction 170 degrees initially.

Follow the path uphill for 400 metres as it leads you to the top of the ridge. Make for the fence that runs along the ridge top. On a clear day you can see the sea on your right with Newhaven prominent at 220 degrees and Seaford just visible at 190 degrees.

Turn left and walk along the ridge top, with the fence on your right-hand side going east. You now follow the South Downs Way for the next 5.5km all the way to Alfriston.

In more detail: Go uphill for 400 metres until you come to a wooden gate which takes you through a barbed-wire fence. Through the gate, continue along the ridge-top path. Another 300 metres brings you to the high point of **Firle Beacon** where there is an Ordnance Survey triangulation point marking 217 metres, the highest point you reach on the walk.

Continue ahead for 1km and then go through a wooden gate with a metal fieldgate to its right. In 50 metres go through another similar gate and straight on, parallel to the tarmac road and car park on your left. **[4]**

At the end of the car park go through a wooden gate with a metal fieldgate to its left and carry straight on along a wide flinty track.

After about 1km make for the four-armed post ahead, forking left on a grassy path (and leaving the flinty track 80 metres before it curves away to the right). Continue, following the South Downs Way, to the brow of the hill.

300 metres further on go through a gate and follow the fence on your left, your direction 110 degrees. In less than 1km the path starts to wend its way downhill and you can see the village of Alfriston nestled in a valley down to your left.

[5] In another 350 metres you come to a crossroads and follow the direction of the wooden footpath sign marked 'South Downs Way' straight ahead through the bushes. In another 40 metres your way joins a car-wide track and you continue in the same direction.

Keep on this road, ignoring ways off and, in less than 1km, you come down into the residential street called Kings Ride and keep straight on down the hill to a crossroads.

Go straight over with Alfriston Motors on your left and walk the 100 metres down to the T-junction. Directly opposite you will see the **George Inn**, Alfriston, the suggested pub for your lunch stop. Opposite the George Inn is the **Star Inn**. Some 70 metres further up the High Street, at Waterloo Square, is **Ye Olde**

Smugglers Inn. At the southern end of the High Street is the **Wingrove Inn**. Alternatively for the **Chestnuts Tea Room** turn right when you are facing the George Inn and carry on for 100 metres; after lunch cross the road and go left 80 metres to reach the alley on the right signposted to 'St Andrews Church/ The Tye/War Memorial Hall'. Or for the **Singing Kettle**, turn left when facing the George Inn and continue to the far end of the square; after lunch retrace your steps to the pub.

After lunch at the George Inn, turn left and, after 70 metres, *go left down the alley* following the sign saying 'St Andrews Church/The Tye/War Memorial Hall' and in 35 metres you will come out opposite the United Reformed Church Memorial Hall. Turn half right to reach the green. Ahead you can see the **Parish Church of St Andrew** and, beyond that to the right, the **Alfriston Clergy House**, both of which are worth a visit.

To continue from the point where you came out on to the green, *turn half left* across the grass towards a path to the right of a small brick building (Southern Water). The path curves right to the White Bridge where you *cross the* **Cuckmere River**.

On the far side of the bridge *turn right* through the kissing gate by the wooden footpath sign marked 'South Downs Way Exceat'. There is a sign on the gate saying 'Private land. Access along the riverbank only'.

You now *follow the South Downs Way for a further 5km until the suggested tea place.* In more detail: In 120 metres go through another kissing gate and continue along the raised path with the river on your right-hand side.

The path soon follows the river to the left and in 800 metres it turns sharply left. After 50 metres go through a pair of kissing gates and continue along the river. The path turns to the right and then after 450 metres sharply left again towards the village of Litlington. In 160 metres you reach a kissing gate

on your right. Go through it and continue along the riverbank.

After 180 metres *take the path to the left following the South Downs Way sign,* your direction 120 degrees. (Do not continue straight ahead where a bridge crosses the river to the right.) The path leads through a line of trees into the village of **Litlington**.

In 130 metres you come through an alleyway to the road opposite Holly Tree House. *Turn right,* in 20 metres passing the **Plough & Harrow** pub on your right. 80 metres further on, *turn left* on a road, going up the hill by the side of a house named Thatch Cottage.

In 25 metres **[!]** *turn right* off the road and head for West Dean, following the South Downs Way sign. 5 metres up the path, go though a kissing gate and straight up the path ahead, in 50 metres coming out into an open field. Go up the hill towards the top left-hand corner of the field, your direction 170 degrees and go through a wooden kissing gate.

Go straight on, following the line of the telegraph poles with the hedge on your left. After 260 metres cross a stile, go over a track and cross a second stile to continue following the telegraph poles. The hedge is now on your right.

Continue ahead for 650 metres ignoring ways off and look out for the White Horse on Cradle Hill to your right. At the bottom of the hill you cross a stile to arrive at a T-junction.

Turn left on to a path, your direction 145 degrees. Ignoring ways off, in 110 metres you come to a wooden footpath post. Ignore a blue arrow pointing along the continuation of the path off to the left. Instead, follow the yellow arrows pointing right to steps going uphill. At the top of the steps you come to a crossing of the ways and follow the South Downs Way yellow footpath arrow pointing straight ahead.

Ignoring ways off, continue for 400 metres where the path forks. Take the *left-hand fork,* which is signposted to West Dean and goes quickly into trees.

Again ignoring ways off, continue for 450 metres to a T-junction. Here *turn right* down the hill, your direction 230 degrees, following the footpath post opposite marked 'South Downs Way'. 65 metres down the hill continue straight on, passing a wooden fieldgate on your right. 15 metres further on you come out on to the concrete driveway leading into The Glebe on your right. Continue ahead and in another 45 metres you reach a tarmac lane.

(To visit the fine **West Dean All Saints Church** and **Parsonage** you can detour here by turning left for 100 metres; the church is on your left. Coming out of the churchyard turn right to retrace your steps along the road.)

To continue the main walk, carry straight on down the hill. Another 80 metres brings you down to a junction by the side of Forge Cottage on your right.

Go straight over the road, past the green Forestry Commission sign welcoming you to **Friston Forest** and past the green phonebox on your left. Go straight ahead up the steps of the hill in front of you. At the top of the steps proceed straight on along the path for another 70 metres up to a stone wall where you have a marvellous view over the estuary of the Cuckmere as it meanders its final way down to the sea.

Go left over the wall past a noticeboard on your right about the **Cuckmere Meanders** and through the wooden gate. Go straight down the hill towards the river, your direction 245 degrees. In 150 metres go through the kissing gate at the bottom and down on to the A259.

On your right, set back, you come to the suggested tea place, **Exceat Farmhouse**. You can also go to the **Exceat Visitors' Centre** to view information about the cliffs and river and look at the shepherd's hut on the way to the restaurant.

Coming out after tea on to the A259, cross over the road to the bus stop (for buses to Seaford) and *turn right* along this main road.

In 500 metres the road comes to Exceat Bridge crossing the Cuckmere River. Walk across the bridge with the **Golden Galleon** pub straight ahead of you on the far side. Immediately over the bridge *turn left through the pub car park*. Walk the 90 metres across the car park parallel to the river.

On the far side there is a gate with a yellow arrow on the gatepost next to a wooden fieldgate. Go through the gate, passing a National Trust sign for Chyngton Farm on the left and an information panel on your right. Continue along the path between hedges.

In 270 metres you come to a gate with yellow arrows showing directions ahead and left. Here you have a choice.

Either: For a walk closer to the river, turn left due east and follow the path when after 100 metres it turns right. Continue on the embankment path with the main river channel on your left and a stream on your right until you get to the beach. 20 metres before reaching the shingle, go right on a grassy path and continue to the end of the beach. Rejoin the main route at **[**]**.

Or: To follow the Vanguard Way, go ahead through the gate, your direction due south initially. Ignoring ways off, follow the path for 750 metres to a gate with a wooden fieldgate to its left. Go through the gate and continue along the path in the same direction as before.

In another 800 metres go through a kissing gate to the left of a wooden fieldgate where the path appears to fork and where you can see some cottages on the hillside ahead. Follow the left-hand fork along the edge of the fence to your left.

After 150 metres go through another gate and a further 50 metres brings you down on to the **Cuckmere Haven** beach, where you can have a dip if you are in the mood. There is also a good view to the left of the shoreline of the white cliffs of the **Seven Sisters** with, at the far end, the lighthouse on the top of Belle Tout.

[6] [**] At this point turn right through a gate going uphill behind the cottages which line the seashore, your direction 260 degrees initially. In 150 metres the car-wide track takes you over a cattle grid.

Turn left towards a wooden bench you can just see ahead. You are now on the edge of the coastal cliff and you follow the edge of the coastline all the way to Seaford, taking the main path nearest to the cliffs wherever alternatives appear. After 2km following the coast, the path takes you along the edge of a golf course and soon starts to descend down the hill towards the town. When you get to the brow of the hill looking down into Seaford, again follow the leftmost paths all the way down to the beach.

Walk along the promenade beside the beach. 400 metres along the seafront you come to the **Martello Tower** that is the Seaford Museum of Local History. There are public toilets next to the Tower.

In 350 metres by a pavilion on the esplanade *turn right down the Causeway* heading away from the seafront, your direction 30 degrees. As you walk down this road, you can see the tower of the parish church ahead and to the left.

At the bottom of the road is a mini roundabout with the **Wellington** pub ahead, and to the left of the pub a building with white pillars all along its front, supporting a wooden balcony. Cross over the road and *go left* along the front of this building *and then right* into Church Street.

50 metres up this street you come to a T-junction where you *turn left, going up the hill* and passing the church. Along Church Street you also pass the **Plough Inn** pub, **Trawler's Fish & Chip Restaurant** and other restaurants.

You come to a junction with the A259 at a mini roundabout, with Sutton Park Road to the right and Station Approach Road to the left. *Turn left* for **Seaford station** on your left.

Lunch & tea places

George Inn *High Street, Alfriston, BN26 5SY (01323 870319, www.thegeorge-alfriston.com).* **Open** 11am-11pm Mon-Fri; noon-11pm Sat, Sun. *Food served* noon-

9pm Mon-Fri; noon-9.30pm Sat, Sun. This treacherously low-ceilinged pub, built in 1397, is the suggested lunch stop. Groups of ten or more should phone ahead.

Star Inn *High Street, Alfriston, BN26 5TA (01323 870495, www.thestar alfriston.co.uk).* **Open** 11am-11pm Mon-Sat; noon-10.30pm Sun. *Food served* noon-2.30pm, 6-9pm Mon-Fri; noon-9.30pm Sat; noon-9pm Sun.

Ye Olde Smugglers Inn *Waterloo Square, Alfriston, BN26 5UE (01323 870241, www.yeoldesmugglersinne.co.uk).* **Open** 11am-11pm Mon-Sat; noon-10.30pm Sun. *Food served* noon-9pm Mon-Thur, Sun; noon-9.30pm Sun. Popular with real ale drinkers.

Chestnuts Tea Room *High Street, Alfriston, BN26 5TB (01323 870298, www.chestnuts-alfriston.co.uk).* **Open** 10am-5pm Wed-Sat; 11am-5pm Sun.

Singing Kettle *Waterloo Square, Alfriston, BN26 5UD (01323 870723).* **Open** 10am-5pm daily. *Food served* 10am-4pm daily.

Exceat Farmhouse *Seven Sisters Country Park, Seaford, BN25 4AD (01323 870218).* **Open** *Apr-Nov* 10am-5pm daily. *Dec-Mar* phone for details. Set well back from the A259, the suggested tea place for this walk offers cream teas and other food and drink.

Wellington *33 Steyne Road, Seaford, BN25 1HT (01323 899517).* **Open** 11am-11pm Mon-Thur, Sun; 11am-midnight Fri; 11am-2am Sat. *Food served* 6-9pm Mon-Thur; noon-3pm, 6-9pm Fri, Sat; noon-4pm Sun.

Plough Inn *20 Church Street, Seaford, BN25 1HG (01323 872921).* **Open** 11am-11pm Mon-Thur; 11am-noon Fri, Sat; noon-11pm Sun. *Food served* 11.30am-8.30pm daily.

Trawler's Fish & Chip Restaurant *32 Church Street, Seaford, BN25 1LD (01323 892520).* **Open** 11.30am-2pm, 5-10pm Mon-Sat. Close to Seaford station, this is a superlative fish and chip shop that is popular with locals and walkers alike. It has a restaurant and also does the usual takeaway.

Walk 32

Arundel to Amberley

Arundel Park, River Arun and Burpham.

Start: Arundel station
Finish: Amberley station

Length: 18.8km (11.7 miles)

Time: 5 hours 15 minutes. For the whole outing, including trains, sights and meals, allow at least 10 hours.

Transport: Take the train nearest to **9am** from **Victoria** station to **Arundel** (journey time about 1 hour

25 minutes). Trains back from **Amberley** to Victoria are hourly, with a similar journey time. Buy a day return to Arundel.

OS Landranger Map: 197
OS Explorer Map: 121
Arundel, map reference TQ024063, is in **West Sussex**, 4km north of Littlehampton.

Toughness: 7 out of 10

Walk notes: This South Downs walk requires a relatively early start from London if you want to be in time for food at the lunchtime pub; the distance to this pub in Burpham from the start of the walk is 6 miles, or 2.5 hours of walking.

There are several stretches that are steep (but with excellent views in compensation) and some of the descents on chalky paths can be slippery in the wet or after recent rain. The final leg of the walk, coming down off the South Downs towards Amberley, across the south-western section of Amberley Wild Brooks, should not be undertaken in winter or after periods of heavy rain, as your route over the water meadows is likely to be flooded; instead, take the direct route – **Walk option e)** below – down High Titten to the railway station and the Bridge Inn.

The walk starts and ends along the River Arun. It goes up Arundel's old High Street, lined with ancient buildings, to the Duke of Norfolk's castle. The Norfolk family have been Roman Catholics for centuries, hence you pass the only

church in the UK that is part Catholic and part Protestant (the Catholic part is their chapel, separated off by an iron grille). You pass the Roman Catholic Cathedral then enter the 1,240-acre Arundel Park (the park is closed on 24 March each year, but the public footpaths should remain open on that day). From the Hiorne Tower, you descend to Swanbourne Lake, then go up and through the park to exit it through a gap in the wall, to walk above the River Arun again. The route leads you to the isolated hamlet of South Stoke, with its unusual church. From there you walk beside the river all the way to the village of Burpham, with its church and pub – your lunchtime stop. The afternoon's walk, up, over and down the chalky South Downs, makes a nice contrast to the morning's walk. Amberley is a delightful village with many thatched houses, a pub, tea shop and village store, in addition to its castle and church. Next to the railway station is the Amberley Museum & Heritage Centre.

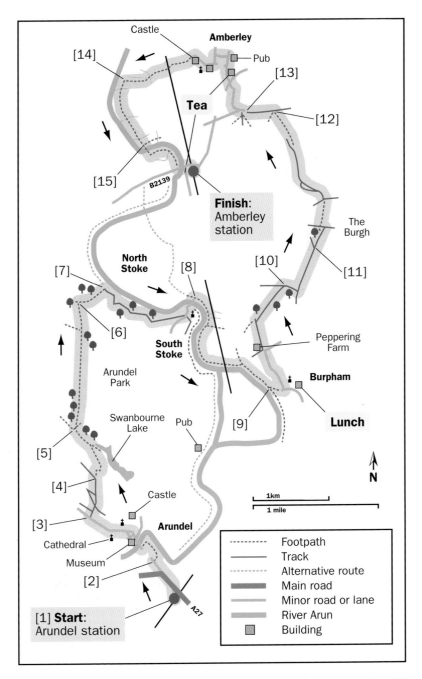

Walk options: There are several opportunities during the walk to cut it short or embark on a different, shorter walk.

Shortening the walk:
a) At point [7] in the directions, on exiting Arundel Park through the tall kissing gate in the wall, instead of turning right, turn left, to follow the path beside the River Arun for the 2.5km to Houghton Bridge and Amberley station, stopping for lunch at the Bridge Inn if you wish. This reduces the walk to some 7.7km (4.8 miles).
b) At South Stoke, instead of crossing the South Stoke bridge, turn right over the stile on your right and then follow the riverside path all the way back to Arundel, stopping for lunch at the Black Rabbit pub. This makes for an easy and pleasant Arundel circular walk of 13.6km (8.5 miles).

c) At South Stoke (point [8] in the directions), instead of turning right over the stile, turn left through the wooden kissing gate, to follow the footpath in a north-westerly direction alongside an old meander of the River Arun (crossing it on a miniature suspension bridge) and up to the hamlet of North Stoke, then along a country lane to Houghton Bridge and Amberley station, stopping for lunch at the Bridge Inn. This reduces the walk to 9.5km (5.9 miles).
d) At the main lunchtime pub in Burpham, you can call for a taxi to take you back to Arundel.
e) Finally, having come down from the South Downs, instead of walking through the village of Amberley before embarking on the home-leg across the Wild Brooks and beside the river, you can take the direct route down High Titten to the railway station. This direct route should be taken in winter and after

August. A full-access ticket costs £16 (2010), but cheaper, restricted-access options are also available.

The lack of labourers after the Black Death in 1349 led to the decay of **St Nicholas Parish Church**, Arundel, which was rebuilt in 1380. There were no pews, but there were stone seats around the side (hence the expression 'the weakest go to the walls'). The building became barracks and stables for the Parliamentarians during the Civil War – their guns laid siege to the castle from the church tower. In 1969, the then Duke of Norfolk opened up the wall between the Roman Catholic and Protestant parts of the church. For ecumenical special occasions, the iron grille dividing them is opened.

The Roman Catholic **Cathedral of Our Lady & St Philip Howard** in Arundel was completed in 1873. Entry is free. St Philip, 13th Earl of Arundel, whose father was beheaded by Queen Elizabeth I, was himself sentenced to death, but died in 1595 after 11 years in the Tower of London, aged 39.

The 11th-century **St Leonard's Church** in the hamlet of South Stoke (population 57) has a thin tower with a 'frilly cap', topped by a 19th-century broach spire with four slatted dormer windows. The church is still lit by candles. Since the last resident Rector left in 1928, the parish has been in the care of the Vicar of Arundel.

A Roman pavement was uncovered in the churchyard of **St Mary the Virgin Church**, Burpham, and parts of the church date from before the Norman Conquest.

Amberley Castle and **St Michael's Church**, Amberley, were both built shortly after the Norman Conquest by Bishop Luffa, using French masons who had been brought over to England to build Chichester Cathedral. The castle, one of three country palaces for the Bishops of Chichester, was considered necessary to defend the Bishops from peasants in

periods of heavy rain, as the Wild Brooks are likely to be waterlogged.

Lengthening the walk:
As a summer extravaganza for fit people who like a very long walk, try returning to Arundel from Amberley on the route of Volume 2's Walk 22 (Amberley to Arundel), making a total circular long walk of some 32km (20 miles).

History: Arundel Castle was built at the end of the 11th century by Roger de Montgomery, Earl of Arundel. The castle was damaged in the Civil War (changing hands twice) and was largely rebuilt in 'idealised Norman' style by Dukes of Norfolk in the 18th and 19th centuries. Parts of the castle – and its grounds and cafe – are open to the public (01903 882173, www.arundelcastle.org) from 10am to 5pm Tuesday to Sunday, Bank Holiday Mondays and Mondays in revolt and from marauding pirates. Today, the castle is an exclusive hotel.

A hundred men once worked at the lime and cement works that now form the **Amberley Museum & Heritage Centre** (01798 831370, www.amberleymuseum.co.uk), next to Amberley railway station. The museum occupies a 36-acre site and is dedicated to the industrial heritage of the south-east. It contains a wide range of exhibits, including vintage modes of transport, tools and telecommunications equipment. The museum is also home to a number of resident craftsmen and craftswomen, working in traditional ways. It is open to the public from mid February to October, 10am to 5.30pm daily; admission is £9.30 (2010).

Walk directions

[1] [Numbers in square brackets refer to the map]
From platform 2 at **Arundel station** go up the steps to the exit on the main road. *Turn left* on this main road to go over the bridge crossing the railway. In 80 metres you pass the access road into the station on your left-hand side. In a further 40 metres you pass Arundel Park Inn on your left-hand side.

In 60 metres cross the busy A-road by the pedestrian traffic lights and turn left to continue down this road. In 50 metres you come to a roundabout where you *fork right*, on The Causeway, signposted Arundel Castle.

In 120 metres **[2]** take the public footpath signposted to the *right*, your direction 65 degrees. In 60 metres go up concrete steps to come to the **River Arun**, where you turn left, your direction 325 degrees, along the top of the bank. Arundel Castle is directly ahead of you, on the horizon.

In 275 metres leave the bank by turning left, on a path between wooden fences. In 8 metres you cross a tarmac drive to go between gateposts and across a parking area, your direction 235 degrees. In 40

metres you come to the main road where you *turn right.*

Go over the river bridge, cross over a mini roundabout and go straight on, up the High Street (the 'no entry' road), with the Post Office on your right. In 60 metres you pass Mill Lane on your right-hand side and in 50 metres you pass the War Memorial on your left. You then pass Tarrant Street on your left and in 40 metres you pass Arundel Museum and Heritage Centre on your left.

Keep on up High Street as it becomes steeper and you pass Maltravers Street

on the left, and then the castle gatehouse on your right. The road now veers left uphill and in 20 metres *fork right*, keeping the castle walls on your right-hand side, heading west, still uphill.

In 90 metres you pass **St Nicholas Parish Church** on your right-hand side. In a further 100 metres, as the road levels out, you pass the entrance to the **Roman Catholic Cathedral of Our Lady & St Philip Howard** on your left-hand side. In 20 metres you pass St Mary's Gate Inn on your left.

The road now swings to the right and downhill, in 125 metres passing St Philip's Catholic School on your left, at the end of which **[3]** you *fork right* off the road, on a path across grass, following the wall on your right-hand side, your direction 340 degrees.

In 70 metres you come to a noticeboard on your left about **Arundel Park**, where you keep ahead, now on a tarmac drive. Ignore the fork on your right to Arundel Estate Offices, and keep ahead up the tarmac drive, with the wall on your right-hand side.

The river and **Arundel Castle**.

In 150 metres go through the wooden kissing gate to the left of the main gates into Arundel Park, with a turreted lodge house on your right. Keep ahead on the tarmac estate road, your direction 10 degrees (or along the top of the bank on its right-hand side, if you prefer).

In 170 metres ignore a road forking to the left and continue ahead. In a further 30 metres, as the road bends to the left, leave it and *turn half right* across the grass and head gently uphill towards **Hiorne Tower [4]** (so marked on the OS map).

In 150 metres, on reaching the Tower, turn 90 degrees right and head for the footpath post (marked by a yellow arrow and a Monarch Way disc), 40 metres away, on a bearing of 50 degrees. At the post, cross a horse ride-cum-training gallop to the fence on your left, from which you can see **Swanbourne Lake** below. *Head downhill,* quite steeply, with the fence on your left-hand side, your direction 45 degrees.

In 30 metres you come down to an earth and chalk car road where you *turn left* to go over a stile, with a fieldgate to its left, your direction 315 degrees. Now continue down this road-cum-track as it swings to the left, then right. Take care during the wet or after periods of heavy rain, as the chalk can be slippery.

The track now swings steadily to the right, downhill, with fine views below to the right and after 450 metres along this track, you reach the valley bottom. **[5]** Cross a major, grassy path junction, with a footpath post on your right and in 10 metres **[!]** *bear left,* steeply uphill, your direction 20 degrees.

In 130 metres you come to a stile and a two-armed footpath sign. Go over the stile and keep straight on (slightly to the left), your direction now 5 degrees, *uphill* on a grassy path.

In 400 metres, still climbing, you come to two oak trees and a two-armed footpath sign on your left. Carry *straight on* (following the direction of the sign)

towards the left-hand edge of the wood ahead, your direction now due north.

In 280 metres, as the way levels out, cross over a stile amongst a cluster of five oak trees, and keep ahead towards the left-hand edge of the wood. In 180 metres your path joins a grass and chalk track coming in from behind and to your right, just before a two-armed footpath sign. Keep ahead along the track, your direction 330 degrees, with the wood to your right.

At the end of the wood on your right, and by a footpath sign, keep ahead down across grass, your direction due north, heading towards a stile. You have fine views of the church in South Stoke on the river to your right (at 85 degrees from you) and three villages lie below you: North Stoke, the closest, on the right; Houghton to its left; and in between and behind these, Amberley, at 40 degrees from you.

In 110 metres cross over the stile, with a wooden fieldgate on its right-hand side) and follow the direction of the footpath sign *downhill*, on another chalky track that can be slippery in the wet.

In 225 metres, at the bottom of the track, at a T-junction **[6]**, follow the footpath sign to the *right,* your direction 110 degrees, on a track, gently downhill.

In 120 metres, as the track swings to the right and by a two-armed footpath sign, follow the sign *left,* with a field fence on your right, your direction 55 degrees, on a narrow path that meanders steadily downhill.

In 225 metres you pass a directional post on your right and continue down, now with the park wall on your right. Pass around a tree in the middle of the path and head more steeply downhill, in 80 metres **[!]** coming to a tall metal kissing gate in the park wall on your right **[!]**, which you pass through to exit Arundel Park.

You are now at a bridleway junction **[7]**, with the **River Arun** some 50 metres ahead and down below you. (Here you have the first opportunity to take a shortcut in your route, by turning left

along the bridleway, to follow the river for 2km to Houghton Bridge.)

But the main walk route is to *turn right* along the bridleway, with the river down below you, over to your left and with the park wall on your right.

In 600 metres you come to a fieldgate and stile, which you cross to keep ahead, following the direction of the two-armed footpath sign. You now come out into the open, with a large field on your right. Follow the line of the fence on your left, downhill and in 220 metres, at the bottom, your path swings sharply to the right, in 35 metres coming to a wooden fieldgate on your left (beside a hidden and overgrown stile). *Turn left* through this (usually open fieldgate, to follow the direction of the footpath sign on your left, along a farm track, on a bearing of 120 degrees.

The track soon heads uphill, with open fields to the right and the river down below, on your left. Some 340 metres along this track (which can be muddy) keep to the main track, passing the first farm buildings over to your left.

In 100 metres you come to an earth road **[!]** where you *turn right,* your direction 145 degrees, with a wall on your right, following the direction of the two-armed footpath sign. (Note: do not take a shortcut across the farm yard to the road – the farmer gets cross with walkers who do not follow the footpath.)

You pass the Gothic-style **Chapel Barn** on your immediate left. 65 metres along the path you reach a tarmac road, where you *turn left,* your direction 55 degrees. Pass **South Stoke Farm** on your left (marked on the OS map). In 70 metres at a minor road junction take the left fork, due north. In 60 metres you pass on your right house no.38 (which used to be an inn), with a postbox in the front wall, and then come to the entrance to **St Leonard's Parish Church, South Stoke**, well worth a visit. After visiting the church, retrace your steps to the road and continue onwards, now on a gravel car-wide track.

In 150 metres, just before the new bridge over the River Arun, ignore the stile on your right. **[!]** (Unless you plan to do an Arundel Circular walk, in which case cross over this stile and follow the riverbank path back to Arundel, stopping at the **Black Rabbit** pub for lunch.)

The main route is to *cross* the new bridge. 5 metres from its end **[!]** you have a wooden kissing gate on your left and a stile on your right.

(**[!]** For a direct, shortcut route to Amberley station, go through the kissing gate, to follow the path to North Stoke, then a lane to Houghton Bridge.)

But the main route is to *turn right* over the stile **[8]** to follow the River Arun, on the path on top of the riverbank, your initial direction 115 degrees, with the river on your right-hand side and the railway line over to your left.

Ignore all ways off, go over two stiles (either side of a coppice) and after some 1.3km cross the railway lines by stiles at either end (with a recently renewed superstructure to the railway bridge over the river on your right). Continue alongside the river.

In 270 metres go over a stile to the left of a new metal fieldgate, cross a builder's access road (built to renew the railway bridge) with a building ruin on your left, and in 15 metres go over a stile to the right of a metal fieldgate, your direction 170 degrees.

Continue ahead beside the river and in 300 metres, go through a new metal swing gate and **[!]** *fork left* **[9]** on a narrow path that heads uphill, your direction 130 degrees. In 90 metres, at a two-armed footpath sign, you *fork left* (not right per the sign), your direction now 55 degrees.

Follow the path uphill beside a wooden fence, coming out on to a car road by the start of houses and, some 150 metres from the path fork, you come to the **George & Dragon**, Burpham, the suggested lunchtime stop.

Coming out of the pub door, turn right, due north, pass to the left of Burpham House and go through the gateway of

St Mary the Virgin Church, which is worth a visit.

Coming out of the church, go *sharp right* through the churchyard, your direction 345 degrees, to exit the churchyard through a metal swing gate. Cross a grassy area with young pine trees to come out on to a tarmac road where you *turn right,* your direction 330 degrees. You have a good view of Arundel Castle, on the horizon over to your left.

In 400 metres you come to **Peppering Farm** (so marked on the OS map) and a tarmac road T-junction. Follow the public bridleway sign *straight on,* your direction 350 degrees, passing barns and sheds on your left-hand side.

Head downhill, then uphill, on a car-wide track with grass down its middle, initially between hedges, then with a large open field on your left. After 400 metres, the track descends and swings to the right. In 70 metres ignore a stile to the left and, in 65 metres, ignore another stile on the left, with a chalk cliff on your right-hand side.

You are now on a grassy track at the bottom of an escarpment, above you on the right, and with a wire fence on your left and water meadows beyond. In 120 metres you pass under mini pylons. In a further 350 metres, with a metal fieldgate and stile directly ahead of you, and by a three-armed footpath sign on your right, **[!] [10]** *turn right* over a stile *to go up steps,* steeply uphill, on a narrow path, your direction 100 degrees.

Go up all 196 steps, after which the gradient of the path becomes less steep, and before long begins to level out, now with an open field on your left. Some 135 metres from the end of the steps you come out on to a bridleway (a flint and chalky car-wide track), with a metal fieldgate on your right.

Turn left on the track, your direction 20 degrees, along the top of the **South Downs**. In 600 metres **[11]**, at a crossing of tracks at an angle, and by a three-armed footpath sign, *cross over* and *keep ahead* (slightly to the right), your direction 30 degrees, now on a car-wide grassy way, gently uphill.

In 150 metres, with a three-armed footpath sign on your right, leave the track **[!]** to *go left* on a possibly overgrown footpath, due north, into trees and brush. In 60 metres, by a four-armed footpath sign, cross a bridleway to continue straight on through brush.

In 30 metres you come out into the open and continue on a grassy, car-wide path, due north, with open fields on your left and a high hedge with blackberry bushes on your right. In 300 metres you come to a four-armed footpath sign, to cross an earth road and *continue ahead* (slightly to the left) on an earth road, with grass down its middle, your direction 350 degrees, downhill.

In 75 metres go through a metal swing gate to the right of a metal fieldgate, and head steadily downhill. In 300 metres, at the bottom of the combe **[!]**, *fork right* to go due north across grass, over a grass track, in 65 metres going through a wooden swing gate to the left of a metal fieldgate, by a two-armed bridleway sign.

Turn left, your direction 290 degrees, on a usually very muddy car-wide earth track, which meanders steadily uphill. In 150 metres you come out into the open and continue uphill, your direction north, following a muddy way by a fence on your left. In 210 metres go through a wooden gate with a metal fieldgate to its right-hand side, and keep onwards, now more gently uphill, with the fence still on your left and with open fields on your right.

In 10 metres ignore the farm track to your left and keep ahead. In 285 metres leave your main earth track, which continues ahead and to the right and take **[!]** *the left-hand fork* beside the fence on your left, your direction 320 degrees.

In 180 metres your way merges with a major farm track from behind and on your right-hand side, with a three-armed footpath sign on your left, and in 60 metres your way is joined by a track from behind and on your left-hand side. There is a pond below you, also to your left, and

Downs Farm (marked on the OS map), off on the other side of the valley.

In 50 metres the track swings to the left through a pair of metal fieldgates, then in another 50 metres you go through another pair of metal fieldgates as the **South Downs Way** joins you from the right. **[12]** Now keep ahead (left) on the South Downs Way. In 50 metres, as the track swings left towards the farm by a three-armed footpath sign, **[!]** *fork right,* your direction 280 degrees, to head downhill, on a narrow path between fences, with the village of Amberley visible below on your right-hand side.

In 240 metres go through a wooden swing gate. In 50 metres you drop steeply down to a tarmac lane where you *go right,* your direction 320 degrees. The lane swings to the left and in 100 metres you come to a lane junction. **[13]**

For the direct route to Amberley station (recommended when the Amberley Wild Brooks are waterlogged, or if it is getting dark and or you wish to get to the railway station in a hurry), take the *left fork,* down High Titten. In 600 metres, at the junction with the B2139 road, *turn left,* and in 400 metres you come to the access road to the railway station on your left-hand side.

But continuing on the full walk route, which takes you through Amberley village and over the water meadows of Amberley Wild Brooks: At the lane junction take the *right-hand fork* (Mill Lane), downhill on tarmac road, your initial direction due west.

In 400 metres you cross the busy B2139 road to go straight on into Amberley Village.

In 170 metres, having passed a school on your right, you come to **Amberley Village Tea Room** on your right-hand side (a possible tea stop). In 20 metres ignore the road to your left and keep ahead, gently uphill. In 50 metres you pass the **Village Store & Post Office** on your right-hand side. In 35 metres you pass the **Black Horse** pub on your right-hand side (another possible refreshment stop).

Turn left by the pub along the tarmac road, your direction due west, walking past thatched cottages on both sides. In 100 metres ignore a footpath sign to the right beside the Thatched House (a track which heads north across Amberley Wild Brooks) and keep ahead. In a further 100 metres you pass the thatched Old Place House on your right-hand side and, at this T-junction, you turn right, your direction west, passing the front of Old Place House.

In 60 metres you pass the Pottery on your left-hand side. In a further 110 metres you may wish to enter St Michael's churchyard. Exit the churchyard by the entrance you came in and continue along the tarmac road, now downhill.

In 80 metres you are below the walls of **Amberley Castle**. In a further 100 metres continue ahead, now on a footpath below the castle walls on a path between fences, your direction 260 degrees. At the end of the walls above keep ahead along the path, now in the open, in 160 metres going over stiles across the railway lines, to continue onwards, with Bury Church visible ahead.

In 210 metres go over a stile to the left of a metal fieldgate, and head a quarter left, following the yellow arrow on the footpath post. In 120 metres cross another stile to the left of a metal fieldgate and keep ahead, across water meadows. In a further 130 metres go over a stile and across a stream and head for the raised path beside the River Arun, directly ahead.

In 150 metres you come to the raised path **[14]**, where you turn left along the top of the riverbank, by a three-armed footpath sign, with the river to your right, your initial direction 220 degrees.

Keep ahead on the path on top of the bank as it sweeps to the left in a semi-circle. In 550 metres cross a stile and keep ahead. In another 550 metres cross the substantial South Downs Way footbridge **[15]** and, on its far side, turn left along the riverside as the path now swings to the right.

In 550 metres you come to the B2139 road and go left over the bridge, **[!]** taking

great care as there is no pavement and the narrow road is quite busy. On the far side of the bridge is a lane on your left, leading to the **Riverside Café**, a possible tea stop. Ahead and on your right-hand side is the **Bridge Inn**, another possible refreshment stop.

Continue ahead along the road, go under the railway bridge and in 40 metres turn right up the station access road, uphill, passing **Amberley Museum & Heritage Centre** on your left, with **Amberley station** on your right. Cross the footbridge for trains back to London.

Lunch & tea options

George & Dragon Inn Main Street, Burpham, BN18 9RR (01903 883131, www.georgeanddragoninnburpham.com). **Open** noon-3pm, 6-10.30pm daily. Food served noon-2pm, 6-9pm daily. The suggested lunch stop is a pub with an extensive menu of quality main courses, (fairly expensive) specials and substantial snacks. It is a very popular place, so booking is advised at weekends and on Bank Holiday Mondays, although in summer it is usually possible to find space at an outdoor table. There are also some benches outside the churchyard where you can sit with a picnic and a pint.

Amberley Village Tea Room The Square, Amberley, BN18 9SR (01798 839196, www.amberleyvillagetearoom. co.uk). **Open** Mar, Oct 10am-5.30pm Sat, Sun. Apr-Sept 10am-5.30pm Mon, Tue, Thur-Sun. Stop for tea here if you are doing the full walk through Amberley.

Black Horse High Street, Amberley, BN18 9NL (01798 831700, www.black horseamberley.co.uk). **Open** noon-11pm daily. Food served noon-3pm, 6.30-9pm Mon-Thur; noon-3pm, 6.30-9.30pm Fri; noon-9pm Sat; noon-8.30pm Sun.

Bridge Inn Houghton Bridge, Amberley, BN18 9LR (01798 831619, www.bridge innamberley.com). **Open** 11am-11pm Mon-Sat; noon-10.30pm Sun. Food served noon-2.30pm, 6-9pm Mon-Sat; noon-4pm, 5.30-8pm Sun. Serves coffee, tea and alcoholic drinks, as well as good-value meals.

Walk 33

Mortimer to Aldermaston

The Roman town of Calleva.

Start: Mortimer station
Finish: Aldermaston station (or Theale station for the extended walk)

Length: 14.8km (9.2 miles)

Time: 4 hours. For the whole outing, including trains, sights and meals, allow at least 8 hours.

Transport: Take the train nearest to **10am** from **Paddington** to **Mortimer**, changing at Reading (journey time 45-50 minutes). Trains back from **Aldermaston**, changing at Reading for Paddington, are hourly (every two hours Sunday). Journey time is 1 hour. On the extended walk, **Theale** has twice as many trains, including (Mon-Sat) an hourly direct service to Paddington.

Buy a day return to Mortimer. In practice this is usually accepted on the return journey, but you might be required to buy a single from Aldermaston (or Theale) to Reading.

This is not a good walk for drivers, as the two stations are on different lines. You could do it by changing at Reading West, but you might have a long wait for the connection.

OS Landranger Map: 175
OS Explorer Map: 159
Mortimer, map reference SU673641, is in **Berkshire**, 10km south-west of Reading. Aldermaston is also in Berkshire. Silchester and the Roman town of Calleva are in **Hampshire**.

Toughness: 3 out of 10

Walk notes: From St Mary's Church in Stratfield Mortimer, the route follows a clear stream – Foundry Brook – to the amphitheatre and the 2.5km of Roman walls surrounding the 107-acre site of the Roman town of Calleva Atrebatum, and the whitewashed 12th-century church at its entrance. The lunch stop is at a pub on Silchester Common, and the afternoon route is mainly through woods of Scots pine and commons of gorse bushes and birch trees. Aldermaston, the teatime destination, is reached over the weirs of the River Kennet.
Walk options: There are buses about every hour on Saturdays from near the

lunchtime pub in Silchester, going to Mortimer (15 minutes) or Reading (50 minutes).

The walk can be extended by nearly four miles to Theale along an enjoyable canalside path, making a total walk of 21km (13 miles).

History: The layout of the **Roman town of Calleva Atrebatum** has survived intact, having been completely abandoned when the Romans withdrew from Britain (the Saxons hated walled towns). However, all the buildings, carefully excavated, have now been reburied to protect them from vandals and the elements. Only the town walls and the **amphitheatre** are visible. The amphitheatre was built in about AD 50, with space for up to perhaps 9,000 spectators. It would have been used for public executions and shows with wild animals, but only sparingly for gladiatorial contests, since gladiators, dead or alive, were expensive. The town walls required some 160,000 wagon-loads of flint and bonding stones, and were built in about AD 260 as part of a general move to protect the Roman Empire from growing unrest. Many exhibits from Calleva are displayed in Reading Museum. The tiny Calleva Museum, half a kilometre beyond the site, closed in 2006.

The earliest part of **St Mary the Virgin Church, Silchester**, dates from about 1125, its walls built with reused Roman bricks. There are two Roman temples underneath the church and graveyard. John Bluett may have contributed to the building of the church, as the price of escaping a vow to join the Crusades. Records show that the church had half a dozen rectors in 1349; most were probably killed by the plague, although one was removed for 'trespass of vert' (taking timber from Pamber Forest).

Walk directions

[1] [Numbers in square brackets refer to the map]

Coming off the London train on platform 1 at **Mortimer station** *go over the footbridge* to exit the station. *Turn right* and, in 50 metres, at a junction (where to go right takes you over the railway bridge), *go left,* your direction 315 degrees. In 70 metres follow the road over **Foundry Brook**. Bear left at the roundabout, *to head towards the church.*

In 70 metres you pass the Cinnamon Tree Indian restaurant on your right-hand side. In 165 metres, by a two-armed byway sign, turn left, your direction 210 degrees.

In 75 metres you pass the lychgate entrance to **St Mary's Church, Stratfield Mortimer** (probably locked), on your right-hand side. In 25 metres you

cross Foundry Brook again and go straight on, with a tarmac drive on your right.

In 35 metres go through a gap in the fence (with a metal fieldgate to its left-hand side) and *turn right, following a yellow arrow footpath sign,* your direction 235 degrees, with the field fence – and soon the banks of the brook – on your right-hand side. Stay on the path following the yellow arrow signs.

In 400 metres turn right, *crossing the brook* by a footbridge with metal railings and *then immediately go left on the other side,* now on a path with the brook on your left-hand side. In 200 metres you pass a wooden platform bridge on your left.

In 230 metres *turn left through a metal gate* (with footpath markers on the far side), your initial direction south, then follow the path along the left-hand side of the field by the edge of the brook. In 365 metres go through a gate and over a ditch on a wooden-planked bridge.

In 100 metres do not go through a gate on your left, but turn right, following the yellow arrow to the right, still with the brook on your left-hand side, your direction 310 degrees. Follow the path as it curves gradually to the right, following the sweep of the brook for 320 metres. Go through a kissing gate in the far corner of the field and on to a path through a copse. In 35 metres you come to a tarmac road [2] *where you turn left, over a bridge,* your direction 230 degrees.

In 400 metres ignore a road to the right and keep straight on, past **Brocas Lands Farm** (as marked on the OS map).

In 200 metres *leave the tarmac road (which veers left) and go straight on, along an earth road,* your direction 250 degrees. In 200 metres, where this earth road bears left, *follow the footpath sign straight across a large field towards pylons,* your direction 275 degrees.

In 450 metres, before going under the pylon cables, *turn left* towards a stile in the hedge, 55 metres away, due south. *Go over the stile* and downhill towards a stile in the valley (which may initially be obscured by crops), your direction 190 degrees. (You are

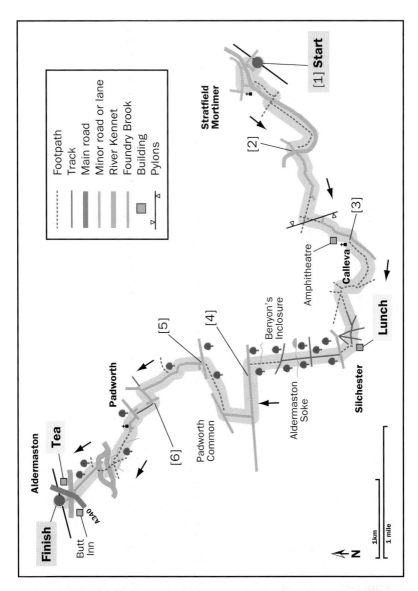

Map legend:
- Footpath
- Track
- Main road
- Minor road or lane
- River Kennet
- Foundry Brook
- Building
- Pylons

[1] Start

Stratfield Mortimer

[2]

[3]

Calleva

Amphitheatre

Benyon's Inclosure

Lunch

Silchester

Aldermaston Soke

[4]

[5]

Padworth

Padworth Common

[6]

Tea

Aldermaston

Finish

Butt Inn

A340

1km
1 mile

N

heading towards the left of a timber-framed thatched house on the hillside opposite.) In 45 metres you pass under the pylons.

In 80 metres go on a two-plank bridge over a stream and over the stile the other side. Once over the stile, continue in the same direction, aiming about 100 metres to the left of the timber-framed house.

In 175 metres, the footpath leaves the field through a concealed exit in the hedge and rejoins the earth road you left earlier. *Turn right uphill,* your direction

205 degrees. (If you miss this exit, continue up the left-hand side of the field towards a vehicle barrier and join the earth road there.

In 85 metres you pass the entrance driveway to the thatched house (The Mount). Keep forward and in 90 metres, although your onward route is straight on, *detour right on Wall Lane,* your direction 340 degrees, and *immediately go through the wooden kissing gate on your right-hand side,* to visit the **Calleva amphitheatre** (next to The Mount).

Retrace your steps and *continue on the tarmac road you were on previously, southwards.* In 100 metres ignore a road to the left and carry straight on, your direction 215 degrees, on Church Lane. In 80 metres you come to the **Roman walls of Calleva** and a pond on your right-hand side. To the right is the entrance to **St Mary the Virgin** church in **Silchester. [3]** Before visiting the church, you might like to go up to the Roman walls to read an information panel about the history of the site.

Coming out of the church, *turn left and then left again* to head south-west on a path through the churchyard, leaving it through a wooden swing gate. *Veer left* to continue on a path along the top of the Roman walls.

In 85 metres go down steps, but at the next gap in the wall go back on top again.

You could continue along the top of the walls for the next 1km to the West Gate, but the suggested route is to come down at the next gap (after 300 metres) and continue below them. On this route there are information panels about the South Gate and the earlier **Iron Age** settlement (whose ramparts are visible in the field on your left after a further 300 metres). For the final 350 metres the path winds through woodland, still with the Roman walls on your right and now a wide ditch down on your left. Eventually you go through a wooden swing gate at the site of the West Gate.

Turn left here and go through a second gate on to a wide path signposted to Silchester Village, your direction 285 degrees, with a hedge on the left and fence on your right.

In 135 metres ignore a stile on your right-hand side. In a further 200 metres, continue through a wooden side gate alongside a fieldgate. In a further 350 metres you go past a green wooden hut, which was the Calleva Museum. Continue across a tarmac lane and along a gravel track.

In 60 metres you come to *another tarmac road and cross over it to continue on a path.* In a further 120 metres, you come to a gravel path, with Silchester Primary School on your right-hand side. *Turn left on to the path and in 20 metres keep left, your direction 190 degrees, and cross the common.* In 250 metres you reach the **Calleva Arms**, the suggested lunchtime stop.

After lunch, *retrace your steps across the common, your direction due north from the pub.* You pass a pavilion on your left-hand side. *Turn left on to the car park beyond the pavilion and take the exit at the far end leading into a copse* (ignore a turning left into playing fields) and in 30 metres you are back at Silchester Primary School. *Turn left, with the school fence on your right-hand side,* your direction due west.

In 30 metres, at the end of the school fence, do not take the forest track to the right of the fence, but keep ahead on a more substantial bridleway, your direction 265 degrees. In less than 100 metres **[!]** *fork right on to a faint path,* into a landscape of gorse and silver birch. In 80 metres your way is joined by another path from behind, on your left-hand side. Continue forward, your direction 30 degrees.

In 100 metres, you come to a *tarmac road. Cross the road and continue on an earth car-wide road,* past a wooden fieldgate, into **Aldermaston Soke woods** (as marked on the OS map), your direction 5 degrees. Heather Brae House is on your right-hand side. Go straight on through these woods, mainly of Scots pine, ignoring all ways off.

In 1.6km **[4]** you come out on to a tarmac road.

(The original route continued ahead for 750 metres across what was Burnt Common and then Padworth Common,

Silchester.

but much of this area has been lost to gravel workings. For a time it was possible to use a diverted public footpath and temporary paths around the disused gravel pits, but these have become overgrown and difficult to follow. The detour around this area involves an unavoidable amount of road walking.)

Turn left on to the road, your direction 265 degrees. In 650 metres *turn right* into Chapel Lane. Walk up Chapel Lane for 200 metres to reach another road with a red postbox on your right.

Turn half right here along the road, your direction 40 degrees. In 400 metres (just before a 50mph sign), *turn half right past a metal barrier* on to Padworth Common and take the signposted public footpath, your direction 60 degrees.

Follow this wide grassy path for 500 metres, ignoring ways off, until you reach a road. Cross over the road-side ditch on wooden planks and *turn left,* your direction 250 degrees.

In 65 metres **[5]** you come to Birch Cottage and *take a signposted bridleway to the right,* marked 'The Croft', your direction 350 degrees, along a rough road.

In 50 metres ignore a turn to the left (to the Croft, House & Stables). In a further 80 metres you pass the thatched Yew Tree Cottage. In 300 metres, with a pond on

your left-hand side, *keep left,* avoiding a driveway ahead. In 35 metres you pass the Croft Cottage on your left-hand side and continue straight on. In 45 metres *veer right with the main path,* your direction 345 degrees, keeping a hedge on the right.

In 270 metres ignore a path on the right and keep straight on, slightly to your left, your direction 320 degrees. In 30 metres a high fence of barbed wire starts on your right-hand side, guarding a buried BP petrol depot.

In 340 metres you come to a *tarmac road where you turn left,* your direction 235 degrees, uphill. In 65 metres you pass the entrance drive to the Jubilee Day Nursery on your left-hand side, where an unofficial path alongside the wire-mesh fence should allow you to avoid walking on the road.

Either way, in 240 metres **[6]**, where the road bends left, *turn right on to the gravel drive to Upper Lodge Farm,* your direction 345 degrees. Keep straight on this public footpath, your direction due north, continuing on a grassy track between a fence on your left and woodland on your right.

In 300 metres go through a fieldgate to come out on to a *tarmac road, opposite Padworth College.* Turn left on this road, your direction 225 degrees.

In 80 metres *turn right on to an earth road, which is a signposted footpath* to Padworth Church, your direction 315 degrees. In 80 metres, in front of the lychgate, *follow a path to the left,* your direction 280 degrees.

In 50 metres you come to a tarmac road where you *turn right and continue forward* with fields on both sides, your direction 300 degrees. In 60 metres *turn left,* your direction 250 degrees, towards five small concrete mushrooms. *By these mushrooms, turn right, on a signposted footpath,* your direction 335 degrees.

In 65 metres go over a stile (a metal fieldgate on its right-hand side) and through a potentially very muddy, horse-churned field, with the fence on your right-hand side. In 190 metres you pass a redundant stile and take the left fork, your direction 290 degrees.

In 210 metres go over a bridge with metal railings and onwards, your direction 295 degrees. In 160 metres, by a four-armed footpath sign, go on three planks over a stream and straight on.

In 100 metres go through a wooden swing gate and on to a bridge over **River Kennet** Weir. You then cross several other bridges in quick succession (passing a notice about the Salmon Pass Project, which allows fish to get past the weirs) and continue on a path between fencing.

You come out *on to an earth car road,* by a three-armed footpath sign where you *go left,* your direction 310 degrees. In 400 metres you pass the Rudolf Steiner **Alder Bridge** centre. In 130 metres you come to a lock and the main road.

At this point you have four choices. You can stop for tea at a pub, go directly to Aldermaston station, stop at the Kennet & Avon Canal Trust's Information Centre for tea, or continue past it along the canal for a further 6.5km (4 miles) to finish in Theale.

If you are going to the **Butt Inn** for tea (open from 6pm), you *go left,* your direction 210 degrees, coming to the pub in 120 metres. Afterwards, retrace your steps to this point.

Take the road over the bridge, your direction 355 degrees.

If you are going to **Aldermaston station**, *turn left on to Station Road,* your direction 320 degrees. In 60 metres fork right, signposted **Aldermaston station**. In 120 metres you need to cross over the footbridge to platform 1 for trains to Reading (where you can get a cup of tea while changing trains) and onwards back to London.

If you are going to the **Canal Trust's tea room** or **continuing along the canal to Theale**, *turn right on the path to the left of the canal,* signposted to Padworth Bridge. In 80 metres you reach the Trust's Information Centre, which has a tea room. After tea, retrace

your steps for Aldermaston station, or *continue straight on* for Theale.

After 2.5km on the towpath on the northern side of the canal, you reach **Ufton Bridge**, where you swap to the southern side of the canal.

Thence you continue along the towpath or paths across fields beside the canal for another 3.5km, passing a number of locks, including Sulhamstead swing bridge and lock.

When you reach *Sheffield Bottom swing bridge, turn left over the bridge into Station Road.* Do not overshoot: there are some white cottages immediately in front of you when you reach this bridge.

Proceed down Station Road. **Theale station** is over the bridge on your right.

If time permits a tea stop, go past the station and on over the bridge, over a roundabout and underneath the A4 until you reach the **Crown Inn**, or use the convenience store almost opposite (about 400 metres from the station).

Lunch & tea places

Calleva Arms *London Road, Silchester, RG7 2PH (0118 970 0305, www.the calleva.com).* **Open** 11am-3pm, 5.30-11pm Mon-Thur; 11am-3pm, 5.30-11.30pm Fri; 11am-11.30pm Sat; noon-11pm Sun. *Food served* noon-2pm, 6.30-9pm Mon-Sat; noon-2pm, 7-9pm Sun. Staff appreciate advance warning for groups at this suggested lunchtime stop.

Butt Inn *Station Road, Aldermaston, RG7 4LA (0118 971 2129).* **Open** noon-3pm, 6-11pm Mon-Sat; noon-10.30pm Sun. *Food served* noon-2pm, 6.30-9pm Mon-Sat; noon-3pm, 6.30-8.30pm Sun. One possible tea stop.

Kennet & Avon Canal Trust Information Centre *Aldermaston Wharf, Padston, RT7 4JS (0118 971 2868).* **Open** 9am-6pm Tue-Sun. The tea room here is the suggested tea stop.

You can also visit the pub or buffet on the Reading station platform while waiting for a connection on the return journey.

Walk 34

Balcombe to East Grinstead

Wakehurst Place, Priest House and Weir Wood.

Start: Balcombe station
Finish: East Grinstead station

Length: 17.2km (10.7 miles)

Time: 5 hours. For the whole outing, including trains, sights and meals, allow at least 9 hours.

Transport: Take the train nearest to **9.40am** from **London Bridge** station to **Balcombe** (journey time 40 minutes); on Sundays, the service is from Victoria (journey time 50 minutes). Trains back from **East Grinstead** go to Victoria and are half-hourly (hourly on Sundays); journey time 55 minutes. Buy a day return to Balcombe. East Grinstead is on a different line and, in theory, you could be asked to pay for a single back to East Croydon of the return journey, but in practice a Balcombe ticket seems to be accepted.

This walk is not recommended for car drivers unless you are prepared to take a taxi back to your car, as there is no convenient public transport link (train or bus) from East Grinstead back to Balcombe.

OS Landranger Map: 187
OS Explorer Map: 135
Balcombe, map reference TQ306302, is in **West Sussex**, 7km south-east of Crawley.

Toughness: 6 out of 10

Walk notes: This walk has a fair number of relatively gentle uphills and downhills, but is well worth the effort. It starts in the old village of Balcombe, passes Balcombe House, and then goes through the woods and by the lake of Balcombe Estate, up to a farm that can be extremely muddy in wet weather, to reach the National Trust gardens and Tudor mansion at Wakehurst Place around mid morning. From there, the route passes through further woods to the Priest House Museum, Norman church and the lunchtime pub in West Hoathly, the second-highest point in Sussex.

After lunch, the route is through Giffard's Wood, then past the Stone Farm climbing rocks (sandstone rocks formed from the bodies of plants and invertebrates, and used as shelters in Mesolithic and Neolithic times), leading to the shoreline of the Weir Wood Reservoir and nature reserve (home to the great crested grebe, heron and osprey). The very energetic could at this point detour to the National Trust estate at Standen. The route finally reaches the station via a walk along a stream and through potentially very muddy fields that mark the outer edges of East Grinstead.

The **Bluebell Railway** (01825 723777) is nearby, and it would be possible to combine the first half of this walk with a trip on a period train hauled by a steam locomotive. You would need to take a taxi to Horsted Keynes for the train journey to Kingscote station. The company is planning to restore the final section of line to East Grinstead, but at present there is a bus service (sometimes a period omnibus) to convey passengers into the town.

Walk options: There is a bus service (not Sundays) about every two hours from the shelter outside the Cat Inn in West Hoathly to East Grinstead and (in the other direction) to Three Bridges station, which is on the same line as Balcombe.

History: The poet **Shelley** lived for a time in Balcombe's Highley Manor. The present queen was a bridesmaid at a wedding in Balcombe Church before the war. **Balcombe House**, privately owned, was part-gutted by fire in 1995.

Wakehurst Place (01444 894066) dates from Norman times, but the Tudor manor house with its sandstone walls was built in 1590 by Sir Edward Culpeper, a distant relative of the Nicholas Culpeper who published a famous herbal compendium in 1651. The gardens (managed by the Royal Botanic Gardens, Kew) are divided into geographical themes, such as Himalayan, Chinese and North American; plants and trees suited to high altitude and extra rainfall can be grown here (Wakehurst Place won a £10 million lottery award for its seed-bank plans). Admission (2010) is £10.75, but National Trust members have free admission to the gardens. Opening hours are 10am to 6pm daily, March to October and 10am to 4.30pm daily, November to February (the place is closed for Christmas).

The timber-framed **Priest House Museum** in West Hoathly is managed by the Sussex Archaeological Trust. Admission (2010) is £3.50. The house and garden are open from 10.30am to

5.30pm Tue-Sat and noon-5.30pm Sun, March to October (also Mondays in August and Bank Holidays).

St Margaret's Church in West Hoathly has a magnificent coffin-shaped chest, probably 13th century, which was used to collect money for the Crusades; it also has a brass memorial to Ann Tree, the last woman to be burned at the stake in England. There are fine views from the terraced churchyard, which is well worth a visit.

The **Cat Inn** once had a tunnel under it, which a past murderer is said to have used to reach the pub for refuge. There is also a well under one of the rooms, which can be seen through a circular glass panel in the floor.

Walk directions

Note: *There is a circuitous route at the outset to avoid walking along a main road, but this involves going down some steps that are very slippery in wet weather. If you would rather avoid these steps, leave the station by the main exit and turn left on to the main road, heading north; in 350 metres, turn right into Bramble Hill and continue the directions at* [*] *below.*

[Numbers in square brackets refer to the map]

For the main route: [1] Coming off the train from London at **Balcombe station**, go over the footbridge and down the platform on the other side. Exit to the right just before the tunnel, then go through the car park, due south. Where this approach road meets the B2036, *take the signposted footpath to the right,* downhill and heading south-west. Go down the steps carefully and across two stiles to a lane.

Turn right on to this lane, due north initially. Continue along it for 600 metres, back past the station on your right-hand side, under the railway line and steeply up to the main road.

Cross diagonally over the B2036 and [*] continue straight on up Bramble Hill,

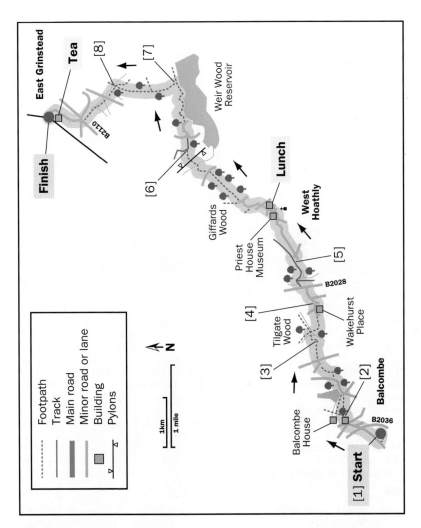

signposted with an arrow to the Tea
Rooms, your direction 40 degrees.

Go up into the village, past the
Balcombe Tea Rooms on your left,
to the crossroads. *Take the second turning
on the left,* passing the Half Moon Inn
on your left-hand side. At the end of
this road is a gate marked 'Balcombe
House. Private'.

[2] *Turn right along a signed footpath,*
your direction 60 degrees. In 100 metres,

by a two-armed footpath sign, *go
through the kissing gate on your left-
and side* and take the path to the left,
your direction initially 10 degrees,
with **Balcombe House** to your left.
Go down the field, staying close to the
left-hand field edge and later following
the path into an overgrown area (if
you stray to the right here, you will
eventually come to a corner of the
field with no exit).

At the end of the field, go through a wooden kissing gate and continue ahead into the woods. After 100 metres, you come to a three-armed footpath sign and *turn right,* your direction 120 degrees. Follow the footpath signs, ignoring other turn-offs. You are walking parallel to stream below you and twice in quick succession you cross a small stream by footbridges. Follow the well-worn path, with **Balcombe Lake** glimpsed below through the trees. Soon you are walking near the edge of this lake (which connects with Ardingly Reservoir). The path swings round to the right to head due south.

A stile takes you out of the trees and into a field. Follow the barbed-wire fence on your left-hand side. In 100 metres, by a three-armed footpath sign, *take the footpath sharply to the left,* over a stream and a stile, your direction 70 degrees. At the far side of the field, by a four-armed footpath sign, bear left on to the tarmac lane, with the lake on your left-hand side and a stepped waterfall on your right, your direction 60 degrees. The lake, which belongs to the Balcombe Estate, is said to be good for fishing: pike and bream in winter; carp, bream, tench and roach in summer.

Carry on up this farm lane. 400 metres beyond the lake, you come to a two-armed footpath sign on your left-hand side. *Take the footpath to the right,* your direction 100 degrees (for what can be an extremely cow-churned muddy stretch in wet weather).

Cross over the stile and go along the left-hand field edge. In 200 metres you come to a fieldgate and stile on your left, with a two-armed footpath sign. Go over the stile, your direction due north, and up past the large cow barn on your left-hand side. Go over the stile and turn half right, following the footpath sign, with the field hedge on your right-hand side, your direction 50 degrees. At the top you come to a three-armed footpath sign and rejoin the farm lane.

Take the lane straight on, your direction 60 degrees. After a bend to the right you come to a T-junction. *Turn right* on to the road and in 10 metres *go over a stile on your left* to continue down a signed footpath, due east, with a fine view over the valley. On the hills beyond you can see a huddle of buildings marking the outskirts of Wakehurst Place.

Keep the fence and a large house on your right-hand side. In 400 metres, **[3]** at the bottom of the field, *veer left,* with the edge of the woods now on your right-hand side and your direction 25 degrees.

At a footpath sign in 150 metres, *turn right through a kissing gate* to go down

a gully into **Tilgate Wood**. Soon it is steeply downhill with a stream visible below you.

Cross two wooden bridges (the second over Ardingly Brook) and follow the footpath sign up the other side, over more streams and eventually through a wire-mesh kissing gate into **Wakehurst Place** gardens (with only a notice to discourage walkers from gaining free access to these National Trust gardens). The public footpath, which is clearly signed, crosses a gravel path and in 200 metres comes to another wire-mesh kissing gate. The path now climbs steeply and at the top goes between high electrified fences on both sides (to keep the deer in). The path soon becomes a wide avenue.

You come out on to a car lane, with cottages on the left behind you, and carry straight on, with garden walls on your right-hand side. In 200 metres **[4]** turn half left on to a wide road, following the footpath sign. For those not visiting the gardens or cafe, the route is straight along the road for 200 metres, through a wooden gate to the right of a cattle grid and, in another 200 metres, reaching the main road (the B2028) by 1 Yew Tree Cottage, where you *turn left.*

(Many walkers with time to spare, however, will be tempted to visit **Wakehurst Place** or the **Seed Café** in its Visitor Centre. To do this, continue ahead on the path signposted 'carpark and exit' up to the Visitor Centre, which contains the ticket office and cafe. Afterwards, rejoin the main walk by going down the car exit road to the B2028 T-junction and *turning left,* coming in 300 metres to the main walk's exit by 1 Yew Tree Cottage.)

Carry on along an embankment to the left of the busy B2028, passing Stonehurst Nurseries (famous for its camellias in early spring) on your right-hand side. In 225 metres cross the road carefully and *go down a clearly signposted bridleway* between cottages, your direction 135 degrees, and so into the woods.

In 100 metres *turn sharp left* on to a car-wide mud track, and in 60 metres *veer right* at another bridleway sign, your direction 125 degrees.

In 100 metres you come to a three-armed sign and *take the bridleway on the left* between ponds, your direction due east. In 250 metres, a stream tumbles noisily under the path, after which it can be treacherously muddy uphill.

In 400 metres **[5]**, *turn right with the bridleway,* where the path ahead is a footpath. You pass several houses and come out, slightly left, on to a car-wide lane signposted as a public bridleway, your direction 105 degrees.

In 40 metres you *fork left* (following another bridleway sign), your direction now 65 degrees. Follow this lane in roughly the same direction for 1km, passing Philpots Quarry on your left-hand side, to meet Hook Lane at a bend.

Continue straight ahead on Hook Lane to go into the village of **West Hoathly**. After a bend to the left you pass the **Priest House Museum**, then several other interesting old houses on your left. The suggested lunch stop, the **Cat Inn**, is ahead of you, just past **St Margaret's Church**.

After lunch, *turn right* out of the pub and *right again by the bus shelter.* Carry on up this tarmac road for 400 metres, your direction 20 degrees, past the village school on your right-hand side and ignoring a public footpath off to the left.

When you come to the main road, *cross straight over into the entrance to West Hoathly Garage* (with its collection of vintage cars). *Go immediately left,* following a public footpath sign down a narrow lane, with the garage on your right-hand side, heading north.

In 200 metres, the lane becomes unasphalted and, at the fork in this lane, you continue straight on into the wood through a kissing gate. In 70 metres you come to a three-armed footpath sign. *Take the right fork,* slightly downhill. In another 50 metres again take the right fork, your direction now 40 degrees.

You now continue gently downhill on this public footpath through Giffard's Wood for over 1km, heading north-east.

In more detail: In 500 metres, having ignored any ways off, your path merges with a car-wide earth track from the right.

[!] 100 metres further on, before this track curves away to the left, *bear right on to a footpath* to resume your original direction, 45 degrees. In 300 metres go across a car-wide grass track and continue downhill.

In 200 metres go over a stile and across an open field, keeping more or less in the same direction, now 30 degrees, with a line of trees and a stream on your left-hand side and a couple of houses off to the right.

At the end of the field cross a stile on to a car lane and follow the sign to the left, your direction 330 degrees. In 40 metres you come to a three-armed footpath sign set back from the lane on your right-hand side where you *take the footpath to the right,* your direction 40 degrees. This takes you up an embankment, over the **Bluebell Railway** and down the other side. Go over a stile into the woods and follow the path, your direction 35 degrees, parallel to the stream below you to your right.

In 100 metres follow a footpath sign towards an electricity pylon 150 metres away. Just to the right of this pylon, *cross a wooden stile and bridge over a stream.* Go into the next field and *follow the grassy path half left uphill,* heading north-east.

In 250 metres, at the edge of a wood at the top of the hill, you come to a three-armed footpath sign. **[6]** Cross over the stile next to a wooden swing gate and head into these woods, your direction 80 degrees.

About 300 metres along this bridleway, you come to **Stone Farm Rocks**: soft sandstone used for rock climbing. They are covered with a profusion of climbers' bolts and are lined with rope marks, and provide platforms for fine views of the valley below, including **Weir Wood Reservoir** away to your left. (Alternatively, you could scramble down and walk along the base of the rocks if you wish to observe the climbers.)

The path eventually comes to a notice warning climbers not to damage the rocks (if you were at the base of the rocks, you would rejoin the main path here). 100 metres from this notice, you come to a car road, with Stonehill House opposite. *Turn right* and walk downhill on this busy road, taking great care. In 50 metres, cross over and *go left on a side road, which leads down to the reservoir.*

350 metres along the lane, you pass under pylons. Ignore a turning on the left leading into a car park, but where you come to a large gate blocking the road, *follow the footpath sign left. You will now be more or less following the side of the reservoir on the Sussex Border Path for the next 1.5km, until your turn-off to the left at [7].*

In more detail: 200 metres along this winding path, just before going under the pylons again, you come to a Countryside Commission information panel describing Standen Rocks and Weir Wood. There is a footpath off to the left here, which you could take if you want to visit **Standen House**, but the main walk route continues straight on.

In 250 metres, and again almost under the pylons, ignore another footpath sign to the left to stay on the Sussex Border Path. In a further 40 metres, go over a stile with the Countryside Stewardship badge on it to continue alongside the reservoir.

In 300 metres, cross a stile near another Countryside Commission information panel, again close to pylons. Continue along the path, in the next 80 metres ignoring two metal gates on the left leading into fields.

150 metres from the second gate, your path bends left to run parallel to the reservoir shore again and passes a wooden bench. You soon cross a pair of stiles to reach a large field, and can now see the far wall of the reservoir up ahead in the distance.

In about 200 metres **[7]**, leave the Sussex Border Path by *forking left on a grassy path towards a gap in the hedge*

(this little shortcut just saves you doubling back slightly from the footpath sign at the end of the field, 50 metres away). You are now heading away from the reservoir, and *1.75km in this direction (roughly northwards) will bring you to the outskirts of East Grinstead at [8].*

In more detail: Go through the hedge into a field and continue uphill, passing to the right of a pylon in 100 metres and then going through a metal fieldgate. In 150 metres, at the top-left corner of the next field, go over a stile between two metal gates.

Ignore another stile into the wood on your left and continue along the left-hand field edge. In 150 metres you pass a pond on your left. In another 100 metres, go over a stile into a strip of woodland by a two-armed footpath sign.

In 40 metres exit this wood by a stile and head north across the field, gently downhill, towards a stile 150 metres away leading into another wood.

Enter the wood, following the footpath sign. In 20 metres ignore a footpath off to the left, then in a further 50 metres take the right fork. In 100 metres, go down to a plank to cross a stream and then up steps on the other side to exit the wood through a gate.

Turn half right to follow the field edge, with a hedge and later a fence on your right-hand side. In 100 metres the path goes down into a dip and up the other side, then in another 150 metres you go through a wooden fieldgate on to a broad path through a strip of woodland.

As you leave this wood by another fieldgate, East Grinstead church is visible on the horizon up ahead, slightly to the right. Aim slightly to the right of the church to pick up a faint grassy path across the field. In 160 metres you pass a small pond on your right. In another 100 metres go through a wooden gate by a two-armed footpath sign and cross a ditch on a plank.

In 150 metres you pass under some power lines and go through a wooden gate. **[8]** *Do not continue down to the metal footbridge over a stream, but turn*

*left on to a narrow path with a hedge on
your left and woods on your right.* In 25
metres there is a plank over a ditch and in
another 20 metres you have a choice: the
official footpath appears to be straight on
along the overgrown path, but in practice
it is much easier to turn left into the field
and take a well-trodden path along the
right-hand field edge.

In 120 metres rejoin the footpath at
a gap in the hedge, passing a concrete
post. Continue through the woods, with
a stream on your right. In 40 metres you
pass between metal barriers to come out
on to a tarmac path, with a playground
behind a wooden fence on your left.

In 160 metres the path comes out on
to Dunnings Road opposite the **Old Mill**
pub, the suggested tea place. Coming
out of the pub, *turn right* to go past
Dunnings Mill Snooker and Social Club,
then *turn right again* on to a footpath
going alongside this building. Follow the
footpath sign at the end to pass a car park
and then another building on your right,
then go over a metal stile into a field.

Continue along the right-hand field
edge. In 140 metres cross a stile, then
in another 150 metres cross a stream
on a wooden bridge. Continue in the
same direction, north-west, for another
400 metres, crossing more stiles and
eventually passing a duck pond on
your left (with some unusual species).

In a further 100 metres, after crossing
a concrete track by some wooden sheds
on your right, *go over an unmarked stile
on your right* on to a narrow path, and
continue up to the road which you can see
ahead (if you miss the stile you will have
to hurdle a locked gate to exit the field).

Turn right on to the main road
(the B2110). In 50 metres, *go left at the
roundabout,* following the sign saying
'Station'. Keep uphill on this road
(Brooklands Way), following it round
to the right and all the way up the hill,
ignoring turn-offs. **Starbucks**, in
Sainsbury's supermarket on your left-
hand side, is the easiest place to stop
for refreshment at this point.

Coming out of Sainsbury's, *turn
right* along the edge of the building.
At the corner *turn right* to go along
the supermarket's access road. **East
Grinstead station** is ahead of you,
on your left.

Lunch & tea places

Balcombe Tea Rooms *Bramble Hill,
Balcombe, RH17 6HR (01444 811777).*
Open 10am-4pm Tue-Sat; 10.30am-4pm
Sun. This cafe serves a good selection
of cakes, should you be in the mood for
elevenses. The owners prefer large groups
to call in advance.
Seed Café *Wakehurst Place, Ardingly,
RH17 6TN (01444 894040, www.kew.
org).* **Open** *Jan, Feb* 10am-4pm daily.
Mar-Oct 10am-5.15pm daily. *Nov, Dec*
10am-4.15pm daily. Located in the Visitor
Centre of Wakehurst Place.
Stables Restaurant *Wakehurst Place,
Ardingly, RH17 6TN (01444 894040,
www.kew.org).* **Food served** *Mar-Oct*
10am-5pm daily. *Nov-Feb* 10am-3.45pm
daily. An lunch alternative for those
visiting the gardens at Wakehurst Place.
Cat Inn *Queen's Square, West Hoathly,
RH19 4PP (01342 810369, www.cat
inn.co.uk).* **Open** noon-3pm, 6-11pm Mon-
Thur; noon-3.30pm, 6-11pm Fri, Sat; noon-
3.20pm Sun. *Food served* noon-2pm, 6-9pm
Mon-Thur; noon-2.30pm, 6-9pm Fri, Sat;
noon-2.30pm Sun. The suggested lunch
stop, serving good (though fairly
expensive) pub food.
Old Mill *Dunnings Mill, Dunnings Road,
East Grinstead, RH19 4AT (01342
326341, www.theolddunningsmill.co.uk).*
Open 11am-midnight Mon-Sat; noon-
11pm Sun. *Food served* noon-9.30pm
Mon-Sat; noon-9pm Sun. About 2km
(just over a mile) before the end of
the walk, this is the suggested tea
stop. Allow 30 minutes from here to
reach the station.

The only place for resfreshments near
the station is the **Starbucks** at the East
Grinstead Sainsbury's (Brooklands Way,
01342 315869, http://starbucks.co.uk).

Walk 35

Crowhurst to Battle

Battle of Hastings and its abbey.

Start: Crowhurst station
Finish: Battle station

Length: 20.0km (12.4 miles)

Time: 5 hours 45 minutes. For the whole outing, including trains, sights and meals, allow 11 hours.

Transport: Take the train nearest to **9.15am** from **Charing Cross** station to **Crowhurst** (journey time 1 hour 30 minutes). Trains back

from **Battle** run about twice an hour until 6pm, and then hourly (journey time about 1 hour 20 minutes). Get a day return to Crowhurst.

OS Landranger Map: 199
OS Explorer Map: 124
Crowhurst, map reference TQ760128, is in **East Sussex**, 6km north-west of Hastings.

Toughness: 4 out of 10

Walk notes: Down the road from the station are the church and ruined manor of Crowhurst, and from farmland nearby – on a clear day – you can see Beachy Head and the sea. This potentially muddy route goes through the woodlands and golf course of Beauport Park, to the church and lunchtime pub in the village of Westfield. It is 9.3km (5.8 miles) to this lunch stop.

In the afternoon the route is mainly alongside streams or the River Brede, and passes through the parkland of the Pestalozzi International Village. Soon the town, church and abbey of Battle are visible ahead, lining the horizon.

You may like to end the day wandering over the site of the Battle of Hastings, by the ruins of the abbey that William the Conqueror built in honour of his victory, and so to the tree marking the spot where King Harold is supposed to have been slain.

Walk options: There are a few ways to shorten this route. You could get a bus

or taxi from near the lunchtime pub in Westfield (turn left out of the pub on Main Road and walk 50 metres), or from near the pub in Sedlescombe (5km further on). For bus information, phone 0871 200 2233. Otherwise, a shortcut to the station, as you enter Battle, is detailed in the walk directions (*see p276*).

History: The **churchyard in Crowhurst** has a perhaps 2,500-year-old yew tree. Next to the church is a **ruined manor house**, built in the 12th century by Walter de Scotney, supposedly a gentleman of substance, who made do with this dwelling which was a mere 6 metres by 12 metres.

In 1100, **St John the Baptist Church** in Westfield, along with a pit for the ordeal of trial by water, was given into the care of Battle Abbey. Some of its church bells are thought to have been cast in a pit dug in the churchyard, so as not to have to transport the finished bells. The church lost its stained-glass windows in World War II.

The **Battle of Hastings** was fought on 14 October 1066, starting at 9am with Harold's unmounted forces on top of Senlac Hill (Battle) under attack from William's mounted knights, protected by infantry and archers. The Normans feigned a retreat to get the English to break ranks, and at dusk King Harold was killed. The **abbey site** (01424 775705) is open daily until 6pm in summer (April to September), 4pm in winter. Admission (2010) is £7.

The **Pestalozzi International Village** is a 170-acre estate in Sedlescombe. It opened in 1959 as an education charity, based on the principles of Swiss educationist and philosopher Johann Pestalozzi, who believed young people would fulfil their potential if they were given a balanced, holistic education to develop their intellectual and practical skills (head, heart and hands). Young students, chosen from developing countries and with disadvantaged backgrounds, but already showing a commitment to helping their own communities, come to study at the Village for the International Baccalaureate. After their studies, and any subsequent university courses, the students return home, where they contribute to the development of their own countries.

Walk directions

[1] [Numbers in square brackets refer to the map]
Coming off platform 2 at **Crowhurst station**, cross the footbridge to exit the station.

Take the tarmac road *away from the station,* your direction 150 degrees, ignoring all ways off.

In 600 metres, and 35 metres before the T-junction, your onward route is **[2]** *left uphill* on a concrete farm drive, a footpath, your direction 130 degrees. (But first, you may like to detour to the **Parish Church of St George**, Crowhurst, visible ahead, and the remains of the **manor house**.)

Going up the farm drive, in 35 metres you *fork left off the drive,* your direction 70 degrees, with a field fence on your left-hand side. In 45 metres continue straight on, with a barn on your right-hand side, on a vehicle-wide earth farm track.

In 400 metres go over a bridge with ponds either side, to follow the footpath (initially) up across the next field. In 200 metres go under an isolated, disused railway bridge that looks like a majestic Roman ruin, and only 80 metres later, go through its degenerate modern alternative: *a corrugated-iron drainpipe tunnel* under the working railway lines.

10 metres beyond the end of the tunnel, go through concrete gateposts the other side and onwards, emerging from the wood in 180 metres, to continue with the wood's edge on your left-hand side, and an open field on your right-hand side.

In 200 metres, at the corner of the field, continue along the (now enclosed) car-wide track. (Once past the wood on your right, you can see the sea far away.) In a further 200 metres, you come to an earth roads crossing (where you cross a public footpath). You continue *straight on* down the track.

In 220 metres ignore a farm track up to your left-hand side. In 60 metres cross over a tiny stream. The track curves to the right uphill towards a house. In a further 80 metres, at a T-junction, *turn right,* your direction 190 degrees.

In 150 metres you pass this house on your left-hand side, and continue on through the farmyard of **Park Farm** (marked on the OS map), along a concrete car-wide track between barns, your direction 120 degrees.

In 100 metres you come to an earth lane T-junction **[3]** *where you go left,* your direction 30 degrees, up a lane (ignoring a stile and public footpath ahead). You soon pass the entrance to Park Farm on your left. Soon Beachy Head is sometimes visible behind you on your right-hand side. In 1.25km you come out to the A2100 T-junction, where you cross the road and *go left* alongside the walls of **Beauport Park**.

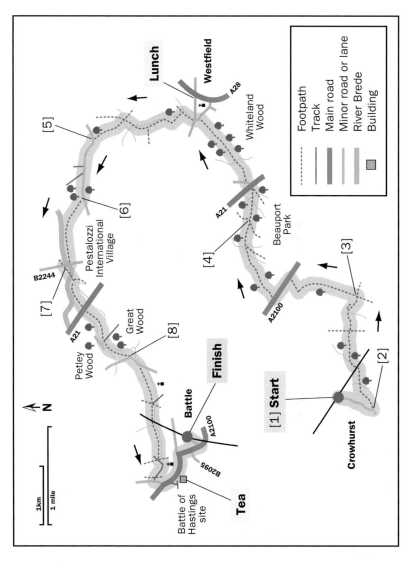

After 450 metres of this unpleasant road, and 30 metres before the water tower on the left-hand side, by a wooden footpath post on your right-hand side, *go right,* your direction 40 degrees, past a metal fieldgate on a wide gravelled track (not the wooden fieldgate and track parallel to yours, to its left).

In 50 metres you pass a corrugated shed on your right-hand side.

35 metres past the shed, *take the left of the two tracks,* with fencing off to your left-hand side.

[!] In a further 80 metres (having emerged on to a golf fairway), *fork left* down into a wood by a public footpath sign, your direction 30 degrees. (Westfield village, the lunchtime destination, may already be visible ahead at 65 degrees, although the walk takes longer than you might imagine to get there.)

In 25 metres *fork right,* your direction 60 degrees. (Ignore the left fork, which goes sharply downhill and then off in the opposite direction.)

Keep on parallel to the fairway on your right-hand side, ignoring ways off, until in a further 150 metres **[!]** *you fork right* on a faint path, marked by a yellow marker on a wooden post, where the main path forks left and sharply downhill (where it continues to go left). Your direction is 80 degrees, keeping to the right-hand side of the wood. In 120 metres you pass a sizeable oak tree off to your right, with a dozen main branches.

After 25 metres go over a crosspaths to continue down through the narrow wood. In 120 metres go over a car-wide track, your direction now 110 degrees. After a further 150 metres go over a car-wide track to continue down through the narrow wood between fairways, your direction 70 degrees.

After 140 metres you reach a car-wide track.

At the time of writing (summer 2010), the footpath ahead through the wood is blocked due to tree felling, although at some stage the path should be cleared. There are two route options: **(i)** continue on the standard original route, or **(ii)** take the alternative temporary route.

(i) The original route through the wood: Continue down through the wood, your direction 80 degrees. After 250 metres at a path T-junction *turn right for 5 metres* to go over a wooden plank bridge over a stream, *to immediately turn left* down a path, marked by a metal footpath signpost, your initial direction 120 degrees. Rejoin the directions at the asterisk **[*]** below.

(ii) Diversion around the blocked path: *Turn left* along the car-wide track.

In 10 metres you come to a fairway, which *you cross over* (with a green just on your right-hand side). In 30 metres you come on to a path where *you go down to the right,* your direction 40 degrees.

In 25 metres you pass the same green on your right-hand side.

In 30 metres you come out to another fairway (with a pylon 300 metres off to your left). *You go down to the right,* your direction 70 degrees, along the wooded edge of this fairway.

In 120 metres ignore a fork going down to the right (into the wood).

In a further 60 metres, you pass a tee and come to a T-junction, *where you go right,* your direction 170 degrees. In 10 metres you pass a public footpath sign (which may still point right into impenetrable blackberry bushes!) and in 5 metres you go across wooden planks over a stream, *to immediately turn left down a path,* marked by a metal public footpath signpost, your initial direction 120 degrees.

[*] In a further 70 metres, you go over a stream.

In 220 metres you come to an earth road T-junction **[4]** by a house with ground-floor lattice window shutters you *go left* on this earth road, downhill, your direction 80 degrees.

In 55 metres *fork right* on to a car-wide gravel track to then *immediately fork left* along a footpath down into a wood, your initial direction 110 degrees.

In 150 metres, at a crosspaths with a car-wide track, continue ahead with rhododendrons on both sides, your direction 100 degrees.

Keep to the waymarked path ignoring turnings off (head towards the traffic noise).

In 300 metres go over a two-plank railed footbridge across a small stream. After 30 metres go past a redundant stile and in a further 25 metres go over a stile. In 10 metres cross a wooden footbridge over a stream.

In 100 metres you come out on to the verge of the A21.

Cross the A21 road to continue on Moat Lane, your direction 60 degrees. In 110 metres, just before Cherrycot House on your right-hand side, *you go right into the park* (by a stile and a concrete footpath marker, with a metal fieldgate on your left-hand side), your direction east, to follow the left-hand edge of the park.

In 400 metres at the left-hand corner of the park you enter **Whiteland Wood** on a bridge over a stream, with a dilapidated fence on your left-hand side. In 200 metres, ignore a way off to the right.

In 150 metres the fencing on your left-hand side comes to an end.

In a further 170 metres, you cross a car-wide way. In 150 metres you cross another way.

In 80 metres, having crossed a stream, you exit the wood to the left of a metal fieldgate and carry on, along a farm track, between a hedge on your right-hand side and a fence to your left-hand side, your direction 20 degrees.

In 180 metres you come out on to a tarmac lane *where you go right,* uphill, your direction 140 degrees.

In 150 metres, immediately after a road leading left into a housing estate, you go quarter left up a grass bank towards a churchyard, and in 30 metres go through its metal swing gate to **St John the Baptist Church**, Westfield.

In 100 metres you come to the main church entrance on your left-hand side. Continuing onwards brings you out on the A28, opposite a bus stop, where you *go left,* your direction 10 degrees.

Walk up for 250 metres to the **Old Courthouse** pub at the crossroads with Wheel/Moor Lane. (The **Plough Inn**, an alternative for lunch, is down Moor Lane to the right; it was changing management in early 2011, so call 01424 751066 in advance if you're planning to eat here. Retrace your steps after lunch.)

After lunch, head down Wheel Lane. In 450 metres ignore Vicarage Lane to the left. In 15 metres you pass the thatched Wheel Cottage on your right-hand side. In a further 25 metres, on the other side of the stream, passing between poles to the right of a diagonal metal car gate, *you go right* through Wheel Farm business park, keeping alongside a stream on your right-hand side.

In 270 metres ignore a wooden bridge with railings on your right-hand side, to *go slightly left away from the stream,* your direction 290 degrees. In 100 metres, go over a stile with a yellow footpath arrow (and a red '1066 Country Walk' marker) with a metal fieldgate to your left, to continue straight on, your direction 340 degrees.

In 90 metres you rejoin the side of the stream on your right-hand side, as you pass under mini pylons.

In 80 metres go through a wooden kissing gate with a 1066 walk marker (a metal fieldgate on its left-hand side).

In 250 metres ignore a grassy vehicle-wide bridge on your right-hand side to carry straight on, with a stream on your right-hand side.

In 80 metres, by a mini waterfall on the right-hand side, you go over a stile (with a metal fieldgate to its left). There is a three-armed footpath post here. Follow this on, ignoring a possible left turn.

In a further 240 metres, go on a wooden bridge, with wooden railings and a stile at both ends, over a stream. Keep to the right-hand side of the field to reach after 220 metres a footpath T-junction with a three-arrow footpath post. *Go left here,* across the end of this narrow field, your direction 320 degrees.

In 30 metres you come to a wooden footbridge (with a metal scaffolding-pole railing). Carry straight on from the other side, with the field fence on your right-hand side, towards a line of pylons, your direction 320 degrees.

In 110 metres, you go over a (broken) stile. In 45 metres you then pass under mini pylons. In a further 250 metres, you may have to negotiate an insulated section

of electric fence (a proper stile has been requested) to cross a farm track, slightly left, continuing on over a stile, with a field hedge on your right-hand side.

In 100 metres you pass under a cable run. In 45 metres go to the right of a stile into a wood (with a pond, visible in winter, away on your left-hand side), your direction 350 degrees.

In 50 metres you come on to a tarmac road **[5]** *where you go left,* your direction 280 degrees.

In a further 320 metres, you pass an entrance to Westfield Place on your left-hand side.

In 220 metres ignore a parking area signposted Brassets Wood, on your right-hand side, with an inviting track leading off it.

In 200 metres you pass another entrance to Westfield Place and a lodge on your left-hand side.

In 25 metres, as the road bends slightly left, *take the path to the right,* by a wooden footpath signpost **[6]**, into a wood (opposite the entrance to the Lodge Nursery). 4 metres inside the wood at a T-junction, *turn left,* your direction 270 degrees.

In 150 metres you *veer down to the right* with the path. In 10 metres you cross a path to go through a wooden kissing gate into the parklands of the **Pestalozzi International Village**, your direction now 300 degrees, *aiming towards the left edge of the woodlands below you* (and well to the right of the house visible ahead).

In 250 metres you come to the fence below you, where you go over a stile with a public footpath yellow arrow on it (there is a metal fieldgate in the fence 100 metres away to your left) *and turn half left into a wood,* your direction 310 degrees. The path may be somewhat overgrown.

In 80 metres cross a plank footbridge to go over a stile to emerge from the wood to continue in a similar direction (310 degrees), across a field. In a further 250 metres, go through a wooded field boundary and through a metal fieldgate to carry straight on, direction 300 degrees, along the right-hand side of a field.

In 55 metres you pass a small utility building off to your right-hand side. In a further 80 metres, go over a stile in the fence on your right-hand side, under an oak tree, to *cross a stream and turn left along the left-hand side of the field,* your direction west.

In a further 120 metres, you pass by the clean waters of the **River Brede** down below you on your right-hand side. Go straight on towards the village of **Sedlescombe**.

In 110 metres go through a metal kissing gate to follow the river on your right-hand side. In 300 metres leave Sedlescombe sports field by a wooden kissing gate and *go right, over a bridge. In 70 metres* (where straight on would take you to a bus stop and, beyond that, to a pub, should you wish to drop out at this point), you *turn left* by a concrete footpath marker **[7]**, just before a garage, on a car-wide tarmac track, your direction 250 degrees.

In 70 metres, by the entrance to a private garden, you *fork left,* your direction 220 degrees. In a further 70 metres, go over a wooden bridge with railings through a bridleway metal gate and *turn right* to continue with the river on your right-hand your direction 280 degrees.

In a further 520 metres, go over the A21 and over a stile (with a metal fieldgate on its left-hand side) *to continue on a path* with a stream on your right-hand side.

In 400 metres *you fork left* away from the stream (to cut short a bend in the stream), your direction 240 degrees. In 110 metres go over a stile (the path may be somewhat overgrown with nettles at this point) to enter a wooded area, to continue with a stream on your right-hand side.

In 40 metres you emerge from the wooded area.

In a further 150 metres, you come to a T-junction *where you go right for 5 metres, then go left,* over a stile to continue on, your direction 220 degrees, with a stream on your left-hand side. In 25 metres you pass under mini pylons.

In 250 metres you come to the first of seven stiles at the bottom of private gardens, which you cross, keeping the stream on your left-hand side.

The last of the seven houses is a thatched barn-house away on your right-hand side. The owner has positioned his fence beside the stream, so that, immediately after crossing the seventh stile, you *cross an eighth, and turn half right across a field towards a wooden footbridge on the far side,* your direction 230 degrees. After 100 metres go over the footbridge *to veer right* aiming for a metal fieldgate on the far side which leads out on to the road, your direction 240 degrees.

In a further 200 metres, you come to a tarmac road **[8]** (with a sign for Great Wood on your left-hand side). There is a concrete public footpath marker pointing back the way you have come. *Turn left* on this main tarmac road, your direction 240 degrees.

In 180 metres *take the farm-track fork right,* your direction 280 degrees. In 20 metres you pass a concrete public footpath marker (half-hidden in summer) at the corner of a field, your direction now 250 degrees.

In a further 170 metres, go over a stile into a wood, now with a fence on your left-hand side.

At the end of the sewage farm fence on your left-hand side, *turn left for 15 metres* and immediately before a car-wide bridge, *turn right,* your direction 310 degrees.

In 120 metres go through a tunnel under the railway line.

In a further 30 metres, you go through a metal fieldgate and onwards, your direction 250 degrees, with a stream on your left-hand side and the buildings of Battle visible on the horizon ahead.

In a further 80 metres, go over a stile, with a field hedge on your right-hand side. In 200 metres go on a plank over a stile and straight on, ignoring the track up to the house. In 70 metres, continue over a stile.

In 40 metres you pass **Little Park Farm** (so marked on the OS map) on your right-hand side and keep straight on.

In 40 metres go over a stile and on across a wooden bridge with a railing over a stream.

In a further 70 metres, you come out on to a farm road. *Go left* on the road, your direction 255 degrees. In 20 metres ignore a stile to the left. (The path southwards from this stile, however, would be a **shortcut to the station**, should you need to get there in a hurry: at a fork, after 100 metres, take the left-hand path; follow the lower edge of the hill; then cross on a long line of wooden planks and go uphill, slightly to your right, coming out by the fork right to the station on the A2100, mentioned in the last paragraph.)

The main suggested route, though, continues on the farm road. In 320 metres, as you go uphill, you cross over a footpath by a footpath sign and continue on, with a Battle Town Council garden on your right-hand side.

In 60 metres you come out on to Mount Street, *where you go left,* your direction 190 degrees.

In 35 metres you pass **Bayeux Cottage**, which serves cream teas. In 35 metres you pass the King's Head. In 30 metres, at the T-junction, *turn left* into the High Street, your direction 150 degrees.

In 25 metres you pass the Bull Inn & Wine Bar on your right-hand side. In a

further 25 metres you pass the **George Hotel** on your right-hand side.

In a further 90 metres, you come to the **1066** pub. In 65 metres more, you come to the gateway of Battle Abbey School. Sometimes admission to the **Battle Abbey** grounds and to the **Battle of Hastings site** is through this gateway.

Alternatively, turn right here on a tarmac lane, passing the Pilgrim's Rest on your right-hand side, your direction 260 degrees.

In 40 metres you come to a car park on your left-hand side and another entrance to Battle Abbey. (There is a wooden swing gate into the abbey grounds beyond the entrance tills, which sometimes remains open after official opening hours – one that is possibly intended for use by local people?)

After visiting the abbey and battlefield, *retrace your steps* to the 1066 pub. To get to the station, coming out of the pub, *turn right,* in 150 metres passing the **Parish Church of St Mary the Virgin** on your left-hand side.

In 120 metres *fork right to the station,* on the A2100. In 200 metres, just before the Senlac Inn (the last opportunity for refreshments), *turn left* for **Battle station**, 200 metres away, your direction 60 degrees, for trains back to London.

Lunch & tea places

You can buy picnic food at the **Londis Red Square** supermarket in Westfield.

Old Courthouse *Main Road, Westfield, TN35 4QE (01424 751603, http://old courthousepub.com).* **Open** noon-11pm Mon-Sat; noon-10.30pm Sun. *Food served* noon-9pm daily. The walk's suggested lunch stop.

Simply Italian *23 High Street, Battle, TN33 0EA (01424 772100, www.simply italian.co.uk).* **Open** noon-10pm daily. A possible tea stop.

Bayeux Cottage *11 Mount Street, Battle, TN33 0EG (01424 772593).* **Open** 10am-3pm Wed-Fri; 11.30am-4.30pm Sun. If you arrive in Battle early, this 17th-century cottage serves cream teas.

Walk 36

Borough Green to Sevenoaks

Plaxtol, Ightham Mote and Knole House.

Start: Borough Green station
Finish: Sevenoaks station

Length: 15.0km (9.3 miles)

Time: 4 hours 30 minutes. For the whole outing, with trains, sights and meals, allow 8 hours 30 minutes.

Transport: Take the train nearest to **10am** from **Victoria** station to **Borough Green** (journey time 40-45 minutes). There are frequent trains back from **Sevenoaks**. Journey time is 35 minutes to Charing Cross, or about an hour to Victoria.

Borough Green and Sevenoaks are on different lines, which diverge at Otford. The simplest advice is to get a day return to Borough Green. In practice this might be accepted for the return journey from Sevenoaks, but you could be asked to buy a single to Otford.

OS Landranger Map: 188
OS Explorer Map: 147
Borough Green, map reference TQ608573, is in **Kent**, 9km east of Sevenoaks.

Toughness: 4 out of 10

Walk notes: The walk goes south from Borough Green through woods and along streams to the old village of Plaxtol, with its Cromwellian church. Then you head through the park of Fairlawne House to Ightham Mote, a beautiful moated medieval manor, and take lunch in its National Trust restaurant. The route onwards is up a potentially muddy bridleway, through orchards and along shaded woodland paths leading to the 1,000-acre Knole Park and 365-room Knole House. Finally, the route goes up by footpaths to tea in Sevenoaks, with the station some way downhill from the centre.

Walk options: To shorten the walk, you could order a taxi from Plaxtol or from Ightham Mote. There are occasional buses from Plaxtol to Borough Green station, but not at weekends.

History: The Cromwellian **Plaxtol Parish Church**, built in 1649, has a fine 17th-century hammer-beam roof that was originally painted blue. Thomas Stanley of Hamptons, later beheaded for his part in the execution of Charles I, contributed money for repairing the church. There is a slab in the nave floor that records the death, within one month in 1771, of four young children of the Knowles family.

    Knole House, built in the 15th century (and so huge that it has a room for every day of the year), was visited by Elizabeth I in 1573, who granted it to Thomas Sackville. It remained in the Sackville family and was the childhood home of Vita Sackville-West, featuring in Virginia

Woolf's *Orlando*. The house, with its tapestries, paintings and collection of 17th-century furniture, is open to visitors from mid March to the end of October, Wednesday to Sunday (plus Bank Holiday Mondays and August Tuesdays), with last entry at 3.30pm and admission (2010) costing £9.50; the garden is open on Tuesdays only. The house stands in a park of 1,000 acres. There is no charge for walking in the park and, in any case, the route described in the walk directions follows public rights of way.

Ightham Mote (pronounced 'item') is a lovely Tudor and medieval moated manor house and garden (01732 810378). Although the building can be seen clearly from the public way, it is well worth a full visit. It is open between 11am and 5pm Thursday to Monday from March to October, with more restricted opening times in November and December. Tickets (2010) cost £11.

Walk directions

[1] [Numbers in square brackets refer to the map]

Turn right uphill (eastwards) out of **Borough Green station** to a T-junction (Wrotham Road) and *turn right* to go over the railway bridge, your direction 205 degrees initially.

In 60 metres you come to the main Western Road turn-off to the right; cross it carefully. Carry straight on, soon passing the driveway to the village hall and public toilets on your left. In 150 metres cross over the A25 (there is a pedestrian crossing to your left) and carry straight on, now on Quarry Hill Road, your direction 220 degrees.

[2] In 50 metres, opposite the church on your right-hand side, *go left* into The Landway, following the public footpath sign on to a tarmac car road, downhill, your direction due south.

In 175 metres you come to a car road and cross it to continue straight on along a public footpath, now a path between fences, soon going gently uphill. In 280 metres cross a car road to carry straight on between wooden fences. In 275 metres the path bends left, going steeply downhill for 160 metres to cross a stream by a brick-and-concrete bridge.

[3] 80 metres further on you come up on to a car road. Go on this road, leftwards (due south initially) with a wide grassy bank and then a lake on your left. Next there is a residential development on the left where the pavement starts. After 120 metres the pavement ends but go straight on (along Basted Mill), ignoring the Mill Lane right turn opposite. Instead, continue on past a grassy area and then Bridge House on your left; in another 20 metres **[!]** *turn right* on to Mill Lane at the junction with Plough Hill, your direction 205 degrees. **[4]**

Pass Orchard Cottage on your right with the stream on your left. In a further 80 metres you pass Basted Cottage on your right. Another 130 metres brings you past Woodruff Cottage, also on your right, after which the earth road becomes a potentially muddy path.

In 350 metres you come to a concrete public footpath marker with an arrow to the right and a tiny stream behind it, but keep on your path as it bends left.

In 325 metres ignore a fork left (which crosses the stream) to come to a T-junction with a car road where you *go right* uphill, your direction 275 degrees. **[5]**

In 115 metres, once over the steepest part of the hill, *turn left* over a stile with a concrete public footpath marker, your direction due south, to go through the orchard.

In 150 metres, at the end of the orchard, continue ahead. In 30 metres, at the corner of the field, you enter a wood downhill, your direction 140 degrees. In 25 metres cross a stream and a wooden bridge with wooden rails, then go over a stile and up the other side to emerge from the wood in 50 metres.

Go ahead on the enclosed path, your direction 220 degrees. You then continue in more or less the same direction for

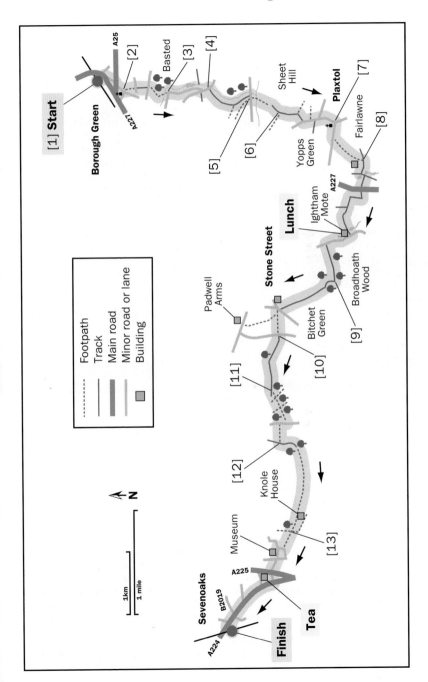

Ightham Mote.

1.3km until you come to the church in Plaxtol.

But in more detail: After 180 metres go through a gap to the left of a wooden fieldgate and pass a bungalow on your right. In 600 metres ignore a footpath to the left. In a further 200 metres your earth car track meets a tarmac car road. **[6]** Continue in the same direction, due south initially. In 40 metres pass an oast house on your right. In another 100 metres ignore a car road to the left called Grange Hill to continue on your road, now called Tree Lane. After a further 150 metres you come to **Plaxtol Church** on the right. **[7]**

Here *turn right* up Church Hill, also known as Plaxtol Lane, your direction due west. 300 metres up this hill and with the strange, disused, isolated gateways of **Fairlawne Estate** 150 metres off to your

left, *turn left* over a stile on a signposted footpath, your direction 170 degrees.

Continue on a faint path to go past the large gateways on your right. You can now see a yellow post ahead, which you soon reach. Continue ahead, passing a second yellow post after 100 metres and after a further 50 metres a third yellow post by a stile, which you cross. Head towards a fourth yellow post some 150 metres away. Impressive **Fairlawne House** can be seen on your right-hand side.

[8] At the fourth post **[!]** *turn right on the bridleway,* westwards (ignore the yellow arrow pointing ahead). Follow the bridleway as it curves right and in 200 metres go through a wooden swing gate. *Turn right* down a tarmac lane towards a pond and buildings, but in 20 metres *turn left* on a tarmac lane away from the houses, your direction 205 degrees, with a garden on your left-hand side.

In 70 metres by the wooden bridge on your left, *turn right uphill* on a tarmac lane, your direction 290 degrees. In 225 metres exit by a wooden swing gate (a wooden fieldgate to its left) and cross the A227 with care to keep straight on, along the earth road opposite, your direction 290 degrees.

In 150 metres *turn right* on a car-wide earth road, your direction 15 degrees, and 30 metres further on go through a wooden swing gate (a wooden fieldgate to its right) into a field where you continue straight on. In 150 metres *go left* over a stile with a stone step (next to a wooden fieldgate on its left) to go on a bridleway, your direction 280 degrees.

In 650 metres you come to a tarmac road and the entrance on your right to **Ightham Mote**, the suggested lunch stop (but see the note on opening hours in the introduction). Follow the signs to the restaurant. After lunch, return to the entrance and *turn right* up the lane, your direction 250 degrees, passing along the side of the manor. Follow the lane as it turns left away from the house and in 50 metres go out through the gateway and *turn right* on the car road, your direction 300 degrees, passing Mote Farm on your left and then a row of cottages on your right.

450 metres along this car road and just before a cottage on your right-hand side [!] *turn left* on a signposted potentially muddy public bridleway, your direction 285 degrees.

[9] After 600 metres, with a wooden barrier ahead and a pond to the left, ignore the permissive path next to the barrier and *turn right* following a Greensand Way blue arrow up a what becomes a steep and potentially muddy, slippery path, your direction 330 degrees; as you go uphill a way can be found parallel to the bridleway, a metre or so above it to the right, which may be slightly less muddy.

After following the narrow path through an intermittently wooded area for 250 metres your way becomes more open and you continue ahead, your direction 350 degrees, on a wide track passing to the left of orchards, ignoring all ways off. In 900 metres you come out on to a car road junction. Cross both roads to a gap opposite with a metal fieldgate on its left.

(To reach the alternative lunch stop, the **Padwell Arms**, go ahead down the wide track – formerly signposted as a bridleway but the words have been greened out – your direction 330 degrees for 450 metres to a road; the pub is just opposite. After lunch retrace your steps to the beginning of the track.)

For the main route: take the path that leads diagonally across the field, your direction due west. At the corner of the field, continue on a narrow path next to a field with a fence to the left and a hedge to your right. In 150 metres you go over a stile and cross a car road. [10]

Go straight on along an earth car road signposted as a public bridleway, your direction 280 degrees, past Lord's Spring Farm Cottage on your right and in another 100 metres past Lord's Spring Oast, also on your right.

About 1km further on, you come to two small houses on your right and you carry straight on, going along the earth driveway of these houses. In 90 metres ignore a turning to the left (which has a concrete public footpath marker) but in a further 50 metres, opposite some wooden stables, take the footpath *left into the wood* (it too has a concrete public footpath marker), your direction 220 degrees. [11]

Go more or less straight on for the next 500 metres. In more detail: In 160 metres cross a path and then another in a further 185 metres; continuing straight on, you have black chain-link fencing on your right for 180 metres. You come out on a tarmac driveway and follow this for 50 metres to a car road.

Turn right on this car road, your direction 345 degrees and in 100 metres *turn left* on a signposted public footpath across the playing fields of Sevenoaks Preparatory School, your direction 260 degrees.

Turn right at the top of the playing field and continue for 50 metres to the corner of the field with a copse on your left. Exit between the three posts to the road. Here you *turn left,* your direction 210 degrees, to go gently downhill. [12]

In 200 metres you pass two houses on your left and then *bear right* with the road. When the tarmac ends, you continue on a path uphill. In a further 100 metres you enter **Knole Park** through a fenced kissing gate.

You have two paths forking ahead of you: *take the wider one to the right,* your direction 265 degrees (not the path to the extreme right). In 75 metres leave the fence to *fork left* between two huge trees, your direction 245 degrees. There is immediately a swathe of grassland on your left.

In 85 metres, having passed a fallen tree on your right, you come to a tiny pond (winter only) on your left and then a large dead tree trunk on your right. Keep *straight on,* your direction still 245 degrees. You can just see the garden wall of Knole House at 260 degrees by the top of the far hill. Note your onwards path, which leads steeply downhill from you, then uphill towards the house.

175 metres down from the tree trunk cross a wide avenue and continue up the other side on the wide grass path, going due west. 200 metres up from the avenue pass through a cluster of ten oak trees.

In a further 85 metres cross a tarmac path to continue straight on despite a 'Danger – Golf Course' sign on your right. In 90 metres you cross a fairway (beware golf balls coming from the right). After a further 50 metres, you see Knole House's garden walls on your left. Carry on along these walls. You pass the entry to the **Brewhouse Tearoom**. At the end of the walls *turn left* for the **Knole House** entrance if you want to go inside.

To continue the walk from the end of the high wall *go straight ahead* on to the grass, heading with no clear path for a clump of trees at the top of the hill, your direction 315 degrees. You will probably need to weave your way round parked cars. Once there, following a footpath sign to the right, continue ahead, your direction 310 degrees. In 150 metres, having passed another footpath post, you pass a crater depression on your right. You are now on a clear path that leads to a tarmac drive. Cross it, passing a footpath post on your right, to carry *straight on,* along a path initially downhill, your direction 300 degrees. [13]

In 200 metres leave Knole Park by a fenced kissing gate *to go steeply uphill,* your direction 265 degrees. In 5 metres you pass the entrance to Sevenoaks Environmental Park on your right.

In a further 200 metres keep to the tarmac path as you pass the Sevenoaks Leisure Centre car park on your right. Continue past the end of the car park with a wall on your right and railings on your left, coming out opposite Waitrose. Cross the road and continue to the right of the toilets (Akehurst Lane), your direction 255 degrees. This leads out to **Sevenoaks High Street**.

(Alternatively you could cross the Sevenoaks Leisure Centre car park diagonally to the opposite corner, where you turn left, following the sign for the Tourist Information Office. After 50 metres you come to a road: cross it and carry on straight ahead past the bus stops to arrive at Sevenoaks High Street.)

There are various possibilities for tea in Sevenoaks. For **Caffè Nero**, turn right down the High Street. For **Costa Coffee**, cross the High Street, turn right and continue to Blighs Road on your left.

After tea, you will need to get to London Road, which runs west of the High Street for the station. From Costa Coffee, cross the car park to the far side, where steps lead down to London Road; then turn right downhill. From Caffè Nero,

carry on along the High Street to the traffic-light junction, where you turn left along Pembroke Road; when you reach London Road, turn right.

Continue for 800 metres (600 from Pembroke Road) down London Road to reach **Sevenoaks station** on the left. Just before the station, at the beginning of a parade on the left of the road, **Alpinia Patisserie** is another possible tea option.

Lunch & tea places

Ightham Mote restaurant *Mote Road, Ivy Hatch, Sevenoaks, TN15 0NT (01732 810378, www.nationaltrust.org.uk).* **Open** *Mar-Oct* 10.30am-5pm Mon, Thur-Sun. *Nov, Dec* 11am-3pm Thur-Sun. The suggested lunch place is the National Trust restaurant at Ightham Mote. You do not need to pay the entrance fee to eat at the restaurant.

Padwell Arms *Stone Street, Seal, TN15 0LQ (01732 761532).* **Open** noon-3pm, 6.30-11.30pm Mon, Wed-Fri;

6.30-11.30pm Tue; noon-11.30pm Sat, Sun. *Food served* noon-2.30pm, 6.30-9pm Mon, Wed-Sun. An alternative (except on Tuesdays) for those who would prefer a pub lunch. If you intend to eat here, it's worth taking an earlier train, since the diversion adds just over 1km (half a mile or so) to the walk.

Brewhouse Tearoom *Knole House, Sevenoaks, TN15 0RP (01732 450608, www.nationaltrust.org.uk).* **Open** times vary; phone for details. Despite having an entrance in the north wall of Knole House, there is no need to pay the entrance fee when visiting this suggested tea stop. It provides cream teas.

Alpinia Patisserie *Tubs Hill Parade, Sevenoaks, TN13 1DH (01732 454669).* **Open** 7.30am-6.30pm Mon-Sat.

Branches of **Caffè Nero** (112 High Street, 01732 779050, www.caffenero.com) and **Costa Coffee** (2 Blighs Road, 01732 462159, www.costa.co.uk) provide further tea options in the centre of Sevenoaks.

Walk 37

Southbourne to Chichester

A Chichester Harbour walk.

Start: Southbourne station
Finish: Chichester station

Length: 18.5km (11.5 miles)

Time: 5 hours. For the whole outing, including trains, sights and meals, allow at least 11 hours.

Travel: Take the train nearest to **9.30am** from **Victoria** station to **Southbourne**. The journey time is 1 hour 40 minutes (longer on Sunday).

Trains back from **Chichester** run about twice an hour, with a journey time of 1 hour 35 minutes (again, longer on Sunday). Buy a day return to Southbourne.

OS Landranger Map: 197
OS Explorer Map: 120
Southbourne, map reference SU770060, is in **West Sussex**, 9km west of Chichester.

Toughness: 3 out of 10

Walk notes: There are no hills at all on this walk. On a clear day you can enjoy marvellous views for miles – inland to Chichester Cathedral and south across the harbour. Birdwatchers should bring binoculars. The lunchtime stop is the popular old village of Bosham (pronounced 'Bozzum'), which appears deceptively close quite early on, except that there is a long detour around the water to get to it. In the afternoon, the walk goes via Fishbourne (there is a Roman palace nearby) and approaches Chichester Cathedral through the lovely Bishop's Palace Gardens. The suggested tea place is opposite the cathedral.

Walk options: A 2km walk north along the road out of Bosham after lunch will take you to Bosham station, which is on the line back into Chichester, and thence to London. Or you could end the walk in Fishbourne, visit the Roman palace

there, have a cup of tea and take a bus into Chichester to see the cathedral.

History: The **Parish Church of St Mary**, Chidham, which dates from the 12th century, was built on the site of a wooden Saxon church. The Saxon font once had a locked cover (obligatory in the 13th century), to prevent witches from stealing the holy water. In 1847, the vicar destroyed a 16th-century tomb within the church because no descendant was willing to pay for its repair.

Bosham is, by tradition, the site of a villa belonging to the Roman Emperor Vespasian, and was an important port in the medieval period. **Holy Trinity Church**, Bosham, is the oldest site of Christianity in Sussex. According to tradition, King Canute's daughter was buried in the church. Holy Trinity also appears in the Bayeux tapestry, on which King Harold is shown entering Bosham Church prior to

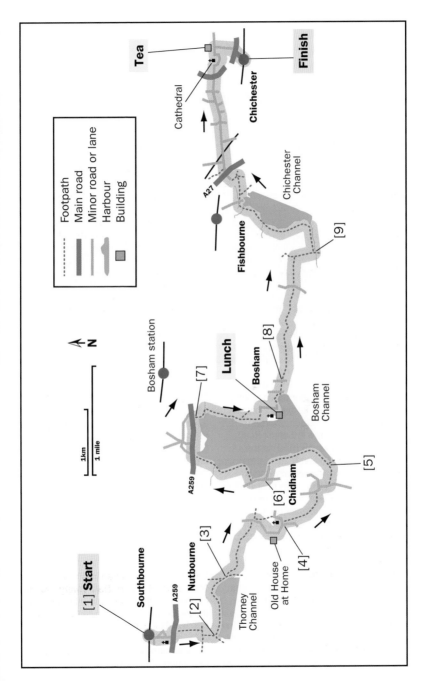

Southbourne to Chichester

Tea

Finish

Cathedral

Chichester

Chichester Channel

A27

Fishbourne

[9]

Footpath
Main road
Minor road or lane
Harbour
Building

N

Bosham station

1km
1 mile

Lunch

[7]

Bosham

[8]

Bosham Channel

Southbourne

[1] **Start**

A259

Nutbourne

[2]

[3]

Thorney Channel

[6]

Chidham

[5]

Old House at Home

[4]

sailing to Normandy in 1064. There are cross marks on the inner porch where Crusaders, returning from the Holy Land, ritualistically blunted their swords.

The **Roman palace** in Salthill Road, Fishbourne (01243 785859) is the largest Roman building to have been found in Britain – the remains include mosaic floors and the underfloor heating system. In summer, it is open daily until 5pm; in winter (mid December to February), weekends only until 4pm. There is a cafeteria. Admission (2010) is £7.60. Buses run from here into Chichester.

Chichester Cathedral (01243 782595), dedicated in 1108, contains many ancient and modern wonders: a stained-glass window designed by Chagall; a painting by Graham Sutherland; a tomb with the Earl of Arundel hand-in-hand with his wife (the tomb inspired the Philip Larkin poem 'What will survive them is love'); a shrine of St Richard, Bishop of Chichester; a 12th-century carving of the raising of Lazarus; and a Roman mosaic from the 2nd century (Chichester was previously the Roman town of Noviomagus). The cathedral has friendly and welcoming helpers, and there is no entrance fee. It is open daily until 7pm in summer, and until 5pm in winter; evensong is at 5.30pm Monday to Saturday, and 3.30pm on Sunday.

Five minutes south-east of the cathedral is **Pallant House** (9 North Pallant, 01243 774557), a Queen Anne townhouse that is open to visitors Tuesday to Sunday; last entry 4.45pm. Admission (2010) is £7.50 during the temporary exhibitions, but free at other times. Chichester is also famous for its **Festival Theatre** (01243 784437). If you want to see a show after the walk, there is normally a late-night train back to London afterwards.

Walk directions

[1] [Numbers in square brackets refer to the map]
At **Southbourne station**, walk down the platform to the road and *turn left, going south.*

350 metres brings you down to a junction with the A259, where you *cross over the road and turn left,* following the signs for Bosham and Chichester. On the corner, on your right-hand side, is the **Parish Church of St John the Evangelist**. In 50 metres *turn right off the road,* following the public footpath sign, with the Southbourne Farm Shop and, soon, a tall hedge on your left-hand side and a ditch on your right-hand side, your direction 205 degrees.

In 200 metres you come to the end of the hedgerows and out into an open field. At the three-armed footpath sign to your right, ignore the way to the left. Carry on straight ahead and in 30 metres follow the footpath as it curves around to the right, with the edge of the field on your right-hand side. In another 60 metres, there is another three-armed footpath sign on your right-hand side and a stile facing you.

Turn left, 5 metres before the stile, and continue in a southerly direction. 260 metres brings you to the far right-hand corner of the field and you follow the path as it continues on through some bushes between fences, carrying on south.

In another 60 metres, **[2]** you come to another public footpath sign, and out on to the edge of the harbour. *Turn left, take the path on the raised bank and follow the water's edge,* your direction 170 degrees initially.

In 600 metres you come to a wooden barrier and continue walking along the water's edge, in the same direction.

In 270 metres pass a metal fieldgate and continue along the water's edge.

In another 300 metres, there is three-armed footpath sign with a footpath going off to the left, but you continue straight on along the water's edge.

In another 270 metres, there is another three-armed footpath sign, on the left-hand side of the path. Ignore this path and continue straight

on along the water's edge, your direction 170 degrees initially.

In 220 metres **[3]** you will find a Chichester Harbour information board and some steps going down off the track to the left. *Go down these steps and, at the bottom, follow the path as it parallels your original course,* continuing in a southerly direction along the edge of the field. There is a drainage ditch on your left-hand side.

In 120 metres you come to the corner of the field where you *turn left,* along the right-hand edge of the field, going inland away from the harbour, your direction 85 degrees initially.

In 300 metres the path takes you over a wooden footbridge across a drainage ditch and you continue straight on across the next field, in the same direction as before.

In 170 metres the path comes up to a line of Lombardy poplar trees and you carry straight on with the trees and a barbed-wire fence on your left-hand side.

In 250 metres the path brings you out on to the road where you *turn right,* your direction 185 degrees. In 35 metres you pass the entrance to Chedeham House on your left-hand side. **[!]** *Watch out for a path,* 20 metres beyond that; where you *turn left off the road,* just before the drainage ditch. Follow the path along the edge of the field as it parallels the road. In 30 metres there is a short three-armed public footpath sign, pointing to the left and ahead. You continue straight ahead, along the right-hand side of the field, your direction 190 degrees initially. You can see the steeple of Bosham Church off to the left across the fields and creek.

After 380 metres of walking around the edge of the field, the path brings you out on to the roadway and you continue walking straight ahead along the road, past the high brick wall to the Manor House on your right-hand side. In 90 metres the road curves around to the right, past the Old Rectory dead ahead. 35 metres further on, you come to the **Parish Church of St Mary**, Chidham.

30 metres past the church, there is a road going off to the left. **[4]** *Turn left off the road just before this turning,* down a grassy path marked by a public footpath sign, your direction 145 degrees initially.

(If you are going to the early pub/restaurant, the **Old House at Home**, follow the road round to the right. The pub is on the left after 200 metres. Coming out of the pub turn right to retrace your route towards the church and turn right down the grassy path.)

The path takes you around the back of the houses and in 125 metres it curves around to the right, due south initially.

In 240 metres stay on the same path as it takes you through some trees and then around to the left, your direction 105 degrees initially. In another 25 metres, you come up on to the edge of a field and continue along this edge, in the same direction. Follow the line of the overhead cables on your right-hand side. Through the bushes on your left-hand side you can catch glimpses of a lake.

In 270 metres **[!]** *your path goes down to the left away from the field,* through some trees and another 40 metres brings you out on to a narrow country lane.

Turn right and walk along the road, with an orchard on your left-hand side. In 90 metres ignore a turning off to the right, signposted to 'Cobnor House and Farm. Private road'. In a further 10 metres turn right through a small car parking area. In 60 metres *turn left* in front of a hedge on to a permissive path, your direction 100 degrees. Follow the edge of the field with the hedge on your right-hand side.

To your half left across the field, and across the water, you can see Bosham Church, the suggested lunchtime destination.

[5] In 400 metres the path takes you to the water's edge. *Turn left here,* heading for Bosham Church.

In 700 metres follow the path along the edge of a fence – which can be a bit tight if the tide is in. In 50 metres you come to a two-armed public footpath sign where you *turn left* along the side of the garden of the large thatched house to the right of the path, due west.

In 70 metres this brings you out by a grass roundabout, outside the entrance to Grey Thatch. Walk across to the other side of the roundabout and down the road opposite, in the same direction as before. In 90 metres you pass the thatched Rithe Cottage on your right-hand side.

[6] 300 metres further on, you come out through a wooden gate at a T-junction on to a road. *Turn right* here, and in 35 metres you *follow the narrow, unmarked track going up the bank on the right-hand side of the road, up to the water's edge.* Walk along a gravel path with the water on your right-hand side, parallel to the road on your left.

In 140 metres you come down to the corner of a field and *turn right,* following the public footpath sign, continuing along the water's edge, your direction 50 degrees initially.

Follow the water's edge for the next 1.3km until it brings you out on to the main road, the busy A259.

On the far side of the road by the property 'Water Edge', *turn right along the pavement and in 30 metres go left up the old road.* Brookside Cottage is on your left-hand side. After 200 metres, you pass the entrance gate to Newells House on your left-hand side and 30 metres further on you go straight over the crossroads into the dead end.

In 150 metres you go past a metal barrier in the road and past Colnor House. [!] *250 metres further on, just before the old road comes back up to the main road there is a small clump of trees on your right-hand side, at the edge of the field. Turn right here, cutting across the end of the field, back to the A259.* 15 metres brings you up to this A road, where you cross straight over.

[7] On the far side of the road, you will see some stone steps, which you follow down past a public footpath sign. Cross a small wooden bridge out into the field and follow the footpath sign, taking you straight across the field towards the

water on the far side, your direction 190 degrees initially.

150 metres brings you across to the other side of the field and over the stile, up to the edge of the water. *Turn left,* following the path around the water's edge. 150 metres brings you past a footpath sign and you continue along the path as it heads off right along the right-hand edge of a field. You are still following the water's edge on your right-hand side but there is now a hedge between you and the water. 550 metres brings you to a three-armed footpath sign. *Take the right-hand fork* continuing along the water's edge. (At very high tides this path may be awash, in which case take the left fork and rejoin the route at [*] below.)

In 200 metres – some of the route is right along the very edge of the water – you come to a three-armed footpath sign. Turn left here up a steep concrete ramp and then immediately right to continue along the car-wide track which is parallel to your previous waterfront path.

In 150 metres you walk through a metal fieldgate which has a number of signs on it (such as 'Please keep your dog on a lead whilst on our premises'). Walk straight past this gate into the boatyard and straight across to the far side. *Turn left up the car-wide gravel track going into the village.* In 175 metres you come out on to a residential street where you *turn right.*

[*] In 40 metres you pass the entrance to the **Mill Stream Hotel** on the left. 35 metres further on you come out on to the main road (Bosham Lane) through **Bosham**.

Turn right, in 25 metres passing the United Reformed Church on your right-hand side. 200 metres brings you down past **Bosham Walk Arts & Crafts Centre**, with its cafe, on your right-hand side. 90 metres beyond that, *turn right* by **Mariners Coffee Shop** and you pass the **Cumberland Gallery**. 70 metres down here, on the left, is the **Anchor Bleu** pub, which is the suggested lunch place. If you continue on up the road, you can visit Bosham's **Holy Trinity Church**.

To continue the walk after lunch, *turn right out of the pub and retrace your steps back to the junction with Bosham Lane. Go straight across the road into the alleyway opposite.* Walk all the way along this footpath. This is raised above the roadway on your right-hand side, along the water's edge (an area that floods at high tides).

In 550 metres you come to the end of the path, with the long, white 1834 National School building ahead of you and you *turn sharp left* into The Drive (underneath the dead end sign, it says 'public footpath'). 35 metres down this cul-de-sac, *turn right off the road,* following the public footpath sign along a path between hedgerows, your direction 110 degrees initially.

In 200 metres the path brings you out through the driveway of a cottage (Byways) and you cross straight over the road on to the footpath on the other side.

[8] *You follow this path going east for the next 1km until you come to another road.* In more detail: From the road, go straight across the field ahead of you. In about 300 metres, the path bends right and then left over a couple of small footbridges, returning to its original course along a car-wide track, following the two-armed footpath sign. When the track leads up to a house on the left, you follow the footpath to the right of the house.

Another 500 metres brings you out on to the road. Just before this, on your left-hand side, there is a metal public footpath sign pointing straight over the road.

Cross the road and carry on along the path on the other side, in the same direction as before. In 650 metres you come *to a T-junction* with a three-armed public footpath sign. Here you *turn right,* your direction 185 degrees.

In 270 metres, you come to a three-armed public footpath sign where **[9]** you *turn left,* walking along the next side of the field, with a hedgerow on your right-hand side, your direction 80 degrees initially.

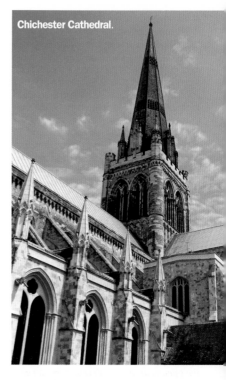

Chichester Cathedral.

After 300 metres going straight along this path, you come to a two-armed public footpath sign and in a further 100 metres to some planks taking you across a small creek, which makes its way out into the channel on your right-hand side. Once over the planks, follow the path as it wends through woodland around to the left, following the distant edge of the water. From here, you can see Chichester Cathedral across the water on your right-hand side.

In 200 metres you climb up a short slope with a step, and then the path proceeds along a ridge which becomes the sea wall ahead. In 60 metres you get to the sea wall and continue on along its top. The sea wall has been rebuilt in places and can be very muddy.

In 700 metres you come to a two-armed public footpath sign and some steps down, immediately after which you cross a small creek on a wooden footbridge. (Between this footbridge and the next one is where you may need your gumboots at very high tides.) Continuing along the path for another 40 metres, you then cross a delightfully clear stream on a larger wooden footbridge going through reeds. 50 metres further on, go across another wooden footbridge.

80 metres further on, the path brings you out besides a picturesque duck pond with weeping willows and a thatched cottage on its far side. This is the village of **Fishbourne**. Another 30 metres brings you out by the entrance to The Mill on the right, and a road going off to the left. Go straight across the road and follow the sign for the public footpath through a metal kissing gate. Follow the path along the bank of a stream to your left, and in 80 metres go through a metal gate and continue along the path. 20 metres further on, to your left, there is a sign giving information about Chichester Harbour and Fishbourne Meadows.

Cross over a stream on the wooden planks and **[!]** immediately turn left off the boardwalk to *follow a grass path as it heads around to the left.* Do not be tempted to stay on the boardwalk straight ahead, but keep close to the hedgerow on your left-hand side, your direction 110 degrees initially. In 20 metres you go over another wooden bridge and walk straight ahead, keeping the stream on your left-hand side.

In another 100 metres, cross a concrete bridge with a metal railing. Walk straight ahead for 25 metres and then turn left through a wooden fieldgate going initially along the right-hand edge of the field, and then straight across the field.

In 35 metres the path forks and you *take the left-hand fork* continuing straight ahead towards the far left-hand corner and a four-armed metal footpath sign. Then *take the left-hand path* going through a wooden kissing gate, and into the trees which form a tunnel, your direction 355 degrees initially. In 75 metres a concrete bridge with

metal railings takes you over a small brook. 100 metres further on, you come out through another kissing gate on to a main road. Cross the road carefully. On the far side, *turn right* along the pavement.

(However, if you want to detour to visit the **Roman palace**, go straight ahead, following the public footpath sign, instead of turning right. This soon becomes a tarmac cycle path. In 250 metres, ignore a stile on your right-hand side and follow the path as it bends sharp left. In a further 250 metres, go through a swing gate on your left with a wooden fieldgate to its left-hand side, and follow the tree line past the café to the museum entrance. Afterwards, retrace your steps to the main road.)

In 100 metres, keep to the pavement. It leads into a footpath to Fishbourne Road East *through the tunnel under the A27 Chichester bypass,* next to a cycle path. On the other side of the tunnel, continue walking straight ahead down Fishbourne Road East.

Follow the roads for the next 1.75km, straight into the heart of Chichester. In more detail: 500 metres after the tunnel, the road curves around to the right and you stay on the left-hand pavement going straight ahead. Cross the railway line ahead.

On the other side of the tracks, walk straight down the road ahead. In 40 metres you see a sign on your right (to the city centre and station). 200 metres further on, you come to a crossroads with a mini roundabout at the end of Sherborne Road and you go straight over into Westgate, in the same direction as before.

Keep straight on down this road until you come to Westgate roundabout. *Turn right here into Avenue de Chartres, cross straight over the road and go right,* past the Old Cottage Indian Restaurant on your left-hand side. 40 metres down the road, there is a tall brick-and-flint wall with a small black plaque pointing off to the left (to Bishop's Palace Gardens). *Turn left down the footpath by the side of the wall* and then right through the gate into the gardens. If the gardens have closed for the day, retrace your steps to the roundabout and turn right to get to the cathedral along the roadside.

Once through the gate into the garden, walk straight ahead, your direction 150 degrees, along the path taking you through the gardens, with the cathedral away on your left-hand side. Keep to the path ahead for 150 metres, as it curves around to the left between low hedges and go through the doorway in the stone wall ahead. Follow the path around to the left and then, in 10 metres, follow it around to the right. In another 20 metres there is a view of the **Bishop's Palace** through the wrought-iron gate on your left and 20 metres further on you go left through the wooden gate into the grounds of the palace. Go immediately right through a stone archway, and walk straight down the street, your direction 105 degrees, with the cathedral on your left-hand side. 40 metres down here, you will see the Deanery on your right-hand side. Turn left down St Richard's Walk, which leads you into the cathedral cloisters. Here you turn immediately left and walk outside to go around to the West Door, where you can enter **Chichester Cathedral** itself.

Out of the West Door, continue on up to the road, past the Bell Tower on your right. Turn right into West Street and walk along the north side of the cathedral.

The **Dolphin & Anchor Hotel** is on the other side of the street, just before the Market Cross at the main crossroads. (If everywhere in the centre is closed, there are a **Café Rouge** and a **Slug & Lettuce** on Southgate, before the station.)

The station is eight minutes away. Coming out of the tea place, cross over the road and go down the left-hand side of the cathedral to the first exit on the left, The Close, which brings you into South Street, where you turn right. (The next left, West Pallant, would take you to **Pallant House**, on the corner with North Pallant, should you want a slight detour.)

Continuing on the main suggested route down South Street, in 200 metres you cross over a busy road, using a pedestrian crossing. Continuing in the same direction, in 100 metres you come to the station approach road on your right-hand side, and so finish at **Chichester station**.

Lunch & tea places

Old House at Home Cot Lane, Chidham, PO18 8SU (01243 572477, www.theold houseathome.co.uk). **Open** 10.30am-11pm daily. Food served noon-2.30pm, 6.30-9.30pm Mon-Sat; noon-9.30pm Sun. A gastropub that offers excellent food at reasonable prices.

Bosham Walk Arts & Crafts Centre café Bosham Walk, Bosham Lane, Bosham, PO18 8HX (01243 572475, www.bosham-walk.co.uk). **Open** 10am-4pm daily.

Mariners High Street, Bosham, PO18 8LS (01243 572960). **Open** Summer 10.30am-5pm daily. Winter 10.30am-4pm daily. **No credit cards**. This coffee shop is an option for refreshments in Bosham.

Anchor Bleu High Street, Bosham, PO18 8LS (01243 573956, www.bosham. org/anchor). **Open** Summer 10.30am-11.30pm Mon-Sat; noon-10.30pm Sun. Winter 11am-3pm, 5-10.30pm Mon-Wed; 11am-3pm, 5-11pm Thur; 11am-11.30pm Fri, Sat; noon-10.30pm Sun. Food served noon-2.30pm, 6.30-9.30pm daily. Superbly located and busy all year round, this pub is the suggested lunchtime stop.

Cloisters Café Chichester Cathedral, Chichester, PO19 9PX (01243 782595, www.chichestercathedral.org.uk). **Open** 9am-5pm Mon-Sat; 10am-4pm Sun. If you get here in time, the cafe serves tea, coffee, home-made cakes and more substantial meals.

If you're stuck, there are also branches of **Café Rouge** (no.30, 01243 781751, www.caferouge.co.uk) and **Slug & Lettuce** (nos.27-28, 01243 792012, www.slugandlettuce.co.uk) on Southgate, just before you reach Chichester station.

Walk 38

Hanborough to Charlbury

Blenheim Palace and Cornbury Park.

Start: Hanborough station
Finish: Charlbury station

Length: 20.5km (12.7 miles)

Time: 6 hours. For the whole outing, including trains, sights and meals, allow at least 11 hours.

Transport: Take the train nearest to **9am** from **Paddington** station to **Hanborough** (journey time about

1 hour 10 minutes). Trains back from **Charlbury** are hourly (journey time about 1 hour 20 minutes). Buy a day return to Charlbury.

OS Landranger Map: 164
OS Explorer Map: 180
Hanborough, map reference SP433142, is in **Oxfordshire**, 7km north-west of Oxford.

Toughness: 6 out of 10

Walk notes: The River Evenlode and its soft, easy hills and fertile countryside inspired Tolkien's Shire, home to the hobbits. At lunchtime, you could take a dip in the river and picnic in the meadow by the Stonesfield Ford and the old slate quarries.

Before lunch, there are the 2,100 acres of the Great Park, leading to Blenheim Palace, its lake and the Column of Victory that the first Duke of Marlborough had placed on the horizon so that he could see it from his bedroom. Once over the wall out of the park, the route is along Akeman Street, the old Roman road from Alchester to Cirencester, with big stone slabs from the old road still visible in places. This is now part of the Oxfordshire Way. The leg of over a mile to Stonesfield is through open farmland and progress can be hard work if you're walking into the wind. You pass through the delightful stone villages of Stonesfield, Finstock

and finally Charlbury, entering it from a footpath beside Lord Rotherwick's deer park, Cornbury Park.

Walk options: At point **[7]** in the walk directions, you can turn right to go directly into Stonesfield for lunch, without going down to the riverbank. After lunch, you can walk straight along the Oxfordshire Way into Charlbury (see the double asterisk **[**✱✱**]** in the walk directions). Alternatively, you could take one of the infrequent buses from Stonesfield to Charlbury or Oxford, or phone for a taxi.

History: The Royal Estate of **Woodstock** was granted to the first Duke of Marlborough in 1704. The old medieval palace had been the birthplace of the Black Prince in 1330 and Elizabeth I was imprisoned there during Queen Mary's reign. It was extensively damaged by the Parliamentary army in the Civil War.

Blenheim Palace was built for the first Duke in recognition of his victory over the French at the Battle of Blenheim in 1704, and the **Column of Victory** has some 6,000 words engraved on it in honour of the Duke. Designed by Vanbrugh, the palace is a fine example of English baroque, set in parkland landscaped by Capability Brown. The palace was the birthplace of **Sir Winston Churchill** in 1874, and there is a permanent exhibition of Churchilliana in the palace.

The palace and gardens are open to the public from 10.30am to 5.30pm daily from mid February to the end of October, and 10.30am to 5.30pm Wednesday to Sunday from November to mid December. Entry costs (2010) £18 to the palace, park and gardens, or £10.30 to the park and gardens only; family tickets and other reduced tickets are also available.

The walk through the park is on public footpaths or permissive paths, however, so there are no admission charge if you keep to the directions below. For more details (and for information about what's on), phone 0800 849 6500.

The village of Stonesfield is the home of **Stonesfield slates**, the stone roof-tiles characteristic of villages and towns in Oxfordshire and of many of the Oxford Colleges. The slates are no longer mined, so only second-hand tiles can be obtained – at great expense.

Cornbury Park is a private estate, the deer park of which was carved out of **Wychwood Forest** (as was Blenheim). The forest was once a vast royal hunting ground that extended over much of western Oxfordshire; in pre-Norman times, it stretched all the way to London. Now the sole surviving remnant of the forest lies within Cornbury Park estate. The imposing 17th-century mansion was built for Edward Hyde, who was Viscount Cornbury and the first Earl of Clarendon. As one of Charles II's chief advisors and Lord Chancellor, he became the virtual head of the government in 1660.

Walk directions

[1] [Numbers in square brackets refer to the map]
Coming out of **Hanborough station**, walk the 100 metres up the access road to the A4095, dead ahead. *Cross over* the road by the pedestrian traffic lights and *turn left* along the pavement. Down in the valley on your right-hand side you can just make out the River Glyme. In 100 metres you cross over a bridge over the railway line. Continue along the road, uphill, towards the village of Hanborough.

In 300 metres you pass a large stone cottage (no.153) on your right-hand side. 100 metres beyond that, you come to a turning on your right-hand side (Park Lane), which is a dead end. **[2]**

Turn right into Park Lane, gently downhill. In 200 metres, you come to the end of the houses. Continue straight on along the path ahead, indicated by a bridleway sign, your direction initially 325 degrees, with a stone wall on your right-hand side.

In 20 metres you pass on your left the entrance to High Thatch. Over the wall, ahead on your right-hand side, you can see the tower of Combe Church.

In 100 metres the path brings you out into a field and you follow it along the right-hand edge of the field, going downhill in the same direction as you were just previously.

In 150 metres, on approaching a wide gap in the hedge ahead, *turn right* through a narrow gap in the hedge to your right and *immediately turn left* along the left-hand edge of that field, still downhill.

In 300 metres you come to the far corner of this field, with a metal field-gate on your left-hand side. *Turn left* through the gap to the left of the fieldgate (where there used to be a wooden swing gate) to go down the car-wide track with a stone wall on your left-hand side, your direction 250 degrees. The **River Evenlode** runs alongside the track, down below on your right-hand side.

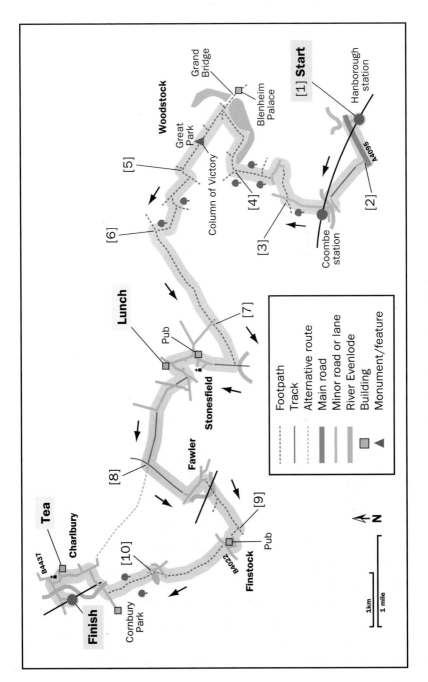

Hanborough to Charlbury

Woodstock

Grand Bridge

Blenheim Palace

Great Park

[1] **Start**

Hanborough station

A4095

[2]

Column of Victory

[5]

[4]

[3]

Coombe station

[6]

Lunch

Pub

[7]

Stonesfield

Footpath
Track
Alternative route
Main road
Minor road or lane
River Evenlode
Building
Monument/feature

Fawler

[8]

Tea

Charlbury

B4437

[9]

Pub

Finstock

B4022

[10]

Cornbury Park

Finish

N

1km
1 mile

In 115 metres you come up to a road. *Turn right* along this road, in 15 metres crossing the river on a stone bridge. In a further 125 metres you pass Blenheim Palace Sawmills Eco-Business Centre on your left-hand side.

In 90 metres pass under the railway bridge and keep straight on, steadily uphill, ignoring ways off and with Combe Church visible on the horizon ahead on your left-hand side. In 450 metres you come to the top of the hill, where there is a house on your right.

In a further 200 metres (and 25 metres after another house on your right-hand side), there are footpath signs pointing off to the left and right. **[3]** *Turn right* off the road, over a stile, following the footpath sign ('East End half a mile'), your direction 85 degrees initially, along a grassy path.

In 200 metres you come to the far left-hand corner of the field. Cross over the stile in the hedge and *turn right,* walking along the right-hand side of the next field, with the hedge on your right, towards a house in the distance, your direction 110 degrees initially.

In 300 metres you come to the far side of the field. Cross a stile and continue straight across the next field, to cross a stile 50 metres away, next to a stone building. *Turn left* up the drive for 30 metres to the road.

Turn left along the road. In 225 metres you come to the Combe Gate entrance to the Blenheim Estate. *Turn right,* following the footpath sign through the high wooden kissing gate to the left of the main gate, to go straight ahead up the estate road. In 50 metres you come to a T-junction and *turn left.* Follow the road as it bends around to the right and down the hill through the trees. The road then swings left then right.

In 350 metres you come to a clearing; if you stop just before the tree-line and look to the right, you may just be able to see

Blenheim Palace.

the top of Blenheim Palace through the trees. The road now swings to the left then right downhill, through some conifers.

300 metres further on, you come **[4]** to the edge of the trees on the right-hand side, where the road ahead goes around to the left and down to a cattle grid. Straight ahead on the hillside opposite are half a dozen copper beeches in two clusters. On your right-hand side here, there is a green and white public footpath sign. **[!]** *Turn off the road* and walk around the tree-line on your right, following the grassy path as it (initially) parallels the wooden fence on the left, your direction 55 degrees. Keep ahead as the path converges with the fence on your left.

In 200 metres you come down near to the edge of the lake, with a 'Private – No Public Access' sign over to your right. Follow the path left to *go over the stile on your left* or go through the wooden swing gate 5 metres to its right. Beyond the stile/gate, keep ahead along the edge of the lake, your direction 70 degrees initially. In 70 metres you come to a junction in the track and follow the wide track *around to the right,* along the side of the lake, gently uphill.

In 600 metres the path curves sharply to the left and up a rise. From this point, you have a fine view over to your right across the lake to the Grand Bridge and your first real view of Blenheim Palace, a view that will slowly unfold as you continue along this path, around the lake towards the bridge.

Keep to this path for the next 600 metres, mostly uphill, ignoring ways off down to your right to the lake, until the path brings you down to a wooden swing gate at a T-junction with a tarmac drive. *Turn right* down the drive and in 85 metres, at a junction in the drive, go through a wooden swing gate in the electric cattle fence on your *left-hand side.*

If you want to visit **Blenheim Palace**, which is highly recommended, instead of turning left through this gate, *continue ahead* down the drive to cross over the

Grand Bridge and keep ahead for the Palace.

But to continue the walk: Having gone through the swing gate, head across the grass, gently uphill, towards the **Column of Victory**, your direction 325 degrees. In 500 metres, at the Column, pass it and continue ahead across the grass in the same direction as before and in 70 metres cross the wooden fencing ahead at a part lowered for walkers.

[!] The suggested way ahead may not be an official public footpath, but it is well used and appears to be permitted by the Blenheim Estate. **[!]** *Keep ahead* across the grass, your direction 325 degrees, keeping parallel to the wooden field fence 150 metres over to your left. In 400 metres the path across the grass comes down to a tarmac estate road, coming in from your right. There is a public footpath down this estate road.

You can now *either* continue along this estate road for 300 metres, in the same direction as before, then *make your way left* across the grass to the stile in the wooden fence over to your left, or to ensure that you don't miss this stile *turn left* immediately on joining the estate road and make for the farm gate in the wooden fence now ahead of you.

On reaching the farm gate, *turn right* along the fence-line and keep ahead beside the fence on your left-hand side. In 300 metres the fence turns half left (45 degrees) and in a further 70 metres **[!]** *you turn left* over the stile in the fence, marked with a yellow footpath arrow. **[5]**

Continue ahead beside the wooden fence on your left-hand side, your direction 210 degrees. In 250 metres you come to a copse of trees surrounded by a wooden fence. *Turn right* and follow the fence around the trees in a circle.

After walking around the circle of the fence for some 75 metres **[!]** you head *half right* across the field, aiming for the wooden kissing gate in the fence ahead of you, with a copse of copper beech trees ahead, slightly left, on the far side of this fence, your direction 235 degrees.

In 110 metres go through this wooden kissing gate and follow the direction indicated by the Blenheim Park footpath arrow (white on a black background). You are now aiming for a gate in the wooden fence on the far side of this field, to the right of a second clump of copper beech trees in the middle of the field, your direction 320 degrees.

In 130 metres you pass the clump of trees on your left-hand side and in a further 200 metres you go through the wooden kissing gate in the fence ahead. You now *bear half left* across a paddock to go through another wooden kissing gate, coming out on to a car-wide track, with a double wooden fieldgate opposite. *Turn right* along this track and in 50 metres go through a narrow band of trees at a field boundary.

On the far side [!] *turn sharp left,* following the yellow arrow along a car-wide track, your direction 235 degrees, with a hedge and tree-line on your left and an open field to your right. The track (muddy in winter) curves to the right and then begins to swing left.

[!] In 150 metres you come to a post on your right-hand side marked with multiple Blenheim Park footpath arrows. Here *turn right* and pass through a wooden swing gate, keeping ahead beside a wooden fence on your left-hand side, your direction 305 degrees, between large fields.

In 400 metres, as the wooden fence on your left ends and before an electric cattle fence starts on your right, *go through* the wooden fieldgate ahead of you, marked with Blenheim Park footpath arrows. 15 metres ahead at the edge of the wood is a footpath post with a yellow arrow. Follow the direction of the arrow along a narrow path between the edge of the wood on your left and the electric cattle fence on your right.

In 60 metres [!] you *turn left* through the trees on an unmarked but clear path into the wooded area: in a further 40 metres follow a yellow footpath arrow on a wooden bridge with wooden railings to cross over this bridge. 20 metres further on, you come to a stony car-wide track. *Turn right,* your direction 350 degrees, though the wood.

In 200 metres you come to another track at a crossroads. *Turn left* on to a footpath and in 25 metres go up wooden steps over a high stone wall [6], and leave the Great Park down the steps on the far side, going into the large field beyond.

Walk straight ahead with a very ancient hedgerow (at least 500 years old) on your left-hand side, your direction 260 degrees along a path that was once the Roman **Akeman Street**.

You are now on the **Oxfordshire Way**, which you will follow straight ahead for the next 2km.

But, in more detail: In 500 metres you go straight over a road and continue along the footpath on the opposite side, still with the hedgerow on your left-hand side. Soon you can see the rooftops of the village of Stonesfield, the suggested stopping place for lunch. In about 800 metres the path switches to the other side of the hedgerow and you continue ahead, now with the hedge on your right-hand side.

In 700 metres you come to another road. [7] If you do not intend to picnic beside the River Evenlode, you can head direct to your lunchtime pub by *turning right* along this road (Combe Road), to rejoin the 'picnic route' at the asterisk [*] below.

The direct route: Head up Combe Road and, in 475 metres, you come to a T-junction with Woodstock Road by Stonesfield's War Memorial. Here *turn left* and in 100 metres you come to the junction with Pond Hill, on your right. The Black Head pub is 45 metres down the road on your left.

To head for the River Evenlode: Cross over the road and continue straight on, keeping a hedge and valley on your left, your initial direction 240 degrees. At the end of the first field, pass through the field boundary with a stone wall on your right and *turn right,* then *immediately left* to continue ahead, still following the hedge and valley on your left, in the same direction as before, but now with a vast field on your right.

Continue along the Oxfordshire Way, ignoring all ways off, for a distance of 650 metres from Combe Road, and then go through a metal kissing gate to the **Stonesfield Ford** meadows by old stone quarries, to swing right on a wide grassy path down to the **River Evenlode**. In 100 metres go through a metal kissing gate and *turn right* – where to go left takes you over the Evenlode footbridge. (30 metres further along the river, on this side and right of the footbridge, is a good spot to swim. This whole area is good for a picnic.)

Having turned right, your onward path into Stonesfield is relatively steeply upwards, away from Stonesfield Ford, initially in a cutting, your direction 10 degrees. Go up some steps in the path

and after 200 metres up this path go through concrete bollards. In a further 25 metres pass on your left-hand side an Oxfordshire Geology Trust notice about Stonesfield's fossils and slates. Here the Oxfordshire Way branches off to the left on a grassy path, but your route is *directly ahead.* The path soon levels out and becomes a track (Brook Lane) between hedges, as you come into the outskirts of **Stonesfield**.

In 200 metres you come to a churchyard on your left-hand side. The track is now a surfaced road (Church Street). Keep ahead and, in a further 175 metres, the road swings to the right at the junction with High Street on your left.

In 30 metres you pass the **Black Head** pub, a possible lunchtime refreshment stop (liquid only), on your right-hand side. In 45 metres you come to a T-junction where you continue more or less straight on, slightly to the left, along Pond Hill. **[*]**

Continue down Pond Hill and ignore all roads off to the left and right. You soon pass on your right-hand side **'Best One' Convenience Store**, a possible stop for basic picnic provisions. Some 400 metres along Pond Hill from the junction with Church Street, you come to a T-junction with the Ridings. Opposite, slightly to your right, is the **White Horse** bistro-pub-restaurant, another possible lunchtime stop.

At the T-junction *turn left, downhill,* following the sign to Fawler and Charlbury. In 160 metres ignore the Boot Street fork, uphill to the left, and 125 metres further on down the hill, you pass a 1722 house called Clockcase on your right-hand side. 30 metres further on **[!]** *turn right* off the road up a car-wide track, rejoining the Oxfordshire Way, your direction 330 degrees initially. Note the traditional slates on the building on your right-hand side at the start of the track and looking back, on other buildings in the village.

In 350 metres you come to the top of the hill next to a barn (Highfield Farm). 100 metres further on you come to a crossroads where you can look back for a panoramic view of the village of Stonesfield. Take the tarmac lane going *straight ahead,* on the Oxfordshire Way, heading in the same direction as before, initially with a hedge on your left and open fields to your right. Once over the brow of the hill, you have open fields on both sides of you.

In 500 metres you come to a building on the right-hand side, where the lane curves sharply around to the right ahead. *Turn left* off the track. In 15 metres you pass Hill Barn Switchgear Station on your right, with a wooden fieldgate on its left. *Turn right* through the wooden swing gate next to the fieldgate, with a blue (faded) Oxfordshire Way arrow on it. Continue *straight ahead,* downhill, along the left-hand edge of the field, following a hedge and fenceline, your direction 290 degrees initially.

In 150 metres you come to the bottom, left-hand corner of the field. Go through the (missing) wooden gate and *turn right* up the car-wide track, following the sign for the Oxfordshire Way. The track heads down into a dip then up the other side, before levelling out, with a hedge on your left and open fields to your right.

After 750 metres along this track you come to a crossroads, opposite a clump of trees **[8]** where the Oxfordshire Way goes straight ahead through the trees. **[**]** (To take the **shortcut** continue straight on at this point, along the Oxfordshire Way, all the way into Charlbury. In 1.45km the path comes out on to a road, *turn left* along the road into the village, and follow the instructions below for getting to the suggested tea stop or to the railway station via the churchyard.)

The main route is to *turn left* on to the car-wide track going into a field on your left, with a footpath post with multiple blue arrows on your right. Walk along the right-hand edge of the field, initially with a hedgerow and later a stone wall on your right-hand side, your direction 220 degrees. Ahead, on the hillside opposite, you can see the village of Finstock, which is on the route of the walk (and further to the right, on the horizon, the Wychwood Forest).

In 900 metres you come to a T-junction with the main road (do not turn right and head for Finstock station: there are no trains at weekends and only one a day in each direction on weekdays). Instead, *turn left* at this T-junction to go down the hill into the village. In 70 metres you pass Manor Barn, a restored farm building, on your right-hand side.

200 metres further on, you pass a postbox on your right-hand side. 40 metres beyond the postbox, as the road starts to go uphill, and opposite a bus stop, *turn right* down a tarmac lane, going past Corner Cottage on your left-hand side, your direction 160 degrees.

In 100 metres, at the end of the tarmac, keep ahead, slightly right, and in 80 metres go over a stile to the right of a padlocked wooden swing gate. Cross the field ahead towards the ironstone railway bridge and in 55 metres you go over a stile or through the wooden swing gate to its right, to go under the archway beneath the railway. 10 metres beyond the archway, *turn left* and cross the footbridge over the **River Evenlode**. On its far side, *turn right* along the riverbank, your direction 245 degrees. (In summer, the first 75 metres of this path are often overgrown.)

After 150 metres along the riverbank, go through a metal kissing gate. 15 metres further on, follow the path as it bends *sharp left,* away from the river, your direction 240 degrees.

Walk along the bottom of the valley on a grassy way and in 250 metres you come up a gentle incline to go through a metal kissing gate. 8 metres further on you come up to a meeting of paths, with a footpath post ahead. *Turn left* for 5 metres and then at a T-junction *turn right* on to a valley path going gently uphill, in the same direction you were going in before (245 degrees), between hedges and barbed-wire fences. The path can be muddy in winter.

After 400 metres along this rutted path with an uneven footbed (unpleasant to walk along), you pass under mini pylons, and 10 metres beyond you pass a metal fieldgate on your right-hand side. In a further 20 metres by a footpath post with a yellow Circular Walk arrow **[9] [!]** you *turn right* through a gap into a field. Follow the path up the left-hand edge of the field, your direction 315 degrees, steeply uphill. In 70 metres pass through bushes, *bear right, then left,* and keep ahead now with the hedgerow on your left-hand side and a vast field to your right, your direction 300 degrees. (Note: if you stay on the path straight ahead between hedgerows, you will find it very overgrown in places.)

In 140 metres you come up to a white farmgate on your left-hand side. Pass through a gap to its *left* and follow the path around to the left as it becomes a car-wide track (Wards Lane), with allotments on your left and properties on your right, heading into the village of **Finstock**, your direction 255 degrees.

In 50 metres you pass a cottage on your right called Madeleine. 200 metres further on, you come to a T-junction with the main street going through the village. *Turn right* into School Road, in 20 metres passing a Parish Council & Village noticeboard on your right-hand side. In a further 100 metres you pass the Village Shop and Post Office on your right-hand side.

Next door to the shop and post office is the **Crown** pub (closed down when we went to press), and 20 metres beyond the pub, you pass the village War Memorial on your right-hand side and come out to a T-junction with the B4022 road. On the opposite side of the road is Manor House. *Turn right,* following the sign for Charlbury and Chipping Norton.

50 metres down this busy and sometimes dangerous road, **[!]** *turn left* over the unusual stone stile, marked by a footpath sign 'To Charlbury'. Go through the hedge archway beyond, across to the far right-hand corner of the lawn. Go through the leftmost of the two fieldgates ahead, to walk straight down the track ahead, your direction 315 degrees, ignoring all ways off.

In 650 metres you come out to a car-wide track with a stone wall to the right. Here *bear right,* your direction 30 degrees.

In 60 metres you join a main track coming in from the left. Here **[!]** *turn half left* off the track, heading across the grass to a footpath post with a yellow arrow, your direction due north. In 60 metres you pass the post to go straight on down the avenue of trees ahead of you.

Head down the avenue of trees, passing a footpath post on your left-hand side. In 440 metres you come down through the trees to bear right on to a tarmac road. **[10]** *Turn left* on this road, opposite Southill Business Park, along the side of a trout lake, your direction 340 degrees.

In 115 metres you come to a green-coloured metal gate into Cornbury Park. *Go through* the green-coloured metal swing gate on its right, marked 'Footpath gate'. Keep ahead, uphill along the path, your direction 350 degrees, and in 90 metres bear left to go through a metal kissing gate.

Now follow the footpath ahead, going between a high metal railing (deer-protection fence) on your left and a lightly wooded area on your right.

In 450 metres, the wooded area on your right-hand side ends and you keep ahead along the path, still beside the high metal railing on your left-hand side, in the same direction as before. Deer can sometimes be seen in the park on your left-hand side. On your right-hand side, as you walk along, you will see the village of Charlbury.

In 350 metres you come to the end of the path, and in the top left-hand corner of the field go through a metal kissing gate. Now walk along a flagstoned path for 25 metres, to exit the park through a high wooden gate, which brings you out by the main entrance to **Cornbury Park**. To your left you have a view of the house. Turn right down the drive, towards the village, your direction 40 degrees.

In 90 metres you cross a stone bridge over the **River Evenlode**, way below. 150 metres further on, the drive crosses over the railway line. On the left you can see the tower of Charlbury Church. 100 metres further on, you come up on to the road. Cross over to the pavement on the far side and *turn left* towards the village, your direction 330 degrees.

In 550 metres you come up past **St Mary the Virgin Church**, Charlbury, where the road curves sharply round to the right. You can take a shortcut through the churchyard down to the railway station, or (for tea) *turn right* up Church Street.

In 80 metres you come to the suggested tea place, the **Bell Hotel**, on your right-hand side. To get to the railway station after tea, coming out of the hotel, retrace your steps to the churchyard, enter the churchyard and follow the tarmac path around the back of the church to the right. Follow the path straight out the other side of the churchyard, through a metal swing gate, past the Old Rectory on your left-hand side and down the road ahead. In 150 metres you come to a T-junction with the main road. *Turn left* down the hill towards the railway station.

In 130 metres the road crosses over the river. 85 metres further on, turn left on the station approach road for the train back to London. **Charlbury station** is a listed building, designed by Isambard Kingdom Brunel.

Lunch & tea places

In summer, we suggest you **picnic** beside the River Evenlode or in the village of Stonesfield. The village has a convenience store, should you need provisions.

White Horse *The Ridings, Stonesfield, OX29 8EA (01993 891063)*. **Open** noon-3pm, 4-11pm Tue-Fri; noon-3pm, 6-11pm Sat; noon-3pm Sun. *Food served* noon-2pm, 6.30-9pm Tue-Sat; noon-2.30pm Sun. Following its reopening in August 2009, this lunch option is now as a bistro-cum-gastropub, serving sandwiches, light meals and main courses in formal and informal dining areas. This is only the latest in a long line of reinventions, punctuated by lengthy periods spent out of business; given the pub's history of closures, it is best to phone ahead.

Bell Hotel *Church Street, Charlbury, OX7 3PP (01608 810278, www.bellhotel-charlbury.com)*. **Open** 10am-10.30pm Mon-Thur, Sun; 10am-12.30am Fri, Sat. *Food served* noon-2.30pm, 6-9pm daily. A comfortable and pleasant tea stop near the end of the walk.

Bull *Sheep Street, Charlbury, OX7 3RR (01608 810689, www.bullinn-charlbury.com)*. **Open** noon-2.30pm, 6-11pm Tue-Sat; noon-3.30pm Sun. *Food served* noon-2pm, 6.30-9pm Tue-Fri; noon-2.30pm, 6.30-9pm Sat; noon-2.30pm Sun.

Rose & Crown *1 Market Street, Charlbury, OX7 3PL (01608 810103)*. **Open** noon-1am daily.

Walk 39

Manningtree Circular

The River Stour – Constable country.

Start and finish: Manningtree station

Length: 17.3km (10.7 miles)

Time: 5 hours. For the whole outing, including trains, sights and meals, allow at least 9 hours 30 minutes.

Transport: Take the train nearest to **9.30am** from **Liverpool Street** station to **Manningtree** (journey time about 1 hour). Trains back from Manningtree run two or three times an hour.

OS Landranger Maps: 168 & 155
OS Explorer Map: 196
Manningtree, map reference TM094323, is in **Essex**, 10km north-east of Colchester. East Bergholt, in the second half of the walk, is in **Suffolk**, 3km north-west of Manningtree.

Toughness: 4 out of 10

Walk notes: This is a walk through the Stour valley that Constable loved, passing by the settings of some of his most famous paintings, a landscape now protected as the Dedham Vale Area of Outstanding Natural Beauty. Lunch is in the beautiful village of Dedham. In the afternoon, the route goes past Dedham Lock and Mill, and from Essex into Suffolk, along the River Stour to Stratford St Mary and its church. From there, you walk to East Bergholt, Constable's birthplace, which has a church with an unusual bell cage and an old friary that is now an organic farming community. Tea is by Flatford Mill, with more Constable connections.

After prolonged heavy rain, the river may overflow and you might have to make a detour to avoid flooded water-meadows.

Walk options: There are bus services connecting Stratford St Mary, East Bergholt and Dedham with Manningtree and Colchester, or you could get a taxi from any of these villages.

You can shorten the walk by 4km by not going to Stratford St Mary after lunch. Directions for the shortcut are given in the text.

History: **John Constable** was born in 1776 in East Bergholt, and his successful corn-merchant father owned Flatford Mill and eventually Dedham Mill. Though supposed to take over the family business, Constable became a landscape painter and much of his work reflects his attachment to Suffolk scenes. The love of his life, Maria Bicknell, was the granddaughter of the rector of East Bergholt, known to him from childhood, but Constable had to overcome opposition due to their difference in social class before they could marry. When Maria died of tuberculosis in 1828, Constable had to bring up their seven children alone. He died in 1837, at the age of 61. Constable never went abroad, concentrating on painting landscapes in Suffolk, Hampstead, Salisbury and Brighton (the Constable family moved south for the sake of Maria's health). This walk passes the buildings in Dedham where Constable was a grammar-school pupil and the scenes for many of his paintings, including *The Hay Wain, The Cornfield, Dedham Vale, Dedham Mill, Flatford Mill* and *The Valley of the Stour.*

St Mary's Church, Lawford, has long views over the River Stour and its estuary. It was probably built by Sir Benet de Cokefield, Lord of the (Lawford) Manor, in about 1340. It has a fine chancel in the Decorated Gothic style, and a timber roof typical of the area. The discovery of treasonable correspondence led to the church's forfeiture by the Crown during the Reformation.

The village of **Dedham** prospered with the wool trade in the 15th and 16th centuries. Work started on the **Parish Church of St Mary**, Dedham, in 1492. Constable attended services at this church, and its tower is a feature in his paintings. The church was renowned for its preaching and contains a 17th-century monument that depicts a preacher known as 'Roaring Rogers' with a book in his hands.

Stratford St Mary contains a henge, a circular sanctuary dated around 4,000 BC; it can only be detected from the air. The church, a fine example of Decorated Gothic, is far larger than needed by the village, which had a peak population of 673 – it was built as big as their prosperity from agriculture could afford, to honour God. The letters of the alphabet are depicted around the exterior, to remind passers-by that all the sacred scriptures can be composed from these letters. The oldest house in the village dates from 1334 and the timber-framed

Priest's House has solid oak beams, four to five inches thick.

The **Parish Church of St Mary the Virgin, East Bergholt**, contains a possibly 15th-century inscription that reads: 'What ere thou art, here reader see, in this pale glass what thou shalt be, despised wormes and putrid slime, then dust forgot and lost in time.' In its churchyard is the tomb of Constable's parents. The tower was never completed, it is said because of the death in 1530 of the church's benefactor, Cardinal Wolsey. The bells were therefore 'temporarily' housed in a **bell cage**, built in 1531 – one that is still used and is unique in that the bells are rung, not by wheel and rope, but by force of hand.

Old Hall, East Bergholt, has had many incarnations: a country house (painted by Constable), a nunnery and then a friary. In 1972, it was set up as a commune by a group who advertised in the *Guardian* for middle-class Greens. It has matured into a stable community.

Walk directions

[1] [Numbers in square brackets refer to the map]
Coming off the train from London go under the tunnel to exit **Manningtree station** and *turn right downhill* with a car park on your left, your direction 255 degrees.

At the bottom of the slope *turn left,* following the footpath sign to Flatford and Dedham. In 25 metres you reach a gravelled track and *turn right,* your direction 275 degrees.

In 50 metres at a three-way footpath post, *turn left uphill* as signed to Lawford. *Continue on a footpath,* with a field fence on your left and a ditch on your right, direction 190 degrees.

In 215 metres bend right and then left with the path to continue on. After a further 400 metres you come to the churchyard. Ignoring a stile on the left, continue on the path which enters the churchyard. Lawford Hall (marked on the OS map) is away on the right.

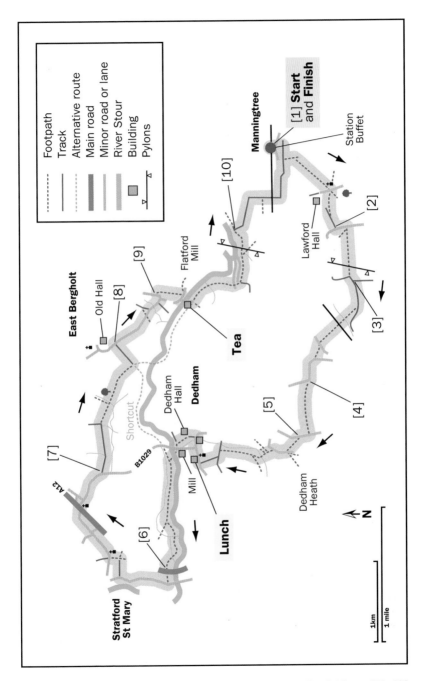

East Bergholt

Stratford
St Mary

Manningtree

[1] Start and Finish

Station Buffet

Lawford Hall

[2]

[3]

[4]

[5]

[6]

[7]

[8]

[9]

[10]

Old Hall

Flatford Mill

Tea

Dedham Hall

Dedham

Mill

Lunch

B1029

Shortcut

A12

Dedham Heath

N

1km
1 mile

Legend

Footpath
Track
Alternative route
Main road
Minor road or lane
River Stour
Building
Pylons

8 metres inside the churchyard *fork left and then right* to go past the side of **Lawford Church** to its entrance. Continue past the church door (or, if you visit the church, turn right when you leave), going westwards.

In 45 metres go out by the wooden swing gate beside a cottage. Cross the tarmac road and take the footpath ahead *signposted half right* (ignore another signpost 15 metres to the left).

In 30 metres go through a gap in the hedge and in another 30 metres go through a kissing gate with an Essex Way sign. Follow it half right and after 100 metres go through another kissing gate with a metal fieldgate on its left-hand side. Ahead is a gravelled lane where you *turn left,* your direction 255 degrees.

In 240 metres go through a defunct kissing gate (with a wooden fieldgate on its left-hand side) to go left on a tarmac road, your direction due south. **[2]**

In 150 metres *turn right* into a field and follow the path along its left edge. After 400 metres you pass under a line of pylons (with more pylons in front of you) and at the corner of the field turn right. After 150 metres turn left at a post with yellow arrows and in 10 metres cross into the next field through a gap.

Follow the path with a hedge on your left and a fence on your right. In 160 metres go past a wooden pole to reach a tarmac track. *Turn left* and in 10 metres *curve right with the road* to continue in the previous direction.

[3] In 40 metres ignore a turn to the left. In 25 metres you pass a corrugated hay barn on your right. In a further 80 metres *bear right* with the road downhill, passing a house entrance on the right after 40 metres and then a clapboard barn.

8 metres beyond the barn *fork right* on a path marked with a yellow arrow, your direction 315 degrees. In 20 metres you pass a wooden shed on your left and keep on down, through the wood.

At the bottom, pass on to a wooden bridge covered with chicken wire across the stream and then over a stile.

Continue on and in 60 metres *cross the railway line* with a stile at each end and then go through a metal kissing gate.

Carry straight on, your direction 310 degrees, through the middle of the field. After 215 metres go through a pair of metal kissing gates and onwards between the fences of horse paddocks.

In 110 metres go through a metal kissing gate. In 55 metres you come to a tarmac road. Cross it *slightly to the right* and go through a metal kissing gate on a signposted footpath. *Turn half left,* your direction 305 degrees, with a view over the River Stour valley on your right-hand side.

In 140 metres go though a metal kissing gate in the far corner of the field to reach a tarmac road. *Turn right,* your direction 340 degrees. In 35 metres you pass Frostwood House on your left.

[4] In 220 metres, where the road veers right, you *go left* through a gate along a signposted footpath uphill, your direction 250 degrees. In 65 metres go through a gate and straight on with the field edge on your left.

In 60 metres go through a gate and onwards with Dedham Church now visible to your right.

In a further 80 metres go through a gate and through a gate again after 160 metres and straight on.

In 230 metres go through a fieldgate out on to a driveway, passing a pantiled clapboard building.

Carry straight on for 75 metres to a car road T-junction *where you go right,* due north, with Lombardy poplars on both sides of the road.

[5] In 80 metres *go left* over a stile, your direction 280 degrees, downhill, slightly to the right. In a further 125 metres go down some steps and after 25 metres cross a stile with an Essex Way sign.

Continue along a narrow path with a private garden on your left and then down through the front garden of a house. Then *go right* on its gravelled drive to a tarmac road where you *turn right,* your direction 20 degrees, uphill.

In 200 metres take the tarmac lane, signposted public footpath *to your left,* just after a cream-painted cottage.

In 20 metres you pass the timber-framed Old House. In a further 30 metres *fork right* and go through a wooden swing gate (a metal fieldgate to its right) and across the tarmac front garden of a house. Just in front of a metal fieldgate on the far side, *turn right* through a metal swing gate, your direction 30 degrees.

In 8 metres go over a stile and keep close to the farmyard on your left. In 30 metres you pass a notice on your left in memory of two horses, Fred and Shem: 'Now forever in Trapalanda'.

In a further 90 metres go over a stile and plank bridge with a scaffolding pole railing over a stream. Either cross the field diagonally to the right to the opposite corner or, if that is not possible because of growing crops, go straight ahead and when you come to a footpath crossing after 65 metres turn right (without going through the hedge) for 110 metres.

Either way you come to a two-plank bridge over a stream. Cross it and continue ahead, your direction 20 degrees, through Lower Park (marked on the OS map) towards an old oak tree.

In 135 metres go through a metal kissing gate and onwards. In a further 115 metres go through another metal kissing gate and continue with the fence on your right-hand side.

In 110 metres go over a stile into a playing field where you *turn left,* your direction 280 degrees. In 80 metres, past the children's roundabout, exit the playing field and *turn right,* with trees on your left, then a fence and finally a breeze-block wall.

In 60 metres you come out on to a gravel lane and go onwards, in 20 metres passing the Old School House on your right. In a further 60 metres you come out on to Dedham High Street where you *turn right.*

In 80 metres you come to the **Sun Hotel**, one of the suggested lunch stops, on your left. In another 30 metres you pass the **Parish Church of St Mary,**

Dedham on your right. In a further 35 metres the **Essex Rose**, also a lunch option is on your left and the war memorial on your right. Continue straight on and just beyond the war memorial are the buildings on the right that were once the grammar school attended by Constable. 120 metres past the war memorial you come to the Dedham Arts and Crafts Centre which includes the **Dedham Centre tea room**, the other suggested lunch stop.

Coming out of the Arts and Crafts Centre after lunch, *turn right,* your direction 85 degrees (or if you have lunched at the Sun Inn or Essex Rose turn left on leaving and continue up the High Street). 70 metres after the Arts and Crafts Centre, where the road veers right, *take the first left fork,* a tarmac lane between fences, your direction 25 degrees, towards a pink house (Dedham Hall on the OS map).

In 65 metres *go left* through a kissing gate along a signposted public footpath, your direction 335 degrees, beside a pond on your left. In 100 metres the path continues through a small meadow and in a further 50 metres go through a kissing gate with a stream on your left.

In 30 metres you pass a car park on the left. In a further 75 metres go over a stile to reach a road that fords the stream. *Go left,* crossing over the streams on two footbridges, your direction 275 degrees.

In 30 metres you come to the main road (the B1029) opposite a converted mill. *Turn right.* In a further 75 metres go over a watercourse and almost immediately *go left* following a concrete public footpath sign, your direction 245 degrees.

In 50 metres, with the converted mill now on your left, cross the bridge over the weir and in 20 metres go over the lockbridge of **Dedham Lock.** Then continue down the steps and after 15 metres through a metal kissing gate.

Here you have a choice. To take the shortcut, which misses out Stratford St Mary, *turn right* along the River Stour. In 100 metres you cross a road, and carry on along the river bank, with the river on your right. Initially the river curves to the right, but after 1km it curves sharply to the left. 150 metres after this, there is a footbridge across the river to the right. Shortly before you come to the bridge, the path is enclosed by bushes. When you get to the bridge, you can either cross it and turn left on its far side, to reach Flatford Mill in another 1km (and pick up onward directions from there); or, to visit East Bergholt Church, do not cross the foot-bridge, but keep on up the enclosed path, which soon becomes a car-wide track. In 200 metres, keep left on the track at a path junction, and keep on this broad track, ignoring ways off as it climbs uphill for around 400 metres to a T-junction with a road. You can now resume the main walk directions at point [8].

But to continue on the main route: After crossing the lockbridge, *turn left* with the field edge nearby on your left, your direction 245 degrees. After 240 metres you pass a Greek temple boathouse on the other side of the river and shortly afterwards go through a metal kissing gate. You are now on the riverside Stour Valley Path.

In 225 metres go through a metal kissing gate and onwards. In a further 420 metres go over a small bridge and through a metal kissing gate. Keep alongside the river for another 300 metres and again go through a kissing gate. 20 metres beyond it go *through a tunnel* under the A12.

[6] On the other side, after 20 metres go through a metal kissing gate and on to a tarmac road where *you turn right,* due north, soon entering Suffolk.

In 200 metres you come to **Stratford St Mary** with a timber-framed house on your left and the Black Horse pub, a possible late lunch option, on your right. In 50 metres you pass a footpath signposted left which would take you in 25 metres to a lock that Constable painted.

Keep on the road and in a further 70 metres you pass the Valley House with its glass lookout roof chamber on your right. In a further 80 metres *turn right* immediately beyond the Swan

pub to go down an earth road, your direction 100 degrees.

In 200 metres go straight through the garden of the house at the end of the road to come through a gate to a T-junction. *Turn left,* northwards. In 5 metres ignore a stile on your right to go straight on through a defunct metal kissing gate.

In 115 metres you come to the main road where you *turn right,* your direction 100 degrees. In 125 metres you pass the Tudor timber-framed **Priest's House**.

In a further 80 metres you pass the Anchor pub on your left-hand side, another late lunch possibility. In 220 metres ignore a turning left to Higham and carry straight on the B1029 signposted to Dedham, parallel to the A12 which is to your right.

In 200 metres you go under the A12 and come in 115 metres to the **Church of Stratford St Mary**.

In a further 60 metres, *turn right* on the B1029 (signposted to Dedham). In a further 230 metres you pass Haywards Cottage on your left. After another 115 metres you pass Ravenys on your left and *immediately turn left* on a tarmac lane, soon a track, your direction 105 degrees. **[7]**

In 500 metres ignore the path to your left to continue straight on, your direction 115 degrees, with a hawthorn hedge on your right. You are skirting the water meadows, which stretch away to Dedham in the distance.

In 340 metres you come to a potentially muddy T-junction where you *turn right* following a yellow arrow, due south. In 40 metres *turn left* to go on two planks over a stream. Ignore a stile to the right on the other side to continue ahead, initially very close to the fence on your right and then veering towards a stile ahead, which you reach after 30 metres. Cross it (with difficulty, as it is broken) and continue ahead.

In 100 metres go over another stile to carry on, your direction 130 degrees, through a water meadow, with a field fence on your left. Ackworth Manor

House (which Randolph Churchill used to own) is visible to the left.

In 90 metres ignore a path continuing to the right and go over a stile to enter a fenced path. In 215 metres go over a stile and *turn left* with a river backwater to the right and a field edge on your left towards a cottage, your direction 105 degrees.

In 40 metres go over a stile to reach an earth road where you *go left,* your direction 50 degrees.

In 110 metres you pass a fork to the left (which leads to a field where, 10 metres in, Constable painted *The Cornfield* – although the stream is now gone). Carry on up the road and in 240 metres you come to a road junction with a bench opposite. **[8]**

Here, if you do not want to want to visit the East Bergholt Church, *turn right*. After 15 metres take the signposted footpath left, resuming the directions at **[*]** below.

Otherwise, to continue on the recommended route, *turn left,* your direction 320 degrees. In 135 metres you pass a private back entrance to Old Hall Community on the right.

In 115 metres you come to the **Parish Church of St Mary the Virgin, East Bergholt**, and its bell cage in the churchyard on the far side of the church.

After visiting the church, retrace your steps southwards down the lane opposite the church beyond the war memorial for 250 metres. Ignore the private road on the right marked as a footpath to Dedham and Stratford opposite a bench (this was the path from which you previously emerged on to the road).

[*] In a further 15 metres take a signposted public footpath *left,* your direction 160 degrees, to go alongside the road. In 265 metres you rejoin the road and in 15 metres start again following a footpath alongside the road.

In 65 metres you cross a footpath. In a further 155 metres you cross a driveway to a sewage works and go straight on. After 130 metres you come down to the road and continue on it with a stream to your left.

In 170 metres you come to a road junction with a car park on the right. *Go left uphill,* your direction 70 degrees, past the thatched Hay Barn on the right.

[9] In 100 metres *go right* on a signposted footpath, over a stile with a metal fieldgate on each side. Continue ahead with a fence on your left, again passing the Hay Barn on the right.

In 80 metres go over a stile to enter the National Trust Flatford estate. Continue ahead with a fence on the right.

In 80 metres zigzag 5 metres to the right to continue on, now with a hedge to your left. In 280 metres you come to a car road T-junction where you *turn left,* your direction 135 degrees.

In 35 metres you come to the thatched and black timber-clad building, The Granary (a bed and breakfast establishment). In a further 60 metres you come to Flatford Mill where Constable painted *The Hay Wain.* (It is now a field centre for nature studies.)

Turn back, retracing your steps. Continue beyond The Granary to reach **Bridge Cottage tea room, Flatford**, the suggested tea place, where there is also a National Trust shop and a small exhibition about Constable. Toilets are in the car park on the opposite side of the road.

After tea, *turn left* out of the Bridge Cottage complex and just beyond it, *left again* to go over the bridge. On the other side *turn left* with the River Stour on your left, direction 140 degrees.

In 50 metres you come to **Flatford Lock**, the subject of another Constable painting.

In 500 metres ignore the earth road to your left to *go straight on,* passing to the right of a concrete **flood-defence barrier**, your direction 175 degrees. In 40 metres cross a stream on a bridge and pass through a metal kissing gate. There is a National Trust sign on the right for Dedham Vale. In 60 metres more, at the far end of the flood-defence barrier, *go up the embankment and turn left* through a kissing gate following the signpost to Manningtree station. Beyond this, carry straight on along a raised embankment, a potentially muddy path.

In 260 metres pass through a metal kissing gate, and 20 metres later a wooden one. In a further 70 metres, you pass under pylons and keep on along the estuary defence dyke, with the River Stour on your left.

In 300 metres go through a wooden kissing gate to reach a three-way footpath sign. *Turn right* following the sign to Manningtree station, away from the river, your direction 150 degrees. [10]

In 60 metres go through a wooden kissing gate. In a further 70 metres, veer left with your track, following a yellow arrow, your direction 105 degrees.

In 300 metres *veer right* with the track and follow it under the railway tunnel, 275 metres away. *Go through this tunnel* and 15 metres beyond it *turn left* on a gravelled track, parallel to the railway lines on your left, due east.

In 600 metres you come to **Manningtree station**, for the last 150 metres retracing the morning's route. The **Buffet** is on the nearest platform.

Lunch & tea places

Sun Hotel *High Street, Dedham, CO7 6DF (01206 323351, www.thesuninn dedham.com).* **Open** 11am-11pm daily. *Food served* noon-2.30pm, 6.30-9.30pm Mon-Thur; noon-2.30pm, 6-10pm Fri; noon-3pm, 6-10pm Sat; noon-3pm, 6.30-9.30pm Sun.

Essex Rose *High Street, Dedham, CO7 6DE (01206 323101, www.trooms.com).* **Open** *Summer* 10am-5.30pm daily. *Winter* 10am-4.30pm daily.

Dedham Centre tea room *Arts & Crafts Centre, High Street, Dedham, CO7 6AD (01206 322677, www.dedhamartand craftcentre.co.uk).* **Open** 10am-5pm daily. A good lunch option for vegetarians.

Bridge Cottage tea room *Flatford, East Bergholt, CO7 6UL (01206 298260, www.nationaltrust.org.uk).* **Open** *Jan, Feb* 11am-3.30pm Sat, Sun. *Mar* 11am-4pm Wed-Sun. *Apr* 11am-5pm daily. *May-Sept* 10.30am-5.30pm daily. *Oct* 11am-4.30pm daily. *Nov, Dec* 11am-3.30pm Wed-Sun.

Manningtree Station Buffet *Station Road, Lawford, Manningtree, CO11 2LH (01206 391114).* **Open** 5.30am-9pm Mon-Thur; 5am-11pm Fri; 8am-11pm Sat; 8am-2pm Sun.

Walk 40

Gerrards Cross to Cookham

Bulstrode Park, Burnham Beeches and Spencer.

Start: Gerrards Cross station
Finish: Cookham station

Length: 15.4km (9.6 miles)

Time: 4 hours 30 minutes. For the whole outing, including trains, sights and meals, allow 7 hours 30 minutes.

Transport: Take the train nearest to **10.15am** from **Marylebone** station to **Gerrards Cross** (journey time 21-30 minutes). Trains back from **Cookham** to Paddington are hourly, changing at Maidenhead (journey time just over an hour).
   As the two stations are on different lines, you cannot get a return ticket for the full walk. Instead, buy an All Zones Travelcard, plus a single from the Zone 6 Boundary to Gerrards Cross. On the return journey, you will need to buy a single in addition from Cookham to the Zone 6 Boundary.
   This walk is not recommended for car travel unless you are prepared to take a taxi back to your car, since there is no convenient public transport link (train or bus) from Cookham back to Gerrards Cross.

OS Landranger Maps: 176 & 175
OS Explorer Map: 172
Gerrards Cross, map reference TQ002887, is in **Buckinghamshire**, 9km north of Slough and 12km east of Cookham, which is in **Berkshire**.

Toughness: 2 out of 10

Walk notes: Near the start, this walk crosses Bulstrode Park and, from there, heads past woods and lakes to a cratered moonscape where the route crosses the M40. Then it goes through the Hedgerley Green Nature Reserve to the church at Hedgerley, and on through Egypt Wood and Burnham Beeches to a pub in Littleworth Common. 8.8km of this walk is covered before lunch. In the afternoon, there are more woods and fringes of woods. You can also take an optional detour to the hilltop Church of St Nicholas in Hedsor, for a fine view over the Thames Valley and across to a late 18th-century folly, a ruined castle.

The walk ends alongside the Thames, going over Cookham Bridge to Cookham Church, the Stanley Spencer Gallery and tea. Finally, you walk across the National Trust's Cookham Moor to Cookham station.

Walk options: There are no convenient bus services on the route, but you could get a taxi from the lunch pub.

History: The 400 acres of **Bulstrode Park** were bought in 1686 by Judge Jeffreys, who built a house here. It was confiscated when he was sent to the Tower of London. The present manor was completed by the 12th Duke of Somerset in 1870. Since 1963 it has been the headquarters for the missionaries and administrative staff of the Worldwide Evangelization Crusade.

Egypt Wood is thought to be so-called because it was a frequently used encampment for gypsies prior to 1880 (the name 'gypsy' derives from 'Egyptian', although gypsies probably originate from India). Since 1880, Egypt Wood (which is a part of Burnham Beeches) has been owned and managed by the Corporation of London.

The **Church of St Nicholas** was mentioned in land records in 1218 and is unusual in that it is entirely set within the grounds of the landowner, Lady Wantner, with the only right of access being for walkers. The church is open on Sunday afternoons in June, July and August.

Cookham was inhabited by ancient Britons, Romans and Saxons. In the Domesday Book it is listed as containing '32 villagers, 21 cottagers, 4 slaves, 2 mills, 2 fisheries and woodland at 100 pigs'. In 1140, a Norman church was built on the site of **Holy Trinity Church**, Cookham. The north wall of the church is built of chalk blocks, probably quarried at Cookham.

The artist **Sir Stanley Spencer** (1891-1959) lived in Cookham and there is a memorial stone to him in the graveyard. Spencer was born in a Victorian semi-detached house in Cookham High Street. He attended services at the Wesleyan Chapel, also in the High Street, which is now the **Stanley Spencer Gallery** (01628 471885). It opens 10.30am-5.30pm daily from April to October, and 11am-4.30pm daily from November to March. There is a small admission fee.

Walk directions

[1] [Numbers in square brackets refer to the map]

Coming off platform 1 at **Gerrards Cross station** go over the footbridge to exit the station building. Cross the pedestrian crossing outside the building and *go left uphill* on a tarmac path, your direction 320 degrees.

In 75 metres *go straight on,* now on the pavement of a tarmac road, walking parallel to the station car park down below. In a further 140 metres, where this road veers sharply to the right and there is a car park on your left, *carry straight on,* along a narrow tarmac footpath, your direction 305 degrees.

In 210 metres turn left to go on a footbridge back over the railway lines. This brings you out on to a road (Laytes Way) where you *turn right,* passing Cedar House on your right-hand side. In 75 metres *bear left* with this road which in a further 140 metres reaches a T-junction.

Cross this road and pick up a signposted footpath opposite, your direction 260 degrees. In 200 metres you come out on to the A40. Cross the road and *turn left* for 25 metres, then *turn right* on to a path (by a green footpath signpost) between concrete posts, down concrete steps and between wooden fences, your direction 220 degrees.

In 110 metres you reach a gravelled road opposite Main Court House. *Turn right,* heading towards the park, your direction 255 degrees.

In 30 metres go through a metal kissing gate by a two-armed footpath sign and yellow path arrows and follow a wide grass path *straight on* across **Bulstrode Park**, your initial direction 255 degrees, slightly uphill and gradually veering right. Bulstrode Manor is just visible behind trees on the hillock to the left in the distance. As you reach the top of the hill, continue on a rough tarmac path in the same direction, now veering slightly to the left.

In 730 metres you go through a wooden kissing gate. *Turn right* on to a gravel car road. In 20 metres you cross **[2]** the entrance driveway to **Bulstrode Manor** and *go straight on* over a cattle grid on a tarmac road.

In 50 metres, just after a left-hand turning, *fork left* on to a path with a fence

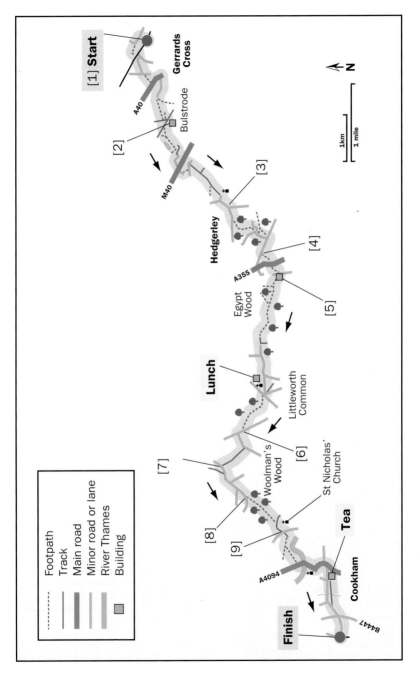

Gerrards Cross to Cookham

[1] **Start**

Gerrards Cross

A40

[2]

Bulstrode

M40

[3]

Hedgerley

[4]

A355

[5]

Egypt Wood

Lunch

Littleworth Common

[6]

[7]

Woolman's Wood

St Nicholas' Church

[8]

[9]

Tea

A4094

Cookham

Finish

B4447

N

1km
1 mile

Footpath
Track
Main road
Minor road or lane
River Thames
Building

to your right-hand side, following yellow arrows. In 225 metres this path comes to a T-junction at the edge of a wood. *Turn left,* your initial direction 255 degrees.

In 80 metres you pass a lake on your right-hand side. Soon the path re-enters a wooded area, with the lake still to your right. In 340 metres you come out into a rough, open scrubland area close to large pylons away to your left.

Continue on the path, going under the overhead cables, your direction 245 degrees. In 50 metres you pass a metal fieldgate on your right, your direction now 225 degrees. In 100 metres, go through a kissing gate and down steps to a tarmac road, where you *turn right,* your direction 315 degrees. In 70 metres you pass Moat Farm on your right-hand side and continue on the road which bears left on to a bridge crossing the M40.

Immediately after crossing the bridge, go over a stile on your left and follow the signposted footpath, your initial direction 100 degrees. Continue down the hill and half-right, your direction 145 degrees.

In 45 metres you reach a high fence. *Turn right* on a car-wide grassy way, your direction 195 degrees; soon there is another fence on your right-hand side. In 40 metres you join a tarmac road and pass houses. In a further 60 metres at a T-junction *turn left,* your direction 100 degrees.

In 75 metres, at the Circular Walk footpath sign opposite Bulstrode House, *turn right* on an earth car-wide road, your direction 220 degrees, through a **nature reserve** (so marked on the OS map). In 200 metres, when your road bends left towards Sherley Close, *leave it to carry straight on* along a bridleway, following a blue arrow on a post, your direction 230 degrees.

In 500 metres ignore a stile off to the right. In a further 200 metres, you come to a church on your left-hand side, **St Mary the Virgin**, Hedgerley, which is likely to be locked. *Bend right* with the tarmac path.

In 85 metres you come out on to a road, Village Lane (near the **White Horse** pub on your right), where you *turn left,* following the circular walk sign, your direction 195 degrees, past Old School Cottage on your left-hand side.

In 80 metres you pass a pond on the left and Hedgerley's 'Buckinghamshire Best Kept Village' sign on the right. In 60 metres *turn right* **[3]** on to Kiln Lane.

In 200 metres *turn left* through a wooden barrier on to a footpath

signposted Circular Walk, your direction 240 degrees. In 30 metres go through the large framework of a broken wooden gate and follow a path uphill through a wood. In a further 300 metres go through a large gate and bear left between fences, your direction 190 degrees. Soon there is a wooden fence on the left.

In 145 metres, at the end of the footpath, *turn left* on a signposted narrow public footpath to the right of Old Nursery Court by a yellow water-marker in the ground, your direction 155 degrees. In 70 metres you enter a wood. In 40 metres, at a post with yellow arrows, *fork right,* your direction 230 degrees. Continue on, in 80 metres passing through a slightly more open area of the wood and straight ahead, ignoring a path to your left, your direction now 250 degrees. In 25 metres go through a broken wooden barrier and onwards, ignoring a path to the right.

In 100 metres you reach a road junction, where you *turn right.* Pass Andrew Hill Lane on your right and Christmas Lane to the left. Continue forward on the main road.

In 100 metres you pass Top Farm on the right-hand side. In a further 85 metres you pass the large gate of Pond's Wood Farm on your left-hand side.

In 130 metres **[4]** *turn left* on to a path signposted Circular Walk, into a wood. Keep forward, your direction 190 degrees, with a fence on your left. In 170 metres cross a stile just before the A355.

Cross the road and continue on a Circular Walk signposted footpath between fences, your direction 230 degrees initially, into **Egypt Wood** (so marked on the OS map). In 250 metres you reach Egypt Lane **[5]** (marked on a Corporation of London signboard).

Cross the road and *go straight on, slightly to the right,* signposted Circular Walk, on a concrete lane, your direction 295 degrees. In 100 metres you pass houses and then concrete garages on your left-hand side.

Keep straight on into the wood through a metal kissing gate to the right of a gate, along a broad earth track running roughly east–west through the wood. Ignore all ways off and keep straight ahead; you will pass three posts with yellow arrows confirming your direction. In 900 metres you reach a junction with two low Circular Walk signs. *Keep straight on, slightly to the left* (ignoring the Circular Walk arrows pointing right and left), now on the edge of the wood, with open fields to your right, your direction due west.

Ignore paths off to the left. In 140 metres go over a stile (with a wooden fieldgate to its left) to exit the wood and continue along the right-hand side a field, with a field hedge on the right.

In 160 metres go through a wooden kissing gate (a wooden fieldgate to its right), and continue straight on, along an earth road. In 100 metres *go straight on,* along a tarmac road, due west.

In 160 metres, at a junction, *keep straight on* (the signpost when repaired will indicate Burnham and Taplow) on Boveney Wood Lane.

In 260 metres you pass Boveney Wood Farm on your right-hand side. Ignore a fork left, and go straight on. n 15 metres ignore a bridleway to the right but in a further 80 metres turn down another bridleway to the *right,* and *bear left* with it after 30 metres. After passing a large bungalow you reach the **Jolly Woodman** pub, the suggested lunchtime stop.

Coming out of the pub door after lunch, *go straight on* along a bridleway opposite the front door, your direction 205 degrees. In 45 metres you come to a tarmac lane and *turn right,* your direction 265 degrees.

In 40 metres you come to the front gate of the Parish Church of St Anne, Dropmore, which is likely to be locked. *Turn left here* across the road, on to a path into the wood, between a wooden post to your left and a metal post on your right, your direction 170 degrees. In 40 metres, at a crosspaths T-junction, *go right,* your direction 295 degrees.

In 55 metres you reach Dorney Wood Road, which you cross. Turn right and in 25 metres you come to a car road T-junction, signposted Beaconsfield to the right. Cross this T-junction carefully, slightly to the left, and pick up a **Beeches Way** signposted footpath to the left of a cottage called Brissels Wood, through a wooden kissing gate, your direction 295 degrees. The path runs between a hedge and wood on the right and a fence and field on the left.

In 460 metres you cross a stile and continue across a large field on a clear path between fences, your direction 280 degrees, with a house visible across the field to the right.

In a further 360 metres, after crossing a farm track, go over a stile (or round the edge of it), and in 80 metres you reach a car road. **[6]** *Turn right* on this road, your direction 320 degrees. In 45 metres you pass the entrance to Hales Cottage on your right-hand side. In a further 140 metres *take the left turn* on to Sheepcote Lane, your direction 245 degrees.

In 310 metres, where the road bends to the left, take the bridleway signposted Beeches Way to the *right*, on a car-wide track (without tarmac after 25 metres), your direction 330 degrees. In 150 metres you pass a cottage on your left-hand side. Continue forward on a narrow bridleway.

In 370 metres you come out on a tarmac road **[7]** where you follow Beeches Way, signposted to the *left*, your direction 255 degrees. In 80 metres ignore a bridleway to the right. In 210 metres you cross Wash Hill to your right and Hedsor Lane to your left to go straight on.

In 180 metres, where the main road bends right, *fork left* on Branch Lane **[8]**, which is marked 'Unsuitable for motors', following the Beeches Way arrow, your direction 230 degrees.

In 200 metres *fork left,* signposted Beeches Way and the Chiltern Way Berkshire Loop, past a metal fieldgate on a gravelled track, your direction 225 degrees, into **Woolman's Wood**.

In 80 metres *fork right* following the Beeches Way arrow and one saying 'Church path' on a post, steadily downhill between fences.

In 620 metres go through a metal kissing gate and straight on along a tarmac road with Lord Boston's 18th-century mock castle folly up on the hill to the right.

In 200 metres it is worth detouring up steps and through a kissing gate on your left-hand side, to take a path across a field steeply uphill, your direction 125 degrees, heading to the right of the **Church of St Nicholas**. From the top, the view over the valley makes the climb worthwhile. There is a kissing gate into the churchyard, but the church is only open on Sunday afternoons from June to August.

Retrace your steps and continue on the road below. In 110 metres you cross a road **[9]** and continue past an unusual thatched house with columns on your right-hand side. Go ahead through a wooden pedestrian gate to the left of a vehicle one, your direction 235 degrees.

In 60 metres, by double gates in front of new houses, *turn right,* your direction 290 degrees and continue with the wall on your left and soon another on your right. In 40 metres go through a pedestrian gate to the left of a double gate on to a path. Keep left between a wooden fence on the left-hand side and metal fence on the right.

In 120 metres go over a stream on a large wooden bridge with railings that lean outwards. At the other end of the bridge, in the corner of a large field, *fork left,* following the Beeches Way arrow, your direction 235 degrees. In 80 metres you pass an obelisk behind the fence on your left-hand side (it may not be visible in summer).

In a further 40 metres your path reaches the bank of the **River Thames** on your left-hand side. Continue for 130 metres, then *veer away from the river,* following a path slightly to the right across the field, your direction 235 degrees.

In 300 metres go over a stile marked by the last of the Beeches Way signposts and *turn left* on the busy A4094, due south, into **Cookham**. Cross this road when traffic permits and continue over the bridge. 20 metres beyond the bridge, immediately opposite steps to the Ferry Inn on your left, *turn right and go down steps* with metal railings (a signposted public footpath) and then straight on, along a gravelled path (which looks like a dead end), your direction 285 degrees.

In 25 metres you come into the churchyard of **Holy Trinity Church**, Cookham, through a wooden swing gate. The church entrance is around the far side. Coming out of the church, take the path *right* from the front door, *then left* in 20 metres at a crosspaths, in 25 metres passing **Stanley Spencer's memorial stone** to the right of a bench.

At the end of the churchyard *bear left*, passing Churchgate House on your left. In 20 metres you reach the A4094 again, where you *turn right*. Stay on this road as it bends to the right.

In 60 metres you come to the **Stanley Spencer Gallery** opposite, at the junction with the High Street. *Turn right* (or if you visit the gallery, turn left when you come out) along the High Street, your direction 260 degrees. The **Bel & the Dragon** pub is opposite the gallery. In 70 metres you pass the **Kings Arms** pub on your left-hand side (the entrance is through the courtyard). Further on, Cookham Arcade is on the right-hand side of the road; go down the passage to find the entrance of **Culinary Aspirations** on the right, the alternative suggestion for tea.

Allow 15-20 minutes to reach the station after tea. Continue to the end of the High Street to reach the War Memorial on your left-hand side. Carry on across **Cookham Moor** on a tarmac lane to the left-hand side of the main street, your direction 265 degrees, and in 200 metres go over a bridge.

100 metres beyond the bridge, you rejoin the main road and *go straight on* at a small roundabout. Continue past the White Oak pub (where you can use the pedestrian crossing to go over the road) and the Old Swan Uppers pub on

your right-hand side. At another roundabout keep forward, following the sign to the **station**, which you reach in 200 metres. The **Station Hill Deli**, on the right just before the station, is another possible place to have tea on weekdays.

Lunch & tea places

White Horse *Village Lane, Hedgerley, SL2 3UY (01753 643225).* **Open** 11am-2.30pm, 5-11pm Mon-Fri; 11am-11pm Sat; 11am-10.30pm Sun. *Food served* noon-2pm Mon-Fri; noon-2.30pm Sat, Sun. A possible stop for an early lunch if you set out late, or a good choice for a morning coffee.

Jolly Woodman *Littleworth Road, Littleworth Common, SL1 8PF (01753 644350, www.thejollywoodman.co.uk).* **Open** 11am-11pm Mon-Fri; 11am-midnight Sat; noon-6pm Sun. *Food served* noon-2.30pm, 6.30-9.30pm Mon-Sat; noon-4pm Sun. This pub, the suggested lunch stop, has a good menu and speedy service. Groups of more than seven should phone ahead.

Bel & the Dragon *High Street, Cookham, SL6 9SO (01628 521263, www.belandthedragon-cookham.co.uk).* **Open** noon-11.30pm Mon-Sat; noon-10.30pm Sun. *Food served* noon-3pm, 6-9.30pm Mon-Thur; noon-3pm, 6-10pm Fri; noon-10pm Sat; noon-8.30pm Sun.

Kings Arms *High Street, Cookham, SL6 9SJ (01628 530667, www.thekingsarms cookham.co.uk).* **Open** 10am-11pm Mon-Sat; 10am-10.30pm Sun. *Food served* 10am-10pm Mon-Sat; 10am-9.30pm Sun. This 17th-century hostelry is another option for refreshments.

Culinary Aspirations *Cookham Arcade, High Street, Cookham, SL6 9TA (01628 523904, www.culinaryaspirations. com).* **Open** 10.30am-4.30pm Tue-Sat. A fantastic selection of cakes makes this a good alternative for tea.

Station Hill Deli *Station Hill, Cookham, SL6 9BT (01628 522202, www.station hilldeli.co.uk).* **Open** 7am-5pm Mon-Fri; 8.30am-3.30pm Sat; 9.30am-1.30pm Sun. An attractive tea place that is handy for Cookham station.

Walk 41

Bow Brickhill to Leighton Buzzard

The Greensand Ridge and the River Ouzel.

Start: Bow Brickhill station
Finish: Leighton Buzzard station

Length: 14.7km (9.1 miles)

Time: 4 hours. For the whole outing, including trains, sights and meals, allow at least 8 hours.

Transport: Take the train nearest to **9.50am** from **Euston** station to **Bow Brickhill**, changing at Bletchley on to the Bedford branch line (journey time about 1 hour). Trains back from **Leighton Buzzard** to Euston run about three times an hour, with a journey time of 35-50 minutes. Buy a day return to Bow Brickhill. Note that there is currently no train service on the Bletchley–Bedford branch line on Sundays.

OS Langranger Map: 165
OS Explorer Map: 192
Bow Brickhill, map reference SP896347, is in **Buckinghamshire**, 9km north of Leighton Buzzard, which is in **Bedfordshire**.

Toughness: 2 out of 10

Walk notes: This is a short and straightforward walk, but it does have a potentially muddy bridleway near the start. In wet weather, you may prefer to begin your walk on the more strenuous but usually less muddy route described in Walk 17 (Bow Brickhill to Woburn Sands, see p129), starting at the same railway station. Walk 17 joins this route by the sequoia trees in Back Wood (see the asterisk [*] in the walk directions below). After Back Wood, this route heads south through Duncombe Wood to take lunch in a pub in Great Brickhill. After lunch, the route joins the Greensand Ridge Walk, with fine views out over the River Ouzel, and heads on for tea in a pub on the Grand Union Canal. You then continue along the canal towpath into Leighton Buzzard.

Walk options: There are infrequent buses – about three a day – from the lunchtime pub in Great Brickhill to Leighton Buzzard or Bletchley. Alternatively, you could call a taxi from Great Brickhill or from the teatime pub near Leighton Buzzard.

History: **Lower Greensand** is very different from the surrounding claylands and consists of marine sands with few fossils – a terrain that supports a tree population dominated by pine.
   Great Brickhill was a centre of the curious coprolite industry: the mining of phosphatic nodules used to manufacture super-phosphatic fertiliser.
   The **Globe Inn**, the suggested teatime stop, was first licensed in 1830 as a beer shop that was intended to serve passing trade on the Grand Union Canal.

Bow Brickhill to Leighton Buzzard

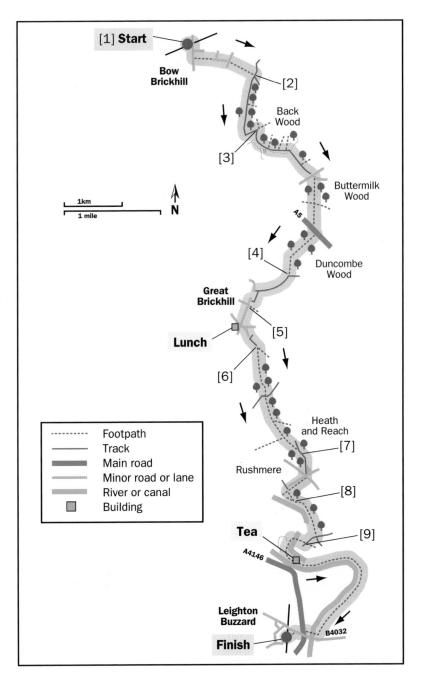

[1] **Start**

Bow Brickhill

[2]

Back Wood

[3]

Buttermilk Wood

A5

[4]

Duncombe Wood

Great Brickhill

[5]

Lunch

[6]

Heath and Reach

[7]

Rushmere

[8]

Tea

A4146

[9]

Leighton Buzzard

B4032

Finish

1km
1 mile

N

- - - - - Footpath
———— Track
Main road
Minor road or lane
River or canal
☐ Building

Walk directions

[1] [Numbers in square brackets refer to the map]
Coming off the platform of **Bow Brickhill station** *turn left* southwards, back over the railway level crossing, on the road V10 Brickhill Street.

In 75 metres you come to a mini roundabout. Ignore the turn left towards Bow Brickhill, cross over and keep ahead along the grass verge on the left-hand side of the busy Brickhill Road.

In 80 metres take the signposted footpath to *the left* over a stile, turning right then immediately left, to continue ahead, due east, on a car-wide grassy way, with the field edge on your right-hand side and a post and wire fence on your left-hand side. In 345 metres cross a farm track to continue straight on through a wooden kissing gate, on a path between fences and houses.

In 40 metres this path comes out on to an estate road and you keep straight on up this road, gently uphill, ignoring a turn-off to the left. In 170 metres you come to a T-junction where you *go right,* your direction 150 degrees. In 45 metres pick up a signposted path to continue in your previous direction (105 degrees).

In 25 metres go through a wooden kissing gate, swing right, then left, to continue in the same direction as before, ignoring the grassy path to your right, across a field of mounds (a remnant of the old ridge-and-furrow field system). In 55 metres, at a path junction, keep ahead, with the field edge on your left-hand side, your direction 120 degrees.

In 80 metres go over a stile to the left of a metal fieldgate (or pass through the fieldgate when open) and keep straight on between timber fences. The path soon starts to go uphill.

In 260 metres, by a three-armed footpath sign on your left (obscured by bushes in summer), **[2]** follow a bridleway sign to *the right,* upwards on an earth car road, your direction 160 degrees. In 30 metres ignore forks off to the left (the routes for Walk 17 – Bow

Brickhill to Woburn Sands; *see p129*) and *bear right (almost straight ahead)* on the earth car road, with a view to the right over Bletchley and with **Back Wood** on your left-hand side.

In 290 metres ignore an avenue off to the left and go straight on, with woods (some cleared) on both sides. Continue ahead, gently uphill and in 270 metres ignore a footpath on the left, steeply uphill, marked by a yellow arrow. The track now starts to go downhill and in a further 60 metres ignore an unmarked earth road-turning on the left uphill and instead **[!]** *swing right* on what is now a grassy track, downhill.

In 220 metres, as you go downhill through a potentially muddy stretch, ignore a possible way off to the left (by a corner fencepost) to follow the blue arrow straight on, downhill, your direction 170 degrees.

In 80 metres, at what seems like a T-junction, near the bottom and 5 metres

Bow Brickhill to Leighton Buzzard

before you reach a fieldgate and stile
which exit the wood, [!] you *turn left* on
a bridleway going gently uphill, marked
by a yellow arrow on a post, your
direction due east.

In 200 metres [3] at a path T-junction
[!] *turn right* and in 12 metres, at a path
crossing, *turn right again* (almost turning
back on yourself) on a car-wide, grassy
bridleway, your direction 200 degrees.

In 475 metres, with ponds on your
right-hand side, cross a footpath
(ignoring a footbridge away to your
right-hand side) to keep straight on,
eastwards. In 185 metres keep straight
on, ignoring ways off uphill to the left,
with sequoia trees now visible ahead
on your right-hand side.

[*] In 60 metres ignore a footpath
uphill on the left, marked by a yellow
arrow and *go right,* continuing on the
bridleway, over a stream (dried up in
summer), and keep ahead, uphill, your
direction 120 degrees.

In 150 metres you can touch the soft
and furry bark of the sequoia trees on
the right-hand side of the path. Keep
ahead, ignoring all ways off, and in 200
metres you come out into an open area.
Ignore a footpath stairway up to the left
and keep ahead, uphill.

In 225 metres go through a wooden
swing gate, with a metal fieldgate to its
left, to come out on to a main road, where
you *turn left,* your direction 125 degrees.
Ignore a road to the left that is signposted
Woburn Golf Club.

Continue on the main road and in 50
metres *go right* on a signposted footpath
over a stile, your direction 200 degrees,
and ahead through a pine wood. In 210
metres you cross a grassy path to keep
straight on. In a further 130 metres cross
a stile with a wooden fieldgate to its left
to leave the wood.

Continue straight ahead on along
the right-hand edge of an open field,
in 55 metres passing a pond and a stile
to the right-hand side, which you ignore.
The field edge bends to the right and left
and in a further 250 metres (the field edge

having continued parallel to the A5 road
for some 100 metres) *turn right* to go
through a 6-metre-wide gap in the hedge
marking the field boundary.

Keep the hedge on your right-hand side
for 40 metres until you reach a track
beside the A5 road. *Turn left* parallel
to the road, your direction 155 degrees.
In 65 metres you pass a footpath sign
on your right-hand side and in a further
150 metres the track passes through a
field boundary.

In 50 metres you reach a part-hidden
stile on your right-hand side. Cross over
the stile and cross the busy A5 road with
extreme care.

On the far side of the A5, beside
an interesting milestone, go straight
on across a stile to cross a minor road.
Continue ahead through a gateway
to cross a house drive (Wood Lodge),
your direction 230 degrees.

Go through a wooden swing gate,
with a hedge arch over, into **Duncombe
Wood** (as marked on the OS map) to go
straight ahead on a broad, grassy track,
following a yellow arrow (the Duncombes
used to be the most important family
in the area). In 280 metres go to the
right-hand side of a fenced-in pond
and keep straight on, ignoring a minor
fork to the right.

In 165 metres you ignore a fork to
the right to bear slightly left with the
main path, following a yellow arrow,
your direction 195 degrees. In 175 metres
[4] go through a wooden kissing gate on
to an earth car road where you go straight
on, your direction 205 degrees.

In 400 metres you pass the entrance
to a farm on your left-hand side. In 225
metres you enter the outskirts of **Great
Brickhill**. In 30 metres, by a public
footpath sign, and 20 metres before
the main road T-junction, *turn left* on an
estate road, your direction 210 degrees.

In 210 metres, at the end of the road,
take the concrete pathway with railings
down to the right. Continue straight
on uphill, on the more main road, your
direction 215 degrees.

In 40 metres **[5]** ignore a footpath to the left and Rotten Row to the right, to go over the brow of the hill and down Pound Hill to the **Old Red Lion** pub, the suggested lunch stop, visible 270 metres ahead at the bottom of the hill on the right-hand side of the road.

Coming out of the pub after lunch, cross straight over the main road to continue on Heath Road, signposted to Heath and Reach and to Leighton Buzzard. In 55 metres *fork right,* downhill on Cuff Lane, your direction 140 degrees. In 110 metres the lane narrows to become a track and in 70 metres ignore a footpath sign and stile to the right to keep straight on, your direction 155 degrees.

In 100 metres you pass the entrance to a sewage treatment plant on your left-hand side. The track is now a footpath and in 55 metres go over a stream on a plank bridge. In 15 metres **[6]** go straight on through a wooden swing gate, your direction 195 degrees, on a way marked CW into woods, ignoring a fork uphill to the left.

In 300 metres, at a path junction, **[!]** *take the fork to the right* (almost straight on), to follow a Millennium Walk arrow. In 150 metres you cross a path to go straight on downhill. The path drops steeply and after 115 metres, at a four-armed footpath sign, follow the yellow arrow ahead for the Bucks Circular walk (or Greensand Ridge Walk (GRW) sign; the common markings for the Greensand Ridge Walk are either the letters GRW or the muntjac deer symbol.

In 160 metres you pass a pond on your left-hand side to go over a stream. Note the decorative log carving and seat on your right-hand side. Ignore a fork left to go straight on, following a CR arrow. In 15 metres go through a kissing gate. In a further 170 metres, by marker posts which advise that you are now on the edge of Rushmere Park, ignore a fork to the left to follow GRW and CW arrows straight on.

In 160 metres you ignore a kissing gate on the right and in a further 150 metres you pass by a disused, broken stile to leave the woods for a time, to continue ahead.

In 200 metres, with a solitary fence post ahead of you, at a minor fork in the path, **[!]** *fork right* with the main path, your direction 145 degrees.

In 215 metres the path drops down and *swings to the right.* **[7]** The path soon has a wooden post-and-rail fence on its left and after 230 metres you pass sequoia trees and a lake on your left-hand side. In a further 140 metres you come out through a kissing gate on to a tarmac road and follow the CW arrows and deer signs *left,* your direction 135 degrees, walking on Bragenham Lane. In 25 metres you come to the main road, with the gateway to Rushmere Park on your left-hand side.

At the main road, *turn right,* then in 15 metres, *go left,* opposite Rushmere House, to pick up the Greensand Ridge Walk signpost, up wooden steps past a barrier, into the beech woods. You then follow the path *right,* your direction 235 degrees, parallel to the road below on your right-hand side.

Follow deer signs along this woodland path and in 340 metres exit the woods and follow the deer signs *left,* uphill, on a grassy way, your direction 135 degrees, with the edge of the wood on your left-hand side. In 145 metres ignore a turning left, back into the woods. In a further 30 metres, at the end of the field, bend left, with your main path, up into the wood, your direction 85 degrees. In 25 metres, at a crosspaths, with a post on your left-hand side, *turn right* on the path going downhill towards the river, your direction 150 degrees.

In 70 metres **[8]** you come down to within 50 metres of the River Ouzel, to reach a clear, broad and level path where you *turn left,* your direction 110 degrees. Stay on this path and in 500 metres you come out on to a driveway and go uphill, your direction 160 degrees.

In 150 metres *turn right* over a cattle grid (or go through the metal kissing gate next to it) on to a tarmac lane signposted

Greensand Ridge Walk and marked Corbetts Hill Farm, downhill, your direction due west. In 100 metres ignore a shortcut path straight on, along a line of telegraph poles, to stay on the tarmac lane, bearing left.

In 160 metres, with a stile in the boundary and deer signs on your left **[9]** *fork right* off the path, across a grassy field, your direction 310 degrees, aiming for a footbridge, with Linslade Church visible in the distance ahead.

In 190 metres you cross the **River Ouzel** on the bridge, on the other side *turning left* along its banks, your direction 240 degrees. In 50 metres you cross a stream-bed on a plank bridge to carry on with the river on your left-hand side.

In 220 metres you come to a marker post marked with a yellow top **[!]** where you *keep ahead* (slightly right) across a field, often waterlogged in winter, aiming for a wooden plank bridge in the field boundary ahead, your direction 200 degrees. In 150 metres turn left to cross the wood plank bridge, 60 metres in length, with a handrail on its left-hand side, and at its far side follow the path ahead, with a field hedge on your right-hand side, your direction due east.

In 80 metres go up a bank to exit the field through a metal kissing gate on your right-hand side on to a tarmac lane. *Turn left,* along the tarmac towpath to the Grand Union Canal, coming in 80 metres to the suggested tea place, the **Globe Inn**.

After tea, *turn left* and continue along the towpath with the canal on your right-hand side. After 1.5km, at the first bridge, with a Tesco car park on your left-hand side, take the ramp up to the road bridge and turn right to cross the canal.

Beyond the mini roundabout at a nearby fork, you see a traffic sign for the railway station and Soulbury (which is a little confusing, as it appears the sign is for Soulbury station, when in fact it is for Leighton Buzzard railway station and the village of Soulbury). Follow this sign uphill along Old Road.

At the Buckingham Arms pub, *fork left* to stay on Old Road, while the main road turns slightly to the right. In 80 metres, at the next mini roundabout, make a ninety-degree turn left past the old Railway Hotel, on your left (now derelict). Follow the road for 100 metres to **Leighton Buzzard station**.

Lunch & tea places

Old Red Lion *Ivy Lane, Great Brickhill, MK17 9AH (01525 261715).* **Open** noon-11pm daily. *Food served* noon-2.30pm, 7-9.30pm Mon-Sat; noon-8pm Sun. This suggested lunchtime stop has a beer garden from which you can enjoy lovely views over a valley to the west.

Globe Inn *Globe Lane, Leighton Buzzard, LU7 2TA (01525 373338).* **Open** 11am-11pm daily. *Food served* noon-10pm daily. Located on the Grand Union Canal, this is the recommended tea place. It is about half an hour from the end of the walk.

There is also a variety of pubs and coffee shops in the centre of Leighton Buzzard.

Walk 42

Holmwood to Gomshall

Leith Tower, its woodlands and its heathlands.

Start: Holmwood station
Finish: Gomshall station

Length: 16.7km (10.4 miles)

Time: 4 hours 40 minutes. For the whole outing, including trains, sights and meals, allow at least 8 hours 30 minutes.

Transport: Take the train nearest to **9.30am** from **Victoria** station to **Holmwood** (journey time 55 minutes). Note that there is no service on this line on Sundays and some Bank Holiday Mondays. Trains back from **Gomshall** run every two hours to Guildford (where you change for Waterloo) and, in the other direction, to Dorking and Redhill (you can change at either station for a train back to London). The journey time is about 1 hour via Guildford, longer on the other routes. If you find you have a long wait for a train at Gomshall, you could take the hourly bus outside the Compasses

Inn to Guildford or Dorking (Monday to Saturday only).

Holmwood and Gomshall are on different lines, with trains operated by different railway companies. If you want the option of travelling back via Guildford, you will need to buy a day return to Gomshall and specifically ask for a ticket that is valid via Guildford. This will be valid as far as Dorking on the outward route and might be accepted to Holmwood, although you could be asked to pay a small supplement. A cheaper alternative is to buy a day return to Holmwood and then a ticket from Gomshall to Dorking (by train or bus) on the return journey, catching a train from there to London. If you are not sure which ticket to buy, ask at your local railway station.

OS Langranger Map: 187
OS Explorer Maps: 145 & 146
Holmwood, map reference TQ175437, is in **Surrey**, 6km south of Dorking.

Toughness: 6 out of 10

Walk notes: Much of this walk is through National Trust land, the broadleaf woods and heathland of Coldharbour, Leith Hill and Abinger Common. Leith Hill, with its tower, is the highest point in south-east England, with views out across the Weald to the English Channel. The hamlet of Friday Street is the suggested lunch place, and then the walk follows the Tillingbourne stream to within sight of Wotton House. From there it goes through the National Trust's Deerleap Wood, and so to the picturesque village of Abinger Hammer. Tea is at the mill at Gomshall, its functioning waterwheels serving to oxygenate the water, attracting trout. Short parts

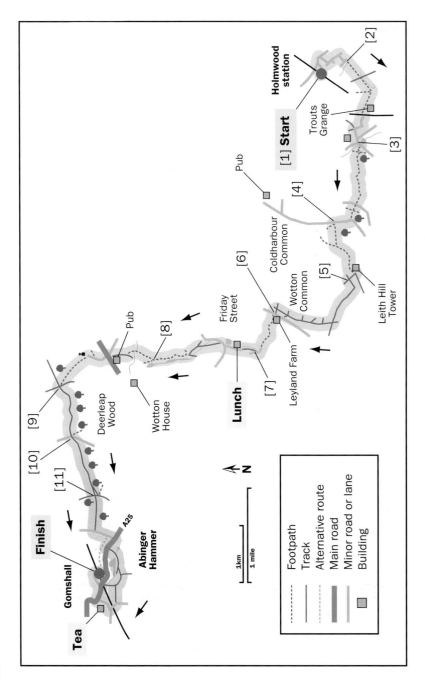

Holmwood station

Trouts Grange

[1] Start

[2]

[3]

[4]

Pub

Coldharbour Common

Leith Hill Tower

[5]

[6]

Wotton Common

Friday Street

Pub

[8]

Leyland Farm

Lunch

[7]

Wotton House

Deerleap Wood

[9]

[10]

[11]

Finish

Abinger Hammer

A25

Gomshall

Tea

N

1km
1 mile

Footpath
Track
Alternative route
Main road
Minor road or lane
Building

of the walk are very steep, but mostly it is easy going, mainly on sandy ways.

Walk options: There are two different approaches to varying this route.

a) Shortening the walk: You could catch a bus from Coldharbour, or a 21 or 22 bus (operated by London & Country) from opposite the lunchtime pub in Friday Street, going to Guildford or Redhill. Alternatively, catch a taxi from the Wotton Hatch pub in Wotton. You could also have tea slightly earlier, in Abinger Hammer, as detailed in the book's walk directions, then simply turn right, westwards, and stay on the A25 to Gomshall station.

b) Lengthening the walk: If you want a long walk, try adding on Walk 14 (Gomshall to Guildford, *see p106*), making an overall walk of some 19 miles.

History: **Leith Hill**, the highest point in south-east England, is based on sandstone bedrock 70 million years old. This bedrock was formed by a cementing amalgam of sand and the silica from seashells. It was on the summit of Leith Hill, in AD 851, that **Ethelwulf** (father of Alfred the Great) defeated the Danes who were heading for Winchester, having already sacked Canterbury and London.

In 1765, **Richard Hull** built Leith Hill Tower with the intention, it is said, of raising the hill above 1,000 feet. He is buried underneath it. The tower is open for people to clamber up on weekends and bank holidays, and Wednesday to Friday from April to October; admission (2010) is £1.20. It has drinks for sale, and maps and information about the area.

The **Stephan Langton Inn**, which is in Friday Street, takes its name from an Archbishop of Canterbury who is said to have spent his childhood in this hamlet. Born in 1150, Archbishop Langton was a subscribing witness to the Magna Carta, supporting the barons against King John and refusing to publish their excommunication by the Pope.

The **Church of St John the Evangelist**, near Wotton (open Sunday only) is of Saxon origin. It contains the tomb of John Evelyn, the essayist (author of, among other works, *Fumifugium, or the Inconvenience of the Air and Smoke of London Dissipated*). Evelyn was born at Wotton House in 1620. His diaries were discovered in an old clothes basket there in 1817.

The **monument to Samuel Wilberforce** in Abinger Roughs marks the spot where this Victorian bishop fell from his horse and died in 1873. Known as 'Soapy Sam', he vigorously opposed Darwin's new theory of evolution, most notably in a famous debate with Thomas Huxley in 1860. Hearing of his death, Huxley is said to have waspishly remarked that 'Wilberforce's brains had at last come into contact with reality, and the result had been fatal'.

Abinger Hammer village is named after the Hammer Pond, which enabled the working of the iron-industry furnaces here from the time of the Tudors. The commemorative iron-master's clock (seen on this walk) has Jack the Smith striking the hours. John Evelyn inveighed against the widespread felling of trees as fuel for the ironworks. In *Sylva*, first published in 1664, he suggested exploiting the developing world instead: ''Twere better to purchase all our iron out of America, than thus to exhaust our woods at home.'

Gomshall Mill is mentioned in the Domesday Book, but the present mill dates from the 17th century. The **Tillingbourne** stream (which springs out of the north slope of Leigh Hill) passes directly under the mill.

Walk directions

[1] [Numbers in square brackets refer to the map]

Leave **Holmwood station**, platform 2, not by the stairs but by the swing gate halfway along the platform. In 5 metres *turn left* on a quiet lane, your direction 65 degrees initially, before the lane swings to the right. In 105 metres you come to the main road where you *turn right,* with a pond on your right-hand side.

In 75 metres, at the other end of the pond, *turn right* by the phone box, on Merebank. In 40 metres ignore the fork right to the village hall. In 35 metres ignore Leith Road to the right, bearing left with the road, your direction 145 degrees. In 40 metres ignore Leith Grove to the right. Then in a further 140 metres *turn right* on Woodside Road.

Ignore all ways off. In 160 metres, at the Highland Road T-junction **[2]**, *carry straight on,* following a signposted footpath, with a timber fence on your left, your direction 210 degrees. In 50 metres you ignore a path off to the right.

In a further 25 metres go down four steps and over a wooden bridge with railings, across a stream, over a stile, and follow the yellow arrow to the left, your direction then 145 degrees.

In 60 metres, by a two-armed footpath sign, *fork right* with the path across fields, your direction 240 degrees.

In 575 metres, having ignored all ways off and crossed three stiles and a farm drive, you go up steps to cross the railway line.

On the other side, you cross a stile to continue ahead, your direction 285 degrees. In 65 metres go over two stiles with steps in between and continue upwards, with a field hedge on your left-hand side.

In a further 125 metres you pass a manor house on your left-hand side (Trouts Grange).

In 80 metres go over a stile beyond the tennis court (a metal fieldgate to its right-hand side) and in 15 metres *turn right* on a tarmac driveway, your direction 300 degrees.

Stay on this tarmac driveway all the way as it turns left, right and left again. Ignore a footpath to the right in 330

metres, passing Minnickfold manor house (which is marked on the OS map) on your right-hand side.

In 240 metres pass between white gates and out on to a tarmac road (Henhurst Cross Lane) **[3]**, which you cross, your direction 240 degrees, to enter Bearhurst estate on a public footpath, with its lodge on your right-hand side.

In 35 metres, immediately after crossing a bridge with its stone parapet on your right, **[!]** *take the footpath to the right* between fences (the signpost may be half-hidden in a hawthorn bush), your direction 310 degrees.

In 100 metres go over a stile and t*urn half left* uphill, a field fence on your left-hand side, your direction due west.

In 240 metres *turn left over a stile* (a metal fieldgate to its side) to continue straight on, slightly to the right, following a yellow arrow, heading for the stile in the top right-hand corner of the field, your direction 300 degrees (not the stile due west into the wood, 80 metres to the left).

In 170 metres cross the stile and then another (a metal fieldgate to its left) to follow the yellow arrow uphill, your direction 255 degrees.

In 215 metres go over a stile (a wooden fieldgate to its right) and follow the yellow arrow on, initially downhill then up, your direction 305 degrees, aiming 50 metres to the right of the house ahead.

In 250 metres go over a stile (a wooden fieldgate to its right) and in 20 metres you go through or around a wooden fieldgate to cross a tarmac road, slightly to your right, **[!]** *continuing on a public footpath uphill,* with a footpath signpost 5 metres ahead and to your right, your direction 265 degrees.

In 12 metres you cross a path to continue on up into the National Trust **Leith Hill Area** woodland.

Follow the yellow arrows on posts on the path ahead and in 300 metres you come to a tarmac road where you *go right.*

In 120 metres a sign indicates that you are entering Coldharbour. (There is a pub,

Walk 42

the **Plough Inn**, 750 metres up the road, should you want an early lunch.)

In 80 metres you pass the entrance to Mosses Wood Cottage on your left-hand side. In 20 metres **[4] [!]** *turn left* and take the signposted public footpath (not the path through the wooden barrier, but the less clear path to the left of it), due west and *very steeply up* into the National Trust's **Coldharbour Common**. This is a 1-in-3 path and a scramble in places. An alternative is the less steep route up past the wooden barrier. If taking this alternative route (particularly advisable if the ground is slippery after wet weather) ignore ways off and in 280 metres you come to a major path crossing and you *go left,* following the Coldharbour Walk arrows. In 260 metres you then rejoin the main suggested route at the asterisk **[*]** below.

The very steep (main) route: In 40 metres or so your path is now a gully, still going very steeply upwards. At the top of the gully, in 40 metres, you follow a less steep, clear path, straight onwards, keeping due west. In a further 40 metres

Leith Hill Tower.

you come to a path crossroads *where you go left,* your direction 190 degrees; there is a yellow arrow on a post here.

In 20 metres **[*]** you follow the National Trust Coldharbour Walk arrow to the *right,* your direction 250 degrees.

Following the NT arrows keep ahead in 20 metres, through chestnut trees (the woodland was being cleared at the time of this walk update).

In 60 metres by post 7 your path is joined by one from the right. In another 85 metres follow the arrow by *forking right,* your direction 245 degrees, as your path merges with the ridge path coming in from the left. Proceed along the undulating ridge path with a view over the Weald and the far line of the South Downs on your left-hand side.

In 150 metres you pass post 8 on your right and keep ahead. In a further 170 metres, by a post with indicators left to Landslip car park and right to Leith Tower, you *go right* passing a wooden barrier, your direction due west, on a downhill path. In 10 metres, *take the middle of three tracks* towards Leith Tower.

In 150 metres you pass a sign on your right side saying 'Dukes Warren', and you ignore a car-wide wooden bridleway barrier straight ahead to go left uphill, your direction 240 degrees, and so to **Leith Hill Tower**.

Enjoy the panoramic views from the Tower and, if the kiosk is open, you can buy hot and cold drinks and snacks.

Just 10 metres beyond the Tower, continuing westwards, you *fork right* on a bridleway, your direction 320 degrees.

In 8 metres you pass a bench, 10 metres away on your right-hand side. In a further 90 metres, ignore a fork to the left. In 25 metres you cross a path.

In a further 60 metres **[5]** while going downhill, **[!]** *take the left fork* by a post on your right, gently uphill, your direction 310 degrees (the right, equally main way, would have made your direction 5 degrees). 450 metres from this fork, your path having bent left, you come to a T-junction where you *go right,* your direction 5 degrees.

In 100 metres ignore a car-wide track to the right. Continue gently downhill and in 25 metres ignore paths to the left. In 150 metres your way is joined by another earth car-wide way from behind on your right.

Continue ahead, gently downhill, and in a further 350 metres, at a three-way fork (where the right fork has a car-wide wooden barrier marked footpath) *take the middle fork,* your direction 355 degrees.

In 200 metres, by a three-armed footpath post, a path joins from behind and to your left.

[!] In a further 100 metres, at a crossing of paths with a four-armed footpath post on your right, take the clear but zigzag path *to the left uphill,* your direction 285 degrees.

In 60 metres you come out on to a tarmac road, with Leylands farm opposite. *Go right* on the road, your direction 25 degrees. In 35 metres [6] *go left* on a signposted public footpath, your direction 280 degrees.

In 150 metres you come to wide open fields where you *turn right,* by a two-armed footpath post, with the field edge on your right-hand side and a new wire fence to your left, your direction 5 degrees.

In 65 metres go through a metal kissing gate and *turn left* with the path to keep a field hedge on your right-hand side, your direction 275 degrees. Keep to this path downhill and in 90 metres go through a metal kissing gate ahead and continue down a closed-in path, passing a house on your right-hand side. In 75 metres [!] *turn right* through a gap in the hedge by a two-armed footpath sign, into the wood, your direction 330 degrees.

In 45 metres (where the fork right heads to a driveway in 10 metres) *fork left,* following the metal two-armed footpath sign over to the right, downhill, your direction 285 degrees. In 100 metres you pass sheds on your left-hand side.

In 100 metres you continue on a tarmac house driveway, downhill. In 50 metres

you come to a road T-junction – the end of a loop of road – and you *go left, downhill,* with Spring Cottage on your left-hand side, your direction 305 degrees.

In 70 metres ignore a bridleway signposted to the left, and a footpath signposted straight on, to swing right with a tarmac road, your direction due north.

In 70 metres, by a car entrance to St John's House on your left-hand side [7], you *fork right* on a bridleway marked by a post with dragon and oak leaf symbols, your direction 15 degrees.

In 35 metres ignore a footbridge to your right. You keep the stream on your right-hand side all the way to Friday Street.

In 400 metres ignore another footbridge on your right.

In 140 metres your way becomes a lane between houses, leading in 50 metres to the **Stephan Langton Inn** in **Friday Street** on your right-hand side, the suggested lunchtime stop.

After lunch, coming out of the pub, *turn right* to carry on up the lane, due north. Ignore other ways off. In 110 metres you have a pond on your right-hand side. In 40 metres you come to a T-junction which you cross over, going slightly to the right, to follow a public footpath sign, on a tarmac driveway downhill, your direction 35 degrees.

In 25 metres you pass Pond Cottage on your right-hand side. In a further 75 metres, you cross a stream on a low footbridge, where cars ford it.

In a further 65 metres, by Yew Tree Cottage on your left-hand side, keep left with your road, joined by a driveway from the right, with the stream on your left-hand side.

In 140 metres cross a path, ignoring the bridge on your left-hand side, to keep on over a stile (with a wooden fieldgate to its left-hand side) into the parkland of Wotton Estate and to a series of ponds created by dams.

In 320 metres you pass wooden fieldgates to your right and left, both marked 'Private'.

In 65 metres **[8]**, by a three-armed footpath sign, take the footpath fork *to the right, steeply up a gully* into the woods, your direction 25 degrees, between fencing.

In 320 metres cross a car-wide way marked 'Private', to carry on downwards, your direction 30 degrees. In 160 metres go over a stile to exit the wood on a path between wire fences, **Wotton House** visible away on your left-hand side.

In 65 metres go over a stream. In 30 metres go up three steps into the wood. In a further 85 metres go over a stile (with a road 5 metres below on your left-hand side) and carry on bearing *half right* across the field towards the left of the house ahead, your direction 5 degrees. (Ignore the stile in the left-hand fence, 75 metres away.)

In 240 metres go over a stile (a metal fieldgate on its right-hand side) and in 12 metres carry straight on across a car park towards the A25. The **Wotton Hatch** pub (a late lunch option) is to the left.

In a further 60 metres, you cross the A25 and *continue on the lane* to the **Church of St John the Evangelist** in **Wotton**.

In 80 metres ignore a stile on your right-hand side. In 200 metres you come to the (locked) front door of the church and either take the new footpath diversion to the left and around the churchyard, or fork left through the churchyard, in 25 metres passing a tombstone table supported by griffins. In 15 metres exit the churchyard by a stile on your left-hand side. *Go right* on the other side, on a clear path downhill between fences, your direction 320 degrees.

In 140 metres go over a stile. In 80 metres you enter **Deerleap Wood** (marked on the OS map).

In 200 metres you exit the wood over a stile and continue straight on across a field. In 120 metres you come out on to earth road crossings **[9]** with a three-armed footpath post on the left where you *fork left (but not sharp left)*, your direction 210 degrees. In 30 metres you pass a timber-framed barn (held up by wooden posts) on your right-hand side and in 20 metres the entrance to Park Farm Cottage, also on your right-hand side.

Keep straight on, following a blue arrow, with the edge of Deerleap Wood on your left-hand side.

In 700 metres *veer right* with the path. In 65 metres continue in your previous direction (due west).

In 190 metres you come to a tarmac road **[10]** where you *go left* for 10 metres, your direction 220 degrees, and then join the public bridleway *to the right* (whose signpost is 10 metres ahead) going past a metal fieldgate, your direction 250 degrees. In 25 metres you pass the National Trust sign for **Abinger The Roughs**. In a further 80 metres ignore a fork to the left to follow the blue arrow onwards.

In 70 metres you pass the **monument to Samuel Wilberforce**. Keep to the main path. In 360 metres ignore a sharp turn left and ignore a fork left in a further 18 metres, to *bear right uphill,* following the main trail.

Keep on this, ignoring ways off. In 550 metres, at the other end of an open section, with a multiplicity of ways on offer **[11]**, ignore the fork left, with its green arrow, and keep to the way that is to the right of this (the main blue arrow car-wide trail), your direction 260 degrees.

In 10 metres ignore a way to the left, marked with a green arrow.

In 125 metres cross a path to continue on, a field fence now on your right-hand side and a farm visible down on your right-hand side (marked Hackhurst Farm on the OS map).

In 145 metres you cross a farm track to carry straight on, following the blue NT arrow, through a wooden swing gate (to the right-hand side of a wooden fieldgate), still due west, with a hedge on your left-hand side and a wire fence to your right.

In 160 metres go through a wooden swing gate. In 15 metres you come to a tarmac lane where you *go left, downhill,* your direction then 185 degrees.

In 300 metres you come down to the A25, the **Abinger Arms** pub on your right-hand side (a possible early tea stop).

For the Abinger Hammer tea rooms, turn left along the A25; the tea rooms are down the road on the left-hand side, just before the post office. After tea here, retrace your steps to the junction by the pub.

[!] To head direct to Gomshall railway station (ignoring the loop into Gomshall), stay on the A25 for some 600 metres, until 100 metres before you reach the railway bridge, where you take the clear signposted path to your right which leads up to the railway station.

Continuing on the main walk: *Turn right,* your direction 300 degrees. In 200 metres, just past the red-brick, timber-framed house, *turn left* on a signposted public bridleway (a car-wide earth road), your direction 220 degrees.

In 80 metres you pass The Willows on your right-hand side. In a further 105 metres, you go over the Tillingbourne stream. In 45 metres *fork left (not sharp left)* off the concrete road, your direction 265 degrees (following *the right* of two blue bridleway arrows).

In 190 metres you come out on to an earth driveway. In 30 metres you come to an earth road T-junction, where you *go right,* your direction 285 degrees.

In 225 metres you pass the entrance to Twiga Lodge on your left-hand side and in 10 metres you *take the second left,* a narrow bridleway heading due west. In 150 metres, the bridleway having merged with a farm track, you pass a farmhouse on your left-hand side. In 60 metres you pass a manor house on your right-hand side, then a barn on your left. In 60 metres you come to a car road T-junction where you *go right* on Tower Hill Road. In 20 metres you go under a railway bridge and on to the T-junction, by a timber-framed house (no.4), where you *go right* on Goose Green Road.

In 260 metres you come to **Gomshall Mill** on your right-hand side. The **Compasses Inn,** your suggested tea place, is to your left.

After tea, *turn right* on the A25. In 225 metres *fork left uphill,* your direction 60 degrees. In 160 metres you come to **Gomshall station**. Cross over the railway to platform 2 for trains to Guildford, or stay on this side for Redhill.

Lunch & tea places

Plough Inn *Coldharbour, Surrey, RH5 6HD (01306 711793, www.ploughinn. com).* **Open** 11.30am-11.30pm Mon-Thur; 11.30am-12.30am Fri-Sun. *Food served* noon-3pm, 6.30-9pm Mon-Thur; noon-3pm, 6.30-9.30pm Fri, Sat; noon-4pm Sun. This atmospheric 17th-century pub is a possible early lunch stop and a good choice for early starters.

Leith Hill Tower kiosk *Leith Hill, nr Coldharbour, Surrey (01306 712711, www.nationaltrust.org.uk).* **Open** *Apr-Oct* 10am-5pm Fri-Sun. *Nov-Mar* 10am-3.30pm Sat, Sun. Elevenses can be taken at the kiosk within Leith Hill Tower. Note that the kiosk is also open Tuesday to Saturday during school holidays.

Stephan Langton Inn *Friday Street, Abinger Common, Dorking, RH5 6JR (01306 730775).* **Open** 11.30am-3pm, 5.30-11pm Tue-Fri; 11am-11pm Sat; 11am-8pm Sun. *Food served* noon-2.30pm, 6.30-9.30pm Mon-Sat; noon-4pm Sun. The suggested lunchtime pub.

Wotton Hatch *Guildford Road, Wotton, Dorking, RH5 6QQ (01306 887694, www.wottonhatch.co.uk).* **Open** 11am-11pm Mon-Sat; 11am-10.30pm Sun. *Food served* noon-3pm, 6-10pm Mon-Fri; noon-10pm Sat, Sun.

Compasses Inn *50 Station Road, Gomshall, GU5 9LA (01483 202506, www.thecompassesinn.co.uk).* **Open** 11am-11pm Mon-Sat; noon-10.30pm Sun. *Food served* noon-9pm Mon-Sat; noon-6pm Sun. This suggested tea place is friendly to walkers and serves drinks and meals all afternoon. There is a pleasant beer garden with a stream outside.

Other options for tea are the **Abinger Hammer tea rooms** and the **Abinger Arms** pub.

Walk 43

Otford Circular

Romney Street, Shoreham and the Darent Valley.

Start and finish: Otford station

Length: 12.0km (7.5 miles)

Time: 3 hours 30 minutes. For the whole outing, including trains, sights and meals, allow 7 hours 30 minutes.

Transport: Take the train nearest to **10.45am** from **Victoria** station to **Otford** (journey time 35 minutes). Fast trains back to Victoria are half-hourly (hourly on Sundays); there are also half-hourly slow trains, from which you may be able to change at Bromley South for a faster service. If you are driving, Otford station car park costs £4 (less at weekends). Alternatively, there is a free public car park in the village, opposite the Bull pub.

OS Landranger Map: 188
OS Explorer Map: 147
Otford, map reference TQ532593, is in **Kent**, 4km north of Sevenoaks.

Toughness: 5 out of 10

Walk notes: This would make a good, brisk, shortish autumn or winter walk, with a late start possible. The route at the outset is steeply uphill, for a time following the North Downs Way, with views back over Otford and the valley, then going through Greenhill Wood, with a glimpse of Oak Hall, before heading north to the pub in Romney Street. In the afternoon, Shoreham village is worth visiting, with its four pubs and 12th-century church (the station building houses the Shoreham Countryside Centre, run by volunteers and open on some weekend afternoons). The route onwards is the Darent Valley Path into Otford, which offers a tea room, a palace (in ruins), a church and many ancient buildings. It is also home to the Otford Solar System: claimed to be the only scale model of its kind in the world, it shows the relative position of the sun and planets at the start of the new millennium.

Walk options: You can cut 0.8km off the end of the walk by following the shortcut at [*] in the walk directions. This alternative route has the advantage of going close to the centre of the Otford Solar System (*see above*). It is also possible to get a train back to London from Shoreham instead of completing the circuit.

History: **Shoreham** is the remote village that the painter **Samuel Palmer** chose as a refuge from London's pollution. He was the leader of a group who followed William Blake and called themselves **The Ancients**. Palmer's father, also called Samuel, rented the **Water House** by the river.

The **Church of St Peter & St Paul** in Shoreham has many interesting features, including an outstanding wooden rood screen, which spans the width of the building, and a stained-glass window by the **Pre-Raphaelite** artist **Edward Burne-Jones**.

Otford Circular

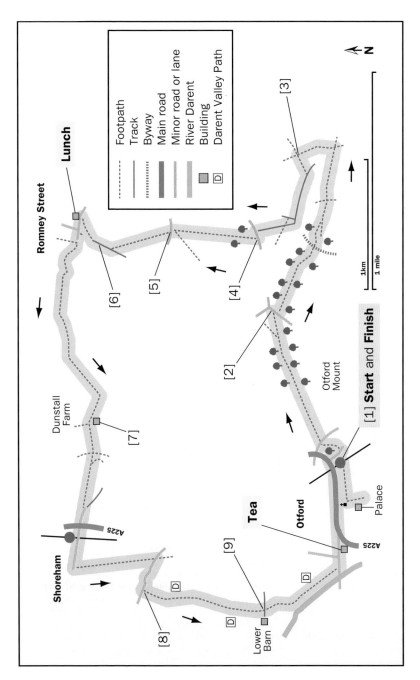

N

Footpath
Track
Byway
Main road
Minor road or lane
River Darent
Building
Darent Valley Path

1km
1 mile

[3]

Lunch

Romney Street

[6]

[5]

[4]

[2]

Dunstall
Farm

[7]

Otford
Mount

[1] Start and Finish

Palace

Tea

Otford

A225

[9]

A225

Shoreham

[8]

Lower
Barn

Otford goes back to the 6th century, when the Anglo-Saxons called their settlement Ottanford ('Otta's ford'). Offa and Canute fought battles here. The village pond, where the duckhouse is Britain's smallest listed building, was the main source of water for local people until the early 20th century.

The Bull pub in Otford has magnificent fireplaces, brought there from the ruined Otford Palace. Opposite the Bull is the Arts and Crafts-style Church Hall. It was designed by Edwin Lutyens, who waived his fee – after all, it had been commissioned by his brother William, who was then vicar of Otford.

Otford Palace once occupied four acres, but it fell into decay after Archbishop Cranmer was forced to surrender it to Henry VIII in 1537. A few fragments remain and are on open view.

Construction of St Bartholomew's Church, Otford, began in 1060, with the tower being added in around 1185. The church contains large marble memorials to Charles and David Polhill, great-grandsons of Oliver Cromwell.

Walk directions

[1] [Numbers in square brackets refer to the map]

From the middle of platform 2 at Otford station, exit up steps with blue-painted metal handrails, then bear right on to a tarmac lane heading east away from the station. In 40 metres *turn left* past a metal fieldgate on an unasphalted public footpath, soon passing a Chalk Pit sign on your right-hand side. Veer left when you reach an open area and in 40 metres go up steps to pass through a wooden kissing gate on to a road.

Turn right on the road for 10 metres, then *go left uphill* on a signposted footpath, the North Downs Way, your direction 40 degrees. The path soon climbs more steeply uphill and eventually comes to a bench, with views back down to Otford and the Darent valley.

Carry on up the path. Near the top, where it levels out, go through a wooden kissing gate and follow the right-hand edge of the large open common. In 300 metres you pass a chest-high Ordnance Survey Marker, 100 metres away on your left-hand side, and in another 100 metres you go through a gate. [2] *Turn right downhill* on a tarmac road signposted Otford and Kemsing, leaving the North Downs Way.

In 100 metres you *go left over a stile* with a public footpath sign (a metal

fieldgate to its left-hand side), your direction 75 degrees, past Row Dow mini reservoir on your left, and parallel to the vale below. Keep to the main path. In 650 metres go through a wooden barrier and across a track to carry straight on through another wooden barrier, past a Kent Wildlife Trust panel for Kemsing Down.

The path curves round to the right and then back left, with another path merging from the right. 100 metres from this path junction, continue past a large dead tree trunk and ignore a path to the right going downhill. In a further 125 metres, *turn right downhill* at a path crossing, rejoining the North Downs Way. In 25 metres go through a wooden kissing gate just below a wooden bench.

Turn left along the hillside, your direction 70 degrees, keeping to the main path. In 125 metres go through a metal kissing gate, leaving Kemsing Down.

In another 200 metres, *bear left uphill* at a fork, following the North Downs Way sign, in 100 metres re-entering the wood. In a further 15 metres, *turn left* at a main path crossing, leaving the North Downs Way to head north uphill. Keep straight on over a drive with the courtyard and wooden part of Oak Hall on your left. In 40 metres go over another drive and, after another 40 metres, go over a stile into the corner of a large field. **[3]**

Turn left to go along the left-hand field edge to the next corner, 200 metres away. (On the OS map the right of way is shown as going into the field, then turning left at a path crossing to go diagonally across the field to the corner. But the path along the edge of the field is widely used and there seems no reason not to use it.)

Leave the field over a stile, to the right of a fieldgate. In 80 metres this path ends and you cross a stile on your left on to a tarmac lane which is the driveway leading to Oak Hall. Turn right here, resuming your westerly direction.

Out past the drive's entrance columns, and past Thatched Cottage on your right-hand side, the road curves to the right and

you continue along it, now heading due north. In 60 metres ignore the North Downs Way signposted off to the left and continue along the road, past Shorehill Farm, Shorehill Cottage and then derelict farm buildings on the right, with a large modern house and barn at the bottom of a field on the left.

You come to a road T-junction and *turn left downhill*, past Primrose Cottage on your right-hand side. 70 metres from the junction, **[4]** *turn right* on to a signposted public footpath, heading north. 350 metres down through the wood, cross a stile into a field and continue in the same direction, soon going uphill.

Exit the field by a stile (with two metal fieldgates on its left-hand side) and carry straight on, with the field fence and wood on your left-hand side. Then go down across a field to the right of a house shielded by a wooden fence and trees, still heading northwards. Exit by a stile (with a fieldgate to its left-hand side) out on to a tarmac road.

[5] *Turn left downhill* on the road. In 20 metres *turn right* over a stile to go uphill on a signposted public footpath, heading northwards. In 30 metres go over another stile and straight on along the edge of a field.

In 100 metres go over a stile into another field. Continue northwards with a wood on your right-hand side (or, if the field is churned up and very muddy, you could look for a path just inside the wood). Exit the field by a stile (a metal fieldgate to its right-hand side) and then *fork right off the main track,* through a metal gate, following a blue bridleway arrow, still heading northwards.

[!] In 60 metres **[6]** you *cross a stile on your right,* at a gap in the hedge. Then go half left over the field towards two white buildings, on a path that is a shortcut to the pub, the **Fox & Hounds** in **Romney Street**, the suggested lunchtime stop.

Coming out of the pub, *turn right* and cross a stile to the left of the Romney Street Farm entrance on to a potentially muddy path between fences, signposted as a public bridleway. In 100 metres the bridleway turns off to the left, but you continue ahead on a footpath.

In 60 metres go over a stile and ignore a yellow arrow pointing to the right. Just behind the boundary hedge to your right is a large field used as a private landing strip, where you can occasionally see light aircraft taking off or landing. You are now away from the last building and carry straight on downhill, your direction initially 300 degrees, with Canary Wharf visible in the distance. Keep to the right of a small island of trees in a crater in the middle of the field.

Exit the field by a stile, go across a car-wide track, and continue over another stile and steeply downhill towards a golf course.

At the bottom of the field go over a stile and continue across the golf course through a tunnel of overarching trees, then steeply uphill to cross a stile and enter a wood.

Exit the wood through a gap in the fence and turn half left on a path across the corner of a large field, your direction 240 degrees. In 80 metres continue across another field on a wide path.

At the end of the field, another farm track merges from the left and you turn half right to join it, going downhill. Keep on this farm track as it goes uphill into Dunstall Farm. **[7]** Go more or less straight on through the farmyard, following a yellow arrow to veer to the right of the far barn, then continue across a field, your direction 260 degrees.

On the far side go down into the wood, in 50 metres crossing a path to carry on down a long flight of earth steps. 350 metres from the end of the steps, your path merges with a bridleway and you carry on downwards, slightly to the right.

In 200 metres, you come to a road junction with the A225. Cross this main road carefully and head west on Station Road, signposted Golf Course and Shoreham Village (or you could detour along the station's access road to visit the Countryside Centre, later going down steps to join Station Road). 100 metres after going under the railway bridge, ignore the main entrance left into Darent Valley golfcourse. But in a further 70 metres **[8]**, your onward route is to *turn left* to head south on a footpath signposted Darent Valley Path.

(However, a detour to visit **Shoreham village** is recommended: Staying on the car road brings you, in 200 metres or so, to the Church of St Peter & St Paul and to Ye Olde George Inne, and beyond that to the River Darent. Either return the same way, or take a 1.5km clockwise circuit of the village: cross the bridge and go along Church Street, High Street and Mill Lane to come back alongside the river; this route will take you past three more pubs and a tea room, the Honeypot.)

Coming back to the main route, the Darent Valley Path: this leads through the golf course on an enclosed path. After 370 metres, *take care when crossing an open fairway.* 40 metres beyond the fairway, go through a metal kissing gate and onwards, now with a cricket pitch and a pavilion on your right-hand side, to follow a path between fences, still heading south. 100 metres along this enclosed path, you come to a major path junction.

(**[*]** For a shorter route back to Otford, you can continue ahead at this point. In 1.5km this path comes out directly opposite the Hospices of Hope tea room, but 300 metres before this, opposite farm buildings, you can cross a stile on your right into the Recreation Ground. The centre of the **Otford Solar System** is in front of you, with an information panel 50 metres away by the hedge on your right.)

For the main route, however, turn sharp right to head north-west on a tarmac lane, still following the signposted Darent Valley Path. In 250 metres, by a crossing of many paths, turn left through wooden barriers, following the Darent Valley Path, signposted 'Footpath to Otford', your direction 200 degrees.

Continue on an enclosed path through a narrow strip of woodland with glimpses of the golf course on either side.

Carry straight on, following the Darent Valley Path signs. Once you are past the golf course, cross a stile into a field and continue along its left-hand edge, with the distant hum of M25 traffic across the valley to the right. Exit the field across a stile and ignore a public footpath sign off to the left, continuing ahead over another stile [9] to carry on towards Otford, now visible in the distance, your direction 150 degrees.

In 230 metres go over a stile to continue on with the clear waters of the River Darent now on your right-hand side, later bearing left with the river's fork by a house on the far bank with unusual round brick chimneys. Go through a wooden swing gate to pass between gardens and houses to the main road and *turn left* towards the village pond and station.

You soon pass Pickmoss, a medieval half-timbered yeoman's house, on your right-hand side. Immediately next door is the old Baptist Chapel (at which Samuel Palmer's father was minister); and, a bit further on, the **Bull** pub (some of which dates to the 16th century). Beyond this, also on your right and opposite a footpath signposted to Shoreham, you come to the **Hospices of Hope** tea room, the suggested tea place.

Further along the High Street, overlooking the village pond, you come to the **Pond View Tea Rooms** (formerly the Willow Tea Rooms) and the **Crown** and **Woodman** pubs. Head towards the **Church of St Bartholomew** on the far side of the pond (where a short detour to the right of the church would take you to the gatehouse and north-west tower, virtually all that remains of **Otford Palace**).

To get to the station without going along the main road, take the tarmac path leading to a wooden gate in front of the church (to look inside, use the new entrance on its north side). Continue along the path on the south side of the church, with the churchyard to your right and later a brick wall to your left, and so through a wooden gate. You continue eastwards, in a further 250 metres reaching the car park of **Otford station**. The station's near platform is for London trains.

Lunch & tea places

Fox & Hounds *Romney Street, Sevenoaks, TN15 6XR (01959 525428, www.foxnhounds.co.uk).* **Open** noon-midnight Mon-Sat; noon-11pm Sun. *Food served* noon-3pm, 7-9pm Mon-Fri; noon-4pm, 7-9pm Sat; noon-4pm Sun. Serves simple pub food. Groups of ten or more should phone ahead to book.

Hospices of Hope tea room *11a High Street, Otford, TN14 5PG (01959 524322, www.hospicesofhope.co.uk).* **Open** 10am-3.45pm Mon-Sat. The recommended stop for tea is a charity shop that uses its profits to support hospices in Romania and surrounding countries.

Pond View Tea Rooms *6 High Street, Otford, TN14 5PQ (01959 522150).* **Open** 9am-2pm Mon, Tue; 9am-4.30pm Wed-Fri; 10am-4.30pm Sat; 11am-4.20pm Sun. A good alternative tea stop, these tea rooms do indeed overlook the village pond.

Bull *High Street, Otford, TN14 5PG (01959 523198).* **Open** noon-11pm daily. *Food served* noon-10pm daily. Stronger libations are on offer at this historic pub, run by Chef & Brewer.

Crown *10 High Street, Otford, TN14 5PQ (01959 522847, http://crownpuband restaurant.co.uk).* **Open** noon-11pm Mon-Thur; noon-11.30pm Fri; 11am-11.30pm Sat; 11am-11pm Sun. *Food served* noon-3pm Mon, Tue; noon-3pm, 6-9pm Wed-Fri; 11am-3pm, 6-9pm Sat; 12.30pm, 2.30pm, 4.30pm Sun.

Woodman *2 High Street, Otford, TN14 5PQ (01959 522195).* **Open** 11.30am-11pm Mon-Fri; 11.30am-11.30pm Sat; noon-11pm Sun. *Food served* 11.30am-2.30pm Tue-Sat; noon-3pm Sun.

Walk 44
Witley to Haslemere

Chiddingfold and the Crown Inn.

Start: Witley station
Finish: Haslemere station

Length: 14.2km (8.8 miles)

Time: 4 hours. For the whole outing, including trains and meals, allow 8 hours.

Transport: Take the train nearest to **10.10am** from **Waterloo** station to **Witley** (journey time about 55 minutes). There are four trains an hour back from Haslemere (two on

Sundays), with a journey time of 50-60 minutes. Buy a day return to Haslemere.

Parking at Witley is easier than at Haslemere, and the station car park is free at weekends. Trains back to Witley are hourly and take 5 minutes.

OS Langranger Map: 186
OS Explorer Map: 133
Witley, map reference SU948379, is in **Surrey**, 12km south-west of Guildford.

Toughness: 2 out of 10

Walk notes: This is an easy but interesting walk from Witley (where walking sticks used to be made – hence the local copses of ash and sweet chestnut). You will pass Lockwood Donkey Sanctuary (now only open to the public on four Sundays a year) and Combe Court manor house, with its 15th-century farmhouse, and head through the churchyard of St Mary's to the medieval village of Chiddingfold, where the Crown Inn is the suggested lunch stop. After lunch, the walk is through Frillinghurst Wood and various National Trust estates, coming out into Haslemere High Street near a tea room.

Walk options: You could shorten the walk by catching the bus to Haslemere (approximately one an hour) from outside the lunchtime pub in Chiddingfold.

History: Chiddingfold's main splendour is the lunchtime pub, the 12th-century **Crown Inn**. In the late 14th century,

the publican was convicted of selling ale 'contrary to the assize' (courts tested ale by pouring some on to a wooden bench, then sitting on it – if it had a sticky quality, it was pronounced good). In 1552, Edward VI stayed at this inn, while his 4,000-strong retinue camped on the green.

Chiddingfold was the centre of the stained-glass industry between the 13th and 17th centuries, and the village was isolated enough to be able to keep working through the plague years, supplying stained glass for St Stephen's Chapel at Westminster in the 1350s.

In the churchyard of the 13th-century **St Mary's Church** in Chiddingfold, there is a 1776 epitaph to Arthur Stedman, one shared with many blacksmiths across the country: 'My fire is out, my forge decay'd...'.

The town of **Haslemere** is lucky to be surrounded by National Trust land in almost every direction, thanks to the campaigns in the early 1900s of

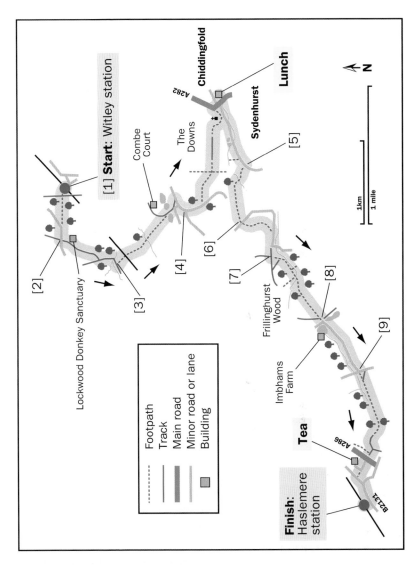

Map legend:
- Footpath
- Track
- Main road
- Minor road or lane
- Building

Start: Witley station [1]

Combe Court

The Downs

A282

Chiddingfold

Lunch

Sydenhurst

[5]

[2]

Lockwood Donkey Sanctuary

[3]

[4]

[6]

[7]

Frillinghurst Wood

[8]

Imbhams Farm

[9]

Tea

A286

Finish: Haslemere station

B2131

N

1km
1 mile

Sir Robert Hunter. He was one of the National Trust's founders, and lived in Haslemere.

In Tudor and Stuart times, **Haslemere** was a centre for the iron industry. With the coming of the railway in the mid 19th century, it became a popular spot for literary people. The poet Tennyson's house, Aldworth, is on the slopes of Black Down, where he loved to walk, and George Eliot wrote *Middlemarch* in Shottermill.

The town has an interesting **museum** up the High Street, just north of Darnleys tea room. The museum is open 10am to 5pm Monday to Saturday, and has important natural history collections, including a fine explanatory display of local wild flowers in the foyer. Other highlights include an Egyptian mummy, Zulu beadwork and Eastern European peasant art.

The **Lockwood Donkey Sanctuary** (01428 687749) in Sandhills is one of the oldest donkey sanctuaries in the UK, having been established by a Mr and Mrs Lockwood in the 1950s. On Mrs Lockwood's death in 2005, the sanctuary was bequeathed to the RSPCA, who now manage the centre. It has become a rescue and rehabilitation centre for horses and ponies, in addition to being a sanctuary for donkeys. Currently (2010) the centre is only open to the public on its four annual open days, usually Sunday. However, if the sanctuary receives sufficient local support, the RSPCA is hoping to open to the public once a week. A visit to the sanctuary early on in the walk is a delightful added feature.

Walk directions

[1] [Numbers in square brackets refer to the map]
On arrival at **Witley station**, cross the footbridge to platform 1. At the bottom of the steps keep straight on to the end of the platform where you join a public footpath, your direction 260 degrees, shortly bending right, your direction north. 100 metres from the bend, immediately after passing a house called Inglewood on your right-hand side, at a crosspaths you *turn left,* your direction west.

Then in 600 metres you come to a road. Cross the road, slightly to your right, to go up a sand shingle drive, your direction 300 degrees. In 15 metres *fork right uphill* on a path marked GW (Greensand Way), your direction 350 degrees. But, 50 metres up the slope, ignore a GW sign to the right, *to turn left* (slightly downhill), your direction 260 degrees.

In 120 metres your path merges with a driveway and in 30 metres it comes out on to a road, by a red phonebox.

Turn right on this road, your direction 280 degrees.

In 60 metres *turn left* down Hatch Lane [2], a tarmac lane signposted public bridleway.

In 150 metres you pass the **Lockwood Donkey Sanctuary**. In a further 400 metres, keep straight on as you enter a wood, passing by a double metal fieldgate to your left.

In 110 metres, by a post offering a public footpath or a public bridleway, follow the public bridleway straight on down through the wood. In 200 metres *bear right* with the path to cross a wooden footbridge over a stream.

80 metres from the bridge, you come to a fork where you go *left uphill* [3], your direction southwards. In 70 metres cross a ditch on two sleepers to go straight on across a field, your direction 140 degrees.

In 160 metres you cross a stile, then the railway lines, and you go over a stile the other side, then across an earth road and over another stile. *Continue straight on* with the field fence on your left-hand side.

In 130 metres you go over a stile, still straight on, down along the edge of a wood. In a further 230 metres, down in the wood, you cross a stream by a brick bridge to go up the other side. In 30 metres you cross a car-wide earth track to keep straight on, your direction 120 degrees. In 160 metres cross a stile to leave the wood, going straight on across a field, your direction 140 degrees, with **Combe Court** (marked on the OS map) visible ahead to your left.

In 120 metres go over a stile, straight on, your direction 145 degrees, passing Combe Court (behind a hedgerow) on your left-hand side. In 180 metres go over a stile in a metal fence to continue down with a wall on your left-hand side. In 280 metres go through a gate to the left of a car-wide black-painted metal gate.

In 20 metres at the main road *turn right,* your direction 250 degrees.

In 230 metres take the first car road *to the left* [4] called Pook Hill.

Follow this road for 300 metres, ignoring ways off, to Langhurst Manor (on your right-hand side, just over the crest of the hill). Then in 50 metres *turn left,* following a public footpath sign over a stile, your direction 80 degrees.

In 300 metres cross a stile to go straight across a driveway (a modern cottage on your left-hand side) and continue *straight on,* with a fence to your right-hand side, your direction 145 degrees. In 30 metres you *fork left,* with the hedge of a more substantial house on your right-hand side.

In 60 metres go through a metal kissing gate. 25 metres further on, go over a stile and straight on across a field, with the field boundary up to your left, your direction 140 degrees. In 300 metres ignore a stile up to the left. In 150 metres go over a stile and another, now with fences to both sides. In a further 100 metres, continue on, now on a tarmac lane with houses on both sides. In 230 metres, when this comes to an end, continue straight on through a metal kissing gate.

In 200 metres you pass a burial ground on your right-hand side to then go through a metal kissing gate with a metal fieldgate and a wooden swing gate to its right.

Turn right at this point through the wooden swing gate into the burial ground and straight on, your direction 200 degrees, with some of the paving stones underfoot made of old headstones. In 110 metres you turn left, with a wall on your right-hand side, in 80 metres coming to **Chiddingfold**'s **St Mary's Church** (usually open). Beyond the church, in 30 metres you go through the lychgate and opposite is the **Crown Inn**, the suggested lunch stop. (The **Swan** pub in Chiddingfold also serves lunch.)

Coming out of the Crown Inn after lunch, *turn left* to then cross the busy A283 with care and *turn left.* In 10 metres, *turn right* up Mill Lane.

Continue along this road for 900 metres to pass the Ukrainian Home, Sydenhurst, on your left-hand side. In a further 230 metres, just beyond the end of Orchard

Cottage's garden on your right-hand side **[5]**, *turn right* through a metal kissing gate (with a metal fieldgate to its right-hand side), your direction 310 degrees, to follow the right-hand side of the field.

In 150 metres cross a stile to *veer left,* your direction 280 degrees, with the fence on your right-hand side. In 80 metres turn right through a metal kissing gate into a wood, a garden fence to your right for 25 metres; then bending *sharp left* with the path, your direction now 310 degrees.

In 220 metres cross a stile to the left of a metal fieldgate, keeping the field fence on your right-hand side, your direction west.

In 300 metres you pass a house on your right-hand side and in a further 50 metres, where the edge of the field goes sharp right (as you pass under mini pylon cables) you continue *straight on* across the field towards another part timber-framed house visible ahead.

In 120 metres **[6]** go across a lane via stiles to continue *half left,* your direction 200 degrees, towards a stile visible in the distance. In 200 metres you go over a pair of stiles to *veer right* across the next field, your direction now 210 degrees.

In a further 320 metres you go over a stile (hidden in the right-hand corner) into a wood; in 30 metres, *turn right* down a tarmac road, your direction 260 degrees.

In 130 metres ignore a left turn over a bridge to continue up towards Frillinghurst Mill, Manor and Farm.

In 330 metres, and 40 metres past a large corrugated barn on your right-hand side **[7]**, you go *left over a stile,* your direction 190 degrees, towards a stile visible in a wooden fence (some 50 metres to the right of where the fence comes out of the wood). Once over it, carry on in the same direction to the edge of the wood, which you then follow along, with the edge on your left-hand side.

In 80 metres you pass a three-armed footpath sign and a stile to your left; in 20 metres go over a stile into **Frillinghurst**

Wood (marked on the OS map), straight on, your direction 250 degrees.

In 35 metres ignore a turn up to the right and keep to the main path. In a further 120 metres, cross a stream by a wooden bridge. **[!]** In a further 120 metres at a path junction, *fork left,* your direction 240 degrees, through the wood along a well-defined path marked by footpath posts along the way. In 400 metres you emerge into the corner of a field to go along its left-hand side towards a cottage on the far side, your direction 230 degrees.

In 260 metres, some 60 metres away from the cottage ahead, you cross over into the next field to continue on in the same direction as before but now with the field hedge on your right-hand side and your path now a bridleway. In 100 metres at a car-road T-junction **[8]** *turn left,* your direction 130 degrees and in 20 metres *turn right,* your direction 220 degrees, with the lake on your right-hand side.

In 130 metres *veer right* with the road, the barns of **Imbhams Farm** (marked on the OS map) on your left-hand side.

600 metres beyond these barns, you come out on to a car road **[9]**, which you cross, slightly to the left, to continue on a signposted public footpath, through a wooden kissing gate, with Holdfast Cottage on your right, your direction 230 degrees.

In 220 metres go through a wooden kissing gate and *turn right (not sharp right)* along a track, keeping a white-painted house on your left-hand side.

In 100 metres you enter the National Trust's **Swan Barn Farm** by a wooden kissing gate to the right of a wooden fieldgate and keep the field edge on your right-hand side. In 110 metres you go through a wooden kissing gate, over a stream and up through another wooden kissing gate.

In 100 metres go through a wooden kissing gate and over another little bridge over the stream and through another wooden kissing gate after 30 metres. In 110 metres go through a wooden kissing gate to enter the National Trust's **Witley Copse** and **Mariners Rewe**.

[!] In 230 metres veer right at a path junction (with a 2-metre-high chain-link fence on your right-hand side). In 100 metres cross over a stream via a wooden bridge and continue up the path through the wood in a westerly direction.

[!] In 300 metres *fork left downhill* to where the main path turns right, uphill, for 25 metres to a small wooden bridge that you cross to go through a wooden gate to enter a field. *Turn right* along the lower side of the field. In 80 metres, at the lower corner of the field, go through a car-wide gap and *veer left* up across the next field. In 100 metres you pass by a wooden gate on your left-hand side to veer round and *up to the right*.

In 150 metres you enter the National Trust's **Swan Barn Walk** by its sign and a wooden kissing gate and *turn right* along a gravel path, your direction 30 degrees, with fine views across the meadows to wooded slopes. In 80 metres *turn left* between buildings to reach **Haslemere High Street**. *Turn left* in the High Street for 50 metres to **Darnleys**, the main suggested tea place, on the other side of the road. (Or you could go to the **White Horse** further down the High Street on the left-hand side.)

Coming out of Darnleys tea room, *turn right* and, in 25 metres, *turn right again* down West Street, signposted to the police station. In 120 metres, where the main street curves to the right past the police station (which is on your right-hand side), take the street *straight on* to the fire station but then *not* the tempting path straight on; instead, *turn left* in front of the fire station and take the footpath that goes *down the left-hand side* of the building (signposted 'Footpath to the station'), your direction 315 degrees. Follow this path, with a stream to your right and later a playground to your left, until you come out on to a tarmac road with Redwood Manor opposite. *Turn left* on this road and, in 40 metres, *turn right*

on to the B2131, leading in 260 metres to **Haslemere station** on your right-hand side. **Metro Café** is on your right just before the station and **Inn on the Hill**, with its bar, is opposite the station. The London platforms (2 and 3) are over the footbridge.

Lunch & tea places

Crown Inn *The Green, Petworth Road, Chiddingfold, GU8 4TX (01428 682255, www.thecrownchiddingfold.com).* **Open** 7am-11.30pm Mon-Sat; 8am-10.30pm Sun. *Food served 7-11am, noon-2.30pm, 6.30-10.30pm Mon-Fri; 8-11am, noon-3pm, 6.30-10.30pm Sat, Sun.* The suggested lunch stop is situated approximately 6km (nearly 4 miles) into the walk. Groups of more than ten should phone to book.

Swan Inn *Petworth Road, Chiddingfold, GU8 4TY (01428 684688, www.theswan innchiddingfold.com).* **Open** noon-10.30pm Mon-Thur; noon-11pm Fri-Sun. *Food served noon-3pm, 6.30-10pm Mon-Sat; noon-3pm, 6.30-10pm Mon-Sat; noon-3pm, 6.30-9pm Sun.*

Darnleys tea room *High Street, Haslemere, GU37 2JZ (01428 643048).* **Open** 9.30am-5pm Mon-Fri; 9am-5pm Sat; 10am-4pm Sun.

White Horse Hotel *High Street, Haslemere, GU27 2HJ (01428 661276, www.thewhitehorsehaslemere.co.uk).* **Open** noon-11pm Mon, Sun; noon-11.30pm Tue; noon-midnight Wed-Sat. *Food served* noon-9.45pm daily.

Inn on the Hill *Lower Street, Haslemere, GU27 2PD (01428 642006, http://tm steaks.co.uk).* **Open** 7am-11pm Mon-Thur; 7am-midnight Fri; 8am-midnight Sat; 8am-10.30 Sun. Conveniently located near the station, Inn on the Hill has a bar – it isn't always walker-friendly, however.

Metro Café *Lower Street, Haslemere, GU27 2PD (01428 651535).* **Open** 6.30am-3pm Mon-Fri; 7.30am-3pm Sat, Sun.

Haslemere, confusingly, also has a **Swan Inn** (01428 641747, www.jdwetherspoon. co.uk) – a back-up option for tea.

Walk 45

Princes Risborough to Great Missenden

The Chilterns, a windmill and Bryant's Bottom.

Start: Princes Risborough station
Finish: Great Missenden station

Length: 15.1km (9.4 miles)

Time: 4 hours 30 minutes. For the whole outing, including trains, sights and meals, allow 8 hours.

Transport: Take the train nearest to **9.45am** from **Marylebone** station to **Princes Risborough** (journey time 40-45 minutes). Trains back from

Great Missenden run twice an hour (journey time 50 minutes). Buy a day return to Aylesbury, where the two Chiltern branch lines converge.

OS Langranger Map: 165
OS Explorer Maps: 172 & 181
Princes Risborough, map reference SP799027, is in **Buckinghamshire**, 11km south of Aylesbury.

Toughness: 6 out of 10

Walk notes: This walk across the Chilterns – the walker's heaven – is through sloping fields and beech woods and hamlets, past upmarket farms and upgraded cottages. The walk is not difficult, but it does have two short, steep hills (with fine views) near the lunch stop, which account for the relatively high toughness rating. The walk directions do, however, offer an alternative route that avoids the first of the inclines. Small sections of the route can be muddy in wet weather, particularly the leg through Monkton Wood before the lunch stop.

Walk options: You could order a taxi from the suggested lunchtime stop, the Gate Inn in Bryant's Bottom, or from the Polecat Inn 2.5km further on. Both places may also have rare buses on weekdays (for information, call Traveline on 0871 200 2233).

History: **Princes Risborough** derives its name from the Black Prince, who is said to have been Lord of the Manor there in 1343.
   Lacey Green Windmill (01844 343560, www.laceygreenwindmill.org.uk) is the oldest smock mill in the country, built in 1650 and moved to this site in 1821. It was in use until 1918, milling corn, wheat, oats and barley. The interior is only open for viewing from 2pm to 5pm on Sundays and Bank Holiday Mondays from May to September.
   The popular children's writer Roald Dahl lived and worked in Great Missenden for 36 years. On the High Street, the **Roald Dahl Museum** (nos.81-83, 01494 892192, www.roalddahl museum.org) aims to inspire a love of stories and creative writing. Its sign tells us it is 'swizzfigglingly flushbunkingly gloriumptious' – so it must be worth a visit! The museum is open until 5pm

Princes Risborough to Great Missenden

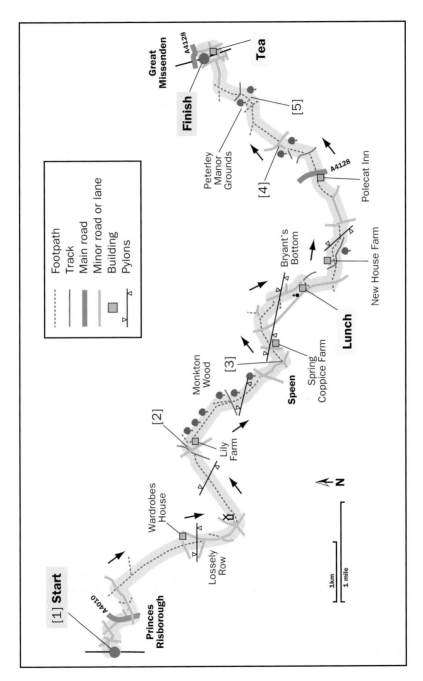

(last entry 4.30pm), weekdays and weekends, but it is closed on Mondays apart from Bank Holidays. Admission (2010) costs £6 for adults, £4 for children or £19 for a family ticket. Its café – Café Twit (no entrance fee) – is the suggested tea stop on this walk.

Walk directions

[1] [Numbers in square brackets refer to the map]

Coming out of **Princes Risborough station**, turn left. In 65 metres veer right with the road, away from the station. At a T-junction in 90 metres, *turn right* on Station Road, signposted High Wycombe and Aylesbury.

In 95 metres ignore the first turn on the right (Picts Lane) and *veer left* with the road. In 90 metres take the next road on the right, Poppy Road (the B4444), signposted High Wycombe.

Keep straight on, past the Poppyseed freehouse, bar and Indian restaurant (formerly the Black Prince pub) on your left-hand side and come out to the A4010 road, where you *bear right*. Cross over the road and continue along it in the direction of High Wycombe.

In 160 metres *turn left* up a tarmac lane, the historic **Upper Icknield Way**, signposted the Ridgeway, your direction 60 degrees initially. Keep straight on up this lane, steadily uphill. In 120 metres ignore a turn right by a power line and, in a further 20 metres, just after the tarmac ends, ignore the turn to your left.

In 300 metres, at a path crossing, *turn right* at a four-armed footpath sign through a metal kissing gate, your direction 150 degrees. Your onward route is more or less straight on for the next 1.5km until you reach a car road junction.

In more detail: Follow the path down-hill, with a fence on your right-hand side, and up the other side, ignoring turn-offs. In 600 metres pass under pylons and go through a gap in a field boundary. Continue ahead, now across an open field, and after 300 metres, at the end of the field, you cross a stile to turn *half left*

down a slope, in 70 metres (at its bottom) crossing another stile. Then head up the other side, following a clear path, proceeding half left uphill.

In 170 metres you come up to a hedge on your left-hand side and continue ahead. In a further 130 metres, cross a tarmac drive (which leads on the left to **Wardrobe House**, marked on the OS map) with redundant stiles on either side of the drive. In 50 metres, as the path and hedge swing to the right **[!]**, *turn left* over a stile to go *half right* and ahead (at right angles to the telephone cables you pass under), your direction 150 degrees.

In 100 metres cross a stile in the hedge ahead. Now follow the clear path across a field, half left, and in 100 metres you pass a redundant stile to come out on to a car road junction. Follow the road Woodway uphill into **Loosley Row Village**.

Stay on this road, uphill, and in 300 metres ignore Lower Road on the right, which forks downhill to Saunderton. In a further 300 metres you come to the top of the hill, at a crossroads, with the **Whip Inn** on your left-hand side. On the right-hand side of this pub is a gravel, car-wide lane which leads to **Lacey Green Windmill**.

Continue ahead along the road into Lacey Green and, some 25 metres beyond the pub, *turn left* on a signposted path, the Chiltern Way, beside a metal bus shelter, your direction 65 degrees, with a field hedge on your left-hand side.

Your route ahead remains more or less straight on for 800 metres until you go under some cables, but in more detail: In 90 metres cross a stile, with the windmill away to your left. In a further 130 metres cross another stile and keep ahead, soon leaving the hedge on your left-hand side as you head across an open field towards another stile.

In 150 metres cross this stile and follow the direction of an arrow, *half right,* your bearing 70 degrees, and head down, then up this field – with horse paddocks to your left and right – towards a new stile in the field-fence boundary directly ahead.

In 85 metres cross this stile and *turn left* on a cinder car-wide track, between new wooden fences, uphill, your direction 40 degrees. In 70 metres cross a cinder track and keep ahead as the track levels out. In 50 metres, at another track crossing, cross over and keep ahead (slightly right) on a car-wide earth track between fences, your direction 55 degrees, heading towards power cables.

In 110 metres cross a new stile to the right of a metal fieldgate and keep ahead, soon with a hedge on your left. In 35 metres go under the power cables and continue straight on, keeping the field hedge on your left-hand side, your direction 30 degrees.

In 300 metres you come to the end of this field with a hedge directly ahead of you and a fieldgate on your left-hand side. Here [!] *turn right* to follow the hedge, which is now on your left-hand side, your direction 130 degrees.

In 100 metres [!] cross a stile in the hedge *on your left* and follow an arrow and clear path, half right, downhill, your direction 80 degrees. In 160 metres cross a stile by a Chiltern Way footpath sign, down into a wooded avenue and on to a bridleway, where you *turn left,* your direction 25 degrees.

Head downhill on this bridleway (on the line of Grim's Ditch, very muddy in wet weather) and in 100 metres you pass **Lily Farm** (marked on the OS map) on your right-hand side, and come out on to a tarmac car lane [2] where you *turn left.*

In 15 metres [!] *turn right* on to a car-wide track, signposted public bridleway, pass Iron Beech Cottage on your right, your direction 60 degrees, into **Monkton Wood**. In 50 metres, by a two-armed footpath signs, some 15 metres before a four-armed footpath sign, *turn half right,* to pass through a wooden barrier in 10 metres.

Your route is more or less straight on along the edge of this mainly beech wood for about 2km, in a south-easterly direction, avoiding as best you can any muddy sections by taking parallel paths on your left.

In more detail: In 1km go straight on through wooden fence barriers at a major path crossing. In a further 500 metres go through a wooden swing gate to pass Cedar Cottage on your right-hand side. In another 80 metres, cross a car road (Hampden Road) and continue straight on along a car-wide lane, Coleheath Bottom, signposted as a bridleway.

In 500 metres you pass Ringwood House on your right-hand side and then, 30 metres before a road T-junction **[3]**, *turn left* on a signposted footpath, uphill into woods, your direction 50 degrees.

In 300 metres you come out on to a car road by **Spring Coppice Farm** (marked on the OS map), where you *turn left*. In 125 metres *turn right* through a wooden kissing gate to join a signposted footpath, your direction 85 degrees.

In 130 metres go through another wooden kissing gate after passing between two small copses of trees, to follow a fence with concrete posts on your left-hand side. Head downhill and in 200 metres go under pylons, then in 10 metres go through a wooden kissing gate. Now go straight on through the grounds of a house called Balnakeil, passing the house on your left-hand side, to head down its driveway and exit the driveway through its gates. In 50 metres you come down to a car road.

[!] At this point, if ground conditions have been very muddy or you are feeling weary and in need of your lunch, you can take a shortcut to the lunchtime pub by turning right along the road for about 850 metres, coming to the Gate Inn on your left-hand side.

But the suggested route is to cross the road and go over a stile into the wood, climbing steeply uphill on a potentially muddy path, your direction 65 degrees. In 100 metres, ignoring forks off, cross another stile and keep ahead, still steeply uphill, following a fence line on your left.

In 150 metres the path starts to level out and you go over a stile to the left of a wooden fieldgate where you *turn right* on to a car-wide earth track (with grass down its middle), your direction 160 degrees. In 100 metres you pass **Denner Farm** on your left-hand side and in a further 20 metres go over a stile to the left of a wooden fieldgate and continue straight on, down the middle of a field, your direction 145 degrees.

In 200 metres go through a metal swing gate to the right of a metal fieldgate to

Lacey Green Windmill.

follow a bramble hedge on your left-hand side. In 150 metres, and some 80 metres before you reach the end of the field, exit the field by a metal swing gate on your left-hand side and head across a field towards a kissing gate and a footpath sign, half right, your direction 105 degrees.

In 80 metres pass through this metal kissing gate to the right of a metal fieldgate, to *turn right* on to car lanes and *take the right fork,* signposted a public bridleway, to go past a shed on the left, your direction 170 degrees, gently downhill.

In 300 metres you pass a renovated flintstone house, Springfield Cottage, on your right-hand side and, by a footpath post on your left-hand side, *turn right* down its far wall, to go steeply downhill on a path through a lightly wooded area, your direction 250 degrees, which in 225 metres comes down to the car road again. The **Gate Inn** at **Bryant's Bottom**, the suggested lunchtime stop, is on your left-hand side.

Coming out of the pub after lunch, *turn left* on the road. In 250 metres, by a two-armed footpath sign on your left-hand side, *turn left* over a stile to the right of a metal fieldgate, to head uphill, quite steeply, bearing half right, up a grassy bank, your direction 105 degrees.

In 200 metres cross a stile to the right of a metal fieldgate and continue uphill, still half right. In a further 50 metres, cross a stile to exit the field on to a tarmac car lane, where you *turn right,* your direction 135 degrees.

In 50 metres pass through metal gates marked 'Private – Denner Hill House' to bend to the left and pass Hughenden Chase, a substantial house on your right-hand side. 50 metres past its main gates (black, between white wing walls), *bear left* over a grass verge towards a stile, as indicated by a footpath sign. Go over the stile and *immediately turn right,* your direction 80 degrees, to follow the path downhill, parallel to the drive, with the field fence on your right-hand side (ignoring the direction shown by a second footpath sign beside the stile).

In 100 metres cross a stile in the field corner to carry on, downhill. In 125 metres *veer left,* following the hedges, down towards the hamlet. In 120 metres, at the bottom and under pylons, go over a stile and *turn right* on the car road. (The entrance to **Prestwood Local Nature Reserve** is 50 metres along the road to the left – a fine piece of chalk downland rich with butterflies, worth a detour in summer.)

Having gone right on the car road, in 20 metres *turn left* into Perks Lane, your direction 70 degrees. Go up this straight, residential road for 600 metres, climbing steadily, and just past the last house on the right (White Lodge), where the road veers to the right [!], keep ahead and go through a metal kissing gate, to follow the direction of the footpath sign, 70 degrees, half right, up a grassy bank.

In 175 metres go under a mini pylon and carry on uphill, now bearing half right, your direction 55 degrees, initially parallel to another set of power cables going your way. With a fine view back over your route, in a further 200 metres you leave the field near its top left-hand corner by a metal kissing gate, some 20 metres to the left of a telegraph pole in the hedge.

Carry on with blackberry bushes on your left-hand side and, in 80 metres, go through a gate to reach the **Polecat Inn** on your right-hand side. Walk through the pub's car park and *turn right* on to the A4128 road. In 30 metres cross this road and *turn left* to follow a signposted footpath between fences and hedges, your direction 65 degrees.

In 250 metres go through gateposts (where once there was a stile) and head slightly leftwards, down into the wood. In 20 metres, *turn left* on to a wider bridleway, your direction northwards, keeping to the main track.

In 70 metres your track merges with a wider track from the right. In 60 metres you pass a deep crater with exposed beech-tree roots on your right-hand side. [!] The suggested route ahead through the wood is to follow the bridleway, marked by periodic signs (a disc with a blue arrow on a white background). [!] Continue ahead with the bridleway discs, along the left-hand edge of the wood.

In 400 metres, with an open field ahead, *turn sharp right* at a path junction to follow a path with the wood now to your right and a fence and the open field to your left, your initial direction 95 degrees.

Follow the bridleway discs and, in 300 metres, leave the wood on an earth driveway beside a footpath and bridleway sign to pass Woodcot, the end house of the row on your right, your direction 35 degrees. Continue on the earth driveway, Church Path, and, in 150 metres, you come to a T-junction [4], where you *turn right* on to a car road.

In 15 metres *turn left* on a signposted footpath. In a further 10 metres, go through a metal swing gate to the left of a rusting metal fieldgate to continue on a clear path over open, mostly flat arable fields, your direction 45 degrees.

In 450 metres the path descends to enter a wood by a footpath post and follow the path, gently downhill, close to the wood's right-hand edge, your direction

100 degrees. In 300 metres go through a metal kissing gate **[5]** and *turn left* uphill, your direction 60 degrees, on a car-wide earth track between post and wire fences.

In 100 metres ignore a kissing gate on your right and in 15 metres ignore a further metal kissing gate on your left, to continue straight on along what is now a wooded path, passing plantations of trees to your left and right.

In 275 metres you come out through retractable bollards on to a tarmac farm road, with **Angling Spring Farm**, a modern house, on your left-hand side in timber and red brick. 25 metres downhill past the farm's entrance, as the tarmac road swings to the right, *fork left* on to a gravel path going along the right-hand side of the farm, your direction 320 degrees.

In 35 metres, at a path junction, *take the right fork* (almost straight on) to follow a footpath arrow on a post, past a Chiltern District Council woodland management sign and map on your right, your direction 330 degrees, downhill.

Keep to the edge of the wood as the path goes steadily downhill and in 200 metres you reach the bottom of the hill to exit the wood through a wooden kissing gate to the right of a wooden fieldgate, and take the earth lane towards Great Missenden, your direction due east.

The lane soon becomes a grassy way along the edge of an open field and in 400 metres you come out on to an earth drive, with a cemetery on your right-hand side, behind a hedge. At a T-junction, *turn right* on an earth road, your direction 160 degrees. In 30 metres, *turn left* on a narrow tarmac path and go under a railway arch.

In 40 metres from the far side of the arch, carry straight on along a gravel drive, Twitchell Road, between houses, in 80 metres coming to a T-junction, opposite the car park of the George Inn, where you *turn left*. In 30 metres, with a car park barrier facing you, *turn right* on a tarmac path between walls, in 50 metres coming to the **George Inn**, a possible tea place.

Turn left along the High Street. In 75 metres you pass the **Café Twit** on your

right-hand side, the suggested tea stop. Coming out of the café, turn right to continue along the High Street, passing the Old Red Lion on your left (now a delicatessen), then the White Lion on your right (now a wine bar). Continue up the High Street, passing the **Cross Keys** pub on your left.

Some 350 metres along the High Street (from the George Inn) *turn left* into Station Approach, uphill, to reach **Great Missenden station** on your left in 80 metres. Just before the station on your left-hand side is a Co-op convenience store.

Lunch & tea places

Gate Inn *Bryant's Bottom, HP16 0JS (01494 488632).* **Open** 11am-11pm Mon-Sat; noon-10.30pm Sun. *Food served* noon-2.30pm Mon; noon-2.30pm, 6-9.30pm Tue-Sat; noon-2.30pm, 7-9pm Sun. Located 9.3km (5.8 miles) into the walk, the Gate is the suggested place to stop for lunch. This walker- and family-friendly pub serves reasonably priced food – main meals, pub favourites and snacks. There is a large outdoor dining area for the summer, at the far end of which is a refurbished children's playground.

George Inn *94 High Street, Great Missenden, HP16 0BG (01494 862084).* **Open** noon-midnight Mon-Sat; noon-10.30pm Sun. *Food served* 1-4pm, 6-9pm daily.

Café Twit *Roald Dahl Museum & Story Centre, 81-83 High Street, Great Missenden, HP16 0AL (01494 892192, www.roalddahlmuseum.org).* **Open** 9.30am-5pm Tue-Sat; 10am-5pm Sun. This café, part of the Roald Dahl Museum (*see p244*), has an outdoor courtyard eating area – behind the 'Wonka' gates. It is the suggested tea place for this walk.

Cross Keys *High Street, Great Missenden, HP16 0AU (01494 865373).* **Open** 11am-11.30pm Mon-Sat; 11.30am-11.30pm Sun. *Food served* noon-3pm, 6.15-9.45pm Tue-Sat; noon-4pm Sun. A traditional pub, well situated by the station for a last drink before heading home.

Walk 46

Wakes Colne to Bures

The Colne valley.

Start: Chappel & Wakes Colne station
Finish: Bures station

Length: 17.7km (11.0 miles)

Time: 5 hours 30 minutes. For the whole outing, including trains, sights and meals, allow at least 9 hours 30 minutes.

Transport: Take the train nearest to **9.30am** from **Liverpool Street** station to **Chappel & Wakes Colne**, changing at Marks Tey (journey time 1 hour).

Trains back from **Bures** are hourly, again changing at Marks Tey (journey time about 1 hour 10 minutes). Buy a day return to Bures (pronounced 'Bewers').

OS Langranger Map: 168
OS Explorer Maps: 195 & 196
Chappel & Wakes Colne station, map reference TL897288, is in **Essex**, 11km north-west of Colchester and 5km south of Bures.

Toughness: 5 out of 10

Walk notes: Many walkers associate Essex with flat landscapes, surly pubs and badly maintained footpaths. This walk suffers only from this last failing – in summer, one 400-metre stretch near the end (just past point **[8]**) can be invaded by almost head-high nettles or vegetation, so wear long trousers and take a walking pole and compass if possible. Other paths on this walk can also be overgrown in high summer. For the rest, the walk is delightful. Since the last edition of this book, there have been some path diversions and a new route is now recommended between Chalkney Wood and Earls Colne. Chappel & Wakes Colne, the station where the walk starts, is a railway museum on every side, with old carriages on display. The village and church at Chappel are a foretaste of the lovely architecture to come along the

Colne Valley, including fine thatched barns and cottages, and the neo-Tudor mansion of Colne Priory. The lunch pub at Colne Engaine is just past the church, and then the route follows the side of a fishing lake (not marked on old OS maps, as it was only created in 1995). Brooks, farms, woods and undulating hills lead into tea at one of the pubs in Bures.

Walk options: There are two different approaches to varying this route.

a) Shortening the walk: It is a short walk after lunch down to the main road (the A1124). From there, buses go hourly via Wakes Colne viaduct, which is just down the road from the station at which you began the walk. Otherwise, call for a taxi from the lunch pub.

b) Lengthening the walk: If you are fit and would like a very long walk, try adding Walk 8, Bures to Sudbury (the shortened version, bypassing Bulmer Tye; *see p60*) on to the end of this walk, making an excellent long walk of more than 30km (some 20 miles).

History: **Colne** is an old English word that means 'roaring river', and thus there are Colne (or Calne) rivers in various parts of the country.

The station at Chappel & Wakes Colne forms the **East Anglian Railway Museum** (01206 242 524). It is open daily from 10am to 4.30pm (or dusk, if earlier). Admission (2010) is £4-£8, depending on which events are on. You get to see a lot of the museum just by coming off the train, and there is a bookshop selling everything for railway enthusiasts.

The impressive **Chappel Viaduct**, adjacent to the station, is the longest in East Anglia, 75 feet high and made with 7 million bricks. It opened in 1846.

The small church in **Chappel** dates from 1352, although it may incorporate earlier Norman work. In the 14th century, the local bishop granted indulgences – remissions of punishment for sins – to all who contributed to the church's repair. It has a tiny wooden steeple and is constructed of stone in the Early English style, with walls of flint rubble and dressings of cement and local materials.

Margery Allingham, the crime novelist, lived in the Chappel area. One of the local walks is named after her.

Colne Priory in Earls Colne was rebuilt with its high neo-Tudor chimneys by the enterprising local vicar in the 1940s.

The sarsen stones in the tower of **St Andrew's Church** in Colne Engaine are sandstone boulders brought down by ice in the glacial period. They were probably previously used as ritual marker stones in a Stone Age temple on the site. Some of the other building material came from a Roman villa nearby. The church dates

back to the early 12th century and the reign of Henry I.

Walk directions

[1] [Numbers in square brackets refer to the map]
After looking round the museum, exit **Chappel & Wakes Colne station** via the booking hall; if the booking hall is closed or you are not visiting the museum, follow the 'Way Out' sign at the end of the platform. Walk down the approach road, as it bears right and in 120 metres you come down to the road T-junction where you *turn left* into Station Road, going downhill into the village.

In 300 metres you come to a crossroads with the A1124 (formerly the A604), with the railway viaduct on your left-hand side and the general store opposite. Cross straight over the main road into the village of Wakes Colne on a road called The Street. In 30 metres cross the bridge over the **River Colne** and immediately beyond the bridge you pass the **Swan Inn** on the left-hand side.

In 130 metres, at the end of the houses on the right-hand side, ignore a public footpath sign pointing off to the left towards the viaduct. Opposite the sign, *turn right* off the road, down the surfaced car-wide track alongside the half-timbered Raynham House, your direction due west.

In 40 metres you pass the entrance to **St Barnabas Chapel** on the right-hand side. In 30 metres go through or pass to the left-hand side of a metal fieldgate. 75 metres further on, ignore a footbridge some 30 metres off to your right, going over the river. Continue *straight on* and in 50 metres you come to a metal fieldgate and cross the stile to its left-hand side into a field. Continue *straight on,* along the left-hand edge of the field, your direction 250 degrees.

In 170 metres go through a wooden kissing gate in the left-hand corner and *turn right* into the next field. Follow the path towards the far side of the field in the same direction as before. In 75 metres you come to a footpath post (hidden in the

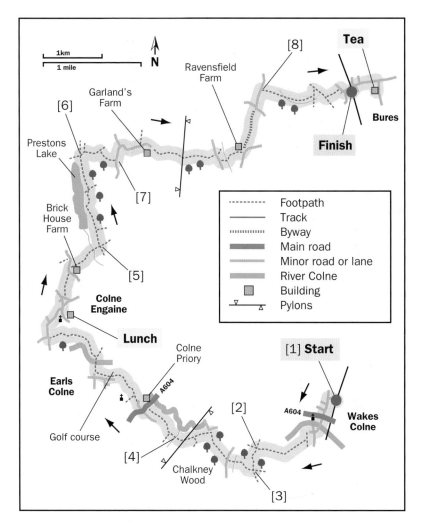

hedge to your right), indicating the
continuation of the path straight ahead,
with the hedge on your right-hand side.
In 60 metres further on, go through a
wooden kissing gate at the far side of the
field and go *straight on* in the next field
on a wide grassy path with a wire fence
to your left and a hedge on your right.

In 200 metres go through a wooden
kissing gate, cross a stony path and then
a wooden bridge with a metal gate on its

far side and keep ahead, your direction
255 degrees. In 100 metres you come to
the start of a lake on your right-hand side.
In a further 120 metres you come to the
far side of the field. *Turn right* through
a metal gate down towards the lake and
turn left down the path with the lake on
your right-hand side. In 50 metres cross
over a stream and then a wooden bridge
with a metal gate on its far side into the
next field. Follow the direction for the

East Anglian Railway Museum.

Colne Valley Path straight ahead along the left-hand edge of the field, with the trees now on your left-hand side.

[2] In 200 metres the fence goes sharply left, following the tree line. On the corner there is a footpath post and here **[!]** you leave the Colne Valley Path and *turn left* through the metal gate on a way known as the Marjory Allingham Walk.

Walk up the footpath going along the edge of the wood, your direction 220 degrees initially. In 120 metres the path bears right and then left, to continue on a bearing of 200 degrees. In 100 metres you pass a footpath post on your right. In 50 metres, by another footpath post on your left, bend with the path round to *the right,* your direction now 195 degrees, slightly uphill between trees, an open field beyond to your right-hand side. In 30 metres pass a footpath post on your right and keep ahead, uphill.

[3] In 180 metres at a path crossing there is a footpath post with many arrows on your right-hand side. *Turn right* along the clear path going up and over the field, your direction 310 degrees initially. In 100 metres you come down to the edge of a

small lake and you follow the footpath sign *straight ahead,* around the right-hand side of the lake. Past the far side of the lake, carry straight on towards the gate ahead, with fruit bushes on your left. In 90 metres pass through the metal gate into the next field. On your right-hand side, looking north, there is a fine view across the valley to a distant church spire. Your path continues straight ahead, down the field. 100 metres straight down the hill, go through a metal gate and then cross a wooden footbridge over a stream. Follow the footpath up the hill ahead, through the trees.

In 100 metres you come out to a lane T-junction. *Turn right* down the lane, your direction 30 degrees. In 25 metres **[!]** *turn left* off the road, following a public footpath sign next to a wooden fieldgate part hidden by bushes, along a path into the trees, your direction 295 degrees initially. In 80 metres you go through the remnants of a wooden fieldgate that has a sign on the gatepost welcoming walkers to **Chalkney Wood**. In 70 metres the path converges with a wider track and you go *straight ahead* (slightly to the right), ignoring a way to the left, your direction 320 degrees initially.

In 150 metres you pass a sign on the right-hand side of the track, which provides information about the management of the forest. In 80 metres ignore a fork right marked by a low post with a red band. In 20 metres further on, you come to a crossing of car-wide tracks. *Take the right fork,* gently downhill, your direction 340 degrees initially.

In 250 metres you come down the hill towards a wooden fieldgate into a farmyard, with a white wooden farmhouse directly ahead. **[!]** Immediately before this fieldgate, *turn left* to cross a partially collapsed platform bridge to take a path through the woods along the edge of the field. Follow this path as it winds through woodland and scrub for about 150 metres, until you reach the hedge at the far end of this field, by a path crossing with a low post with red band directly ahead. *Turn right* over a ditch, via some planks, and use the stile to climb into the next field and carry straight on, your direction 355 degrees, keeping the hedge on your right-hand side.

In 100 metres, on reaching the far corner of the field, ignore the other path coming in from the right. *Turn left* here and continue along the right-hand edge of the field, your direction 250 degrees initially. In 170 metres you walk underneath an electricity pylon. 30 metres beyond the pylon, go through into the next field and continue straight on along its right-hand edge.

In 60 metres you come to the far right-hand corner of this field, with a number of metal fieldgates and rusted gates ahead. **[4]**

Follow the field boundary to the left. In 30 metres *turn right* over a stile, cross a three-plank footbridge into a field, where you *turn right* for 30 metres, *then left* at a footpath post, with a wire fence on your right, your direction now 315 degrees. Proceed ahead along this fence **[!]**, but note that later you need to be on its other side.

In 125 metres you come to a footpath post on your right, with directions pointing left and ahead (with a kink right). Ignore this post (unless you wish to turn left across the field, direction 195 degrees, in 250 metres going over a stile to turn right down Tey Road, in 650 metres arriving at the former Carved Angel pub). But the recommended route is to *keep ahead* at this footpath post, and in a further 125 metres (and 25 metres before a metal fieldgate) *turn right* over a stile and bear left. In 25 metres go through a hotchpotch of gates and barriers to *turn left* along the edge of the field ahead (you are now on the other side of the field edge as required). *Keep ahead* along this field and head towards its left-hand corner.

In 400 metres at this left-hand corner, go through a metal gate and proceed along a fenced-in path, your direction 335 degrees. In 100 metres come out on to a gravel drive, turn left for 15 metres to reach the main road, A1124 (formerly A604) and *turn left.*

In 175 metres you reach a road junction with ahead the former Carved Angel pub, Earls Colne, long closed and most recently a banqueting hall. Here *turn right* over the A1124 with **Colne Priory** directly ahead of you. Follow the public footpath sign along the side of Colne Priory. Walk along the footpath with a metal-railing fence on your right-hand side and a hedge on your left. Soon you can see the church of Earls Colne on your left-hand side. In 130 metres you ignore a path going off up the hill to your left. Continue straight on through the metal kissing gate ahead.

In 120 metres you come out on to a **golf course**. The next section of the route takes you across this golf course (beware of flying golf balls), Walk straight ahead across the course towards the right of a large oak tree directly ahead, your direction 305 degrees.

In 120 metres you pass the oak on your left and continue straight on towards a track, with the main golf course on your right. Keep ahead along this track and in 225 metres you pass under overhead cables. Bear left and gently uphill on the now grassy track and, 250 metres further on, you ignore a wooden kissing gate and a concrete lane going off to the left.

In 200 metres you *bear right,* with the edge of the golf course, not following the fork left with the edge of the houses, and come back on to the left-hand edge of the course proper. Proceed along this boundary and 150 metres further on you come to a finger of hedgerow sticking out into the golf course. **[!]** Here you *turn right* and take a path that has come down from the road on the left to go *straight down the hill* on a bearing due north towards and over the footbridge 300 metres away at the bottom. Take great care as you cross a number of fairways during the descent to the bridge.

Once over this metal bridge and across the river, ignore the path that you can see going off through the trees when you look half left. Instead, *turn sharp left* along the riverbank towards the stile that you can see ahead, your direction 315 degrees initially.

In 110 metres you cross the dilapidated stile. Going straight ahead under the metal barriers would be the simplest shortcut (under the old dismantled railway bridge), but the official way is to go slightly right and *up and over* the dismantled railway line. Then go down again and over the next stile back to the riverbank on your left-hand side, having negotiated an overgrown path. The old railway line is now managed as a nature reserve.

In 80 metres ignore a track to the right and, in a further 30 metres, you pass a mini weir. After a further 120 metres ignore a left-hand fork going into a field, to *bear right* and to the right of an oak tree, your direction 330 degrees. In 30 metres you go across a three-plank bridge through the hedgerow to follow a wooded path before entering the next field. Continue straight on along the left-hand edge of this field, your direction 310 degrees. In a further 140 metres the path crosses over into the next field and you

follow the left-hand edge of this field, heading in the same direction as before.

On your right-hand side, up the hill, you can now see the tower of St Andrew's Church in Colne Engaine. In 100 metres ignore a stile on your left-hand side where the fence turns sharp left to follow the clear path *straight across* the field, towards the right of a copse of trees directly ahead, aiming for the red house on the far side of the field, your direction 300 degrees. 150 metres further on, you come to the corner of the copse, and follow the path as it *bears round to the left,* along the edge of the wood.

In 300 metres you come out on to a road at a T-junction. The road opposite is signposted to Buntings Green. *Turn right* up the road. (This is the official way, although there is a more pleasant, well-used local footpath that runs parallel to the road, to its right-hand side, which brings you to the church via a climb up a bank and over a football pitch.) But following the road uphill, ignoring ways off, you come into Church Street, following the sign for Pebmarsh and Bures. In 10 metres further on, you *turn right* off the road, through the entrance to **St Andrew's Church**, Colne Engaine.

Walk straight through the churchyard, past the church entrance and straight down the path on the far side, down to the road. To your right is the **Five Bells** pub, the suggested lunchtime stop.

After lunch, come out of the pub and *turn right.* This is Mill Lane. In 80 metres you pass a turning on the left for Halstead and Earls Colne. Go straight on and in 60 metres you pass the village store and post office on your left-hand side. 20 metres beyond that, you come to the village green. Walk across the middle of the green and cross the road on the far side. Walk *straight down* the path ahead, between houses, your direction 15 degrees initially. The path is indicated by a concrete public footpath sign that may be obscured by a bush.

In 150 metres you come out into the corner of a large, flat field and follow the

along the right-hand side of the field, gently downwards, your direction 85 degrees.

400 metres downhill, you come to the bottom of the field and go across a concrete footbridge with metal railings across a stream. Go straight on through the trees and, 20 metres further on, you come out into a field next to a footpath post pointing to the left and right.

[5] *Turn left,* following a path along the left-hand side of the field as it goes up the hill beside trees. In 25 metres, around the edge of the field, there is another footpath post, partly hidden in bushes. *Turn left* into the trees, your direction 340 degrees initially. In 340 metres, along a clear, winding path through the trees, occasionally clambering over fallen tree trunks, you come out into a large field. There is a wooden footpath post on your right-hand side, part hidden in undergrowth. Ignore the path to the right and follow the path ahead along the left-hand side of the field, your direction 340 degrees initially.

In 140 metres, ignore a footpath post to the left. In a further 20 metres *bear left* by another footpath post (partly hidden) and cross a three-plank bridge across a stream into the next field. Walk along the left-hand edge of this field, gently uphill. In 120 metres you come to the end of the trees on your left-hand side. *Turn right* up the hill, as per the footpath post on your left-hand side. Aim to the right of a bench, halfway up the hill, your direction 60 degrees. Past the bench, *turn left,* your direction 340 degrees initially, on a path above and parallel to the edge of the large fishing lake called **Prestons Lake**, down on your left-hand side, keeping ahead parallel to the gravel track below. (Alternatively, if you prefer, walk along this track and through the car parking area on its far side.)

In 230 metres, with a footpath post on your left, cross the car-wide track that goes uphill, and pass between a gap in the hedge ahead, past a Portaloo on your left, dog-leg right and continue along a grassy

clear path straight ahead along its right-hand edge. 300 metres further on, the path curves to your right, down on to a road. *Turn left* along the road, in the same direction as before.

In 270 metres there is a footpath post hidden in bushes, 50 metres before a brick farmhouse. *Turn right* off the road, cross over a stile to the left of wooden fieldgates, and go straight across a fenced-in horse paddock with electrified fences towards the stile on the far side, your direction 90 degrees. In 60 metres go through a stile in a wooden fence into the next field and follow the wooden fence and horse-training ground on your left-hand side. 65 metres further on, *turn left* over a stile in the corner of the field. Follow the path along the line of overhead cables, around the back of the farm buildings.

In 40 metres *turn right* over the stile into the next field. Follow the path ahead path with a hedge on your left. In 400 metres you come to the far edge of the field. *Turn right* following the direction of the yellow pointer on a post along the hedgerow. In 40 metres *turn left* through the trees, your direction 10 degrees initially.

For the next 600 metres, follow this recently diverted footpath, which is intermittently fenced on both sides, until you reach a post on your left-hand side with many yellow arrows on it. (The far side of the post has arrows numbered 14 pointing to both left and right.) **[!]** 3 metres before this post, *go right* through a metal fieldgate (its left-hand edge hinged on another metal fieldgate) out of the wood to follow a footpath with a hedge on your left-hand side, your direction 90 degrees.

In 200 metres, after a gap in the hedge and the hedge then resuming, you come to a yellow arrow on a post (partly hidden in the hedge), pointing you to the right of the hedge. Here you keep ahead.

150 metres beyond this **[6]**, you come to another footpath post and *turn right,* following the direction of the arrow.

Walk with the edge of the field and trees on your left-hand side, gently downhill, your direction 140 degrees.

In 160 metres you come to the far edge of the field. Cross over the stile into the next field and ignore the track uphill (half left) to follow the way slightly to the right towards another footpath post 60 metres away on the far side, your direction 140 degrees. Continue gently uphill along the left-hand side of the field, your direction 130 degrees initially, with a hedge on your left and a low fence on your right. In 200 metres the path curves around to the left and takes you out to a road T-junction. **[7]** *Turn left* along the road, your direction 350 degrees.

In 300 metres, where the road curves around to the left towards a pretty thatched cottage, *turn right* along the road signposted Valiants and Garlands Farms only.

In 170 metres you pass the entrance to Valiants Farm on your right-hand side. Follow the road as it continues around to the left. 350 metres further on, ignore a public footpath sign pointing off to the left. In a further 180 metres

you pass Garlands Cottage on your right-hand side.

Keep on this track, now gravel, following it round to the right, with ponds on your left-hand side, a drive lined with lime trees, until within 80 metres of the very substantial **Garlands Farmhouse**, at which point, by a footpath post, you *turn left* away from the track, opposite the first farm building, along the right-hand side of the farmhouse front garden, your direction 75 degrees. In 25 metres *bear right* on a car-wide grassy path, your direction 145 degrees, with a hedgerow separating the path from the farmhouse on your right-hand side. 90 metres further on, you come out into open fields and follow the grassy track as it continues along the left-hand edge of the field, your direction 105 degrees, with a hedge on your left.

Ignore ways off and, 340 metres further on, you come underneath overhead cables to the left-hand corner of the field. Go straight ahead for 10 metres through the trees into the next field and walk straight ahead along the right-hand edge of the field, your direction due east initially. Do not go down the track to the right into the trees.

In 280 metres along the field edge, by a post on your right **[!]**, *turn right* and cross over the ditch via a bank into the trees. In 5 metres *bear left* through the

trees and in 15 metres go on two planks across another ditch. *Turn left,* following the direction of the footpath post with hedges to your left-hand side, your direction 55 degrees. Walk straight ahead along the left-hand edge of the field.

200 metres further on, with a pretty thatched barn ahead of you on your right-hand side, you come to the left-hand corner of the field, down a couple of steps, across some planks and out on to a narrow country lane T-junction. *Turn right* along the road, your direction 195 degrees. In 40 metres you pass the thatched barn and the entrance to a pink farmhouse on your left-hand side.

50 metres further on, *turn left* following the footpath sign, your direction 75 degrees, between new trees on an alleyway between two fields, ignoring the field entrance on your left. In 200 metres you bear left, by a footpath post on your right, your direction 90 degrees, a brick hut to your left-hand side. You make for the footbridge that is 90 metres ahead of you. Cross this wooden footbridge with metal railings.

Go over the stile on the far side of the bridge into a field. Keep ahead, your direction 80 degrees, ignore the horse jump to your left and go through a metal gate. Proceed uphill along the left-hand edge of the field with a hedge on your left towards a large farmhouse at the top of the hill. 150 metres up and over the brow of the hill, you can see a metal fieldgate on your right-hand side. *Turn half right* across the field, towards the gate, your direction 120 degrees. In 60 metres cross the stile to the right of the gate and walk through the gap in the wooden fence ahead.

Go straight ahead through the farm buildings of **Ravensfield Farm** (marked on the OS map) towards double metal gates on the far side. When you get to the gates, *turn right* along the gravel drive down to the road T-junction. There may be peacocks in the garden on your right.

Turn left into the road and in 10 metres *turn left again,* with a sign saying 'Public byway', a car-wide path, your direction 20 degrees.

In 200 metres you come out into a field and continue along the track on the right-hand side of the field in the same direction.

650 metres further on, you come out to a road T-junction where you *turn left,* past the gateway into Horne's Green Cottage, a very pretty 1821 thatched cottage on your left-hand side. In 35 metres *turn right* down the road signposted to Lamarsh, direction 20 degrees.

In 300 metres **[8]** *turn right* off the road, following the direction of the concrete public footpath sign, down a grassy car-wide track between two hedgerows and a ditch on your right, your direction 120 degrees.

In 370 metres you come to a wooden footpath post pointing you straight ahead into the trees. Follow the narrow, potentially very boggy and overgrown footpath through the trees in the same direction as before, direction 140 degrees.

400 metres further on, however lost you may have felt wading through a sea of vegetation, you come out on to the edge of a field, *bear left* on a farm track and follow the direction of the tree-line away to your right, your bearing 90 degrees.

In 200 metres, as the track bears half left uphill, *keep ahead.* In 150 metres go up steps and come out on to a road at a T-junction. There is a grassy triangle at the junction and you follow the right-hand edge of the triangle to pick up the blue bridleway arrow pointing *down the road ahead,* your direction 75 degrees.

125 metres further on, you come to another T-junction, with a horse chestnut tree in the middle of the junction. *Go right* on a track downhill, signposted Ferriers Barn, your direction 140 degrees. In 50 metres you pass Ferriers Barn on your right-hand side and carry straight on down the road.

100 metres further on, you ignore the footpath going over a bridge to your right.

450 metres further on, you come down to the bottom of the track and out on to a

residential street T-junction. The sign to your left says 'Lamarsh Hill'. *Turn right,* going into the village of **Bures**. In 50 metres you pass a turning on the right signposted White Colne, and go straight ahead under the railway bridge. After the bridge you pass Water Lane on your left. 25 metres beyond that is the turning on the right, The Paddocks, which takes you up to **Bures station**.

If you wish to have tea in Bures, continue straight on down the road. 100 metres further on, you pass the other end of Water Lane on your left. After another 40 metres, the **Bures Swan**, one of your options for tea, is on your right-hand side. Just past the Swan, at the junction with Colchester Road, turn right to get to the **Eight Bells**, your other possible tea stop in Bures.

To return to Bures station, just retrace your steps.

Lunch & tea places

Five Bells *7 Mills Lane, Colne Engaine, CO6 2HY (01787 224166, http://five bells.net).* **Open** noon-3pm, 6pm-midnight Mon-Wed; noon-midnight Thur-Sun. *Food served* noon-2.30pm, 6.30-9.30pm Mon-Fri; noon-9.30pm Sat, Sun. Walkers are welcome at this pub, the suggested lunch stop. It offers a good selection of cooked meals and snacks, and has informal eating areas, a separate restaurant space and a beer garden. In winter, aim to leave here no later than 2pm to avoid walking to Bures station in the dark.

Bures Swan *1 Station Hill, Bures, CO8 5DD (01787 228121).* **Open** 3-11pm Mon; 11.30am-11pm Tue-Thur, Sun; 11.30am-midnight Fri, Sat. *Food served* noon-2.30pm, 6.30-9.30pm Tue-Sat; noon-6pm Sun. One of two tea options on the walk. Open in the afternoon for tea, coffee and alcoholic drinks.

Eight Bells *6 Colchester Road, Bures, CO8 5AE (01787 227354).* **Open** 11am-3pm, 5-11pm Mon-Fri; noon-midnight Sat, Sun. *Food served* noon-2pm, 7-9.30pm daily. An alternative tea stop, with a beer garden for summer walkers.

Walk 47
Ockley to Warnham

Woods and rural delights.

Start: Ockley station
Finish: Warnham station

Length: 16.5km (10.3 miles)

Time: 5 hours. For the whole outing, including trains, sights and meals, allow 8 hours 40 minutes.

Transport: Take the train nearest to **9.30am** from **Victoria** station to **Ockley** (journey time 1 hour 5 minutes). Note that there is no service on this line on Sundays and some Bank Holiday Mondays. Direct trains back from **Warnham** are hourly, but you can also catch one of the hourly trains in the other direction and change at Horsham; the journey time for both routes is about 1 hour 10 minutes. Note that the last direct train back is currently around 8pm (weekdays) and 6pm (Saturdays), with the last train via Horsham about 30 minutes later. Buy a day return to Warnham or, better, to Horsham (thus leaving more options for your return journey).

OS Landranger Map: 187
OS Explorer Maps: 134 & 146
Ockley, map reference TQ165404, is in **Surrey**, 9km north-west of Horsham and 7km north of Warnham, which is in **West Sussex**.

Toughness: 3 out of 10

Walk notes: This is a beautiful walk through unspoiled countryside of fields, woods and gentle hills. In this sleepy corner on the Surrey–Sussex border, it seems as if nothing exceptional has happened through the ages. You go through no bustling towns, pass no grand country houses and there are no particularly interesting historical events to relate. Just mile after mile of oak woods and rural delights. Note that there is no evening service on this line (for last train times, *see above*) and it is 1.4km (nearly a mile) to the station from the village pub in Warnham.

Walk options: You could call a taxi from either of the lunch pubs to Warnham or Horsham station.
    If you make the detour to the Punch Bowl pub, the diversion and onward route reduces the length of the walk by 1.5km (1 mile).

History: The **Parish Church of St John the Baptist** in Okewood has 13th-century wall paintings and an unusual arrangement of roof beams.
    Warnham's best-known son is the poet **Percy Bysshe Shelley**, who was born at Field Place, just south of the village, in 1792. Expelled from Oxford for his pamphlet *The Necessity of Atheism* and having eloped with 16-year-old Harriet Westbrook, he was forbidden by his father Sir Timothy Shelley ever to visit the family seat – in case he corrupted his sisters.

Walk directions

[1] [Numbers in square brackets refer to the map]

Come out of **Ockley station** and go through the car park, *turning right* down the tarmac station approach road. In 100 metres you come down to the road where you *turn right* under the railway arch. 10 metres beyond the railway arch, *turn left* off the road, following the public footpath sign, on a path between fences, your direction 200 degrees initially. In 150 metres go over the metal bridge across a brook and bear right with the path. 250 metres further on you come out on to a narrow road. *Turn right* on to the road. In 25 metres you come to the entrance to a house called Weavers on your left-hand side. *Turn left,* off the road, cross the house's driveway, and continue along the path, following the public footpath sign on the corner of the driveway, your direction 250 degrees initially. In 230 metres, having initially walked parallel to a driveway, the path takes a *sharp left turn,* going around the back of the garden of the big house on your left. 25 metres further on, it goes right again and continues in the same direction as before.

In 100 metres you come to the edge of the trees and follow the path alongside a barbed-wire fence in the same direction as before. 300 metres further on, at the far side of the field, ignore a crosspath. Continue straight ahead, going slightly downhill, with a recent plantation of trees on your left-hand side. 90 metres down the hill, go over a wooden bridge across the stream. Ignore a fork off uphill to the left in 10 metres, to continue along the bridleway as it makes its way through the trees, uphill.

Ignore ways off and in 340 metres go through a metal fieldgate into the field beyond. Walk across the field, your direction 260 degrees, in 100 metres passing some 40 metres to the right of a strange, metal contrivance in the middle of the field (an old water pump). Over the brow of this small hill, you now head for the stile visible directly ahead, and just before the edge of a wood. (The farmer from time to time connects field fencing to this stile, at other times not.) In 100 metres cross this stile, or walk around it, and *turn left,* your direction 190 degrees, with the edge of the wood on your right-hand side.

In 100 metres **[!]** you go over a stile in the right-hand corner of the field (part hidden in summer) into the next field. Walk along the right-hand edge of the field, gently uphill, your direction 195 degrees initially. In 90 metres cross a stile and walk along the edge of the next field, in the same direction as before. In 25 metres follow the path as it bends around to *the right,* your direction 260 degrees initially. In 50 metres you come down to a lane, leading up to a wooden fieldgate on your left-hand side, with a gate marked 'Private'. **[2]**

Go *straight across* the lane, following the public footpath sign next to the right-hand gatepost, past a large oak tree, your direction 200 degrees. In 40 metres cross over a stile to the right of a metal fieldgate. On your right-hand side you can soon see the village of **Ockley**. Walk along the left-hand edge of the field, gradually descending as your way curves to the left. In 100 metres go over a stile to the left of a metal fieldgate. Continue downhill. In 200 metres cross a path junction by a four-way sign and ignore a stile to the left. In a further 100 metres enter the wood by a rusty metal fieldgate.

Keep ahead, ignoring all ways off, your initial bearing 200 degrees, on a broad path which starts level then gently rises. In 300 metres a path joins you from the left. In a further 100 metres the path begins to descend.

In 190 metres at a T-junction with a new tree plantation to your left **[!]** and a beech tree 10 metres to the left (with 'Anthony Annette Adam' carved on it nearly 2 metres up) *bear right* with the path, your direction 255 degrees, entering Birches Wood. After 45 metres by a cypress tree *take the left-hand fork* and in a further 45 metres by a small signpost with two yellow arrows on it **[!]** take a clear path *left, steeply downhill,* due south. 80 metres down the hill, with a

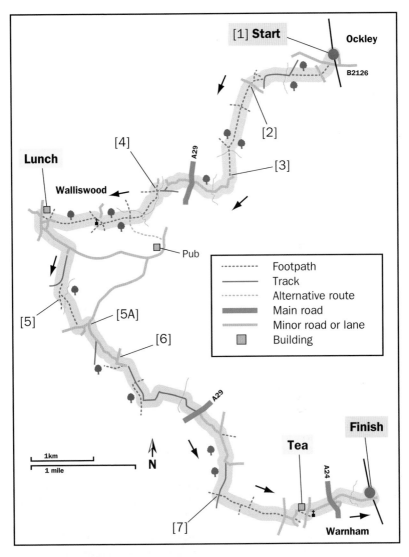

[1] **Start**

Ockley

B2126

[2]

[4]

[3]

Lunch

A29

Walliswood

[5]

[5A]

[6]

Pub

<table>
<tr><td>..........</td><td>Footpath</td></tr>
<tr><td>————</td><td>Track</td></tr>
<tr><td>- - - - -</td><td>Alternative route</td></tr>
<tr><td></td><td>Main road</td></tr>
<tr><td></td><td>Minor road or lane</td></tr>
<tr><td>▨</td><td>Building</td></tr>
</table>

1km

1 mile

N

A29

Finish

Tea

A24

[7]

Warnham

three-armed footpath sign on your right, cross a wood and metal bridge going over the stream. Over the bridge, follow the path *left* for 15 metres and then *around to the right* up the hill, heading southwards. In 150 metres cross over a stile and walk along a grassy bank and then a field with a hedgerow on the right-hand side, your

direction 190 degrees. In 200 metres you come to a metal fieldgate. Go through (or cross over the stile away to its left-hand side) on to a car-wide track.

[3] Eversheds Farmhouse (marked on the OS map) is straight ahead of you. *Turn right* with the farm buildings to your right-hand side. Then simply follow the track through its bends: in 90 metres the track goes sharply around to the left; 140 metres further on, sharply around to the right. In a further 350 metres you come down to the bottom of a slight incline, sharply around to the right, over a concrete bridge (with wooden and makeshift metal railings on its left-hand side and metal railings on its right) and *continue uphill,* your direction 305 degrees.

300 metres further on, you come up to a concrete road, pass through a metal fieldgate (usually open) to come to a crossing of farm tracks with farm buildings off to the left. [!] *Turn right,* through a (usually open) metal fieldgate on to a farm track, which in 125 metres *swings left.* Continue past Mill Cottage on your left and down to the A29 road, which you cross over to follow the public bridleway sign on the far side. In 15 metres, East Standon Lodge is on your right-hand side. Follow the car-wide track *to the left,* your direction 230 degrees initially and in 450 metres you come to a wooden gate (leading to a house called Middle Lodge). Follow the wooden fence of this house *round to the left.* In 70 metres, at the end of the fence, keep on the path as it *bears left,* your direction 200 degrees.

In 100 metres, you go through a metal fieldgate with a tall handle on the edge of Oakwood Mill Farm, with another metal fieldgate on its right-hand side. *Turn right,* down the car-wide track just beyond this gate, your direction 265 degrees initially. In 40 metres go over the river [4] and through or over a metal fieldgate, ignoring any 'keep out' sign on the gate.

Stay on the track and in 20 metres *take the left-hand fork.* Follow the track as it curves around to the left, in the same general direction as the river down on your left-hand side. In 70 metres follow the track sharply around to the right and up the hill, your direction 290 degrees initially. In a further 100 metres there is a metal fieldgate directly ahead at the top of the hill. Follow the track around to the *left,*

your direction 220 degrees initially. Follow the line of the fence on your right-hand side, with the river down below on your left-hand side.

In 300 metres, the next turning can be easily missed. [!] Turn *sharp right,* on to a path going up the hill with a fence to your right-hand side, your direction 300 degrees initially. In 60 metres you come up into a field. Walk alongside the barbed-wire fence on the right-hand edge of this field, your direction due west initially. In 200 metres cross over the stile into the wood and follow the woodland track, in the same general direction as before. In 50 metres you come to a footpath post and *fork left,* your direction due west. 30 metres further on, there is another footpath post, where you ignore the fork slightly to the left to continue straight on (slightly to the right), your direction still due west.

St John the Baptist, Okewood.

(To detour to the Punch Bowl pub in Oakwood Hill, take the fork slightly to the left (ahead), your direction 230 degrees. Follow this path as it swings to the left, then descends a dip to go up the other side, now along the edge of the wood. 475 metres along this path you come out onto a road, opposite a road sign for 'Oakwood Hill'. *Turn right,* uphill, in 425 metres coming to the **Punch Bowl** pub on your right-hand side. After lunch, *turn right* and in 80 metres at a road junction (where to keep ahead would take you to Rosehill Cottage in 1km) you *bear left* with the road (Honeywood Lane), in 1km coming out at point [5A] in the main directions, where you rejoin the main route by turning left down the tarmac lane signposted to Monks Farm and Honeybush Farm.)

But continuing with the main route: In 400 metres the path leads you down through the trees to the **Parish Church of St John the Baptist** in **Okewood**. Go through the wooden gate into the churchyard and walk around to the front entrance of the church, which is usually open and well worth a visit. Coming out of the church, *go down the path* with stepping stones *directly opposite* the entrance to the church, your direction 260 degrees. In 25 metres go through the gate and descend steps to go over a wooden bridge. In 40 metres at a T-junction, *bear left,* due west. In 30 metres cross over a wooden bridge, ignoring the similar bridge to the right. *Continue ahead,* bearing 270 degrees, gently uphill.

Ignoring ways off, in 480 metres you come to a footpath post on your left-hand side. Ignore the way ahead into a field, which is anyway fenced and gated. *Turn right* here, following the arrow on the tree, your direction 305 degrees initially.

Go straight on for 550 metres, ignoring ways off, to come out through a wooden kissing gate on to a road, where you *turn right* into the village of **Walliswood**. In 50 metres, you reach the **Scarlett Arms** pub on your right, the suggested lunch stop.

Coming out of the pub after lunch, *turn left,* back down the road. In 60 metres you pass a turning on the right to Ewhurst. In 120 metres further on, you pass a dead-end turning on your left called Oakfields. 60 metres beyond that, *turn left,* following signs to Oakwood Hill, Ockley and Dorking. You pass a house on your right-hand side called Charles Copse.

In 400 metres you come to Rosehill Cottage on your right-hand side. Just beyond this, on the right-hand side of the road, there is a public bridleway sign pointing to the right. *Turn right* off the road, along a car-wide gravel track, your direction 200 degrees. In 25 metres go through a wooden fieldgate into Rosehill Farm. Keep ahead, passing through the farmyard and then along the left-hand edge of a field, on a grassy path with woodland to your left.

In 300 metres, on the far side of the field, you go through a gap in the hedgerow into the next field. Walk *straight ahead* along the edge of this field, with the wood on your left, direction as before. In 250 metres you come to the corner of the field. Follow the yellow arrows, along the barbed-wire fence on your right-hand side, keeping ahead, with the edge of the wood on your left. This narrow path is usually very overgrown and you should take care as there is a ditch close to its left edge, waiting to catch your ankle.

In 150 metres you come out from this overgrown path into an open field on the edge of the wood and here [5] you have a choice. *Either keep ahead* to the stile in the wooden fence, 30 metres directly ahead, cross it and *turn left* along the fence as far as the first stile noted below. *Or* you can turn *half left,* your bearing 120 degrees and aim for the (first) stile 100 metres away, which you cross and head for another stile 40 metres away, go over it and keep ahead, uphill, over a large field, on a bearing of 135 degrees, heading to the right of a copse.

In 200 metres you come up to trees where you will see that there is a barbed-wire fence going all around the copse. You should come up to the right-hand corner of this copse. Walk *straight on,* with the barbed-wire fence and trees on your left-hand side, in the same direction as before. In 100 metres you come to the far side of the copse, where one fence goes sharply off to the left. Continue *straight on* across the field ahead, with the barbed-wire fence on your left-hand side, in the same direction as before. Aim for the gap in the hedgerow, a line of small trees ahead. In 20 metres you walk underneath overhead cables. 80 metres further on, cross over a concrete bridge, go over a wooden step and through the gap in the trees into the next field. *Aim half left* towards the far side of the field, your direction 125 degrees, and in 130 metres go over a stile and out on to a car road where you *turn left.*

In 125 metres you will see a postbox on your left-hand side and on your right-hand side North Lodge, the gatehouse for Tanglewood. On the left-hand side of the road is a metal footpath sign pointing right across the road to the wooden sign to Tanglewood, within the lodge's driveway. Ignore this path (The Sussex Border Path) and *turn right* down the tarmac lane **[5A]**, signposted Monks Farm and Honeybush Farm, your direction 205 degrees initially.

In 250 metres you come to a three-armed signpost on your right-hand side. Follow the bridleway *straight ahead* through a metal fieldgate. In 450 metres you pass between two farmhouses and pass a barn on your right, and up to a T-junction **[6]** where there is a three-armed signpost, by a large oak tree. Ignore the Sussex Border Path 1989, which goes left at this point along the course of Stane Street (an old Roman Road). *Turn right* down the public bridle-way. **[!]** Beware of unruly dogs here.

In 40 metres follow the track *sharply around to the left,* with a wooden fence on your left-hand side. 50 metres further on there is another three-armed signpost. Follow the public bridleway sign going

straight ahead. 30 metres further on there are two metal fieldgates. Go through the left-hand gate (white and rusting) and down the bridleway between hedges and treelines, your direction 75 degrees initially. In 150 metres follow the bridleway sharply around *to the right,* your direction 190 degrees initially, with a wire fence on your left. 170 metres further on, where there is a metal fieldgate directly ahead and another on your left, follow the bridleway as it curves around to the left, your direction 155 degrees initially.

60 metres further on, there is a three-armed signpost on your right. Follow the public footpath sign and **[!]** *turn right,* due south, through a wooden gate, then *turn half left* down the footpath to the left-hand corner of the field, where you can see another footpath sign. In 80 metres you pass a three-armed footpath sign by a wire fence on your left and in 20 metres you come to the far side of the field and go through the wooden fieldgate on the left. Walk down the path through the trees, which is signposted public footpath, your direction 145 degrees.

In 300 metres, following a clear path through the trees, you come to another two-armed signpost. Follow the public footpath, going *slightly round to the right.* 35 metres further on, look out for the three-armed public footpath signpost on your left-hand side. Go to it and follow its direction due east to go over a stile in 30 metres. Walk straight ahead, your direction due east, with a field fence on your left-hand side, along the top of a bank and out into a field.

In 150 metres you come to a two-armed footpath sign on your left-hand side. Follow the direction of the footpath, *going left* towards some farm buildings, your direction 10 degrees. Keep ahead, passing the farm buildings on your right (the two stiles that you used to have to cross have now gone). In 90 metres, there is a two-armed footpath sign on your left, by a metal fieldgate. *Go right* across the field, following the sign's direction (85 degrees) towards another footpath sign 200 metres away, 100 metres to the right of the red farmhouse.

Once at this three-armed wooden footpath sign, go through a wooden fieldgate. Follow the sign for the public bridleway, going straight ahead, your direction 100 degrees initially. In 150 metres you pass metal fieldgates on both sides of the path and continue straight on down the hill. 125 metres further on, cross over a wooden bridge over North River. On the other side of the bridge, do not go through the gate ahead but *turn right* along the riverbank, following the direction of the public bridleway sign. In 60 metres cross over a stone bridge with wooden railings going over a stream and continue straight on uphill up the path on the other side.

In 250 metres you pass a gatepost and come out on to the main road (the A29). Cross straight over the road and follow the public bridleway sign up the car-wide track on the other side. In 30 metres go through a wooden fieldgate and *bear left* with the track. In 120 metres follow the direction of a two-armed signpost on your right, directly ahead, along the bridleway through the trees. In 100 metres you pass Pear Tree Farm on your right-hand side. 250 metres further on, you come out on to a road, alongside a rather sinister half-timbered old building of mixed styles called Maltmayes on your left-hand side. *Turn right* on to the tree-lined road and walk up the hill. In 20 metres ignore the public footpath going off the road to the left. 300 metres further on, you pass a driveway on the left-hand side, leading to a very tall clock tower (an old water tower, built in 1891 for the Warnham Lodge Estate and redundant since the mid 1930s).

200 metres beyond the tower, the road curves sharply around to the left. Ignore the first way off to the right (a track between wooden posts) but just beyond it you *turn right* off the road, following a new bridleway sign on the corner, going straight ahead, due south. Follow the path

to the left of the bridleway, making its way through the trees, beside railings along the left-hand edge of the wood (or in non-muddy conditions just walk up the bridleway).

After 500 metres along this winding, narrow path, keeping near to the railings on your left-hand side whenever there is a choice, the path goes steeply downhill. 25 metres from the start of this hill, your way is rejoined by the at-times muddy bridleway coming in from the right. Follow the bridleway straight across the bottom of the depression and straight up the far side, your direction 235 degrees initially. Ignore a path that forks off to the right.

In 200 metres you come over the hill and down to a four-armed sign on your right. 10 metres before this sign **[!]** *turn left* off the bridleway, **[7]** go up a bank of tree roots and up on to a footpath along oak trees lining the left-hand edge of a field, your direction 125 degrees initially.

In 400 metres you come to the far side of the field, where there is a three-armed public footpath sign, going past a broken metal fieldgate to *bear left,* following the path along the left-hand edge of the field, your direction 70 degrees initially. In 80 metres you come to another three-armed public footpath sign where you *bear right,* carrying on around the field, your direction 105 degrees initially.

In 80 metres you come to a two-armed public footpath sign on your left. Follow the sign, *half right* across the field towards Warnham, your direction 120 degrees. In 140 metres by a two-armed footpath sign, go through a gap in the hedge and continue in the same direction. 120 metres further on, you come to the edge of this field and continue straight on through the gap in the hedge and trees. When you come into the next field, you can see a recent development of red-brick houses on your right-hand side. Continue on, with the fence surrounding this development on your right, down the hill, in the same direction as before. In a further 100 metres, you come to the edge of this field. Follow the path ahead through the trees. The path takes you down through the trees and out on to a road.

Cross straight over the road (Tillets Lane) and down Lucas Road opposite. In 150 metres, you pass Hollands Way on the right. 100 metres further on, you come to a dead end at Warnham Church of England Primary School. Go down a concrete footpath *to the right* of the school. 150 metres down this footpath you pass a three-armed footpath sign on the right-hand side and continue straight on. In another 100 metres you come out on to the road opposite the church. 50 metres down the road, on your right-hand side, is the village store and post office, which can be relied on for ice-cream, cakes and snacks. In the opposite direction, on the left-hand side of the road, is the **Sussex Oak** pub, the suggested tea place.

To get to the station, walk down Bell Road, directly opposite the Sussex Oak,

signposted 'Horsham 2 miles'. In 500 metres you come to a T-junction on to a major road (the A24). Cross straight over the road and *turn left,* in the direction of London and Dorking. In 30 metres *turn right,* following the sign for **Warnham station**. As you walk along this road, you can see the brickworks up on the left. Just walk straight up the road for 700 metres until you come to the station. The platform for trains to London is the one on the left, before the level crossing.

Lunch & tea places

Punch Bowl *Okewood Hill, Ockley, RH5 5PU (01306 627249, www.punchbowl-inn.co.uk).* **Open** noon-11.30pm Mon-Sat; noon-7pm Sun. *Food served* noon-2.15pm, 6.30-9.30pm Mon-Fri; noon-9.30pm Sat; noon-5pm Sun. The Punch Bowl's menu covers main courses, specials and sandwiches with generous fillings. The pub is reached via a detour beginning in the woods in Walliswood; the main walk can then be rejoined at point [5A].

Scarlett Arms *Horsham Road, Walliswood, RH5 5RD (01306 627243, www.scarlettarms.com).* **Open** 6-11pm Mon; noon-3pm, 6-11pm Tue-Fri; noon-11pm Sat; noon-6pm Sun. *Food served* noon-3pm, 6-9pm Tue-Sat; noon-3pm Sun. The suggested lunch stop, this is a small, walker-friendly, old-fashioned, homely pub with an inglenook fireplace for cold winter days and a garden for sitting outside in the summer. It has a good menu of sandwiches (with generous fillings) plus main courses.

Sussex Oak *Church Street, Warnham, RH12 3QW (01403 265028, www.the sussexoak.co.uk).* **Open** 11am-11pm Mon-Sat; 11am-10.30pm Sun. *Food served* noon-2.30pm, 6-9.30pm Mon-Fri; noon-9.30pm Sat; noon-8pm Sun. The suggested tea place, serving alcoholic and hot drinks, as well as food.

Warnham Village Store *3 Church Street, Warnham, RH12 3QP (01403 265132).* **Open** 7am-6.30pm Mon-Fri; 7am-6pm Sat; 7am-2pm Sun. There is a bench outside for those looking for a rest.

Walk 48

Whitchurch to Andover

Longparish, thatched cottages and the River Test.

Start: Whitchurch station
Finish: Andover station

Length: 19.0km (11.8 miles)

Time: 5 hours. For the whole outing, including trains, sights and meals, allow at least 9 hours.

Transport: Take the train nearest to **9.30am** from **Waterloo** station to **Whitchurch (Hants)**. Journey time is about 1 hour. Trains back from

Andover run twice an hour (hourly in the evening and on Sundays), with a journey time of about 1 hour 15 minutes. Buy a day return to Andover.

OS Langranger Map: 185
OS Explorer Maps: 131 & 144
Whitchurch, map reference SU464489, is in **Hampshire**, 16km north of Winchester.

Toughness: 3 out of 10

Walk notes: This is a longish walk that is neither steep nor particularly prone to getting muddy. Several changes have been made to the walk route and the directions since the last edition of this book – some enforced due to footpath closures and diversions, others desirable to avoid dangerous crossings of the A303 road.

Just before Tufton, you cross a field that in summer can be very overgrown with nettles – so wearing trousers, rather than shorts, is recommended.

At lunchtime, the walk comes to so many thatched cottages that a visitor to this country might suppose thatch to be the most popular roofing material for English country villages.

The route initially follows the line of a dismantled railway and passes the Church of All Hallows in Whitchurch to go along the River Test – 'England's most famous trout stream'. Then it's on to the

village of Tufton, with its interesting church. A new path detour returns you to the route of the dismantled railway as you bypass Paper Mill Farm (where the footpath is closed). Next, you go on to Longparish, with a lunch stop at one of its two pubs. The church at Longparish, with punishment stocks beside it, is your first stop after lunch. The walk then goes via a hamlet of more thatched cottages along the River Test, before following a new detour over the A303 road to go up into Harewood Forest, past a vast piggery. A new part of the route takes you through a tunnel under the A303, before you rejoin the original route by Bere Hill Farm to continue on a straight footpath all the way into Andover, with its tea rooms, pubs, church and museum.

Just before Longparish is a three-storey, brick-built, working flourmill (Longparish Upper Mill) on the River Test. If you give the owner a call (and some advance warning: 01264 720344), they might open it up for a guided tour, which is not normally available to the general public. One walker has described it as 'fascinating and well worth the detour'.

Walk options: The first part of this walk is perhaps the more interesting, so you could catch one of the hourly buses to Andover at lunchtime (after 8km of walking) from the Plough Inn at Longparish. Otherwise, phone for a taxi from either of the pubs in Longparish.

There is also a shortcut from All Hallows Church, Whitchurch, to Tufton (although this misses out the enjoyable leg beside the River Test). You could also take the original road route from Tufton to Britwell Priors. Both these options can be found on the Saturday Walkers' Club website (www.walkingclub.org.uk).

History: Whitchurch has a working **silk mill**, still powered by a waterwheel; visiting this involves a 1km detour from the main route. The Mill (28 Winchester Street, 01256 892065, www.whitchurch silkmill.org.uk) is open 10.30am to 5pm daily (closed Mondays, but open Bank Holidays). Admission (2010) is £4.

All Hallows Church, Whitchurch, has Norman arches and pillars with Victorian embellishments and a gruesome 1602 story picture about those who disobeyed the Commandments (for instance, 'one stoned for gathering stocks on the Sabbath Day').

St Mary's Church, Tufton, has a late Saxon chancel arch and an 800-year-old wall painting of St Christopher, depicted unrealistically so as not to infringe the commandment 'Thou shalt not make any graven images'.

Stocks for the punishment of offenders were erected in every village during the reign of Edward III. Those in Longparish are among the few still remaining. The **Church of St Nicholas**, Longparish, was perhaps used as a stable by Cromwellian troops. It has a stained-glass window in remembrance

of Major Hawker VC, an air-force pilot shot down in 1916.

Andover had its ancient heart of timber-framed buildings removed courtesy of a Greater London Council Town Development Scheme in the 1960s. The town has a museum (6 Church Close, 01264 366283, www3.hants.gov.uk/andover-museum), just to the east of the church. It is open 10am to 5pm Tuesday to Saturday; admission is free. The **church** closes at 4pm. It is made of Caen stone brought up the old canal from France; the stone was wrongly faced, so the church is crumbling. George II used to stay at the **Danebury Hotel** in Andover on the way to his beloved Weymouth. Lord and Lady Nelson also stayed there.

Walk directions

[1] [Numbers in square brackets refer to the map]
On exiting **Whitchurch station**, go *straight ahead,* then bear left on Greenwoods cul-de-sac, passing the closed and boarded-up Railway Hotel on your left-hand side, your direction 195 degrees. You come to a car road T-junction with a ten-foot-high railway station sign on your right-hand side.

Turn right downhill on Evingar Road. In 200 metres, as the road bends left, *turn right* downhill on Ardglen Road. In 100 metres you pass an ambulance station on your left-hand side. At the end of this building, **[!]** you should not follow the path to the right down into allotments as this is not a public footpath.

Instead, *continue along* Ardglen Road, soon passing light-industrial premises on your left, then on your right. This road ends in a cul-de-sac, but 90 metres before the dead end, *turn right,* your direction west, and in 25 metres go through a metal barrier on to a tarmac path. In 35 metres you come out on to Bloswood Drive, where you *turn left.* You pass a row of bungalows on the right-hand side and in 160 metres you come to a car road T-junction. **[2]**

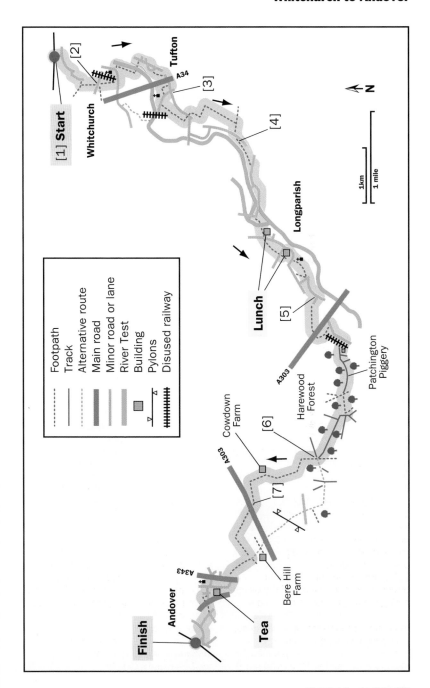

Whitchurch to Andover

Legend:
- Footpath
- Track
- Alternative route
- Main road
- Minor road or lane
- River Test
- Building
- Pylons
- Disused railway

[1] Start
[2]
[3]
[4]
[5]
[6]
[7]

Whitchurch
Tufton
A34
Longparish
Lunch
A303
Harewood Forest
Patchington Piggery
Cowdown Farm
A303
Bere Hill Farm
Tea
A343
Andover
Finish

N

1km
1 mile

Cross *straight over* the road and cross a stile in a wooden fence to the right of a wooden barrier and locked wooden field gates. Take *the left* of two signposted public footpaths. In 15 metres you go over a stile and follow the direction of the yellow arrow, half right towards a field exit, at 165 degrees from you, which adjoins the embankment of the disused railway line.

In 200 metres go through a metal swing gate and onwards, uphill on an earth and gravel path, with the embankment on your left-hand side and a fence to a new housing development on your right. In 25 metres you pass on your left-hand side a pedestrian tunnel under the embankment.

In 35 metres the path *goes up* on to the embankment and straight on, with the old railway station (now a private house and garden) behind a fence on your left-hand side. In 45 metres the path swings left, then right, and now has a tarmac surface. In a further 15 metres you come out to a T-junction with a new cul-de-sac (Park View). Here *turn left,* and in

25 metres you come to a T-junction with a main road, Wells Lane.

Turn right on Wells Lane (by a house called The Mount), gently downhill, your direction 190 degrees. In 180 metres you come to a road junction (the B3400), with **All Hallows Church**, Whitchurch, on your left-hand side. *Turn left* along the B3400 beside All Hallows Church and in 90 metres you come to the entrance to the church on your left-hand side. After visiting the church continue along the road in the same direction as before.

(If at this point you wish to detour to the **Silk Mill**, continue on this road for 450 metres and then turn right – the fourth turning – at a roundabout on to a road for 150 metres. Coming out of the Mill, continue on this road and in 1km rejoin the main route below.)

Continuing on the main route, in 20 metres the road swings to the left just past St Cross House on the right-hand side. Here *turn right* on a signposted footpath, a car-wide track between walls, your direction 130 degrees.

Whitchurch Silk Mill.

In 85 metres you come to the river where you *veer right* with the path, now with the clean **River Test** (only about 8km from its source in Overton) on your left-hand side. Keep on this riverside path, with a fence on your right-hand side and, in 400 metres, as you approach Fulling Mill ahead of you, cross over a concrete bridge with wooden railings.

15 metres beyond the end of the bridge, you pass the entrance to Fulling Mill on your right-hand side. Here *turn left* over a concrete bridge with wooden handrails and immediately *turn right* to continue straight on, your path parallel and 10 metres to the left of your previous path, your direction 140 degrees.

In 20 metres cross a concrete-slab bridge with a wooden handrail on its right-hand side and keep ahead on a grassy path, your direction 120 degrees. In 20 metres go over a grassy path crossing and soon pass a Meadow Sluice noticeboard on your left-hand side.

You now cross this 'Millennium Greens' project, which is regenerating this meadow from its previous wasteland state. In 30 metres cross a concrete-slab bridge and keep ahead on the grassy path. In a further 70 metres make for a wooden kissing gate to exit the meadow and come out on to a tarmac road, where you *turn right,* your direction 210 degrees. (The route from the Silk Mill rejoins here.)

In 165 metres *turn right* on a crescent drive towards houses. In 65 metres you pass the rebuilt Ivy Cottage on your right-hand side.

In a further 65 metres *go over* a signposted stile to your right (half-hidden by a cypress tree) to continue on, diagonally across this field, half left, your direction 200 degrees, in 240 metres coming to the furthest corner of the field. (**Note**: this field can be very overgrown with nettles in summer: to avoid them, stay on the road for a further 200 metres, then turn right under the A34, then right again, and head into Tufton.)

Go over a stile (with a metal fieldgate to its left-hand side) and in 30 metres you come out on to a road where you *turn right,* in 30 metres going under a bridge (the A34), your direction 220 degrees. 20 metres past the bridge, *turn right* on a signposted footpath, your direction 320 degrees.

In 40 metres, by a metal fieldgate to your left-hand side, *carry on* along a narrow path between fences, your direction 350 degrees. In 130 metres, follow the path to the *left,* your direction now 255 degrees. In 100 metres the field on your right ends and you keep ahead along a path with a hedge on your right. In 70 metres, at the end of the path and just before a private property sign, **[!]** go over the stile on your *right-hand side.*

Go left on a surfaced driveway, your direction 240 degrees, in 20 metres coming to a churchyard on your right-hand side and in a further 30 metres a phonebox on your left. **[3]** Here you *turn right* on the road, your direction 320 degrees, passing **St Mary's Church, Tufton** on your right-hand side (well worth a look inside).

Coming out of the church, *turn right* along the road which heads towards Manor Farm. At the farm, the road swings left and in 150 metres you pass on your right-hand side a two-armed finger post with a path on your right leading to a footbridge.

In 35 metres follow the Hampshire County Council (HCC) footpath post *left,* up through a metal kissing gate to *turn right* along a field edge with the embankment to the dismantled railway on your right-hand side, your initial direction 230 degrees.

This new footpath follows the railway embankment for the next 600-plus metres. In 325 metres pass through a field boundary and keep ahead, your direction 200 degrees, staying alongside the fence and field edge on your right. In a further 300 metres the field comes to an end and you *turn left* along its bottom edge.

In 80 metres *turn right* through a metal kissing gate and in 20 metres drop down to the road junction, where turning right heads to Hurstbourne Priors and Paper

Mill Farm, and the road ahead towards Longparish. **[!]** *Do not turn right* down the road, as the footpath through Paper Mill Farm is now closed. Instead **[!]** *cross the road* and *turn right* through a metal kissing gate, to turn *half right* between new saplings, your direction 160 degrees.

In 100 metres pass through a gap in the fence and *turn right,* following the direction of the footpath post, 220 degrees, and go along the right-hand edge of a large, open field.

In 90 metres, at the end of this field, *turn left,* your direction now 120 degrees, down the edge of the field with a post and wire fence on your right-hand side.

In 250 metres, at the bottom of the field, go through the field boundary and *turn right,* following the direction of the footpath post, 220 degrees.

In 100 metres go through a field boundary and the gap in the fence, to follow the path, at first right, then left, the latter bearing 210 degrees. You have a hedgerow on your right-hand side as the path goes gently downhill to a dip, then starts to rise. Some 250 metres along this path, you pass an open barn on your right behind the hedge to come out to a junction with a gravel farm track.

[!] *Turn right* – following the direction of the footpath post – and in 20 metres, with a metal fieldgate ahead of you (and a pair of metal fieldgates at right angles to it) **[!]** *turn left* to follow the direction of a footpath post, due south, along the right-hand edge of a field, with a post-and-wire fence on your right.

In 350 metres go through a metal kissing gate and down the ramps to your left, then right, to come out on to a farm track (Firgo Lane).

Go under the bridge (to the disused railway) and keep ahead along the farm track, your direction due west, and in 150 metres you come out to the road, with Garden Cottage on your left-hand side. *Turn left,* to walk along the road.

In 100 metres you pass the rather beautiful **Britwell Priors** and garden on your left-hand side. (In 1927 a colonel and his wife had these timber-framed farm cottages moved here from Oxfordshire, with – in those days – unhealthy water piped in directly from the River Test; at the previous site of the cottages, the well came up into the dining room.)

Some 60 metres past the front gate of Britwell Priors **[4]**, **[!]** *fork right* on a signposted footpath, your direction 235 degrees, going through three wooden posts to go along a path through brush heading down to the river below on your right-hand side. In 400 metres you come out on to a tarmac road and *turn right* to follow it alongside the river, your direction 280 degrees.

In 145 metres, *fork left* with the road, ignoring a path to the right leading to a footbridge. You now have a shallow stream on your right-hand side.

In 325 metres, by a mini weir and a farmhouse to the right-hand side, follow your road over a bridge with white railings and in 45 metres go over a second such bridge, with the farmhouse and old mill closer now on your right-hand side. In 20 metres go over a third (smaller) bridge with white railings.

At the far end of the millhouse, the road swings right to cross a bridge over a weir. Do not cross this bridge but keep ahead, in 5 metres going *through a gap* to continue on the path, with the river on your right-hand side, your direction 315 degrees.

In 80 metres go over a wooden bridge with wooden railings and, at its end, go through a wooden kissing gate. Follow the direction of the yellow arrow on the gatepost and, in 50 metres, go through a wooden kissing gate to continue between post-and-wire fences, your direction due west. In 125 metres go over a wooden bridge with railings, with the moderately imposing **Longparish House** (marked on the OS map) away on your right-hand side.

In 80 metres go through a wooden kissing gate and on to a 40-metre-long wooden bridge between wooden railings (the bridge can be slippery), over the River

Test, and through another wooden kissing gate at the end of the bridge. Now head for the wooden kissing gate to the right of a stile less than 100 metres ahead of you, your direction 260 degrees, in the direction of the thatched buildings beyond. Once through the kissing gate, continue across the grass towards the thatched buildings, your direction still 260 degrees.

In 130 metres your path bends right, hugging the field edge on your right-hand side, and in a further 90 metres you exit the field through a wooden kissing gate and keep ahead, in 20 metres coming out on to the B3048 road, by the thatched Yew Cottage.

Turn left on this B road, your direction 225 degrees. In 30 metres you pass a Londis Convenience Store on your right-hand side and in a further 25 metres you come to the **Cricketers Inn** pub, **Longparish**, on your left, the first of your possible lunch stops. 130 metres past the pub, and by Little Newton thatched cottage on your left-hand side and Aston thatched cottage on your right, **[!]** you *turn right* up a driveway (that runs to the left of Aston Cottage), your direction 315 degrees.

In 40 metres, by a garage shed, *go left* on a clear grassy footpath, your direction 240 degrees, with the field edge now on your left-hand side. In 385 metres ignore a wooden kissing gate on your left-hand side to continue straight on. In a further 155 metres go through a wooden kissing gate (a metal fieldgate to its right-hand side) to continue straight on, across a field, in 100 metres passing a long wooden shed on your left-hand side, then a house. In 50 metres go through a metal kissing gate to come out on to a tarmac road where you *turn left,* your direction 130 degrees.

In 10 metres **[!]** *turn right* on a signposted footpath (opposite Lower Farm House), passing the front gardens to a terrace of houses on your right-hand side, your direction 205 degrees. In 60 metres go through a high wooden panel gate and *turn left* around the edge of a soccer pitch, then right. In a further 60 metres, directly behind one of the goals, *turn left* through a gap in the hedge, your direction 145 degrees. Follow the path ahead through trees and in 25 metres you come out into the car park of the **Plough Inn**. The entrance to the pub is some 30 metres ahead on your right-hand side. This is your second pub-lunch option.

Coming out of the pub, *turn right* on the main road, opposite a bus shelter, your direction 210 degrees. In 150 metres, as the road swings to the right, fork left, your direction 235 degrees, on the driveway now shared with the new Longparish Church of England Primary School on your left and the **Church of St Nicholas**, Longparish. In 70 metres

you go through the lychgate into the churchyard – but before going through the gate, note the punishment stocks 3 metres to its right.

Take the *left fork* through the churchyard, passing the entrance to the church on your right. Leave the churchyard by the far (western) lychgate and pick up the clear, grassy footpath *going right* (past a thatched barn on your right-hand side), your direction 255 degrees. In 90 metres you go through a wooden kissing gate and continue on, across a field, with the river over to your left.

Follow the line of telegraph poles and in 225 metres go through a wooden kissing gate in the direction of the Test Way long-distance path (a TW green arrow) *to the left,* on a tarmac road, your direction 215 degrees. (Your onward route follows these Test Way green arrows into Harewood Forest.)

In 30 metres you pass a large building (Buckclose House) on your right-hand side and soon a haven of more thatched cottages. 440 metres further along this tarmac road, it swings to the right, with a farm track ahead leading to Forton Farm Cottages and Lyewoods.

[!] You now follow the TW detour to avoid a dangerous crossing of the A303 road. [5] Follow the TW detour sign *right,* gently uphill, your direction 310 degrees.

In 200 metres, at the top of the hill, you come to a T-junction with another road. *Cross over* and go through a wooden kissing gate, to follow the TW sign across a large field, your direction due west, initially downhill. In 75 metres go under electricity cables and now keep ahead up the other side of this field. In 150 metres, at the far side of this field, by a footpath post, follow the TW sign *left,* your direction 145 degrees, on a broken-surfaced farm track.

In 40 metres cross a stile to the left of a pair of metal fieldgates and in 25 metres you come to a T-junction with a road. *Turn right,* your direction due west and

follow the road as it swings around to the left, in 120 metres going over the A303 road on a road bridge.

On the far side of the bridge, ignore the turning right into Harewood Forest Industrial Estate, and *continue down* the road as it bends to the left. In 80 metres you come down to a T-junction with the B3048 road, where you *turn right,* signposted to Wherwell (there is also a TW sign on your right).

Stay on this road, uphill, and in 160 metres, at the top of the hill, you pass Smallwood Lodge on your right-hand side. In 100 metres as the road descends and swings left, *turn right* off the road at a footpath and TW sign beside a sign to Pachington Copse and Middleton & Portway Estate, on to a surfaced road, your direction 295 degrees.

In 20 metres you pass through the old railway embankment into **Harewood Forest** (so marked on the OS map). In a further 20 metres, by a Pachington Copse sign, *keep ahead.*

In 25 metres *turn left* on a gravel track and in a further 15 metres go through a metal fieldgate, to *turn right* up a concrete track, your direction 310 degrees, following TW signs, gently uphill. In 125 metres the track swings to the left.

In 50 metres you pass two large blue-coloured circular tanks on your left-hand side. In 15 metres you pass two silos at the end of a piggery shed. In 50 metres, as the track turns sharply to the left, [!] you follow the arrow on a post directly *ahead,* your direction 240 degrees, into Harewood Forest.

Follow green arrows on trees through the wood and in 275 metres pass to the right of a metal fieldgate to come out on to a concrete track, where you *turn right,* your direction 260 degrees. Now follow green TW arrows on posts as the concrete track starts to descend and then swings to the right.

In 270 metres you pass on your right-hand side the first of three large piggery sheds – in turn, nos.4, 5 and 6, each with a feed silo attached to its end with Calor gas tanks to the side. After the last of these sheds (shed no.6), you continue *straight on,* your direction 290 degrees, following a TW sign on a post on your left-hand side, as the path enters woodland.

In 130 metres you come to a junction of paths, just after a metal cable barrier that you need to walk around. Continue *straight on,* taking the middle path, following a footpath sign, your direction 255 degrees. In 35 metres you pass to the left of a metal gate across a car-wide track.

Keep ahead, following TW arrows through the forest and, in 480 metres, you come to a track crossroads, with a footpath post on your left-hand side. Here you leave the Test Way and **[!]** *turn right,* a car-wide concrete track, your direction due north.

In 150 metres you come to a fork in the concrete roads and you *take the left fork* (the five-foot concrete pillar by the right fork has now lost its top two feet), your direction 330 degrees. Now progress steadily uphill on this concrete track and after 800 metres you come to a crossroads of tracks and paths. **[6]**

[!] In order to avoid the second dangerous crossing of the A303 road, your onward route is now as follows: At the crossroads, do *not* turn left as directed in previous editions of this book, but instead *cross over* and take the grassy track opposite, passing to the right of a circular drum tank, your direction due north. This track can be muddy in winter.

Continue ahead, between Furzy Croft Copse on your left and Popple Hill Copse on your right. In 220 metres the track merges with a gravel track and swings to the right, your direction now 20 degrees. Keep ahead and in 90 metres you come to a crossroads. Here you *turn left,* on a gravel track with grass down its middle, gently uphill, your direction 260 degrees.

In 380 metres, just before the end of the wood, you come to a T-junction of tracks. **[!]** Here *turn left* on the concrete drive and in 10 metres **[!]** *take the faint path to your right,* your direction 245 degrees. In 30 metres you exit the wood and come out

on to a gravel track, with large open fields now in front of you.

Turn right on this gravel track and head gently uphill towards **Cowdown Farm Buildings**, your direction 350 degrees. In 400 metres, just before the farm buildings, *turn left* with the track and come down on to Cowdown Lane.

Turn right on the lane and in 100 metres **[!]** *turn left* off the lane on a clear car-wide track, initially downhill, your direction 350 degrees, towards the A303 road. In 320 metres the path swings to the left and levels out as you approach the road. In a further 280 metres, at the end of the field, beside the embankment of the A303 road, *turn left* along the bottom edge of this field.

In 110 metres pass to the right of a metal fieldgate and head down a surfaced track, in 65 metres *turning right under a bridge* carrying the A303 road above. **[7]**

On the far side of the bridge *turn left,* uphill along the track. At the end of the track, you are faced with a number of path options. **[!]** Take the grassy track *half left,* your direction 310 degrees, with a hedgerow soon on your right-hand side. In 60 metres pass under telegraph wires and *keep ahead,* gently uphill.

In 360 metres, at the top of the incline, as the hedge on your right ends, the track *turns left* and heads towards **Bere Hill Farm**, your direction now 225 degrees. In 170 metres the track comes to a field boundary which you pass through, to continue ahead now on a grassy path. (**Note**: the alternative grassy path heading half right leads down to the metal pipe stile in your route below, but this path is not an official right of way.)

In 120 metres *turn right* on a path that swings left around the outbuildings of Bere Hill Farm. In 50 metres, just before the field boundary, *turn right* downhill, with a fence on your left-hand side, your direction 320 degrees.

In 120 metres, at the bottom left-hand corner of the field, you cross over an unusual metal pipe stile with metal footplates, and go over a footpath to continue straight on, *down steps,* following a footpath sign, your direction 320 degrees.

Keep straight on all the way down to the main road (Eastern Avenue). In more detail: Ignore all ways off and in 125 metres you have allotments on your left-hand side and a playing field to your right on the far side of a hedge. At the end of the allotments go down a path between hedges and in 60 metres you come to a tarmac estate road and cross it, your onward path now visible for some distance ahead.

In 40 metres go through concrete bollards and in 60 metres cross an estate road: the sign on your left tells you that the path is Dene Path. In 200 metres cross a road and keep ahead. In a further 80 metres Dene Path comes to an end but you *continue straight on* along a tarmac road, towards the church soon visible in the distance. In 100 metres you reach the T-junction with Eastern Avenue.

Cross Eastern Avenue by the lights to your right and *go down* London Street (slightly to the left on the other side of Eastern Avenue), past the Life Cinema, Café & Bar on your left-hand side and in 100 metres passing the Forresters Arms pub on your left-hand side.

In 30 metres, *turn right* into the High Street, in 50 metres, *turning left* under the archway of Shaws Walk to the **Copper Kettle**, which is the suggested tea place.

Coming out of the Copper Kettle, you *return* to the High Street via the archway and *turn left*, carrying on uphill towards the church, taking the slightly right-hand fork in the High Street which passes to the right of the **Lower Guildhall**.

At the top of the hill you pass the Angel pub on your left-hand side and you continue ahead, now slightly downhill. In 60 metres you come to a **Norman arch** on your right-hand side, with steps up to the **church**. To visit Andover **museum**, turn right at the church to get to Church Close, then left to the museum at 6 Church Close.

To get to the railway station, however, [!] *turn left* into Chantry Street, just 15 metres before the church. Carry on down this road and in 100 metres cross the junction with West Street on your left and *turn right* into Andover Leisure Centre. At the end of the centre, *turn left* down its flank wall, pass the pond on your right to *turn right* in front of the courthouse buildings. At their far end, with Cricklade College & Theatre ahead of you, *turn left* down the flank wall of the courthouse.

Keep ahead to go over the river and under the underpass. In 60 metres, at a T-junction with a car road, *go right* following the pedestrian sign to the station, your direction 315 degrees.

In 40 metres *turn left* up Bishopsway. In 400 metres, at a T-junction, *turn left uphill* on Cross Lane, and in 20 metres you *fork right* for **Andover station**, now visible ahead. Go under the tunnel for trains to London (platform 1).

Lunch & tea places

Cricketers Inn *Longparish, Andover, SP11 6PZ (01264 720335, www. cricketersinnlongparish.co.uk).* **Open** noon-3pm, 6.30-11pm Tue-Sun. *Food served* noon-2.15pm, 6.30-9.15pm Tue-Sat; noon-2.15pm, 6.30-8pm Sun. An extensive menu of main courses, lighter meals (such as ciabattas) and starters to share is offered at the suggested lunchtime stop on this walk. Food is served in comfortable surroundings, which include a large beer garden. The owners like diners to phone ahead and book, and have been known to refuse to serve walkers who turn up without prior notice, even when tables are available.

Plough Inn *Longparish, Andover, SP11 6PB (01264 720358, www.theploughinn. info).* **Open** *Summer* noon-3pm, 6pm-midnight Mon-Sat; noon-9pm Sun. *Winter* noon-3pm, 6pm-midnight Mon-Sat; noon-5pm Sun. *Food served* noon-2.30pm, 6-9.30pm Mon-Sat; noon-8pm Sun (in winter, food served until 4pm Sun). Specialises in seafood. Groups of six or more are advised to book ahead.

Copper Kettle *Shaws Walk, Andover, SP10 1LJ (01264 351175).* **Open** 8.30am-4pm Mon-Sat. Cream teas are available at the suggested tea stop for this walk.

Walk 49

Box Hill to Leatherhead

River Mole, Juniper Top and White Hill.

Start: Box Hill & Westhumble station
Finish: Leatherhead station

Length: 11.5km (7.1 miles)

Time: 3 hours 30 minutes. For the whole outing, including trains, sights and meals, allow at least 6 hours 30 minutes.

Transport: Take the train nearest to **10.15am** from **Victoria** station to **Box Hill & Westhumble** (journey time 50 minutes). There are six trains an hour (four on Sundays) back from **Leatherhead** to Victoria or Waterloo (journey time about 45 minutes). Buy a day return to Box Hill & Westhumble.

OS Langranger Map: 187
OS Explorer Map: 146
Box Hill & Westhumble station, map reference TQ167518, is in **Surrey**, 5km south of Leatherhead.

Toughness: 7 out of 10

Walk notes: Box Hill derives its name from the box trees there; yew trees are also found on its chalky slopes, with beech and oak up on top where the ground is clay and flint. The suggested route involves crossing the River Mole on stepping stones (or detouring if these are under water), before going steeply up steps on the North Downs Way to the top of Box Hill, to enjoy views out over the valley. The route then follows woods before you drop down Juniper Top, which also enjoys fine views, and steeply up White Hill on to Mickleham Downs. You head down to lunch in one of Mickleham's two pubs. After lunch, the route is along the River Mole valley, through Norbury Park, into the centre of Leatherhead.

This route can be slippery at times when wet and has two steep climbs, one up to the top of Box Hill and one – very steep – up White Hill.

Walk options: You could call for a taxi from the Smith & Western Bar Grill, on top of Box Hill, or from one of the lunchtime pubs. Buses go from outside the Smith & Western, and there is a half-hourly bus service from Mickleham to Leatherhead and Kingston (hourly on Sundays).

After lunch in Mickleham, instead of walking to Leatherhead, you could loop back to Box Hill through Norbury Park.

In the morning, instead of following the directions down Juniper Top, you could follow the more direct route to White Hill car park, by descending Juniper Bottom (this was the route in previous editions of this book, but it lacks the views from Juniper Top). For details of these options, refer to the Saturday Walkers' Club website (www.walkingclub.org.uk).

History: **Box Hill & Westhumble station**
was built in 1867 in polychrome brick
with stone dressings, as part of an
agreement with the landowner that it
should be 'of an ornamental character'.

Box Hill, 172 metres above sea level,
contains Bronze Age burial mounds.
Daniel Defoe described scenes of
drinking, dancing and debauchery
on the hill; Jane Austen placed the
picnic scene in *Emma* here; John Keats
climbed Box Hill by moonlight while
composing *Endymion*; and John Logie
Baird conducted his TV experiments
from the summit. The area was given
to the nation by Leopold Salomons of
Norbury Park in 1914 and is now in the
care of the National Trust. Box trees
used to be in demand for making
wood-cut blocks and mathematical
rulers – boxwood is heavy and does
not float in water.

St Michael & All Angels Church,
Mickleham, has Saxon and Norman
origins and was renovated by the
Victorians. Its chancel is noticeably
out of alignment with the nave –
'a weeping chancel, to suggest the
head of Christ leaning on the cross'.

The poet and novelist **George
Meredith** lived at Flint Cottage
in Mickleham.

The **River Mole** is thought to have
got its name from a tendency to
disappear underground in dry weather
near Dorking. It rises near Crawley in
Sussex, to join the Thames near
Hampton Court.

Thorncroft Manor was completed
in the 1770s when Capability Brown
worked on the gardens, creating a bridge
and island on the river. It was used by
Canadian troops during World War II.

Walk directions

**[1] [Numbers in square brackets
refer to the map]**
Coming out of **Box Hill &
Westhumble station**, *turn left* up
the concrete steps, your direction 345
degrees. In 30 metres *turn left* over the

bridge to cross the railway line, your
direction 295 degrees.

Carry on uphill on this main road,
Chapel Lane. In 25 metres you pass
an arch gateway on your right-hand
side (it has a plaque dedicated to Fanny
Burney, diarist and novelist) and the
timber-framed Westhumble Chapel.
Carry on up the road and in a further
30 metres you *fork left* by Chaucer Cottage
on a tarmac path that runs parallel to
the road at its right-hand side.

In 115 metres you rejoin the main road,
passing Pilgrim's Way on your left-hand
side. **[!]** In a further 25 metres take a
signposted (but somewhat concealed)
public footpath *left*, between fences,
your direction 220 degrees.

In 150 metres cross a tarmac lane by a
house called Kearsney, to carry *straight
on,* now on a narrow path between a
hedge and fence.

In 200 metres go through a wooden
kissing gate and straight on, across a
field. In 50 metres go through another
wooden kissing gate. In 15 metres, by a
four-armed footpath sign **[2]**, with a large
vineyard ahead of you, *turn left* on a car-
wide way, signposted North Downs Way.

(For elevenses at **Denbies**, instead
of turning left, *cross over* this path
and in 15 metres go through a wooden
swing gate to keep ahead along a path
between vines, your direction 170
degrees. In 280 metres, where this
path meets a main access road,
turn left to Denbies visitor centre
and restaurant. After elevenses retrace
your steps to the junction with the
North Downs Way.)

Continue on the North Downs
Way, gently downhill, ignoring paths
off. In 300 metres go through a wooden
swing gate to the left of a wooden farm
gate. The track is now a tarmac lane. In
65 metres go under the railway bridge.
In 150 metres go through a metal gate
and in a further 15 metres cross – with
care – both carriageways and the central
reservation of the busy A24 road, slightly
to the left, to pick up the continuation of

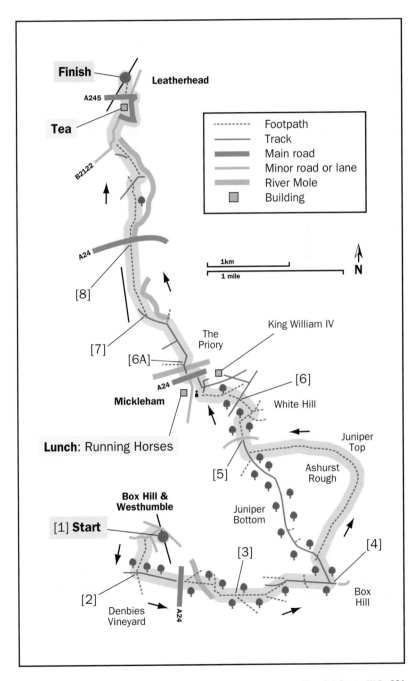

Box Hill to Leatherhead

Finish

Leatherhead

A245

Tea

B2122

Footpath
Track
Main road
Minor road or lane
River Mole
Building

1km
1 mile

N

A24

[8]

[7]

King William IV

The Priory

[6A]

A24

[6]

White Hill

Mickleham

[5]

Juniper Top

Ashurst Rough

Lunch: Running Horses

Juniper Bottom

Box Hill & Westhumble

[1] **Start**

[3]

[4]

[2]

Denbies Vineyard

A24

Box Hill

the North Downs Way straight on, down into a car park area. At the other end of the car park, you fork right, marked towards 'Stepping Stones', your direction 115 degrees.

Carry on, straight down. In 100 metres go over the **River Mole** on these **stepping stones**. Carry straight on the other side of the river, on the main path, your direction 120 degrees. (If the river is running high, and there is a danger of its flooding and covering the stepping stones, retrace your steps to the car park. Here take the left-hand fork marked 'footbridge'. Having crossed the bridge, turn right and follow the path by the river for 150 metres to return to the stepping stones – but now on the eastern side of the River Mole.)

In 120 metres you ignore a fork to the left. In 60 metres you start *going up steps* following the North Downs Way acorn signs on footpath posts and keep on following the main path. In 70 metres ignore the path ahead and take the flight of steps to the *left*, your direction 50 degrees.

Follow the acorn signs as you continue steeply up another five flights of steps. At a T-junction, near the top of the hill, follow the acorn sign to the *right*, your

direction 120 degrees, with a fine view over Dorking and the Mole Valley below.

Keep on the main path along the ridge, gently uphill, ignoring ways off. In 225 metres you come to the **stone memorial** and lookout point **[3]** to **Leopold Salomons** of Norbury Park, who gave Box Hill to the nation in 1914. There is a trig station pillar just below the lookout that has fine views over Gatwick, Leith Hill and Hindhead. 65 metres past this lookout point, *fork left uphill* by a multi-branch oak tree on your right-hand side, your direction 35 degrees.

In 110 metres *bear right* with the path (there is a car park and a road on your left-hand side). Keep *straight on,* ignoring all ways off, following North Downs Way acorn posts.

In 225 metres go through a wooden swing gate. In 110 metres go through another. *Keep ahead,* ignoring ways off, following acorn signs and in 230 metres *turn right* by a footpath post with acorn sign, your direction 150 degrees, to go down four steps and up five steps on the other side. In 30 metres go down four steps to an earth car road crossing your path. *Turn left uphill,* your direction 70 degrees.

In 40 metres this brings you up to the **Smith & Western** bar and grill **[4]**, a possible elevenses or early lunch stop. Walk through its car park and *turn left* on to a road. In 20 metres *turn right* at a signpost bridleway, your direction 325 degrees, into **Ashurst Rough** (so marked on the OS map).

Ignore all ways off and keep on the main path, initially to the edge of the wood then through the wood. In 400 metres cross a car-wide earth road and in a further 15 metres you come to a four-way path junction.

At this path junction *turn right,* your direction 20 degrees, in 30 metres joining a path from your right by a footpath post. Keep ahead, now on a gravel and earth road, gently downhill, and ignore all ways off.

In 800 metres go through a wooden gate to the right of a metal fieldgate and come out on to **Juniper Top**. Keep ahead and in 100 metres *bear left* on a broad, grassy path, your bearing 300 degrees.

Descend Juniper Top, enjoying fine views ahead. In some 500 metres, the grassy path narrows to an earth and stony path; in a further 100 metres, go through a wooden kissing gate to the right of a metal fieldgate, with a three-way footpath sign and a National Trust donation cairn to your right. *Turn right* to join a track, your bearing 330 degrees, to pass in 30 metres a Box Hill notice-board. In a further 15 metres go through White Hill car park to cross the Headley Road. **[5]**

Follow the public footpath sign directly ahead on the other side of the road to climb steeply up the steps of **White Hill** (so marked on the OS map).

Beyond these steep steps, the path bears right and becomes less steep and in 150 metres comes to a fork, with a bench to your left and by footpath post no.5. Here *keep ahead, slightly left,* on a bearing of 45 degrees, through woods. In 45 metres, at a T-junction, by the remains of a fence's metal corner post, *go left,* following the 'Long Walk' arrow on a post, your direction 330 degrees. In 40 metres, by post no.6, bear left for 8 metres, then turn left by a footpath post to follow its Long Walk direction, your bearing again 330 degrees, your path ahead soon going downhill.

In 200 metres you come to a car-wide bridleway crossing **[6]** with a **Box Hill Estate** noticeboard on your right-hand side.

Your way ahead depends on which pub in Mickleham you target for lunch.

To **go direct to the King William IV pub**, bypassing Mickleham village and St Michael's church:

Turn right at the car-wide bridleway, your direction 20 degrees, gently uphill on a chalky track, passing on your right a National Trust Mickleham Downs sign. In 100 metres a path joins from your left-hand side. In a further 130 metres, at a path crossing **[!]** take an indistinct path on your *left downhill,* your direction 300 degrees. In 65 metres, the path swings left and a path joins from the right. The path descends more steeply now and in 200 metres it narrows and starts to descend steeply through brush. In a further 150 metres cross a main path junction and keeping ahead, *descend steps,* in 80 metres coming to the entrance to the **King**

William IV pub on the hillside on your left-hand side. After lunch, turn left down steps to the un-made-up road, Byttom Hill. *Turn left,* downhill, to the A24 road, where you turn left for 200 metres, to cross the A24 and rejoin the route below.

To **go to the Running Horses pub and St Michael's Church**:

At the car-wide bridleway crossing [6], *cross over,* to continue *straight on* down, following the Long Walk arrow, due west. In 150 metres at a fork, and by a footpath post, *bear left,* downhill, your direction 250 degrees. In 110 metres you pass a tennis court on your right-hand side. In 80 metres cross a stile to join a gravel driveway towards the church. In a further 120 metres you *enter the churchyard* and in 40 metres, at the other side of the churchyard, you *turn left* towards the front door of **St Michael & All Angels Church**. Opposite the church is the **Running Horses** pub. Next door is a convenience store if you wish to purchase refreshments for a picnic. Coming out of the pub after lunch, *turn left* on to the Old London Road, which you follow down, passing Box Hill School on your left-hand side, to come out to the A24 road.

Cross both carriageways and the central reservation with care, slightly left, to pick up a tarmac lane bridleway ahead. [!] (**Note**: an alternative route to the King William IV pub is to turn right down the A24 for 200 metres, to turn right up Byttom Hill to the pub on your right-hand side.)

Cross the *River Mole* on a humpback bridge, your direction 345 degrees, into **Norbury Park. [6A]**

Ignore all ways off and in 400 metres you pass Norbury Park Farm on your right-hand side. In 50 metres *fork left,* your direction 300 degrees, on an earth car road.

In 40 metres go through a wooden kissing gate to the left of a metal fieldgate and continue straight on. In a further 215 metres, you are back alongside the River Mole on your right-hand side. You more or less follow the river all the way to Leatherhead. In more detail: When you see a cottage 90 metres ahead of you on

your left-hand side, climb over a low wire fence on your *right-hand side* **[7]** and follow the river on your right-hand side for 40 metres until it bends off to the right. You can see, straight ahead of you, a fieldgate on a lane (which you would have come to if you had simply gone to the cottage and turned right, by a footpath sign). Head towards this fieldgate, your direction 330 degrees.

In 240 metres you go through a wooden kissing gate to the right-hand side of the fieldgate, to continue on the lane.

In 95 metres carry *straight on,* along a path near the river, your direction 15 degrees. In 400 metres you exit this large field by a kissing gate (with a fieldgate to its left-hand side). Ignore the path to the left and carry *straight on,* with the river on your right-hand side.

In 30 metres you pass a **River Mole Local Nature Reserve noticeboard** and in 50 metres go over a metal pipe barrier and then onwards under the concrete bridge carrying the A246. **[8]**

In 45 metres ignore a fork to the left. In a further 85 metres, go through a wooden kissing gate with a metal barrier on its right and with a vineyard on your left-hand side. In 20 metres *bear right* with the path and in 30 metres you pass a bridge carrying pipes. In a further 320 metres, you go through a metal kissing gate (with a metal barrier to its left-hand side). In 20 metres you come to an earth car road and by a four-armed footpath sign, you *turn right* on the road (now surfaced) signposted Gimcrack Hill, your direction 65 degrees. In 175 metres you pass the entrance to **Thorncroft Manor** on your left and you are back alongside the River Mole.

In 100 metres, 5 metres before a bridge, by a three-armed footpath sign, you *go left,* signposted Town Bridge, through a wooden barrier and on to a stony and gravel path, alongside the River Mole on your right-hand side.

In 20 metres you pass another River Mole Local Nature Reserve noticeboard and, in 400 metres, yet another. In 120 metres *turn right* over the town bridge, your direction 60 degrees. Go over a mini roundabout and carry straight on up Bridge Street, passing the Running Horse pub on your left as you head into **Leatherhead**. At the top of Bridge Street you pass **Gourmet Delis** on your right, a possible tea stop. Bear slightly right into the pedestrianised High Street and in 45 metres *go through* the lower (main) entrance to the Swan Shopping Centre on your left. In 80 metres you come to a **Costa Coffee**, another possible tea stop, on your right-hand side (**Starbucks** and **Annie's** are further up the High Street and nearer the upper entrance to the shopping centre).

Coming out of Costa Coffee, exit the shopping centre northwards through the alleyway, keeping Sainsbury's on your right-hand side. In 55 metres go up steps on to the main road (the A245).

Cross this A road, slightly to the left, to pick up a narrow tarmac lane (Middle Road) and *go straight on upwards* between houses, your direction 330 degrees (with house no.4 immediately on your right-hand side).

In 100 metres you come to a tarmac road T-junction where you *go left,* your direction 230 degrees. In 70 metres, at the far end of the car park, *turn right,* your direction 300 degrees, with a large building just ahead of you. In 15 metres you come to a public garden (**King George V Memorial Gardens**) where you *take the right fork,* a tarmac lane, downhill.

In 65 metres take the second fork right, your direction 25 degrees, now parallel with the main road below, and still within the public garden.

In 80 metres exit the public garden through brick piers and down four steps, to come down to the main road, which you cross with care to go *straight on,* your direction 290 degrees, on Randalls Road.

In 120 metres, just before a railway bridge, *turn right* to go to **Leatherhead station**, your direction 15 degrees. After a further 70 metres, go under the railway lines to reach platform 1 for trains to

London (which go back to Victoria or Waterloo).

Lunch & tea places

Denbies Wine Estate Conservatory Restaurant *London Road, Dorking, TH5 6AA (01306 876616, www. denbies.co.uk).* **Open** *Apr-Oct* 9.30am-5pm Mon-Sat; 10am-5.30pm Sun. *Nov-Mar* 9.30am-5pm Mon-Sat; 10am-5pm Sun. For those in need of a very early tea or coffee, Denbies restaurant is around 1km (about half a mile) into the walk.

Smith & Western Bar Grill *Boxhill Road, Tadworth, KT20 7LB (01737 841666, www.smith-western.co.uk).* **Open** noon-11pm Mon-Sat; noon-10pm Sun. A potential lunch stop, at the summit of Box Hill, for late starters.

King William IV *Byttom Hill, Mickleham, RH5 6EL (01372 372590, www.king-williamiv.com).* **Open** 11am-3pm, 6.30-11pm Mon-Sat; 11am-10.30pm Sun. *Food served* 11.45am-2pm Mon; 11.45am-2pm, 7-9pm Tue-Fri; noon-2pm, 7-9pm Sat; noon-5pm Sun. A cosy pub, with good food and beer. One of two options for lunch in Mickleham.

Running Horses *Old London Road, Mickleham (01372 372279, www.the runninghorses.co.uk).* **Open** noon-2.30pm, 7-9.30pm Mon-Fri; noon-3pm, 7-9.30pm Sat; noon-3pm, 6.30-9pm Sun. The other option for lunch in Mickleham, serving an excellent range of main meals and deep-filled sandwiches. There's a log fire in winter. The management like walkers to take off their walking boots, so please comply.

Gourmet Delis *5 Bridge Street, Leatherhead, KT22 8BL (01372 386108).* **Open** 7.30am-4pm Mon-Sat. A possible tea stop.

Annie's Tea Room *37 High Street, Leatherhead, KT22 8AE (01372 373399).* **Open** 8am-5pm Mon-Sat; 9am-2pm Sun. A possible tea stop, located near the upper entrance to the shopping centre.

There are a number of pubs in **Leatherhead** if you prefer a tipple at the end of the walk.

Walk 50

Yalding to Borough Green

Mereworth and the Kentish Weald.

Start: Yalding station
Finish: Borough Green station

Length: 16.8km (10.4 miles)

Time: 5 hours. For the whole outing, including trains, sights and meals, allow 9 hours.

Transport: Take the train nearest to **10am** from **Charing Cross** station to **Yalding**, changing at Tonbridge or Paddock Wood (journey time about 1 hour 5 minutes). Trains

back from **Borough Green** to Victoria run twice an hour (hourly on Sundays), with a journey time of 45 minutes. Buy a day return to Yalding; although on a different line, this is acceptable for the return journey from Borough Green.

OS Landranger Map: 188
OS Explorer Map: 148
Yalding, map reference TQ685502, is in **Kent**, 10km north-east of Tonbridge.

Toughness: 3 out of 10

Walk notes: This is an easy walk through the woods and fields of the Kent countryside, without too much in the way of hills. You will, however, need gumboots in muddy weather. The walk starts beside the River Medway, follows the Greensand Way to Roydon Hall (once the self-styled Maharishi's 'Capital of the Age of Enlightenment') and then goes on to the lunch stop in Mereworth, a village dominated by its massive Palladian church, the steeple of which is visible for miles around. After lunch, the walk is principally through the vast Mereworth Woods (very muddy in winter) on the Wealdway, then up – following a stream – to Borough Green. You will need long trousers for one short stretch in late summer (due to the nettles).

Walk options: You can get a bus about once an hour to either Maidstone or

Tunbridge Wells from a stop on the way into Mereworth, near the church.

History: **Roydon Hall** is a Tudor manor house, built in 1535, which has changed ownership only three times: in 1834, from the Roydon/Twysden family to William Cook, a city merchant who accepted it in settlement of debts; in 1974, from the Cook family to the Maharishi for his Transcendental Meditation centre, until it again changed hands much more recently. In the 19th century, a water diviner told the Cook family to dig into the lawn – where they found a collection of large silver dishes, probably buried in the Civil War.

The **Church of St Lawrence**, Mereworth, has been described as 'one of the most remarkable neo-classical churches in Europe'. It has a portico supported by six Tuscan columns and

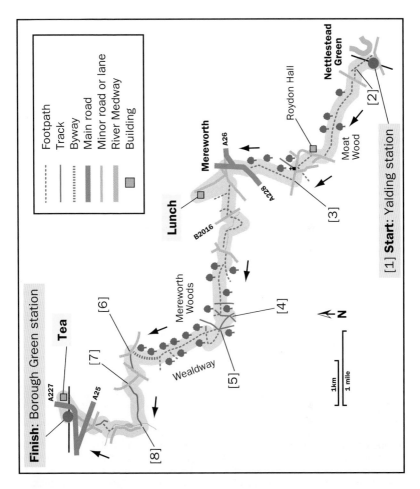

a steeple 'so tall', wrote Horace Walpole, 'that the poor church curtsies under it'. Admiral Charles Lucas, who won the first Victoria Cross in 1854 for throwing overboard a live shell that had hit his ship, is buried in the churchyard.

Walk directions

[1] [Numbers in square brackets refer to the map]
Coming off the London train, go over the bridge and exit **Yalding station** by a gate in the new fence. Go out through the station car park to the main road, and

turn left (where to turn right goes over the railway crossing), your direction 75 degrees. In 120 metres, just before the bridge over the **River Medway**, *turn left* on a signed Medway Valley footpath on the left-hand bank of the river, your direction 15 degrees. (Your route will follow the Greensand Way and its arrows as far as the church beyond Roydon Hall.)

In 110 metres *fork left* away from the river, following the Greensand Way arrow, your direction 340 degrees and between concrete fences. In 100 metres cross the railway line and go up the steps the other side, over a stile and then *straight on,* slightly to the right, your direction 325 degrees, across a large field.

In 280 metres cross a stile and, after a further 100 metres, another, leading to a field where you go half left **[2]**, your direction 280 degrees. Follow a barbed-wire fence on your left-hand side and in 230 metres you exit over a stile and go straight across the B2015 to continue *straight on* to the left of no.1 White Cottage, your direction 290 degrees. In 55 metres go over a stile and straight on across a field of ponies, donkeys and ducks, exiting the field in 160 metres, by a stile in its top left-hand corner, to continue in your previous direction (280 degrees) towards the woods.

In 160 metres you have an edge of the wood on your right-hand side. In a further 150 metres you come (via a break in the wood of 50 metres) to a large wood-enclosed field and continue straight across it, your direction 315 degrees. Exit the field in 450 metres over a stile, straight on into **Moat Wood** (marked on the OS map).

In 275 metres *bend sharp left* with your main path (following the Greensand Way arrow). In a further 175 metres the wood becomes a dark pine forest, your direction now due west. In a further 75 metres you step across a tiny stream (in summer, possibly dried up); in a further 100 metres, exit the wood by a new stile to go straight on.

In 60 metres cross a (private) car-wide road to continue straight on along a car-wide grass path, your direction 295 degrees initially, between blackberry bushes on both sides.

In a further 150 metres you get a first sight of Roydon Hall ahead to your right, your path following the fence on your right-hand side. At the end of this fence go straight on up the grass verge and off the road, which bends left towards the main gate, also ignoring any vague path off to the right (a detour down this, for 100 metres, would give you a close-up view of Roydon Hall and its garden). Follow the fence on your right-hand side until, in 80 metres, you are down on a tarmac road where you *turn right,* your direction 40 degrees. In 110 metres

you pass a side entrance to Roydon Hall and, in a further 120 metres, come to the front entrance. (Note: the sign once there, announcing the building as the 'Capital of Enlightenment', has gone; the Hall is no longer open to visitors, as it is under new ownership.)

[!] Your onward path is opposite the front entrance, a Greensand Way footpath, your direction 305 degrees, skirting twin ornamental garden ponds and, in 90 metres, becoming a path between fences. In a further 120 metres go over a stile, with a pond on your right-hand side, following a fence to your right, uphill. By the Greensand Way marker on a post, *veer left,* your direction 320 degrees, uphill towards the now visible church. You exit this field by a stile to an enclosed path leading in 30 metres to the graveyard of St Michael's Church; though not open for regular worship, St Michael's is now a consecrated building that is sometimes open to the public and cared for by the Churches Conservation Trust. After exiting the church (or passing to its left-hand side), exit the churchyard by a stile in its far corner, down steps and straight on downhill on a car road (the one with a dead-end sign), your direction 320 degrees.

200 metres down the road [3], by the end of the wood (and just before gravelled approaches to fieldgates to your left and right) *turn right* on a signposted public footpath, your direction 25 degrees, with the edge of the wood on your right and a fence on your left.

In 300 metres go over a stile and straight on, on a path across a giant field, your direction 25 degrees.(This path can be very muddy when ploughed.) The church in Mereworth is ahead, to the north.

In 500 metres your path becomes a car-wide earth track and you *bend left* with this towards the church. This leads down on to the A228, where you *turn right.* In 100 metres cross a bridge over a river and, in a further 100 metres along this A road, ignore a tarmac drive off to your left, then take the left fork (northwards) signposted

Mereworth and West Malling. In 165 metres *turn left* on to The Street into the village of **Mereworth**. Detour to the suggested lunchtime stop by taking the *first right,* Butcher's Lane, to the **Queens Head** pub, some 500 metres up the lane on your left-hand side.

Return to Mereworth after lunch and *turn right* to the **Church of St Lawrence**. 100 metres further on, you come to the site of the old Torrington Arms pub (now called Torrington House). *Turn right* on a signposted footpath, a tarmac lane, your direction 325 degrees. You go into a narrow path between fences by house no.103. In 180 metres you ignore a fork up to the right (going north). Continue on the main path (now 265 degrees). In 130 metres go round to the right of an old stile to continue *straight ahead* (275 degrees) on a car-wide earth track through a network of fields.

Take the *left fork,* in 250 metres, for 10 metres by a corrugated water mini reservoir and *immediately fork right,* your direction now 230 degrees, until in a further 80 metres a stile (to the left of a metal fieldgate) leads you out on to the main B2016. (To detour to **Beeches** restaurant, turn right.) The main route is to cross the B2016 to continue *straight on* along a tarmac lane to the left of Libbits Cottage. [!] In 40 metres *go left* by a post marked 'FP' to take the faint footpath to the left of a fieldgate (since gone), with a fence on your right-hand side, parallel and to the left of the main track, your direction 175 degrees. This is a potentially very muddy area – there is now a boardwalk for some of it, possibly because one reader wrote 'on the day we did it, it was impassable, we had to continue along the track to the right and clamber down an earth mound building site to regain the woods and the path'.

In 180 metres go over a metal fieldgate to continue straight on, your direction 210 degrees initially, towards buildings, with the chimneys of **Yotes Court** mansion

Walk 50

house (marked on the OS map) visible in the distance. Exit the field in 175 metres, by its far-left corner, through a metal fieldgate. *Turn right uphill* on an earth farm road, your direction 320 degrees, away from the houses.

In 30 metres take a footpath to the right of metal fieldgates, your direction 350 degrees. In 20 metres you are between hedges on both sides. In a further 270 metres your path crosses over a stream and then it follows the stream (with the stream to its left). In 160 metres you come to what looks almost like a low wooden horse-jump and you go round this, to the left, leaving the stream banks to continue straight on, with a fence on your left-hand side, your direction 285 degrees. In 130 metres there are duck ponds on your left-hand side.

Go past what used to be a mini stile, part of another 'horse jump', and in 10 metres you are on a tarmac road where you *turn left,* your direction 210 degrees. Opposite Yew Tree Cottage, in a few metres, *turn right* on an earth car road (there is a pond on your right-hand side), your direction 295 degrees.

Keep straight on. In 100 metres you pass a cottage on your left-hand side – apparently you are on a private drive. In a further 100 metres, go out through its metal fieldgate and continue *straight on,* your direction 250 degrees, until you reach the woods. There you *swing to the right,* bearing 295 degrees, on a wide avenue to the right of the woods. In a further 250 metres, go up left through a metal fieldgate on an earth car road, your direction 300 degrees.

In 100 metres this road has an avenue of small redwood trees on both sides of the road. You are now in **Mereworth Woods** (as marked on the OS map). In 650 metres you cross a bridleway and continue *straight on* (due west). In a further 375 metres, you come to a T-junction of paths and *turn left,* your direction 245 degrees, and in 15 metres you ignore an unofficial

bridleway off to the right (310 degrees) to continue straight on.

In a further 150 metres you come to a post with blue arrows **[4]** and here you *turn sharp right,* your direction 330 degrees, on a path marked with a public bridleway concrete marker.

It is normally possible to skirt the muddy areas ahead by little detours into the woods. In a further 125 metres keep to the main path, your direction 300 degrees, ignoring all turn-offs until you reach an earth road with a wooden post covered with yellow arrows. *Go right* on this earth road (MR 315), your direction 355 degrees.

In 65 metres, at a road junction **[5]**, *take the middle fork* with yellow WW arrow indicating the **Wealdway** (so marked on the OS map), your direction 330 degrees.

Your route for the next 2km or so is more or less straight on, following the Wealdway, until you come to a tarmac car road.

In more detail: In 275 metres you cross paths to continue on, following the WW arrow on a post. In a further 360 metres, you come to a three-way fork and *take the leftmost fork* (the one that is the most straight on for you), your direction 330 degrees.

In a further 200 metres, you ignore a fork off to the right, to continue *straight on,* your direction 325 degrees. In 300 metres you ignore a footpath going left, marked MR 316 on a post, and keep straight on, your direction 340 degrees, with the field fence (and oast house beyond) on your left-hand side and the wood to your right. In a further 140 metres you cross a path that goes off left into orchards (and right into a field for horses).

In a further 800 metres **[6]**, you come out on to a car road (by a WW arrow on a post) and *turn left* on this for 1 metre, **[!]** *immediately going left again* on to a public bridleway (with a concrete marker), your direction 285 degrees.

A green way, soon running parallel to your path in a field to the left and with regular openings from your path, offers an unofficial refuge from the potentially muddy bridleway. You come out by a wooden fieldgate in 400 metres on to a car road, where *you turn left uphill,* your direction 230 degrees. In 200 metres, *turn right, downhill,* on Crouch Lane (signposted to Borough Green and Ightham), your direction 325 degrees. (If it is getting dark, you can follow this road all the long way to the A25, then turn left into town.)

In 250 metres you pass Sotts Hole Cottage on your left-hand side. 15 metres past this cottage **[7]**, DO NOT turn left on a private tarmac driveway (to go 30 metres down towards a wooden fieldgate with a grass road beyond it), **[!]** *but keep ahead* down the road *for just a few metres* past the driveway to a hedge with a gap. Here you *turn left* to go down a few steps, to pick up a clear, narrow bridleway, your direction 235 degrees, to continue parallel to the grass car road on your left-hand side.

Follow this path for 1km.

In more detail: In 70 metres you follow the way through two zigzags to the right. 90 metres beyond these, you pass a wooden fenced gate (marked 'Private') on your right-hand side. Descend through the woods until, in 110 metres, you come out to an open glade, ignoring a minor fork straight on, to *fork right* on the main bridleway, ignoring any ways off until, after a further 600 metres or so, having passed through a housing-estate site, you reach a car road. *Turn right* here. There is a small waterfall to your right-hand side.

[8] Continue on, now with a lake on your right-hand side.

[!] In 450 metres, just beyond the end of the green open space on your right-hand side, you *fork right* on an unmarked path, your direction 5 degrees.

In 50 metres you pass a small orchard on your left-hand side and immediately go over a stream on a concrete-and-brick bridge (if you forked right off the tarmac road 50 metres too soon, you will have come to the wrong bridge, consisting of three wooden planks).

The route is then steeply up the other side. In 450 metres you cross a car road to continue on your path between fences, your direction 15 degrees.

In 260 metres, having passed a telephone exchange on your left-hand side, you cross a housing-estate road to carry *straight on, still uphill,* your path now tarmac. In a further 185 metres you come up to the Church of the Good Shepherd and a car road, where *you turn right,* your direction 55 degrees.

In 40 metres you pass a fish-and-chip shop on your left-hand side and cross the A25 to go straight on, now on **Borough Green** High Street. In 220 metres you come to the railway bridge. 5 metres before the bridge, a tarmac lane to the left leads down between metal railings to platform 1 of **Borough Green station**, for trains to London. On the other side of the railway bridge is the recommended tea stop, the **Henry Simmonds** pub.

Lunch & tea places

Queens Head *Butchers Lane, Mereworth, ME18 5QD (01622 812534, www.queensheadmereworth.co.uk).* **Open** 3-11pm Mon-Fri; noon-10.30pm Sat, Sun. *Food served* noon-3pm Sat, Sun. The suggested lunchtime pub has a spacious dining room at the rear and currently specialises in Seychelles Creole cuisine. If walkers phone ahead, arrangements can be made for food to be served during the week.

Beeches *Seven Miles Lane, Mereworth, ME18 5QY (01622 813038, www.beeches restaurant.co.uk).* **Open** noon-2.30pm, 6.30-10pm Tue-Sat; noon-6pm Sun. This alternative lunch stop requires a detour. Having become a restaurant, it may not be suitable for muddy walkers.

Henry Simmonds *Wrotham Road, Borough Green, TN15 8BD (01732 882016).* **Open** 11am-11pm Mon-Sat; noon-10.30pm Sun. *Food served* 11am-6pm Tue-Sat; noon-5pm Sun. The suggested tea stop for this walk.

Walk 51

Henley to Pangbourne

The River Thames, beech woods, pubs and alpacas.

Start: Henley station
Finish: Pangbourne station

Length: 19.2km (11.9 miles)

Time: 5 hours 40 minutes. For the whole outing, including trains, sights and meals, allow at least 9 hours 30 minutes.

Transport: Take the train nearest to **9am** from **Paddington** station to **Henley-on-Thames**, changing at Twyford (journey time 65 minutes). Trains back from **Pangbourne** to Paddington are every half hour (hourly on Sundays), with a journey time of 1 hour 15 minutes (or just under an hour if you change at Reading for a faster service).
    Buy a day return to Pangbourne. In practice this is usually accepted on the Henley branch line, but you may be required to buy an additional single from Twyford to Henley.

OS Landranger Map: 175
OS Explorer Map: 171
Henley, map reference SU764823, is in **Oxfordshire**, 10km north-east of Reading. Pangbourne, map reference SU633766, is in **Berkshire**, 8km west along the River Thames from Reading.

Toughness: 6 out of 10

Walk notes: This walk starts beside the Thames in Henley, goes down one of Henley's most ancient streets, out into a broad valley, to the church and first pub at Rotherfield Greys. It then goes to the church at Rotherfield Peppard, and thereafter through fields, beech woods and small villages. This walk suffers from no shortage of refreshment stops, including three pubs ideally located for lunch, plus others. The route also takes in an alpaca farm, just outside Whitchurch, where you can watch hundreds of the exotic ruminants grazing, a true highlight towards the end of the walk. On its final leg, the walk carries on to the Whitchurch parish church beside the Thames, to the toll bridge over the Thames, and finally into Pangbourne for a last refreshment stop.

Walk options: The walk can be shortened to just under 13km (8 miles) by catching a bus just outside the Palm Tree restaurant at Cane End. However, by taking this option you miss the alpacas towards the end of the walk. From just outside the Palm Tree, buses X39/X40 run into Reading every 20-30 minutes Monday to Saturday (hourly on Sunday), taking about 20 minutes for the journey. For more bus information, phone 0871 200 2233. Alternatively, you could order a taxi from any of the pubs en route.

Henley to Pangbourne

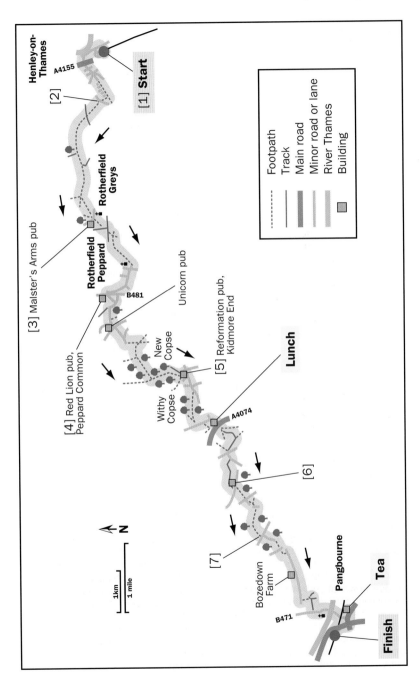

Legend:
- Footpath
- Track
- Main road
- Minor road or lane
- River Thames
- Building

Henley-on-Thames
A4155
[2]
[1] Start
Rotherfield Greys
Malster's Arms pub
Rotherfield Peppard
[3]
B481
Unicorn pub
[4] Red Lion pub, Peppard Common
New Copse
Withy Copse
[5] Reformation pub, Kidmore End
Lunch
A4074
[6]
N
1km
1 mile
[7]
Bozedown Farm
B471
Pangbourne
Tea
Finish

History: **Henley,** with its 300 listed buildings, is said to be the oldest settlement in Oxfordshire.

St Nicholas' Church in **Rotherfield Greys** (if you should be lucky enough to find the door unlocked) contains the ornate tomb of Robert Knollys, counsellor to Elizabeth I and a friend of Mary Queen of Scots.

The building of **All Saints Church,** Rotherfield Peppard, began in the 12th century. Its stained-glass windows – designed by Meredith Williams, son of a rector of the parish – date to the early 20th century. At the start of the 20th century, Mirabel Grey, another local artist, made the Last Supper picture behind the altar and the other panels of inlaid wood.

St Mary's Church, Whitchurch, dates from the 12th century. St Birynius is said to have landed at the ferry crossing at Whitchurch and, on seeing how fine the place was, decided to build a church.

An Act of Parliament in 1792 allowed the building of **Whitchurch Toll Bridge** to replace the ferry. The ten proprietors were given the right to charge tolls: one halfpenny for every sheep and lamb, for instance. The present iron bridge, built in 1902, replaced two previous wooden toll bridges.

The earliest mention of **Pangbourne** is in a Saxon charter of 844 as 'Paegingaburnam' (meaning 'streams of sons of Paega'). In 1919, DH Lawrence stayed in Pangbourne, commenting: 'Pleasant house – Hate Pangbourne – Nothing happens.' Kenneth Grahame, author of *The Wind in the Willows,* lived in Church Cottage.

Walk directions

[1] [Numbers in square brackets refer to the map]

Coming out of **Henley station,** *turn right* and walk 50 metres to the main road. Here, opposite the Imperial Hotel, *turn right* on to the main road. In 120 metres, bear left and you are walking

along the Thames, with the water on your right-hand side.

In 120 metres, *turn left* up Friday Street, soon passing the Anchor Inn on your left-hand side. Go straight on, ignoring all turn-offs. In 200 metres, cross Reading Road to continue on Greys Road with the Queens Head pub on your right. Go straight on.

In 240 metres, *fork right* on to Deanfield Avenue. In a further 15 metres you *fork left* on to a car lane, signposted on the right-hand side as a public footpath (the sign might be obscured by bushes at certain times of the year), your direction 230 degrees. Go straight on, ignoring ways off.

In 350 metres the path ends and you come out at a tarmac road. Go along the road in the same general direction as before, now 245 degrees. In 80 metres, *turn right* on Tilebarn Close.

In 100 metres, *turn left* due west on a footpath (sign-marked Rotherfield Grey) between fences, with a car park on your right-hand side, ignoring the wider footpath to the left. **[2]**

In 50 metres, go through a defunct rusted metal kissing gate; soon you pass tennis courts on your right-hand side. In 480 metres cross over a bridleway to go over a stile and straight on, your direction 320 degrees. Soon you are going through a delightful valley.

In 650 metres, go over a stile into a small copse. Continue on, slightly to your right, following a couple of white arrows on trees, your direction 295 degrees (ignoring a path to the right going uphill on the side of the field). In 125 metres go over a stile to continue ahead on a potentially muddy track. In a further 200 metres, you come to a path junction and carry straight on through a field, your direction 265 degrees.

After 400 metres, at a footpath post with yellow arrows *fork right* to go over a stile 20 metres to the right, following a yellow arrow, with a field fence on your left-hand side, your direction 280 degrees (ignoring the path to the left, which goes

into an avenue of chestnut trees). In 300 metres you pass a redundant stile on the left and follow a yellow arrow straight on, ignoring an arrow to the right.

In 55 metres, *go left over a stile* to follow the direction of its yellow arrow westwards to the right, with a field hedge on your right-hand side. In 75 metres, *fork left uphill,* your direction 210 degrees initially, with a field fence on your left-hand side. When you reach the top of the rise, it is worth looking back for a great view.

In 520 metres, *bear left* to come out through a wooden kissing gate on to a tarmac road, where you *go right*. In 20 metres, you pass the lychgate of **St Nicholas' Church**, Rotherfield Greys.

[3] In a further 25 metres, with the **Maltster's Arms** pub ahead of you to the right, *turn left* on a signposted public footpath, your direction 180 degrees, keeping to the edge of the churchyard on your left-hand side. In 70 metres, go through a swing gate and *veer right,* your direction 220 degrees. In 20 metres, go through another swing gate to continue

in the same direction across a field. In 220 metres, go through a metal swing gate, then *go half right* across another field.

In 140 metres, go through a metal swing gate and *turn left* on a wide path between hedges, your direction 185 degrees.

In a further 150 metres, go through a wooden swing gate (with a metal field gate to its left) and *turn right* on an earth car road, your direction 280 degrees.

In 80 metres, by a public bridleway sign, *go left* through a metal swing gate (a metal fieldgate to its right), your direction 160 degrees, on a potentially muddy path that winds its way along the fringe of the wood. Ignore ways off.

[!] In 200 metres, at a footpath crossing, *go through* the metal kissing gate to the right, on a path due west with trees on either side, ignoring all ways off. After 600 metres, go straight across a track to pass through a metal kissing gate and carry onwards between the fences of Rectory Farm.

In 200 metres, go over a stile on to an earth car-road where you *turn right,* your

direction 300 degrees. In 130 metres, you come to the fine **All Saint's Church**, Rotherfield Peppard. Beyond the church, carry straight on along the road, Church Lane, ignoring ways off.

In 350 metres, with School House on your right and Slaters Farm on your left, *fork right,* still on a tarmac road, your direction 330 degrees. **[4]** Head towards the **Red Lion** pub, Peppard Common, visible 240 metres ahead and reached after crossing the main road. This is the first of three possible lunch stops.

At the pub, turn left (or, if leaving the pub, turn right) on the minor tarmac road, your direction 240 degrees. Carry along this road for 1km (ignoring all ways off), when you will arrive at the **Unicorn** pub on the right-hand side, the second of the three suggested lunch stops.

At the Unicorn pub, turn left (or, if leaving the pub, go straight ahead). In 35 metres, cross the main road into Wyfold Lane, your direction 240 degrees. Continue ahead, ignoring all ways off.

In 300 metres, you take the signposted footpath through the metal kissing gate *to your left* to go due south, with a field hedge on your right-hand side. In 200 metres, go through a gap with a metal fieldgate on the right. Continue along the enclosed path.

In 150 metres, go over a stile and *turn sharp right,* your direction 310 degrees, with the field hedge on your right-hand side, then bending left with the path at the field corner.

In 130 metres, go through a metal gate and after another 20 metres pass through a metal kissing gate to enter a beech wood, **New Copse** (so marked on the OS map). 5 metres after the metal kissing gate, *fork left* (ignoring the path straight ahead). In a further 10 metres, *take the right fork,* due west. Keep straight on, ignoring ways off, your path marked intermittently by white arrows on trees.

[!] In 850 metres, there is a T-junction marked on a tree, just ahead of a multiple footpath junction, with part of a wooden fence directly in front of you and four

possible ways onwards. (You can see a fieldgate and the edge of the wood visible 50 metres away to the right.) At this intersection *go left,* your direction 165 degrees.

In 300 metres, at a crossroads in a clearing, keep straight on, your direction 170 degrees. In a further 370 metres, having ignored all ways off, you come out through wooden barriers on to a car lane lined with houses, where *you go left,* your direction 110 degrees.

In 70 metres, you pass the interesting cogwheel of a well on your left-hand side and, in 15 metres, you come to the main road. There you *turn right,* your direction 250 degrees. **[5]** In 50 metres, you arrive at the **Reformation** pub in Kidmore End, the last of the three possible lunch stops.

Continue past the pub (or, if leaving it, turn right) along the main road. In 270 metres you pass Wyfold Road on the right and, in another 200 metres, *turn right* on to a path that is 10 metres further on from a footpath post. Pass a scaffolding-pole barrier in front of you and, in 10 metres, follow a white arrow marked on a tree by *forking left,* your direction 270 degrees. This is **Withy Copse** (so marked on the OS map).

Continue along this footpath (which can be faint and overgrown at times, but is marked by occasional white arrows) as it winds its way through the trees, ignoring all ways off. In 700 metres, you reach a fence and metal fieldgate with the garden of a house to the right.

Veer left to go through a metal gate with a yellow arrow (marking a diverted route). Continue half left for 50 metres through a small field and go through another metal gate with a yellow arrow. Follow the arrow direction half left through the next field, which you exit at the top left-hand corner, through a gate on to a *road, where you turn left.*

In 60 metres take the signposted footpath over the stile to *your right,* your direction 220 degrees. Keep the field hedge on your left-hand side at this point (a timber-framed cottage is visible ahead of you to your right).

In 165 metres, *take a stile to your left in the fence* to continue on an entrance driveway (ignoring an earlier footpath signpost on the left, about halfway along this field edge). In 35 metres, *turn left* on the A4074, your direction 130 degrees.

In 105 metres, you pass the **Palm Tree**, Cane End, on your left. The bus stop for the X39/X40 route to Reading is in front of this Indian restaurant.

40 metres past the restaurant, where a lane comes in from the left, cross the main road carefully to go on to an earth track opposite, leading to a metal swing gate by a metal fieldgate. Ignore the track straight ahead and follow the blue and yellow arrow marked bridleway half left, your direction 170 degrees.

In 50 metres go through a metal swing gate and *then half right,* your direction 205 degrees. In 30 metres, go through another metal swing gate. Keep straight on along the right side of a field.

After 120 metres, at the corner of the field, continue ahead with trees on the left and a hedge on the right. In another 80 metres, follow a path to the right. In a further 70 metres, you enter the wood, your direction 240 degrees. Keep on the main car-wide track. In 100 metres, at a path junction, follow a M3 arrow (this stands for Mapledurham footpath 3) to keep straight on along a track, with the edge of the wood to your right, your direction 295 degrees.

In 100 metres, you cross a farm track to continue on into the wood, following white arrows on the trees. In 210 metres, follow the path *to the left,* your direction 250 degrees, ignoring a faint path to the left.

In 135 metres, at a junction, go straight on along a tarmac road (ignoring tracks to the right and left), your direction 240 degrees. In 10 metres, you pass Crossways Cottage on your left-hand side. In a further 160 metres, by concrete bollards on your left-hand side, take the signposted bridleway *to your right* into the wood, your direction 280 degrees, on a wide muddy

track (part of the Hardwick Estate). **[!]** In 25 metres, *veer left* on to a narrower track going deeper into the woods (ignoring a wide track going off to the right). Ignore all ways off through the woods.

In 150 metres, you cross a track and *turn left,* going gently downhill, following intermittent white arrows on the trees, your direction initially 240 degrees. Ignore ways off. In 150 metres, your route is gently uphill. In 120 metres, near the top, follow a white arrow on a tree straight on (ignoring ways off), your path slightly narrower now.

In 400 metres, you come to a tarmac road, where you *turn left,* your direction 120 degrees. In 100 metres you come, on the left, to a house called the King Charles' Head (formerly a pub). **[6]**

Opposite this house, you *go right* on a footpath over a stile, signposted Path Hill (the stile and sign may be hidden by bushes at certain times), your direction 230 degrees. In 100 metres, having passed a redundant stile on the right, go over a stile to the left of a wooden gate to follow the edge of the wood on your left-hand side, your direction 250 degrees.

In 125 metres, go over a stile. In 65 metres, your way merges with a driveway and you continue between fences, past a flint cottage on your left-hand side. In a further 145 metres, cross a tarmac lane to go straight on along a very wide earth avenue.

In 150 metres, *turn left* on a car-wide earth road, your direction 190 degrees. In 50 metres, where there is a yellow arrow on a corner-post on your left-hand side, you *go right* between sheds, your direction 290 degrees. Then, in 25 metres, go through a metal kissing gate to the right of a metal fieldgate and *veer slightly to the left* across a small field (usually with horses) towards a gap in a fence, in about 20 metres, leading into an adjacent larger field (usually with geese). Continue half left downhill across this next field in the same direction, 250 degrees.

In 80 metres, you go through a metal kissing gate straight into the wood. In a further 110 metres, you exit the wood through a metal swing gate to continue downhill across a field, due west.

In 80 metres, go through a metal kissing gate and left uphill, your direction 245 degrees, with the edge of the wood fairly near you on your left-hand side. In a further 120 metres, go through a gap, then a gate and straight on.

In 75 metres, go through a fieldgate on to a tarmac road with farm buildings opposite. **[7]** Cross the road and carry straight on along a tarmac lane, signposted footpath, your direction 220 degrees. In 200 metres, you pass the entrance on your left-hand side to a house with turrets.

In 45 metres, you go through a wood barricade *slightly to your right* (level with the house's garden gate) to go downhill, ignoring a wider path downhill to the left.

In 230 metres, you come to a tarmac road which you cross to continue straight on, past a broken stile and through a metal fieldgate. Continue onwards with a field hedge on your left-hand side.

In 60 metres, you go through a metal kissing gate. In 25 metres, by a post with yellow arrows, *turn left downhill,* your direction 165 degrees, with a field hedge on your left-hand side. In 150 metres, you come to a tarmac road, where you *go right.* Continue along the road, from which – through occasional breaks in the hedge

on your left – you can see a large number of grazing alpacas.

In 500 metres, you come to the **Bozedown Alpaca Farm** on the right. Continue on and, at the end of the farm buildings, *go right* off the road at a bench on to a signposted path parallel and above it. In 300 metres, the path rejoins the road for the second time (having previously dipped down very close to it to cross a driveway). 20 metres after the path rejoins the road for good, *turn left* at a signposted footpath beside a wooden fieldgate on to a wide track, your direction 170 degrees.

In 190 metres, *turn right* on the tarmac driveway of a primary school, your direction 235 degrees. In 50 metres, bear right on a lane and, in a further 440 metres, you come to the main road, with the **Greyhound** pub, **Whitchurch**, on your right-hand side. You *turn left,* due south.

In 35 metres, *take the footpath right to the church,* signed Thames Path, on the tarmac driveway of Walliscote House. In 15 metres you fork left, your direction 225 degrees. In 65 metres, you enter the lychgate of the **Parish Church of Whitchurch-on-Thames,** which is worth visiting.

Veer left on the faint path through the churchyard (or turn right out of the church). Leave the churchyard through a

gap to go down a narrow path between brick walls. In 30 metres, *turn left* on a gravel road by a mill house, with the Thames on your right-hand side.

In 65 metres, you come back to the main road and *turn right* to cross Whitchurch Toll Bridge over the Thames. Keep on this main road, which continues on a bridge over the Thames. (If you do not wish to go into Pangbourne for tea, you can take the signposted path to the station, on your right 40 metres after the bridge.)

Otherwise continue on the road. In 250 metres, go under the railway bridge. In 75 metres, with the George Hotel on your right-hand side, you come to the main road T-junction. Turn left along Reading Road and, in 25 metres, you arrive at **Lou La Belle Café** on your left-hand side, one of the suggested tea places. Coming out of the café, turn right, cross over the mini roundabout and keep ahead, in 85 metres coming to another mini roundabout at the junction with the A329. The **Elephant Hotel** – another possible tea/late meal stop – is opposite. If you turn left, you come to the **Cross Keys** pub on your left-hand side in 60 metres.

But to get to the railway station, at the road junction opposite the Elephant, *turn right,* to pass the Parish Council Offices and Village Hall on your left-hand side (with a useful WC block in the front of the car park).

In a further 100 metres, just before the railway bridge, *turn left* up the lane to **Pangbourne railway station**. Pass under the tunnel to reach platform 2 for trains to London. (Alternatively, you can walk under the railway bridge and take the access road on your left-hand side, which leads to the station. Platform 2 is now on your near side.)

Lunch & tea places

Maltster's Arms *Rotherfield Greys, Henley-on-Thames, RG9 4QD (01491 628400, www.maltsters.co.uk).* **Open** noon-3pm, 6-11pm Mon-Thur; noon-3pm, 6-midnight Fri, Sat; noon-10.30pm Sun. *Food served* noon-3pm, 6-10pm Mon-Sat; noon-

4pm Sun. For those doing the shorter, 13km (8 mile) version of the walk, the Maltster's Arms is a good option for lunch, although it can get very busy.
Red Lion *Peppard Common, Henley-on-Thames, RG9 5LB (01491 628329).* **Open** 11am-11pm daily. *Food served* noon-9pm daily. The first of three possible lunchtime stops for the main walk comes after 6.8km (4.2 miles).
Unicorn *The Cross Roads, Kingwood, RG9 5LX (01491 628303, http://the-unicorn.co.uk).* **Open** noon-3pm, 5-11pm Mon-Fri; 11am-11pm Sat, Sun. *Food served* noon-3pm, 6-9pm Thur-Sun. 7.8km (4.8 miles) into the walk, this is the second option for lunch. It doesn't serve food early in the week.
Reformation *Horsepond Road, Gallowstree Common, RG4 9BP (01189 723126, www.brakspear.co.uk).* **Open** noon-3pm, 5.30-11pm Mon-Thur; noon-midnight Fri, Sat; noon-9pm Sun. *Food served* noon-2.15pm, 6-9pm Mon-Thur; noon-9.30pm Fri, Sat; noon-5pm Sun. The final lunch option, coming 10.4km (6.5 miles) into the main walk.
Lou La Belle Café *3-5 Reading Road, Pangbourne, RG8 7LR (01189 842246, www.loulabellefinefoods.co.uk).* **Open** 8am-5pm Mon-Sat. A suggested tea stop.
George Hotel *The Square, Pangbourne, RG8 7AJ (0118 984 2237, www.thegeorge hotelpangbourne.com).* **Open** 10am-11pm Mon-Thur; 10am-midnight Fri, Sat; 10am-10.30pm Sun. *Food served* (Bar) 10am-7.30pm daily.
Elephant Hotel *Church Road, Pangbourne, RG8 7AR (0118 984 2244, www.elephanthotel.co.uk).* **Open** 11am-11pm Mon-Thur; 11am-midnight Fri, Sat; 11am-11pm Sun. *Food served* noon-3pm, 6-10pm daily. Formerly called the Copper Inn, the Elephant offers cream teas and proper meals.
Cross Keys *Church Road, Pangbourne, RG8 7AR (0118 984 3268).* **Open** noon-10.30pm Mon-Wed; noon-midnight Thur; noon-1.30am Fri, Sat; noon-10.30pm Sun. *Food served* noon-3pm, 6-9.30pm Mon-Sat; noon-6pm Sun.

Walk 52

Princes Risborough to Wendover

The Ridgeway Path through Chequers.

Start: Princes Risborough station
Finish: Wendover station

Length: 14.9km (9.3 miles)

Time: 4 hours 30 minutes. For the whole outing, including trains, sights and meals, allow 8 hours.

Transport: Take the train nearest to **10.15am** from **Marylebone** station to **Princes Risborough** (journey time 40-45 minutes).

Trains back from **Wendover** run twice an hour (journey time 50 minutes). Buy a day return to Aylesbury (where the two Chiltern branch lines converge).

OS Langranger Map: 165
OS Explorer Map: 181
Princes Risborough, map reference SP799027, is in **Buckinghamshire**, 11km south of Aylesbury.

Toughness: 6 out of 10

Walk notes: This walk is easy to follow, being mainly along the Ridgeway, and although very much uphill and downhill, it isn't strenuously so. The way is predominantly through high beech woods and chalk downlands, including the Grangelands Nature Reserve. There are views from Coombe Hill over the Vale of Aylesbury and surrounding counties. The walk ends by descending into the pleasant old town of Wendover.

Walk options: There are buses back to Princes Risborough from near the lunch pub in Great Kimble. You could also shorten the walk by staying on the Ridgeway and not detouring via Dunsmore.

History: The town of **Princes Risborough** derives its name from the Black Prince, who in 1343 was Lord of the Manor.

This area was first settled by farmers in Neolithic times, around 4,000 BC. It was defended by a line of hilltop forts, linked by the broad **Icknield Way**, which can be traced from Dorset to Norfolk. On this walk, it survives as the narrow Ridgeway. Remains of such forts can be found on **Pulpit Hill** and **Coombe Hill**.

Whiteleaf Cross, carved into a hillside, is thought to commemorate a victory over the Danes.

Chequers, the prime minister's country retreat, was given to the nation for this purpose by Lord and Lady Lee of Fareham in 1921. Lady Mary Grey, sister of Lady Jane Grey, was imprisoned in Chequers in 1566. The house was later owned by a grandson of Oliver Cromwell.

Wendover's name comes from the Anglo-Saxon 'wand' (winding) 'ofer' (bank). In 1600, the town had one pub for every 50 inhabitants. Wendover became the property of the Crown and was given by

Henry VIII to his wife Catherine of Aragon. It had John Hampden as its MP during the five parliaments leading up to the Civil War: he was one of the MPs whose attempted seizure by Charles I led to the Civil War.

Walk directions

[1] [Numbers in square brackets refer to the map]
Coming out of **Princes Risborough station**, turn left. In 65 metres, veer right with the road, away from the station. At a T-junction in 90 metres *turn right* on Summerleys Road, signposted to High Wycombe and Aylesbury.

In 95 metres, ignore the first turn on the right (Picts Lane) and *veer left* with the road. In 90 metres take the next road on the right, Poppy Road (the B4444), signposted to High Wycombe.

Keep straight on, past the Poppyseed freehouse, bar and Indian restaurant (formerly the Black Prince pub) on your left-hand side, and come out to the A4010 road, where you *bear right.* Cross over the road and continue along it in the direction of High Wycombe.

In 160 metres *turn left* up a tarmac lane, the historic **Upper Icknield Way**, signposted the Ridgeway, your direction 60 degrees initially. **[2]**

Keep straight on up this lane for 1km, ignoring footpaths off to the right and left.

After passing a school and playing fields, cross over a road and continue *straight on* along the Ridgeway Path (still called the Upper Icknield Way). Keep on this lane, ignoring a footpath sign off to the left.

[3] In 350 metres, as you reach the end of playing fields on your left-hand side, take the Ridgeway footpath to your *right* at a three-armed footpath sign, your direction 95 degrees, uphill. The Whiteleaf Cross becomes visible on the hillside to your left at 40 degrees. Keep on this main way all the way up, with a field fence on your right-hand side. Ignore a fork to the left at the top right-hand corner of this first field.

At the top, follow the acorn sign (the Ridgeway Path symbol – and the symbol for all National Trails) *up steps* into the wood. In 15 metres you ignore a footpath sign to the left to *keep on up the steps* of the Ridgeway Path.

Near the top of the hill, go through a kissing gate (with a view back over Princes Risborough). In order to stay on the right of way, follow the acorn sign straight on upwards, eastwards (less leftwards than the arrows by the kissing gate might lead you to believe), going between bushes 15 metres up from this gate.

In 200 metres, at the top right-hand corner of the field, there is a car lane on your right. Some 10 metres before the kissing gate out on to this tarmac lane, you instead follow the Ridgeway Path sign to your *left,* staying within the field close to its right-hand edge, your direction 15 degrees. Exit a further 50 metres on, through a kissing gate, and carry straight on, your direction 25 degrees.

In 100 metres you come down on to a car road and follow the Ridgeway Path sign upwards on this road, your direction 115 degrees.

In 15 metres *go sharp left* by a four-armed sign, up on to the Ridgeway bridleway, your direction 345 degrees, past a car park and picnic tables on your right-hand side.

At the nearby path junction *turn right,* following the blue arrow for the bridleway that goes along the ridge of the hill.

In some 350 metres, go through a swing gate with a large wooden gate on its right-hand side. Immediately after the gate, there is a Neolithic mound a few metres to your left. In 50 metres you reach a three-armed sign. Here you *go right* with the Ridgeway Path, your direction 80 degrees. (However, you may first like to detour left for 50 metres to the top edge of the **Whiteleaf Cross** to enjoy a lovely view.) In 50 metres, go through a swing gate with a sign to Whiteleaf Hill. 100 metres past the swing gate, as your path starts going steeply downhill, you *veer left* with the

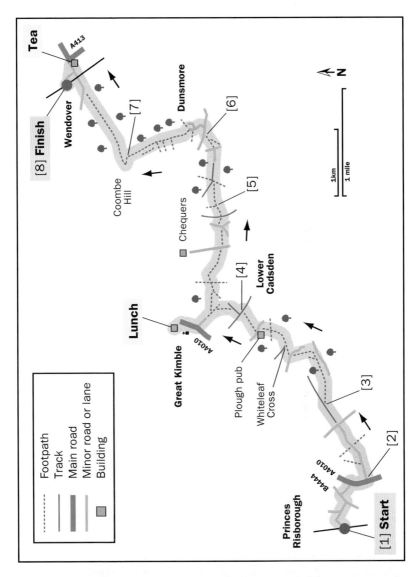

main path downhill, past a knee-high concrete post, your direction 60 degrees.

Keep on the main path downhill through the woods, with a golf course away on your left-hand side. In 500 metres, go through a metal kissing gate (next to a metal fieldgate to its left).

In 70 metres *turn left* on a tarmac road, passing on your left-hand side the **Plough** pub in Lower Cadsden, a possible early lunch stop. 110 metres beyond the pub, you cross a more substantial road. 10 metres beyond this junction, leave the Ridgeway Path to [!] *turn right* through a wooden barrier by an electricity pole, your direction 45 degrees.

In 150 metres, go through a wooden kissing gate (not the bridlegate away to its left) and up into the **Grangelands Nature Reserve**. Ignoring forks to the left, keep to the path upwards, your direction predominantly 35 degrees.

[4] In 500 metres, at the edge of the reserve, *turn right*, soon to reach a wooden kissing gate. Go through and *turn left* downhill on a car-wide track, your direction 310 degrees.

Ignore a stile to the left in 130 metres. Then in 70 metres, at a three-armed footpath sign, *take the Ridgeway Path* through a metal kissing gate to your right, your direction 15 degrees. Ignore a footpath that you cross in 150 metres. Soon there are fine views on your left-hand side, out over the Vale of Aylesbury.

Some 400 metres beyond this footpath, go up steps beyond a kissing gate.

In 40 metres, by a four-armed footpath sign (saying 'North Bucks Way – Wolverton 35 miles'), you leave the Ridgeway Path to

go *left,* your direction 260 degrees. Keep going downhill, soon on a straight car-wide track. Ignore all ways off, in 700 metres coming down to the main road (the A4010), where you *turn right, uphill*.

In 150 metres you pass the **Church of St Nicholas** and reach the suggested lunchtime stop, the **Bernard Arms** in **Great Kimble**.

After lunch, *retrace your steps:* Go right out of the pub, 150 metres downhill on the main road, then left up the lane you came down, signposted North Bucks Way and public bridleway.

400 metres up this path, **[!]** *take the footpath to the left* by a post with two blue arrows on it, going through a metal kissing gate and taking a right fork to go *half right, uphill,* your direction 110 degrees.

Keep to the main path that goes just to the left of the hilltop ahead. 500 metres from your fork off the lane, you come to a T-junction, the well-trodden Ridgeway Path, where you *turn left,* eastwards.

Some 65 metres after crossing a gully, go past a three-armed footpath sign,

Boer War monument.

ignoring a footpath to the left, and keep on the Ridgeway Path along the top of an old rifle range, the valley on your left-hand side.

In a further 110 metres, ignore a stile and footpath off to the left and go on for 75 metres, up to a metal kissing gate (next to a metal fieldgate and a stile off to the left). **[!]** Go *straight on* along the Ridgeway Path, due east.

In 250 metres, by a three-armed footpath sign, go out through a kissing gate (a wooden fieldgate to its right) and go to your *right,* following the Ridgeway sign, your direction 140 degrees, with the wood's edge on your right-hand side.

You now have your first glimpse of **Chequers** to your left (at 70 degrees). In 450 metres you *turn left* by a two-armed footpath sign and a stile, towards the Chequers gatehouse, your direction 115 degrees, through kissing gates, over the Chequers entrance drive and straight on the other side, through another kissing gate.

In 350 metres, leave Chequers through a kissing gate. Carefully cross the car road and continue *straight on,* following the Ridgeway bridleway sign, your direction 75 degrees.

In 130 metres you pass a barn on your right-hand side.

Go up into a narrow strip of woodland, following the acorn and blue arrow on a post. In 100 metres (at a sign marked 'alternative footpath for walkers only') *fork left* (the right fork merges again with your way in 100 metres).

Some 45 metres beyond where these ways merge, by a four-armed footpath sign, ignore the South Bucks Way to your right and carry *straight on up* the Ridgeway footpath.

[5] In 250 metres you come to a three-armed footpath sign, more or less at the top of the hill, a potentially muddy patch. Leave the Ridgeway Path here (which goes left) and *carry straight on,* following the footpath sign, on a car-wide track, your direction 65 degrees.

Carry on, soon downwards, through the woods, ignoring ways off. In 450 metres

you ignore a footpath that crosses yours, staying on your car-wide track. In 300 metres, ignore a yellow-signed footpath up to your left. Go down past the house and stables on your left-hand side, to go over the road at a three-armed path sign.

Carry straight on, along a signposted footpath uphill, over a stile, your direction 70 degrees, between fences. Then go over a stile into a field, following the path *half left* to the next stile. Go over this stile towards the upper left-hand corner of the field, which you exit just to the left of a mini pylon. **[6]**

Turn right on a car road. In 80 metres, just past a pond on your right-hand side, *turn left,* signposted 'Dunsmore Village only'.

Ignore a footpath sign off to the right in 60 metres. In a further 20 metres, a bridleway sign points your continuing way, straight on up the tarmac car lane.

In 90 metres, continue past Apple Tree Cottage on your right-hand side and the Beeches slightly further on. Ignore a stile to the left to carry on.

The path has by now narrowed and, in 100 metres, you **[!]** *fork left* on a wide path, between fences to your left and right, through woods. Continue on for 50 metres.

Your path shortly meets a rusting metal fence to your right (you continue to walk alongside this fence for 1km or so until the fence ends at the edge of a field). Go *straight on,* your direction 320 degrees, on a route that in winter can be very muddy in places.

In 100 metres, cross a bridleway. In a further 500 metres, you ignore a bridleway that goes through a gap in the fence to your right.

In a further 250 metres you ignore a footpath off to the left and (100 metres away on the other side of the fence to your right) you pass a house with a conservatory. In a further 250 metres, at the point when the fence ends, you continue *straight on* between the remains of a rusted fence, your direction 315 degrees.

In 250 metres **[7]** there is a tree on your left-hand side with a railing partly embedded in it. **[!]** Go straight on through a gap in the bank to cross a wide track and continue ahead (slightly left – more or less your previous direction, 320 degrees) on a **[!]** narrow winding path, beside a straight row of trees to your right-hand side.

In 150 metres, at a bridleway T-junction marked by a post with a blue bridleway badge, *turn left,* your direction 240 degrees.

In 70 metres *turn right* through a metal kissing gate and go past a National Trust sign saying **Coombe Hill**. Carry straight on, your direction 285 degrees, with a fence on your left-hand side. In 450 metres you come to a **Boer War** monument.

At the monument, there is a concrete pillar indicating directions to distant points. Follow more or less the direction it marks to Edlesborough Church to your *right*, to pick up the Ridgeway Path (marked with acorn posts) down towards Wendover, your direction 80 degrees.

Exit the Coombe Hill grounds by a metal kissing gate to go over a bridleway and through another kissing gate and *straight on* along the Ridgeway Path, your direction 70 degrees.

In 300 metres, by a sign for **Bacombe Hill**, you *fork left,* following the Ridgeway Path down, in 100 metres passing through a kissing gate, then straight on, your direction 70 degrees. There are fine views out on to the Vale of Aylesbury below.

Keep to the main path. Further on, a fine view of Halton House appears ahead of you on your left-hand side. 400 metres on from the kissing gate, follow an acorn-marked post to *fork to the left*.

Carry straight on along this path downhill, ignoring a further fork to the left into woods by a bench some 300 metres on. In 200 metres go through a metal kissing gate marked with the acorn and carry on down.

In 80 metres *turn right* on the car road and carry on down under pylons into **Wendover**, passing the train station off to your left and coming to South Street on your right. Further down the High Street are **Rumsey's** chocolaterie on the left-hand side and the **Red Lion Hotel** on the right-hand side.

After tea, to get to the station, turn left out of the cafe, retracing your steps as you go. In 70 metres, you pass the **Shoulder of Mutton** pub on your right, and take the road to the right (Station Approach), which leads down to **Wendover station. [8]** The platform nearest to you is the one for London.

Lunch & tea places

Plough *Cadsden Road, Lower Cadsden, nr Princes Risborough, HP27 0NB (01844 343302, http://plough-at-cadsden.co.uk).* **Open** 11am-2.30pm, 5-11pm Mon-Fri; 11am-11pm Sat; 11am-10pm Sun. *Food served* noon-2pm, 6.30-9.30pm Mon-Sat; noon-2.30pm Sun. For those starting late, or not wishing to make a detour, the Plough is a good early lunch option.

Bernard Arms *Risborough Road, Great Kimble, HP17 0XS (01844 346172, http://bernardarms.com).* **Open** noon-3pm, 5-11pm Tue-Fri; noon-11pm Sat; noon-5pm Sun. *Food served* noon-2.30pm, 5-9pm Tue-Fri; noon-9pm Sat; noon-4pm Sun. Foreign dignitaries tend to visit this pub, the suggested lunch stop, when staying at Chequers. Groups of more than ten should phone ahead to book.

Rumsey's of Wendover *The Old Bank, 26 High Street, Wendover, HP22 6EA (01296 625060, www.rumseys.co.uk).* **Open** 9.30am-6.30pm daily. As well as making fancy chocolates, Rumsey's serves hot drinks, cakes and light lunches.

Red Lion Hotel *9 High Street, Wendover, HP22 6DU (01296 622266, www.redlionhotelwendover.co.uk).* **Open** 7am-11pm Mon-Fri; 8am-11pm Sat, Sun. *Food served* noon-9pm daily. The 17th-century bar of the Red Lion serves tea and coffee as well as main meals.

Shoulder of Mutton *20 Pound Street, Wendover, HP22 6EJ (01296 623223).* **Open** 11am-11pm Mon-Sat; noon-10.30pm Sun. *Food served* 11am-10pm Mon-Sat; noon-9pm Sun. Another option providing tea, coffee and full meals.

Walk 53

Wye Circular

The Crundale Downs and the River Great Stour.

Start and finish: Wye station

Length: 18.1km (11.2 miles)

Time: 5 hours. For the whole outing, including trains, sights and meals, allow at least 9 hours 30 minutes.

Transport: Take the train nearest to **9.10am** from **Charing Cross** station to **Wye** (journey time 1 hour 30 minutes). For a premium, you can reduce the journey time to 1 hour by taking the High Speed Train from St Pancras and changing at Ashford International. Trains back to Charing Cross run twice an hour; change at Ashford for the High Speed Train to St Pancras.

OS Langranger Map: 189
OS Explorer Map: 137
Wye, map reference TR048470, is in **Kent**, 6km north-east of Ashford.

Toughness: 7 out of 10

Walk notes: This walk goes high up on the Crundale Downs ('crun', in Old English, meant chalk; 'dala' meant dell or valley), with breathtaking views. The walk comes to an isolated Norman church at Crundale, then on to a 15th-century inn for lunch. The walk next passes Crundale House and the manor of Olantigh, crosses the River Great Stour and returns to Wye through its churchyard, for tea at a teashop at the bottom of Church Street or at a pub next to the railway station.

Beware that parts of the route can be very muddy in wet weather: be prepared.

Walk options: You could call a taxi from the lunchtime pub. Otherwise, you could save 2km by not having lunch at the pub and instead descending on a byway from Crundale church, your direction 290 degrees, to rejoin the main route beside Crundale House. Or you could turn left at the T-junction just after point **[9]** and walk along the road into Wye.

History: The **Crown Memorial**, cut into the hillside outside Wye, is a unique landmark constructed in mid June 1902 out of flintstones to commemorate the Coronation of King Edward VII. The King viewed the Crown illumination from Eastwell Park on 2 July 1904. The Crown is part of a Site of Special Scientific Interest (SSSI), surrounded by rare downland herbs, orchids and butterflies.

To mark the Millennium, a **Crown Millennium Stone** was added just above the Memorial.

The **Church of St Mary** in **Crundale** is thought to be on a Roman site. It retains Norman parts. Inside is a nearly life-sized memorial slab commemorating the Reverend John Sprot, who died in 1466 and is depicted in his full vestments.

The **Church of St Gregory & St Martin** in **Wye** dates from the 12th or early 13th century. It was once larger than it is now – the tower collapsed in 1686. **Wye College**, next to the church, was founded in 1447 by John Kempe, the Archbishop of York, and is now part of Wye Agricultural College, University of London.

Walk directions

[1] [Numbers in square brackets refer to the map]
Walk to the end of platform 2 at **Wye station**, towards the footbridge, to exit the station through the white wooden gate at the far end of the platform. *Turn left* and cross over the level crossing to pass the station building on your left-hand side.

In 40 metres you cross a bridge over the **River Great Stour**, then pass the Tickled Trout pub on the other side. (You can return to the pub for tea at the end of the walk.) 30 metres past the pub *turn left* on Churchfield Way.

In 80 metres, as the road curves right, ignore the first lane off to the left by a house called Kelston. In 55 metres *turn left* on an estate road (Abbots Walk).

The road swings to the right and, in 115 metres, at a crossroads with a green space ahead and to your right, **[!]** *turn left* on a concrete road that looks like a dead end, heading due north, with house no.44 on your left-hand side. In 30 metres, at the end of the road, *turn right,* due east, with house no.52 on your left-hand side.

In 55 metres the road bears left, and by a concrete public-footpath marker, go through a wooden gate, cross a field enclosure and, in 8 metres, go through a wooden kissing gate. *Keep ahead* across a field, your direction 45 degrees, on a clear path.

In 160 metres go through a metal fieldgate and, in 6 metres, through a wooden swing gate, to *turn right* on a tarmac lane **[2]**, your direction 130 degrees. In a further 40 metres, cross over a cattle grid. In 200 metres you pass another cattle grid. In 20 metres, go over a tarmac road **[3]** to continue *straight ahead* on Occupation Road, following a North Downs Way (NDW) sign.

You pass buildings of Imperial College London on your left-hand side. *Keep ahead,* now with a tall hedge on your left and

single-storey business units on your right. In 175 metres the hedge ends. In a further 110 metres, go through a metal gate to the left of a metal fieldgate, with a NDW sign on its post.

In 60 metres you cross Wibberley Way (a permissive path) to continue straight on, with an open field on your left and a tree-line on your right, steadily upwards towards the Crown Memorial, carved into the hillside.

In 270 metres, by a footpath post on your right, ignore the Stour Valley Walk going off to the left. In a further 275 metres, cross a tarmac lane and *continue uphill* with a hedge on your left and an open field on your right, your direction 85 degrees, signposted NDW.

In 250 metres there is a fine view back over the valley just before you enter a wood through a wooden swing gate, to continue steeply upwards. Follow the NDW post sign. In 20 metres, cross a path junction and keep ahead.

In 90 metres, ignore the Wibberley Way path off to the right. In 20 metres, as the path levels out, cross another path junction. In a further 20 metres you come to a tarmac road with a view ahead (northwards). Ignore the wooden kissing gate directly ahead and instead **[!]** *turn right* along the road, following the NDW sign, uphill.

In 225 metres, **[!]** *go right, up steps,* signposted NDW, your direction 220 degrees.

In 30 metres, go through a metal squeeze stile to the right of a wooden fieldgate to continue on a grassy farm track beside a line of trees. In a further 60 metres, go through another metal squeeze stile (or go over the low wooden stile) to the right of a metal fieldgate, and *turn left,* following the NDW arrow, to continue along the Ridgeway, your direction 170 degrees, the valley out beneath you on your right-hand side.

In a further 100 metres, at the corner of a fence on your left-hand side, carry straight on, *slightly to the left,* then *turning right,* with a small hollow on

Wye Circular

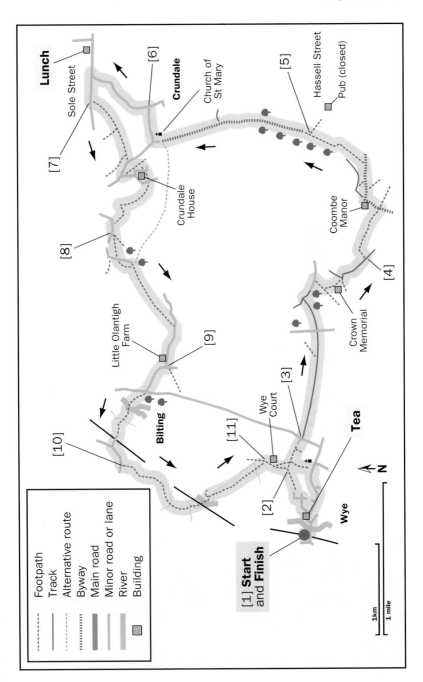

Lunch

Sole Street

[6]

[7]

Crundale

Church of
St Mary

Hassell Street

Pub (closed)

[5]

Crundale
House

Coombe
Manor

[8]

[4]

Little Olantigh
Farm

Crown
Memorial

[9]

Bilting

[3]

[10]

[11]

Wye
Court

Tea

[2]

Wye

[1] **Start**
and **Finish**

N

Footpath
Track
Alternative route
Byway
Main road
Minor road or lane
River
Building

1km
1 mile

your right and the **Crown Millennium Stone** just below you, above the **Crown Memorial** on the hillside below.

Carry on, along an undulating grassy path, your direction 150 degrees, keeping the hillside on your right. In 165 metres, go through a metal kissing gate, to follow the NDW arrow, with a fence on your left-hand side, your direction now 145 degrees.

In 250 metres **[4]** leave the North Downs Way **[!]** to go through a metal kissing gate on your *left,* marked with a yellow circular walk arrow, your direction 80 degrees, to cross a field on an indistinct path. In 110 metres, go through a metal kissing gate to the left of a metal fieldgate to go down into a wood on a footpath used by horses, your direction 135 degrees.

In 115 metres, at the other end of the wood, *go straight on* with the edge of the wood now on your right-hand side and **Coombe Manor** ahead on your left-hand side, initially downhill.

The path levels out and in 275 metres you come to a tarmac lane, with a metal fieldgate opposite and a post with yellow arrow on your right. Here *turn left* down the lane, your direction 25 degrees.

In 145 metres *turn right* through an open wooden fieldgate, following a footpath sign, gently uphill, your direction due east. In 120 metres, at the top of the field, *turn left* through a metal fieldgate. In 30 metres, ignore the gate 20 metres directly ahead, and instead follow the footpath sign, to your *right,* up the hillside on a wide, grassy path, with the edge of the wood over to your left.

In 225 metres (and 15 metres before the metal fieldgate ahead of you), *drop down* the bank to your left and *go over a stile* into the wood, your direction 25 degrees. In 35 metres, exit the wood through a metal kissing gate to continue down a field with the edge of the wood on your left-hand side, your direction 60 degrees.

In 140 metres, pass through a field boundary and keep ahead. Stay close to the field edge and, in a further 340 metres, go through a metal kissing gate to come out on to an earth lane.

Go left and then **[!]** *immediately fork right* by a new Byway sign **[5]**, along the car-wide earth lane, your direction 350 degrees. Stay on this byway, uphill, through the wood of beech and chestnut trees, ignoring all ways off. The path

eventually levels out and passes through several muddy sections (passable by detouring into the wood on your left-hand side).

In 680 metres you have a view out over the valley to your left. In a further 150 metres you come to an open field on your right-hand side, with views now over to your right. In a further 160 metres, ignore a stile on your right-hand side.

In 20 metres go through a metal fieldgate ahead of you and keep straight on, your direction 345 degrees, between field fences. The path at first goes downhill, then uphill, and then downhill again, in 700 metres coming out into the car park of the **Church of St Mary, Crundale**, on your right.

After visiting the church, leave the churchyard by its main gate, by the war memorial, and *turn right* on the tarmac lane, downhill, your direction 105 degrees.

In 450 metres, at a T-junction **[6]**, follow the sign to the Compasses Inn to the *left,* along a tarmac lane. In 600 metres, having climbed steeply for the last part, you come to a T-junction where you *turn right,* due east. In 250 metres this brings you on your left to the suggested lunch pub, the **Compasses Inn**.

After lunch, turn right out of the pub. In 250 metres, ignore the lane on your left on which you came up before lunch. In 125 metres, ignore the dirt road that forks to the right uphill.

In 170 metres, ignore a path to the right marked by a new Byway sign; but then, in 40 metres **[7]**, as the road swings to the right, follow the footpath sign **[!]** to *fork left* through a wooden swing gate to the left of a wooden fieldgate in a tractor-wide gap in the hedge. Then *go downhill* on a path, *half right* across a field, your direction 235 degrees.

In 150 metres, at the edge of this field, cross an old hedge-line and a path crossing to continue *straight on,* now gently downhill, on a car-wide path, your direction 250 degrees.

In 145 metres the car-wide path swings to the right **[!]** *but you keep ahead* on a

narrow path uphill between fields, your direction 240 degrees. In 230 metres the path leads you along the left-hand edge of a wood.

In 80 metres, just before the field corner, *turn right* and cross a stile into the wood. In 10 metres, at a path junction, ignore the stile directly ahead of you, some 20 metres away, but instead *bear left,* downwards, through the wood, your direction 290 degrees.

In 70 metres you come out on to a tarmac road where you *go right.* In 110 metres, *turn sharp left* on the driveway of Crundale House, your direction 175 degrees. In 10 metres, *fork left* on a footpath by a concrete public-footpath marker, your direction 120 degrees (the way has been overgrown at times in the past).

In 25 metres, go over a stile between two metal fieldgates and follow the path between hedges. In 85 metres, ignore the wooden gate on your left-hand side and keep ahead, now with a barbed-wire-topped post and wire fence on your left-hand side.

In 160 metres, by a stile on your left-hand side, **[!]** *go right, steeply down steps,* your direction 280 degrees. In 15 metres, go over a stile and across a field, your direction 250 degrees, aiming for a footpath post to the left of an industrial shed and stables.

In 65 metres, go through a metal fieldgate and over a concrete farm road, with stables on your right-hand side. In 10 metres, go through a metal fieldgate (usually kept open) and keep straight on, your direction 260 degrees, with a field hedge and fence on your right-hand side.

In 100 metres **[!]** you go over a stile on your *right-hand side.* In 5 metres, drop down to a road, which you cross to continue straight on uphill, on an earth road, your direction 240 degrees initially.

In 35 metres, at the end of the wooden fence on your right-hand side, follow the yellow arrow to the right, your direction 320 degrees, on a clear grassy path with the hedge and then the back garden of **Crundale House** on your right.

At the end of the garden hedge, *swing right* with the fence for 50 metres, then *bear left* across the field ahead, following the line of telegraph poles, your direction 300 degrees. In 180 metres, keep ahead through a field boundary, now with a wire fence on your right.

In 90 metres, when the path reaches the garden hedge ahead of you, *turn left alongside it,* your direction 250 degrees, with the garden hedge on your right-hand side. In 100 metres, and 8 metres beyond the house, you *go right* through a wooden gate, your direction 335 degrees. In 25 metres, go straight on, now on the driveway of Farnley Little Barn.

In 40 metres you come to a tarmac road where you *go left,* uphill, your direction 255 degrees. In 120 metres **[8]** take the signposted footpath *left.* In 15 metres, ignore the footpath to the left and follow the footpath ahead up into the wood, your direction 260 degrees.

Keep ahead as the path winds its way uphill and, in 125 metres, you come to a crossing with an earth car-wide track, where you *turn right,* your direction 300 degrees. In 45 metres you come out on to a tarmac road, which you cross to go through a wooden kissing gate, then *turn left,* your direction now 210 degrees, with the field fence on your left-hand side.

In 150 metres you bear slightly to the right to make for the bottom, far right-hand corner of the field. There you go over a stile and across a field, slightly to the left, aiming for a footpath post on its far side, your direction 275 degrees.

In 160 metres you enter a wood. In a further 20 metres you come to an earth track, where you *go left,* due south. In 40 metres you leave the wood and *go half right* across a vast field, your direction 230 degrees.

In 340 metres, you cross a stile by a footpath sign (if it's overgrown, go through the gate 40 metres to its left) and come out on to a car road, where you *go right,* your direction 300 degrees.

In 280 metres you pass Ripple Farm Organics on your left-hand side and **Little Olantigh Farm** on your right. In 20 metres **[9]** ignore a fork left to Brook and *turn right,* signposted Wye.

In 300 metres you come to a T-junction where you *go right,* signposted Crundale. (To **shorten the walk**, turn left here and walk along the road for 2km into the centre of Wye.)

In 30 metres **[!]** *turn left* through a metal kissing gate to the left of a wooden swing gate on a signposted footpath, your direction 320 degrees, downhill, and head towards the footbridge ahead. The **Chapel & Manor of Olantigh** (as marked on the OS map) are visible, away on your left-hand side.

In 215 metres you cross the River Stour on the steel footbridge with wooden gates at both ends. On the far side, *turn half right,* your direction 300 degrees, across a field. In 125 metres you pass through a metal fieldgate into the next field. *Keep ahead,* your direction now 310 degrees.

In 200 metres you pass Finches House on your left-hand side. In a further 25 metres you go through a wooden swing gate to cross the railway line. On its other side, go through a wooden kissing gate and keep ahead along an access drive. In 120 metres you come to a T-junction by Home Farm House where you *go left,* your direction 260 degrees, gently uphill.

In 200 metres (and 30 metres before a phonebox on the far side of the A28 road) **[10]** *go left* on an earth car-road, your direction 200 degrees. In 40 metres you come out into a field to go straight across it, your direction 205 degrees.

In 250 metres, at the left-hand corner of a wood, go over a stile to continue in your previous direction (205 degrees), now with a fence and the wood on your right-hand side.

The field boundary swings left and in 255 metres **[!]** you *turn right* over a stile. Follow the yellow arrow and continue *onwards, slightly right,* your direction 220 degrees across a vast field.

In 385 metres, cross a stream on a plank bridge, some 15 metres to the right of a hedge corner, and then *fork left,* due south. In 90 metres, go through a gap in the hedge and onwards across another field, your direction 140 degrees.

In 215 metres, go through a field boundary to cross the river and its tributary on two double-plank bridges. On the far side, *turn right* along the riverbank on an often overgrown path, your direction 165 degrees.

In 120 metres, go over a stile and cross the railway line, then over another stile and a concrete bridge with metal railings over the River Great Stour. On the other side of the bridge, *turn right* with the path, your initial direction 160 degrees, and continue as the path soon swings *to the left.*

In 60 metres, take the path to the right of a redundant gate, with a ditch to your left, your direction 150 degrees. In 300 metres you cross a drain on a concrete, tractor-wide platform, to go through a metal fieldgate. *Keep ahead,* following a yellow arrow, your direction 170 degrees, towards a house, keeping close to the left-hand field fence.

In 160 metres [11] you pass the side of the house over to your left and keep ahead, aiming for the left-hand corner of the field. In 50 metres, go through a wooden swing gate in the field corner and *go slightly left* along a tarmac lane, your direction 155 degrees.

In 45 metres, ignore a path off to the right (though a wooden swing gate). In 35 metres, go over a cattle grid. In a further 60 metres, *turn right* through a wooden swing gate to go along a path, with a hedge on your left-hand side and a fence on your right, your direction 220 degrees.

In 150 metres you come into the churchyard of the **Church of St Gregory & St Martin** in Wye.

For a drink at the **Kings Head** pub, cross over the road and walk ahead down Church Street. The pub is 60 metres along on the right-hand side and there's a cafe another 70 metres down the road, on

your right, at the junction with Upper Bridge Street.

For the railway station and/or refreshments at the Tickled Trout pub: Coming out of the churchyard, *turn right* on the main road (High Street). This soon becomes Churchfield Way and, in 400 metres, you pass Abbots Walk on your right. Now retrace your steps at the beginning of the walk, to pass the **Tickled Trout** pub on your right.

Cross back over the bridge over the River Great Stour to **Wye station**. The platform for trains to Ashford and London is on your near side.

Lunch & tea places

Compasses Inn *Sole Street, Crundale, CT4 7ES (01227 700300, www. compassesinncrundale.co.uk).* **Open** noon-3pm, 6-11pm Tue-Sat; noon-6pm Sun. *Food served* noon-2pm, 6.30-9pm Tue-Sat; noon-3pm Sun. The suggested lunch place for the walk, with a varied menu – main courses, specials and lighter snacks – internal seating areas and a pleasant rear garden. Visitors wishing to eat their own sandwiches in the pub's outside areas, having first purchased a drink from the bar, should seek the pub management's permission to do so.

Kings Head *Church Street, Wye, TN25 5BN (01233 812418, www.kingsheadwye. co.uk).* **Open** 11am-3pm, 6-11pm Mon-Wed; 11am-11pm Thur-Sat; noon-10.30pm Sun. *Food served* noon-2pm, 6-9pm Mon-Sat; noon-3pm Sun. On returning to Wye, through the churchyard of the Church of St Gregory & St Martin, instead of turning right and heading for the railway station, you can take the road directly ahead to bring you to this old coaching inn.

Tickled Trout *2 Bridge Street, Wye, TN25 5EB (01233 812227).* **Open** 11am-3pm, 6-11pm Mon-Fri; 11am-3pm, 6-midnight Sat; noon-4pm, 7-11pm Sun. *Food served* noon-2pm, 6-9pm Mon-Sat; noon-3pm, 7-9pm Sun. The suggested tea stop has a pleasant beer garden overlooking the River Great Stour and is conveniently located, adjacent to the railway station.

Index